France For Dummies,® 1st Edition

Cheat Sheet

French Numbers

English	French	Pronunciation
zero	zéro	*zare*-oh
one	un	oon
two	deux	duh
three	trois	twah
four	quatre	*kaht*-ruh
five	cinq	sank
six	six	seess
seven	sept	set
eight	huit	wheat
nine	neuf	nuhf
ten	dix	deess
eleven	onze	ohnz
twelve	douze	dooz
thirteen	treize	trehz
fourteen	quatorze	kah-*torz*
fifteen	quinze	kanz
sixteen	seize	sez
seventeen	dix-sept	deez-*set*
eighteen	dix-huit	deez-*wheat*
nineteen	dix-neuf	deez-*nuhf*
twenty	vingt	vehn
thirty	trente	trahnt
forty	quarante	ka-*rahnt*
fifty	cinquante	sang-*kahnt*
sixty	soixante	swa-*sahnt*
seventy	soixante-dix	swa-sahnt-*deess*
eighty	quatre-vingts	kaht-ruh-*vehn*
ninety	quatre-vingt-dix	kaht-ruh-venh-*deess*
one hundred	cent	sahn
one thousand	mille	meel
one hundred thousand	cent mille	sahn meel

Hungry Minds™

For Dummies: Bestselling Book Series for Beginners

BESTSELLING
BOOK SERIES

France For Dummies
1st Edition

W9-CSJ-303

A List of Handy French Words and Phrases

English	French	Pronunciation
Thank you	Merci	mair-*see*
Please	S'il vous plaît	seel voo *play*
Yes/No/and	Oui/Non/et	wee/nohn/ay
Do you speak English?	Parlez-vous anglais?	par-lay-voo-ahn-*glay*
I don't understand	Je ne comprends pas	jhuh ne kohm-*prahn* pah
I'm sorry/Excuse me	Pardon	pahr-*dohn*
Good day/Good evening	Bonjour/Bonsoir	bohn-*jhoor*/bohn-*swahr*
My name is . . .	Je m'appelle	jhuh ma-*pell*
Miss	Mademoiselle	mad mwa-*zel*
Mr.	Monsieur	muh-*syuh*
Mrs.	Madame	ma-*dam*
Where is/are . . . ?	Où est/sont . . . ?	ooh-eh?/ooh-sohn ?
. . . the toilets?	. . . les toilettes?	lay twa-*lets*?
. . . the bus station?	. . . la gare routière ?	lah gar roo-tee-*air* ?
. . . the hospital ?	. . . l'hôpital?	low-pee-*tahl* ?
to the right/to the left	à droite/à gauche	ah drwaht/ah goash
straight ahead	tout droit	too-drwah
a ticket	un billet	uh *bee*-yay
one-way ticket	aller simple	ah-*lay sam*-pluh
round-trip ticket	aller-retour	ah-*lay* ree-*toor*
I want to get off at . . .	Je voudrais descendre à . . .	jhe voo-dray day-son-drah-ah
I would like . . .	Je voudrais . . .	he voo-dray
a room	une chambre	ewn *shahm*-bruh
the key	la clé	lah clay
a phonecard	une carte téléphonique	ewn cart tay-lay-fone-*eek*
aspirin	des aspirines	deyz ahs-peer-*eens*
How much does it cost?	C'est combien?	say comb-bee-*ehn*?
Do you take credit cards?	Est-ce que vous acceptez cartes de credit?	es-kuh voo zak-sep-*tay* lay kart duh creh-*dee* ?

For Dummies: Bestselling Book Series for Beginners

France

FOR

DUMMIES®

1ST EDITION

By Cheryl A. Pientka and Laura M. Reckford

Hungry Minds™

Best-Selling Books • Digital Downloads • e-Books • Answer Networks
e-Newsletters • Branded Web Sites • e-Learning

New York, NY ◆ Cleveland, OH ◆ Indianapolis, IN

France For Dummies® 1st Edition

Published by:
Hungry Minds, Inc.
909 Third Avenue
New York, NY 10022
www.hungryminds.com
www.dummies.com

Library of Congress Control Number: 2001089306

ISBN: 0-7645-6292-4

ISSN: 1534-5033

Printed in the United States of America

10 9 8 7 6 5 4 3 2 1

1B/QY/QW/QR/IN

Distributed in the United States by Hungry Minds, Inc.

Distributed by CDG Books Canada Inc. for Canada; by Transworld Publishers Limited in the United Kingdom; by IDG Norge Books for Norway; by IDG Sweden Books for Sweden; by IDG Books Australia Publishing Corporation Pty. Ltd. for Australia and New Zealand; by TransQuest Publishers Pte Ltd. for Singapore, Malaysia, Thailand, Indonesia, and Hong Kong; by Gotop Information Inc. for Taiwan; by ICG Muse, Inc. for Japan; by Intersoft for South Africa; by Eyrolles for France; by International Thomson Publishing for Germany, Austria and Switzerland; by Distribuidora Cuspide for Argentina; by LR International for Brazil; by Galileo Libros for Chile; by Ediciones ZETA S.C.R. Ltda. for Peru; by WS Computer Publishing Corporation, Inc., for the Philippines; by Contemporanea de Ediciones for Venezuela; by Express Computer Distributors for the Caribbean and West Indies; by Micronesia Media Distributor, Inc. for Micronesia; by Chips Computadoras S.A. de C.V. for Mexico; by Editorial Norma de Panama S.A. for Panama; by American Bookshops for Finland.

For general information on Hungry Minds' products and services please contact our Customer Care department; within the U.S. at 800-762-2974, outside the U.S. at 317-572-3993 or fax 317-572-4002.

For sales inquiries and resellers information, including discounts, premium and bulk quantity sales and foreign language translations please contact our Customer Care department at 800-434-3422, fax 317-572-4002 or write to Hungry Minds, Inc., Attn: Customer Care department, 10475 Crosspoint Boulevard, Indianapolis, IN 46256.

For information on licensing foreign or domestic rights, please contact our Sub-Rights Customer Care department at 212-884-5000.

For information on using Hungry Minds' products and services in the classroom or for ordering examination copies, please contact our Educational Sales department at 800-434-2086 or fax 317-572-4005.

Please contact our Public Relations department at 212-884-5174 for press review copies or 212-884-5000 for author interviews and other publicity information or fax 212-884-5400.

For authorization to photocopy items for corporate, personal, or educational use, please contact Copyright Clearance Center, 222 Rosewood Drive, Danvers, MA 01923, or fax 978-750-4470.

Hungry Minds™ is a trademark of Hungry Minds, Inc.

About the Authors

Cheryl A. Pientka is a freelance journalist and assistant literary agent. She's the author of *Paris For Dummies* and co-author of *Frommer's Paris from $80 a Day*. A graduate of Columbia University Graduate School of Journalism and the University of Delaware, she lives in Paris when she's not in New York. For *France For Dummies,* Cheryl wrote Chapters 11 to 13 and collaborated on Chapters 1 to 10.

Laura M. Reckford has traveled around France frequently over the past 20 years, visiting friends and family and exploring the country. She lives on Cape Cod and is a newspaper reporter and freelance writer. She's also the author of *Frommer's Cape Cod, Martha's Vineyard & Nantucket.* For *France For Dummies,* Laura wrote Chapters 14 to 22 and the Appendix and collaborated on Chapters 1 to 10.

Dedication

Cheryl A. Pientka: For my father, Philip E. Pientka (1936 – 2000), the wind beneath my wings.

Laura M. Reckford: This book is dedicated to all those lucky people planning a trip to France. Bonne vacances!

Author's Acknowledgments

Cheryl A. Pientka: I'd like to thank the following on this side of the pond: Mary Anne Pientka and John Pientka, Sean Stevens, Jen and Henry at the Henry Dunow Literary Agency, Alicia Patterson Giesa, G and G, Jean-Christian Agid and Patricia Gaviria Agid, Alice Alexiou, Daniel Simmons, Kelly Regan, Kimberly Perdue, and Ron Boudreau. In Paris, thanks go to Siobhan Fitzpatrick and Margie Rynn, Karen Fawcett, and Anne Deleporte.

Laura M. Reckford: Many thanks to my editor, Ron Boudreau, who with patience, skill, and a sense of humor turned this into a book. Also thanks go to Margaret Russell at the Falmouth Enterprise for holding my job while I cavorted around France. I am grateful to the staff of Centre Hospitalier Landerneau, who taught me a lot about the charm of Brittany. I thank my parents for teaching me about perseverance, and my French family, David, Laurence, Simon, and Matilda, who gave me a place to sleep and many tips along the way. Thanks to Tom, Kate, Dave, Edie, Guy, and Mado for moral support. And finally, I thank my friends Jonathan Akasten and Catherine Kelly, who traveled around with me, for better or worse.

Publisher's Acknowledgments

We're proud of this book; please send us your comments through our Hungry Minds Online Registration Form located at www.dummies.com

Some of the people who helped bring this book to market include the following:

Editorial

Editors: Ron Boudreau, Linda Brandon

Copy Editor: Greg Pearson

Cartographer: Roberta Stockwell

Editorial Manager: Christine Beck

Editorial Assistant: Jennifer Young

Senior Photo Editor: Richard Fox

Assistant Photo Editor: Michael Ross

Cover Photos: The Stock Market, ©Bo Zaunders

Production

Project Coordinator: Emily Wichlinski

Layout and Graphics: Amy Adrian, Joyce Haughey, LeAndra Johnson, Julie Trippetti

Proofreaders: Linda Quigley, TECHBOOKS Production Services

Indexer: TECHBOOKS Production Services

Special Help: Kathy Cox, Esmeralda St. Clair

General and Administrative

Hungry Minds, Inc.: John Kilcullen, CEO; Bill Barry, President and COO; John Ball, Executive VP, Operations & Administration; John Harris, CFO

Hungry Minds Consumer Reference Group

Business: Kathleen A. Welton, Vice President and Publisher; Kevin Thornton, Acquisitions Manager

Cooking/Gardening: Jennifer Feldman, Associate Vice President and Publisher

Education/Reference: Diane Graves Steele, Vice President and Publisher; Greg Tubach, Publishing Director

Lifestyles: Kathleen Nebenhaus, Vice President and Publisher; Tracy Boggier, Managing Editor

Pets: Dominique De Vito, Associate Vice President and Publisher; Tracy Boggier, Managing Editor

Travel: Michael Spring, Vice President and Publisher; Suzanne Jannetta, Editorial Director; Brice Gosnell, Managing Editor

Hungry Minds Consumer Editorial Services: Kathleen Nebenhaus, Vice President and Publisher; Kristin A. Cocks, Editorial Director; Cindy Kitchel, Editorial Director

Hungry Minds Consumer Production: Debbie Stailey, Production Director

◆

The publisher would like to give special thanks to Patrick J. McGovern, without whom this book would not have been possible.

◆

Contents at a Glance

Cartoons at a Glance

By Rich Tennant

page 7

"And how shall I book your flight to France — First Class, Coach, or Medieval?"

page 55

"It says, 'children are forbidden from running, touching objects, or appearing bored during the tour.'"

page 105

"Now THAT was a great meal! Beautiful presentation, an imaginative use of ingredients, and a sauce with nuance and depth. The French really know how to make a 'Happy Meal.'"

page 229

"Funny — I just assumed it would be Carnmes too."

page 283

"I'M PRETTY SURE YOU'RE SUPPOSED TO JUST SMELL THE CORK."

page 325

"Here's something. It's a language school that will teach you to speak French for $500, or for $200 they'll just give you an accent."

page 475

Cartoon Information:
Fax: 978-546-7747
E-Mail: richtennant@the5thwave.com
World Wide Web: www.the5thwave.com

Maps at a Glance

Table of Contents

Introduction

*Y*ou're going to *la belle France*. Bravo! Let us be the first to commend you on your excellent choice. France is a traveler's dream, with so many places to visit, sights to see, and things to do and with so much fabulous food and wine to savor. It's old Europe's cobblestone streets and soaring Gothic cathedrals mixed with new Europe's contemporary art and architecture. The French have mastered — and in some cases invented — the art of living well, and as a visitor you get to learn some of their tricks, like loitering in sidewalk cafes and lingering over five-course meals.

Sure, you'll probably want to start with Paris, one of the world's most romantic and sophisticated cities. Then you may have to make some choices. Will it be the castles of the Loire Valley, the chic towns of the French Riviera, or the historic sites in Normandy? Will you be spending time in the dappled sunshine of Provence or along the rocky coast of Brittany? This book helps you make those choices and nail down all the details for a perfect trip. So wrap a scarf around your neck and get ready to go to France!

About This Book

France For Dummies is a reference book, a critical tool for the first-time traveler, as well as a useful guide for those who've visited France before. There's no need to read it from front to back — just dive in wherever you want details on hotels, restaurants, sights, or travel tips. It would take a lifetime of travel to see all of France, so this book helps you make choices and narrow down your itinerary. In addition, it gives plenty of insider advice (the kind you'd get from a good friend) about the best places to visit, hotels to stay in, restaurants to try, and some pitfalls to avoid.

We tell you which fancy hotels and restaurants are worth a splurge and which cheap ones will do in a pinch. Planning a trip can be lots of fun, but we think the actual travel part is the best. So this guide is full of hints that help you with the nitty-gritty reality of travel, including some of those unexpected events that can't be planned for ahead of time. Likewise, we don't bog you down with unimportant details or mediocre sights; we give you just the good stuff — really the best of France.

Conventions Used in This Book

France For Dummies is a reference book, meaning you may read the chapters in any order you wish. We use some standard listings for hotels, restaurants, and sights. These listings allow you to open the book to any chapter and access the information you need quickly and easily.

Other conventions used in this book include the following:

- The abbreviations for credit cards: AE (American Express), DC (Diners Club), MC (MasterCard), and V (Visa).

- Hotels, restaurants, and sometimes attractions are listed in alphabetical order so that moving among the maps, worksheets, and descriptions is easier.

- Street abbreviations used throughout the book include *rue* (street), *bd.* (boulevard), and *av.* (avenue).

- The Paris *arrondissement*, or administrative district, is included in each address to give you a better idea of where each place is located. Paris is divided into 20 *arrondissements,* which are indicated by an ordinal number from first (in the very center of Paris, abbreviated *1er* in French) to 20th (on the outer edges of the city, abbreviated *20e* in French). They appear after the street address in each citation in this book. For example, "123 bd. St-Germain, 6e," indicates building number 123 on boulevard St-Germain in the 6th *arrondissement.* To get an idea of where each *arrondissement* is located, consult the "Paris Arrondissements" map in Chapter 11.

- For orientation in the Paris section, we list the nearest subway (or Métro) stop for all destinations (for example, Métro: Pont Marie).

- Two prices are provided for everything — first in the local currency (the franc) and second in U.S. dollars, rounded to the nearest dollar. Though exchange rates can and will fluctuate daily, and the rate probably won't be the same when you visit, the price conversions in this book were calculated at the rate of seven francs to one U.S. dollar.

All hotels and restaurants in this book are rated with a system of dollar signs to indicate the range of costs for one night in a double-occupancy hotel room or a meal at a restaurant, from "$" (budget) to "$$$$$" (splurge). Check out the following table to decipher the dollar signs.

Cost	Hotel	Restaurant
$	Under 700F ($100)	Under 125F ($18)
$$	700–1,000F ($100–$143)	125–200F ($18–$29)
$$$	1,000–1,500F ($143–$215)	200–300F ($29–$43)
$$$$	1,500–2,100F ($215–$300)	300–500F ($43–$71)
$$$$$	Over 2,100F ($300)	Over 500F ($71)

Foolish Assumptions

As we wrote this book, we made some assumptions about you and what your needs might be as a traveler. Maybe this is your first trip to France. Or maybe you've been to France but don't have a lot of time to spend on trip planning and don't want to wade through a ton of information. Perhaps you've been frustrated with other guidebooks that bore you with background but don't give enough of the helpful info you really need. If any of these apply, then *France For Dummies* is the perfect guide for you.

How This Book Is Organized

France For Dummies is divided into seven parts. The first two cover everything you need to plan your trip. Part III covers Paris and its environs. The other parts tackle the top regions of France, with all the best sights. You can read these parts independently if you want to zero in on the areas that interest you. Following are brief summaries of each of the parts.

Part 1: Getting Started

The five chapters that comprise Part I introduce France and touch on everything you need to consider before planning a trip. You find out the pros and cons of each season and region, develop a realistic budget, and discover a host of options available to travelers with special needs or interests. We also suggest some itineraries that help you see some of France's highlights.

Part II: Ironing Out the Details

In Part II are the nuts and bolts of trip planning, to help you answer questions such as, Should you use a travel agent or go it alone? How do you find the best flight to France? What's the best way to get around the country? What kind of accommodations should you use in France? We also advise you on how to tie up those frustrating last-minute details that can unnerve the most seasoned traveler.

Part III: Paris and the Ile de France

Chapters 11 to 13 make up Part III, which guides you through this most magical of cities and the surrounding area. After exploring all the ins and outs of Paris, we take you on day trips to Versailles, Fontainebleau, Chartres, Disneyland Paris, and Giverny.

Part IV: Tours and the Loire Valley Châteaux

In Part IV, we visit this beautiful region full of history and enchantment. Chapter 14 explores Tours, a lively college town and a good base for exploring the region. Chapter 15 visits eight château towns: Azay-le-Rideau, Chinon, Ussé, Chenonceaux, Chaumont, Blois, Amboise, and Chambord, with tours of the royal residences. Finally, we visit charming Orléans, another good base for exploring the region.

Part V: Normandy and Brittany

Part V is a tour of these authentic regions on the western coast of France. In Normandy, we visit Rouen, a city of half-timbered houses rich in history; Bayeaux, the site of the famous tapestry telling the adventures of William the Conqueror; the D-Day beaches, where allied forces dared to invade the mainland in 1944; and Mont-St-Michel, Europe's most famous abbey. In Brittany, there's Quimper, home of famous pottery; Carnac, site of France's most extensive Neolithic remains; and Nantes, a historic center between Brittany and the Loire Valley.

Part VI: Provence and the French Riviera

Two of France's best-loved regions are covered in Part VI. In Provence, we hit the famous towns of Avignon, Arles, and Aix-en-Provence, as well as the quaint village of St-Rémy. We also take a quick, safe look at Marseille. Along the Riviera, we stop in at ten towns: St-Tropez, Cannes, Biot, Antibes, Vence, St-Paul-de-Vence, Nice, St-Jean-Cap-Ferrat, Beaulieu, and Monaco.

Part VII: The Part of Tens

And no *...For Dummies* guide would be complete without The Part of Tens, a quick collection of fun tidbits: a list of French foods you *must* try and recommendations for the best gifts to buy in France.

Icons Used in This Book

Throughout this book, you'll notice in the margins little pictures called icons. Consider them signposts or flags to alert you to facts or information of particular interest.

This icon is a catchall for any special hint, tip, or bit of insider's advice that may help make your trip run more smoothly. Really, the point of a travel guide is to serve as one gigantic "tip," but this icon singles out the nuggets o' knowledge you may not have run across before.

This icon pegs the best bargains and juiciest money-saving tips. You may find a particularly value-conscious choice of hotel or restaurant, a discount museum or transportation pass, or simply a way to avoid spending more than you have to.

When you need to be aware of a rip-off, an overrated sight, a dubious deal, or any other trap set for an unsuspecting traveler, this icon alerts you. These hints also offer the low-down on the quirks, etiquette, and unwritten rules of the area — so you can avoid looking like a tourist and get treated like a local.

This icon, in addition to flagging tips and resources of special interest to families, points out the most child-friendly hotels, restaurants, and attractions. If you need a baby-sitter at your hotel, a welcoming and relaxed atmosphere at a restaurant, or a dazzling sight that delights your child, look for this icon. We include information regarding larger, family-sized rooms at hotels and restaurants that serve meals that go easy on your little one's tummy.

Sometimes a great hotel, restaurant, or sight may be located in a town or area that we don't have the room to include in this book. We let you in on these secret finds, and you can rest assured, we don't include any spots that aren't truly worth the energy.

Where to Go From Here

To France! And *France For Dummies* takes you there. If you're at the beginning of planning for your trip, you'll want to dig in to the next couple of chapters for tips on when and where to go. If you're ready to start picking hotels, skip right over Part I and jump into the rest of the book. To brush up on your French, flip to the back, where you'll find a glossary. As the French say, *Bonne continuation.*

Part I
Getting Started

In this part...

Planning the perfect trip to France is easy, especially if you answer a few basic questions. Where should I go? When should I go? How much will it cost? These opening chapters help you answer these questions so you can fine tune plans for your trip. Think about what you're most interested in seeing and experiencing. If it's French culture, you may want your trip to coincide with a festival or celebration. If it's the ultimate in food and wine, you should budget for a couple of splurge meals. If it's contemporary art, you'll want to hit the Riviera, which has the country's best selection of modern art museums.

Chapter 1 is an overview of the best France has to offer, so you can chose what you like most and focus your trip. Chapter 2 outlines the regions and seasons, then gives a list of the country's best annual festivals and events. Those who need help planning an itinerary can check out Chapter 3's five possibilities, which depend on your interests. Chapter 4 tackles budget issues, and Chapter 5 lists tips for those with special interests and needs.

Chapter 1

Discovering the Best of France

• •

In This Chapter

▶ Taking in the sights in Paris

▶ Reveling in France's art and architecture

▶ Enjoying French food and wine

▶ Perusing a brief history of France

• •

*F*rance is one of the most popular vacation sites for people traveling abroad, and its reputation for combining sophistication and
the art of fine living is unmatched. The country has long been at the
heart of European culture, with its elegant language, excellent cuisine,
and old-world charm. Traveling through France is like taking a crash
course in European history, because you can encounter everything
from Roman ruins and medieval villages to Gothic cathedrals,
Renaissance castles, early-1900s villas, and postmodern office blocks.
You can visit vineyards where the world's most prestigious wines are
made, or you can travel along the fabled French Riviera, a region long
frequented by the rich and famous.

Many travelers to France start with Paris and then, via planes or the
French rail system, visit areas like the Riviera or the Loire Valley.
France has such a multitude of diverse sites and distinct regions that
many French people spend every vacation exploring their own country.
However, because a typical tourist has only one or two weeks of vacation, you'll want to maximize the experience. The following is a handful
of essential aspects of France that you won't want to miss on your trip,
whether it's a long weekend in Paris or two weeks traveling around the
country.

Exploring the City of Light

The first stop for almost every first-time visitor to France is Paris,
one of the world's most beautiful and exciting cities. From the Arc de
Triomphe to Sacré-Coeur to the Tour Eiffel, Paris boasts France's most
recognizable and famous sites, as well as some of the world's top art
museums, such as the Musée du Louvre and the Musée d'Orsay. Paris

is a majestic city, laid out in the Middle Ages but fine-tuned to regal proportions in the eighteenth and nineteenth centuries, particularly under Napoléon III, who was emperor from 1851 to 1871.

Part of sightseeing in Paris is discovering its distinct neighborhoods, from the student-filled St-Germain-des-Prés on the Left Bank, to the stylish, gay-friendly Marais on the Right Bank, and up to the old artist haunt, Montmartre, which seems to sit above Paris. Though Paris has much to see and do, this is also a city that demands time for just strolling in parks and gardens and sitting in cafes, watching impossibly elegant people walk by as you sip coffee or wine. Shopping in Paris is lots of fun, whether you're seeking over-the-top luxury or something a little funkier (and cheaper). In the evenings, you can dine at a famous brasserie, enjoy an opera in the recently restored Opéra Garnier, and then hit the jazz clubs or discos for the late-night scene. But Paris nights are also the time when lovers can walk arm-in-arm beside the Seine, watching the moon rise over the soaring towers of the Cathédrale Notre-Dame. (See Chapters 11 and 12 for details on Paris.)

Paris is part of the Ile de France region, and nearby is a wide choice of day trips from the capital (see Chapter 13). You can see the extraordinary Château de Versailles, once home of the Sun King (Louis XIV); Fontainebleau, which served French monarchs from François I to Napoléon I; the High Gothic Cathédrale Notre-Dame in Chartres; Disneyland Paris, where you and your kids can party with Mickey and Minnie; and Giverny, the house and gardens where the Impressionist artist Claude Monet painted his famous series of waterlilies.

Viewing France's Art and Architecture: From Roman Ruins to Modern Masters

France has long embraced art in all its forms, and its museums contain some of the top collections anywhere. You can find everything from Roman antiquities to daring contemporary art — this is a culture that preserves the old but is still concerned about staying on the cutting edge. In Paris, you can visit the old masters at the Musée du Louvre, the Impressionists at the Musée d'Orsay, and the contemporary art at the Centre Pompidou, and then check out more intimate museums such as the Musée Picasso, the Musée National Auguste-Rodin, and the Musée National du Moyen-Age. The Riviera is another area rich in art museums, particularly those focusing on the Impressionists and twentieth-century art (see Chapter 19). From the Fondation Maeght in St-Paul-de-Vence to the Musée Matisse in Nice, art lovers will enjoy discovering these gems. You can also follow in the footsteps of artists like Gaugin in Pont-Aven, Matisse in Nice, Cézanne in Aix-en-Provence, and van Gogh in Arles.

From prehistoric stones to glass pyramids, you can find a host of historic sites and architectural treasures in France. Brittany offers France's most ancient site, the awesome field of megaliths at Carnac (see Chapter 17). You'll find a number of Roman ruins in Provence, especially in the towns of Arles, Orange, and St-Rémy (see Chapter 18). Medieval abbeys are scattered through the provinces, but the mother of all abbeys is Mont-St-Michel in Normandy (see Chapter 16). And throughout France are many awe-inspiring churches, including the Cathédrale Notre-Dame and Sainte-Chapelle in Paris; the Cathédrale Notre-Dame in Chartres, just 97 km (60 miles) southwest of the city; and the Cathédrale Notre-Dame in Rouen, which captivated painter Claude Monet. When people think of French villages, they may picture those quintessentially charming half-timbered houses of Normandy or the hilltop villages along the Riviera. But France contains wondrous modern structures, many of which are in Paris, such as the glass pyramid at the Louvre, the Grand Arche de la Défense, the Cité des Sciences et de l'Industrie, and the Bibliothèque National de François Mitterrand.

Tasting the Food and Sipping the Wine of France: A Moveable Feast

The French pride themselves on their food and wine, and you'll have a great time eating and drinking in the country. The first thing you may notice is how fresh everything is. Perhaps it's the soil (*le terroir,* as the French call it) that seems to invest all produce with rich flavor. Almost every town holds a daily fruit-and-vegetable market, so chefs throughout France have an abundance of fresh produce at their disposal. And this means you can stop at any market to soak in the atmosphere and gather the fixings for a memorable *pique-nique.*

While in France, you'll learn how to pace yourself through multi-course meals, to look forward to the cheese course, and to never skip dessert. There's virtually no turnover of tables in French restaurants, and customers are expected to settle in for at least a two-hour meal. Service usually moves at a leisurely pace because the idea is not to rush through the meal but to linger and enjoy the experience.

Throughout this book, I provide recommendations on top restaurants and medium-priced places that offer good value, so you can enjoy this most special cuisine.

Then there's the wine. First made by monks in wineries in the south, French wine is now big business, yet it's still essentially controlled by relatively small-time farmers. Most restaurants have a good selection of local vintages on hand, and you may be surprised at how reasonable the prices are when compared to what you'd be charged for a similar bottle at a restaurant outside France. House wines, available by the glass and the carafe, tend to be very reasonably priced as well.

After dinner, many towns in France offer exciting nightlife, but —
outside Paris — the biggest party takes place nightly along the Riviera.
Lovers of opulence and glamour won't want to miss the fabled Monte
Carlo Casino in Monaco, but exciting discos, nightclubs, bars, and
cafes flourish throughout the region. The late-night cafe scene is
always lively in university towns like Tours in the Loire Valley (see
Chapter 14), Aix-en-Provence in Provence, and Nantes, Brittany's historic capital. You'll find even more great cafes harborside in St-Tropez,
at the top of the village in St-Paul-de-Vence, and among the winding
streets of the old town of Nice (see Chapter 19).

Discovering Landmarks of History: From the Loire Valley Châteaux to the D-Day Beaches

France is full of intriguing historic sites, and every cobblestone street
seems to lead to a piece of history. But perhaps no region is as integral
to French royal history as the Loire Valley, where kings and queens
married, plotted, cheated, feuded, and generally carried on for 1,200
years. Today you can visit the castles where some of these events took
place. Whether you're interested in the largest castle, Chambord, or
the most beautiful, Chenonceau, in Sleeping Beauty's castle at Ussé, or
in the castle of Henri II's mistress at Chaumont, you'll get a taste of the
lifestyles of the rich and infamous from a distant age. Those who want
to see where today's royalty live can travel to the tiny principality of
Monaco on the French Riviera, where the Grimaldis' home, the Palais
du Prince, is perched high on a rock above the city.

Many other great historic sights are in France, including Normandy's
Bayeux Tapestry, a medieval scroll that tells the tale of William the
Conqueror's conquest of England. One of France's most popular historic attractions is the immense Palais des Papes in Avignon, where for
a short period in the fourteenth century France was the seat of the
leaders of Christendom. Those in search of the fifteenth-century story
of Joan of Arc can find parts of her tale in Chinon in the Loire Valley,
where she convinced the dauphin Charles VII to follow her into battle,
and in Orléans, where she led a French army that expelled the English.
Her tale ended in Rouen in Normandy, where she was burned at the
stake; a number of tributes to her are there, including a church dedicated to her. The most visited modern historic sights in France are the
D-Day beaches in Normandy. On this desolate coast, thousands of
brave men from England, Canada, and the United States participated in
some of the seminal battles of World War II.

Buying Beautiful Things: Bringing Back a Bit of France

One of the joys of purchasing anything in France, from a fruit pastry to a summer dress, is watching the salespeople wrap the package with great care and style. The French believe in the precious qualities of all objects and treat purchases with an almost sacred regard. You'll enjoy shopping in France, from the great department stores like La Samaritaine and Galeries Lafayette to the tiny boutiques and specialty stores. You can find famous French-made items like perfume, soap, and haute couture in Paris, of course, but every region also has its own craft or specialty item that will be a perfect memento of your trip. Whether it's pottery from Quimper (see Chapter 17) or hand-blown glass from Biot (see Chapter 19), you'll be able to find top-quality products everywhere. Shopping for high-end items on the Riviera is a pleasure in Cannes, Nice, St-Tropez, and Monaco, but you may have even more fun exploring the weekly flea markets and antiques markets in towns and villages.

Frolicking in the French Countryside

From the gardens and parks of Paris to the beaches of the Riviera, France offers a wide range of ways to explore the beauty of the country. In Paris, the periphery of the city is surrounded by the great parks, the Bois de Boulogne and Parc Monceau, where you can rent boats, horses, or bikes. People heading to the Atlantic coast will be able to take in the beaches of Normandy and Brittany. On the French Riviera, you can take walking tours of pedestrian-only hilltop villages like Biot, St-Paul-de-Vence, and Les Baux. Then there's the option of beaching it at the famous Riviera resorts of Antibes, Cap-Ferrat, Beaulieu, and the quintessentially hip St-Tropez.

Getting a Brief Taste of French History

France — with its centuries of monarchies, its fiery Revolution, its native son trying to conquer all of Europe, and its role in two world wars — has an extraordinarily complex and fascinating history. Countless influential artists, writers, and philosophers have emerged from this culture, which is both one of the most sophisticated and one of the most traditional of Western nations. The following brief overview may come in handy when you're sightseeing and trying to sort out just who did what to whom and when.

The area now known as France was originally called Gaul. In the first century B.C., it was conquered by the powerful **Romans,** led by Julius Caesar, and was ruled from Rome for 400 years. During that time, the Romans established their colony of **Lutetia** on the Ile de la Cité, an island in the Seine River in the center of what's now Paris. The French language evolved from the Latin of these early invaders. For the next 500 years, the **barbarians,** who were Germanic tribes, invaded Gaul and eventually settled there. One of these tribes, known as the Franks, gave their name to France.

Reigning over France

Clovis I (reigned A.D. 481–511) is considered the first king of France, though his influence was really restricted to the north of the country. He converted to Catholicism, united territories, and selected Paris as the capital. A couple hundred years later, along came **Charlemagne,** who reigned (768–814) over an area that extended from the Baltic to the Mediterranean and included parts of France, Germany, and Italy. Now here was a king the people could rally behind, a great general and bold ruler. The pope in Rome crowned Charlemagne Holy Roman Emperor in 800, giving a spiritual legitimacy to his rule. These were good times for scholarship and the arts.

France and Germany didn't become separated until 843, when Charlemagne's grandsons, Louis, Lothair, Pepin, and Charles, split the kingdom. **Charles the Bald** got France. He and **Louis** united against Lothair by taking the *Oath of Strasbourg,* the first known document written in French and German, instead of the usual Latin. Charles, who ruled over a region whose borders resembled the France of today, developed a complex feudal system.

In 1066, William, duc de Normandie, known in history as **William the Conqueror,** began a campaign to conquer England, and the Bayeux Tapestry in Normandy tells the dramatic tale. In 1152, **Eleanor of Aquitaine** stirred things up again between France and England when she divorced the king of France (Louis VII) and married the king of England (Henry II), placing western France under English rule. War between the two countries continued on and off for hundreds of years.

During the Middle Ages, the Catholic church was a powerful force in France. Holy men preached the **Crusades** in the twelfth and thirteenth centuries, inciting armies of men to journey to foreign lands in the name of the church. These so-called **holy armies** set off to conquer lands for the Holy Roman Emperor.

Over the next 700 years, five dynasties held the French crown and built the monarchy into one of Europe's most powerful. Of these kings, several stand out for their achievements in bringing about the France of today. An especially long and fruitful reign was that of **Louis IX** (1226–1270), called St-Louis. During his reign, Notre-Dame cathedral and Sainte-Chapelle were built on the Ile de la Cité in Paris. The arts of tapestry weaving and stone cutting flourished.

Philippe IV (the Fair), who reigned from 1285 to 1314, was instrumental in France gaining independence from the pope in Rome. Philippe had a French pope elected, **Clement V,** who transferred the Holy See to Avignon, where it remained from 1309 to 1378. For a brief period, two popes — one in Rome and one in Avignon — jockeyed for power. Rome eventually won out. In 1348, the Bubonic Plague, called the **Black Death,** wiped out a third of Europe's population. Meanwhile, the **Hundred Years' War** between France and England waged from 1337 to 1453. Things looked bad for the French until 1431, when a peasant girl named **Joan of Arc** led an army to take back Orléans and then accompanied Charles VII to Reims, where he was crowned king. In revenge, the English burned Joan at the stake in Rouen, a town they controlled, in 1431.

François I (1515–1547) brought the Italian Renaissance to France by becoming a patron to Leonardo da Vinci and other great Italian artists and architects. Around this time, the Protestant religion was gaining popularity, which led to discrimination by the ruling Catholics against the Protestants. From 1559 to 1598, the Wars of Religion pitted Catholics against the Protestant minority, reaching a crescendo when **Catherine de Médici,** widow of Henri II, ordered the St. Bartholomew's Day massacre, killing hundreds of Protestants on August 14, 1572. **Henri IV** (1589–1610) earned a place in the history books by signing the Edict of Nantes that guaranteed religious freedom to Protestants. The edict was revoked in 1685.

The sinister Catholic-cardinal-turned-prime-minister, **Cardinal Richelieu,** gained power from 1624 until his death in 1642 and paved the way for the absolute monarchy. **Louis XIV,** who had the longest reign in the history of France (1643–1715), became one of its greatest kings, expanding the kingdom and amassing great wealth. In 1664, he began construction of the palace of Versailles. During his reign, great writers (Pierre Corneille, Molière, Jean Racine) and architects (François Mansart) were celebrated. During the long reign of his great-grandson, **Louis XV** (1715–1774), great thinkers and philosophers like Voltaire, Jean-Jacques Rousseau, Montesquieu, and Denis Diderot voiced their opinions in the period known as the Age of Enlightenment.

Louis XV's grandson, **Louis XVI** (1774–1791), married **Marie Antoinette** of Austria in 1770, and their ostentatious manners proved to be the downfall of the French monarchy. From 1776 to 1783, following the maxim "the enemy of my enemy is my friend," France supported the North American colonists' quest for independence from England.

On June 20, 1789, representatives of the National Assembly met in the Versailles tennis court and swore **"The Tennis Court Oath"** to put together a Constitution for France with a legislative government. But impatient for reform, the people of Paris stormed the **Bastille** prison on July 14, 1789. The **Declaration of the Rights of Man** and the **Constitution** were drawn up later that year, and these documents are still cited as models of democratic values. But the mob couldn't be stopped. They arrested Louis XVI in 1791 and put him on trial. He was executed in 1792, the year France was declared a Republic, and Marie Antoinette was executed in 1793. The dreaded Revolutionary radical Robespierre led this **Reign of Terror,** in which over a thousand people were beheaded, that finally ended in 1794.

It took the short but powerful Corsican-born general **Napoléon Bonaparte** (1804–1815) to restore order to France after the Revolutionary fervor. In a 1799 coup d'état, Napoléon was named one of three in a ruling Consulate, but by 1802, he was made First Consul for life. In 1804, Napoléon crowned himself emperor and his wife, **Joséphine,** empress as the pope looked on. The following year, he was crowned king of Italy. By 1808, having occupied Vienna and Berlin and invaded Portugal and Spain, Napoléon seemed on his way to conquering Europe and brought great pride to the French. But after his disastrous retreat from Moscow in 1814, he abdicated and was exiled to Elba. Napoléon returned to power the following year and was defeated at Waterloo on June 18, 1815. After that crushing defeat, Napoléon was deported to the island of St. Helena in the South Atlantic and died there in 1821.

The monarchy was restored with **Louis XVIII** (1814–1824) and then **Charles X** (1824–1830). In 1830, **Louis-Philippe I,** descended from a branch of the Bourbons that ruled France on and off since the sixteenth century, was called king of the French, not king of France, under a more liberal constitution, but he was forced out of office in 1847. During these politically tumultuous but fairly prosperous years, Victor Hugo, Stendhal, and Honoré de Balzac wrote great novels. In 1848, Napoléon's nephew, **Louis-Napoléon Bonaparte,** was elected President of the Second Republic. In 1852, he assumed the title of emperor as Napoléon III and, with the help of **Baron Haussmann,** designed Paris's grand boulevards. In July 1870, a dispute over a telegram escalated into France declaring an ultimately unsuccessful war on Prussia. As a result of the military defeats and invasion of France by Prussia, Napoléon III was removed from office. The period of 1875 to 1940 is known as the Third Republic. Meanwhile, on the cultural scene, the artists known as the **Impressionists** scandalized the French Academy and forever changed art. And in 1889 at Paris's Universal Exposition, the **Eiffel Tower** was unveiled. Many Parisians hated it at first, but now it's the universally beloved symbol of Paris.

Creating a nation

World War I (1914–1918) was devastating for France, as 1.4 million of its people were killed and 300,000 wounded. The world-wide economic depression that followed severely weakened the government while

Germany gained power under the charismatic and acquisitive **Adolf Hitler.** France declared war on Germany in 1939, following the German invasion of France's ally, Poland. In 1940, the German army invaded France; the French army rapidly collapsed, and the Germans occupied the country. The period called the **Collaboration** is one of France's most shameful. The government was transferred first to Bordeaux and then, under the Nazi-approved President Pétain, to Vichy. French General Charles de Gaulle refused to accept the Armistice with Germany and Italy and broadcast a call for resistance from London on June 18, 1940. However, everything changed on June 6, 1944, when thousands of allied troops from the United States, the United Kingdom, and exiles from the invaded nations landed on the wind-swept shores of Normandy in the **D-Day** invasion. Brilliant allied military maneuvers led to the eventual surrender of Germany on May 8, 1945.

After the war, the **Fourth Republic** was set up in 1946. Insurrection in France's African and Asian colonies caused huge problems for the government. After suffering great losses, France withdrew from most of its colonies, including Indochina in 1954 and Algeria in 1962. In 1958, General de Gaulle returned to power with the **Fifth Republic.** In May 1968, university students joined with workers to create uprisings that paralyzed Paris and spread through the country. These led to de Gaulle's resignation in 1969. In 1969, Georges Pompidou became president, followed by Valéry Giscard d'Estaing in 1974. In 1981, the left came to power with the election of **François Mitterrand,** the first Socialist president since World War II. Mitterrand served two terms and bestowed on Paris famous *grands projets* like the Louvre pyramid, Opéra Bastille, and Grand Arche de la Défense.

Over the past decade, France has been heavily involved in the development of the **European Union,** the 12 countries that have banded together with a single currency and no trade barriers. In 1993, voters ousted the socialists and installed a conservative government that's now headed by **Jacques Chirac** as president. A decade of bombings, strikes, and rising unemployment all faded into the background on December 31, 1999, as **Paris's salute to 2000** with spectacular fireworks over the Eiffel Tower was one of the world's most spectacular celebrations.

In the past year, headlines of government scandals involving high-ranking officials have competed with news about Mad Cow disease, a virus that seemed to have originated in England and spread across Europe through greed and government misdeeds. At press time, about 90 people in Europe, mostly in the United Kingdom, have died from the human form of the virus, and thousands of cattle have been slaughtered to prevent its spread. News of the disease has captivated the public, as the quality of France's cherished food is at stake.

Chapter 2

Deciding When and Where to Go

* *

In This Chapter

▶ Exploring France's main areas of interest

▶ Choosing the best season to visit

▶ Finding events that suit your interests

* *

This chapter will help you decide which parts of France you want to visit and when to go. We give you the pros and cons of each season so you can time your trip to make the most of your visit. We also provide a calendar of the most memorable annual events in France — you may want to consider planning your trip to coincide with (or avoid) one of these festivals, sporting events, or celebrations.

Checking Out France's Points of Interest

France For Dummies is a book of highlights, so you won't find all of France's regions inside. What follows are short sketches of each of the regions covered in this book, in order to help you choose where you want to go. These are the ones with the best and most interesting sites, the blockbusters of France.

Falling in love with Paris: From the Tour Eiffel to Montmartre

France's capital is one of the world's most beautiful, romantic, and exciting cities. **Paris** is so full of things to see and do that you can't possibly cover everything in one trip, even one *long* trip. So don't even try. You may have to limit your sightseeing to the greatest hits — the Tour Eiffel, Cathédrale Notre-Dame and Sainte-Chapelle, the Musée du Louvre, the Musée d'Orsay, and Montmartre and Sacré-Coeur — in order to have plenty of time for strolling, shopping, and enjoying cafe society. If you start to get overcome by all the choices, chill out with a boat ride on the Seine or a picnic in the Luxembourg Gardens. One thing to consider about Paris: Expect rain every day and you won't be disappointed. (See Chapters 11 and 12 for details on Paris.)

Then check out the famous sights just outside the city (see Chapter 13), such as Louis XIV's breathtaking Château de Versailles, the Cathédrale Notre-Dame in Chartres, the Renaissance castle of Fontainebleau, Monet's house at Giverny with its famous waterlily pond, and even Disneyland Paris.

Exploring the Loire Valley Châteaux

The **Loire Valley**, an hour's train ride from Paris, is where France's royalty lived for hundreds of years, and their castles, many of them Renaissance masterpieces, are a lot of fun to visit. Because more than a dozen famous châteaux are within about 97 km (60 miles), this region is easy to explore. You'll even see plenty of people biking from castle to castle. We give you the lowdown on eight wonderful castles, including Chambord, the largest, and Chenonceau, the most beautiful (see Chapter 15). Remember not to overdo it: Two to four castles in one trip is about right before châteaux fatigue kicks in. We also introduce you to Tours (see Chapter 14) and Orléans, cities that bookend the region and are good bases to begin your exploration of the Vallée de la Loire.

Traveling through Normandy and Brittany

Normandy and Brittany, two regions on the west coast, offer a wealth of historic sites, as well as captivating coastal views. **Rouen,** just under an hour from Paris by the fast train, is a good place to see the Norman architecture that many people think of as quintessentially *ye olde world:* half-timbered houses on cobblestone pedestrian-only streets. In Rouen, you also find several interesting museums and historic sites, many relating to Joan of Arc, who was burned alive at the stake in the central square. And fans of Impressionism will enjoy seeing the elaborate Rouen Cathedral, which Monet, fascinated by its intricate façade, painted countless times.

Normandy is also the place to see two of France's most famous historic sights (see Chapter 16): the Bayeux Tapestry, in the charming village of Bayeux, and Mont-St-Michel, the most famous of all abbeys, set high on a rock just off the coast. (Mont-St-Michel is very popular with tourists, so we give you hints on how to avoid being trampled.) Many

The Regions of France

tourists go to Normandy just to see the D-Day beaches, where thousands of American, British, and Canadian troops bravely made their way to shore, paving the way for the allies' defeat of the Nazis in World War II. The soldiers' graveyards, white crosses stretching as far as the eye can see, may be the most moving site you'll ever see. The best season to see Normandy is in the fall, when the apple orchards are in bloom, the weather is fairly mild, and there are fewer tourists.

Brittany's rocky coast juts out along France's western edge, and the region is steadfastly proud of its unique culture and language, which is actually closer to Welsh than French (see Chapter 17). The coast is dotted with unassuming fishing villages, as well as pricey resorts. In Brittany, I take you to **Quimper,** home of the famous pottery; **Carnac,** which has thousands of aligned stones dating to Neolithic times; and **Nantes,** a lively city between Brittany and the Loire Valley. Brittany is a more remote region, a little harder to get to, which for some people makes it all the more attractive. Coastal towns in Brittany are popular summer resorts, and if you want to swim in the ocean, you'll need to go during the height of summer when the waters are warm enough. The fall and spring can be a desolate but appealing time to see this area, when the crowds are few and villages seem more peaceful.

Seeing the best of Provence and the Riviera

Provence and the Riviera may be France's most popular regions, and you also find the most tourists in the south of France. But that's because these are lovely areas to visit, full of interesting sites, wonderful food, and friendly people who have a bit of Italian *joie de vivre* mixed in with the classic French hauteur. And of course there's the weather: marvelous sunny days with refreshing sea breezes year-round. In **Provence** you see the great French towns of **Avignon,** home of the Palais des Papes; **Arles,** with Roman ruins and memories of the artist Van Gogh; and **Aix-en-Provence,** a beautiful city full of sparkling fountains. You can also visit the quaint village of **St-Rémy,** with more Roman ruins and more memories of Van Gogh. I also make a quick tour of **Marseille,** a rough town but a major transportation hub in the south. (See Chapter 19 for more on Provence.)

The **Riviera** has so many terrific towns that it's hard to choose which to visit (see Chapter 20). We guide you through the nine top French towns to visit plus the tiny country of Monaco. Along the coast from west to east are **St-Tropez, Cannes, Antibes, Nice, St-Jean-Cap-Ferrat, Beaulieu,** and **Monaco.** In the hills are **Biot, Vence,** and **St-Paul-de-Vence.** You can hang out at the most fashionable beaches, stroll through cobblestone villages, see some of France's best modern art museums, and participate in the glamorous nightlife. From the Monte Carlo Casino to the beaches of St-Tropez, this slice of France is a slice of heaven.

Knowing the Secret of the Seasons: What to Expect

As in much of Europe, *high season* in France is summer and *low season* is winter, leaving the *shoulder seasons* of spring and fall as good times to visit (fewer crowds, decent weather). One exception to this is winter on the Riviera, which is popular with retirees. Paris is a rainy city much of the year and quite cold and bleak in winter, but during those dark days of February, the crowds are low and so are the airfares.

The French government has mandated that store sales happen twice a year, in January and in late June/early July. They last for two weeks, first in the north (Paris and environs) and then in the south (the Riviera and environs). Every French person takes a vacation in August, so you find the biggest crowds that month, as well as a number of closings at restaurants, particularly in Paris. Many stores, restaurants, and hotels throughout the country also close for a few weeks in December or January. But one of the best things about a summer visit is you can bask in daylight that lasts until 10 p.m. Table 2-1 gives you an idea of what the temperatures are like in Paris throughout the year.

Table 2-1   Average Daytime Temperatures for Paris

Jan	Feb	Mar	Apr	May	June	July	Aug	Sept	Oct	Nov	Dec
38°F	39°	46°	51°	58°	64°	66°	66°	61°	53°	45°	40°
3°C	4°	8°	11°	14°	18°	19°	19°	16°	12°	7°	6°

Spring

George Gershwin sang "I love Paris in the springtime," and with good reason. The parks and gardens of Paris (as well as those at Versailles, Fontainebleau, and Claude Monet's Giverny) are at their colorful, fragrant best in early May. But keep in mind that April in Paris isn't as temperate as Gershwin would have you believe. Count on the weather being very fickle, so pack for warm, cold, wet, dry, and every other eventuality (bring layers and don't even think about coming without an umbrella).

In the rest of France, particularly the coastal areas of Normandy, Brittany, and the Riviera, spring is off-season, so you'll be blessed with short lines for sites and museums. You may also be able to get reservations in the country's top restaurants, which are fully booked come summer. Airfares have yet to reach their summertime highs, and you may even find a bargain. Nearly every Monday in May is a holiday in France, so stores may be closed and other venues affected. Unless you're a race car fanatic, don't go anywhere near Monaco during the **Grand Prix** in mid-May. Hotel prices in Monaco and surrounding towns are at their highest and are booked well in advance.

Summer

Wonderfully long and sultry days are summer's hallmark — we're talking 6 a.m. sunrises and 10 p.m. sunsets — so you're afforded additional hours to wander and discover. Historic sites, museums, and shops keep longer hours and are usually open during lunch, unlike the rest of the year. You can find discounts of 30–50% in most stores during late June and early July, one of the two big months for shopping sales (January is the other). But remember that an influx of tourists during summer means long lines at museums and other sites throughout the country. Because most French people take their vacations in August, you find tourist areas packed throughout the country.

In Paris, the city's cultural calendar slows down, and some shops and restaurants still close for the entire month of August. But in areas like Provence and the Riviera, the cultural calendars are at their fullest. Late June to early August is the time of many of the country's top festivals in the south, like Nice's **Grand Parade du Jazz** and **the Festival d'Avignon** and **Festival d'Aix-en-Provence.** The summer is also the time to see cultural festivals throughout the country. And let's not forget the great bike race **Le Grand Tour de France** in July. Keep in mind that on July 14, **Bastille Day,** stores and most sites throughout the country are closed; in Paris, however, festivals are held and terrific fireworks take place at the Eiffel Tower.

Fall

Fall is a wonderful time to visit France. The wine harvest starts mid- to late September, and by mid-October the country's vineyards are a golden color. The days are often clear and crisp. Paris crackles back to life come September, one of the most exciting times of the year, when important art exhibits open along with trendy new restaurants, shops, and cafes. Airfares drop from summertime highs. But keep in mind that finding a hotel at the last minute in fall can be difficult due to the number of business conventions and trade shows happening in Paris and other cities like Orléans, Tours, Rouen, Nantes, Cannes, and Nice. And transportation strikes of varying intensities traditionally occur during fall — some may go virtually unnoticed by the average traveler, but others can be a giant hassle. Be aware that in some seashore areas, like Brittany, some restaurants close for a couple of weeks in October to take a breather from the busy summer.

Winter

You can find great airfare deals during winter, when airlines and tour operators often offer unbeatable prices on flights and package tours. Lines at museums and other sights are mercifully short. And if shopping is your bag, you can save up to 50 percent during the January sales.

In Paris, winter is gray (sometimes the sun doesn't shine for weeks), dreary, and often bone-chillingly damp. And look out for those wind tunnels that lash up and down the city's grand boulevards. Bring a warm, preferably waterproof, coat.

Hitting the Big Events: A France Calendar

Running into one of France's great festivals is truly a joy when you're traveling, but unless you plan ahead, you have no guarantee. The following is a list of just the very best special events around the country.

January

Monte Carlo Motor Rally. Mid-January; Monaco. This is one of the world's most famous car races. For more details, call ☎ **92-16-61-66.**

International Ready-to-Wear Fashion Shows (Le Salon International de Prêt-à-porter). Mid-January to mid-February; Paris. Taking place at the Parc des Expositions, Porte de Versailles, this is one of the premier fashion shows in the city that practically invented fashion. For more details, call ☎ **01-44-94-70-00.**

February

Carnival of Nice. Mid-February to early March; Nice. France's biggest Mardi Gras celebration is the renowned Carnival of Nice, attracting hundreds of thousands of revelers. The highlight of the event is the Mardi Gras parade with dozens of giant floats, but smaller parades occur during the daytime and evenings, as well as boat races, concerts, street music and food vendors, masked balls, and fireworks. The Niçoise's love of flowers is celebrated in the Battle of Flowers, when opposing teams throw flowers at each other. For details, call ☎ **04-92-14-48-00** (Fax: 04-92-14-48-03; Internet: www.nicetourism.com).

March

Foire du Trône. Late March to end of May; Paris. Tacky and fun, this annual carnival has a Ferris wheel, rides and games, hokey souvenirs, and fairground food all set up at the Pelouse de Reuilly in the Bois de Vincennes. For details, call ☎ **01-46-27-52-29.**

April

Paris Marathon. Mid-April; Paris. One of the most popular athletic events during the year, this race runs past a variety of the city's most beautiful monuments. Held on a Sunday, the marathon attracts enthusiastic crowds. For details, call ☎ **08-36-68-31-12** or 01-49-52-53-35 (Fax: 01-49-52-53-00; Internet: www.paris-touristoffice.com).

May

Cannes Film Festival. Mid- to late May; Cannes. The world's most famous film festival takes over this seaside resort for almost two weeks in May. With thousands of reporters and photographers jockeying for position, it's not easy for a civilian to get close to the stars. The town also becomes very expensive, with hotel rooms at a premium and booked far in advance. Most film screenings are by invitation only, so don't count on seeing the latest films. Your best bet for a star search is to have lunch at one of the expensive beachfront restaurants attached to the grand hotels along the coast. For more details, call ☎ **01-42-66-68-85** (Fax: 01-45-61-97-60). If you need info less than two weeks before the festival, call ☎ **04-93-39-01-01.**

Monaco Grand Prix. Mid-May; Monaco. This is Monaco's biggest event of the year, and with the crowds and the noise, you have to really love car racing for this one. Hundreds of race cars speed through Monaco to the fascination of thousands of fans. For details, call ☎ **01-42-96-12-23.**

French Open. Last week in May and first week in June; Paris. Tickets are hard to come by for this major tennis tournament, held in the Stade Roland Garros in the Bois de Boulogne on the western edge of the city. Tickets go on sale two weeks before the competition starts. The stadium is at 2 av. Gordon Bennett, 16e. For details, call ☎ **01-47-43-48-00** or visit www.fft.fr.

June

Fireworks at La Villette. Mid-June; Paris. Once a year, by invitation, a famous architect or designer plans a fireworks celebration along the banks of the canal de l'Ourcq between the modern museums and gardens of the Musée de la Musique and the Cité des Sciences et de l'Industrie. For details, call ☎ **08-36-68-31-12** or 01-49-52-53-35 (Fax: 01-49-52-53-00; Internet: www.paris-touristoffice.com).

Festival Chopin à Paris. Mid-June to mid-July; Paris. The Orangerie in the beautiful Bagatelle gardens on the edge of the Bois de Boulogne is the backdrop for this much-loved annual series of daily piano recitals. For details, call ☎ **01-45-00-22-19.**

Fête de la Musique. June 21; country-wide. The entire country becomes a concert venue in celebration of the first day of summer, and you can hear everything from classical to hip hop for free in squares and streets around Paris and other cities. A big rock concert usually happens in place de la République in Paris, and a fine classical concert generally takes place in the gardens of the Palais Royal. For details, call ☎ **08-36-68-31-12** or 01-49-52-53-35 (Fax: 01-49-52-53-00; Internet: www.paris-touristoffice.com).

Paris Air Show. Mid-June; Paris. One of the most distinguished aviation events in the world takes place in odd-numbered years (2001, 2003) at Le Bourget Airport just outside Paris. You can check out the latest aeronautic technology on display. For details, call ☎ **08-36-68-31-12** or 01-49-52-53-35 (Fax: 01-49-52-53-00; Internet: www.paris-touristoffice.com).

Gay Pride. Late June; Paris. Art exhibits and concerts as well as a fantastic parade are held in the Marais neighborhood and in other Paris streets, including boulevard St-Michel. For details, call ☎ **01-43-57-21-47.**

July

Les Baroquiales. Early July; towns near the French Riviera and Italian border. This cultural festival spotlights the baroque style, the seventeenth-century mode of art and architecture that features elaborate ornamentation. Events are presented cooperatively by tourism bureaus in France and Italy with music, theater, and dance concerts, as well as walking tours and village fairs. Because this annual event is relatively new, you won't find as many crowds or problems with reservations. For details, call ☎ **04-93-04-92-05.**

Bastille Day. July 14; country-wide. The biggest party on Bastille Day is in Paris. Citywide festivities begin on the evening of June 13, with street fairs, pageants, and feasts. Free *bals* (dances) are open to everyone and held in fire stations all over the city. (Some of the best bals are in the fire station on rue du Vieux-Colombier near place St-Sulpice, 6e; rue Sévigné, 4e; and rue Blanche, near place Pigalle, 9e.) On July 14, a big military parade starts at 10 a.m. on the Champs-Elysées; get there early if you hope to see anything. A sound-and-light show with terrific fireworks is held that night at the Trocadéro; rather than face the crowds, many people watch the fireworks from the Champs de Mars across the river, from hotel rooms with views, or even from rue Soufflot, in front of the Panthéon.

Tour de France. Three weeks in July; country-wide. The most famous bicycle race in the world covers more than 2,000 miles throughout France and always ends in Paris on the Champs-Elysées. Spectators need special invitations for a seat in the stands near place de la Concorde, but you can see the cyclists farther up the Champs-Elysées and, depending on the route (which changes each year), elsewhere in the city, too. Check the newspapers the day before. For details, call ☎ 01-41-33-15-00.

Nice Jazz Festival (Grand Parade du Jazz). Ten days in early to mid-July; Nice. Inspired by the great American jazz performers, this international jazz festival is one of the Riviera's biggest annual events. It draws famous soloists and bands to the spectacular site of the Roman Amphitheater and gardens of Cimiez, the hill north of the city. In the past, performers like Dizzy Gillespie and Herbie Hancock have brought down the house. For details, call ☎ 04-93-92-82-82 (Fax: 04-93-92-82-85).

Festival d'Avignon. Mid-July to early August; Avignon. This world-class cultural event presents works in theater, dance, and music from international troupes. The focus is usually on the avant-garde; the festival is prestigious, and tickets are pricey. During the same period as the festival, another festival called Festival Off takes place, sort of the off-off-Broadway version with less expensive events and less established performers. For details, call ☎ 04-90-82-65-11 (Fax: 04-90-82-95-03).

Festival d'Aix-en-Provence. Mid-July; Aix-en-Provence. This is primarily a music festival with a wide range of styles, from medieval to contemporary. The events are more affordable at this festival than those in the previously described neighboring festival at Avignon. For details, call ☎ 04-42-17-34-34 (Fax: 04-42-66-13-74).

September

Journées Portes Ouvertes. Weekend closest to September 15; Paris. Off-limits palaces, churches, and other official buildings throw open their doors to the public for two days. Long lines can put a damper on your sightseeing, so plan what you want to see and show up early (with a good book, just in case). Get a list and a map of all the open buildings from the Paris Tourist Office, reachable at ☎ 08-36-68-31-12 or 01-49-52-53-35.

Festival d'Automne. September 15 to December 31; Paris. This arts festival held around Paris is recognized throughout Europe for its innovative programming and the high quality of its artists and performers. Obtain programs through the mail so that you can book ahead for events you don't want to miss. For details, call ☎ 01-53-43-17-00.

International Ready-to-Wear Fashion Shows (Le Salon International de Prêt-à-porter). Late September; Paris. Taking place at the Parc des Expositions, Porte de Versailles, this is one of the premier fashion shows in the city that practically invented fashion. For more details, call ☎ 01-44-94-70-00.

October

Fêtes des Vendanges à Montmartre. First or second Saturday of October; Paris. Celebrate the harvest of the wine produced at Montmartre's one remaining vineyard, Clos Montmartre, and watch as the wine is auctioned off at high prices to benefit local charities. (Word of advice: *Don't bid!* The wine isn't very good.) Locals dress in period costumes, and the streets come alive with music. For details, call ☎ 08-36-68-31-12 or 01-49-52-53-35 (Fax: 01-49-52-53-00; Internet: www. paris-touristoffice.com).

Les Voiles de St-Tropez. Early October; St-Tropez. This wonderful event is an antique wooden sailboat regatta in glamorous St-Tropez on the Riviera. It's a tossup whether the most beautiful sight is when all the boats in the bay are under full sail or when they're all docked in the harbor so you can get a close look at their gleaming hulls. During the week-long festival, the town is full of youthful sailors from all over the world and evenings are very lively. For details, call ☎ 04-94-97-45-21.

FIAC (Foire Internationale d'Art Contemporain). Early October; Paris. One of the largest contemporary art fairs in the world, the FIAC has stands from more than 150 galleries, half of them foreign. As interesting for browsing as for buying, the fair takes place in Espace Eiffel Branly, near the Eiffel Tower. For details, call ☎ 08-36-68-31-12 or 01-49-52-53-35 (Fax: 01-49-52-53-00; Internet: www.paris-touristoffice.com).

November

Les Trois Glorieuses. Third week in November; Clos-de-Vougeot, Beaune, Meursault, Burgundy. France's most prestigious wine festival is held annually in three towns in Burgundy, featuring wine tastings galore and lots of street fairs. The biggest event is the wine auction in Beaune, which attracts wine connoisseurs from around the world. Getting a room in Beaune or nearby villages is very difficult during this event. For details, call ☎ 03-80-26-21-30.

Lancement des Illuminations des Champs-Elysées. Late November; Paris. The annual lighting of the avenue's Christmas lights makes for a festive evening, with jazz concerts and an international star who pushes the button that lights up the avenue. For details, call ☎ 08-36-68-31-12 or 01-49-52-53-35 (Fax: 01-49-52-53-00; Internet: www.paris-touristoffice.com).

December

La Crèche sur le Parvis. December 1 to January 3; Paris. Each year a different foreign city installs a life-sized Christmas manger scene in the plaza in front of the Hôtel de Ville (City Hall). The crèche is open daily 10 a.m. to 8 p.m.

The Boat Fair (Le Salon International de la Navigation de Plaisance). Early December (lasts for eight days); Paris. The Boat Fair is Europe's most visible exposition of what's afloat and of interest to wholesalers, retailers, and individual boat owners. The fair takes place at Parc des Expositions, Porte de Versailles, Paris, 15e (☎ **01-41-90-47-10;** Fax: 01-41-90-47-00; Métro: Porte de Versailles).

Fête de St-Sylvestre (New Year's Eve). Nationwide, December 31. In Paris, it's mainly celebrated in the Latin Quarter near the Sorbonne with crowds of merrymakers in the streets. Wide streets like boulevard St-Michel and the Champs-Elysées are filled with pedestrians.

Trip-Planning Tips

When visiting France, a large country with so many diverse sights, the biggest challenge may be deciding what regions you want to visit. You can't do it all, but you can see and do quite a lot in just a week. Here are some things to keep in mind when planning your trip:

- ✔ **Make choices.** Choose one region or at most two adjoining regions to visit in addition to Paris, unless you're planning a long trip. You'll get a much better feel for the region you visit, and you won't spend so much time en route to places. Good regions to combine are Normandy and Brittany and Provence and the Riviera.

- ✔ **Take the train.** France's train system is exceptionally fast and efficient. And in 2001, new TGV (high-speed) trains to the Riviera are running up to half an hour faster. The best way to travel to the regions described in this book is to catch a train from Paris and then either rent a car or rely on public transportation if you plan to travel to several smaller towns. If possible, you want to avoid driving in and out of large cities such as Paris, Nantes, Rouen, and Nice. The outskirts of these cities aren't at all scenic, and the complex highways and tailgating drivers can make you loony. Our advice is to take the train from Paris to explore large cities and then rent a car. That way, you'll at least avoid driving in and out of Paris, which can be a nightmare. You could also choose to take a train to a small town in the region and rent a car from there. In contrast to city driving, you'll find that driving along country roads in France can be a real pleasure. Roads are well marked and are often uncrowded.

✔ **Avoid disappointment and book ahead.** Many people visit France regularly to stay at the top hotels and dine in the top restaurants. If you're planning to splurge on an expensive hotel or a three-Michelin-star meal, be sure to book well ahead of time. A week or two in advance isn't too early to make a reservation for the country's top restaurants, and booking a couple months in advance is a good idea for the best hotels.

✔ **Expect strikes.** France is infamous for its strikes, and oddly the French have a very blasé attitude toward what can be a major inconvenience. The more common strikes usually have to do with transportation. Here are some examples from 2000: Railroad pullmen on strike meant no food or water on long train rides. Air traffic controllers on strike meant cancelled flights into, out of, and around the country. Gas delivery trucks on strike meant no gas at gas stations for two weeks. Subway strike in Paris . . . Well, you get the point. The possibility of strikes means you shouldn't cut it close with travel plans. If you absolutely *must* be at a meeting back home on Monday morning, you'd better plan to leave Saturday, not Sunday, night.

✔ **Enjoy the lifestyle.** One reason French people may not be as annoyed by strikes as other nationalities may be is that they have a fairly laid-back attitude toward life. To the French, certain pleasures — like great food, fine wines, and beautiful art — make life worth living. How does this affect you, the visitor? Instead of filling every second of your day running from sight to sight, try to slow down a little and appreciate the details. Spend an afternoon writing postcards in a cafe or strolling through a historic neighborhood. Amble through a village market or visit an unusual monument. And, above all, don't skip meals.

✔ **Adjust to French mealtimes.** The French eat a light continental breakfast, and you can learn to love a scrumptious *pain au chocolat* and *café au lait* first thing in the morning. You'll find that many things are closed between noon and 2 p.m., as that's when many French people have a long lunch. Although you can probably find a museum or a shop open during this time in most of the country, do yourself a favor and have lunch then, too. Dinner starts after 7:30 p.m. That long lunch should tide you over until then. The more you fit yourself into the French timetable, the more you'll enjoy your trip and feel like one of the natives.

Chapter 3

Four Great Itineraries

● ●

In This Chapter

▶ Touring France in one or two weeks

▶ Visiting France with your kids

▶ Reviewing a tour for art lovers

● ●

*I*n this chapter, we've put together several itineraries to help you plan your trip if you're unsure how to do it on your own. If you're a first-time or time-pressed traveler with one or two weeks to spend in France, you may find it helpful to have some must-see destinations and sights laid out in an easy-to-follow order. Or if you've been to France before, perhaps you'd like to concentrate this visit on food and wine or on great art. You can have an extraordinary taste of the country in just one or two well-planned weeks.

Most of the regions in this book are within a short train ride of Paris. That means you can easily combine a few days in the capital with visiting the highlights of Normandy and the Loire Valley, both are just one or two hours away by train. Brittany and Provence are slightly longer trips by train (three to four hours). If you're traveling from Paris to Nice on the Riviera (6½ hours), you may want to take a very early train, so you don't waste the whole day traveling.

 While traveling, give yourself the freedom to be flexible: If you end up loving a town that you were supposed to stay in for just one night, you can change things around and stay for two nights or more. We once ran into a couple in St-Tropez who were supposed to be traveling all along the Riviera and decided to stay in St-Tropez for their entire trip because they loved it so much!

The following itineraries take you through some wonderful towns and past some great sights. The pace may be a bit breathless for some people, so be sure to skip a sight occasionally in order to spend some down time. Of course, you can use any of these as a jumping-off point to develop your own itinerary that perfectly matches your interests.

Seeing France in One Week

Use the following itinerary to make the most of your week in France, but feel free to leave out a sight or two in order to explore a charming village or stay an extra day just to relax. One week is a perfect amount of time to get an introduction to Paris and see the sights of Normandy, a region on the west coast of France not too far from Paris.

Get a flight that arrives in **Paris** as early as possible on **Day One.** Check into your hotel and hit the nearest cafe for a pick-me-up *café au lait* and croissant before sightseeing. Try to see one major and one minor (less time-consuming) sight your first day in Paris. Major sights include the **Musée de Louvre, Tour Eiffel, Musée d'Orsay,** and **Cathédrale Notre-Dame.** Minor attractions include the **Arc de Triomphe, Sainte-Chapelle** and the **Conciergerie, Musée Rodin, Centre Pompidou,** the **Tuilleries** and **Luxembourg Gardens,** and **Montmartre** and **Sacré-Coeur.** Buy and send postcards and wander around to get your bearings. That night, enjoy dinner at the famous brasserie **Bofinger** or one of the many restaurants in the stylish Marais district.

On **Day Two,** try to see one major and two minor sights. Of course, on the way to these sights, in particular Notre-Dame and Sainte-Chapelle, you'll inevitably have quintessential Paris experiences like walking along the **quais of the Seine** and visiting the **St-Germain neighborhood** on the Left Bank.

On **Day Three,** take an early-morning train to **Versailles.** You need several hours to tour the palace and the gardens. Return in the afternoon for tea at **Angelina,** shopping at the fancy food shop **Fauchon,** and a late dinner. (See Chapter 12 for details on exploring Paris.)

On **Day Four,** take an early train to **Rouen** in Normandy (see Chapter 16), check your bags at the train station, and walk around the city for a couple of hours, seeing the half-timbered buildings. After lunch, rent a car and drive to **Bayeux,** where you'll spend the night. On the way, you can stop to explore beautiful **Abbaye de Jumièges.**

On the morning of **Day Five,** see the famous **Bayeux Tapestry** and then drive to the **D-Day beaches,** stopping at the **American Cemetery** and the **Caen Memorial.** That evening, drive to **Mont-St-Michel** (less than two hours) and stay overnight in the pedestrian village on the rock. If it's summer, you can take an illuminated night tour of the abbey — after most of the other tourists have gone home. Or you can do the first tour in the morning on **Day 6** before all the tour buses arrive. Then drive back to Rouen and take the train back to Paris and your flight home.

Seeing France in Two Weeks

With two weeks to explore France, you won't feel too rushed and will be able to have some breathing room. You'll also be able to see several regions: Paris, two Loire Valley castles, a couple of towns in Provence, and several towns on the Riviera, including Monaco.

You can spend **Day One, Two,** and **Three** in **Paris,** as covered under "Seeing France in One Week." On **Day Four,** leave Paris on an early train to **Orléans** (trip time 1¼ hours). Rent a car in Orléans and drive to see the **Château de Chambord,** the largest of the Loire Valley castles. That afternoon, drive to **Amboise** to stay overnight and visit the **Château d'Amboise** and **Leonardo da Vinci's home.** (See Chapter 15 for details on exploring the Loire Valley.)

On **Day Five,** get an early start and return the rental car in Orléans. You have a choice now: You can take a morning train from Orléans to Paris's **Gare d'Austerlitz** and then take the Métro or a taxi to the Gare de Lyon, where you'll hop on a TGV (fast train) to **Avignon** (3 hours, 20 minutes). Or you can take a train from Orléans to **Lyon** and change to a train for Avignon. Check into your hotel in Avignon. You should have time to wander through the town to get your bearings, buy some colorful Provençal fabrics, and see one of the smaller sites in Avignon, such as the **Pont St-Bénézet** (also known as the Bridge of Avignon) or the **Musée du Petit-Palais.** (See Chapter 18 for details on Provence.)

On the morning of **Day Six,** see the **Palais des Papes**. After lunch, rent a car and drive to **St-Tropez,** wander around the village, and people-watch from one of the cafes along the harbor. Spend the night in St-Tropez.

On **Day Seven,** hit the beach in St-Tropez or visit the **Musée de l'Annonciade,** with its lovely selection of Impressionist paintings. In the afternoon, drive to **Nice** (108 km/67 miles). Check into your hotel, wander through the **old town,** stroll on the **promenade des Anglais,** lie on the beach, walk through the **Marché aux Fleurs,** or visit one of the less time-consuming sights, such as the **Palais Lascaris, Musée International d'Art Naïf Anatole-Jakovsky, Musée of Beaux-Arts, Cathédrale Orthodoxe Russe St-Nicholas à Nice, Musée d'Art Moderne et d'Art Contemporain,** or **Musée d'Art et d'Histoire Palais Masséna.** During the day, stop for a snack of *socca,* a round crêpe made with chickpea flour that's sold steaming hot by street vendors. Have dinner at one of the charming restaurants in Nice's old town. You'll find a number of Italian restaurants, as well as restaurants offering traditional Niçoise cuisine, which has Italian influences. You can also take the **Train Touristique de Nice** for a 40-minute sightseeing ride past the major sights. (For detailed information on towns in the Riviera, go to Chapter 19.)

On **Days Eight and Nine,** see more of Nice and head up to the suburb of **Cimiez** to see the **Musée Matisse, Monastère de Cimiez,** and **Roman ruins,** all next to one another, and the **Musée National Message Biblique Marc Chagall,** a short drive away. On **Day Ten,** drive to **Monaco.** On the way, stop in **Beaulieu** for lunch and to see the **Villa Kérylos,** a replica of an ancient Greek residence that overlooks the sea. Arrive in Monaco, check into your hotel, get decked out, have dinner at the **Café de Paris** and head to the **Monte Carlo Casino** for a night of glamorous gambling. On **Day Eleven,** explore Monaco's many sights, like the changing of the guards in front of the **Palais du Prince** (and the interior, called the **Grands Appartements du Palais);** the **Jardin Exotique,** a cactus garden built into the side of a rock; the **Musée de l'Océanographie,** which includes one of Europe's best aquariums; the **Collection des Voitures Anciennes de S.A.S. le Prince de Monaco,** Prince Rainier's personal antique car collection; and the **Musée National de Monaco,** with a large antique doll collection. On **Day Twelve,** head back toward Avignon to return the rental car, stopping for an overnight on the way in one of three towns: **St-Paul-de-Vence,** a hilltop village of art galleries; **Grasse,** an ancient town and the perfume capital of France; or **Aix-en-Provence,** one of France's most beautiful cities. After your stay in one of these charming towns, drop off the car in Avignon on **Day Thirteen** and then take the TGV train back to Paris for your return flight home.

Enjoying France with Kids

France offers many attractions that kids will enjoy. Perhaps your main concern with kids along is pacing yourself with museum time. Many of Paris's attractions are fascinating for children, like the **Tour Eiffel** (they'll love the elevator) and **Notre-Dame** (be sure to point out the gargoyles at the top). Of course, Paris is full of parks and gardens with playgrounds for children. Two favorites are the Jardin du **Luxembourg,** with a popular playground and puppet shows, and the Jardin des **Tuilleries,** with a fountain used for toy boats, and in summer a *grand roue* (Ferris wheel).

One suggestion is to take parts of the itinerary that I recommend for two weeks and bring your kids to the **Loire Valley castles** and/or to the **Riviera.** You can fit a Loire Valley castle or a town on the Riviera into a one-week trip. If you have two weeks, you can travel around more extensively. Most kids enjoy a beach vacation, and the Riviera has plenty to entertain them. The people-watching alone is likely to leave them wide-eyed (be aware that they'll see plenty of skin; topless bathing is rampant), and there's always lots of free entertainment in summer along the boardwalk in **Nice,** called the **promenade des Anglais.** In the tiny principality of **Monaco** on the Riviera, kids will enjoy the formal changing of the guard ceremony at the palace and the tour of the interior apartments. But the best part of Monaco for kids is the **Musée de l'Océanographie,** one of Europe's best and biggest aquariums, with lots of sharks and other exciting sea creatures. Monaco also has the **Collection des Voitures Anciennes de S.A.S. le Prince de Monaco,** Prince Rainier's personal antique car collection, and the **Musée National de Monaco,** with a large antique doll collection.

Taking the Art Buff's Tour

The art buff's tour of France definitely must begin in **Paris,** one of the world's great cities for art. You could spend two weeks at the **Musée de Louvre** and still not see everything, but you'll certainly want to spend at least a half a day there. Then you can move on to the **Musée d'Orsay** for the Impressionists. (Don't attempt these huge museums on the same day though.) For contemporary art, you can hit the **Centre Pompidou.** Then if you want to hang out at some artists' haunts, head to St-Germain on the Left Bank or take the Métro up to Montmartre, where you'll still find a few hopeful, hungry artists with easels set up in place du Tertre. Paris offers many more wonderful art museums, from the recently remodeled medieval collection at the **Musée de Cluny** to the **Musée Picasso** and **Musée Rodin.** The **Grand Palais** usually has a blockbuster art exhibit going, for which you'll probably need to reserve a ticket in advance.

After you've had a taste of Paris's art offerings, take a day trip to see Monet's house and garden at **Giverny,** where you can ponder the famous lily pond. Then take a high-speed TGV train south to **Nice** on the Riviera. All along the Riviera are wonderful modern art museums. For a selection of Nice's art museums, see the two-week itinerary earlier in this chapter. Matisse and Chagall buffs will enjoy the museums devoted to those artists in the suburb of Cimiez. Easy day trips west by rental car will take you to the **Chapelle du Rosaire** designed by Matisse in Vence, **Fondation Maeght** in St-Paul-de-Vence, which has one of the country's best modern art collections, the **Musée National Fernand-Léger** in Biot, and the **Musée Picasso** in Antibes.

Chapter 4

Planning Your Budget

. . . .

In This Chapter

▶ Developing a workable budget

▶ Uncovering hidden expenses

▶ Cutting costs

. . . .

*S*oit raissonable (be reasonable), the French say, and being reasonable is the key to budgeting a trip to France. A good way to figure out a budget is to mentally walk through the trip, from the minute you leave to the minute you get back home (figure in your transportation to and from the airport). Then add in the flight cost (see Chapter 6 for tips on how to fly to France for less), the price of getting from the airport to your hotel, your hotel rate per day, meals, public transportation costs, admission prices to museums and the theater, other entertainment expenses, and souvenir costs. Afterward, add 15 to 20 percent for good measure. To help you record your estimates, we include several budget worksheets — look for our very own "yellow pages" at the end of the book.

Adding Up the Elements

Cities are rarely cheap or expensive across the board; Paris tends to be pricey for dining but reasonable for accommodations. Other cities, towns, and villages in France are much less expensive than Paris for both dining and lodging, though prices for historic sites are similar all over the country. In addition, outside Paris, your franc goes further. For example, a four-course dinner in the provinces will cost the same as a two-course dinner in Paris.

This section covers some guidelines for what you're likely to spend while in France.

Getting to and around France

The biggest item in your budget will probably be your airline ticket to France, and that can range from those great deals that pop up in winter (like $99 each way, New York to Paris) to $500 each way if you don't shop around for bargains. Make sure you check out our money-saving tips before you buy your airline tickets.

Transportation within France offers many options. Almost every town mentioned in this book can be accessed by public transportation, either train or bus. If you're traveling long distances by train (say from Paris to the Riviera), consider buying a French Rail Pass (see Chapter 7). In Paris, the Métro has been the model for subways around the world since its inauguration in 1900 — it's one of the best transit systems around in terms of price and efficiency. Getting across town in less than half an hour is no problem, and the cost is lower if you purchase one of several discount tickets, such as a *carnet* of ten tickets (see Chapter 11 for options and prices).

Renting a car gives you more flexibility than using public transportation does, but it's expensive, mainly because of the high cost of gas in Europe, which will set you back about $50 per tank for a medium-sized car. (That's not a misprint.) You also have to pay to park a car in most French cities and towns. That said, several regions lend themselves to driving, like the Loire Valley. And if you want to see some of the smaller towns on the Riviera, a rental car is the best way.

As for cars in Paris — well, expect your heart to be in your throat the entire time you drive in Paris — unless, of course, you thrive on dealing with labyrinthine one-way streets, a dearth of parking spaces, hellish traffic, and the statistically worst drivers in Europe. If you want to rent a car to see other parts of France or make a day trip outside Paris, do it on your way out of the city (see Chapter 11 for addresses and phone numbers of Paris car-rental agencies).

Looking for lodging

Before you start shelling out money for lodging, think about how much time you'll actually spend in your room. For 300 to 500F ($43 to $71) in Paris, and slightly less in the rest of the country, you can rent a clean but functionally furnished hotel room with a private bathroom and cable TV. Though these kinds of budget rooms are normally comfortable and have the basic furnishings and decor, they're supplied with thin but serviceable towels and a less-than-stellar array of toiletries (often just a bar of soap). For 700F ($100) and up, the upper-tier hotels offer bigger rooms and more services, such as room service and air-conditioning.

Regional variations in hotel rates occur, from the most popular areas to the least popular. In addition, hotels in virtually all the regions covered in this book have higher rates in summer. The prices are highest in Paris, especially compared to what you can get for the same price in other regions. The prices are also high on the Riviera, which happens to offer some of France's most famous palace hotels. Nevertheless, you can find medium-priced and even cheap hotels in every town in this book, and we give you a wide range of choices. You may want to plan one or two splurge nights, just to get a feel for how wonderful the service is and how exquisite the accommodations are in France's top hotels.

You can certainly save money by not having breakfast at your hotel, which normally runs 40 to 60F ($6 to $9) for a continental breakfast (hot beverage, bread, croissant) at medium-priced hotels. You can get the same thing for less by bellying up to the counter at a cafe nearby — and you can feel more like a native.

All the hotel reviews in this guide list the high-season rack rates (the rate the hotel quotes you) and use a specific number of dollar signs to indicate the general price range. The dollar signs correspond to the following amounts:

$ up to 350F (up to $50)

$$ 350–700F ($50–$100)

$$$ 700–1050F ($100–$150)

$$$$ more than 1050F ($150 and up)

Keep in mind, however, that because of exchange rates, these prices can change quite a bit. A hotel that at press time costs $$$ may be $$ when you get to France if the dollar is strong or $$$$ if the dollar is weak. And what was $$$ at press time may be $$$$ when you arrive in France because the hotel may have completed a renovation and raised prices. Table 4-1 gives you a taste of what things will cost in Paris, while Table 4-2 shows you the cost of similar items in one of France's provinces.

Table 4-1	What Things Cost in Paris
Taxi from Charles de Gaulle Airport to the city center	$31
Taxi from Orly Airport to the city center	$24
Public transportation for an average trip within the city (from a Métro *carnet* of 10)	80¢
Local telephone call	35¢
Glass of wine	$2.60
Coca-Cola (at a cafe)	$3.45
Café au lait	$4.00
Roll of ASA 100 color film, 36 exposures	$8
Average hotel room for two	$180
Dinner at a medium-priced restaurant, per person	$30
Admission to the Louvre	$6
Movie ticket	$8
Concert ticket (at the Salle Pleyel)	$11

Table 4-2	What Things Cost in Chinon, Loire Valley
Local telephone call	35¢
Coca-Cola (at a cafe)	$2.57
Café au lait	$2.14
Roll of ASA 100 color film, 36 exposures	$7
Rental car for a weekend	$80
A play in the nearby city of Tours	$9
Average hotel room for two	$43
Dinner at a medium-priced restaurant, per person	$28
Admission to the castle at Chinon	$4

Dining out

Unless you like expensive hotels, you should expect to pay more for dining in France than for lodging. The French consider dining out one of the finer joys in life, and they pay for it. But you can get a memorable five-course meal with wine at a medium-priced restaurant anywhere in France, except Paris, for about 200 to 250F ($29 to $36) per person. In Paris, that gets you a decent three-course meal. Paris also has a wide range of cheaper dining options (in addition to the most expensive restaurants in France). For example, you can find restaurants serving satisfying two-course meals for as little as 125F ($18) and wonderful ethnic food and sandwich shops that help you save even more money.

The best way to save money on meals in France is by choosing what's called *le menu,* the fixed-price meal with two or three choices for each course (first course, main course, dessert). The fixed-price menu often includes the cheese course or a choice between the cheese course and the dessert course. At the better restaurants, the fixed-price menu includes two main courses: a fish course and a meat course. At top res-taurants, you'll see a very expensive *menu dégustation* or tasting menu, which includes all the chef's specialties. Choosing a fixed-price menu is always cheaper than ordering à la carte, and it's a much better value.

Alas, *le menu* isn't as common at Parisian restaurants as in the rest of the country, where you find at least a couple and sometimes five or six menus to choose from. If you choose a medium-priced menu (not the cheapest, not the most expensive), you'll usually get an excellent meal, which often includes chef's specialties and high-quality items like the "catch of the day." Sometimes menus include a glass of wine with one or more courses, and some even include coffee at the end of the meal. Needless to say, to get your money's worth, you need to be hungry!

If your budget is limited, consider buying a picnic lunch or dinner at a town or village market. You'll be wowed by the selection of fresh pro-duce, breads, meats, and cheeses on display. Buy a bottle of wine at a grocery store and you're all set for a wonderful French meal. For this type of meal, a Swiss army knife with corkscrew comes in very handy.

Seeing the sights

Entry fees to museums and other sights can add up quickly. First refer to the money-saving advice at the end of this chapter and in Chapter 9; then make a list of must-dos to get a feel for how much money to set aside. Many towns in France, including Paris, offer special museum passes that'll save you money if you plan to see more than a couple of attractions. These passes are always available at tourist offices and sometimes at historic sites as well. Throughout this guide, we let you know if these passes are available. Keep in mind that occasionally sights are free on certain days (like the first Sunday of every month). You can get this info at the local tourist office.

Shopping without breaking the bank

France (especially Paris) is a shopping paradise, and French shopkeep-ers arrange their wares in windows so enticingly that you'll be tempted to splurge. Shopping is the most flexible part of your budget, and you'll certainly save a lot of money if you skip a few shopping excursions. But France has wonderful things to buy, and in each chapter we list some great shops to look for if you're in the mood for souvenirs. You can find some amazing deals during the semi-annual sales held in January and July, but remember that a steep 20.6 percent tax (TVA or value-added tax) is added to most goods. If you live outside the European Union, you're usually entitled to get back part of the tax, if you meet certain requirements. See Chapter 9 for more information.

Spending a night on the town

Budget big if you plan to visit clubs and other nightspots; nightclubs and bars aren't cheap in France, because cover charges and those drinks really add up. But nightlife is also one of the great pleasures of France, particularly in Paris and other larger cities. So don't forego the spectacles at the Moulin Rouge or Folies Bergère in Paris if you've always wanted to see them. Just know beforehand that they charge a small fortune for entry and alcoholic beverages. Plan on seeing the show without dinner and you'll save some money. In addition, some cities have great free nightlife, such as street performers and musicians along the beach promenade in Nice. In fact, just wandering around the old cobblestone streets of some French towns in the evening can be quite entertaining.

Keeping a Lid on Hidden Expenses

It tends to be the small things that you don't think about that add up and burst your carefully planned budget. But if you keep the following tips in mind, you can avoid some of the most common money-wasting traps.

In restaurants, the tip is already included (*service compris* — the 15 percent is already figured into the bill), and though technically unnecessary, a small additional tip for satisfactory service (10F/$1.45 per person for a moderately priced meal) is considered appropriate. Don't tip a bartender for each round of drinks — instead leave 5 to 10F (70¢ to $1.45) at the end of the night. Hotel service personnel should get 5F per luggage item or service performed, and taxi drivers generally are tipped 10 percent of the fare. If an usher shows you to your seat in a cinema or theater, tip 5F.

Don't think a cafe is a cheaper alternative to a restaurant. A simple meal of *croque monsieur* and *pommes frites* (a toasted ham-and-cheese sandwich with french fries) accompanied by a beer or soda can set you back $15 or $20. You can get a much tastier meal at the same price or less at a restaurant.

Here are some cost-cutting strategies to keep in mind:

- ✔ **Fly during the week rather than on weekends.** Also you can save on airfare and dining if you travel during the off-season, the period from approximately October to March.

- ✔ **Try a package tour.** By making one call to a travel agent or searching the Internet for package deals, you can book airfare, hotel, ground transportation, and even some sightseeing for many destinations, especially the Riviera, for a lot less than if you tried to put the trip together yourself. (See Chapter 6 for specific companies to call.)

- ✔ **Pack light.** You won't need a cart or a taxi to carry your load.

- ✔ **Take the cheapest way into Paris from the airport.** You can save around $30 by taking a train or bus instead of a cab from Charles de Gaulle and about $15 from Orly, both located in Paris.

- ✔ **Book your hotel room early.** Those at the best prices fill up quickly.

- ✔ **Negotiate the room price, especially in the low season.** Ask for a discount if you're a student or over 60; ask for a discount if you stay a certain number of days.

- ✔ **Reserve a room with a kitchen.** It may not seem like much of a vacation if you do your own cooking and dish washing, but you can save a lot of money by not eating in restaurants three times a day. Even if you only make breakfast and pack an occasional bag lunch, you may have a little extra cash for those gifts for your family and friends back home. And you won't need to fret about a hefty room service bill.

- ✔ **Stay at a hotel that doesn't insist you take breakfast and dinner.** Breakfast can add at least $5 a day to your bill, and dinner at a hotel restaurant in a resort area (those are the ones that usually insist on two-meal-a-day plans in season) will run you at least another $35. Instead, buy a croissant or a *pain au chocolat* (croissant filled with chocolate) from a *boulangerie* (bread bakery) for about $2. By all means go out to dinner, but give yourself the freedom to choose a less expensive place or substitute a picnic occasionally.

- ✔ **Make lunch your main meal.** Many restaurants offer great deals on a fixed-price (*prix fixe*) lunch. After two or three courses at midday, you won't want a big dinner. Lunch is definitely the way to go for those splurge meals you've budgeted for. Lunch at a fancy French restaurant is almost half the price of dinner.

- ✔ **Try the ethnic neighborhoods in Paris or the larger cities.** In Paris, you can get terrific Chinese food in the 13e *arrondissement* (neighborhood) between place d'Italie and porte de Choisy; and the 10e, 18e, and 20e have North African, Turkish, Vietnamese, and Thai. Couscous is on the menu at many restaurants and is usually an inexpensive offering. Throughout the book, I've listed less expensive restaurants and neighborhoods where you can find cheap ethinic meals in larger cities.

✔ **Remember that the plat du jour is usually the cheapest main dish at a budget restaurant.** Often the special of the day will include a starter and a main course or a main course and dessert.

✔ **Remember that a glass of house wine is cheaper than soda.** Also some mineral waters are less expensive than others. Ask for tap water (*une carafe d'eau*), which is free.

✔ **Know the tipping rules.** Service is usually included at restaurants; don't double-tip by mistake.

✔ **Have drinks or coffee at the bar.** You pay twice as much when you're seated at a table.

✔ **In Paris, use the Métro or else walk.** When in Paris, buy a *carnet* of ten Métro tickets at a time — a single ticket costs10F ($1.35), while a carnet ticket is 6F (85¢). Better yet, if you know you're going to be in Paris from one to five consecutive days, buy a **Paris Visite pass,** good for unlimited subway and bus travel.

✔ **If you plan to visit two or three museums a day in Paris, buy the Carte Musées et Monuments.** Most cities in France have similar museum passes. The pass costs 80F ($11) for one day, 160F ($23) for three days, and 240F ($34) for five days.

✔ **Take advantage of the reduced admission fee at museums.** The reduced price usually applies after 3 p.m. and all day Sunday.

✔ **For discounts on fashion in Paris, try rue St-Placide in the 6e arrondissement.** Look for stylish inexpensive clothes at Monoprix or Prisunic, located all over the city.

✔ **In Paris, buy half-price theater and other performance tickets.** You can find them at one of the kiosks by the Madeleine, on the lower level of the Châtelet–Les Halles Métro station, or at the Gare Montparnasse.

✔ **At clubs, avoid weekends if you want to save money.** Also you can save money by sitting at the bar instead of at a table. Some clubs are cheaper than others, and some are cheaper during the week.

Finally, in general, *always ask for discount rates.* Membership in AAA, frequent-flyer plans, trade unions, AARP, or other groups may qualify you for savings on car rentals, plane tickets, hotel rooms, even meals. Ask about everything; you could be pleasantly surprised.

Chapter 5

Planning Ahead for Special Travel Needs

• •

In This Chapter

▶ Visiting France with children

▶ Getting discounts for seniors

▶ Locating wheelchair-accessible attractions and accommodations

▶ Identifying resources for gay and lesbian travelers

▶ Travelling solo

• •

*W*hether it's the food, the history, the breathtaking art and architecture, or that inimitable French *joie de vivre* (joy of living), France ranks among the most visited of all tourist destinations, and more resources than ever make it available — and enjoyable — to all. This chapter covers the how-to guides, tour companies for disabled travelers, and English-speaking baby-sitters that are only some of the ways that travelers with special needs are making the most of France these days.

Taking the Family Along

France has a very family-oriented culture, so you should feel free to bring your kids along. They'll undoubtedly be wide-eyed by the cultural differences and interested in the unusual historic sights. However, you may want to reconsider taking children to the fanciest hotels and restaurants unless they're very well behaved. Some of these establishments have a somewhat inhospitable reaction to screaming tots. Throughout the book, the Kid Friendly icon lets you know which hotels and restaurants are best for kids. Your best indication for kid-friendly restaurants is if they have *enfant* (child) menus, which will be posted outside. Many historic sights and museums are free or half-price for kids. In addition, you'll be pleased to know that children are well cared for in most of France.

Don't let anyone talk you out of taking your kids to Paris. The City of Light is full of attractions worthy of your children's attention, and your kids will only benefit from the experience — probably longer than you will! Parks and playgrounds and kid-specific sights and museums abound, along with interesting boat rides and bike tours. Paris is also safer than most big cities.

Getting kids ready for France

If you plan your trip well in advance, your kids may get a kick out of learning the language from one of the many French-language video-tapes on the market. Books like Ludwig Bemelmans's *Madeline* series, Albert Lamorisse's *The Red Balloon,* and Kay Thompson's *Eloise in Paris* are great for kids under 8. You can order them from the **Forum Français** in Wellesley, Massachusetts (☎ **781-239-0658;** Fax: 781-237-9083; Internet: www.forumfrancais.com), or the **Librairie Française** in New York, New York (☎ **212-581-8810;** Fax: 212-265-1094). Older teens might appreciate Ernest Hemingway's *A Moveable Feast,* Victor Hugo's *Les Misérables,* Rose Tremain's *The Way I Found Her*, and Peter Mayle's books about Provence.

Preview some of the museums and other sights that you want to visit (see the sidebar "Ten Web sites to browse with your children" below) by checking out their Internet sites. Children under 18 are admitted free to France's national museums (though not necessarily to Paris's city museums). If you stay long enough, consider a day trip to Disneyland Paris, easily accessible by public transportation (see Chapter 13 for more information).

Ten Web sites to browse with your children

Checking out some of the following Web sites with your children is a wonderful way to introduce them to the sights they'll find in Paris and the rest of France.

- **Avignon and Provence:** www.avignon-et-provence.com
- **Brittany:** www.brittany-guide.com
- **Châteaux in the Loire Valley:** www.chateauxandcountry.com
- **Cité des Sciences et de l'Industrie:** www.cite-sciences.fr
- **Disneyland Paris:** www.disneylandparis.com
- **The French Riviera:** www.beyond.com
- **Les Catacombes:** www.multimania.com/houze
- **Musée de Louvre:** www.louvre.fr
- **Musée d'Orsay:** www.musee-orsay.fr
- **Tour Eiffel:** www.tour-eiffel.fr

If your children are under 12 and you're traveling by rail through France, check out the **Carte Enfant Plus.** Available at any SNCF (French National Railroads) station, it offers a 50-percent discount for the child and up to four adult travel companions. The card costs 330F ($47) and is good for a month, but only a limited number of seats are available and the discounts aren't offered for periods of peak travel or on holidays. Reserve in advance.

Although the French people love kids and welcome them just about everywhere, they do expect them to be well-mannered. Proper behavior is expected, especially in restaurants and museums. French children are taught at an early age to behave appropriately in these settings, and French adults expect the same from your kids.

Bringing along baby

You can arrange ahead of time for such necessities as a crib, bottle warmer, and, if you're driving, a car seat (small children are prohibited from riding in the front seat). Find out if the place you're staying stocks baby food; if not, take some with you for your first day and then plan to buy some. Plenty of choices are available. Transportation in Paris isn't as stroller-friendly as in the United States. Be prepared to lift your child out of the stroller to board buses and climb up and down stairs and/or walk long distances in some Métro stations. The upside to all of this is that you and your child can be strolling in some of the world's prettiest parks and gardens.

Locating some helpful resources

If you need a baby-sitter in Paris, consider one of the following agencies that employ English-speaking caregivers: **Ababa** (8 av. du Maine, 15e; ☎ 01-45-49-46-46); **Allo Maman Poule?** (7 villa Murat, 16e; ☎ 01-45-20-96-96); or **Kid Services** (17 rue Molière, 9e; ☎ 01-42-61-90-00). Specify when calling that you need a sitter who speaks English. If you need a babysitter anywhere else in France besides Paris, check with the local office of tourism and they'll be able to make recommendations.

The books *Family Travel* (Lanier Publishing International) and *How to Take Great Trips with Your Kids* (The Harvard Common Press) are full of good general advice that can apply to travel anywhere. Another reliable tome with a worldwide focus is *Adventuring with Children* (Foghorn Press).

You can also check out *Family Travel Times,* published six times a year by Travel with Your Children, 40 Fifth Ave., 7th floor, New York, NY 10011 (☎ 888-822-4FTT or 212-477-5524; Internet: www.familytraveltimes. com). It includes a weekly call-in service for subscribers. Subscriptions are $39 a year. A free publication list and a sample issue are available on request.

Teenagers will be fascinated by the beach scene on the Riviera, or any other beach scene in France for that matter. In addition, older children may enjoy some of the more spectacular attractions like the Palais des Papes in Avignon and the Château de Chambord in the Loire Valley. Teens also seem to love France's cafe society, where you can find a central spot to sit and people-watch for hours on end.

Searching Out Bargains for Seniors

While in France, don't be shy about asking for senior discounts and always carry a form of ID that shows your date of birth. And mention that you're a senior when you first make your travel reservations. People over age 60 qualify for reduced admission to theaters, museums, and other attractions, as well as for other travel bargains like the 285F ($41) **Carte Senior,** which entitles holders to an unlimited number of train rides and reductions of 20 to 50 percent on train trips (except during holidays and periods of peak travel). The Carte Senior also allows some discounts on entrance to museums and historic sites. It's valid for one year, and you can buy it at any SNCF station anywhere in France. Be prepared to show an ID or a passport as proof of age when you buy the card.

If you're not already a member, join the **American Association of Retired Persons** (AARP), 601 E St. NW, Washington, DC 20049 (☎ 800-424-3410; Internet: www.aarp.org), for discounts on hotels, airfares, and car rentals. As a member, you're eligible for a wide range of special benefits, including *Modern Maturity* magazine and a monthly newsletter.

You get discounts on hotel and auto rentals and a magazine that's partly devoted to travel tips if you join the nonprofit **National Council of Senior Citizens,** 8403 Colesville Rd., Suite 1200, Silver Spring, MD 20910 (☎ 301-578-8800; Internet: www.ncscinc.org). Annual dues are $13 per person or couple.

Members of **Mature Outlook,** P.O. Box 9390, Des Moines, IA 50306 (☎ 800-265-3675), receive discounts on hotels and a bimonthly magazine. Annual membership is $19.99, which includes discounts and coupons for discounted Sears merchandise.

Available by subscription ($30 a year), *The Mature Traveler,* a monthly newsletter on senior travel, is a valuable resource. A free sample can be had by sending a postcard with your name and address to GEM Publishing Group, Box 50400, Reno, NV 89513, or by e-mailing your information to maturetrav@aol.com. GEM also publishes *The Book of Deals,* which lists more than 1,000 senior discounts on airlines, lodging, tours, and attractions around the country, and can be purchased for $9.95 by calling ☎ 800-460-6676. *101 Tips for the Mature Traveler* is another useful publication and is available from

Grand Circle Travel, 347 Congress St., Suite 3A, Boston, MA 02210 (☎ **800-221-2610;** Internet: www.gct.com).

Hundreds of travel agencies currently specialize in senior travel, one of which is Grand Circle. However, many of these vacations are of the tour-bus variety, which may cramp the style of an independent senior. One bonus of these tour-bus packages is that free trips are often thrown in for organizers of groups of 20 or more. Obtain travel information from **SAGA International Holidays,** 222 Berkeley St., Boston, MA 02116 (☎ **800-343-0273**), which offers inclusive tours and cruises for those 50 and older.

Accessing France: Advice for Travelers with Disabilities

Alas, features that make French towns so beautiful — uneven cobblestone streets, quaint buildings with high doorsills from the Middle Ages, and sidewalks narrower than a wagon in some areas — also make using a walker or a wheelchair a nightmare. According to French law, newer hotels with three stars or more are required to have at least one wheelchair-accessible guest room. However, most of the country's budget hotels, exempt from the law, occupy older buildings with winding staircases and/or elevators smaller than phone booths and are generally not good choices for travelers with handicaps. On the bright side, many hotels have at least one ground-floor room, which may suffice. In addition, the tourist office in the town you're visiting will be able to give you information on hotels with facilities for people with disabilities.

In Paris, the public transportation system isn't the most accessible to folks with mobility problems. Few Métro stations have elevators, and most feature long tunnels, some with wheelchair-unfriendly moving sidewalks and staircases. Escalators often lead to a flight of stairs, and many times when you climb up a flight of stairs, you're faced with another set of stairs leading down. Wheelchair lifts are currently not standard equipment on city buses, and they don't "kneel" closer to the curb to make the first step lower.

But don't let these inconveniences change your mind about visiting France.

Before your trip, contact the **French Government Tourist Office** for the publication (with an English glossary) *Touristes Quand Même.* It provides an overview of facilities for the disabled in the French transportation system and at monuments and museums in Paris and the provinces. You can also get a list of hotels in France that meet the needs of disabled travelers by writing to **L'Association des Paralysés de France,** 22 rue de Père Guérion, 75013 Paris (☎ **08-00-85-49-76**).

You can contact the **Groupement pour l'Insertion des Personnes Handicapées Physiques** (Help for the Physically Handicapped), Paris Office, 98 rue de la Porte Jaune, 92210 St-Cloud (☎ 01-41-83-15-15), and Les Compagnons du Voyage of the **RATP** (☎ 01-45-83-67-77; Internet: www.ratp.fr/voy_q_eng/f_travel_eng.htm) for help in planning itineraries using public transportation.

In Paris, the newly built line 14 of the Métro is wheelchair accessible, as are the stations Nanterre-Université, Vincennes, Noisiel, St-Maur–Créteil, Torcy, Auber, Cité-Universitaire, St-Germain-en-Laye, Charles-de-Gaulle–Etoile, Nanterre-Ville, and several others. Bus no. 91, which links the Bastille with Montparnasse, is wheelchair accessible, as are new buses on order. Some high-speed and intercity trains are also equipped for wheelchair access, and a special space is available in first class (at the price of a second-class ticket) for wheelchairs, though you must reserve well in advance.

A good English-language guide for disabled travelers is *Access in France,* which you can obtain by calling ☎ 020-1250-3222 or writing to **RADAR,** Unit 12, City Forum, 250 City Road, London EC1V 8AF. It costs £13.95 (approximately $10).

More options and resources for disabled travelers are available than ever before. Check out *A World of Options,* a 658-page book of resources for disabled travelers, which covers everything from biking trips to scuba outfitters around the world. The book costs $35 and can be ordered from **Mobility International USA,** P.O. Box 10767, Eugene, OR, 97440 (☎ 541-343-1284, voice and TYY; Internet: www.miusa.org). Another place to try is **Access-Able Travel Source** (Internet: www.access-able.com), a comprehensive database of travel agents who specialize in disabled travel and a clearinghouse for information about accessible destinations around the world.

Travelers with disabilities may also want to consider joining a tour that caters specifically to them. One of the best operators is **Flying Wheels Travel,** P.O. Box 382, Owatonna, MN 55060 (☎ 800-535-6790; Fax: 507-451-1685), offering various escorted tours and cruises, as well as private tours in minivans with lifts. Another good company is **FEDCAP Rehabilitation Services**, 211 W. 14th St., New York, NY 10011. Call ☎ 212-727-4200 or fax them at 212-727-4373 for information about membership and summer tours.

Vision-impaired travelers should contact the **American Foundation for the Blind,** 11 Penn Plaza, Suite 300, New York, NY 10001 (☎ 800-232-5463), for information on traveling with Seeing-Eye dogs.

Tips for Gay and Lesbian Travelers

France is one of the world's most tolerant countries toward gays and lesbians, with no laws discriminating against them. In fact, many French cities — including Paris, Nice, and St-Tropez — are meccas for gay travelers. In Paris, where famous gay people like Oscar Wilde, James Baldwin, and Gertrude Stein once lived, same-sex couples are treated with polite indifference by everyone from hotel clerks to servers.

If you're looking for detailed coverage of the hottest gay areas in France, check out *Frommer's Gay & Lesbian Europe* (Hungry Minds, Inc.), with fabulous chapters on Paris and Nice and the Côte d'Azur.

In Paris, the gay center is the **Marais neighborhood,** stretching from the Hôtel de Ville to place de la Bastille. The biggest concentration of gay bookstores, cafes, bars, and clothing boutiques is here, as well as the best source of information on Parisian gay and lesbian life, the **Centre Gai et Lesbien** (3 rue Keller, 11e; ☎ 01-43-57-21-47; Métro: Bastille). The center's staff coordinates the activities and meetings of gay people around the world. Centre Gai et Lesbien is open daily 2 to 8 p.m.

Another helpful source in Paris is **La Maison des Femmes** (163 rue Charenton, 12e; ☎ 01-43-43-41-13; Métro: Charonne), which has a cafe and a feminist library for lesbians and bisexual women. It holds meetings on everything from sexism to working rights and sponsors informal dinners and get-togethers. Call Monday, Wednesday, or Friday 3 to 8 p.m. for more information.

In Paris, gay magazines that focus mainly on cultural events include *Illico* (free in gay bars, about 12F/$1.70 at newsstands) and *e.m@le* (available free at bars and bookstores). *Lesbia* is a magazine that caters to lesbians. You can find these magazines and others at Paris's largest and best-stocked gay bookstore, **Les Mots à la Bouche** (6 rue Ste-Croix-la-Bretonnerie, 4e; ☎ 01-42-78-88-30; Métro: Hôtel-de-Ville). Open Monday to Saturday 11 a.m. to 11 p.m. and Sunday 3 to 8 p.m., the store carries both French- and English-language publications.

In most large cities in France, there are gay bars and we've listed those in the nightlife sections.

For advice on HIV issues, call **F.A.C.T.S.** (☎ 01-44-93-16-69) Monday, Wednesday, and Friday 6 to 10 p.m. The acronym stands for Free Aids Counseling Treatment and Support, and the English-speaking staff provides counseling, information, and doctor referrals.

Going It Alone

Many people prefer traveling alone. The only downside is the relatively steep cost of booking a single room, which is usually well over half the price of a double. You'll find that restaurants in France welcome single travelers — maybe because they're more likely to concentrate on and delight in the cuisine! — and you're likely to be given an excellent table and terrific service.

Travel Companion (☎ 516-454-0880) is one of the oldest roommate finders for single travelers. Register with them and find a trustworthy travel mate who'll split the cost of the room with you and be around as little or as much as you like during the day. Several tour organizers cater to solo travelers as well. **Experience Plus** (☎ 800-685-4565; Fax: 907-484-8489) offers an interesting selection of singles-only trips.

Travel Buddies (☎ 800-998-9099 or 604-533-2483) runs single-friendly tours with no extra charge because you're traveling solo. And the **Single Gourmet Club,** 133 E. 58th St., New York, NY 10022 (☎ 212-980-8788; Fax: 212-980-3138), is an international social club for singles, with offices in 21 cities in the United States and Canada and one in London.

Part II
Ironing Out the Details

The 5th Wave   By Rich Tennant

"And how shall I book your flight to France —First Class, Coach, or Medieval?"

In this part...

Part I covers the basics, but this part gets down to specifics: the detailed information you need to book your trip. Chapter 6 covers the various ways of getting to France and saving some money in the process. Chapter 7 gives you information about getting around France after you arrive. Chapter 8 discusses different styles of accommodations to choose from and booking a room. Chapter 9 discusses money (with the arrival of ATMs all over France, there are more options than ever). Chapter 10 takes care of details that you too often leave to the last minute, such as getting a passport, thinking about medical and travel insurance, and packing.

Chapter 6

Getting to France

● ●

In This Chapter

▶ Picking a travel agent

▶ Deciding on a package or escorted tour

▶ Making your own arrangements

▶ Saving money on the Web

● ●

*P*lanning a trip abroad used to be a science so exact that only travel agents, with their numerous contacts and extensive experience, could get you fantastic trips at low prices. These days, the Internet — with its online travel agents; airline, lodging, and car rental Web sites; and myriad of information about your destination — has drastically changed travel planning. Still, don't negate entirely the idea of the travel agent, because there *are* times that an agent will be better at handling your arrangements than you will be. That's why you need to decide what kind of travel best suits you — are you an independent traveler, or do you prefer the comfort of a tour group where everything is planned for you? In this chapter, I show you how to get to France simply and easily — whether you do it yourself or have someone do it for you.

Using a Travel Agent

A travel agent can help you find a bargain airfare, hotel, or rental car, but these days many people are choosing to forego this route entirely in favor of acting as their own agents by using the Web (see "Making Your Own Arrangements" later in this chapter). If you have a complicated itinerary with multiple stops and not much time to plan, a travel agent may be your best bet. And a good agent knows how to balance price with value. Travel agents can tell you how much time you should budget for a destination, find a cheap direct flight, get you a better hotel room at a lower price, and even give restaurant and sightseeing recommendations.

To make sure you get the most out of your travel agent, do your homework. Read about your destination and pick out some accommodations and attractions that you think you'd like. Visit travel-planning Web sites like Expedia (www.expedia.com) and Travelocity (www.travelocity. com) for the latest airfares and special hotel promotions. Does your travel agent know about them? Let him or her know that you've got a good feel for what's out there and what it costs and ask for more deals and discounts. Your travel agent still has access to more resources than even the most complete Web travel site (though the Web is quickly catching up) and should be able to get you a better price than you could get on your own. An agent can also issue your tickets and vouchers right on the spot, and if he or she can't get you into the hotel of your choice, can recommend a good alternative.

Remember, however, that travel agents work on commission. You don't pay it; the airlines, hotels, resorts, and tour companies do. Because of this payment, however, some travelers have turned to the Web to avoid agents who push vacations designed to net them the highest commission. If you have plenty of time — and it does take some time — go ahead and explore your Web options. I provide some helpful travel sites (later in this chapter) to get you on your way.

Understanding Package and Escorted Tours

What kind of traveler are you? Do you like listening to a tour guide tell you about a city's important sights, or would you rather discover those sights and lesser-known attractions on your own? Do you like avoiding the stress of getting to unfamiliar places, or do you prefer to make an adventure of finding your way in a foreign destination? Is meeting people one of your goals, or do you shrink at the idea of sharing so much time with strangers? How you answer these questions will let you know whether you'd prefer an escorted tour or a package tour.

Taking an escorted tour

The most inclusive kind of travel, an *escorted tour* spells out nearly everything in advance: your flights, your hotels, your meals, your sight-seeing itineraries, and your costs. It's the least independent way to travel, but some travelers find the escorted tour to be liberating — no hassles with public transportation, no deciphering maps, and the comfort of knowing what you're getting. Others fervently despise escorted group tours, feeling that they're being herded from one sight to the next and missing the element of surprise and individuality that independent travel affords.

If you choose an escorted tour, ask the following questions before
you buy:

- ✔ **What is the cancellation policy?** Do you have to place a deposit?
Can the tour organizers cancel the trip if they don't secure enough
people? How late can you cancel if you're unable to go? When do
you pay? Do you receive a refund if you cancel? If they cancel?

- ✔ **How jam-packed is the schedule?** Do tour organizers try to fit 25
hours into a 24-hour day, or will you have ample time for relaxing
and/or shopping? If you don't enjoy waking at 7 a.m. every day
and not returning to your hotel until 6 or 7 p.m., you may not
enjoy certain escorted tours.

- ✔ **How big is the group?** The smaller the group, the more flexible
the schedule and the less time you'll spend waiting for people to
enter and exit the bus. Tour operators may be evasive about this,
because they may not know the exact size of the group until
everybody makes their reservations, but they should be able to
give you a rough estimate. Some tours have a minimum group size
and may cancel the tour if they don't book enough people.

- ✔ **What's included in the package?** Don't assume that anything's
included. For example, you may have to pay to get yourself to and
from the airport. Or an excursion may include a box lunch, but
drinks may cost extra, or the meal may include beer but not wine.
How much choice do you have? Can you opt out of certain activities or does the bus leave once a day, with no exceptions? Are all
your meals planned in advance? Can you choose your entree at
dinner or does everybody get the same *boeuf bourguignon*?

 With an escorted tour, think strongly about purchasing travel insurance, especially if the tour operator asks you to pay up front. But don't
buy insurance from the tour operator! If they don't fulfill their obligations to provide you with the vacation that you've paid for, don't
expect them to fulfill their insurance obligations either. Buy travel
insurance through an independent agency.

Some companies specialize in escorted tours of France. Here's a brief
list:

- ✔ **Trafalgar Tours,** 11 E. 26th St., New York, NY 10010 (☎ **800-
854-0103**), offers a 14-day Best of France trip starting and ending
in Paris, with stops on the Riviera and in Lourdes, Nice, Monaco,
and other cities. Most meals and twin-bed accommodations in
first-class hotels are part of the package, which is $1,525 per
person for the land portion only. Its nine-day, four-city Treasures
of France tour, also beginning and ending in Paris, has similar
meal and accommodation offerings and costs $925 per person for
the land portion only. Call your travel agent for more information.
Trafalgar takes calls only from agents.

✔ Another good choice is **Globus/Cosmos Tours,** 5301 S. Federal Circle, Littleton, CO 80123-2980 (☎ **800-338-7092**). Globus offers first-class escorted coach tours of various regions of France lasting from 8 to 16 days. Cosmos, a budget branch of Globus, offers escorted tours of about the same length. You must book tours through a travel agent, but you can call the 800 number for brochures.

✔ **Tauck Tours,** 276 Post Rd. W., Westport, CT 06990 (☎ **800-468-2825**), provides superior first-class, fully escorted coach grand tours of France, as well as one-week general tours of specific regions. Its 14-day tour covering the Normandy landing beaches, the Bayeux Tapestry, and Mont-St-Michel among other places of historic interest costs $3,850 per person, double occupancy (land only); a 14-day trip beginning in Nice and ending in Paris costs $3,980 per person, double occupancy (land only).

Taking a package tour

Package tours are a happy medium between hooking up with a group and going it alone, and they're enormously popular because they save you a ton of money. In many cases, a package tour bundles the price of airfare, hotel, and transportation to and from the airport into a "package" that you buy, and the good news is that the package often costs less than the hotel alone would have, had you booked each item separately. That's because packages are sold in bulk to tour operators, who resell them to the public at a cost that drastically undercuts standard rates.

Many travelers confuse the package tour with the escorted tour. On an escorted tour, every detail of your trip is prearranged, from the flight to the hotels, meals, sightseeing, and transportation. Package tours, on the other hand, bundle various elements of the trip — perhaps your flight and hotel or your flight and a rental car, for example. But once you arrive at your destination, your time is your own.

So what's the catch? Packages vary widely. Some offer a better class of hotels than others. Some offer the same hotels for lower prices. Some offer flights on scheduled airlines, while others book charters. In some packages, your choice of accommodations and travel days may be limited. Some packages let you choose between escorted vacations and independent vacations; others allow you to add on just a few excursions or escorted day trips (also at lower prices than you could locate on your own) without booking an entirely escorted tour. Each destination usually has one or two packagers that are cheaper than the rest because they buy in even greater bulk. If you spend the time to shop around, you'll save in the long run.

The best place to start your search is the travel section of your local Sunday newspaper. Also check the ads in the back of national travel magazines like *Arthur Frommer's Budget Travel, Travel & Leisure, National Geographic Traveler,* and *Condé Nast Traveler.* **Liberty Travel** (☎ 888-271-1584 to find a travel agent near you; Internet: www. libertytravel.com), one of the biggest packagers in the Northeast, often runs a full-page ad in the Sunday papers. You won't get much in the way of service, but you will get a good deal. **American Express Vacations** (☎ 800-241-1700; Internet: www.leisureweb.com) is another option. They're pros at bundling flights on big-name carriers with accommodations in mid-priced hotels.

Another good resource is the airlines themselves, which often package their flights with accommodations. (See later in this chapter for airline Web addresses and phone numbers.)

If money is most certainly an object, it's hard to beat the deals offered by **New Frontiers**, 12 E. 33rd St., New York, NY 10016 (☎ **800-366-6387** or 212-779-0600; Fax: 212-770-1007); another branch is at 5757 West Century Blvd., Suite 650, Los Angeles, CA 90045 (☎ **800-677-0720** or 310-670-7318; Fax: 310-670-7707). New Frontiers has its own airline, Corsair (one of the few that fly direct from the United States into Orly Airport, 12.87 km/8 miles south of Paris), and a recent round-trip flight bought five days in advance in the middle of summer cost just $498 before tax. But there's always a catch: The plane was older, with small, uncomfortable seats; meals were small and of poor quality; and the flight was packed.

The French Experience, 370 Lexington Ave., Suite 812, New York, NY 10017 (☎ **212-986-3800**), offers several fly-drive programs through regions of France (the quoted price includes airfare and a rental car). You can specify the type and price level of hotels you want. The agency arranges the car rental in advance, and the rest is up to you. Some staff can seem unfriendly, but persevere for good deals. **American Express Vacations,** P.O. Box 1525, Fort Lauderdale, FL 33302 (☎ **800-241-1700**), is perhaps the most instantly recognizable tour operator in the world. Its offerings in Paris and the rest of Europe are probably more comprehensive than those of any other company and include package tours, as well as independent stays.

Checking Out Special-Interest Vacations

Whether biking, ballooning, or barging, there are a host of options available for special-interest vacations in France. These are a great idea if you are journeying with a large group, say a family reunion, because the organizers take care of all the complex details and itineraries.

People who like to travel with lots of luggage may also enjoy these tours, because they often will help you get your suitcases from one spot to the next.

Ballooning

The world's largest hot-air balloon operator is the **Bombard Society,** 333 Pershing Way, West Palm Beach, FL 33401 (☎ **800-862-8537** or 561- 837-6610; Fax: 561-837-6623). It maintains about three dozen hot-air balloons, some stationed in the Loire Valley and Burgundy. The five-day/ four-night tours — costing $5,494 — incorporate food and wine tasting and include all meals, lodging in Relais & Châteaux hotels, sight-seeing, rail transfers to and from Paris, and a daily balloon ride over vineyards and fields. The **Bonaventura Balloon Co.,** 133 Wall Rd., Napa, CA 94558 (☎ **800-359-6272**), meets you in Paris and takes you via TGV to Burgundy, where your balloon tour begins, carrying you over the most scenic parts of the region. A seven-day trip is $2,395 per person, including a full day of sightseeing in Paris, two balloon excursions, lodging, cooking classes, wine tasting, and at least one meal per day.

Cruising on a barge

Before the advent of railways, many of the crops, building supplies, raw materials, and finished products of France were barged through a series of rivers, canals, and estuaries. On all these trips, you sleep on the barge and are served gourmet meals.

French Country Waterways, P.O. Box 2195, Duxbury, MA 02331 ☎ **800-222-1236** or 781-934-2454) leads one-week tours at $2,895 to $4,395, double occupancy. **European Waterways,** 140 E. 56th St., Suite 4C, New York, NY 10022 (☎ **800-217-4447** or 212-688-9489; Fax: 800-296-4554 or 212-688-3778), operates one-week cruises starting at $1,990 per person. And **Kemwel's Premier Selections,** 106 Calvert St., Harrison, NY 10528 (☎ **800-234-4000** or 914-835-5555; Fax: 914-835-8756), has trips of three nights starting at $1,410 and six nights starting at $2,615.

Biking

Backroads, 801 Cedar St., Berkeley, CA 94710 (☎ **800/-462-2848** or 510-527-1555; Fax: 510-527-1444; Internet: www.backroads.com), runs bike tours of Brittany and Normandy, the Loire Valley, and Provence. Per person rates are $2,498 for six days or $3,098 for eight days. **Bike Riders,** P.O. Box 130254, Boston, MA 02133 (☎ **800-473-7040**; Internet: www.bikeriderstours.com; E-mail: info@bikeriderstours.com), runs seven-day biking tours of Provence starting at $2,800. Participants can bike 15 to 35 miles per day on gently rolling terrain, staying at Relais & Châteaux hotels and eating at several Michelin-starred restaurants.

Learning the language

The **Alliance Française,** 101 bd. Raspail, 75270 Paris (☎ **800-6-FRANCE** in the U.S. or 01-45-44-38-28; Fax: 01-45-44-25-95), is a state-approved nonprofit organization with a network of 1,100 establishments in 138 countries, offering French-language course to some 350,000 students. The international school in Paris is open all year; two-week courses range from 765 to 1,530F ($109 to $219). French is an elegant and complex language and you certainly will find that a knowledge of it will bring satisfaction both to you and to your hosts, the people of France. In fact, the French are very pleased when people make an effort to speak the language and will gladly correct any problems with tenses and vocabulary.

Learning to cook

At the **Ritz-Escoffier Ecole de Gastronomie Français,** 15 place Vendôme, 75001 Paris (☎ **800-966-5758** in the United States or 01-43-16-30-50), you can take a master class on Monday, Tuesday, and Thursday afternoons for 275F ($39) each. There are also 1- to 12-week courses in French and English.

Making Your Own Arrangements

So you want to plan the trip on your own? This section tells you all you need to know to research and book the perfect trip.

Flying to France

Flying time to Paris from New York is about 7 hours; from Chicago, 9 hours; from Los Angeles, 11 hours; from Atlanta, 8 hours; from Miami, 8½ hours; and from Washington, D.C., 7½ hours.

The two Parisian airports — Orly and Charles de Gaulle — are almost even bets in terms of convenience to the city's center, though taxi rides from Orly might take a bit less time than those from de Gaulle. Orly, the older of the two, is 12.87 km (8 miles) south of the center and Charles de Gaulle 22.5 km (14 miles) northeast. Air France's flights from North America fly into de Gaulle (Terminal 2C). U.S.-based airlines fly into both de Gaulle and Orly.

There are also flights from major U.S. cities to Nice on the Riviera, which takes about an hour longer than flying to Paris and costs about the same. Flights from Paris to Nice are very frequent. Air France has 30 flights per day. They take one hour and 20 minutes and can cost about 2,625F ($375).

Most airlines offer the cheapest fares between November 1 and March 13. The shoulder seasons, offering slightly more expensive fares, are mid-March to mid-June and all of October. From mid-June to September, air fare rates to France are at their highest.

Who flies there from the United States and Canada

Following are the phone numbers and Web sites for the major airlines serving Paris. These sites offer schedules, flight booking, and package tours; most have Web pages where you can sign up for e-mail alerts that list weekend deals and other late-breaking bargains.

Air Canada (☎ 800-630-3299; Internet: www.aircanada.ca) flies from Halifax, Montreal, Toronto, and Vancouver.

Air France (☎ 800-237-2747; Internet: www.airfrance.com) flies from Atlanta, Boston, Chicago, Cincinnati, Houston, Los Angeles, Miami, New York City, Philadelphia, and Washington, D.C.

American Airlines (☎ 800-433-7300; Internet: www.aa.com) flies from Boston, Chicago, Dallas, Los Angeles, New York City, and Miami.

British Airways (☎ 800-247-9297; Internet: www.british-airways.com) flies from Atlanta, Baltimore, Boston, Charlotte, Chicago, Cincinnati, Detroit, Houston, Los Angeles, Miami, Orlando, Philadelphia, Phoenix, Newark, New York City, San Diego, San Francisco, Tampa, and Washington, D.C.

Continental Airlines (☎ 800-525-0280; Internet: www.continental.com) flies from Houston and Newark.

Delta Air Lines (☎ 800-221-1212; Internet: www.delta-air.com) flies from Atlanta, Cincinnati, and New York City, and shares flights with Air France from Los Angeles, Philadelphia, and San Francisco.

Iceland Air (☎ 800-223-5500; Internet: www.icelandair.com) flies from Baltimore, Boston, Minneapolis, and New York City.

Northwest/KLM (☎ 800-225-2525; Internet: www.nwa.com) flies from Detroit, Memphis, and Minneapolis.

TWA (☎ 800-221-2000; Internet: www.twa.com) flies from New York City and St. Louis.

United Airlines (☎ 800-241-6522; Internet: www.united.com) flies from Chicago, Los Angeles, San Francisco, and Washington, D.C.

USAirways (☎ 800-428-4322; Internet: www.usairways.com) flies from Charlotte, Philadelphia, and Pittsburgh.

Who flies there from the United Kingdom

These airlines serve Paris from the United Kingdom:

Air France (☎ 0845-0845-111; Internet: www.airfrance.com) flies from London and Manchester.

British Airways (☎ 0845-773-3377; Internet: www.britishairways.com) flies from Edinburgh, Glasgow, London, and Manchester.

British Midland (☎ 0870-6070-555; Internet: www.britishmidland.com) flies from Leeds, London, and Manchester.

Who flies there from Australia

These airlines fly to Paris from Australia and New Zealand:

AOM (☎ 61-92-23-44-44; Internet: www.flyaom.com) flies from Sydney.

Qantas (☎ 13-13-13 anywhere in Australia; Internet: www.qantas.com) flies from Sydney.

Tips for getting the best airfare

Passengers within the same cabin on an airplane rarely pay the same fare — they pay what the market will bear. As a leisure traveler, you should never, *ever* pay full fare. The top price is for business travelers who need fares with unrestricted flexibility. They buy their tickets a few days or a few hours in advance, need to be able to change itineraries at the drop of a hat, and want to be back home for the weekend. Flying unrestricted coach class from New York to Paris on a major airline can cost more than $500 each way during the summer high season.

Most vacation travelers can get a great fare by buying a ticket with restrictions. Book your tickets at least 14 days in advance, travel Tuesday to Thursday and stay over one Saturday night, and you can nab the airline's lowest available fare, typically about $650 in summer or $400 in winter, a huge savings over the full unrestricted fare.

Periodically airlines lower prices on their most popular routes. Check your newspaper for advertised discounts, check the Web, or call the airlines directly and ask if any *promotional rates* or special fares are available. You'll almost never see a sale during July and August or during the Thanksgiving or Christmas seasons. Note, however, that the lowest-priced fares are often nonrefundable, require advance purchase of one to three weeks and a certain length of stay, and carry penalties for changing dates of travel.

Check airfares from secondary or alternative airports. If you live in a city that's close to more than one international airport, check prices on flights going to Paris from all of them. For example, travelers living in the Philadelphia area should check out prices not only from Philadelphia International but also from Newark and Baltimore– Washington International. You may find that lower prices or special promotions are not offered from the airport you regularly use.

Consolidators, also known as *bucket shops,* are also a good place to find low fares. Consolidators buy seats in bulk from the airlines and sell them back to the public at prices below even the airlines' discounted rates. Their small, boxed ads usually run in the Sunday newspaper travel section at the bottom of the page.

Before you pay, however, ask for a confirmation number from the consolidator and then call the airline itself to confirm your seat. If the airline can't confirm your reservation, *don't book with the consolidator.* There are plenty of others from which to choose. Also be aware that bucket shop tickets are usually nonrefundable or carry stiff cancellation penalties, often as high as 50 to 75 percent of the ticket price.

Council Travel (☎ **800-2-COUNCIL;** Internet: www.counciltravel.com) and **STA Travel** (☎ **800-781-4040;** Internet: www.sta-travel.com) are two consolidators that cater especially to young travelers, but their low prices are available to people of all ages. **1800-AIRFARE** (☎ **800-AIR-FARE;** Internet: www.1800airfare.com) also offers deep discounts on many airlines, with a four-day advance purchase. *Rebaters,* such as **Travac** (☎ **877-872-8221** or 212-630-3310), rebate part of their commissions to you.

You can also try booking a seat on a *charter flight* for savings. Discounted fares have knocked down the number available, but they can still be found. Most charter operators advertise and sell their seats through travel agents. Before deciding to take a charter flight, however, check the restrictions on the ticket: Two well-known operators that sell tickets directly to the public are **Travac** (☎ **877-872-8221** or 212-630-3310) and **Council Charters,** 205 E. 42nd St., New York, NY 10017 (☎ **212-822-2800**).

Look into *courier flights.* Couriers relinquish their luggage allowance in return for a deeply discounted ticket. Flights are often offered at the last minute, and you may have to arrange a pre-trip interview to make sure you're right for the job. **Now Voyager,** open Monday to Friday 10 a.m. to 5:30 p.m. and Saturday noon to 4:30 p.m. (☎ **212-431-1616;** Internet: www.nowvoyagertravel.com), flies from New York. If you don't want to fly as a courier, Now Voyager also offers noncourier discounted fares.

Finally, try joining a travel club, such as **Moment's Notice** (☎ 718-234-6295; Internet: www.moments-notice.com) or **Sears Discount Travel Club** (☎ 800-331-0257; ask for code T5D29), to get discounted prices on airfares. You pay an annual membership fee to get the club's hotline number. Of course, you're limited to what's available, so you have to be flexible.

Booking your ticket online

Online travel sites are among the most visited on the Web. The top agencies, including Expedia and Travelocity, offer an array of tools that are valuable even if you don't book online. You can check flight schedules, hotel availability, or car rental prices or even get paged if your flight is delayed. For each of them, the drill is basically the same: You enter your departure city, destination, and travel dates, and the site generates a list of flights, noting the lowest fare. Some sites even search for lower fares leaving from different airports or on different days.

Most online travel sites now have extensive security policies and protect against credit card theft with the most advanced encryption technologies. To be assured you're in secure mode when purchasing with a credit card, look for an icon (such as padlocks in Netscape or Internet Explorer) at the bottom of your Web browser. Most sites also offer toll-free numbers if you prefer to book over the phone.

If the thought of all that comparison shopping gives you a headache, then two options await you. Head for the **Smarter Living** newsletter service (www.smarterliving.com), where every week you'll get a customized e-mail summarizing the discount fares available from your departure city. They track more than 15 airlines, so it's a worthwhile time saver (but keep in mind the majority of low fares quoted are for travel available the weekend immediately following the e-mail). If you'd prefer to let the computer do the work for you, call up **Qixo.com** (www.qixo.com), an airfare search engine that'll check almost a dozen travel sites (including the biggies like Expedia and Travelocity) to find the lowest fares for the dates you have in mind.

Here's the lowdown on what you can expect from the top online sites for discount travel fares:

 ✔ **Travelocity.com** (www.travelocity.com; www.frommers.travelocity.com; www.previewtravel.com) is Frommer's online travel planning/booking partner. It offers reservations and tickets for more than 400 airlines, plus reservations and purchase capabilities for more than 45,000 hotels and 50 car-rental companies. An exclusive feature of the system is its *Low Fare Search Engine,* which automatically searches for the three lowest-priced itineraries based on your criteria. Last-minute deals and consolidator fares are included in the search too. If you book with Travelocity, you can select specific seats for your flights with online seat maps and also view diagrams of the most popular commercial aircraft. Its hotel finder provides street-level location maps and photos of selected hotels. With the Fare Watcher e-mail feature, you can select up to five routes and receive e-mail notices when the fare changes by $25 or more. Travelocity's Destination Guide includes updated information on some 260 destinations worldwide — supplied by Frommer's.

✔ **Expedia.com** (www.expedia.com) lets you book flight, hotel, and rental car reservations on one itinerary. Its hotel search offers crisp maps to pinpoint most hotel properties and you can click on the camera icon to see images of many rooms and facilities. Expedia also offers a service similar to that of Priceline — you name the price for a flight or a hotel room and submit your credit card information. If your price is matched, Expedia makes the reservation and charges your card. Keep in mind, however, that like many online databases, Expedia focuses on the major airlines and hotel chains, so you may not get the lowest prices out there.

✔ **Priceline.com** (www.priceline.com) lets you name your price for domestic and international airline tickets. Select a route, dates, and a preferred rate; make a bid for what you're willing to pay; and guarantee with a credit card. If the hotels and airlines in Priceline's database have a fare that's lower than your bid, your credit card will automatically be charged. You can't say what time you want to fly — you have to accept any flight leaving between 6 a.m. and 10 p.m. on the dates you choose, and you may have to make one stopover. No frequent-flyer miles are awarded, and tickets are non-refundable and can't be exchanged for another flight. So if your plans change, you're out of luck. Priceline can be good for travelers who have to take off on short notice (and who are thus unable to qualify for advance purchase discounts).

But be sure to shop around first — if you overbid, you'll be required to purchase the ticket and Priceline will pocket the difference between what it pays for a ticket and what you bid.

Cheap Tickets (www.cheaptickets.com), **Lowestfare.com** (www.lowestfare.com), **Go4Less** (www.go4less.com), and **Last Minute Travel** (www.lastminutetravel.com) are four sites that sometimes offer exclusive deals not available through more mainstream channels.

Tunneling from London to Paris

The **Eurostar** train (☎ **0990-300-003** in London, **01-44-51-06-02** in Paris, and **800-EUROSTAR** in the U.S.; Internet: www.eurostar.com) runs through the Channel Tunnel (chunnel) and connects London's Waterloo Station with Paris's Gare du Nord and Brussels's Central Station. Both trips take about three hours (you arrive four hours later with the time change). Because the old train-ferry-train route (through

Dover and Calais) takes all day and costs almost the same, the Eurostar option is a great deal.

Reserving a seat on the Eurostar is always a good idea. Tour groups and England's frequent bank holidays (three- or four-day weekends) book the train solid, because many Londoners take short vacations to Paris.

The Eurostar leaves exactly on time, and passengers are not let on less than fifteen minutes before departure. Don't cut it close with this one!

Other Ways to Get There

You can take trains into Paris from any other major city in continental Europe. There are fast train connections from cities in Italy and Germany, and many routes provide night trains. Many people take an overnight train for the route from Rome to Paris, for instance.

You can arrive in France by ferry from Italy or England. The ferry service from Italy is out of Genoa. From Dover, England, a ferry lands in Calais, France. But the chunnel train (see previous section) is so convenient for this route, there's little reason to take the ferry.

If you love driving long distances and have plenty of time, you can drive into France, though the routes around the Alps can be either scary or exhilarating, depending on your disposition.

Chapter 7

Getting Around France

• •

In This Chapter

▶ Flying to and fro

▶ Catching the train

▶ Renting a car

• •

*T*his chapter gives you the details you need about traveling within France. Your best bet for getting around the country is via the speedy and efficient train system, especially the super-fast TGV. If you're pressed for time and need to cover a large distance, then opt for a plane. But if you have lots of time, you can rent a car and tour the countryside. Normandy and the Loire Valley are within a couple of hours of Paris, so taking the train from the capital makes sense; if you want to explore the countryside, rent a car from a city within the region. Brittany and Provence are three to four hours by train from Paris, so the train probably still makes sense. However, if you're going all the way south to the Riviera, you may want to consider a flight.

Traveling by Plane

The French national airline is **Air France** (☎ **800-776-3000** in the United States; 020-8742-6600 in London; Internet: www.airfrance.com), which offers domestic flights to every major city in France. Although you may consider flying from Paris to Nice, you should know that flights within France are occasionally delayed or cancelled because of strikes. There are 30 flights a day from Paris to the Aéroport Nice–Côte d'Azur, which is an easy shuttle from the center of Nice. The flights take one hour and 20 minutes, and the average fare is 2,625F ($375) The train to Nice takes about 6 hours and 40 minutes. See travel times in Table 7-1.

Table 7-1: Travel Times Between the Major Cities

Cities	Distance	Train Travel Time	Driving Time	Air Travel Time
Paris to Tours	241 km/ 150 miles	1 hr.	2 hrs., 45 min.	no direct plane
Paris to Rouen	136 km/ 85 miles	1 hr., 10 min.	1 hr., 40 min.	no plane
Paris to Nantes	387 km/ 240 miles	2 hrs., 10 min.	4 hrs., 10 min.	no direct plane
Nantes to Quimper	234 km/ 145 miles	2 hrs., 30 min.	2 hrs., 30 min.	no plane
Paris to Avignon	710 km/ 441 miles	2 hrs., 40 min.	7 hrs., 15 min.	1 hr.
Avignon to Nice	257 km/ 160 miles	3 hrs., 50 min.	2 hrs., 40 min.	no direct plane
Paris to Nice	966 km/ 600 miles	6 hrs., 40 min.	10 hrs.	1 hr., 20 min.

Taking the Train

Train travel in France is a relative bargain, and the trains are famous for being on time. You can get almost anywhere in the country — service covers 24,000 miles of track and about 3,000 stations — and the super-fast TGVs (pronounced *tay-jay-vay*, meaning Trains à Grand Vitesse), servicing 50 French cities, are continually being improved. Most trains are clean and comfortable. On all TGVs and some other trains, you have a choice of first and second class. First class is generally cleaner and quieter, with slightly larger chairs, and is occupied mainly by business-people. Trains traveling long distances have *couchettes* (sleepers). Most trains have snack bars.

If you plan on much rail travel, get the latest copy of the ***Thomas Cook European Timetable of Railroads.*** This comprehensive 500-plus-page book documents all Europe's mainline passenger rail services with detail and accuracy. It's available in North America from the **Forsyth Travel Library,** 226 Westchester Ave., White Plains, NY 10604 (☎ **800-367-7984**), at a cost of $27.95, plus $4.95 postage (priority airmail in the United States) and $6.95 U.S. for shipments to Canada.

If you're at a train station and are told at the ticket window that a train you want to take is booked, always ask the train conductor. The ticket window computers include bookings for possible no-shows, so a "booked" train could actually have hundreds of seats available.

 Always bring bottled water and a snack on a French train. You never know when a strike is going to mean a closed snack bar.

 Make sure that you get on the right *car*, and not just the right train. Check your ticket for the *voit* (car) and the *place* (seat). Individual train cars may split from the rest of the train down the line and join a different train headed to a different destination. Making sure that you're on the right car is especially important when taking a night train (if you have a reserved spot, you needn't worry). Each car has its own destination placard, which may also list major stops en route. Always check with the conductor.

 If you want to bypass Paris entirely or visit Paris at the end of your trip, consider taking a train directly from Charles de Gaulle Airport to your destination. There are direct trains from the airport to Avignon, Dijon, Marseille, Nantes, and St-Pierre des Corps (just outside Tours) among other cities.

Getting more information

To get more information and to buy rail passes before you leave, check out the following:

In the United States: Contact **Rail Europe,** 500 Mamaroneck Ave., Suite 314, Harrison, NY 10528 (☎ 800-4-EURAIL or **800-677-8585;** Fax: 914-682-3712; Internet: www.raileurope.com.

In Canada: Contact **Rail Europe,** 2087 Dundas St. E., Suite 105, Mississauga, ON L4X 1M2 (☎ 800-361-RAIL or **800-361-7245** or 905-602-4195; Fax: 905-602-4198).

In the United Kingdom: Contact **French Railways,** 179 Piccadilly, London, W1V 1M2 (☎ **0345-48-49-50;** Fax: 020-7491-9956).

To get train information or to make reservations once you get to Paris, call **SNCF (Société Nationale des Chemins de Fer, which is the French National Railroad)** at ☎ **08-36-35-35-39** for English-speaking operators and ☎ **08-36-35-35-35** for French-speaking operators (some of whom may speak a little English). You're charged 3F (50¢) per minute to use this service. You can also go to any local travel agency, of course, and book tickets. A simpler way to book tickets is to take advantage of the *Billetterie* (ticket machines) in every train station. If you know your PIN, you can use American Express, MasterCard, and Visa to purchase your ticket. You can also find out schedule info on the Web at www.sncf.fr.

Buying French rail passes

Working cooperatively with SNCF, Air Inter Europe, and Avis, **Rail Europe** offers two flexible cost-saving rail passes that can reduce travel costs considerably.

The **France Railpass** provides unlimited rail transport throughout France for three days within one month, costing $205 in first class and $180 in second. You can purchase up to six or more days for an extra $30 per person per day. The costs are even more reasonable for two adults traveling together: $328 in first class and $280 in second. Children 4 to 11 travel for half price.

The **France Rail 'n Drive Pass,** available only in North America, combines good value on both rail travel and Avis car rentals and is best used by arriving at a major rail depot and then renting a car to explore the countryside. The best part is there is no surcharge for dropping off at another location, so you don't have to retrace your steps. It includes the France Railpass, along with unlimited mileage on a car rental. The costs are lowest when two or more adults travel together. You can use it during five nonconsecutive days in one month, and it includes three days of travel on the train and two days' use of a rental car. If rental of the least expensive car is combined with first-class rail travel, the price is $204 per person; if rental of the least expensive car is combined with second-class rail travel, the charge is $169 per person. Cars can be upgraded for a supplemental fee. The above prices apply to two people traveling together; solo travelers pay from $255 in first class and $289 in second. Up to six additional rail days can be purchased for $29 per day and unlimited additional car days can be purchased for $35 per day.

Other passes for France from Rail Europe include:

- ✔ **France Saverpass** offers a discount for two or more people traveling together (prices start at $146);

- ✔ **France Seniorpass** gives a discount to people over 60 traveling in first class (prices start at $159);

- ✔ **France Youthpass** gives a discount for youths (prices start at $130);

- ✔ **France Weekender Pass** includes unlimited train travel for four consecutive days including Saturday and Sunday from October 1 to December 31, 2001 (prices start at $119).

Even with a rail pass, you need to make a reservation for TGVs and some other trains. When you make the reservation, you need to specify that you have a rail pass, but only a limited number of seats are available for those with passes. If first class is booked, a seat in second class will probably be available. Be aware that on TGVs, you need to pay a 20F ($2.85) supplement even if you have a rail pass; pay it at the ticket window before boarding the train. If you wait to pay the supplement to the train conductor, he or she may charge you a small penalty.

Getting Around by Bus

The bus system in France, which is separated into about a hundred different small companies, can get you to most out-of-the-way places not reachable by train. The hill towns of the Riviera are particularly well serviced by bus. You can pick up local schedules at tourist offices. Remember that bus service on Sundays is severely reduced. For many bus routes in France, you pay the driver for the trip. Throughout the book, I give you numbers for bus companies servicing individual towns.

Like in most countries, French bus stations tend to be a little less safe than train stations, and you should keep a close eye on your luggage.

Driving Around in a Car

Many of France's most luxurious accommodations lie off the beaten track, so you need a rental car (or a taxi) to get there. And nothing beats the flexibility of a rental car for exploring certain regions of France, particularly Brittany and the Loire Valley. Driving times vary depending on traffic near the major cities and how fast you want to go. Paris to Rouen is about 2½ hours, Paris to Nantes is 3½ hours, and Paris to Marseille can be 7½ hours. (The new fast TGV gets you to Marseille in 3½ hours.)

Knowing the rules of the road

Along with the flexibility of having your own transportation comes the responsibility of following the rules of the road. Here are some things to keep in mind as you traverse the cities and countryside:

- ✔ **Seat belts:** Everyone in the car in both the front and back seats must wear seat belts.
- ✔ **Kids in the car:** Children 11 and under must ride in the back seat.
- ✔ **Yield:** Drivers are supposed to yield to the car on their right, except where signs indicate otherwise, as at traffic circles.
- ✔ **Speed limits:** If you violate the speed limits, expect a big fine. Those limits are about 130 km per hour (80 m.p.h.) on expressways, about 100km per hour (60 m.p.h.) on major national highways, and 90 km per hour (56 m.p.h.) on small country roads. In towns, don't exceed 60 km per hour (37 m.p.h.)

- ✔ **Defensive driving:** The French are known as the most dangerous drivers in Europe — with even worse reputations than the Italians — because of the speed they go. As a result, the French have one of the highest per capita death rates by auto in Europe. You'll be tailgated. Be very careful.

✔ **Gas:** Known as *essence*, gas in France is very expensive for those used to U.S. prices. At press time, *essense super* sold for 6 to 7F per liter, which works out to around 24.50F ($3.50) per U.S. gallon. Depending on your tank, filling a medium-sized car will cost between $45 and $65.

✔ Sometimes you can drive for miles in rural France without encountering a gas station, so don't let your tank get dangerously low.

Understanding the rules of renting

Renting a car in France is easy. You need to present a passport, a valid driver's license, and a valid credit card. You also need to meet the minimum age requirement of the company (for Hertz 21, for Avis 23, for Budget 25; more expensive cars at any of these companies require at least age 25). It's highly unusual in France that you'll be asked for an International Driver's License, but to be safe, you can get one at your nearest AAA office for about $15.

The best deal is usually a weekly rental with unlimited mileage. And to save the most money, reserve the car before you leave home.

All car-rental bills in France are subject to a 20.6-percent government tax.

Unless it's already factored into the rental agreement, an optional *collision-damage waiver (CDW)* carries an extra charge of 110 to 125F ($16 to $18) per day for the least expensive cars. Buying this will usually eliminate all but $250 of your responsibility in the event of accidental damage to the car. If you total the car, expect to pay about $500. Because most newcomers aren't familiar with local driving customs and conditions, I highly recommend you buy the CDW, though you should check with your credit card company first to see if they cover this automatically when you rent with their card. At some rental car companies the CDW won't protect you against the theft of a car, so if this is the case, ask about buying extra theft protection. This cost is 45F ($6) extra per day.

Don't just assume your credit card will cover the collision-damage waiver. I've heard some horror stories of people having to pay the full price of a $50,000 car. Some credit cards cover damage to the car but not liability, so make sure you understand this clearly.

Automatic transmission is considered a luxury in Europe, so if you want it, you'll have to pay about double the cost of the rental car. And renting in one city and dropping off in another city will usually double your rental fee.

Here are the contact numbers for the big car-rental companies:

- **Budget** (☎ **800-472-3325** in the United States and Canada; Internet: www.budgetrentacar.com) maintains about 30 locations in Paris, with its largest branch at 81 av. Kléber, 16e (☎ **01-47-55-61-00**; Métro: Trocadéro). Budget also has offices in Tours, Orléans, Rouen, Nantes, Avignon, Aix, Nice, Marseille, and Cannes, among other cities.

- **Hertz** (☎ **800-654-3001** in the United States and Canada; Internet: www.hertz.com) maintains about 15 locations in Paris, including offices at the city's airports. The main office is 27 rue St-Ferdinand, 17e (☎ **01-45-74-97-39**; Métro Argentine). Hertz also has offices in most major French towns. If you are in France and want to rent a car for anywhere in France outside of Paris, call 08-03-86-18-61.

- **Avis** (☎ **800-331-2112** in the United States and Canada; Internet: www.avis.com) has offices at both Paris airports, as well as an inner-city headquarters at 5 rue Bixio, 7e (☎ 01-44-18-10-50; Métro: Ecole-Militaire), near the Eiffel Tower. Avis also has offices in most major French towns.

- **National**, which is called National Citer in France(☎ **800-227-3876** in the United States and Canada; Internet: www.nationalcar.com) is represented in Paris by Europcar, whose largest office is at 165 bis rue de Vaugirard (☎ **01-44-38-61-61**; Métro: St-Sulpre). It has offices at both Paris airports and about a dozen other locations, including Tours, Nantes, Avignon, Aix, Nice, and Cannes.

Chapter 8

Booking Your Accommodations

* *

In This Chapter

▶ Getting the best room at the best rate

▶ Surfing the Net for hotel deals

▶ Landing a room if you arrive without a reservation

* *

*A*fter you decide where in France you'll be heading, you need to get down to the nitty-gritty of choosing the type of lodging you want and finding a great room at a great price. France tends to charge reasonable hotel rates; many of its hotels offer additional special deals, and this chapter tells you how to find them. Use the money you save on your room for dinners in quality restaurants, spectacular entertainment, or gifts for family and friends (or yourself).

Finding the Price of Comfort

The *rack rate* is the maximum rate that a hotel charges for a room. It's the rate you'd get if you walked in off the street and asked for a room for the night. You sometimes see the rate printed on the fire/emergency exit diagrams posted on the back of your door.

Hotels are happy to charge you the rack rate, but you don't have to pay it! At chain hotels and at other luxury hotels you can often get a good deal by simply asking for a discounted rate. Your odds improve dramatically if you're staying for more than just a few nights.

Also keep in mind that a travel agent may be able to negotiate a better price at top hotels than you can get yourself. (The hotel gives the agent a discount for steering business its way.)

Keep in mind, however, that bartering for a cheaper room isn't the norm in France's budget hotels. Most establishments are small and privately owned; they post their rates in the reception area and may not be willing to negotiate. To be fair, they may not be able to afford to let rooms go for less.

Choosing Accommodations in France: The Basic or the Best?

Hotels in France have their own set of quirks that you may not be familiar with if you're used to hotels in the United States. Things you may take for granted in U. S. hotels — such as closets, shower curtains, washcloths, and window screens — are very rare in France. Many medium-priced hotels don't have air-conditioning, and their bathrooms are usually quite small. Likewise, many charming French hotels are in ancient buildings and don't have elevators. Sometimes the stairways are steep, narrow, winding stone passageways. Forewarned is forearmed. Pack light and consider the inconvenience part of the old-world charm.

Because hotel offerings vary greatly, if some particular amenity is very important to you — air-conditioning, elevator, whatever — ask about it when you're reserving your room.

Hotels

Even the most basic hotel rooms in France have telephones and televisions. But only the higher-priced hotels offer satellite televisions that receive English-language stations.

As a rule, basic and medium-priced French hotels offer fewer amenities than their American counterparts, but they're also far cheaper than medium-priced hotels in similar resort areas. For example, a medium-priced hotel room on the Riviera will run around $100 in season; a medium-priced hotel room on the island of Nantucket in Massachusetts in season will run around $200. On the high end of the scale, you'd be hard-pressed to find a hotel in the United States that has as much elegance and glamour as some of France's top hotels, mainly because the United States doesn't have 300-year-old palaces and other such grand historic locales.

Fortunately, most towns in France offer a wide range of hotel choices, from unassuming hostelries with small, simple rooms to world-famous palaces with super-deluxe suites. Many travelers want a medium-priced hotel, perhaps with some historic charm, that's in a good location, within walking distance of sights, shopping, and restaurants. So I include those types of places throughout the book. I also include inexpensive places for those who want to save a few francs, as well as expensive places for those who are looking to splurge.

Chain hotels are often concrete blocks on the outskirts of cities. Their bargain rates for standard amenities are often popular with business travelers. The big chains are **Mercure** (☎ **800-221-4542** in the United States), which has medium-priced rooms, and **Formule 1** (☎ **01-69-36-75-29** in France), which has inexpensive rooms.

French hotels are government-rated by stars, which are always indicated on the exterior of the building on a government plaque, as well as in all brochures for the hotel. The ratings from highest to lowest are four star deluxe (the best), four star (excellent), three star (very nice), two star (good quality), and one star (budget). "No star" hotels, which means they don't have the minimum amenities to receive one star, are also available. (You probably want to avoid no-star hotels; they often have shared bathrooms in the hallways.) Two-star and three-star hotels are the mid-range options, and though the quality and comfort of these can range quite a bit, they always have a clean room with a simple bathroom (sink, toilet, shower and/or tub, and a bar of soap).

Relais & Châteaux and Logis de France

Relais & Châteaux is a marketing organization for some of the most deluxe privately owned hotels in France and around the world — France contains about 150 of them. In order to qualify for the organization, hotels must adhere to strict hospitality standards, so you're pretty much guaranteed a wonderful room at a Relais & Châteaux hotel, usually occupying a historic building such as a former castle, abbey, or mansion. But these hotels are always very pricey, and some insist on half or full board, meaning you have to take one or two meals at the hotel, which also will be very pricey (though probably very tasty; the restaurants attached to these hotels are usually the best in town).

For an illustrated catalog of these establishments, send $8 to **Relais & Châteaux,** 11 E. 44th St., Suite 704, New York, NY 10017. These booklets are available free at all Relais & Châteaux establishments. For information or to book a Relais & Châteaux hotel, you can call the hotel directly or the organization headquarters at ☎ **800-860-4930** or 212-856-0115 (Fax: 212-867-4968; E-mail resarc@relaischateaux.fr; Internet: www.relaischateaux.fr).

Establishments with the **Logis de France** designation are usually medium-priced family-owned hotels that offer good value and standard amenities. You can send $23.95 to receive a copy of a booklet listing these hotels by contacting the **French Government Tourist Office,** 444 Madison Ave., New York, NY 10022 (☎ **212-838-7800**). Or you can contact the **Fédération Nationale des Logis de France,** 83 av. d'Italie, 75013 Paris (☎ **01-45-84-70-00**).

Bed-and-breakfasts

The term for a bed-and-breakfast in France is *gîte* or *chambre d'hôte*, and these are usually very inexpensive accommodations on a farm or in a village home. Many of them offer a meal of the day, such as lunch or dinner, as well.

At least 6,000 of these accommodations are listed with **La Maison de Gîtes de France et du Tourisme Vert,** 59 rue St-Lazare, 75009 Paris (☎ **01-49-70-75-75**). Sometimes these accommodations are quite nice; you could be in a privately owned castle in the countryside, and madame may let you prepare a meal in her kitchen. In the United States, a good source is **The French Experience,** 370 Lexington Ave., Room 812, New York, NY 10017 (☎ **212-986-1115;** Fax: 212-986-3808). It also rents furnished houses for as short a period as one week.

Condos, villas, houses, and apartments

For longer-term stays in condos or apartments where you don't mind cooking your own meals and cleaning the house, you can obtain a list of real estate agencies from the **French Government Tourist Office,** 444 Madison Ave., New York, NY 10022 (☎ **212-838-7800**). One of the best French real estate groups is the **Fédération Nationale des Agents Immobiliers,** 129 rue du Faubourg St-Honoré, 75008 Paris (☎ **01-44-20-77-00**).

If you want to rent an apartment in Paris, the **Barclay International Group,** 150 E. 52nd St., New York, NY 10022 (☎ **800-845-6636** or 212-832-3777), can give you access to about 3,000 apartments and villas scattered throughout Paris (plus 39 other cities in France) ranging from modest modern units to the most stylish. Units rent for one night to six months and start around $95 per night, double occupancy.

At Home Abroad, 405 E. 56th St., Apt. 6H, New York, NY 10022-2466 (☎ **212-421-9165;** Fax: 212-752-1591), specializes in villas on the Riviera and in the Provençal hill towns. Rentals are usually for two weeks. For a $25 registration fee, they'll send you photographs of the properties and a newsletter.

Getting the Best Room at the Best Rate

In all but the smallest accommodations, the rate you pay for a room depends on many factors — chief among them being how you make your reservation. A travel agent may be able to negotiate a better price with certain hotels than you can get by yourself. (That's because the hotel often gives the agent a discount in exchange for steering his or her business toward that hotel.)

The best room in the house, *s'il vous plait*

After you've made your reservation, asking one or two more pointed questions can go a long way toward making sure you have the best room in the house.

Always ask for a corner room. They're usually larger, quieter, and closer to the elevator and tend to have more windows and light than standard rooms — and they don't always cost more. Also ask if the hotel is renovating; if it is, request a room away from the renovation work. Inquire, too, about the location of the restaurants, bars, and discos in the hotel — these could all be a source of irritating noise. If the room is on a busy street, ask for a room in the back, overlooking the garden or courtyard. And if you aren't happy with your room when you arrive, talk to the front desk. If they have another room, they should be happy to accommodate you, within reason.

Reserving a room through the hotel's toll-free number (this applies only to larger hotels or chains) may also result in a lower rate than if you called the hotel directly. On the other hand, sometimes the central reservations number may not know about discount rates at specific locations. For example, local franchises may offer a special group rate for a wedding or family reunion but may neglect to tell the central booking line. Your best bet is to call both the local number and the toll-free number and see which one gives you a better deal.

Room rates also change with the season, as occupancy rates rise and fall. If a hotel is close to full, it's less likely to extend discount rates; if it's close to empty, it may be willing to negotiate. Room prices are subject to change without notice, so the rates quoted in this book may be different than the actual rate you receive when you make your reservation. Be sure to mention membership in AAA, AARP, frequent-flyer programs, and any other corporate rewards programs when you make your reservation. You never know when it might be worth a few dollars off your room rate (though this usually works only at chain hotels; family-run establishments rarely have such arrangements with large organizations).

Throughout France, as in many tourist centers worldwide, hotels routinely overbook, so booking by credit card doesn't automatically hold your room if you arrive later than expected or after 6 p.m. The hotel clerk will always ask when you expect to arrive, and the hotel usually holds the room until that time. Always pad your expected arrival by a few hours to be safe. But all bets are off after 7 p.m.; the hotel is likely to give away your room to someone off the street unless you call and specifically ask them to hold it. Also, a credit card number holds a room better than just your word over the telephone that you will show up. If you've made a reservation very far in advance, confirm within 24 hours of your expected arrival. If you're experiencing a major delay, alert the hotel as soon as you can.

Here's some advice to keep in mind when trying to save money on a room:

- ✔ Ask about corporate discounts if you'll be staying in one of the chains.

- ✔ Don't forget that your travel agent may be able to negotiate a better price at top hotels than you can get yourself.

- ✔ Always ask if the hotel offers any weekend specials, which typically require you to stay two nights (either Friday and Saturday or Saturday and Sunday). In Paris, you can find this kind of deal from September through March at almost all price levels.

- ✔ *Forfaits* (*fohr*-feh) are discounts that require you to stay a certain number of nights — perhaps a minimum of three or five. Sometimes something else is thrown in (like a bottle of champagne) to sweeten the deal. If you're going to be in a city for more than three days, always ask if there's a *forfait* and then pick the hotel with the best deal.

- ✔ Visit Paris during the summer low season. That's no typo. Room rates in Paris tend to be lower in July and August, which, though big tourist months, are considered low season by Paris hoteliers. November and December are also low season, while October is heavy on conventioneers, making it difficult to find a room.

- ✔ Visit regions outside of Paris during the shoulder seasons of spring and fall when prices can be considerably lower, particularly along the Riviera.

- ✔ In hotels outside of Paris, the best room in a medium-priced hotel is usually much better than the worst room at a high-priced hotel and it is also usually cheaper. Ask for the price of the best room, the room with the best views, or the quietest room.

- ✔ Don't forget about package deals (see Chapter 6) that include airfare, hotel, and transportation to and from the airport.

- ✔ Look on the Internet for deals (see the following section, "Surfing the Web for Hotel Deals").

- ✔ If you're a risk taker, stop in at the **Office de Tourisme de Paris,** 127 av. des Champs-Elysées, 8e, during July and August or November and December — slow season for Paris hotels. At these times, hotels with unsold rooms often sell to the tourist office at reduced rates, and you can stay in a three-star hotel at a two-star price. During the summer slow season, however, you have to wait in a long line and are not guaranteed a room. The office charges a small fee for the service (see "Arriving Without a Reservation," later in this chapter).

Surfing the Web for Hotel Deals

Although the major travel booking sites (Travelocity, Expedia, Yahoo! Travel, and Cheap Tickets) offer hotel booking, using a site devoted primarily to lodging may work best, because you may find properties that aren't listed on more general online travel agencies. Some lodging sites specialize in a particular type of accommodations, such as bed-and-breakfasts, which you won't find on the more mainstream booking services. Others offer weekend deals on major chain properties that cater to business travelers and have more empty rooms on weekends. Therefore, checking out some of the online lodging sites, many of which offer discounts, may be in your best interest.

Hotel Discounts (www. hoteldiscounts.com), a service of the Hotel Reservations Network, offers bargain room rates at hotels in more than two dozen U.S. and international cities. HRN pre-books blocks of rooms in advance, so sometimes it has rooms — at discount rates — at hotels that are "sold out." **TravelWeb** (www.travelweb.com) lists more than 16,000 hotels worldwide, focusing on chains like Hyatt and Hilton, and you can book almost 90 percent of these online. Find weekend deals at many leading hotel chains on TravelWeb's Click-It Weekends. **All Hotels on the Web** (www.all-hotels.com) lists tens of thousands of lodgings throughout the world, and **Hotels and Travel on the Net** (www.hotelstravel.com) offers detailed listings of hotels in more than 150 countries and links to 75,000 travel resources. (The hotels on both these sites pay a fee to list.) **Places to Stay** (www.placestostay. com) lists inns, B&Bs, resorts, hotels, and properties you may not find anywhere else. Privately owned hotels that are part of the Logis de France (www.logis-de-france.fr) marketing organization are usually a very good value. There are 3,600 hotels in the group.

Arriving Without a Reservation

If you arrive in any town in France without a reservation (I don't advise this), you have two choices: You can pick up a phone and start dialing (after you've purchased a phone card at the nearest *tabac*), or you can find the local tourist office and ask them to help. Some charge a small fee for this service, but they will almost always be able to find you a room. The problem is it might be more expensive than you wanted or not in a central location. You can also explore the town and check out the hotel suggestions in this guide to see which one you like best. The trouble is, you may end up dragging your luggage all over town, unless you can check it at the train station. For this option, we suggest you start out early in the day if you need a room for that night. But on the brighter side, last-minute room booking can get you a cheaper price if the hotel is not busy and wants to rent the room to you. That's pretty much at the discretion of the management, but you can frown and shake your head when you hear the price to see if they'll go lower.

In Paris, you can let the multilingual staff at the **Office de Tourisme de Paris** (127 av. des Champs-Elysées, 8e; ☎ **08-36-68-31-12** or 01-49-52-53-35; Fax: 01-49-52-53-00; Internet: www.paris-touristoffice.com; E-mail: info@paris-touristoffice.com; Métro: Charles-de-Gaulle–Etoile or George V) find a hotel for you. It's open daily 9 a.m. to 8 p.m. (Sunday 11 a.m. to 7 p.m. November through April). For a fee, the staff will make a reservation for you on the same day you want a room. The charge is 8F ($1.15) for hostels and *foyers* (homes), 20F ($2.90) for one-star hotels, 25F ($3.60) for two-star hotels, and 40F ($6) for three-star hotels. There are small offices at the airports; their staffs will help you make a hotel reservation, but they work only with hotels that charge more than 350F ($50) per night.

In slow periods, hotels with unsold rooms often sell to the Paris tourist office at a huge discount, providing you with a good way to stay in a three-star hotel at a two-star price. The office is very busy in summer, with lines sometimes stretching outside.

The Office de Tourisme has *auxiliary offices* at the Eiffel Tower (May through September only, daily 11 a.m. to 6 p.m.) and at the Gare de Lyon (Monday to Saturday 8 a.m. to 8 p.m.).

Chapter 9

Money Matters

In This Chapter

▶ Understanding the franc and the new euro

▶ Finding out where to get cash

▶ Reporting a lost or stolen credit card

*A*n important detail to handle when planning your trip is how to carry and access your money. You need to decide whether to use ATM cards, credit cards, or traveler's checks, or perhaps a combination. You also have to get used to the franc, the French standard currency. As of 2000, all businesses in France have been required to include information on the new European currency, the *euro,* so you'll also see euro prices on hotel bills and restaurant menus and in stores. By early 2002, the euro will replace the franc, as well as local currencies in 11 other European Union nations.

How far your dollars go depends on currency rates, which are always changing. France's most expensive city, Paris, is about on par with New York and San Francisco. Outside Paris, prices can seem very reasonable compared to those of top American resorts. But store purchases in France can seem more expensive because merchants add on a 20.6 *détaxe* (abbreviated TVA), which is also called a value-added tax (VAT). Merchants need to pay this amount to the government, so they charge it to the customer.

Making Its Last Stand: The Franc

The unit of French currency is the *franc* (written F or FF), divided into 100 *centimes*. Bills come in denominations of 500F, 100F, 50F, and 20F. Try to avoid getting 500F bills; they're the most commonly forged bill, so some merchants don't accept them, and those that do usually go through a long process of checking to make sure the bill is real. You also must deal with 20F, 10F, 5F, 1F, ½F, and 20-, 10-, and 5-centime coins. Franc coins are silver and heavier, while centime coins are copper and lighter. Franc coins add up quickly, so think twice about emptying your pockets to panhandlers; you may have a dinner's worth of change on you.

 When preparing for the end of your trip, remember that exchange bureaus don't change coins, so if you're weighted down with change on your way out of the country, you're going to be stuck with it.

At this writing, the rate of exchange was at a pleasantly favorable 7F to the dollar. For a look at the most recent rates of exchange (updated each minute), check out www.xe.net/currency or the exchange rate in the financial pages of your local newspaper.

 Note that when writing sums of money, the French use commas where we use decimal points, and vice versa. For example, 1,200.58 francs is written as 1.200,58F.

Introducing the Euro

The year 2001 is the last in which local commerce in France is conducted in the franc. After January 2002, 12 countries in the European Union will begin using the banknotes and coins of the *euro*, the single monetary unit that will eventually make it possible to travel in Europe without changing currency. Today, the euro is used in financial transactions at the fixed rate of 6.55 francs to 1 euro. Many of your sales receipts will show totals in both euros and francs in preparation for the switch.

 The euro is very close in value to the dollar. As long as this balance lasts, you'll have a much easier time of estimating costs throughout France in terms of dollars. For more information and pictures of the new currency, check online at the official site of the European Union: europa.eu.int/euro/.

Taxing matters

The price of all goods in France includes a 20.6 percent sales tax called the *détaxe*, abbreviated TVA. (It's also sometimes referred to as value-added tax.) If you live outside the European Union, you can be reimbursed for part of the TVA you paid, but, as always, a catch is involved: You have to spend at least 1,200F ($171) in the same store *on the same day.* The amount of the refund varies from store to store but generally comes out to about 13 percent of the tax you paid on the item. The department stores Au Printemps and Galeries Lafayette have special *détaxe* desks where clerks prepare your sales invoices, but small shops don't always have the necessary paperwork.

Choosing ATMs, Credit Cards, or Traveler's Checks

Money makes the world go 'round, but dealing with an unfamiliar currency can make your head spin. When it comes to getting cash in France, should you bring traveler's checks or use ATMs? How easy is it to pay with a credit card? You find the answers in this section.

Using ATMs

Before you leave, make a note of these Web sites: **Visa** at www.visa.com/pd/atm and **MasterCard** at www.mastercard.com/atm, which identify the locations of cash machines all over France. Most of the major banks in France, such as Crédit Lyonnais, Crédit Agricole, Banque Nationale de Paris (BNP), Banque Populaire, Crédit Commercial de France (CCF), Crédit du Nord, and even some branches of the post office have automatic cash distribution machines. But you won't be able to check your balance or transfer funds, so keep track of your withdrawals while you travel. These banks are in all major cities and most towns included in this book have at least one major bank. But note that some small villages do not have any major banks.

Make sure your ATM card has a four-digit personal identification number (PIN). French bank cards are issued with PINs of four digits, but most French ATMs still accept PINs of up to six digits. To withdraw cash, your PIN has to be made up of just numbers (French ATMs usually don't have alphanumeric keypads). If your PIN is a combination of letters and numbers, use a telephone dial to figure out the numeric equivalent.

In major cities, ATMs are never far away, so you can walk around with 700F ($100) in your pocket and have enough for eating and most activities. However, before going on a driving tour of the countryside, such as in Brittany or the Loire Valley, which have lots of small towns and villages, make sure you have a good stock of cash in your wallet.

 Remember that each time you withdraw cash from an ATM, your bank hits you with a fee, sometimes as much as $5. Check how much your bank charges before leaving home. On top of this, the bank from which you withdraw cash may include its own fee. Thus, you may save money by taking out larger amounts of money every two to three days rather than small denominations again and again. And remember that your bank places a limit on the amount of money you can take out per day, usually 1,500 to 3,000F ($214 to $430) — check before you leave.

Paying by credit card

You can use credit cards to buy virtually anything in France, as long as it costs a minimum of 100F ($14). You can also get cash advances from your Visa and MasterCard at any bank. You'll need a PIN for withdrawing cash from a credit card, and hefty interest fees are charged from the moment you withdraw the money.

 American Express and Diners Club are not widely accepted at small restaurants, shops, and budget hotels in France. And finally, many credit card companies have begun tacking on additional fees for foreign currency transactions — sometimes up to 4 percent, on top of the 1-percent service charge they already take. Worse, according to Lee Dembart, a writer for *The International Herald Tribune,* is that credit card companies don't expect you to notice the charge. "Recognizing the additional fee requires that the consumer know what the exchange rate was on the day the charge came through and then do the math," he writes, "steps most people don't take." You can find the official rate for dates in the past at www.oanda.com."

If you don't know how much your credit card charges for currency conversion, ask them. If the rate isn't acceptable, consider switching — **MBNA America** (☎ **800-932-2775**; Internet: www.mbna.com), a Delaware-based credit card issuer, still charges only 1 percent for currency conversion.

Leaving home without traveler's checks

Because most cities now have banks with 24-hour ATMs, traveler's checks, which were previously one of the globetrotter's best friends, have become less necessary. Many people find it increasingly difficult to find places that cash traveler's checks. And when you do, well, who wants to stand in a line?

Throughout the country, you can easily exchange traveler's checks in U.S. dollars for French francs, but don't expect to use traveler's checks directly at many budget establishments; change them for francs at a bank or change outlet and use cash instead. Keep in mind that many establishments don't accept traveler's checks in French francs and that, of the places that do accept traveler's checks in U.S. dollars, you normally get a poor exchange rate.

If you're still interested in purchasing traveler's checks, you can get them at almost any bank. Make sure to keep a record of their serial numbers, separately from the checks of course, so you're ensured a refund in an emergency. Your best bet is to buy traveler's checks before leaving home, as well as some French currency — about $50 to $100 worth — unless you don't mind waiting at the exchange offices at the Paris airports.

You can exchange traveler's checks for francs at any of the following banks in Paris: **American Express,** 11 rue Scribe, 9e (☎ **01-47-14-50-00;** Métro: Opéra, Chaussée-d'Antin, or Havre-Caumartin; RER: Auber); **Barclay's,** 24 av. de l'Opéra, 1er (☎ **01-44-86-00-00;** Métro: Pyramides), or 96 rue Turenne, 3e (☎ **01-42-77-24-70;** Métro: St-Paul); **Citibank,** 125 av. Champs-Elysées, 8e (☎ **01-53-23-33-60;** Métro: Charles-de-Gaulle–Etoile); **Thomas Cook,** 194 rue de Rivoli, 1er (☎ **01-42-60-37-61;** Metro: Tuileries), or 25 bd. des Capucines, 2e (☎ **01-42-96-26-78;** Metro: Opéra), and 18 other locations around Paris.

Dealing with a Stolen or Lost Credit Card

Almost every credit card company has an emergency toll-free number that you can call if your wallet or purse is stolen. Not all of these numbers can be used overseas, so you should check with your bank before leaving and have a regular phone number handy just in case. The company may be able to wire you a cash advance off your credit card immediately, and, in many places, can deliver an emergency credit card in a day or two.

Call ☎ **08-36-69-08-80** if you've lost or had your Visa card stolen. **American Express** card and traveler's check holders in France can call international collect (☎ **0800-99-00-11** for an AT&T operator; ☎ **0800-99-00-19** for MCI; ☎ **0800-99-00-87** for Sprint) or ☎ **336-393-1111** for money emergencies; to report lost cards, call ☎ **01-47-77-72-00.** For **MasterCard,** call ☎ **01-45-67-53-53** or 08-00-90-1387.

Be aware that replacing a bank ATM card can take weeks, and there's usually a fee. In contrast, the large credit card companies can replace a card in a day or two at no charge. A bank card has the added disadvantage of allowing a thief to empty out your bank account, if he or she can figure out the PIN.

Chapter 10

Tying Up Loose Ends

*S*ometimes planning for a trip abroad seems to last longer than the actual trip itself. Though this chapter can't go out and do everything for you, it *does* advise and help you organize those innumerable loose ends and last-minute tasks that can frustrate the most seasoned travelers.

Getting a Passport

The only legal form of identification recognized around the world is a valid *passport*. You can't cross an international border without it, though countries that are part of the new European Union aren't as rigid about checking passports for travel between those member countries. Authorities definitely need to see your passport if you arrive by plane or ferry. A passport is the only item you absolutely *must* have in order to travel. In the United States, you're used to your driver's license being the all-purpose ID card. Abroad, it only proves that some American state lets you drive. Getting a passport is easy, but it takes some time to complete the process.

Knowing the rules for U.S. citizens

To apply for a passport for the first time in the United States, you need to go in person to one of 13 passport offices throughout the country; one of the many federal, state, or probate courts; or a major post office (not all accept applications; call the National Passport Information

Center, detailed later in this section, to find the ones that do). You need to bring proof of citizenship, which means a certified birth certificate. You should bring along a driver's license, state or military ID, and any other identifying documents. Bring along two *identical* passport-sized photos (2 inches x 2 inches) you've had taken within the last six months. Get the photos at almost any corner photo shop, where a special camera is used to make them identical. You *cannot* use the strip photos from one of those photo vending machines.

When you get your passport photos taken, have the photo shop make up six to eight total. You may need the extra photos to apply for an International Driving Permit and student or teacher IDs. Take the rest with you. You may need one for random reasons on the road, and — heaven forbid — if you ever lose your passport, you can use one as a replacement photo.

For people 16 and over, a passport is valid for ten years and costs $60 ($45 plus a $15 handling fee); for those under 15, passports are valid for five years and cost $40 total. If you're over 15 and have a passport issued fewer than 12 years ago, you can renew it by mail by filling out the application, available at the places described earlier or at the State Department Web site (http://travel.state.gov). By mail, you bypass the $15 handling fee, so it costs just $45.

Allow plenty of time — at least two months, preferably longer — before your trip to apply. The processing takes four weeks on average but can run somewhat longer during busy periods (especially the spring). To get your passport more quickly — in about five business days — visit an agency directly (or go through the court or post office and have them overnight your application) and pay an additional $35 fee.

For more information, such as finding your regional passport office, visit the State Department Web site at http://travel.state.gov or call the **National Passport Information Center** (☎ 900-225-7778; 35¢ per minute for automated service; $1.05 per minute to speak with an operator).

Keep your passport with you at all times — in your money belt or other secure place. The only times to show it are at the bank for them to photocopy when they change your traveler's checks, at borders for the guards to peruse (or for the conductor on overnight train rides), at gambling casinos, if any police or military personnel ask for it, and *briefly* to the concierge when you check into your hotel.

A valid passport is the only documentation you need as an American to visit France. When you enter the country, your passport is stamped with a temporary tourist *visa* that's good for 90 days of travel within France. If you plan to stay longer, contact any French consulate in the United States before you leave, or any U.S. consulate once you're abroad, to get a specific visa.

Knowing the rules for citizens of other countries

If you're a resident of *Canada,* you can pick up a passport application at one of 28 regional passport offices or most travel agencies. The passport is valid for five years and costs $60. Children under 16 may be included on a parent's passport but need their own to travel unaccompanied. Applications, which must be accompanied by two identical passport-sized photographs and proof of Canadian citizenship, are available at travel agencies throughout Canada or from the central **Passport Office, Department of Foreign Affairs and International Trade,** Ottawa, Canada K1A 0G3 (☎ **800-567-6868;** Internet: www. dfait-maeci.gc.ca/passport). Processing takes five to ten days if you apply in person or about three weeks by mail.

Residents of the *United Kingdom* and *Ireland* need only an identity card, not a passport, to travel to other EU countries. However, if you already have a passport, you can't go wrong by carrying it. *Australian* residents can apply for a passport at a post office or passport office, or search the government Web site (www.dfat.gov.au/passports/). Passports are A$128 for adults and A$64 for those under 18. *New Zealand* citizens can pick up a passport application at the Passport Office or any travel agency, or download the form from www.passports.govt.nz. For more info, contact the Passport Office, Boulcott House, 47 Boulcott St., Wellington (☎ **0800-225-050**). Passports are NZ$80 for adults and NZ$40 for children under 16.

Dealing with a lost passport

Always keep a photocopy of the inside page of your passport with your picture packed separately from your wallet or purse. In the event your passport is lost or stolen, the photocopy can help speed up the replacement process. When traveling in a group, never let one person carry all the passports. If the passports are stolen, obtaining new ones can be much more difficult because at least one person in a group needs to be able to prove his or her identity in order to identify the others.

If you're a U.S. citizen and either lose or have your passport stolen in Paris, go to the Consulate of the **American Embassy** at 2 rue St-Florentin, 1er (☎ **01-43-12-22-22;** Métro: Concorde). Canadians in the same circumstances should visit the Consulate of the **Canadian Embassy,** 35 av. Montaigne, 8e (☎ **01-44-43-29-00;** Métro: Franklin-D-Roosevelt or Alma-Marceau). Australians should go to the **Australian Embassy** at 4 rue Jean-Rey, 15e (☎ **01-40-59-33-00;** Métro: Bir-Hakeim). New Zealanders should visit the **New Zealand Embassy,** 7 rue Léonard-de-Vinci, 16e (☎ **01-45-00-24-11,** ext. 280, 9 a.m. to 1 p.m.; Métro: Victor-Hugo). If you have your passport stolen anywhere else in France outside of Paris, contact the local police (the phone number for police anywhere in France is ☎ **17**), who will direct you on how to get a new passport.

Buying Travel and Medical Insurance

You should consider three primary kinds of travel insurance: trip cancellation, medical, and lost luggage.

Trip cancellation insurance is always a good idea if you pay a large portion of your vacation expenses up front, but the other two types of insurance — *medical* and *lost luggage* — really aren't needed by most travelers. Your existing health insurance should cover you if you get sick while on vacation, but be sure to check your policy before leaving home to see exactly what it promises. Homeowner's insurance should cover stolen luggage if you have off-premises theft. Check your existing policies thoroughly or contact your insurance agent before you buy any additional coverage. The airlines are responsible for $2,500 on domestic flights (and $9.07 per pound, up to $640, on international flights) if they lose your luggage; if you plan to carry anything more valuable than that, keep it in your carry-on bag.

Some credit cards (American Express and certain gold and platinum Visa and MasterCards, for example) offer automatic flight insurance against death or dismemberment in case of an airplane crash.

If you feel that you need more insurance, here's a list of reputable issuers of travel insurance for trip cancellation, medical, and lost luggage: **Access America**, 6600 W. Broad St., Richmond, VA 23230 (☎ **800-284-8300**; Fax: 800-346-9265; Internet: www.accessamerica.com); **Travelex Insurance Services,** 11717 Burt St., Ste. 202, Omaha, NE 68154 (☎ **800-228-9792**; Internet: www.travelex-insurance.com); **Travel Guard International,** 1145 Clark St., Stevens Point, WI 54481 (☎ **800-826-1300**; Internet: www.travel-guard.com); **Travel Insured International, Inc.,** P.O. Box 280568, 52-S Oakland Ave., East Hartford, CT 06128-0568 (☎ **800-243-3174**; Internet: www.travelinsured.com).

Don't pay for more insurance than you need. For example, if you need only trip cancellation insurance, don't purchase coverage for lost or stolen property. Trip cancellation insurance costs about 6 to 8 percent of the total value of your vacation.

Getting Sick Away from Home

Getting sick can ruin your vacation, and finding a doctor you can trust may be difficult when you're away from home. Bring all your medications with you, as well as a prescription for more if you worry that you may run out. If you wear contact lenses, bring an extra pair in case you lose one. And don't forget the Pepto-Bismol for common travelers' ailments like upset stomach or diarrhea.

Keep in mind that sometimes your brand of medication may not exist in France. In that case, any big city pharmacy will have a computer and can research your medication on the Internet and find a similar medication. But of course, this is not ideal, especially with medications for serious illnesses.

For not-so-serious illnesses, you'll find that French pharmacists are highly skilled at providing you with medicines to battle all symptoms. If you go into a pharmacy complaining of the sniffles, you may come out with five different types of medicine to ensure that your sniffles will be vanquished forever.

If you need a pharmacy on a Sunday or at night, you can inquire at the local police station for the nearest 24-hour pharmacy. There is always one in cities. In smaller towns, pharmacies alternate staying open after hours.

 If it is a real emergency, you need to dial ☎ **15** for the SAMU (Service d'Aide Medicale Urgence), which is the ambulance service. You may get even quicker service by dialing the fire department at ☎ **18.** Dial ☎ **17** for the police.

If you have health insurance, check with your provider to find out the extent of your coverage outside your home area. Be sure to carry your ID card in your wallet. And if you worry that your existing policy won't be sufficient, purchase medical insurance (see "Buying Travel and Medical Insurance," earlier in this chapter) for more comprehensive coverage.

If you suffer from a chronic illness, talk to your doctor before taking the trip. For such conditions as epilepsy, diabetes, or a heart condition, wearing a *Medic Alert identification tag* immediately alerts any doctor to your condition and gives him or her access to your medical records through Medic Alert's 24-hour hotline. Membership is $35, with a $15 renewal fee. Contact the Medic Alert Foundation, 2323 Colorado Ave., Turlock, CA 95382 (☎ **800-432-5378;** Internet: www.medicalert.org).

The French government pays 70 percent of the cost of doctor visits, and its national health insurance covers 99 percent of France's population. Visitors needing medical care in France will find that doctors almost always see them the day of the appointment, and patient fees are relatively inexpensive. Patients will almost always have to pay up front, unless they're citizens of European Union countries with reciprocal medical arrangements. Usually, U.S. health insurance companies will reimburse most of the cost of treating illnesses in foreign countries; be sure to keep all receipts.

One benefit U.S. citizens will notice in France is that, with the lack of HMOs to keep an eye on costs, doctors are focused on the patient's comfort rather then the bottom line. For example, injuries for which a U.S. doctor wouldn't check you into the hospital at all may mean five days in a French hospital. Socialized medicine in France also means a lot less paperwork. As long as you have medical insurance in the United States that covers you abroad, you don't have to worry about treatment in France. The medical establishment is of a very high quality, with care for patients the number-one concern.

If you do get sick, ask the concierge at your hotel to recommend a local doctor — even his or her own doctor if necessary. In Paris, you can also call **SOS Help** (☎ **01-47-23-80-80**) between 3 and 11 p.m. for help in English and to ask for an English-speaking doctor. The **Centre Médicale Europe** (44 rue d'Amsterdam, 9e; ☎ **01-42-81-93-33**) is another good option. A host of specialists are located here, and foreigners only pay 115F ($17) for a consultation.

Making Reservations and Getting Tickets in Advance

France's cultural and entertainment scene is hot, and you need to book early for opera and ballet performances, classical music concerts, and some museum exhibits. You also need to reserve ahead if you want to dine at sought-after restaurants. Even popular walking tours of the larger cities get booked up, so you should reserve in advance to avoid getting shut out.

For information on major cultural events, begin from home on the Web with the **French Government Tourist Office** (www.francetourism.com), the **Office de Tourisme et de Congrès de Paris** (www.paris-touristoffice.com), and the **Maison de la France** (www.franceguide.com). You can also try **Culture Kiosque** (www.culturekiosque.com) for excellent magazine-style sites about opera, dance, and major museum exhibits around the world, including schedules, reviews, and phone numbers for ordering tickets. Culture Kiosque also features an online magazine in English, *JazzNet,* which features a calendar of upcoming jazz club dates in Paris and other French cities. In Paris, a free monthly English-language magazine, the **Paris Free Voice** (http://parisvoice.com), features an events calendar and reviews of current opera, dance, and theater.

You can also try these strategies to secure hard-to-get tickets to music, dance, and opera performances:

  ✔ **Call the box office.** Call the venue's box office directly and pay over the phone with your credit card to purchase tickets. Tickets can be sent to your hotel in your name or held at the box office.

✔ **Contact your hotel's concierge.** If you're planning to stay at a hotel with a concierge, phone or fax ahead and ask him or her to obtain tickets for the productions you desire as early as possible, specifying your preferred date with a couple of back-up dates, and the maximum amount you're willing to spend. Expect to pay handsomely for hard-to-land tickets and don't forget to tip the concierge for his or her efforts (50F discreetly slipped into an envelope that you present to the concierge upon receipt of your tickets should be appropriate).

✔ **Try a ticket broker.** One of the most respected international ticket agencies is **Keith Prowse,** 234 W. 44th St., Suite 1000, New York, NY 10036 (☎ **800-669-8687;** Fax: 914-644-8671; E-mail: tickets@. keithprowse.com). Prowse almost always has excellent seats to upcoming musical concerts, ballets, operas, and some sports events. You can also pre-purchase city tours, museum passes, and transportation discounts here.

✔ **Check the Web** for what's going on across France. You can get box office phone numbers, and in some cases, you may be able to link to sites and buy tickets directly. *Time Out*'s Paris Web site (www.timeout.com) lists events in English and updates them weekly. The Web site of the **Paris Office du Tourisme** (www. paris-touristoffice.com) also provides information, in English, on entertainment.

In Paris, you can find several local publications providing up-to-the-minute listings of performances and other evening entertainment. Foremost among these is ***Pariscope: Une Semaine de Paris*** (3F/43¢), a weekly guide with thorough listings of movies, plays, ballet, art exhibits, clubs, and more. It contains an English-language insert written by staff in *Time Out*'s Paris office and can be found at any newsstand. ***L'Officiel des Spectacles*** (2F/30¢) is a weekly guide and ***Paris Nuit*** (30F/$5.10) is a monthly guide; both contain good articles, as well as listings, though neither provides information in English. Costs vary, depending on who is performing what on which day of the week. Call the theaters for information, or consult *Pariscope* and the other entertainment listings.

Many concert, theater, and dance tickets are sold through **FNAC** stores throughout France, as well as at the box office. FNAC outlets number over a dozen in Paris; the most prominent is 74 av. des Champs-Elysées (Métro: George V). You can also reserve by phone (☎ **01-49-87-50-50**) Monday to Friday 9 a.m. to 8 p.m. and Saturday 10 a.m. to 5 p.m. **Virgin Megastore** (52 av. des Champs-Elysées; ☎ **01-49-53-50-00;** Métro: Franklin-D-Roosevelt) is another reputable ticket seller in Paris. The store is open Monday to Saturday 10 a.m. to midnight and Sunday noon to midnight; its tickets-by-phone number listing is ☎ **01-44-68-44-08.**

Packing It Up and Taking It on the Road

Start by taking everything you think you need and laying it out on the bed. Then get rid of half of it — you won't have space, in your suitcase and in your hotel rooms, for that much. Really try to limit yourself to one medium-sized piece of luggage on wheels. And even if it's on wheels, make sure you can comfortably lift it. Many hotels in France don't have elevators, so you may find yourself having to lug your bag up four flights of steps.

The trick to packing light is bringing items that are versatile — the addition of a jacket, a scarf, or jewelry, or the removal of a sweater — allowing you more mileage out of your wardrobe. Bring separates in neutral colors that can make several outfits. You'll never need to worry about something to wear and you'll always look smart. Accessorize with a scarf and you could be mistaken for a local!

If you plan to buy some of those fabulous French clothes as a souvenir of your trip, consider bringing far fewer clothes and leaving some room in your suitcase.

In order to conserve baggage space, you must limit yourself to two pairs of shoes. No exceptions! One pair should be for walking — preferably not sneakers. In Paris and other large cities, sneakers are looked down on in many places, and you feel much more comfortable if you're not over- or underdressed (and nothing screams tourist more than a pair of bright white sneakers). Try for a casual-Fridays-at-work look. The same holds true for evenings. Think a notch dressier than what you'd normally wear out to dinner (even more if your normal evening out attire usually consists of sweats and a ball cap). Even at casual neighborhood bistros, most men wear sport jackets and women wear skirts or smart pantsuits at dinner.

Remember to fill your shoes with small items like socks and underwear to help to save space. Fit the rest of your small items around your shoes, and pack breakable items between several layers of clothing. Dry cleaners' plastic bags are great for protecting items that wrinkle easily. And don't forget those handy resealable plastic sandwich bags — they make great toiletry cases, they solve the problem of leaky items, and if you have small kids, they can hold a damp washcloth to clean up little messes. You can also save space by buying travel-sized plastic bottles at the drugstore to fill with shampoo, conditioner, and other liquid beauty essentials.

Leave your cell phone at home — unless you have one of the new phones that adapt to the GSM norm on which the European cell phone system works. And as for appliances, not only are they clumsy to carry around, you need an electrical adapter to use them — European current runs on 210–220V, while American current is 110V, 60 cycles — along with a transformer to bring the voltage down and the cycles up. If you must bring an appliance, be sure it runs on dual voltage.

 For more tips on packing, consult **Travelite** (www.travelite.org), which also gives advice on packing light, choosing luggage, and selecting appropriate travel wear. Its printable packing lists are very helpful.

Looking Like a Local

Male visitors usually find it easy to look like a local. The staple casual look for Frenchmen is a blazer over a button down shirt and khakis (or sometimes nicely pressed Levis) with loafers or other casual shoes that don't fall into the sneaker category. The tie is optional. Men with more formal careers wear beautifully tailored suits and often carry small leather briefcases also known as "male handbags."

For women, obtaining that French look is a bit harder. In the first place, it seems French women are born understanding how to put outfits together with that *je ne sais quoi* that no foreigner can imitate. In general, French women dress for all occasions in a fancier and sexier way than most American women (rent a Catherine Deneuve flick; she is *très typique!*). Accessorizing is the key, and you may find your most critical item of clothing is a great scarf. Wear it with a white t-shirt during the day and with a little black dress at night. You can't go wrong in France with feminine clothes in neutral colors. For walking during the day, avoid being instantly picked out as a tourist by investing in a pair of comfortable walking shoes that are dressy enough to wear with a casual skirt. Leave the sneakers, fanny pack, shorts, and baseball cap at home. Though Paris is the most visited city in the world, I recently saw an elderly Parisienne stare disapprovingly at two American women wearing shorts on the Métro. If you bring a small purse with long straps, you can wear it diagonally across your body for a fashionable and safe way to carry your belongings.

Sizing Things Up: Size Conversions

Face it — you're probably going to be tempted to buy some clothes while in France. Shopping for clothes in France is a bit easier, now that S, M, and L are used in some cases. Hats and shirt collars, however, are measured in centimeters. To find your correct size, multiply the number of inches you require by 1.34.

Consider that the French are often smaller — and thinner — than Americans. Many women's clothes come in a maximum size of 46 (see Table 10-1), so you have to go to specialty stores to find a larger size, with a very marked change in style. For men, the advantage is that pants are sold without a hem, so you can have them custom tailored for your height.

Here's a size conversion chart to help you with your purchases. However, remember that sizes aren't necessarily standardized among different makers, and that trying clothes on before you buy is always best, especially shoes.

Table 10-1	Size Conversion Chart						
Women's Clothing							
American	6	8	10	12	14	16	
French	36	38	40	42	44	46	
British	8	10	12	14	16	18	
Women's Shoes							
American	5	6	7	8	9	10	
French	36	37	38	39	40	41	
British	4	5	6	7	8	9	
Men's Suits							
American	34	36	38	40	42	44	46	48
French	44	46	48	50	52	54	56	58
British	34	36	38	40	42	44	46	48
Men's Shirts							
American	14½	15	15½	16	16½	17	17½	18
French	37	38	39	41	42	43	44	45
British	14½	15	15½	16	16½	17	17½	18
Men's Shoes							
American	7	8	9	10	11	12	13
French	39½	41	42	43	44½	46	47
British	6	7	8	9	10	11	12

Converting Electricity

The standard voltage throughout France is 200 volts, 50 cycles, as compared to American electricity, which is 110 volts, 60 cycles. In some older establishments, you may find 110 or 115 volts. *Adapters* are needed for all sockets, as France uses a two-pin and sometimes a three-pin socket. For some appliances, you need a *current converter* or *transformer* in addition to an adapter. Unless you absolutely need them, leave the electrical appliances at home.

Travel-size versions of hair dryers, irons, and shavers are dual voltage, which means they have built-in converters (usually you have to turn a switch to go back and forth). Most contemporary laptop computers automatically sense the current and adapt accordingly. Check the manual, bottom of the machine, or manufacturer to make sure you don't damage your machine.

Getting Through Customs

Technically, no limits are placed on how much loot you can bring back into the United States from a trip abroad, but the customs authority *does* put limits on how much you can take in for free (mainly for taxation purposes, to separate tourists with souvenirs from importers).

You're allowed $400 worth of goods duty-free upon reentry to the United States, provided you've been out of the country at least 48 hours and haven't used the exemption in the past 30 days. Among the allowable goods are one liter of an alcoholic beverage (you must, of course, be over 21), 200 cigarettes, and 100 cigars. Goods you mail home from abroad are exempt from the $400 limit, but other limits are still in place. You may mail up to $200 worth of goods to yourself (marked "for personal use") and up to $100 to others (marked "unsolicited gift") once each day, so long as the package does not include alcohol or tobacco products. You must pay an import duty on anything over these limits.

Note that buying items at a *duty-free shop* before flying home does *not* exempt them from counting toward your U.S. Customs limits (monetary or otherwise). The "duty" you avoid in those shops is the local tax on the item (like state sales tax in the States), not any import duty that may be assessed by the U.S. Customs office.

If you have further questions, or to get a list of specific items you can't bring into the United States, look in your phone book (under U.S. Government, Department of the Treasury, U.S. Customs Service) to find the nearest Customs office. Or check out the Customs Service Web site (www.customs.ustreas.gov/travel/travel.htm).

If you're not an American citizen, check with your local Customs department before going abroad to determine your country's policy.

Part III
Paris and the Ile de France

"It says, 'children are forbidden from running, touching objects, or appearing bored during the tour.'"

In this part...

Welcome to Paris and its environs, called the Ile de France! If you've never been to Paris, you'll find so much to like. If you've visited before, you'll find much has changed. The city is a lot friendlier than it's reputed to be; many people are willing to try out their English to help visitors, and warm and helpful service at stores and restaurants is the norm. Monuments have been restored, people talk on cell phones everywhere, and futuristic parks and buildings are popping up all over. Although Paris is a thoroughly modern city, its timeless beauty will take your breath away and have you visiting again and again.

In Chapter 11, I help you get oriented, get you on your way to discovering the City of Light, and give you my top picks for hotels and restaurants. In Chapter 12, you'll learn about the top sights and how much time you should devote to them. You'll find out where to go to see theater, opera, ballet, and concerts and where to dance until the wee hours. In Chapter 13, I tell you about five great side trips — some of the best places to explore in the Ile de France — including magnificent Versailles, impressive Fontainebleau, and one of the world's greatest Gothic masterpieces, the Cathedral of Chartres. I also introduce you to Disneyland Paris and to Giverny, the vibrant gardens and home of Impressionist painter Claude Monet.

Chapter 11

Settling into Paris: City of Light

- -

In This Chapter

▶ Getting to Paris, and getting your bearings once you're there

▶ Traveling around Paris

▶ Choosing where to stay and where to dine

- -

*A*fter you finish reading this chapter, you'll be walking around Paris like a native in no time. I tell you about all the different ways to get to Paris, then I orient you and get you around the city's most happening neighborhoods by bus, Métro, taxi, bike, and on foot. Don't worry about where you'll be resting your weary head or satisfying your appetite — I list some of the best centrally located and reasonably priced hotels and restaurants in Paris. You also find out where you can eat when you just don't have the room for a full-course meal. Finally, I give you some of our picks for cafes and wine bars, where you'll see the Parisian sport of people-watching at its best.

Getting There

It's not difficult to find transportation to Paris, France's capital; the major autoroutes converge there, trains arrive there from all parts of France and Europe, and the city is also served by two airports. This section covers getting to Paris by plane, train, bus, and automobile, as well as by ferry, hydrofoil, and hovercraft.

By air

Paris is a major hub for air transportation. **Aéroport Charles-de-Gaulle** is the larger, busier, and more modern airport, commonly known as CDG and Roissy–Charles de Gaulle. It's located 23.3 km (14.5 miles) northeast of downtown Paris, and nearly all direct flights from North America land there. French domestic flights and intra-European and intercontinental flights arrive at **Aéroport d'Orly**, 13.5 km (8.5 miles) south of downtown Paris.

Arriving at Roissy–Charles de Gaulle

Nearly all direct flights from North America land at Charles de Gaulle (☎ 01-48-62-22-80). Bilevel **Terminal 1 (Aérogare 1),** is the older and smaller of the two terminals and is used by foreign airlines; **Terminal 2 (Aérogare 2),** is used by Air France, domestic and intra-European airlines, and some foreign airlines, including Air Canada. Terminal 2 is divided into halls A through F. A free **shuttle bus** *(navette)* connects the two terminals.

Getting from the airport to your hotel

Paris may be the first stop on your France itinerary, or you may simply land there to transfer planes, collect your rental car, or take the train to another destination. You'll probably need to know how to get to and from **Charles de Gaulle,** so I list the ways in this section. Fortunately, they're all easy.

Probably the easiest, but certainly not cheapest, way to your hotel is by **taxi.** A cab into town from Charles de Gaulle takes 40 to 50 minutes, depending on traffic, and costs about 220F ($31) between 7 a.m. and 8 p.m. and about 40 percent more at other times. Taxis are required to charge the price indicated on the taxi's meter plus 6F (90¢) for each piece of luggage stowed in the trunk. If your French is poor or nonexistent, it's a good idea to write down the name and full address of your hotel. The five-digit postal code is the most important morsel of information; it lets the driver know the *arrondissement* (municipal ward) of your destination (the last two numbers of the code are the arrondissement number). Check the meter before you pay — rip-offs of arriving tourists aren't uncommon. If you feel you may have been overcharged, demand a receipt (which drivers are obligated to provide) and contact the **Préfecture of Police** (☎ 01-55-76-20-00). Here's where you can find the taxi stands at Charles de Gaulle: **CDG 1** (Porte 16, arrivals level), **CDG 2A and 2C** (Hall A, Porte 7), **CDG 2B and 2D** (Hall D, Porte 7), and **CDG 2F** (Porte 1, arrivals level).

The **Airport Shuttle** (2 av. Général Leclerc 14e; ☎ 01-45-38-55-72; Fax: 01-43-21-35-67; E-mail: ashuttle@club-internet.fr; Internet: www.paris-anglo.com/clients/ashuttle; Métro: Denfert-Rochereau) is cheaper than a taxi for one or two people but more expensive than airport buses and trains. As soon as you arrive, call Airport Shuttle's toll-free number (☎ 0-800-50-56-10), while you wait for your bags, to confirm pickup. You'll be picked up in a minivan at Charles de Gaulle or Orly and taken to your hotel for 89F ($13) per person for parties of two or more or 120F ($17) for a single. There's no extra charge for luggage. The **Paris Airport Service** (BP 41, Cedex 94431 Chennevières; ☎ 01-49-62-78-78; Fax: 01-49-62-78-79; E-mail: pas@magic.fr) offers a similar service. It costs 145F ($21) for one person or 180F ($26) for two or more from Charles de Gaulle and 115F ($16) for one person or 135F ($19) for two or more from Orly. Both companies accept Visa and MasterCard.

If you're not overloaded with baggage and you want to keep down your expenses, the best way into Paris is probably the **RER** *(air-uh-air)* **Line B suburban train,** which stops near Terminals 1 and 2. This is how most Parisians get home from the airport, since it's cheap and convenient. The line operates Monday to Friday 5 a.m. to midnight and Saturday and Sunday 7 a.m. to 9 p.m. A free **shuttle bus** connects the terminals to the RER train station. If you land in **CDG 1** (Terminal 1), exit the terminal at Porte 28 on the arrivals level and look for the bus marked "RER." If you land in **CDG 2** (Terminal 2), there's no shuttle bus, since the terminal is linked to the RER by a walkway. Look for the round RER logo or ask an airport employee. At the ticket counter, ask for the **RER plus Métro** ticket, 47F ($7), and hang onto it in case of ticket inspection. (You'll be fined 100F/$14 if you can't produce your ticket to an inspector.) In any case, if your hotel is too far from the RER, you'll need your ticket later to get off the RER system and into the Métro system. From the airport station, trains depart about every 15 minutes for the half-hour trip into town, stopping on the **Right Bank** at Gare du Nord and Châtelet–Les Halles and on the **Left Bank** at St-Michel, Luxembourg, Port-Royal, and Denfert-Rochereau before heading south, out of the city.

A **bus** is better than the RER, if you're not heading into town during a weekly rush hour and your hotel is near one of the drop-off points. If you're staying on the **Right Bank,** in the **8e, 16e,** or **17e** arrondissements, an **Air France coach** stops at Porte Maillot, before ending up at Etoile, the name for the huge traffic roundabout at the Arc de Triomphe. The bus runs every 12 minutes from 5:40 a.m. to 11 p.m. and costs 60F ($9) one way. You don't have to be an Air France passenger to use the service, and you can buy your ticket right on the bus. In light traffic, such as on weekend mornings, it takes about 40 minutes to get from the airport into the city. During weekday morning rush hour, however, the same trip can take twice as long or longer. You can pick up this coach from **CDG 1** (Porte 34, arrivals level), **CDG 2A and 2C** (Porte 5), **CDG 2B and 2D** (Porte 6), and **CDG 2F** (Porte G, arrivals level).

If you're staying on the **Right Bank** near the **Bastille (11e** or **12e)** or on the **Left Bank** in **Montparnasse (14e),** a different **Air France coach** stops at the Gare de Lyon, before ending up near the back of the Gare de Montparnasse. The bus runs every 30 minutes from 7 a.m. to 9 p.m. and costs 70F ($10) one way. In light traffic it takes about 50 minutes to get from the airport into the city. Catch this coach from **CDG 1** (Porte 26, arrivals level), **CDG 2A and 2C** (Hall C, Porte 2), **CDG 2B and 2D** (Hall D, Porte 12), and **CDG 2F** (Porte H, arrivals level). If your hotel is on the **Right Bank** near the **Opéra (2e** or **9e),** take the **Roissybus** that leaves every 15 minutes from 6 a.m. to 11 p.m. and costs 45F ($6). The drop-off point is on rue Scribe, a block from the Opéra Garnier near American Express. It takes 45 to 50 minutes in regular traffic. You can buy your tickets in the little office next to where the bus parks. Pick up this coach from **CDG 1** (Porte 30, arrivals level), **CDG 2A and 2C** (Hall C, Porte 10), **CDG 2B and 2D** (Hall D, Porte 12), and **CDG 2F** (Porte H, arrivals level).

Arriving at Orly

Orly airport (☎ **01-49-75-15-15**) has two terminals — **Ouest (West)** and **Sud (South)** — and English speakers will find the terminal easy to navigate. French domestic flights land at Orly Ouest, and intra-European and intercontinental flights arrive at Orly Sud. Shuttle buses connect these terminals, and other shuttles connect them to Charles de Gaulle every 30 minutes or so. There's a **tourist desk** at Orly Sud, Gate G, where you can pick up city maps and other visitor essentials.

Getting from the airport to your hotel

A **taxi** from Orly into Paris costs about 170F ($24) and takes from 25 minutes to 1 hour, depending on traffic. You'll find the taxi stand just outside Porte H. Remember to write down the full name and address of your hotel for the driver. Also note that cabs charge 6F (90¢) for each piece of luggage that's put in the trunk.

You can also take the **Airport Shuttle** or the **Paris Airport Service** (see "Arriving at Roissy–Charles de Gaulle" earlier in this chapter).

If you're staying on the **Left Bank** near **Les Invalides (7e),** take the **Air France coach,** leaving from Porte F every 12 to 15 minutes. Line 1 leaves from Exit D on the arrival level at Orly Ouest and Exit K at Orly Sud. The trip takes 30 minutes to its final destination, Gare de Lyon, and costs 45F ($6). You can request that the bus stop at Montparnasse-Duroc.

The cheapest trip into town is on the **Jetbus.** It connects Orly with the Villejuif–Louis Aragon Métro station in south Paris and costs 26.50F ($3.80) for the 15-minute journey. The bus leaves every 12 to 15 minutes from Exit G2 in Orly Sud and from Exit C, arrival level in Orly Ouest. The **Orly bus** operates from Exit J, arrival level at Orly Ouest and from Exit H, Platform 4 at Orly Sud to the Left Bank's **Denfert-Rochereau,** for 35F ($5).

You can also take the **RER Line C,** although it's a bit of a hassle. To take it, you catch a free shuttle bus from Porte H, Platform 1 to the **Rungis** station, where RER C trains leave every 15 minutes. A one-way fare is 32F ($4.60), and the trip into the city takes 30 minutes, making various stops along the Seine on the **Left Bank.** If you're staying on the **Right Bank,** you can take the **Orlyval service** using **RER Line B** right from the airport. From Orly Sud, Orlyval departs from Exit K near the baggage-claim area and from Exit W and Exit J on the departure level at Orly Ouest. You'll connect at the **Antony** RER station where you'll board the RER B train to Paris. If your hotel is too far from the RER, you can buy a Métro pass for the subway at the Antony station. You can avoid the line by buying your Orlyval tickets from a machine, if you have French coins with you. Once in Paris, the train stops at **Denfert-Rochereau, Port-Royal, Luxembourg,** and **St-Michel** on the Left Bank and then crosses to the Right Bank and stops at **Châtelet** and **Gare du Nord.** The trip to Châtelet takes about 30 minutes and costs 57F ($8).

By train

If you're already in Europe, you may want to go to Paris by train, especially if you have a **Eurailpass.** For information, call the national train network, **SNCF** (☎ **01-53-90-20-20**), and ask for someone who speaks English, or go to a travel agent or one of the information booths at the stations.

If you come from northern Germany or Belgium (and sometimes London), you'll probably arrive at the **Gare du Nord.** Trains from Normandy come into **Gare St-Lazare,** in northwest Paris. Trains from the west (Brittany, Chartres, Versailles, Bordeaux) head to the **Gare de Montparnasse;** those from the southwest (the Loire Valley, the Pyrénées, Spain) to the **Gare d'Austerlitz;** those from the south and southeast (the Riviera, Lyon, Italy, Geneva) to the **Gare de Lyon.** Trains coming from Alsace and eastern France, Luxembourg, southern Germany, and Zurich, arrive at the **Gare de l'Est.** All train stations are next to a Métro station bearing the same name.

By bus

Buses connect Paris to most major cities in Europe. European Railways operates **Europabus** and **Eurolines.** The companies don't have American offices, so travelers must make bus transportation arrangements after arriving in Europe. In **Great Britain,** contact Eurolines (☎ **0207/730-8235**) at the Victoria Coach station. In **Paris,** the contact is Eurolines (28 av. du Général-de-Gaulle, 93541 Bagnolet; ☎ **08-36-69-52-52** at 2.23F/min). International buses pull into Paris's **Gare Routière Internationale (International Bus Terminal)** at av. Charles-de-Gaulle in the suburb of Bagnolet, just across the *périphérique* (ring road) from the Gallieni Métro station. To go downtown, take Line 3 and change buses according to your final destination.

By ferry and tunnel

About a dozen companies run hydrofoil, ferry, and hovercraft across the English Channel — or *La Manche* ("the sleeve"), as the French say. Services operate daily and most carry cars. Hovercraft and hydrofoils make the trip in 40 minutes; the shortest ferry route between Dover and Calais is about 1½ hours. The major routes are between Dover and Calais, and Folkestone and Boulogne (about 12 trips a day). Depending on weather conditions, prices and timetables can vary. It's always important to make a reservation, because ferries are crowded.

For information stateside, call **Britrail** (☎ **800/677-8585**) or **Britain Bound Travel** (☎ **800/805-8210**). In Britain, contact **Hoverspeed** (☎ **0870/524-0241**). Special fares are offered, but they change frequently. A good travel agent — say, in London — can help you sort out the maze of ferry schedules, find a suitable option, and book your ticket.

The **Channel Tunnel** (Chunnel) opened in 1994, and the popularity of its Eurostar train service has had the happy effect of driving down prices on all cross-channel transport. This remarkable engineering feat means that if you take your car aboard Le Shuttle in Britain, you can be driving in France an hour later. Tickets can be purchased in advance or at the tollbooth. Eurostar tickets start at 690F ($99) for round-trip off-season if you book 7 days in advance and stay over the weekend, but prices rise in April and again in June. Taking your car aboard Le Shuttle trains costs about 60F ($9) extra. For further information and reservations in the United States, call Britrail or Britain Bound Travel; in the U.K., call ☎ 0870/518-6186; in Paris, call ☎ 01-49-70-01-75; in Australia, call GSA:Rail Plus, ☎ 61/3-9642-8644.

By car

If you drive, remember that a road called the *périphérique* circles Paris — its exits aren't numbered. The major highways in Paris are **A1** from the north (Great Britain and Belgium); **A13** from Normandy and other points in northwest France; **A109** from Spain and the southwest; **A7** from the Alps, the Riviera, and Italy; and **A4** from eastern France. Avoid rush hours!

Orienting Yourself in Paris

You've arrived at your hotel, checked in, and maybe unpacked a little. Now it's time to go out and act like a Parisian — have a cup of coffee or a glass of wine at a cafe, check out the passing crowds, and get ready to explore.

Making your way around Paris can be simplified by knowing the arrondissement that your intended destination is in. The city is divided into 20 municipal wards called **arrondissements,** each with its own mayor, city hall, police station, and central post office. Some arrondissements even have remnants of market squares. The river Seine divides Paris into a Right and Left Bank. The Right Bank, **Rive Droite,** is to the north and the Left Bank, **Rive Gauche,** to the south. These designations make sense when you stand on a bridge and face downstream; watching the water flow out toward the sea, to your right is the north bank, to your left the south. Thirty-two bridges link the banks of the Seine, some providing access to the two small islands at the heart of the city, **Ile de la Cité,** the city's birthplace and site of Notre-Dame, and **Ile St-Louis,** a moat-guarded oasis of sober seventeenth-century mansions. These islands can cause some confusion to walkers who think they've just crossed a bridge from one bank to the other, only to find themselves caught up in an almost medieval maze of narrow streets and old buildings.

The key to finding any address in Paris is looking for the arrondissement number, rendered either as a number followed by "e" or "er" (1er, 2e, and so on) or more formally as part of the postal code. The last two digits indicate the arrondissement — 75007 indicates the 7th arrondissement, 75017 the 17th, and so on. Numbers on buildings running parallel to the Seine usually follow the course of the river, east to west. On north-south streets, numbering begins at the river.

Paris by arrondissement

Probably your best introduction to Paris and the way the city is laid out is from the tower at Notre-Dame. The magnificent cathedral is visible from many parts of the city, and a visit will help you get oriented. You'll also realize that the Seine is actually Paris's most important "street." I list the more famous arrondissements here:

- ✔ **1er Arr. (Right Bank, Musée du Louvre/Palais-Royal/Les Halles):** One of the world's greatest art museums (some say *the* greatest), the **Louvre** still lures all visitors to Paris to the 1er arrondissement. You'll see many of the city's elegant addresses along **rue de Rivoli,** as well as arched arcades under which all kinds of touristy junk is sold. You can walk through the **Jardin des Tuileries,** Paris's most formal garden, and then take in the classic beauty of opulent **place Vendôme,** home of the Hôtel Ritz. The **Forum des Halles,** an above-ground and below-ground shopping-and-entertainment center, is also here. This arrondissement tends to be crowded, and its hotels are higher priced in high season because the area is so convenient.

- ✔ **2e Arr. (Right Bank, La Bourse):** Often overlooked by tourists, the 2e houses the **Bourse** (stock exchange). The district, lying between the **Grands Boulevards** and **rue Etienne-Marcel,** is also home to the garment trade; wholesale fashion outlets abound. Beware: there's some prostitution here.

- ✔ **3e Arr. (Right Bank, Le Marais):** Le Marais (the swamp) is one of Paris's hippest neighborhoods, and you'll find one of the city's most popular attractions, the **Musée Picasso,** here. Paris's old Jewish neighborhood is around **rue des Rosiers,** and **rue Vieille-du-Temple** is home to numerous gay bars and boutiques.

- ✔ **4e Arr. (Right Bank, Ile de la Cité/Ile St-Louis/Centre Pompidou):** In the 4e you'll find aristocratic town houses, courtyards, antiques shops, flower markets, the **Palais de Justice,** the **Conciergerie, Notre-Dame, Sainte-Chapelle,** the **Centre Pompidou,** and **place des Vosges.** This is one of the prettiest and most crowded arrondissements.

- ✔ **5e Arr. (Left Bank, Latin Quarter):** Bookstores, schools, churches, nightclubs, student dives, Roman ruins, publishing houses, and expensive boutiques characterize this district. It's called "Latin" because at one time students and professors at the Sorbonne spoke Latin. Stroll along **quai de Montebello,** inspecting the inventories of the *bouquinistes* (booksellers) and wander the shops in the old streets of **rue de la Huchette** and **rue de la Harpe** — but don't eat on either of these streets. The restaurants have people who'll try to pull you in by promising cheap food. They'll hit your wallet, however, with their overpriced drinks and extras. The 5e also stretches down to the **Panthéon,** and to the fun **rue Mouffetard** behind it, where you can visit one of the city's best produce markets or eat at a variety of ethnic restaurants.

✔ **6e Arr. (Left Bank, St-Germain/Luxembourg Gardens):** The art school that turned away Rodin, the **Ecole des Beaux-Arts,** is here, as well as some of the most chic designers around. But the secret of the district lies in discovering its narrow streets and hidden squares. Everywhere you turn, you encounter places with famous historic and literary associations. The 6e takes in the **Jardin du Luxembourg,** probably its residents' most loved park.

✔ **7e Arr. (Left Bank, Eiffel Tower/Musée d'Orsay):** The city's most famous symbol, the **Tour Eiffel,** dominates the 7e, and part of the **St-Germain** neighborhood is here too. The **Hôtel des Invalides,** which contains both **Napoléon's Tomb** and the **Musée de l'Armée** is also in the 7e, in addition to the **Musée Rodin** and the **Musée d'Orsay,** the world's premier showcase of nineteenth-century French art and culture.

✔ **8e Arr. (Right Bank, Champs-Elysées/Madeleine):** The 8e is the heart of the Right Bank, and its showcase is the **Champs-Elysées.** Here, you'll find the fashion houses, the most elegant hotels, expensive restaurants and shops, and the most fashionably attired Parisians. The Champs stretches from the **Arc de Triomphe** to the city's oldest monument, the obelisk on **place de la Concorde.**

✔ **9e Arr. (Right Bank, Opéra Garnier/Pigalle):** Everything from the **Quartier de l'Opéra** to the strip joints of **Pigalle** falls within the 9e, which was radically altered by Baron Haussmann's nineteenth-century redevelopment projects, like his Grands Boulevards radiating through the district. Major attractions include the **Folies Bergère,** where cancan dancers have been high-kicking since 1868, and entertainers like Mistinguett, Edith Piaf, and Maurice Chevalier appeared along with Josephine Baker. Try to visit the **Opéra Garnier** (Paris Opera House), which was expensively restored a few years ago.

✔ **10e Arr. (Right Bank, Gare du Nord/Gare de l'Est):** Though most of this arrondissement is dreary, a few bright spots exist along the **Canal St-Martin** in the east: **Quai de Valmy** and **quai de Jemmapes** are scenic tree-lined promenades on the canal, where the movie *Hôtel du Nord* was filmed.

✔ **11e Arr. (Right Bank, Opéra Bastille):** The 11e has few landmarks or famous museums, but it's become a mecca for hordes of young Parisians looking for casual, inexpensive nightlife. Always crowded on weekends and in summer, the overflow retires to the steps of the **Opéra Bastille,** which opened in 1989.

✔ **14e Arr. (Left Bank, Montparnasse): Montparnasse** is the former stomping ground of the "lost generation": Gertrude Stein, Alice B. Toklas, Ernest Hemingway, and other American expatriates who gathered here in the 1920s. After World War II, it ceased to be the center of intellectual life in Paris, but the memory lingers in its cafes. Some of the world's most famous literary cafes, including **La Rotonde, Le Select, La Dôme,** and **La Coupole,** are in the northern end of this large arrondissement, near the **Rodin statue of Balzac** at the junction of boulevard Montparnasse and boulevard Raspail. At its southern end, the arrondissement contains pleasant residential neighborhoods filled with well-designed apartment buildings, many built between 1910 and 1940.

✔ **16e Arr. (Right Bank, Trocadéro/Bois de Boulogne):** This is where the moneyed live. Highlights include the **Bois de Boulogne,** the **Jardin du Trocadéro,** the **Musée de Balzac,** the **Musée Guimet** (famous for its Asian collections), and the **Cimetière de Passy,** final resting place of Manet, Talleyrand, Giraudoux, and Debussy. One of the largest arrondissements, the 16e is known today for its exclusivity, its BCBG residents *(bon chic bon genre),* its upscale rents, and some rather posh (and, according to its critics, rather smug) residential boulevards. Prosperous and suitably conservative addresses include avenue d'Iéna and avenue Victor Hugo. Also prestigious is **avenue Foch,** the widest boulevard in Paris and home at various times to Aristotle Onassis, Shah Mohammad Reza Pahlavi of Iran, Maria Callas, and Prince Rainier of Monaco. The arrondissement also includes what some visitors consider the best place in Paris from which to view the Eiffel Tower, **place du Trocadéro.**

✔ **18e Arr. (Right Bank, Montmartre): Montmartre,** the **Moulin Rouge,** the **Basilique du Sacré-Coeur,** and **place du Tertre** are only some of the attractions in this outer arrondissement. Take a walk through the winding old streets here, and you'll feel transported into another era. The city's most famous flea market, the **Marché aux Puces de la Porte de St-Ouen,** is another landmark.

Street smarts: Where to get information after you arrive

The prime source of information is the **Office de Tourisme de Paris** (127 av. des Champs-Elysées, 8e; ☎ **08-36-68-31-12** or 01-49-52-53-35; Fax: 01-49-52-53-00; E-mail: info@paris-touristoffice.com; Internet: www.paris-touristoffice.com; Métro: Charles-de-Gaulle–Etoile or George V). It's open daily, 9 a.m. to 8 p.m. (Sunday 11 a.m. to 7 p.m., November to April).There's an **auxiliary office** at the **Eiffel Tower** (open May to September, daily 11 a.m. to 6 p.m.) and at the **Gare de Lyon** (open Monday to Saturday 8 a.m. to 8 p.m.).

Paris Arrondissements

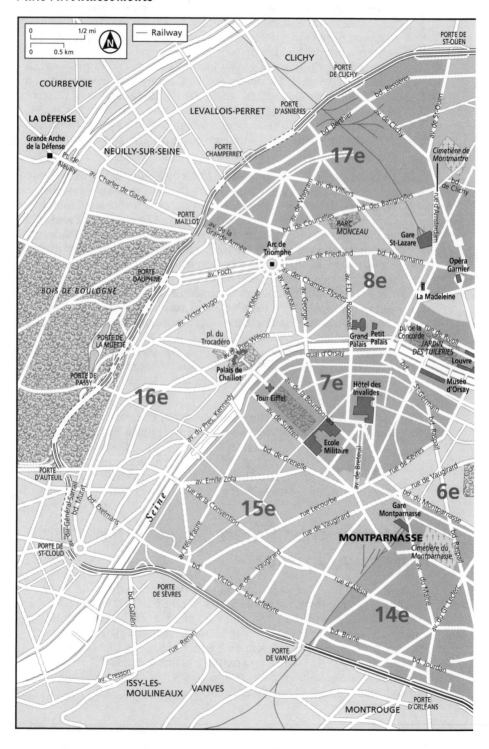

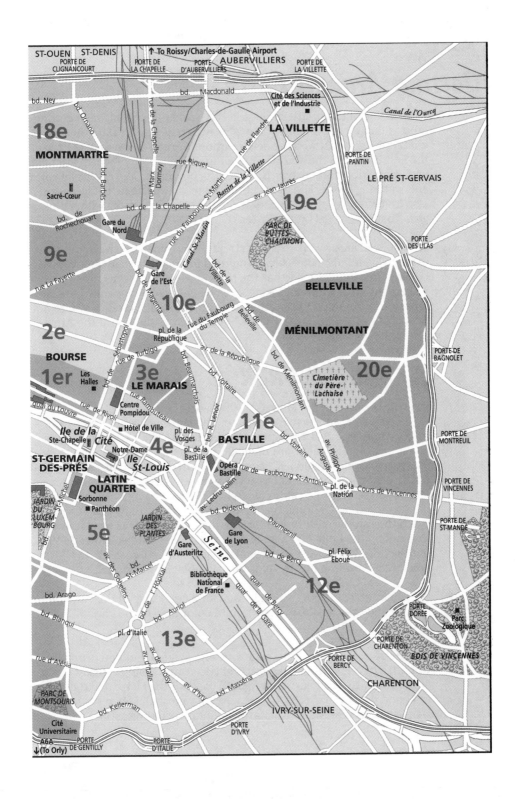

At the main and auxiliary tourist offices, you can also reserve concert, theater, or cabaret tickets without an extra fee.

Getting Around Paris

Paris is one of the prettiest cities in the world for strolling, and getting around on foot is probably the best way to really appreciate the city's character. The best walking neighborhoods are **St-Germain-des-Prés** on the Left Bank and the **Marais** on the Right Bank, both of which are filled with romantic little courtyards, wonderful boutiques, and congenial cafes and watering holes. The quais of the Seine, as well as its bridges, are also lovely, especially at sunset when the sun fills the sky with a pink glow that's reflected on the water.

Take special care when crossing streets, even when you have the right of way. The number-one rule of the road in France is that whoever is coming from the right side has the right of way. This means drivers often make right turns without looking, even when faced with pedestrians at crosswalks. And don't *ever* attempt to cross a traffic circle if you're not on a crosswalk. The larger roundabouts, such as the one at the Arc de Triomphe, have pedestrian tunnels.

By Métro and RER

Over 100 years old, the **Métro** (☎ **08-36-68-41-14**; Internet: www.ratp.fr) is fast, safe, and easy to navigate. The subway is operated by the **Régie Autonome des Transports Parisiens (RATP),** as are city buses, and it has 16 lines and more than 360 stations, so there's bound to be one near your destination. It's connected to the **Réseau Express Régional (RER)** regional trains that connect downtown Paris with its airports and suburbs. Subway trains run daily 5:30 a.m. to 1 a.m., and you'll often witness people running down streets around 12:50 a.m., trying to catch the last train. During off-hours, the RATP operates **Noctambuses** that run on the hour 1:30 a.m. to 5:30 a.m. from Châtelet–Hôtel-de-Ville, but they don't cover every arrondissement. Tickets cost 30F ($4.30). You'll recognize the bus by its yellow-and-black owl symbol.

See the front inside cover of this book for a color map of the Paris Métro system and the back inside cover for a color map of the Paris RER system.

The Métro and RER operate on a zone fare system, but you probably won't travel any farther than the first two zones. A **single ticket** costs 8F ($1.15). A 10-ticket **carnet (booklet),** good for the Métro and the buses, is a good deal for 55F ($8). Carnets are on sale at all Métro stations, as well as *tabacs* (cafes and kiosks that sell tobacco products).

If you plan to use public transportation frequently, consider buying the **Carte Orange.** This weekly or monthly pass is inexpensive — 80F ($11) for a week's unlimited travel *(coupon hebdomadaire)* or 271F ($39) for a month's pass *(coupon mensuel)* — and covers zones 1 and 2. The only catch is that you must supply a little photo of yourself. Bring one from home or visit a photo booth at one of the many Monoprix stores, major Métro stations, department stores, or train stations, where you can get four black-and-white pictures for 25F ($3.60). The weekly Carte Orange is on sale Monday to Wednesday morning and is valid through Sunday. But, the monthly card is sold only on the first two days of the month.

You'll also see ads for the **Paris Visite** card, starting at 55F ($8) per day. It does offer free or reduced entry to some attractions, in addition to unlimited public-transportation travel, but make sure the attractions that interest you are included on the list.

At the entrance to each station, insert your ticket in the turnstile, pass through, and take your ticket out of the machine. When you ride the Métro, you must keep your ticket until you exit the train platform at your destination and pass the *limite de validité des billets* (limit of validity of tickets) . An inspector may ask to see your ticket at any time, and if you fail to produce it, you'll be subject to a steep fine. When you ride the RER, it's especially important that you keep your ticket, because you have to insert it in a turnstile when you exit the station.

Some older Métro stations, such as Porte Dauphine, are marked by elegant art nouveau gateways reading "Métropolitain"; others are marked by big yellow "M" signs. Every Métro stop has maps of the system, which are also available at ticket booths. Once you decide which line you need, make sure you're going in the right direction: On Métro line 1, "Direction: Esplanade de la Défense" indicates a westbound train, and "Direction: Château de Vincennes" is eastbound. To change train lines, look for the "correspondance" signs; blue signs reading "sortie" mark exits.

A *plan du quartier,* a very detailed pictorial map of the streets and buildings surrounding the station, with all exits marked, is usually near each exit. It's a good idea to consult the plan du quartier before you climb the stairs, especially at very large stations — you may want to use a different exit to reach the other side of a busy street or wind up closer to your destination.

For more information on the city's public transportation, stop in at the **Services Touristiques de la RATP** (place de la Madeleine, 1er; ☎ 01-40-06-71-45; Métro: Madeleine), open Monday to Saturday 8:30 a.m. to 7 p.m. and Sunday 8:30 a.m. to noon.

By bus

Buses bear the logo RATP and are conveniently located throughout Paris; all major sightseeing attractions have bus stops nearby. Each bus shelter has a route map, which you'll want to check carefully.

Because of the number of one-way streets, the bus is likely to make different stops, depending on its direction. Métro tickets are valid for bus travel, or you can buy your ticket from the conductor; however, you can't buy *carnets* on board. You must punch your ticket in a machine inside the bus and retain it until the end of the ride.

Though it's a lot slower than the Métro, the bus system is a convenient and inexpensive way to sightsee without wearing out your feet. Bus stops are located throughout the city. Buses are marked with the initials of Paris's transportation system, RATP, and run Monday to Saturday 6:30 a.m. to 8:30 p.m.; service is reduced after that. Look for the AUTOBUS DU SOIR placard; these buses run to 1 a.m. After 1 a.m. the Noctambus takes over (see above). There's also reduced bus service on Sundays and holidays.

To take the bus, you'll need the same kind of ticket used for the subway, which you can buy from the driver. Board at the front, punch the ticket into the gray machine next to the driver, and wait for the machine to spit it back out. To disembark, press one of the red buttons located throughout the bus on the safety poles. Once the bus comes to a complete stop, push the exit button and the side doors will open. For a map of Paris's bus lines, ask for the free Autobus Paris-Plan du Réseau from the tourist office and most subway ticket booths. The free Grand Plan de Paris, available at all Métro ticket booths, is a map of Paris's transportation system, which also contains bus maps and schedules.

Try these bus routes for easy jump-on, jump-off sightseeing: **Bus 69** (Eiffel Tower, Invalides, Louvre, Hôtel de Ville, place des Vosges, Bastille, Père-Lachaise Cemetery); **Bus 80** (boulevard Haussmann's department stores, Champs-Elysées, avenue Montaigne's haute-couture shopping, Eiffel Tower); and **Bus 96** (St-Germain-des-Prés, Musée de Cluny, Hôtel de Ville, place des Vosges).

By taxi

Parisian taxis are expensive, and you need to know a few things before you hail one. First, look for the blue taxi sign denoting a taxi stand. Although you can hail taxis in the street (look for a taxi with a white light on; an orange light means it's occupied), most drivers won't pick you up if you're in the general vicinity of a taxi stand. Check the meter carefully, especially if you're coming in from an airport — rip-offs are very common.

For one to three people, the drop rate in Paris proper is 13F ($1.90); the rate per kilometer is 3.45F (49¢) 7 a.m. to 7 p.m.; otherwise it's 5.70F (81¢). You'll pay supplements from taxi stands at train stations and at the Air France shuttle-bus terminals of 5F (75¢), along with 6F (90¢) for luggage, and, if the driver agrees to do so, 10F ($1.45) for transporting a fourth person. It's common practice to tip your driver

2 to 3F (30¢ to 45¢), except on longer journeys when the fare exceeds 100F ($14); in these cases, a 5 to 10 percent tip is appropriate.

If you feel that you've been overcharged for a cab ride, demand a receipt (which drivers are obligated to provide) and contact the **Préfecture of Police** at ☎ **01-55-76-20-00.**

By car

The streets are narrow, parking is next to impossible, and nerve, skill, and ruthlessness are required — in other words, don't drive in Paris. If you arrive by car, immediately return it to the rental company or stash it in a garage.

If you insist on driving in the city, get an excellent street map and have another person along to navigate, because there's no time to think at intersections.

For the most part, you must pay to park in Paris. Depending on the neighborhood, expect to pay 5 to 15F (75¢ to $2.15) per hour for a maximum of 2 hours. Place coins in the nearest meter, which issues you a ticket to place on your windshield. You can also buy parking cards at the nearest *tabac* (cafes and kiosks selling tobacco products) for meters that accept only cards. Parking is free on Sundays, on holidays, and for all of August.

Drivers and all passengers must wear seat belts, and children under 12 must ride in the back seat. Drivers are supposed to yield to the car on the right, except where signs indicate otherwise, as at traffic circles. Watch for the *gendarmes* (police) , who lack patience and consistently change the lights. Horn blowing is frowned on, except in emergencies. Flash your headlights instead.

If you want to rent a car to explore the Ile de France or travel on from Paris, try one of the following: **Avis** (place Madeleine, 8e; ☎ **01-42-66-67-58;** Internet: www.avis.com); **Budget** (☎ **08-00-10-00-01;** 1.29F/18¢ min.; Internet: www.drivebudget.com); **Hertz France** (123 rue Jeanne d'Arc, 13e; ☎ **01-45-86-53-33;** Internet: www.hertz.com); or **National** (23 bd. Arago, 13e; ☎ **01-47-07-87-39;** Internet: www.nationalcar.com).

By bicycle

City planners have been trying to encourage more cycling by setting aside 99.2 km (62 miles) of bicycle lanes throughout Paris. The main routes run north-south, from the Bassin de la Villette, along the Canal St-Martin through the Left Bank and east-west, from Château de Vincennes to the Bois de Boulogne and its miles of bike lanes. For more information and a bike map, pick up the **Plan Vert** (Green Map) that details Paris's green spaces from the tourist office.

Between March and November, the banks of the Seine are closed to cars and open to pedestrians and cyclists each Sunday 10 a.m. to 5 p.m.; the same is true for the area around the Canal St-Martin. It may not make much of a dent in the air quality, but it's a fun and healthy way to spend a Sunday afternoon.

To rent a bicycle, contact **Paris-Vélo** (2 rue du Fer-à-Moulin, 5e; ☎ **01-43-37-59-22**; Métro: St-Marcel). The charge is 80F ($11) per day and 60F ($9) per half-day. A steep deposit is required. (See Chapter 12 for organized bike tours of Paris.) Open Monday to Saturday 10:00 a.m. to 12:30 p.m. and 2 p.m. to 7 p.m.

Where to Stay in Paris

If this is your first visit to Paris, your expectations about what a hotel room should look like are probably based on what you've seen in your own country. However, rooms here tend to be smaller than you'd expect, even in expensive places (unless you opt for a modern chain hotel). Parisian doubles are almost never big enough to hold two queen-size beds, and there probably won't be a lot of space around the bed to put more than a desk and perhaps a chest of drawers. Welcome to Europe: The story is the same in London, Rome, and most other continental capitals. The buildings date back two, three, or sometimes four centuries, when dimensions — and people! — were smaller.

Parisian hotels also vary widely in their plumbing arrangements. There are units with only sinks and toilets (showers/tubs located down the hall) and units with private bathrooms (sinks, toilets, and shower stalls or tubs). Private bathrooms with tubs often have handheld shower devices — so pay attention to where you aim — and shower curtains are a rarity. In the listings I provide later in this chapter, all units come with private bathrooms, unless otherwise specified.

Acoustics tend to be unpredictable in old Parisian hotels. Your quarreling neighbors may be as annoying as street noise, so bring earplugs or ask for a room in the rear of the hotel. And, be aware that most budget hotels in Paris don't have air conditioning — however, their solid stone walls tend to keep out the summer heat.

You're coming to Paris to see the city, and you want accommodations that put you in the middle of everything. Toss aside any book that recommends a well-run, little hotel next to the Gare du Nord or an adorable *pensione* near place d'Italie. You want to be able to walk out your door and be within walking distance of at least two major sights and a short stroll from the river. You absolutely need a hotel in one of the first eight arrondissements, and I provide you with the best choices here.

If you arrive in Paris without a reservation and can't find a room at one of my choices, note that the staff at the **Office de Tourisme** (127 av. des Champs-Elysées, 8e; ☎ **08-36-68-31-12** or 01-49-52-53-35; Fax: 01-49-52-53-00; E-mail: info@paris-touristoffice.com; Internet: www.paris-touristoffice.com; Métro: Charles-de-Gaulle–Etoile or George V) can make a reservation for you, for a small fee. It's open daily 9 a.m. to 8 p.m. (Sunday 11 a.m. to 7 p.m. November to April). Keep in mind, however, that you need to arrive in person.

Prices for the recommended hotels are designated with dollar signs — the more you see, the more expensive the hotel. The number of dollar signs corresponds to the hotel's rack rates (full rate), from the cheapest double room in low season to the most expensive in high season. The rates run like this:

$	Under 700F (under $100)
$$	700–1,000F ($100–$143)
$$$	1,000–1,500F ($143–$215)
$$$$	1,500–2,100 ($215–$300)
$$$$$	2,100F and up (over $300)

The most noticeable differences between hotels in the budget bracket and the most expensive hotels are better amenities and services, followed by a more luxurious decor.

The top hotels

Castex Hôtel

$ **Le Marais (4e)**

The Castex is a popular budget classic near everything in the Marais. Each large room has a writing table or a desk and chair; some have views over the courtyard. The staff is friendly and accommodating. The rooms don't have TVs, but there's a TV salon. Reserve at least a month in advance.

5 rue Castex. ☎ *01-42-72-31-52. Fax: 01-42-72-57-91. Métro: Bastille or Sully-Morland. Rack rates: 320–360F ($46–$51) double; 410–460F ($59–$66) triple; 530F ($76) quad. Breakfast: Continental breakfast 35F ($5). AE, DC, MC, V.*

Citadines Les Halles Aparthotel

$$ **Louvre (1er)**

Citadines recently bought up the aparthotels of the Orion chain. As in its other properties, the studios and one-bedrooms have fully equipped kitchenettes, and services include a 24-hour reception desk, satellite TVs, air conditioning, housekeeping, baby-equipment rental, and a Laundromat.

Paris Accommodations

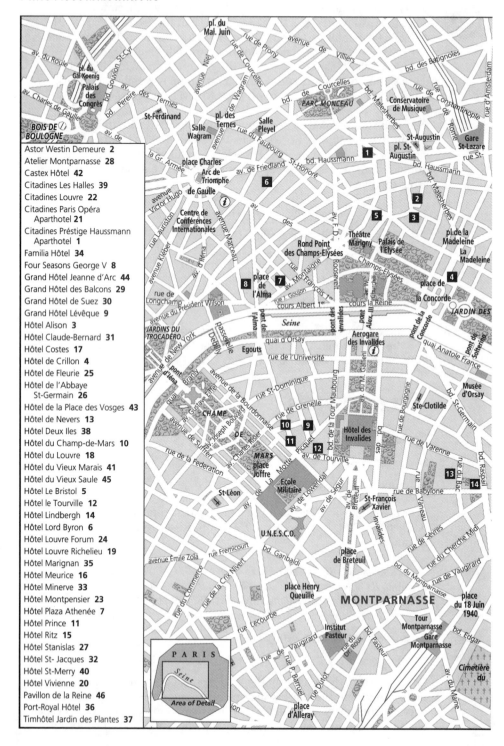

Astor Westin Demeure **2**
Atelier Montparnasse **28**
Castex Hôtel **42**
Citadines Les Halles **39**
Citadines Louvre **22**
Citadines Paris Opéra
    Aparthotel **21**
Citadines Préstige Haussmann
    Aparthotel **1**
Familia Hôtel **34**
Four Seasons George V **8**
Grand Hôtel Jeanne d'Arc **44**
Grand Hôtel des Balcons **29**
Grand Hôtel de Suez **30**
Grand Hôtel Lévêque **9**
Hôtel Alison **3**
Hôtel Claude-Bernard **31**
Hôtel Costes **17**
Hôtel de Crillon **4**
Hôtel de Fleurie **25**
Hôtel de l'Abbaye
    St-Germain **26**
Hôtel de la Place des Vosges **43**
Hôtel de Nevers **13**
Hôtel Deux Iles **38**
Hôtel du Champ-de-Mars **10**
Hôtel du Louvre **18**
Hôtel du Vieux Marais **41**
Hôtel du Vieux Saule **45**
Hôtel Le Bristol **5**
Hôtel le Tourville **12**
Hôtel Lindbergh **14**
Hôtel Lord Byron **6**
Hôtel Louvre Forum **24**
Hôtel Louvre Richelieu **19**
Hôtel Marignan **35**
Hôtel Meurice **16**
Hôtel Minerve **33**
Hôtel Montpensier **23**
Hôtel Plaza Athénée **7**
Hôtel Prince **11**
Hôtel Ritz **15**
Hôtel Stanislas **27**
Hôtel St- Jacques **32**
Hôtel St-Merry **40**
Hôtel Vivienne **20**
Pavillon de la Reine **46**
Port-Royal Hôtel **36**
Timhôtel Jardin des Plantes **37**

The big splurge

In this chapter I supply entries for a couple of deluxe $$$$$ hotels, the **George V** and the **Meurice**. If you're looking for the plushest of the plush and want a few more alternatives, here they are:

Hôtel Costes. 239 rue St-Honoré. ☎ **01-42-44-50-00.** Fax: 01-42-44-50-01. Métro: Tuileries or Concorde.

Hôtel de Crillon. 10 place de la Concorde. ☎ **800-241-3333** in the U.S. and Canada, or 01-44-71-15-00. Fax: 01-44-71-15-02. E-mail: crillon@crillon-paris.com. Métro: Concorde.

Hôtel du Louvre. 1 place André-Malraux. ☎ **800-777-4182** in the U.S., 800-673-1286 in Canada, or 01-44-58-38-38. Fax: 01-44-58-38-01. E-mail: sales-hoteldulouvre@concorde-hotels.com. Métro: Louvre.

Hôtel Le Bristol. 112 rue du Faubourg St-Honoré. ☎ **01-53-43-43-00.** Fax: 01-53-43-43-01. E-mail: resa@hotel-bristol.com. Métro: Miromesnil.
Hôtel Plaza Athénée. 25 av. Montaigne. ☎ **800-448-8355** in the U.S. and Canada, or 01-53-67-66-65. Fax: 01-53-67-66-66. Métro: Franklin-D.-Roosevelt or Alma-Marceau.

Hôtel Ritz. 15 place Vendôme. ☎ **01-43-16-30-30.** Fax: 01-43-16-31-78. E-mail: resa@ritzparis.com. Métro: Concorde, Tuileries, or Opéra.

Here are other Citadines properties in Paris, with similar rates: $$ **Citadines Louvre Aparthotel** (8 rue de Richelieu, a block north of the Louvre, 1er; ☎ **800/755-8266** or 212/688-9489 in the U.S.; Fax: 212/688-9467; Internet: www.citadines.fr; Métro: Palais-Royal or Pyramides); $$ **Citadines Paris Opéra Aparthotel** (18 rue Favart, 2e; ☎ **01-41-05-79-79;** Fax: 01-47-59-04-70; Internet: www.citadines.fr; Métro: Richelieu-Drouot); $$$ **Citadines Préstige Haussmann Aparthotel** (129 bd. Haussmann, 8e; ☎ **01-41-05-79-79;** Fax: 01-47-59-04-70; Internet: www.citadines.fr; Métro: Miromesnil).

4 rue des Innocents (100 yards from the Forum des Halles). ☎ *800-755-8266 or 212-688-9489 in the U.S. Fax: 212-688-9467. Internet:* www.citadines.fr. *Métro: Les Halles. Rack rates: 835-900F ($119-$129) 2-person studio; 1,260-1,360F ($180-$194) 4-person apt. AE, MC, V.*

Familia Hôtel

$ Latin Quarter (5e)

In the hands of Eric and Sophie Gaucheron, this hotel offers many personal touches, such as window boxes full of flowers, a fountain and frescoes in the lobby, restored stone walls in some rooms, and balconies with enchanting views of the Latin Quarter in others. From the fifth and sixth floors, you can see Notre-Dame. The baths are small but modern and tiled. All rooms have cable TV and hairdryers. The Gaucherons also own the Minerve next door (see later in this section).

11 rue des Ecoles. ☎ *01-43-54-55-27. Fax: 01-43-29-61-77. Métro: Cardinal Lemoine or Jussieu. Rack rates: 465–595F ($66–$85) double; 620–695F ($87–$99) triple; 695–750F ($99–$107) quad. Breakfast: 30F ($4). AE, DC, MC, V.*

Four Seasons Hotel George V

$$$$$ Champs-Elysées (8e)

If palatial splendor is business as usual for you, reserve a room at the newly renovated George V. Separated from the public corridors by their own halls, the rooms (starting at 450 square feet) are decorated in Louis XVI style and feature dual phone lines, modem lines, 51-channel TVs, VCRs, Internet access, Sony PlayStation consoles, and stereo systems. The views from the upper floors are truly remarkable, with some rooms offering a stone's throw view of the Eiffel Tower — from their bathtubs. Other amenities include a spa, a bar, and a restaurant overseen by the former chef of three-star Taillevent.

31 av. George V. ☎ *01-49-52-70-00. Fax: 01-49-52-70-10. Métro: George V. Rack rates: 3,734–4,389F ($533–$627) double; 7,860F ($1,123) one-bedroom suite. AE, DC, MC, V.*

Grand Hôtel des Balcons

$$ St-Germain-des-Prés (6e)

This gracious hotel has balconied rooms with modern light-oak furnishings and new beds. Although most rooms — and their wrought-iron balconies — are small, clever use of space has allowed for large closets and full-length mirrors. The baths are small but well designed. The higher-priced doubles, triples, and quads are big and luxurious; some have double-sink baths and separate toilets. Free tea and coffee are available in the lounge.

3 rue Casimir-Delavigne. ☎ *01-46-34-78-50. Fax: 01-46-34-06-27. Internet:* www. balcons.com. *Métro: Odéon. RER: Luxembourg. Rack rates: 505–800F ($72.15– $114.30) double; 950F ($135.70) triple or quad. Breakfast: Buffet breakfast 60F ($9), free on your birthday. AE, DC, MC, V.*

Grand Hôtel de Suez

$ Latin Quarter (5e)

Many guests keep returning for this hotel's many good-sized quiet rooms at a great price. The beds are firm, the storage space is ample, and the modern baths have hair dryers. Don't even think of opening the windows to the street-side balconies — boulevard St-Michel is as noisy as a carnival.

31 bd. St-Michel. ☎ *01-53-10-34-00. Fax: 01-40-51-79-44. Métro: St-Michel. Rack rates: 420–450F ($60–$64) double; 450–535F ($64–$76) twin; 505–590F ($72–$84) triple. Breakfast: Continental breakfast 30F ($4.30). AE, DC, MC, V.*

Grand Hôtel Jeanne d'Arc

$ Le Marais (4e)

Reserve a room well in advance for this great budget hotel, located just off the center of the Marais, near the Musée Picasso. Contemporary artists have hand-painted the walls of the breakfast and sitting rooms in this eighteenth-century building. The decent-sized rooms have large French windows, direct-dial phones, satellite TVs, card-key access, and large baths, though storage space is a bit cramped. If a view is important, request one.

3 rue de Jarente. ☎ *01-48-87-62-11. Fax: 01-48-87-37-31. Internet:* www. hoteljeannedarc.com. *Métro: St-Paul or Bastille. Rack rates: 325–500F ($46–$71) double; 550F ($79) triple; 620F ($89) quad. Breakfast: 38F ($5). MC, V.*

Grand Hôtel Lévêque

$ Eiffel Tower (7e)

This large hotel, with a friendly staff, is on a pedestrian street with a market-place selling fresh fruits, cheese, and wine. The lobby has a comfortable lounge area with a drink and ice dispenser and the daily newspaper. The rooms are a relatively good size and contain new, if not inspired, decorations, satellite TVs, hairdryers, and ceiling fans; safes are available for an extra 20F ($2.85). The baths are small but in excellent condition. Ask about the higher-priced fifth-floor rooms with balconies and partial views of the Eiffel Tower.

29 rue Cler. ☎ *01-47-05-49-15. Fax: 01-45-50-49-36. Internet:* www.interresa.ca/ hotel/leveue/. *E-mail:* leveque@hotelleveque.com. *Métro: Ecole-Militaire or Latour-Maubourg. Rack rates: 400F ($57) double; 420F ($60) twin; 580F ($83) triple. Breakfast: Continental breakfast 40F ($6). AE, MC, V.*

Hôtel Alison

$$ Madeleine (8e)

This hotel has an upscale ambience, in tune with the classy neighbor-hood. The well-appointed large rooms are furnished in modern black furniture set against light walls. Amenities include safes, trouser presses, double-glazed windows, and plenty of storage space. Hairdryers and Roger & Gallet toiletries grace the baths, which have wall-mounted show-ers. You can relax in the plush lobby or enjoy a drink in the bar.

21 rue de Surène. ☎ *01-42-65-54-00. Fax: 01-42-65-08-17. E-mail:* hotel.alison@ wanadoo.fr. *Métro: Madeleine or Concorde. Rack rates: 690–880F ($99–$126) double; 780–880F ($111–$126) twin; 1,000F ($143) triple. Breakfast: 45F ($6). AE, DC, MC, V.*

Hôtel du Champ-de-Mars

$ Eiffel Tower (7e)

This gem is tucked away on a colorful street near the Eiffel Tower. Flowing curtains, fabric-covered headboards, and cushioned high-backed seats make each room a delight in comfort. The baths are in mint condition, with hairdryers, large towels, and good lighting, and those with tubs have wall-mounted showers. Reserve at least four months in advance.

7 rue du Champ-de-Mars. ☎ *01-45-51-52-30. Fax: 01-45-51-64-36. Internet:* www. hotel-du-champ-de-mars.com. *E-mail:* stg@club-internet.fr. *Métro: Ecole-Militaire. RER: Pont de l'Alma. Rack rates: 430F ($61) double; 460F ($66) twin; 550F ($79) triple. Breakfast: Continental breakfast 35F ($5). MC, V.*

Hôtel Claude-Bernard

$$ Latin Quarter (5e)

It's evident from the moment you enter the lobby that the three-star Claude-Bernard keeps high standards. Each spacious room has tasteful wallpaper, a sleek bath, and, often, a charming piece of antique furniture, such as a writing desk. There are also some particularly attractive suites with couches and armchairs. A sauna is available for 50F ($7).

43 rue des Ecoles. ☎ *01-43-26-32-52. Fax: 01-43-26-80-56. Internet:* www.hotelcv. com. *Métro: Maubert-Mutualité. Rack rates: 790–890F ($113–$127) double; 1,190–1,390F ($170–$199) triple; 890–1690F ($127–$241) suite for 1–4 people. Breakfast: Continental breakfast 50F ($7). AE, DC, MC, V.*

Hôtel de Fleurie

$$$ St-Germain-des-Prés (6e)

This charming Left Bank hotel has all the comforts, including marble baths, quality toiletries, and fresh flowers. Some rooms are furnished in a modern style; others are more classical in appearance. There's a computer for guests' use at 20F ($2.90) for 15 minutes. The staff is friendly.

32–34 rue de Grégoire-de-Tours. ☎ *01-53-73-70-00. Fax: 01-53-73-70-20. Internet:* www. hotel-de-fleurie.tm.fr. *E-mail:* bonjour@hotel-de-fleurie.tm. fr. *Métro: Odéon. Rack rates: 900–1200F ($129–$171) double. Breakfast: 50F ($7). AE, DC, MC, V.*

Hôtel de l'Abbaye St-Germain

$$$–$$$$ St-Germain-des-Prés (6e)

Formerly an abbey, this hotel is popular with those looking for chic but cozy air-conditioned surroundings. Some of the rooms have their original oak ceiling beams, and all have nineteenth-century-style furnishings and damask upholstery. The rooftop suites boast terraces. The lobby has a fireplace, and in summer, you can have breakfast in the pretty garden.

10 rue Cassette. ☎ *01-45-44-38-11. Fax: 01-45-48-07-86. Métro: St-Sulpice. Rack rates: 1,030–1,650F ($147–$236) double; 2,100–2,200F ($300–$314) suite. Breakfast: Rates include breakfast. AE, MC, V.*

Hôtel de la Place des Vosges

$ Le Marais (4e)

Henri IV once kept his horses here, but you'd never know this hotel was a former stable by its antiques-filled lobby. The rooms and baths are small but tidy and well maintained. Amenities include TVs suspended from the ceiling, desks, and hairdryers. Most beds are firm, but storage space is lacking. The entrance to the King's Pavilion, on place des Vosges, is only steps away.

12 rue de Birague. ☎ *01-42-72-60-46. Fax: 01-42-72-02-64. Métro: Bastille. Rack rates: 555–620F ($79–$89) double. Breakfast: Continental breakfast 35F ($5). MC, V.*

Hotel de Nevers

$ St-Germain-des-Prés (7e)

This renovated seventeenth-century house provides simple rooms at reasonable prices. In the wood-beamed lobby, the friendly staff will check you in. You'll then be escorted up a tapestry-adorned winding staircase to a room with wood bureaus and wood-framed mirrors. The baths are spotless and well maintained, if not brand new. You have to pay in cash (credit cards are used for reservations only), so save your plastic for shopping in the nearby stores.

83 rue de Bac. ☎ *01-45-44-61-30. Fax: 01-42-22-29-47. Métro: Rue du Bac. Rack rates: 490F ($70) double, 540F ($77) double with terrace; 520F ($74) twin. Extra bed 100F ($14). Breakfast: Continental breakfast 35F ($5). No credit cards.*

Hôtel du Vieux Marais

$ Marais (4e)

This hotel has undergone a total renovation and now has a sparkling, elegant lobby, average-size air-conditioned rooms, a lighted garden, new wardrobes, and tiled baths with a Mexican-inspired design. The Centre Pompidou is a two-minute walk away.

8 rue du Plâtre. ☎ *01-42-78-47-22. Fax: 01-42-78-34-32. Métro: Hôtel-de-Ville. Rack rates: 600–690F ($86–$99) double. Breakfast: Continental breakfast 40F ($6). MC, V.*

Hôtel du Vieux Saule

$ Le Marais/Bastille (3e)

This north Marais hotel offers cheerful, small, air-conditioned rooms with safes, double-glazed windows, luggage racks, satellite TVs, trouser presses, and even small irons/ironing boards. Fifth-floor rooms tend to be bigger. The tiled baths come with hairdryers. Breakfast is served in a vaulted cellar, and there's also a sauna.

6 rue Picardie. ☎ *01-42-72-01-14. Fax: 01-40-27-88-21. Métro: République. Rack rates: 590F ($84) double. Breakfast: Buffet breakfast 50F ($7). AE, DC, MC, V.*

Hôtel le Tourville

$$–$$$ Eiffel Tower (7e)

At this splendid hotel, you get almost all the amenities you'd find in a more expensive hotel — Roger & Gallet toiletries, hairdryers, air conditioning — at prices that are still manageable. The rooms are decorated in pastels or ochres, with white-damask upholsteries, antique bureaus and lamps, and mismatched old mirrors. There are three particularly great rooms with vine-covered terraces — nos. 16, 18, and 112 — and the junior suites come with whirlpool baths. The staff is wonderfully helpful.

16 av. de Tourville. ☎ *01-47-05-62-62. Fax: 01-47-05-43-90. Métro: Ecole-Militaire. Rack rates: 890–1,090F ($127–$156) double; 1,090F ($156) twin; 1,990F ($284) junior suite. Breakfast: 70F ($10). AE, DC.*

Hôtel Lindbergh

$ St-Germain-des-Prés (7e)

Two themes are featured at this hotel: aviation and fine accommodations at fair prices. The rooms range from simple and sweet, with colorful bedspreads and matching baths, to refined and elegant, with floor-length curtains, fabric headboards, and color-coordinated cushioned seats. The owners are eager to talk about their photo collection, which includes Charles Lindbergh in his plane or standing with Blériot (the first man to fly across the English Channel) and Antoine de Saint-Exupéry, the pilot and author of *Le Petite Prince*.

5 rue Chomel. ☎ *01-45-48-35-53. Fax: 01-45-49-31-48. Métro: Sèvres-Babylone. Rack rates: 490–560F ($70–$80) double; 670–820F ($96–$117) larger double for 1–4 people. Breakfast: Continental breakfast 45F ($6). AE, MC, V.*

Hôtel Louvre Forum

$ Louvre (1er)

This modern hotel, on a quiet street, provides comfort at a reasonable price. Best of all, the hotel is only steps from the Louvre. The brightly colored rooms are small but have writing tables, lamps, chairs, and small armoires with hanging space and shelves. The modern tiled baths contain hairdryers.

25 rue du Bouloi. ☎ *01-42-36-54-19. Fax: 01-42-36-66-31. Métro: Louvre-Rivoli. Rack rates: 490–540F ($70–$77) double. Ask about discounts (around 20 percent) for stays* *over 5 nights and in July and Aug. Breakfast: Continental breakfast 40F ($6). AE, DC, MC, V.*

Hôtel Louvre Richelieu

$ Louvre (1er)

You can't beat this hotel's location — halfway between the Louvre and the Opéra. You enter through a corridor with restored stone walls; the pleasant reception area/lobby is on the second floor (no elevator). The two-bed double rooms are dark but spacious and have high ceilings, and each includes a writing table, a small closet, and a luggage rack. Reserve at least two weeks in advance for summer.

51 rue de Richelieu. ☎ *01-42-97-46-20. Fax: 01-47-03-94-13. Métro: Palais-Royal– Musée du Louvre or Pyramides. Rack rates: 420F ($60) double; 490F ($70) triple. Breakfast: Continental breakfast 35F ($5). MC, V.*

Hôtel Marignan

$ Latin Quarter (5e)

Owners Paul and Linda Keniger welcome families and have invested a lot of time in renovating this hotel. They've retained much of the architectural detailing, like the stucco ceiling moldings, while tiling the baths and adding new beds. They don't mind if you bring your own food into the dining room, and in low season, the kitchen is available too. You also have a washer/dryer and iron at your disposal.

13 rue du Sommerard. ☎ *01-43-54-63-81. Métro: Maubert-Mutualité or St-Michel. Rack rates: 270–420F ($39–$60) double; 310–560F ($44–$80) triple; 360–620F ($51–$88) quad. Breakfast: Continental breakfast 20F ($2.90). No credit cards.*

Hôtel Meurice

$$$$$ Louvre (1er)

The newly renovated "hotel of kings" is awe-inspiring, from its eighteenth-century lobby to each of its floors corresponding to a particular period of decor. The spacious rooms are soundproof and air conditioned and boast many luxuries: antique furnishings, fresh flowers, walk-in closets, satellite TVs, computer ports, and more. Amenities include two fine restaurants, a health club/spa, a laundry and dry cleaning, office services (meeting rooms, board room, copying, faxing, and laptop hookups), and translation services.

228 rue de Rivoli. ☎ *01-44-58-10-10. Fax: 01-44-58-10-19. E-mail:* reservations@ meuricehotel.com. *Métro: Tuileries. Rack rates: 3900F–4800F ($273–$336) double; 5900F–16,500F ($413–$1,155) suite; apartments and a royal suite with private terrace are available on request. Breakfast: Continental breakfast 175F ($25); American breakfast 250F ($36). AE, DC, MC, V.*

Hôtel Minerve

$ Latin Quarter (5e)

Owners Eric and Sylvie Gaucheron have extended beyond their Familia Hôtel (earlier in this section) to renovate the slightly more upscale Minerve next door. The rooms here are larger and have wood-beamed ceilings, exposed stone walls, carved mahogany furnishings, and expensive wallpapers. Several rooms contain delightful hand-painted sepia frescos, and ten have large balconies overlooking the street.

13 rue des Ecoles. ☎ 01-43-26-26-04. Fax: 01-44-07-01-96. Métro: Cardinal Lemoine or Jussieu. Rack rates: 460F ($66) double with shower stall; 540–650F ($77–$93) double with shower/tub combo. Breakfast: Continental breakfast 37F ($5). AE, MC, V.

Hôtel Montpensier

$ Louvre (1er)

This was once the residence of Mlle de Montpensier, cousin of Louis XIV. The hotel's high ceilings and windows and the lounge's stained-glass ceiling create a sense of Sun King grandeur. Many rooms on the first two floors boast a wonderful faded elegance, while the fifth-floor rooms have attractive slanted ceilings and good views. Most rooms contain easy chairs, ample closet space, and modern baths with hairdryers (no shower curtains in rooms with tubs).

12 rue Richelieu. ☎ 01-42-96-28-50. Fax: 01-42-86-02-70. Métro: Palais-Royal– Musée du Louvre. Rack rates: 500F ($71) double; 590F ($84) triple. Breakfast: Continental breakfast 40F ($6). AE, MC, V.

Hôtel Prince

$ Eiffel Tower (7e)

The Prince has modern soundproof rooms with double-glazed windows, luggage racks, and ample closets, plus big baths made warm by fluffy towels. (Some baths have hairdryers.) The buffet breakfast, with croissants, fresh fruits, and cereals, is a steal. If you're too tired from sightseeing to stagger out the door, the hotel will arrange for a local restaurant to deliver a meal. There's also a ground-floor room with facilities for travelers with disabilities.

66 av. Bosquet. ☎ 01-47-05-40-90. Fax: 01-47-53-06-62. Métro: Ecole-Militaire. Rack rates: 470–520F ($67–$74) double; 520–625F ($74–$89) twin; 625F ($89) triple. Breakfast: Buffet breakfast 40F ($6). AE, DC, MC, V.

Hôtel Stanislas

$ Montparnasse/St-Germain-des-Prés (6e)

This family-owned hotel between Montparnasse and St-Germain-des-Prés has some of the nicest staff in Paris, as well as a small cafe where you can get breakfast or a light snack until midnight. The clean rooms are in good condition and generally large. Satellite TVs and double-glazed windows are nice extras, at this price. There's no elevator.

5 rue du Montparnasse. ☎ *01-45-48-37-05. Fax: 01-45-44-54-43. Métro: Notre-Dame-des-Champs. Rack rates: 330–350F ($47–$70) double. Breakfast: Continental breakfast 35F ($5). AE, MC, V.*

Hôtel St-Jacques

$ Latin Quarter (5e)

The wall and ceiling murals in the breakfast room and lounge are recent, but several rooms have original nineteenth-century ceiling murals. Most of the high ceilings have elaborate plasterwork, giving the decor an old-Paris feel, accentuated by traditional furniture. The owners have added their own touches in the halls, with stenciling on the walls and *trompe-l'oeil* painting around the doors. Modern comforts include spacious rooms with double-glazed windows and ample closet space, as well as tiled baths with hairdryers and toiletries.

35 rue des Ecoles (at rue des Carmes). ☎ *01-44-07-45-45. Fax: 01-43-25-65-50. Métro: Maubert-Mutualité. Rack rates: 470–630F ($67–$90) double; 700F ($100) triple. Breakfast: 40F ($6). AE, DC, MC, V.*

Hôtel St-Merry

$$ Le Marais (4e)

Next to St-Merri — and once the church's seventeenth-century presbytery — this hotel without an elevator retains some of its medieval atmosphere. The beds have wood screens for headboards, and many of the rooms are dark, with beamed ceilings, stone walls, and wrought-iron chandeliers and sconces. The fabrics are sumptuous, however, and the baths are pleasantly modern and come with hairdryers. Higher prices are for larger rooms with views.

78 rue de la Verrerie. ☎ *01-42-78-14-15. Fax: 01-40-29-06-82. Métro: Hôtel-de-Ville or Châtelet. Rack rates: 480–1,800F ($69–$257) double; 1,100–2,050F ($157–$293) triple; 2,300F ($329) quad; 1,800–2,300F ($257–$329) suite. Breakfast: 55F ($8). AE, V.*

Hôtel Vivienne

$ Louvre/Opéra (2e)

This hotel, between the Louvre and the Opéra, offers comfortable rooms at a good price. The rooms and baths vary in size, from adequate to huge, and all are in good shape; some rooms have views of the Eiffel Tower. The baths have hairdryers and wall-mounted showers in the tubs.

40 rue Vivienne. ☎ *01-42-33-13-26. Fax: 01-40-41-98-19. E-mail:* paris@hotel-vivienne.com. *Métro: Bourse, Richelieu-Drouot, or Grands Boulevards.*

Rack rates: 390–530F ($56–$76) double. Breakfast: Continental breakfast 40F ($6). MC, V.

Port-Royal Hôtel

$ **Latin Quarter (5e)**

The rates of a super-budget motel but the looks of a high-class hotel with an antiques-filled lobby make this location, run by the same family for over 60 years, a dream. The rooms are decorated with flowery pastel wallpaper, and many rooms have nonworking fireplaces. The front rooms' double-glazed windows help cut the noise. There's a breakfast/TV room and a small courtyard for outside dining.

8 bd. Port-Royal. ☎ 01-43-31-70-06. Fax: 01-43-31-33-67. Métro: Gobelins. Rack rates: 260F ($37) double without bathroom, 387–477F ($55–$68) double with bathroom. Breakfast: Continental breakfast 27F ($3.90). No credit cards.

Timhôtel Jardin des Plantes

$$ **Latin Quarter (5e)**

This great two-star hotel boasts a roof terrace, a sauna, a vaulted cellar with a fireplace, and a glass-fronted sidewalk cafe. The floral decor of the rooms on each floor comes from a flower (iris, geranium, mimosa, and so on) featured in the Jardin des Plantes across the street. The more expensive fifth-floor rooms open onto a sunny terrace. All the rooms have tiled baths with hairdryers.

5 rue Linné. ☎ 01-47-07-06-20. Fax: 01-47-07-62-74. E-mail: jardin-des-plants@timhotel.fr. Métro: Jussieu. Rack rates: 700F ($100) double; 900F ($129) triple. Breakfast: Continental breakfast 50F ($7). AE, DC, MC, V.

Runner-up accommodations

If all of the preceding choices are full, you can try one of the following very good hotels:

Astor Westin Demeure

$$$$ **Champs-Elysées (8e)**   This reliable hotel, with spacious rooms, is for families who want to stay near the chain-store madness of the Champs. *11 rue d'Astorg.* ☎ *800-WESTIN1* in the U.S., 01-53-05-05-05 in Paris. Fax: 01-53-05-05-30.

Atelier Montparnasse

$$ **St-Germain-des-Prés (6e)**   Here you'll find deco-inspired elegance within shouting distance of three cafes favored by 1920s artists — Le Dôme, Le Select, and La Coupole. *49 rue Vavin.* ☎ *01-46-33-60-00.* Fax: 01-40-51-04-21.

Hôtel Deux Îles

$$ **Ile St-Louis (4e)** With only 17 rooms, this charming hotel is intimate and superbly located on the Ile St-Louis. *59 rue St-Louis-en-l'Ile.* ☎ *01-43-26-13-35. Fax: 01-43-29-60-25.*

Hôtel Lord Byron

$$ **Champs-Elysées (8e)** Luxurious, quiet, and understated, this is one of the best-value hotels around the Champs-Elysées. *5 rue de Chateaubriand.* ☎ *01-43-59-89-98. Fax: 01-42-89-46-04.*

Pavillon de la Reine

$$$$ **Le Marais (3e)** Each room is unique here — some even have sleeping lofts above cozy salons. *28 place des Vosges.* ☎ *800-447-7462 in the US; or 01-40-29-19-19. Fax: 01-40-29-19-20.*

Where to Dine in Paris

After all that sightseeing has revved up your appetite, you'll thank Escoffier (the Ritz's master chef) that you're in one of the world's best cities for dining. Parisians take dining very seriously. They expect the same freshness and quality in their meals that their ancestors had, and newspapers are full of outrage that American fast-food chains have made inroads into their country. They worry about the consequences of genetically altered fruits and vegetables. And although mad-cow disease hasn't been as prevalent in France as it has been in England, each new case merits mention on the national news.

But this doesn't stop Parisians from dining out. They're on an eternal quest for the perfect meal, and they make a pastime of sharing *les bonnes addresses* (the right addresses) with their friends. And, the number of *bonnes addresses* seems as if it's always increasing these days! In the last decade, the city has seen celebrity chefs open baby bistros — restaurants offering simpler and less expensive meals than those served at their deluxe establishments — and the gifted young apprentices of these celebrity chefs, the young upstarts, open their own restaurants. The best baby bistros are still going strong (examples are Rôtisserie Armaillé and Spoon, Food and Wine, both listed later in this chapter), and the well-prepared home-style food of the young upstarts (like the Provençal cooking of Gilles Ajuelos, protégé of Michel Rostang) has become a trend that everyone appreciates. In addition, the reopening of two palace hotels that had been closed for renovations — the Meurice and George V — has given Paris two new gastronomic restaurants that are drawing raves and are almost sure to win coveted Michelin stars.

French food embraces the specialties from the country's varied regions. Thus, you can encounter on menus a hearty *bouillabaisse* (fish stew), a specialty of Marseille and the south coast of France; *choucroute garni* (sauerkraut with tender slices of pork) with origins in Alsace close to the German border; or *coq au vin* (chicken stewed in red wine with mushrooms), made famous in Burgundy. For more on each region's cuisine specialties, see the sidebars "Sampling the region's cuisine" throughout.

Even the French need a break from French food every once in a while, and you may find your taste buds craving something different and, perhaps, highly spiced. If this is the case, take advantage of the numerous Chinese, Thai, Vietnamese, Indian, Tex-Mex, and Russian restaurants. Try the 13e arrondissement, between place d'Italie and the Porte de Choisy, for terrific and reasonably priced Chinese and Vietnamese food; try the 10e, 18e, and 20e, for North African, Turkish, Vietnamese, and Thai offerings. Probably the most popular ethnic dish in France is couscous from North Africa — steamed semolina garnished with broth, stewed vegetables, and meat; there's at least one restaurant or *couscousserie* on nearly every street.

Saving on dining

Here are some dining tips to help give your wallet a break:

✔ **Order a prix-fixe or formule (fixed-price) meal.** These inclusive meals are up to 30 percent cheaper than ordering the same dishes à la carte. However, your options are more limited with these meals. Review the prix-fixe option carefully to determine what you're getting at that price. Does it come with wine, and if so, how much — a glass or a half bottle? Is dessert or coffee included?

✔ **Make lunch your main meal.** Many restaurants offer great deals on fixed-price lunches. You probably won't be hungry for a full meal after two or three courses at lunch.

✔ **Try a crêperie.** Crêperies offer a great value — you can enjoy meat- or vegetable-filled *galettes* and dessert crêpes, with a bowl of cider, in Brittany-inspired surroundings. There are many crêperies off the boulevard du Montparnasse around square Delambre.

✔ **Join the chain gang.** Chain restaurants like Batifol, Hippopotamus, Léon de Bruxelles, and l'Écluse offer some good-value meals. Sandwich shops like Pommes des Pains and Lina's are another alternative.

✔ **Decline your hotel breakfast (unless it happens to be included in the rates).** Don't eat breakfast at your hotel, unless you want to add at least $5 more per person to your hotel bill. Grab a croissant or a *pain au chocolat* (chocolate-filled croissant) from a boulangerie and save francs.

✔ **Know the tipping rules.** Service is usually included at restaurants, so don't double-tip by mistake. If service is excellent, however, you may want to round up the price with a few francs.

Only the most expensive restaurants enforce dress codes (suit and tie), and in theory, you can dress up or down as you like. Realize, however, that Parisians are a stylish lot, even when dressing informally. Relaxed dressing doesn't mean sloppy jeans and sneakers — *especially* sneakers. The look to aim for is casual Fridays at work. You won't go wrong if you dress in neutral colors — think black, beige, cream, navy, and chocolate. Go a notch dressier than what you'd wear at home. Even at neighborhood bistros, most men wear sports jackets, and women wear skirts or smart pantsuits and the ever-present scarf.

The vast majority of French restaurants are small establishments with limited seating, and tables are scrupulously saved for folks who book ahead. It's almost always a good idea to make a same-day reservation, for even a modest neighborhood bistro. Some top restaurants require several weeks' notice. Remember to call if you're going to be more than 20 minutes late. Showing up late is considered bad form.

If you're staying at a hotel with a concierge, phone or fax ahead and ask him or her to make a reservation at the sought-after restaurant where you'd like to eat. Do this as early as possible, specifying your preferred date, with a backup or two. And don't forget to tip him for his efforts.

Franc-ly speaking: Defining $ to $$$$$

The price ranges for the following restaurant listings reflect the cost of a three-course meal (appetizer, main dish, dessert, coffee), ordered à la carte, for one person. The dollar signs will give you a general idea of how much a meal will cost at dinner:

$	Under 125F ($18)
$$	125–200F ($18–$29)
$$$	200–300F ($29–$43)
$$$$	300–500F ($42–$71)
$$$$$	Over 500F ($71)

The top restaurants

16 Haussmann

$$–$$$ Grands Boulevards (9e)   CLASSIC FRENCH

A daring color scheme and bold concoctions are the hallmarks of this restaurant. The *oeufs coques à la crème d'épices et caramel de xérés* (soft-boiled eggs in sherry-cream sauce with spices) is a good way to start your meal, while the *daube de joue de boeuf* (beef stew with carrots and leeks) is a delicious main course. Even with a tureen of salmon spread as an hors d'oeuvre, the two-course menu may not satisfy a large appetite, so plan on sampling one of the luscious desserts. Wines begin at 85F ($12) per half bottle, and there's a good selection of wines by the glass.

In the Hôtel Ambassador, 16 bd. Haussmann. ☎ *01-48-00-06-38. Métro: Chausée d'Antin or Richelieu-Drouot. Meals: 2-course menu 165F ($24); 3-course menu 200F ($29). AE, DC, MC, V. Open: Mon–Fri noon to 2:30 p.m. and 7–10:30 p.m.*

A la Bonne Crêpe

$ Odéon (6e)   BRETON/CREPES

Sit at picnic-like tables covered in checkered cloths, sip some hard cider (Brittany's answer to beer), and watch mouthwatering crêpes being made on open stoves a few feet away. Savory crêpes filled with cheese, meat, seafood, or other hearty ingredients are the main courses here, and sweet crêpes filled with jam, fruit, or chocolate are a wonderful dessert.

11 rue Grégoire-de-Tours. ☎ *01-43-54-60-74. Métro: Odéon. No reservations. Meals: 2-course lunch (crêpe and glass of cider or wine) 50F ($7); 2-course dinner 63F ($9); à la carte crêpes 16–50F ($2.30–$7). No credit cards. Open: Mon–Sat noon to 2 p.m. and 7–11 p.m. Closed last two weeks of Aug.*

Alcazar

$$$$ St-Germain-des-Prés (6e)   MODERN BRASSERIE

This stylish large restaurant from England's Sir Terence Conran opened a few years ago, and though the reviews have been mixed, it's going strong. Chef Guillaume Lutard (formerly of three-star Taillevent) executes a brasserie menu with platters of shellfish and oysters, Mediterranean-inspired dishes like puff pastry with goat cheese and sun-dried tomatoes, and Pan-Asian staples like soy-infused chicken and duckling. The food is good and the service friendly, but the size of the dining room renders the place deafening. An option is the upstairs piano bar, where you can order wine by the glass and small plates of sushi, oysters, caviar, foie gras, and smoked salmon.

62 rue Mazarine. ☎ *01-53-10-19-99. Métro: Odéon. Reservations required at least two days in advance. Meals: Main courses 140–260F ($10–$18). Open: Daily noon to 3 p.m. and 7:30 p.m.–1 a.m.*

Au Bon Accueil

$$–$$$ Eiffel Tower (7e)   MODERN BISTRO

You get a spectacular view of the Eiffel Tower from the outside tables here, and the daily changing menu is just as amazing. If you're ordering from the prix-fixe menu, you may start with the *filets de sardines mi-cuites à l'huile et romarin méli mélo de legumes provencaux* (sardines lightly grilled in oil with vegetables from Provence), followed by the *steack de thon poélé et son caviar d'aubergine aux olives* (seared tuna steak with eggplant caviar and olives). Main courses could include scallops with asparagus and whole lobster from Brittany, roasted in herbs and tomatoes. End your meal with a fantastic dessert like a fig tart or crème brûlée made with walnuts.

14 rue de Monttessuy. ☎ *01-47-05-46-11. Métro: Alma-Marceau. Reservations recommended. Meals: Main courses 152–245F ($22–$35); 3-course menu 165F ($24). MC, V. Open: Mon–Fri noon to 2:30 p.m. and 7:30–10:30 p.m.*

Au Pied de Cochon

$–$$ Les Halles (1er) CLASSIC FRENCH

Au Pied de Cochon, opened in 1946, is a vibrant part of the history of this old market neighborhood. Boasting marble, murals, elaborate sconces, and chandeliers, as well as tourists, the restaurant provides great fun at manageable prices. You can have a plate of half a dozen oysters or cheesy onion soup to start, then follow with the grilled salmon or *entrecôte maître d'hôtel* (in rich red-wine sauce) or their namesake, *pied de cochon* (pig's feet). Finish with mouthwatering profiteroles.

6 rue Coquillière. ☎ *01-40-13-77-00. Métro: Châtelet–Les Halles. Meals: Main courses 86–180F ($12–$26). AE, DC, V. Open: Daily 24 hours.*

Au Poulbot Gourmet

$–$$ Montmartre (18e) CLASSIC FRENCH

Photos of old Montmartre and original drawings by illustrator Francisque Poulbot adorn the walls, and the burgundy leather banquettes are usually filled with locals savoring the moderately priced classics. Chef Jean-Paul Langevin brings tremendous finesse to the preparation and presentation of dishes like *noisette d'agneau* (lamb slices) with delicate splashes of mashed potatoes and spinach and *marmite de poissons* (assorted fresh fish in a light saffron sauce). As an appetizer, the *oeufs pochés* with smoked salmon is a standout. For dessert, try the *charlotte glacée.*

39 rue Lamarck. ☎ *01-46-06-86-00. Métro: Lamarck-Caulincourt. Meals: Main courses 92–160F ($13–$23); 3-course menu 190F ($27). MC, V. Open: Mon–Sat noon to 1:30 p.m. and 7:30–10 p.m.; Sun noon to 1:30 p.m. only Oct–May.*

Bofinger

$$ Bastille (4e) ALSATIAN/BRASSERIE

Almost 140 years old, Bofinger is one of Paris's best-loved restaurants, with dark wood, gleaming brass, a painted curving-glass ceiling, and waiters, with long white aprons, delivering extraordinary food. The menu features many Alsatian specialties, like *choucroute* (sauerkraut with smoked ham), as well as the oysters and foie gras for which the restaurant is renowned. Best of all, the prices are actually quite moderate for Paris.

5–7 rue de la Bastille. ☎ *01-42-72-87-82. Métro: Bastille. Meals: Main courses 75–196F ($11–28); lunch and dinner menu (with half-bottle of wine) 189F ($27). AE, MC, V. Open: Mon–Fri noon to 3 p.m. and 6:30–1 a.m.; Sat–Sun noon to 1 a.m.*

Brasserie Balzar

$–$$ Latin Quarter (5e)   BRASSERIE

Balzar has played host to some of France's most famous intellectuals, including Jean-Paul Sartre, and it's always full of rich bohemians. People stop here for coffee and pastries between lunch and dinner and drop in for drinks in the evening. Regulars go for the *poulet rôti avec frites* (roast chicken with french fries) or *choucroute garni* (sauerkraut with tender slices of pork), but you can also get *steak au poivre* (steak with pepper and/or peppercorns) and a few fresh fish dishes. The portions are copious. For dessert, try the *gâteau au chocolate amère* (bittersweet chocolate cake).

49 rue des Ecoles. ☎ *01-43-54-13-67. Métro: Cluny–La Sorbonne. Meals: Main courses 75–134F ($11–$19). AE, MC, V. Open: Daily noon to midnight. Closed Aug.*

Brasserie Flo

$$ Gare du Nord (10e)   ALSATIAN/BRASSERIE

This is one of the city's oldest restaurants, built in 1868, and it has a lovely early 1900s ambience. On any given night, you'll find plenty of tourists and a sprinkling of Parisians, who feast on the renowned *choucroute*. Brasserie Flo is also known for its seafood, but that may empty your wallet faster than you can say *bouillabaisse*.

7 cour des Petites-Ecuries. ☎ *01-47-70-13-59. Métro: Château d'Eau. Meals: Main courses 89–168F ($13–$24); 3-course menu (with wine) 189F ($27). AE, DC, MC, V. Open: Daily noon to 3 p.m.; Tues–Sat 7:15 p.m.–1 a.m.; Sun–Mon 7:15 p.m.–12:30 a.m.*

Brasserie Ile St-Louis

$–$$ Ile St-Louis (1er)   ALSATIAN/BRASSERIE

Owned by the same family for over 60 years, this is Paris's last remaining independent brasserie and was once the favorite haunt of writer James Jones *(The Thin Red Line)*, who kept a *chope* (mug) at the bar. Its location is perfect: directly off the footbridge from Ile de la Cité to Ile St-Louis, with an unparalleled view of the eastern tip of Ile de la Cité (including the back of Notre-Dame). The food is quintessentially Alsatian — *choucroute,* with heaps of tender, biting sauerkraut and meaty slices of ham or hearty *cassoulet,* laden with rich beans and tender pieces of lamb and pork.

55 quai de Bourbon. ☎ *01-43-54-02-59. Métro: Pont-Marie. Meals: Main courses 60–130F ($9–$19). V. Open: Fri–Tues noon to 1 a.m.; Thurs 6 p.m.–1 a.m.*

Paris Dining

16 Haussmann **24**
A la Bonne Crêpe **35**
Alain Ducasse **9**
Alcazar **36**
Au Bon Accueil **17**
Au Pied de Cochon **28**
Au Poulbot Gourmet **20**
Berthillon **50**
Bofinger **54**
Brasserie Balzar **43**
Brasserie Flo **25**
Brasserie Ile St-Louis **53**
Café Beauborg **59**
Café de Flore **30**
Café les Deux Magots **33**
Café Mabillon **32**
Café Marly **29**
Caveau du Palais **38**
Cercle Ledoyen **13**
Chantairelle **47**
Chardenoux **52**
Chez Casimir **23**
Chez Maître Paul **41**
Chez Marie **21**
Chez Michel **22**
Closerie des Lilas **46**
Dame Jeanne **55**
Faugeron **10**
Fouquet's **5**
Guy Savoy **3**
Jacques Cagna **39**
Jo Goldenberg **58**
La Bastide Odeon **40**
La Cigale **19**
La Coupole **45**
L'Ambroisie **56**
La Petite Chaise **18**
Lasserre **14**
L'Astor **7**
La Tour d'Argent **49**
Le 404 **60**
L'Ebauchoir **51**
Le Cinq **11**
Le Grand Véfour **26**
Le Grenier de
  Notre-Dame **48**
Le Père Claude **16**
Le Polidor **42**
Le Violon d'Ingres **15**
Lucas-Carton
  (Alain Senderens) **8**
Michel Rostang **1**
Pierre Gagnaire **4**
Restaurant Dane
  Gourmand **57**
Restaurant du
  Palais-Royal **27**
Restaurant Orestias **34**
Restaurant Paul **37**
Restaurant Perraudin **44**
Rôtisserie Armaillé **2**
Spoon, Food and Wine **12**
Taillevent **6**
Vagenende **31**
Web Bar **61**

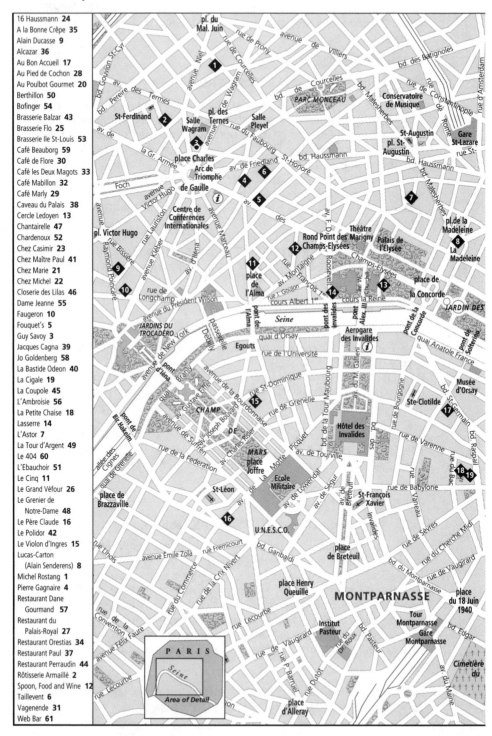

MONTMARTRE 20 21

Moulin Rouge
bd. de Clichy
place Pigalle
bd. de Rochechouart
bd. de la Chapelle
av. Jean Jaurès
rue Armand Carrel
avenue Secrétan
av. Trudaine
rue de Magenta
St-Joseph
St-Georges
PARC DES BUTTES CHAUMONT
Casino de Paris
Ste-Trinité
rue Blanche
rue N.D. de Lorette
Pigalle
rue Condorcet
22
23
Gare du Nord
rue La Fayette
place du Colonel Fabien
quai de Valmy
quai de Jemmapes
Notre-Dame de Lorette
St-Vincent de Paul
rue de Chabrol
Gare de l'Est
St-Laurent
rue du Faubourg St-Martin
bd. de la Villette
rue St-Maur
Lazare
rue La Fayette
Folies Bergère
rue de Paradis
quai de Jemmapes
quai de Valmy
rue de la Grange
rue St-Maur
bd. Haussmann
Opéra Garnier
24
bd. Montmartre
bd. des Italiens
25
rue du Faubourg Poissonnière
rue du Faubourg St-Denis
rue de Strasbourg
St-Joseph
place des Capucines
place de l'Opéra
bd. de Bonne Nouvelle
bd. de Strasbourg
rue du Faubourg du Temple
Bourse des Valeurs
rue du 4 Septembre
rue St-Augustin
N.D. des Victoires
rue de Cléry
rue d'Abukir
rue de Réaumur
bd. St-Martin
place de la République
avenue de la République
place Vendôme
rue des Petits Champs
26
rue du Mail
Conservatoire des Arts et Métiers
rue du Faubourg du Temple
St-Roch
27
Palais Royal
rue de Valois
rue de Sébastopol
rue St-Martin
Turbigo
60
TUILERIES
place A. Malraux
28
St-Eustache
61
St-Ambroise
place du Carrousel
29
Musée du Louvre
rue de Rivoli
Bourse du Commerce
Forum des Halles
59
Centre Georges Pompidou
rue des Archives
LE MARAIS
pont Royal
quai des Tuileries
St-Germain l'Auxerrois
Archives Nationales
St-Denis
rue du Chemin Vert
pont du Carr.
quai du Louvre
Théâtre du Châtelet
St-Merri
58
rue de Turenne
quai Malaquais
pont des Arts
Seine
pont Neuf
St-Gervais
57
Hôtel de Ville
rue St-Antoine
bd. Beaumarchais
Ecole Nationale des Beaux-Arts
pont au Change
pont N. Dame
place des Vosges
56
Théâtre de la Bastille
ST-GERMAIN-DES-PRÉS 36
37 38
ILE DE LA CITÉ
quai de l'Hôtel de Ville
St-Paul
55
St-Germain des Prés
30 31
quai des Grands Augustins
Cloître N. Dame
quai de la Tournelle
place de la Bastille
54
rue du Faubourg St-Antoine
bd. St-Germain
32 33 34 35
39
ILE ST-LOUIS
Opéra Bastille
St-Séverin
quai St-Michel
Notre-Dame
53
St-Louis
50
rue de Charenton
rue du Four
St-Sulpice
40
St-Julien
quai de la Tournelle
52
41 42
43
rue des Ecoles
bd. St-Germain
49
pont de Sully
51
Palais du Luxembourg
Sorbonne
Institut du Monde Arabe
quai Henry IV
bd. Henry IV
quai de Bercy
rue de Vaugirard
QUARTIER LATIN
47
quai St-Bernard
av. L. Rollin Lyon
44
Panthéon
St-Etienne du Mont
Université Paris VII
bd. Diderot
Gare de Lyon
JARDIN DU LUXEMBOURG
rue St-Jacques
rue Gay Lussac
rue d'Ulm
JARDIN DES PLANTES
pont d'Austerlitz
quai de la Rapée
Université Paris V
45
bd. du Montparnasse
rue Claude Bernard
St-Médard
rue Censier
Université Paris III
Gare d'Austerlitz
Seine
quai d'Austerlitz
Mont-parnasse
46
bd. de Port Royal
bd. Saint Marcel
rue de l'Hôpital
pont de Bercy
Observatoire de Paris
bd. Arago

0   1/4 mi

Railway

0   0.25 km

N

The big splurge

Paris is filled with "temples of gastronomy," where master chefs reign and demand a king's ransom for their superlative food. If you want to experience a meal worth cashing in that IRA, try one of these places (remember that reservations are required about two months in advance):

Alain Ducasse. In the Le Parc Hôtel, 59 av. Raymond-Poincaré, 16e. ☎ **01-47-27-12-27.** Fax: 01-47-27-31-22. Métro: Trocadéro.

Faugeron. 52 rue de Longchamp, 16e. ☎ **01-47-04-24-53.** Fax: 01-47-55-62-90. Reservations required 2 months in advance. Métro: Trocadéro.

Guy Savoy. 18 rue Troyon, 17e. ☎ **01-43-80-40-61.** Fax: 01-46-22-43-09. Métro: Charles-de-Gaulle–Etoile or Ternes.

Jacques Cagna. 14 rue des Grands-Augustins, 6e. ☎ **01-43-26-49-39.** Fax: 01-43-54-54-48. Métro: St-Michel.

Lasserre. 17 av. Franklin-D.-Roosevelt, 8e. ☎ **01-43-59-53-43.** Fax: 01-45-63-72-23. Métro: Franklin-D.-Roosevelt.

L'Astor. In the Hôtel Astor, 11 rue d'Astorg, 8e. ☎ **01-53-05-05-20.** Fax: 01-53-05-05-30. Métro: St-Augustin.

La Tour d'Argent. 15–17 quai de la Tournelle, 5e. ☎ **01-43-54-23-31.** Fax: 01-44-07-12-04. Métro: Maubert-Mutualité or Pont-Marie.

Le Grand Véfour. 17 rue de Beaujolais, 1er. ☎ **01-42-96-56-27.** Fax: 01-42-86-80-71. Métro: Louvre.

Le Violon d'Ingres. 135 rue St-Dominique, 7e. ☎ **01-45-55-15-05.** Fax: 01-45-55-48-42. Métro: Ecole Militaire.

Lucas-Carton (Alain Senderens). 9 place de la Madeleine, 8e. ☎ **01-42-65-22-90.** Fax: 01-42-65-06-23. Métro: Madeleine.

Michel Rostang. 20 rue Rennequin, 17e. ☎ **01-47-63-40-77.** Fax: 01-47-63-82-75. Métro: Ternes.

Pierre Gagnaire. 6 rue Balzac, 8e. ☎ **01-44-35-18-25.** Fax: 01-44-35-18-37. Métro: George V.

Taillevent. 15 rue Lamennais, 8e. ☎ **01-44-95-15-01.** Fax: 01-42-25-95-18. Métro: George V.

Caveau du Palais

$$ Place Dauphine (1er)   CLASSIC FRENCH

This cozy Parisian secret is in the heart of tree-lined place Dauphine, a little park nestled at the tip of Ile de la Cité. Begin a memorable meal with the sumptuous *foie gras cru de canard au naturel* (raw duck liver), then dive into the house specialty *côte de boeuf* (grilled giant ribs prepared for two). The *confit de canard et pommes Sarladaise* (duck served with crispy potato bits sautéed in foie gras drippings), is another must.

19 place Dauphine. ☎ 01-43-26-04-28. Métro: Pont-Neuf. Meals: Main courses 90–155F ($13–$22); 2-course menu 140F ($20). AE, DC, MC, V. Open: Mon–Sat 12:15–2:30 p.m. and 7:15–10:30 p.m.

Cercle Ledoyen

$$–$$$ Champs-Elysées (8e)   NORTHERN FRENCH

The less expensive sibling of the two-star Ledoyen, this restaurant offers light, classic cooking supervised by Ledoyen's chef, Christian Le Squer. The menu varies but may include *dos de cabillaud aux pousses d'épinards* (cod filet with baby spinach) and *carré d'agneau roti au romarin* (roasted lamb with rosemary). The desserts, like the pear tart, are wonderful. Although a dinner for two with wine will run over $100, this place is well worth the splurge.

1 av. Dutuit. ☎ 01-53-05-10-02. Métro: Champs-Elysées–Clemenceau. Meals: Main courses 130F ($19). AE, DC, MC, V. Open: Mon–Sat noon to 2:30 p.m. and 7:30–10:30 p.m.

Chantairelle

$–$$ Latin Quarter (5e)   AUVERGNE

This charming place with a back garden offers you a visit to the Auvergne, France's rugged south central region. An old church door and a tiny fountain have been incorporated into the decor, and a sound system plays bird songs and church bells. There are even tiny bottles of essential oils made from native plants, to give you the region's smell. The delicious peasant food comes in enormous portions, so order an appetizer — maybe some of the famous *charcuterie* — only if you're ravenous. Main courses include the wonderful stuffed cabbage and the *potée* (a tureen filled with pork, cabbage, potatoes, turnips, and leeks in broth). Though most dishes use ham or pork, vegetarians will enjoy the *croustade forestière,* mushrooms and eggs poached with Fourme d'Ambert cheese. The best Auvergne wine is the Chateaugay, a fine fruity red.

17 rue Laplace. ☎ 01-46-33-18-59. Métro: Maubert-Mutualité. Meals: Main courses 72–139F ($10–$20). MC, V. Open: Mon–Fri noon to 2 p.m.; daily 7–10:30 p.m.

Chardenoux

$–$$ Bastille (11e)   CLASSIC BISTRO

This charming place tops the list of Parisians' favorite bistros. From the etched-glass windows to the swirling stucco decorations on the walls and ceiling, the early 1900s decor is the essence of old Paris, and the building has been appointed a Monument Historique. The service is friendly and even English-speaking. A variety of French regional dishes appears on the menu. Try the *oeufs en meurette* (a Burgundian dish of poached eggs in a sauce of red wine and bacon) or the *boeuf en daube* (braised beef Provençal style). The desserts are pure comfort food, especially the fruit tarts and nougat in raspberry sauce.

1 rue Jules-Valles. ☎ *01-43-71-49-52. Métro: Charonne. Meals: Main courses 80–125F ($11–$18). AE, MC, V. Open: Mon–Fri noon to 2 p.m.; Mon–Sat 8–11:30 p.m.*

Chez Casimir

$ Gare du Nord (10e)   CLASSIC FRENCH

It's worth the trip from almost *anywhere* to dine at this delightful restaurant, next to the Gare du Nord. Chef Philippe Tredgeu works magic in his kitchen, and his charms emanate into the mod-style dining room with rustic wood tables. Using market-fresh ingredients, he prepares inventive upscale dishes. Start with the refreshing *crème de petit pois au parmesan* (cold green bean soup with slices of Parmesan cheese, served with toasted bread); take as much as you want from the pot placed on your table and then have the *filet de rascasse avec des spaguetti de courgettes* (scorpionfish filet served with spaghetti-style zucchini, tomatoes, and a touch of vinegar). For dessert, indulge in a homemade pastry with raspberries and vanilla cream. The wine list is highly affordable.

6 rue de Belzune. ☎ *01-48-78-28-80. Métro: Gare du Nord. Reservations recommended for dinner. Meals: Main courses 75–80F ($11–$12). No credit cards. Open: Mon–Fri noon to 2 p.m. and 7–11:30 p.m.; Sat 7–11:30 p.m.*

Taking an ice cream break

Without a doubt, while sightseeing (especially in summer), you'll need to fortify yourself with some luscious creamy calories. You can stop at the new Häagen-Daz store, but why do that when you have such a good selection of Parisian shops serving usual and unusual flavors like rhubarb, plum, and cassis? Ask for a *cornet seule* (single scoop cone) or *double* — even the cone is yummy. Most shops are open daily 11 a.m. to sunset or 10 p.m. (remember it stays light a lot longer in France in summer).

You'll find the best ice cream at the famous **Berthillon** (31 rue St-Louis-en-l'Ile on Ile St-Louis, 4e; ☎ 01-43-54-31-61; Métro: Pont-Marie). However, the following will also put soft serve to shame: **Dammam's** (20 rue Cardinal Lemoine, 5e; ☎ 01-46-33-61-30; Métro: Cardinal Lemoine); **La Butte Glacée** (14 rue Norvin, 18e; ☎ 01-42-23-91-58; Métro: Abbesses); **Le Bac à Glaces** (109 rue du Bac, 7e; ☎ 01-45-48-87-65; Métro: Rue du Bac); **Octave** (138 rue Mouffetard, 5e; ☎ 01-45-35-20-56; Métro: Monge); and **Vilfeu** (3 rue de la Cossonerie, 1er; ☎ 01-40-26-36-40; Métro: Les Halles).

Chez Maître Paul

$$ St-Germain-des-Prés   EASTERN FRENCH

The word is out about comfortable Chez Maître Paul, which serves special-
ties from the Comté region of eastern France. Start with a fluffy *rillette de
saumon* (preserved salmon) and follow with *poulet sauté au vin blanc*
(chicken sautéed in white wine with mushrooms and tomatoes). Also
recommended is the *terrine de foie* (liver pâté) and *fricassée de veau* (veal
stew). The 195F ($28) menu offers a choice of cheese or dessert, following
the main dish. Service is friendly and English-speaking.

12 rue Monsieur-le-Prince, 6e. ☎ *01-43-54-74-59. Métro: Odéon. Reservations
recommended. Meals: Main courses 82–160F ($12–$23); 3-course menu 165F ($24);
3-course menu with half-bottle of wine 195F ($28). AE, DC, MC, V. Open: Daily noon
to 2:30 p.m. and 7–10:30 p.m.*

Chez Marie

$–$$ Montmartre (18e)   CLASSIC FRENCH

Some of the cheapest eats in this neighborhood, not exactly known for
bargain dining, are at the base of the steps heading to place du Tertre.
The food is hearty, the owners are charming and friendly, and the room
is cozy, with wood benches, red-and-white tablecloths, and wallpaper in
the style of Toulouse-Lautrec. Stick to the basics like lamb and *frites* or
duck confit, and you'll leave full and with money in your wallet.

27 rue Gabrielle. ☎ *01-42-62-06-26. Métro: Abbesses. Meals: Main courses 38–
136F ($5–$19); 3-course menus (all include an aperitif) 63F ($9), 98F ($14), and 120F
($17). AE, DC, MC, V. Open: Daily noon to 3:30 and 6 p.m.–1:30 a.m. Closed Jan.*

Chez Michel

$$ Gare du Nord (10e)   BRETON/BISTRO

Although it opened only a few years ago, this bistro has already added 70
seats, to accommodate the crowds that come for the excellent, unusual
food at very fair prices. Chef Thierry Breton puts old-fashioned Breton
dishes on his menu — look for succulent scallops, handpicked by scuba
divers, which are served with truffles in winter. For the cheaper menu,
sit in the cellar at wooden tables and eat all the shellfish, patés, and
salads you want. Choose from over 100 wines at retail cost, a truly dizzy-
ing experience.

10 rue Belzunce. ☎ *01-44-53-06-20. Métro: Gare du Nord. Meals: 3-course menu
180F ($26); table d'hôte menu 130F ($19). MC, V. Open: Tues–Sat noon to 2 p.m. and
7 p.m. to midnight. Closed last week of July and first 3 weeks of Aug.*

Closerie des Lilas

$$–$$$$ St-Germain-des-Prés/Montparnasse (6e)   BRASSERIE/ RESTAURANT

This old literary haunt remains one of the city's most romantic sites for a meal. Ernest Hemingway, James Jones, and John Dos Passos once hung out under the shady lilac bushes, while Lenin and Trotsky debated politics over chess. Closerie is split into two dining areas — a more expensive but romantic restaurant, and a cheaper, brighter brasserie. A meal may start with *oeufs dur* (eggs with mayonnaise), oysters in season, a tasty *terrine de foie gras canard avec toasts* (duck liver terrine with toasted bread), or the classic *steack tartare avec frites maison* (marinated raw steak with french fries). Dinners may include a tender *salle d'agneau rotie en crôute dorée* (roasted lamb flank in a golden crust), peppery *filet de boeuf au poivre,* or *homard Breton à votre façon* (Brittany lobster cooked the way you choose). Finish up with a *café* and *pâtisseries du jour* or *crêpes Suzette.*

171 bd. du Montparnasse. ☎ *01-40-51-34-50. Métro: Port-Royal. Reservations required. Meals: Main courses 120F–450F ($17–$64). AE, DC, MC, V. Open: Daily noon to 1 a.m.*

Dame Jeanne

$$ Bastille (11e)   MODERN BISTRO

Chef Francis Lévêque creates memorable, reasonably priced dishes at this restaurant, decorated in autumnal colors and illuminated by soft golden lighting. The fruit-and-vegetable menu may have dishes like *fricassée de légumes au lard et à l'estragon* (sautéed vegetables with cured ham and oregano) and desserts like caramelized brioche topped with sweetened banana. The more expensive menus may offer risotto accented with tapenade and topped with diced steamed salmon. The wine list begins with Dame Jeanne's discoveries — lesser-known wines — for 90F ($13) a bottle.

60 rue de Charonne, 11e. ☎ *01-47-00-37-40. Métro: Lédru-Rollin. Meals: 2-course menu 148F ($21); 3-course menu 178F ($25); seasonal fruit-and-vegetable menu 120F ($17). MC, V. Open: Tues–Sat noon to 2:15 p.m.; Tues–Thurs 7:30–11 p.m.; Fri–Sat 7:30–11:30 p.m.*

Jo Goldenberg

$ Marais (4e)   CENTRAL EUROPEAN/DELI

Jo Goldenberg is adorned with long red banquettes, surrounded by photos of famous patrons, including former French president Mitterrand, and original paintings by up-and-coming artists. Eastern specialties abound, like *poulet paprika* (chicken in paprika sauce), goulash, moussaka, Wiener schnitzel, and typical deli offerings like pastrami and corned beef — allegedly invented right here by Goldenberg senior in the 1920s. Adding to the festive air are the Gypsy musicians who begin playing around 9 p.m. For a final touch, Goldenberg, himself, hands departing patrons gifts, such as a calendar of Jewish holidays, a neighborhood map, and a drawing of the Hebrew alphabet for kids.

7 rue des Rosiers. ☎ *01-48-87-20-16. Métro: St-Paul. Meals: Main courses 70–89F ($10–$13). AE, DC, MC, V. Daily 9 a.m. to midnight.*

L'Ambroisie

$$$$$ Le Marais (4e)   HAUTE CUISINE

Chef Bernard Pacaud has made a name for himself in this gorgeous seventeenth-century mansion. French president Jacques Chirac and his wife, Bernadette, took Bill and Hillary Clinton here when they wanted to impress them. Three-star specialties include fricasée of lobster in wine sauce, roasted free-range chicken with black truffles, and an award-winning *tarte fine* (chocolate pie served with bitter chocolate and mocha ice cream). The decor in the two high-ceilinged salons evokes an Italian palazzo, with terrace dining in summer.

9 place des Vosges. ☎ *01-42-78-51-45. Métro: St. Paul. Reservations required at least 4 weeks in advance. Jacket/tie recommended. Meals: No prix fixe; expect to spend at least 1,100F ($157) per person per meal. AE, MC, V. Open: Tues–Sat noon to 1:30 p.m. and 8–9:30 p.m. Closed two weeks in Feb and three weeks in Aug.*

La Bastide Odéon

$$ Jardin du Luxembourg (6e)   PROVENÇAL

Chef Gilles Ajuelos serves delicious Provençal cooking in a lovely dining room, across from the Jardin du Luxembourg. The menu changes regularly, but the chef's dynamic creations include rabbit stuffed with eggplant as a starter, then *gnocchi* with snails and garlic, and, as dessert, roasted pear with *brousse,* rosemary, honey, and citrus syrup alongside yogurt sorbet. You can also savor an iced tomato soup with grappa or olives from the chef's *cuisine du marché* (from the market).

7 rue Corneille, 6e. ☎ *01-43-26-03-65. Métro: Odéon. Meals: 2-course menu 154F ($22); 3-course menu 194F ($28). AE, MC, V. Open: Tues–Sat noon to 3 p.m. and 7:30– 11 p.m. Closed Aug.*

La Cigale

$–$$ Eiffel Tower   BISTRO

Stylish yet discreet, Le Cigale serves delicious soufflés (among other specialties) to a sophisticated and high-spirited crowd. The food is simply some of the best you'll get in Paris, for these prices. The delicate soufflés are beaten high; brim with camembert, sautéed spinach, or tarragon cream; and melt in your mouth. And that's before dessert, which offers — you got it — soufflés of heavenly citron and sinful chocolate. If you're not in the mood for a soufflé, other tempting entrees include a rump roast and succulent lamb chops.

11 bis rue de Chomel. ☎ *01-45-48-87-87. Métro: Sèvres-Babylone. Reservations recommended. Meals: Main courses 58–112F ($8–$16). MC, DC, V. Open: Mon–Fri noon to 2 p.m.; Mon–Sat 7:30–11 p.m.*

La Petite Chaise

$$ St-Germain-des-Prés (7e)   CLASSIC FRENCH

Built in the mid-seventeenth century, this small gem is allegedly Paris's oldest restaurant. The entranceway, adorned with a smoky antique mirror from the early eighteenth century, leads to a softly illuminated dining room reminiscent of an old country inn. Start with the *escargots bourguignon* (burgundy-style snails cooked in a garlic sauce) or home-made *foie gras de canard maison* (housemade duck liver). As a main dish, the *magret de canard pomme et miel* melts away your appetite — the robust duck tastes supple and sweet under honey and lightly salted potatoes gratinée. A slice of chocolate cake with English cream will top off your meal perfectly.

36 rue de Grenelle. ☎ *01-42-22-13-35. Métro: Sèvres-Babylone. Meals: Main courses (with half-bottle wine) 125F ($18); 2-course menu (with half-bottle wine) 160F ($23); 3-course menu (with half-bottle wine) 195F ($28). AE, MC, V. Open: Daily noon to 2 p.m. and 7–10:45 p.m.*

L'Ebauchoir

$–$$ Bastille (12e)   BISTRO

Tucked into a non-touristy part of the Bastille neighborhood, this restaurant is well worth the visit. A mural pays homage to the working-class roots of the area, and the space is just large enough to render dining here a bit noisy. The waiters rush to show diners to their seats, at the first-come, first served tables. The day's offerings are written on a chalkboard, and once you've sampled lunch or dinner, you'll find that the decibel level is more than made up for by the superb food. Appetizer choices may be warm foie gras or stuffed ravioli, followed by mouthwatering smoked tuna with fennel or steak in a red-wine Bordelaise sauce. For dessert, the *millefeuille* (a flaky multilayered pastry) is divine.

45 rue de Citeaux, 12e. ☎ *01-43-42-49-31. Métro: Faidherbe-Chaligny. Reservations not accepted. Meals: Main courses 75–125F ($11–$18). MC, V. Open: Mon–Thurs noon to 2:30 p.m. and 8–10:30 p.m.; Fri–Sat noon to 2:30 p.m. and 8–11 p.m.*

Le Cinq

$$$$$ Champs-Elysées (8e)   HAUTE CUISINE

Phillippe Legendre, a celebrated three-star chef, is winning raves for his new Le Cinq in the renovated Four Seasons Hotel George V. Every element is in place, from the stately yet serene dining room to the perfect waitstaff. The inventive cuisine includes *crème de cresson de source glacée au caviar Sevruga* (chilled watercress cream with Sevruga caviar), *ris de veau fermier poêlé aux girolles* (seared sweetbreads with chanterelles), and for dessert, the delightful *variations autour de la fraise* (a whimsical assortment of strawberry confections, ranging from strawberry tiramisu to sorbet of strawberry and green tomato).

31 av George V. ☎ 01-49-52-71-54. Métro: George V. Reservations required. Meals: Main courses 249–394F ($36–$56); gourmet tasting menu 984F ($141). AE, MC, V. Open: Daily 5:30–10:30 p.m.

Le Grenier de Notre-Dame

$ Latin Quarter (5e)   VEGETARIAN

Le Grenier is enveloped in green, from the walls and tablecloths to the outdoor patio under a balcony of hanging plants, as if to prove that, yes, this is a vegetarian restaurant. Nevertheless, the food is good, and I especially recommend the *cassoulet végétarien,* with white beans, onions, tomatoes, and soy sausage. The couscous and the cauliflower au gratin are also delicious. Le Grenier has a well-deserved reputation for desserts, such as the *tarte de tofu.* The wine list includes a variety of organic offerings.

18 rue de la Bûcherie. ☎ 01-43-29-98-29. Métro: Maubert-Mutualité. Meals: Main courses 64–89F ($9–$13). MC, V. Open: Mon–Thurs 12:30–3 p.m. and 7–10:30 p.m.; Fri–Sat noon to 2:30 p.m. and 7–11 p.m.; Sun noon to 3 p.m. and 7–10:30 p.m.

Le Père Claude

$$ Eiffel Tower (15e)   CLASSIC BISTRO

This bistro serves well-prepared, hearty dishes. Starters include warm sausage with pistachio and apples, as well as mussel soup with saffron. The rotisserie behind the bar signals that the house specialty is roasted meat, and the *panaché des viandes* is an assortment of perfectly roasted meat served with mashed potatoes. Make sure that you specify how you want the beef cooked, or it'll be served the way the French like it — *bleue,* very rare. Seafood lovers won't be disappointed in the *assiette de pêcheur aux pâtés fraiches* (fisherman's plate with fresh terrine). The large tables and relaxed atmosphere make this a family-friendly place. After dinner, you can stroll up avenue de la Motte-Picquet and take in a view of the dazzlingly lit Eiffel Tower.

51 av. de la Motte-Picquet. ☎ 01-47-34-03-05. Métro: La Motte-Picquet–Grenelle. Meals: Main courses 95–160F ($14–$23). AE, MC, V. Open: Daily 11:30 a.m.–2:30 p.m. and 7 p.m. to midnight.

Le Polidor

$–$$ St-Germain-des-Prés (6e)   CLASSIC BISTRO

For about 150 years, this has been the quintessential Left Bank bistro, perpetually crowded with people, sitting elbow to elbow and surrounded by wood, mirrors, and lace curtains. The cooking is earthy, with all of the desserts and ice creams made on the premises. Begin with a spinach salad with nut oil, followed by solid plates of *rognons en madere* (veal kidneys in madeira), *blanquette de veau* (veal cooked in a cream sauce), *boeuf bourguignon* (beef cooked in a stock flavored with red wine, mushrooms, and onions), or *ragoût* of pork. Save room for one of the fresh tarts and pies. At weekday lunch, you can get a quarter-liter of wine for 7F ($1).

41 rue Monsieur-le-Prince. ☎ *01-43-26-95-34. Métro: Odéon. Meals: Main courses 49–76F ($7–$11). No credit cards. Open: Mon–Sat noon to 2:30 p.m. and 7–12:30 a.m.; Sun 7–11 p.m.*

Restaurant Dane Gourmande

$$ Bastille/Marais (4e)   LYONNAIS

Regulars rave about this tiny bargain, at the edge of the Marais, run by Dane, a 70-something chef from Lyon. With only 16 seats, the brightly-lit plain restaurant fills up quickly each night, as guests feast on starters like the buttery *terrine maison au canard* (homemade duck terrine) and the salad with country ham or anchovies. Main courses may include *canard croustillant de miel* (crispy duck cooked in honey) or *steak au poivre* cooked to your taste and crunchy with green and black peppercorns. Try a homemade *tartelette* for dessert with ice cream. Dane does all the cooking and most of the serving herself.

9 rue du Turenne. ☎ *01-42-77-62-54. Métro: Bastille or St-Paul. Meals: Lunch menu (with half-pitcher of wine) 140F ($20); dinner menu (with bottle of wine) 183F ($26). Open: Daily noon to 2:30 p.m. and 7:20–10 p.m. Closed Mon lunch.*

Restaurant du Palais-Royal

$$ Louvre (1er)   CLASSIC FRENCH

The elegant arcade encircling the Jardin du Palais-Royal also surrounds this restaurant, making it one of the most romantic locations in Paris. Sit at the terrace on sun-filled days and begin with marinated leeks in a beet-juice vinaigrette or scallop salad. Main dishes vary with the season but might include grilled tuna steak with a Basque relish or roast baby lamb. The desserts are delicious, and the house red wine, served Lyonnais style in thick-bottomed bottles, is inexpensive and very good.

43 rue Valois. ☎ *01-40-20-00-27. Métro: Palais-Royal–Musée du Louvre. Meals: Main courses 112–195F ($16–$28). AE, DC, MC, V. Open: Mon–Fri 12:30–2:30 p.m.; Mon–Sat 7:30–10:30 p.m.*

Restaurant Paul

$$ Place Dauphine (1er)   CLASSIC FRENCH

This relaxed restaurant, on the first floor of an eighteenth-century town house, is overshadowed by its charismatic young owners, Thierry and

Chantal. The couple's affection for their restaurant, which they remodeled with wood banquettes and walls hand-painted with Parisian scenes, is palpable, and they extend that same enthusiasm to their patrons. Start with an invigorating lentil salad, tossed with marinated *lardons* (bits of cured ham) or a cool terrine of salmon, asparagus, and dill. Main dishes include a sumptuous haddock in a butter-tarragon cream sauce and a surprisingly delicate casserole of tender veal and mushrooms served with rice. End your lovely evening with a warm *tarte de pomme* (apple tart).

Two entrances at 15 place Dauphine and 52 quai des Orfévres, 1er. ☎ *01-43-54-21-48. Métro: Pont Neuf or Cité. Meals: Main courses 85–110F ($12–$16). AE, MC, V. Open: Tues–Sun noon to 2:30 p.m. and 7–10:30 p.m.*

Restaurant Perraudin

$–$$ Latin Quarter (5e)   CLASSIC BISTRO

It's said that Hemingway went to the Closerie des Lilas, when he was rich, and to Perraudin, when he was broke. You'll enjoy this historic bistro, too, from its red-checked tablecloths and lace lampshades to its bargain lunch menu offering a choice of three appetizers, two main courses, and cheese or dessert. You may start with tomatoes and mozzarella, then have ham with endive or roast beef, followed by *baba au rhum* (a type of rum cake). Classics like duck confit and *gigot d'agneau* (leg of lamb) with *gratin Dauphinois* (potatoes topped with cheese) are on the à la carte menu. At lunch, Mme Perraudin offers a quarter-liter of red wine for 10F ($1.45). Arrive early for a table.

157 rue St-Jacques. ☎ *01-46-33-15-75. Métro: Luxembourg. Meals: Main courses 59F ($8); 3-course gastronomic menu 150F ($21). No credit cards. Open: Tues–Fri noon to 2:15 p.m.; Mon–Sat 7:30–10:15 p.m.*

Rôtisserie Armaillé

$$–$$$ Charles-de-Gaulle–Etoile (17e)   MODERN BISTRO

Jacques Cagna is a celebrity chef with a highly regarded restaurant in St-Germain-des-Prés, and this "baby bistro" is his nod to the current mood for fine dining at a fixed price. Although the decor is pleasant, with light wood paneling and plaid upholstery, it's his modern approach to hearty bistro dishes that draws crowds of businesspeople for lunch and the local chic set for dinner. Freshly baked bread accompanies starters like the *terrine de laperau aux parfums d'agrumes* (terrine of baby rabbits with citrus zest) and main courses of *squab aux raisins de Smyrnes* (squab in raisins from Smyrnes) or tuna carpaccio. The service is fast and friendly.

6 rue d'Armaillé, 17e. ☎ *01-42-27-19-20. Métro: Charles-de-Gaulle–Etoile or Argentine. Meals: 2-course lunch menu 165F ($24); 2-course dinner menu 230F ($33). AE, DC, MC, V. Open: Mon–Fri noon to 2:30 p.m.; Mon–Sat 7:30–11 p.m.*

Spoon, Food and Wine

$$–$$$ Champs-Elysées (8e) MODERN BISTRO

Celebrated chef Alain Ducasse has reinvented the joy of dining out, offering world-class food, reasonable prices, and service bordering on indulgent. A menu of mix-and-match choices — you choose the condiment, side dishes, and vegetables to complement the main dish — presents a variety of international dishes. Take, for example, spare ribs — try a marmalade of stewed meat, red wine, tomatoes, and olives to lavish on the meat, beside a heaping portion of Maxim's potatoes. Spoon also boasts the most international wine list in Paris, with 120 choices from South Africa, Argentina, and New Zealand. Although bubble gum ice cream and Ben & Jerry's are available for dessert, opt for the oozing warm chocolate "pizza." This affordable splurge, organized by a world master chef, ends with a Parisian coffee, the second cup is on the house.

14 rue de Marignan. ☎ *01-40-76-34-44. Métro: Franklin-D.-Roosevelt. Reservations recommended one month in advance. Meals: Main courses 85–225F ($12–$32); 3-course Bento Box menu 135F ($19). AE, MC, V. Open: Mon–Fri 11:45 a.m.–2:30 p.m. and 6:30–11:30 p.m.*

Vagenende

$$ St-Germian-des-Prés (6e) BRASSERIE

Founded in 1904 as a *bouillon* (soup kitchen) by M. Chartier — of the 9e arrondissement restaurant of the same name — Vagenende evolved into a brasserie, now classified as a Monument Historique. The art nouveau decor is authentic — mirrors, frescoes, and swirling floral patterns abound within walls of dark wood, making this the place to live out your belle époque fantasy. Lace curtains, globe lights, and spacious booths enhance the classic atmosphere. The dishes are equally classic — *confit de canard* (duck confit), *sole meunière* (a filet of sole that is rolled in flour and sautéed in butter), and *pavé de morue sauce vierge* (cod with lemon-flavored sauce).

142 bd. St-Germain. ☎ *01-43-26-68-18. Métro: Odéon. Meals: Main courses 68–152F ($10–$220). AE, DC, MC, V. Open: Daily noon to 1 a.m.*

Runner-up restaurants

Le 404

$–$$ **Le Marais (3e)** This restaurant, owned by popular French comedian Smain, serves some of the best couscous in Paris — perhaps it's the hand-rolled semolina. *69 rue des Gravilliers, 3e.* ☎ *01-42-74-57-81.*

Restaurant Orestias

$ Latin Quarter (6e) This pleasant Greek restaurant offers well-pre-pared fresh meals for cheap, cheap, cheap. *4 rue Grégoire-de-Tours, 6e.* ☎ *01-43-54-62-01.*

Tea salons (salons de thé)

If you're tired of all those short blasts of French coffee, you have an alternative. The French are finally appreciating tea, and tea lovers need look no further than a tea salon for a wide range of blends. The pastry selections in these places are usually excellent, but save your full meals for a restaurant — tea salons tend to be expensive.

The belle époque **Angelina** (226 rue de Rivoli, 1er; ☎ **01-42-60-82-00;** Métro: Concorde or Tuileries) gives patrons gilded mirrors and an arched entrance in addition to a wide variety of succulent pastries. It's open daily 9 a.m. to 5:45 p.m. (lunch served 11:45 a.m. to 3 p.m.). At **A la Cour de Rohan** (59–61 rue St-André-des-Arts, actually a passage-way off of rue St-André-des-Arts, 6e; ☎ **01-43-25-79-67;** Métro: Odéon or St-Michel), wicker chairs, flowery wallpaper, chintz curtains, and beamed ceilings give the two rooms an irresistible homespun charm. It's open Sunday to Thursday noon to 7:30 p.m. and Friday and Saturday noon to 11:30 p.m. The American management of **A Priori Thé** (35–37 Galerie Vivienne, enter at 6 rue Vivienne, 4 rue des Petits-Champs, or 5 rue de la Banque, 2e; ☎ **01-42-97-48-75;** Métro: Bourse, Palais-Royal–Musée du Louvre, or Pyramides) has created a harmonious and appealing blend of Parisian and new-world styles in this cleverly named tea salon. It's open Monday to Friday 9 a.m. to 6 p.m., Saturday 9 a.m. to 6:30 p.m., and Sunday 12:30 to 6:30 p.m. Founded during the belle époque, **Ladurée** (16 rue Royale, 8e; ☎ **01-42-60-21-79;** Métro: Concorde and 75 av. des Champs-Elysées ☎ **01-40-75-08-75;** Métro: Franklin-D-Roosevelt) is the most refined tearoom in Paris, and society still gathers there. The tearoom is open Monday to Saturday 8:30 a.m. to 7 p.m.

The Parisian cafe

For many visitors, this will be the most essential section of the book: the best places to read the paper, write postcards, people-watch, soak up the city's atmosphere, relax with a cup of coffee or a glass of wine or beer, and even fill up on delicious food.

In the heart of St-Germain-des-Prés, **Café de Flore** (172 bd. St-Germain, 6e; ☎ **01-45-48-55-26;** Métro: St-Germain-des-Prés) is still going strong, even though the famous writers have moved on, and you now pay high prices for the opportunity to indulge in nostalgia. Sartre is said to have written *Les Chemins de la liberté (The Roads to Freedom)* at his table in Café de Flore, and other regulars included André Malraux and Guillaume Apollinaire. It's open daily 7 a.m. to 2 a.m. Like its neighbor Café de

Flore, **Café des Deux Magots** (6 place St-Germain-des-Prés, 6e; ☎ 01-45-48-55-25; Métro: St-Germain-des-Prés) was a hangout for Sartre and de Beauvoir. The intellectuals met here in the 1950s, and Sartre wrote at his table every morning. With prices starting at 23F ($3.30) for coffee and 12F ($1.75) for a croissant, it's an expensive place for literary-intellectual pilgrims but a great spot to watch the nightly promenade on boulevard St-Germain. The service can be snippy. It's open daily 7 a.m. to 1:30 a.m.

La Coupole (102 bd. Montparnasse, 14e; ☎ 01-43-20-14-20; Métro: Vavin) has been packing them in since Henry Miller came here for his morning porridge. The cavernous interior is always jammed and bristling with energy. Japanese businesspeople, French yuppies, models, tourists, and neighborhood regulars keep the frenzied waiters running until 2 a.m. You won't know which is more interesting, the scene on the street or the parade that passes through the revolving doors. The food is good, too. The cafe is open Monday to Thursday 7:30 a.m. to 2 a.m., Friday 9:30 a.m. to 4 a.m., and Sat 3 p.m. to 7 p.m. and 9:30 p.m. to 4 a.m.

Not far from the Arc de Triomphe, the early-1900s **Fouquet's** (99 av. des Champs-Elysées, 8e; ☎ 01-47-23-70-60; Métro: George V) is an institution. Patrons have included James Joyce, Charlie Chaplin, Marlene Dietrich, Winston Churchill, and Franklin D. Roosevelt. You'll pay dearly for the glitzy associations and nostalgia. Fouquet's is open daily 8 a.m. to 1 a.m.

At the Louvre, the stunning **Café Marly** (93 rue de Rivoli, at the cour Napoléon, 1er; ☎ 01-49-26-06-60; Métro: Palais-Royal–Musée du Louvre) has a gorgeous view of I. M. Pei's glass pyramid. With high ceilings, warmly painted pastel walls, and luxurious red sofa chairs, the rooms could house the museum's latest art collection. Don't let the elegant ambience intimidate you — wonderful food at reasonable prices is on the menu. Choose from the lovely wine list, sit on the balcony, and enjoy the exquisite lighting on the surrounding eighteenth-century facades. Café Marly is open daily 8 a.m. to 2 a.m. After 8 p.m., seating is for dinner only.

Designed by renowned architect Christian de Portzamparc, the hip bi-level **Café Beaubourg** (100 rue St-Merri, 4e; ☎ 01-48-87-63-96; Métro: Rambuteau or Hôtel-de-Ville) boasts large circular columns that soar up to an illuminated ceiling. The walls are filled with books, and a small wooden bridge spans the upper part of the cafe and leads to quieter, artistically designed tables. In summer, sit in a wicker chair on the terrace and become a main attraction yourself, as passersby cast curious glances at you. The cafe is open Sunday to Thursday 8 a.m. to 1 a.m., Friday and Saturday 8 a.m. to 2 a.m.

Café Mabillon (164 bd. St-Germain, 6e; ☎ 01-43-26-62-93; Métro: Mabillon) was a simple cafe until it was renovated a few years ago. Now, during the day, contemporary rock music draws a hip young crowd to relax on the terrace or in the ultramodern interior. At night, the music changes to techno and the bordello-red banquettes fill with a wide assortment of night owls. As dawn approaches, the sound drops to a level just loud enough to keep you from dozing off in your seat. Café Mabillon is open 24 hours.

The tri-level **Web Bar** (32 rue de Picardie, in the Marais, 3e; ☎ **01-42-72-66-55;** Internet: www.webbar.fr; Métro: République) exhibits art, plays experimental music, shows short films, and hosts storytelling, fashion shows, and even an occasional chess tournament. A casual crowd of locals creates a warm mood, in contrast to the rather stark decor. There are 18 computers at 40F ($6) per hour or 25F ($3.60) per half hour. The Web Bar is open Monday to Friday 8:30 a.m. to 2 a.m. and Saturday and Sunday 11 a.m. to 2 a.m.; avoid the Web Bar on weekdays between 5 and 7 p.m., or you may have to wait to use the computers.

Wine bars

Wine bars are great places to sample fine French wines that are normally only available by the bottle. Most wine bars serve one or two *plats du jour* (plates of the day) in traditional bistro style, but the best choices are apt to be the cheeses, terrines, and patés. Most wine bars are closed on Sundays; some are closed week-ends.

Look closely at the exterior of **A la Cloche des Halles** (28 rue Coquillière, 1er; ☎ **01-42-36-93-89;** Métro: Les Halles or Palais-Royal–Musée du Louvre) for the bell that once tolled the opening and closing of the vast food market for which this neighborhood was named. Today the tiny bar/cafe is crowded at lunchtime with people dining on plates of ham and *terrine de campagne* (country-style pâté) or quiche, accompanied by a bottle of wine. This bar is convivial and fun but very noisy and crowded. If you can't find a seat, you can usually stand at the bar and eat. It's open Monday to Friday 8 a.m. to 10 p.m. and Saturday 10 a.m. to 5 p.m.

Le Griffonnier (8 rue des Saussaies, 8e; ☎ **01-42-65-17-17;** Métro: Champs-Elysées–Clemenceau) is noted as much for its first-rate kitchen as for its comprehensive wine cellar. You can sample bistro specialties like *confit de canard maison* (homemade specialty of duck preserved and cooked in its own fat), or try a hearty plate of charcuterie (sliced meats), terrines, or cheese, usually from the Auvergne region of central France. Hot meals are served only at lunchtime and on Thursday evenings. Le Griffonnier is open Monday to Friday 7:30 a.m. to 9 or 10 p.m.

After you settle in at one of the cozy tables at **Le Sancerre** (22 av. Rapp, 7e; ☎ **01-45-51-75-91;** Métro: Alma-Marceau), you'll find some typically French items on the menu, such as omelets of all varieties with a side of fried potatoes. And there's the ubiquitous *andouillette,* the sausage that's decidedly an acquired taste. You also have a choice of Loire wines — including the bar's namesake, Sancerre. Le Sancerre is open

Monday to Friday 8 a.m. to 10 p.m. and Saturday 8 a.m. to 4 p.m. At the **Taverne Henri IV** (13 place du Pont-Neuf, 1er; ☎ 01-43-54-27-90; Métro: Pont-Neuf), a variety of wines by the glass can be accompanied by open-faced sandwiches (including warm goat cheese), pâtés, and cheeses, such as Cantal and Auvergne blue. Although on the expensive side, the wine and food are excellent. This is an authentic old-fashioned bar frequented by men reading the newspaper, discussing the news of the day, and smoking nonstop. Taverne Henri IV is open Monday to Friday noon to 10 p.m. and Saturday noon to 4 p.m. **La Tartine** (24 rue de Rivoli, 4e; ☎ 01-42-72-76-85; Métro: St-Paul) is pure prewar Paris, from the nicotine-browned walls and frosted globe chandeliers to the worn wood furniture. The ambience is funky and working class, but you'll find a broad segment of society throwing back little glasses of wine at the bar or lingering over a newspaper in the spacious back room. La Tartine is open Monday to Friday 10 a.m. to 10 p.m., Sat noon to 10 p.m., and Sunday noon to 7 p.m.

Chapter 12

Exploring Paris

● ●

In This Chapter

▶ Checking out the top attractions in Paris

▶ Taking a guided tour of Paris

▶ Finding the best places to shop

▶ Experiencing Paris's nightlife

● ●

*F*or this chapter, I whittle down Paris's many attractions to only 20 top sights, but that's still probably more than you'll be able to do in a single trip. At the end of this book is a worksheet where you can plot the top sights according to how much you want to see them.

Two passes in Paris are designed especially with busy visitors in mind, but only one is a very good deal. The **Paris Visite** card, available at most Métro and RER stops for 55F ($8) a day, provides free transportation on any of Paris's buses, subways, and RER trains, as well as discounted admission to some sights and excursions. The pass is a good deal only if you plan to take a lot of daily transportation and if the discounted attractions are of interest to you.

If you know you'll be visiting two or three museums a day, purchase the **Carte Musées et Monuments,** on sale at most major museums and Métro stations. The pass costs 80F ($11) for one day, 160F ($23) for three days, and 240F ($34) for five days. If you consider that full-price admission to the Louvre is 45F ($7) and entrance fees to most other museums are the same or a little less, well . . . you do the math. The pass gives you access to 65 museums and monuments in Paris and the Ile de France, allowing you to bypass lines and proceed directly inside — a distinct benefit on a hot day at Versailles.

Paris's Top Attractions

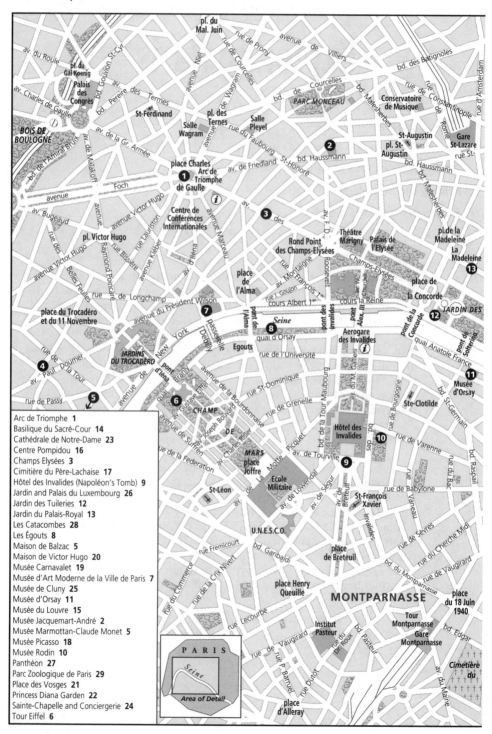

Arc de Triomphe **1**
Basilique du Sacré-Cœur **14**
Cathédrale de Notre-Dame **23**
Centre Pompidou **16**
Champs Elysées **3**
Cimitière du Père-Lachaise **17**
Hôtel des Invalides (Napoléon's Tomb) **9**
Jardin and Palais du Luxembourg **26**
Jardin des Tuileries **12**
Jardin du Palais-Royal **13**
Les Catacombes **28**
Les Égouts **8**
Maison de Balzac **5**
Maison de Victor Hugo **20**
Musée Carnavalet **19**
Musée d'Art Moderne de la Ville de Paris **7**
Musée de Cluny **25**
Musée d'Orsay **11**
Musée du Louvre **15**
Musée Jacquemart-André **2**
Musée Marmottan-Claude Monet **5**
Musée Picasso **18**
Musée Rodin **10**
Panthéon **27**
Parc Zoologique de Paris **29**
Place des Vosges **21**
Princess Diana Garden **22**
Sainte-Chapelle and Conciergerie **24**
Tour Eiffel **6**

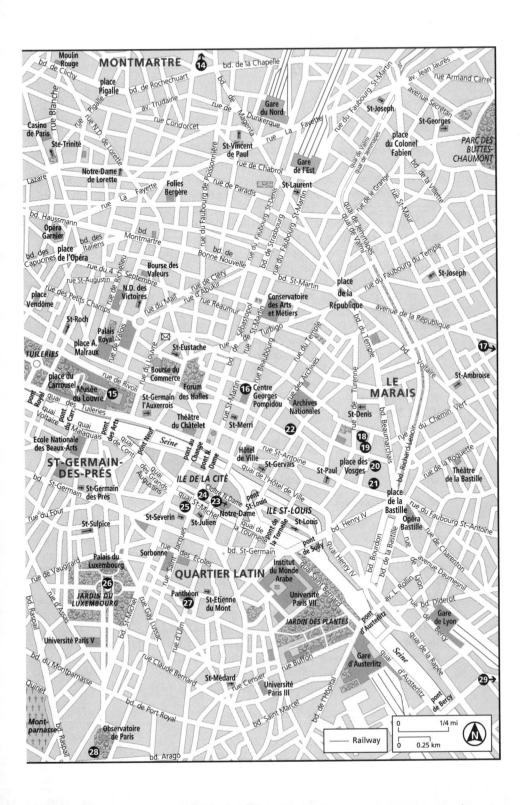

The Top Sights: From the Arc to the Tour

Arc de Triomphe

Champs-Elysées (8e)

The Arc de Triomphe is the world's largest triumphal arch, commissioned by Napoléon in honor of the 128 battles won by his *Grande Armée.* Although it has come to symbolize the thrill of victory, it has also witnessed the agony of defeat — in 1871 and 1940, German armies marched victoriously through the arch and down the Champs-Elysées. Today the arch houses France's Tomb of the Unknown Soldier. Several notable sculptures cover the arch, such as Rude's *La Marseillaise,* on the Champs-Elysées side, and his bas-relief *Departure of the Volunteers.* The real thrill here, though, is the panoramic view. To reach the stairs and elevators that climb the arch, take the underpass using the white Métro entrances. From the top of the Arc de Triomphe, 162 feet up, you can see the Champs-Elysées, the obelisk at the center of place de la Concorde, and the Louvre in a straight line. That big cube (Notre-Dame could fit beneath it) at the far end in the other direction is the Grande Arche de la Défense in St-Denis, built to be the modern equivalent to this arch. (Many think it failed miserably.) Allow an hour to visit.

Place Charles de Gaulle. ☎ *01-43-80-31-31. Métro: Charles-de-Gaulle–Etoile. Bus: 22, 30, 31, 52, 73, or 92. Admission: 40F ($6 adults, 32F ($4.60) ages 12–25, free for children under 12. Open: Apr–Sept daily 9:30 a.m.–11 p.m.; Oct–Mar daily 10 a.m.–10:30 p.m. Closed major holidays.*

Basilique du Sacré-Coeur

Montmartre (18e)

Take the Métro to the Abbesses stop and admire the splendid art nouveau Métro station before catching the *funiculaire* (funicular) to the top of Montmartre's *butte* (hill). There stands the white Byzantine-Romanesque church you've been seeing from all over the city: **Sacré-Coeur** (Sacred Heart). The best reason to come is the city-spanning views — 30 miles across the rooftops of Paris on a clear day — that you can see from its dome. Reaching the dome requires a nail-bitingly steep climb up corkscrew steps. (That's why it's a good idea to take the elevator up from the Métro and ride the funiculaire.) Built from 1876 (after France's defeat in the Franco-Prussian War) to 1919, the church's interior isn't as striking as its exterior and is, in fact, vaguely depressing.

At the back and to the left side of the cathedral is **place du Tertre,** which Vincent van Gogh used as a scene for one of his paintings. (He also once lived there.) The square is usually swamped by tourists and quick-sketch artists in spring and summer. The steps in front of the church come alive around dusk, when street musicians entertain the crowd that gathers to watch the city's lights come on. Allow an hour to visit the church and climb to the tower and half an hour to explore place du Tertre. Any street that leads downhill from place du Tertre brings you to the quiet side of **Montmartre,** where you'll catch a glimpse of Paris from another era — surprisingly unspoiled lanes, quiet squares, ivy-clad shuttered houses with gardens, and even Paris's only vineyard. Together, Sacré-Coeur, place du Tertre, and this quiet neighborhood in Montmartre all create a sense of a rustic village, set apart from the churning metropolis of busy Paris below.

25 rue du Chevalier-de-la-Barre. ☎ *01-53-41-89-00. Métro: Abbesses. Take the elevator to the surface and follow the signs to the funiculaire that runs to the church (1 Métro ticket). Bus: The only bus that goes to the top of the hill is the local Montmartrobus. Admission: Basilica free; dome 15F ($2.15) adults, 8F ($1.15) students 6–24; crypt 15F ($2.15) adults, 8F ($1.15) students 6–24. Open: Basilica daily 6:45 a.m.–11 p.m.; dome and crypt Apr–Sept daily 9 a.m.–7 p.m.; Oct–Mar daily 9 a.m.–6 p.m.*

Cathédrale de Notre-Dame

Ile de la Cité (4e)

Crusaders prayed here before leaving for the holy wars, Napoléon crowned himself emperor and Joséphine empress here, and when Paris was liberated during World War II, General de Gaulle rushed to the cathedral to give thanks. And of course, Quasimodo and Esmerelda hung around here, among the gargoyles, a lot.

Construction of Notre-Dame started in 1163 when Pope Alexander III laid the cornerstone, and it was completed in the fourteenth century. Built in an age of illiteracy, the cathedral's exterior tells the stories of the Bible in its portals, statuary, and stained glass. Angry citizens pillaged Notre-Dame during the French Revolution. They mistook the religious statues above the portals on the west front for representations of kings and beheaded the figures. Nearly 100 years later, when Notre-Dame had been turned into a barn, writer Victor Hugo and other artists called attention to its dangerous state of disrepair, and architect Viollet-le-Duc began the much-needed restoration. He designed Notre-Dame's spire, a new feature. Baron Haussmann (Napoléon III's urban planner) evicted the residents of the houses that cluttered the cathedral's vicinity and tore the buildings down to create better views of the cathedral.

Notre-Dame de Paris

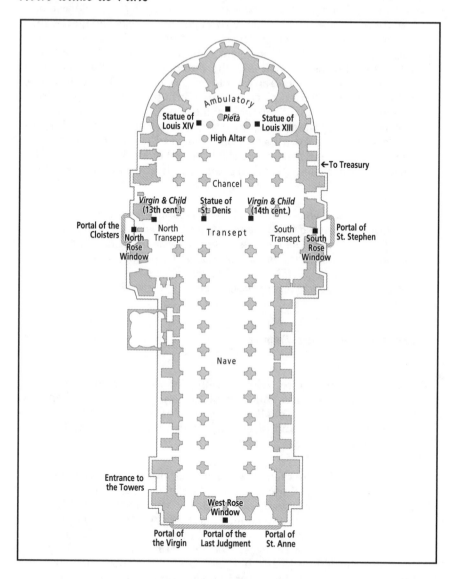

Today, the art of Notre-Dame continues to awe its hundreds of thousands of yearly visitors. The west front contains 28 statues representing the monarchs of Judea and Israel. The three portals depict, from left to right, the Coronation of the Virgin; the Last Judgment; and the Madonna and Child, surrounded by scenes of Mary's life. Before entering the cathedral, walk around to the east end of the church to appreciate the spectacular **flying buttresses** (the external side supports that give the massive interior a sense of weightlessness). The interior, with its slender, graceful columns and high, high ceilings, is impressive, with room for as many as

6,000 worshipers. Visit on a sunny morning to appreciate the giant **rose windows** — to the west, north, and south — which retain some of their thirteenth-century stained glass. The blazing colors are a glory to behold on a sunny day. The cathedral's **treasury,** for which you must pay admission, is just that — a treasure trove of historical items from the cathedral, including gold and jeweled chalices and other objects used to celebrate masses, and robes and headdresses worn by archbishops. For a glimpse of Roman times through the nineteenth century on Ile de la Cité, head down into the **Crypte Archéologique,** the entrance of which is about 200 feet in front of the cathedral. The crypt is fairly new, discovered in the twentieth century by builders digging a parking garage. Before you leave the island, pay a visit to the moving **Mémorial de la Déportatation,** not far behind the cathedral on the island's eastern tip. This garden honors the 200,000 French victims deported to concentration camps by the Nazis, with an eternal flame to the deportees. Take the staircase to river level and see gold triangles with the names of concentration camps where victims lost their lives. You will exit on the upper level by a gate over which reads: "*Pardonne. N'oublie pas.* (Forgive. Don't forget.) Admission is free.

For a great photo-op, cross the pont au Double to the Left Bank and view Notre-Dame from the quay. The highlight for kids will undoubtedly be climbing the 387 steps to the top of one of the towers for a fabulous Quasimodo-eye view of the gargoyles and Paris. For entrance to the towers, you'll line up in front of the north tower. Allow 30 minutes to visit Notre-Dame, longer if you climb the towers.

6 place du Parvis Notre-Dame. ☎ *01-42-34-56-10. Métro: Cité or St-Michel. RER: St-Michel. Bus: 21, 38, 85, or 96. Admission: Church free; towers 35F ($5) adults, 26F ($3.70) ages 12–25, under 12 free; Crypte Archéologique 26F ($3.70) adults, 17F ($2.50) ages 12–25, under 12 free; Treasury 26F ($3.70) adults, 17F ($2.50) ages 12–25, under 12 free. Open: Cathedral daily 8 a.m.–6:45 p.m. (closed Sat 12:30–2 p.m.); Treasury Mon–Sat 9:30–11:30 a.m., 1:30–5.30 p.m.); Towers daily Apr–Sept 10 a.m.– 6 p.m., Oct–Mar 10 a.m.–4:30 p.m.; Crypte winter 10 a.m.–4.45 p.m., summer 10 a.m.–5.45 p.m. Six masses celebrated on Sun, four on weekdays, one on Sat. Free guided visits in English Wed and Thurs at noon.*

Centre Pompidou

Beaubourg (4e)

Escalators, elevators, air-conditioning ducts, and tubular passages resembling a giant gerbil run are on the outside of the colorfully futuristic Centre National d'Art et de Culture Georges Pompidou, while the inside is a spacious haven where visitors can view, touch, or listen to modern art and artists. The newer of Paris's two modern art museums, the Centre Pompidou includes two floors of work (floors four and five) from France's national collection of modern art (to see more of this collection, you can pay a visit to the **Musée National d'Art Moderne de la Ville de Paris** at 11 av. du Wilson, 16e, ☎ 01-53-67-40-00). The Centre

Pompidou also includes the **Brancusi Atelier** (containing nearly 150 drawings, paintings, and other works by Romanian sculptor Constantin Brancusi), a cinema, a huge public library, and spaces for modern dance and music and temporary exhibits that often include video and computer works. Between its 1977 opening and 1997, more than 160 million people visited the Centre Pompidou — and the building began to crumble under the weight of its popularity. After a $100-million renovation, the center reopened to much fanfare on January 1, 2000. Even if you don't want to check out the museum, you can still take an escalator for free to the top floor for a breathtaking view of Paris. Don't miss the nearby Igor Stravinsky fountain, either, with its fun sculptures by Tinguely and Niki de Saint Phalle that include red lips spitting water and a twirling, grinning skull. Dedicate at least two hours to viewing the works and slipping upstairs for the view.

Avoid Georges, the ultrahip top-floor restaurant; it's expensive, the portions are tiny, and the service is slow.

Place Georges-Pompidou. ☎ *01-44-78-12-33. Internet:* www.centrepompidou. fr. *Métro: Rambuteau, Hôtel-de-Ville, or Châtelet–Les Halles. Bus: 21, 29, 38, 47, 58, 69, 70, 72, 74, 75, 76, 81, 85, or 86. Admission: 30F ($4.30) adults, 20F ($2.85) ages 18–26, children under 18 free; guided tours 40F ($5.70). Open: Daily 11 a.m.–10 p.m.*

Champs-Elysées

(8e)

If you were in Paris when the new millennium began or when the French won the 1998 World Cup or when the 2000 Euro Cup soccer championship took place, you'll understand what the Champs-Elysées means to the French. As many as a million singing, flag-waving Parisians spilled onto the avenue — it was said the country hadn't experienced such group euphoria since the days following the Allied Liberation of Paris in 1944. The Champs is also the avenue that the military proudly marches down on each Bastille Day and where cancer-survivor Lance Armstrong won his second Tour de France in July 2000. The scene here is liveliest at night, with people lining up for the cinemas (it's a great place to see English-language films — look for "v.o." for version originale on schedules and posters), floodlights illuminating the Arc de Triomphe and place de la Concorde, and tourists crowding the pavement. The restaurants on the avenue consist mainly of standard chain cafes (Chez Clément, Hippo) and American-style fast-food places (McDonald's, Planet Hollywood, ChiChi's), though there are great restaurants (like Pierre Gagnaire and Taillevent) on the streets surrounding the avenue. The shopping along the Champs ranges from reasonably priced stores (Zara) to luxe boutiques (Louis Vuitton) to chain stores that you'd see in any American mall (Disney Store). Many of the stores are even open on Sunday. Allow an hour to walk the entire distance — about a mile — longer if you want to shop, eat, or dawdle.

*Stretching from place Charles de Gaulle–Etoile to place de la Concorde. Métro:
Concorde, Champs-Elysées–Clémenceau, Franklin-D.-Roosevelt, George V, or
Charles-de-Gaulle–Etoile. Bus: Many lines cross it, but only no. 73 travels its entire
length.*

Cimetière du Père-Lachaise

Ménilmontant (20e)

The world's most-visited cemetery is more like an outdoor museum than
a place of sadness. No wonder Parisians have always come here to stroll
and reflect. With its winding cobbled streets, park benches, and street
signs, the 110-acre Père-Lachaise is a mini-city all its own. Many visitors
leave flowers or notes scrawled on Métro tickets for their favorite
celebrity residents, who include **Isadora Duncan, Edith Piaf, Oscar
Wilde, Frédéric Chopin, Maria Callas, Jim Morrison** (the most popular), **Modigliani, Molière, Colette, Camille Pissarro, Marcel Proust,
Sarah Bernhardt, Gertrude Stein** and **Alice B. Toklas,** and **Yves
Montand** and **Simone Signoret.** If for nothing else, go for the striking and
often poignant statuary, such as the boy who seems to sit up in bed, as
if he'd heard a noise, and the young woman who's frozen mid-dance, as
if turned to stone without warning. Allow at the very least two hours to
visit.

You can obtain a free map from the gatekeeper at the main entrance,
but a better map is sold outside the entrance for 10F ($1.45).

*16 rue du Repos. Main entrance on bd. du Ménilmontant. Métro: Père-Lachaise.
Bus: 61 or 69. Admission: Free. Open: Mar 16–Nov 5 Mon–Fri 8 a.m.–6 p.m., Sat
8:30 a.m.–6 p.m., Sun 9 a.m.–6 p.m.; Nov 6–Mar 15 Mon–Fri 8 a.m.–5:30 p.m., Sat
8:30 a.m.–5:30 p.m., Sun 9 a.m.–5:30 p.m.*

Memorial to a princess

Place de l'Alma (Métro: Alma-Marceau) has been turned into a tribute to the late
Diana, princess of Wales, who was killed in an auto accident on August 31, 1997,
in the nearby underpass. The bronze flame in the center of the park is a replication
of the flame held by the Statue of Liberty and was a 1987 gift by the *International
Herald Tribune* to honor Franco-American friendship. Many bouquets and messages (and even grafitti) are still placed around the flame, which seems to have
come to represent the princess.

Paris has also opened the **Center for Nature Discovery, Garden in Memory of
Diana, Princess of Wales,** at 21 rue des Blancs-Manteaux in the Marais. The small
park, which you can visit daily during daylight hours, is devoted to teaching children about nature and gardening and contains flowers, vegetables, and decorative
plants.

Hôtel des Invalides (Napoléon's Tomb)

Invalides (7e)

The best way to get a sense of the awe that the Hôtel des Invalides inspires is to walk to it by crossing from the Right Bank to the Left via the pont Alexander III. As you proceed toward it through the Esplanade des Invalides, you'll see the dome (gilded with 12 kilograms of real gold) of the **Eglise du Dôme,** one of the high points of classical art, rising 107 meters from the ground and, in the cobblestone forecourt, 16 green copper cannons point outward in a powerful display. The Invalides was built by Louis XIV as a hospital and home for all veteran officers and soldiers who were wounded in battle. It still has offices for various departments of the French armed forces, and part of the complex is still a hospital.

The **Église de St-Louis,** part of the Invalides also known as the Church of the Soldiers, is adorned with a row of enemy flags captured during the military campaigns of the nineteenth and twentieth centuries; But most visitors come to see the red-rock **Tomb of Napoléon,** where the emperor is buried in six coffins, one inside the other under the great dome. The first coffin is iron, the second mahogany, the third and fourth lead, the fifth ebony, and the outermost oak. The emperor's remains were transferred to his final resting place in 1840, almost 20 years after his death on the island of St. Helena, where he was exiled following his defeat at Waterloo.

If you like military lore, you may want to visit the **Musée de l'Armée** — admission is included when you buy your ticket for Napoléon's tomb — one of the greatest army museums in the world. It features thousands of weapons from prehistory to World War II. Allow half an hour for the tomb and an hour for the museum.

Place des Invalides. ☎ *01-44-42-37-72. Métro: Latour-Maubourg, Invalides, or Varenne. Bus: 63, 83, or 93. Admission: 38F ($6) adults, 28F ($4.65) students 12–25, children under 12 free. Open: Oct–Mar daily 10 a.m.–5 p.m.; Apr–Sept daily 10 a.m.– 6 p.m.; Napoléon's tomb June–Sept daily until 7 p.m, Oct–May 10 a.m.–5 p.m. Closed major holidays.*

Jardin and Palais de Luxembourg

St-Germain-des-Prés (6e)

Henri IV's queen, Marie de' Medici, commissioned the Jardin du Luxembourg, one of Paris's most beloved parks. Not far from the Sorbonne and just south of the Latin Quarter, the large park is popular with students and children, who love it for its playground, toy boat pond, pony rides, and puppet theater. Besides pools, fountains, and statues of queens and poets, there are tennis and boules (similar to boccie) courts. Orchards containing 360 varieties of apples, 270 kinds of pears, and grape vines are in the park's southwest corner. Members of the Senate get to eat the fruit, but leftovers go to a soup kitchen. Walk north and you'll come across a bevy of beehives behind a low fence. A beekeeping (apiculture) course is taught here on weekends.

The Palais du Luxembourg, at the northern edge of the park, was also built for Marie de' Medici, who was homesick for the Palazzo Pitti in Florence, where she had spent her childhood. When the queen was banished in 1630, the palace was abandoned until the Revolution, when it was used as a prison. It's now the seat of the French Senate, but it isn't open to the public. Take as long as you like to wander in the garden, soak up the sun by the fountain, or watch the children play.

Main entrance at the corner of bd. St-Michel and rue des Médicis. ☎ *01-43-29-12-78. Métro: Odéon. RER: Luxembourg or Port-Royal. Bus: 38, 82, 84, 85, or 89. Admission: Free. Open: Daily dawn–dusk.*

Jardin du Palais-Royal

Louvre (1er)

Cardinal Richelieu ordered the Palais Royal built in 1630 as his personal residence, complete with grounds landscaped by the royal gardener. Today the royal palace is no longer open to the public, but its statue-filled gardens, including the controversial prison-striped columns built in 1986, remain one of the most restful places in the city. Its square, place du Palais-Royal, is ringed by restaurants, art galleries, and specialty boutiques and is also home to the Comédie-Française.

Entrance on rue St-Honoré. Métro: Musée du Louvre–Palais-Royal. Bus: 42, 69, 72, 73, or 94. Admission: Free. Open: Daily 7:30 a.m. to dusk.

Jardin des Tuileries

Louvre (1er)

Spread out over 63 acres, the city's most formal gardens originally ran between the Louvre and Catherine de' Medici's Palais des Tuileries, which was burned down during the 1871 Paris Commune. In keeping with the French style of parks, the trees are planted according to an orderly design, and the sandy paths are arrow straight. You can catch some rays from one of the chairs surrounding the ponds and fountains and get a light snack at one of the outdoor cafes. During summer, a carnival features an enormous Ferris wheel (with great views of the city), a log flume, a fun house, ice cream stands, and arcade-style games. Come for a stroll before or after visiting the Louvre.

Entrances on rue de Rivoli and place de la Concorde. ☎ *01-44-50-75-01. Métro: Concorde or Tuileries. Bus: 42, 69, 72, 73, or 94. Admission: Free. Free guided visits of the gardens (in French) Sun, Wed, and Fri at 3 p.m. Open: Daily 7:30 a.m. to dusk.*

Musée Jacquemart-André

Champs-Elysées (8e)

Edouard André, heir of a prominent banking family, and Nélie Jacquemart, a well-known portraitist, commissioned architect Henri Parent to build this impressive residence. They then set about filling it with French, Flemish, and Italian paintings, furniture, and tapestries. Now the structure is a paradise for Renaissance art fans, worth visiting as much for a glimpse of how the filthy rich Parisians lived in the nineteenth century as for its Italian and Flemish masterpieces by Bellini, Botticelli, Carpaccio, Uccello, Rubens, Rembrandt, and Van Eyck. Take advantage of the free audioguide that leads you through the mansion with a fascinating narrative. Allow an hour to visit the museum and then take a break in what was Madame's lofty-ceilinged dining room, now a classy tearoom serving light lunches and snacks.

158 bd. Haussmann. ☎ *01-42-89-04-91. Métro: Miromesnil. Bus: 28, 32, 49, or 80. Admission: 49F ($7) adults, 37F ($5) students and children under 18. Open: Daily 10 a.m.–6 p.m.*

Musée du Louvre

Louvre (1er)

You could visit the Louvre every day for a month and still not see each of its more than 30,000 treasures. So to have an enjoyable, nonexhausting experience, you'll need to limit your focus or plan more than one trip. The sheer scale of the Louvre, organized in three wings — **Sully, Denon,** and **Richelieu** — makes it easy to get lost, so grab a map on the way in. The Louvre bookstore in the Carrousel de Louvre sells many comprehensive guides and maps in English; there are even brochures for "visitors in a hurry" and a guidebook, **The Louvre, First Visit.** For a quick orientation to the museum's layout, try the **90-minute tour** with a museum guide for 17F ($2.45) that covers the most popular works. Or you can set your own pace with the four-hour **audiotour** (30F/$4.30), for rent at the entrance to any of the wings. (For more information on the tours, call ☎ **01-40-20-52-09.**)

If you're in a hurry but want to do the Louvre on your own, you can follow this approach; consider it a "best of the Louvre" tour. Start with Leonardo da Vinci's *Mona Lisa* (Denon wing, first floor). Nearby, on the same floor, are two of the Louvre's most famous French paintings, Géricault's *The Raft of Medusa* and Delacroix's *Liberty Guiding the People.* Next, visit the *Winged Victory* and Michelangelo's *Slaves* (both Denon wing, ground floor), before seeing the *Venus de Milo* (Sully wing, ground floor). After that, let your own interests guide you. Keep in mind that only Florence's Uffizi Gallery rivals the Denon wing for its Italian Renaissance collection, which includes Raphael's *Portrait of Balthazar Castiglione* and Titian's *Man with a Glove.* And the revamped Egyptian antiquities department is the largest exhibit of Egyptian antiquities outside of Cairo.

The Louvre

The Pyramid

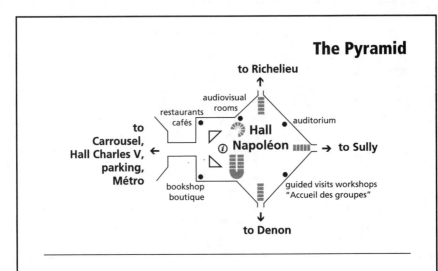

to Richelieu

audiovisual rooms

restaurants cafés

auditorium

to Carrousel, Hall Charles V, parking, Métro

i **Hall Napoléon**

→ to Sully

bookshop boutique

guided visits workshops "Accueil des groupes"

to Denon

The Levels

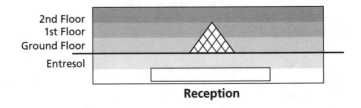

2nd Floor
1st Floor
Ground Floor
Entresol

Reception

The Wings

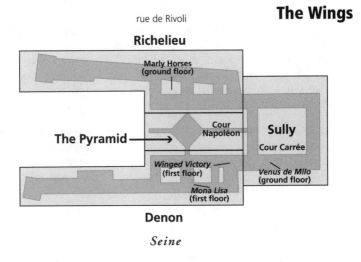

rue de Rivoli

Richelieu

Marly Horses (ground floor)

Cour Napoléon

Sully
Cour Carrée

The Pyramid →

Winged Victory (first floor)

Venus de Milo (ground floor)

Mona Lisa (first floor)

Denon

Seine

Some Louvre tips

Long waiting lines outside the Louvre's pyramid entrance are notorious, but there are some tricks for avoiding them.

- ✔ Order tickets by phone at ☎ 08-03-80-88-03, have them charged to your Visa or MasterCard, and then pick them up at any FNAC store, such as the one at 74 av. des Champs-Elysées (Métro: George V). This gives you direct entry through the Passage Richelieu, 93 rue de Rivoli.

- ✔ Enter via the underground shopping mall, the Carrousel du Louvre, at 99 rue de Rivoli.

- ✔ Enter directly from the Palais Royal–Musée du Louvre Métro station.

- ✔ Buy the Carte Musées et Monuments (Museum and Monuments Pass), allowing direct entry through the priority entrance at the Passage Richelieu, 93 rue de Rivoli. For details on the pass, see the beginning of this chapter.

In April 2000, a new exhibit featuring 120 pieces of art and antiquity from the earliest civilizations in Africa, Asia, Oceania, and the Americas opened on the ground floor near the Denon wing. The exhibit will be housed here until 2004, when the Musée de Quai Branly, to which the pieces belong, opens.

As of 1989, the main entrance to the museum is I. M. Pei's controversial 71-foot glass pyramid — a startling though effective contrast of the ultra-modern against the palace's classical lines. Commissioned by the late president François Mitterrand, it allows sunlight to shine on an underground reception area that contains a complex of shops and restaurants. Avoid this entrance and its long lines by using the rue de Rivoli/Carrousel du Louvre entrance or take the stairs at the Porte des Lions near the Arc du Triomphe du Carrousel. For a restful and elegant break, visit Café Marly (see Chapter 11) in the Louvre's cour Napoléon (☎ 01-49-26-06-60). Its gorgeous view of I. M. Pei's glass pyramid and its high ceilings, luxurious red sofa chairs and light, yet filling lunches will quickly give you a second wind so that you can conquer all the other rooms in the museum you haven't yet seen.

Rue de Rivoli. ☎ *01-40-20-50-50 for recorded message, 01-40-20-53-17 for information desk. Internet:* www.louvre.fr. *Métro: Palais-Royal–Musée du Louvre. Admission: 45F ($6) adults, 26F ($3.70) after 3 p.m. and Sun, 1st Sun of month free; children under 18 free. Mon (certain rooms only) and Wed 9 a.m.–9:45 p.m.; Thurs–Sun 9 a.m.–6 p.m.*

Musée d'Orsay

Musée d'Orsay (7e)

One of Jacques Chirac's greatest achievements as mayor of Paris was turning the abandoned Orsay train station into one of the world's most brilliantly designed museums. To get a sense of this remarkable conversion, take a moment at the top of the central staircase to envision where the trains once pulled into the station, under the arcing iron-and-glass roof. Then enjoy the Musée d'Orsay's real claim to fame — its unsurpassed collection of Impressionist masterpieces. In order to appreciate them, don't visit the museum from bottom to top, because you'll get too tired. Instead, go directly to the top floor and work your way down after soaking up Monet, Renoir, Degas, Cézanne, Gauguin, van Gogh, and their contemporaries. A few standout works are Manet's *Déjeuner sur l'herbe,* Renoir's *Moulin de la Galette,* Monet's *Rouen Cathedral: Full Sunlight,* and Whistler's *Arrangement in Grey and Black: Portrait of the Painter's Mother.* Allow 90 minutes for the Impressionists, longer to see the whole museum. (The art nouveau rooms are extraordinary.) The Café des Hauteurs, which looks out toward the Right Bank through the station's enormous clock, is a terrific place for a light lunch or snack.

62 rue de Lille/1 rue Bellechasse, 7e. ☎ *01-40-49-48-14, or 01-40-49-48-48 for information desk. Internet:* www.musee-orsay.fr. *Métro: Solférino. RER: Musée-d'Orsay. Bus: 24, 68, 69, or 73. Admission: 40F ($6) adults, 30F ($4.30) ages 18–24 and Sun for adults, free for children under 18. Open: Tues–Wed and Fri–Sat 10 a.m.–6 p.m.; Thurs 10 a.m.–9:45 p.m.; Sun 9 a.m.–6 p.m. June 20–Sept 20 opens at 9 a.m.*

Musée Picasso

Le Marais (3e)

In 1973, following Picasso's death, his heirs donated his personal art collection to the state in lieu of paying outrageous inheritance taxes, and the Musée Picasso was created from these holdings. Because the works here are exhibited in rotation, you can pay a visit to this museum on each of your trips to Paris and see something different every time. The spectacular collection includes more than 200 paintings, almost 160 sculptures, 88 ceramics, and more than 3,000 prints and drawings — every phase of his prolific 75-year career is represented. You can view the works chronologically. The museum also displays works by other artists collected by Picasso, including Corot, Cézanne, Braque, Rousseau, Matisse, and Renoir. The seventeenth-century Hôtel Salé (salé means "salty"; the former owner was a salt-tax collector), which houses the collection, has a gorgeous carved stairway and is worth a visit in its own right. Budget at least a few hours, if not more, for this museum.

In the Hôtel Salé, 5 rue de Thorigny. ☎ *01-42-71-25-21. Métro: Chemin-Vert, St-Paul, or Filles du Calvaire. Bus: 24, 68, 69, or 73. Admission: 38F ($5) adults, 28F ($4) ages 18–25 and Sun for adults, free for children under 18; 1st Sun of each month free. Open: Apr–Sept Wed–Mon 9:30 a.m.–6 p.m.; Oct–Mar Wed–Mon 9:30 a.m.–5:30 p.m., Thurs to 8 p.m.*

Musée Rodin

Eiffel Tower and Invalides (7e)

Auguste Rodin, often regarded as the greatest sculptor of all time, lived and worked in what is now this museum from 1908 until his death in 1917. The museum is in the eighteenth-century Hôtel Biron, which was a convent before it became a residence for artists and writers. Matisse, Jean Cocteau, and poet Rainer Maria Rilke lived and worked in the mansion, before Rodin moved there at the height of his popularity. If you don't have a lot of time or money, it's worth the 5F (70¢) admission to visit just the gardens, where some of the artist's most famous works — *The Thinker, The Gates of Hell, Balzac,* and *The Burghers of Calais* — stand among 2,000 rosebushes. The highlight of the indoor exhibits are *The Kiss* and *Eve.* Allow at least an hour to visit, longer if you want to break for coffee in the garden cafe.

In the Hôtel Biron, 77 rue de Varenne. ☎ *01-44-18-61-10. Métro: Varenne. Bus: 69 or 83. Admission: 28F ($4) adults, 18F ($2.60) ages 18–24 and Sun for adults, free for children under 18; 5F (70¢) for garden only. Open: Apr–Sept Tues–Sun 9:30 a.m.– 5:45 p.m.; Oct–Mar Tues–Sun 9:30 a.m.–4:45 p.m. Garden to 5:45 p.m. in summer, last admittance one hour before.*

Panthéon

Latin Quarter (5e)

The Panthéon is to France what Westminster Abbey is to England: a final resting place for many of the nation's great men (and one great woman, Marie Curie, beside her husband). Inside the domed church's barrel-vaulted crypt are the tombs of Voltaire, Rousseau, Hugo, Braille, Zola, and more. André Malraux was the last to be entombed here in 1996. In 1755, Louis XV ordered the Panthéon built as a church in thanksgiving to Ste-Geneviève (its original name) after his recovery from an illness. After the French Revolution, the church was renamed the Panthéon — in remembrance of Rome's ancient Pantheon — and rededicated as a burying ground for France's heroes. All Christian elements were removed and windows were blocked. From 1806 to 1884, officials turned the Panthéon back into a church two more times, before finally declaring it what it is today. You can't miss the Panthéon at night — it's lit from inside with eerie blue lights that give it the appearance of a UFO or a trendy disco. Allow half an hour to an hour for your visit.

Place du Panthéon. ☎ *01-44-32-18-00. Métro: Cardinal-Lemoine or Maubert-Mutualité. Bus: 84, 85, or 89. Admission: 35F ($5) adults, 23F ($3.30) ages 18–25, free for children under 18. Open: Apr–Sept daily 9:30 a.m.–6:30 p.m.; Oct–Mar daily 10 a.m.–6:15 p.m.*

Place des Vosges

Le Marais (4e)

The most beautiful square in Paris sits right in the middle of the Marais. Place des Vosges is a symmetrical block of 36 brick-and-stone town houses, 9 on each side, with handsome slate roofs and dormer windows. Its lovely arcaded walkway is home to galleries, cafes, antiques dealers, and smart boutiques. By locating his palace here in the early seventeenth century, Henri IV transformed this area into France's most prestigious neighborhood, and the square, then called place Royal, quickly became the center of courtly parades and festivities. After the Revolution, it became place de l'Indivisibilité and later place des Vosges, in honor of the first département in France that completely paid its taxes to Napoléon. Victor Hugo lived at no. 6 for 16 years. Allow 30 minutes to walk all the way around the square under the arcades and to briefly stroll in the park.

Métro: St-Paul. Bus: 69, 76, or 96.

Sainte-Chapelle and Conciergerie

Ile de la Cité (4e)

Save Sainte-Chapelle for a sunny day. Its 15 perfect stained-glass windows, soaring 50 feet high to a star-studded vaulted ceiling, will take your breath away. You'll think you've stepped into a kaleidoscope. Louis IX, the only French king to become a saint, had the Sainte-Chapelle built as a shrine to house the relics of Christ's crucifixion, including the Crown of Thorns that Louis bought from the emperor of Constantinople. Building the Sainte-Chapelle cost Louis less than buying the hideously expensive Crown of Thorns, which now resides in the vault at Notre-Dame.

Built between 1246 and 1248, the Sainte-Chapelle consists of two chapels, one on top of the other. Palace servants worshiped at the *chapelle basse* (lower chapel); it's ornamented with fleur-de-lis designs. The *chapelle haute* (upper chapel) is considered one of the highest achievements of Gothic art. If you had the hours and hours it would take to read the stained-glass windows, you'd see that the 1,134 scenes trace the biblical story from the Garden of Eden to the Apocalypse. Read from the bottom of the windows up and from left to right. One of the biblical stories portrayed on the first window to the right is the story of the Crown of Thorns; St. Louis is shown several times. On evenings when the upper chapel becomes a venue for classical-music concerts, the effect of its chandelier lights dancing off the windows is magical. Allow 45 minutes to visit.

Around the corner from the Sainte-Chapelle, the Conciergerie dates from the Middle Ages, when it was an administrative office of the Crown. The far western tower, the Tour Bonbec, came to be known facetiously as the

Tower of Babel because of the frequent screams from the many prisoners tortured there. But the Conciergerie is most famous for its days as a prison during "The Terror" years of the French Revolution, when 4,164 "enemies of the people" passed through here. More than half of them headed for the guillotine on place de la Révolution, now called place de la Concorde. Besides revolutionary ringleaders Danton and Robespierre, Charlotte Corday and poet André Chenier were imprisoned here. Marie Antoinette was kept here in a putrid 11-foot-square cell, to await her fate. When she was taken to her execution, the despised queen was forced to ride backward in the cart, so she'd have to face a jeering crowd. Her cell is now a chapel, and the other cells have been transformed with exhibits and mementos designed to convey a sense of prison life in a brutal era.

Part of the Palais de Justice, 4 bd. du Palais. ☎ *01-53-73-78-50. Métro: Cité or St-Michel. RER: St-Michel. Bus: 21, 38, 85, or 96. Admission: Sainte-Chapelle 26F ($3.70) adults, 7F ($1) ages 12–25, free for children under 12; Conciergerie 35F ($5) adults, 23F ($3.30) ages 12–25, free for children under 12; combined Sainte-Chapelle and Conciergerie 50F ($7.15). Open: Both Apr–Sept daily 9:30 a.m.–6:30 p.m.; Oct–Mar daily 10 a.m.–5 p.m. Closed major holidays.*

Tour Eiffel

Eiffel Tower and Invalides (7e)

You could fill an entire page with fun trivia about Paris's most famous symbol. For starters, it weighs 7,000 tons, soars 1,056 feet high, and is held together with 2.5 million rivets. Gustave Eiffel beat 699 other individuals in a contest to design what was supposed to be a temporary monument for the 1889 *Exposition Universelle* (Universal Exposition). Luckily for us, the advent of radio saved the tower from being torn down — as the tallest human-made structure in Europe at the time, it made a perfect spot to place a radio antenna (now a TV antenna). Praised by some and damned by others, the tower created as much controversy in its time as I. M. Pei's pyramid at the Louvre (see "Musée du Louvre," earlier in this chapter) did 100 years later. The Prince of Wales (later Edward VII) and his family were invited to be the first to ascend it. In 1989, the tower's centennial was celebrated with 89 minutes of music and fireworks, in the 1990s it counted down the days and minutes until the turn of the millennium, and on New Year's Eve 1999 it was the site of a spectacular fireworks show. Allow 2 hours for your visit: one hour to line up and another to take in the panorama. You can ascend the tower two ways — by foot and by elevator. Ascending by foot is cheaper, but definitely more strenuous. There are 704 stairs to the second landing, so if you're in doubt about your fitness for the climb, take the elevators. Climbers will have to take an elevator from the second landing to the third landing (the top); it's the only way to get to the top. Visitors taking the elevators from the ground and first landing must get into a different elevator on the second level for the lift to the top.

Lines are shorter the first thing in the morning, but if you come after dark, you'll be in for a treat: The tower's lights frame the lacy steelwork in a way that daylight doesn't, beneath you the city twinkles, and the Seine reflects it all. Even if you ascend the tower during the day, try to return to the area at night to see Paris's symbol aglow.

Parc du Champ-de-Mars. ☎ *01-44-11-23-45. Internet:* www.tour-eiffel.fr. *Métro: Trocadéro, Bir-Hakeim, or Ecole-Militaire. RER: Champs-de-Mars. Bus: 42, 69, 82, or 87. Admission 24F ($3.50) for elevator to first landing only (188 ft.); 45F ($7) for elevator to first and second landings (380 ft.); 65F ($9) for all three landings (1,060 ft.); 20F ($2.90) for stairs to first and second landings; additional 20F to take the elevator to the third landing. reduced admission for children under 12. Open: Sept to mid-June daily 9:30 a.m.–11 p.m.; late June to Aug daily 9 a.m. to midnight. Fall and winter, stairs close at 6:30 p.m. Closed major holidays.*

More Cool Things to See

Les Catacombes

Montparnasse (14e)

If it's dark and spooky, older kids and teens usually love it, and the Catacombes are perfect for hardy kids over 10. About six million skulls and skeletons are stacked in thousands of yards of tunnels, and a visit is bound to provoke at least a little bit of the fear factor. Les Catacombes, a former quarry, began housing bones in 1785 from the Cimetière des Innocents and an assortment of other overstocked Parisian cemeteries. Les Catacombes earned the nickname *place d'Enfer* ("Hell Square"), which later became place Denfert-Rochereau.

Those prone to claustrophobia should think twice about entering — the deep, dark tunnels close in rapidly and tightly. Equip yourself with flashlights to navigate the poorly illuminated corridors and read the inscriptions, and wear proper shoes (sneakers or hiking boots) to avoid a misstep on the rocky, often slick passageways. A hood of sorts will also protect you from the water dripping overhead.

1 place Denfert-Rochereau. ☎ *01-43-22-47-63. Métro or RER: Denfert-Rochereau. Admission: 33F ($4.70) adults, 17F ($2.45) ages 8–26, free under 8. Open: Tues–Fri 2–4 p.m.; Sat–Sun 9–11 a.m. and 2–4 p.m.*

Les Egouts

Eiffel Tower and Invalides (7e)

Believe it or not, this tour of the city's sewers is so popular that you sometimes have to wait as long as half an hour in line. The tours start with a short film on the history of sewers and are followed by a visit to a small museum and, finally, a short trip through the maze. Paris's sewers are laid out like an underground city, with streets clearly labeled and each branch pipe bearing the name of the building to which it's connected. Don't worry, you won't trudge through anything *dégoutant* (disgusting), but the visit may leave your clothes smelling a bit ripe. Visit at the end of the day and wear something you don't plan to wear again until it's washed.

Entrance at a stairway on the Seine side of the quai d'Orsay, facing no. 93. ☎ *01-53-68-27-82. Fax: 01-53-68-27-89. Métro: Alma-Marceau. RER: Pont de l'Alma. Admission: 25F ($3.60) adults, 20F ($2.85) students and adults over 60, 15F ($2.15) children 5–12, free under 5. Open: May–Sept Sat–Wed 11 a.m.– 5 p.m.; Oct–Apr 11 a.m.–4 p.m. Closed 3 weeks in Jan.*

Maison de Balzac

Western Paris/Bois de Boulogne (16e)

The very modest Honoré de Balzac lived in this very posh residential Passy neighborhood from 1840 to 1847 under a false name to avoid creditors, allowing entrance to only those who knew a password. He wrote some of his most famous novels here, including those that make up his *La Comédie Humaine* (The Human Comedy). His study is preserved, and portraits, books, letters, and manuscripts are on display. You'll also see his jewel-encrusted cane and the Limoges coffee pot that bears his initials in mulberry pink — leaving you to wonder just how bad his money problems really were.

47 rue Raynouard, 16e. ☎ *01-55-74-41-80. Métro: Passy. Admission: 30F ($4.30) adults, 20F ($2.85) adults over 60, 15F ages 8–26, free for children under 8. Open: Tues–Sun 10 a.m.– 5:40 p.m. Closed holidays.*

Maison de Victor Hugo

Le Marais (4e)

If you or your kids have read *The Hunchback of Notre-Dame* and *Les Misérables,* you may want to visit this house. The novelist/poet lived on the second floor of this town house, built in 1610, from 1832 to 1848. You'll see some of Hugo's furniture, samples of his handwriting, his inkwell, first editions of his works, and a painting of his funeral procession at the Arc de Triomphe in 1885. There are also portraits of his family, and the Chinese salon from Hugo's house on Guernsey has been reassembled here. The highlight is more than 450 of Hugo's drawings, illustrating scenes from his own works.

6 place des Vosges. ☎ *01-42-72-10-16. Métro: St-Paul. Admission: 22F ($3.15) adults, 15F ($2.15) children 8–17; free on Sunday. Open: Tues–Sun 10 a.m.–5:40 p.m. (window closes at 5:15 p.m.).*

Musée Carnavalet

Le Marais (3e)

If you like history but are bored by textbooks, this is the place for you. The museum is housed inside two luxurious Renaissance mansions; one is the former home of one of France's greatest letter writers, Mme de Sévigné, and her daughter. The history of Paris comes alive through an impressive selection of paintings and other items. The chess pieces that Louis XVI played with while waiting his turn for the guillotine are here, as are Napoléon's cradle and a replica of Marcel Proust's cork-lined bedroom. Many salons depict events related to the Revolution, and the paintings of what Paris used to look like are fascinating.

23 rue de Sévigné. ☎ *01-42-72-21-13. Métro: St-Paul. Admission: 35F ($5) adults, 25F ($3.60) students; Sun admission 20F ($2.85). Open: Tues–Sun 10 a.m.–5:40 p.m.*

Musée de Cluny (Musée National de Moyen Age/ Thermes de Cluny)

Latin Quarter (5e)

This is the city's foremost example of civil architecture from the Middle Ages and before, and the museum is one of Paris's treasures. Here you'll see ancient Roman baths and the statues that furious revolutionaries tore from Notre-Dame, thinking they represented royalty. Its gorgeous renovated gardens opened to the public in September 2000.

In the nineteenth century, the Hôtel de Cluny belonged to a collector of medieval art; upon his death in the 1840s, the government acquired the house and its contents. The exhibits are absolutely fascinating and include wood and stone sculpture, brilliant stained glass and metalwork, and rich tapestries. The famous fifteenth-century tapestry series of The Lady and the Unicorn is an allegory representing the five senses; the meaning of the sixth tapestry remains a mystery. The gift shop here is a wonderful place for souvenirs.

6 place Paul-Painlevé. ☎ *01-53-73-78-00. Métro: Cluny–La Sorbonne. Admission: 27F ($3.90) adults, 18F ($2.60) ages 18–25 and on Sun, free for children under 18. Open: Wed–Mon 9:15 a.m.–5:45 p.m.*

Musée Marmottan–Claude Monet

Western Paris/Bois de Boulogne (16e)

The Musée Marmottan celebrates painter Claude Monet and contains an outstanding collection of his waterlily paintings, as well as his more abstract representations of the Japanese Bridge at Giverny (see Chapter 13 for an easy trip to Giverny). Here you'll find the painting *Impression— Rising Sun,* from which the term "impressionism" was coined to describe the painting style and subsequent artistic movement. Also on hand is Monet's personal collection that includes works by his contemporaries: Pissarro, Manet, Morisot, and Renoir.

The museum, between the Ranelagh garden and the Bois de Boulogne, is in a nineteenth-century mansion that belonged to art historian Paul Marmottan. When Marmottan died in 1932, he donated the mansion and his collection of Empire furniture and Napoleonic art to the Académie des Beaux-Arts. When Claude Monet's son and heir bequeathed his father's collection to the Marmottan, the museum paid permanent homage to the artist's unique vision. Subsequent donations have expanded the collection to include more Impressionist paintings and the stunning Wildenstein collection of late-medieval illuminated manuscripts.

2 rue Louis-Boilly. ☎ *01-42-24-07-02. Internet:* www.marmottan.com/fr/informations/index.html. *Métro: La-Muette. Admission: 40F ($6) adults, 25F ($3.60) ages 9–25, free for children under 8. Open: Tues–Sun 10 a.m.–5 p.m.*

Parc Zoologique de Paris

Bois de Vincennes (12e)

It's big enough to keep your kids occupied for an afternoon, with lions, tigers, bears, and a cool tower, with a great view of the animals, that they'll love climbing. Most animals live in settings that closely resemble their natural habitats, and you can even watch while some are fed lunch (bears at 11:30 a.m., pelicans at 2:15 p.m., seals and sea lions at 4 p.m.).

In the Bois de Vincennes. ☎ *01-44-75-20-10. Fax: 01-43-43-54-73. Métro: Porte Dorée. Admission: 40F ($6) adults, 30F ($4.30) ages 4–25, free for children under 4. Open: Summer daily 9 a.m.–6 or 6:30 p.m.; winter daily 9 a.m.–5 or 5:30 p.m.*

Parks and Gardens

There are parks for flowers and plants and parks for admiring views. There are parks with puppet shows and pony rides and parks with museums on the grounds. Whatever parks you decide to visit, the beauty and serenity of planted gardens, splashing fountains, and arrow-straight paths are sure to relax you — and your kids will love them. Most parks are open daily until sunset, unless otherwise noted.

The legendary **Bois de Boulogne** in western Paris (16e; ☎ 01-40-67-97-02) was a royal forest and hunting ground. Napoléon III donated it to the city and Baron Haussmann transformed it, using London's Hyde Park as his model. Today, the Bois is not just for picnickers. Its 2,200 acres offer jogging paths, horseback riding, cycling (rentals are available), and boating on two lakes. The **Longchamp** and **Auteuil** racecourses are here, as is the beautiful **Pré Catelan,** a garden containing many of the herbs and plants mentioned in Shakespeare's plays. The

Bois de Boulogne's **Jardin d'Acclimation** contains an amusement park loved by Parisian children. The rose gardens in the Bois's **Parc de la Bagatelle** (16e; Métro: Porte Maillot), are sublime, while the thematic gardens reveal the art of gardening through the centuries. There's even a waterlily pond that pays homage to a certain famous painter. The château here was built by the comte d'Artois in 1775, after he made a bet with his sister-in-law, Marie Antoinette, that he could do it in under 90 days. It took 66 days. Under Napoléon, it was used as a hunting lodge.

Parc Monceau (boulevard de Coucelles, 8e; ☎ **01-42-27-39-56**; Métro: Monceau or Villiers) is beloved by Parisians for its oddities, including a Dutch windmill, a Roman temple, a covered bridge, a waterfall, a farm, medieval ruins, and a pagoda, all designed by Carmontelle. It was a favorite place for Marcel Proust to stroll and contains Paris's largest tree, an Oriental plane tree with a circumference of almost 23 feet. It's open Tuesday to Sunday. Have a picnic here with supplies from the nearby rue de Levis, a pedestrian shopping street open Tuesday to Sunday.

The **Parc de La Villette** (19e; Métro: Porte de la Villette) is an enormous high-tech urban cultural park, resplendent with theaters and music and science centers. In summer, you can catch an outdoor movie or listen to a concert and watch kids play on the giant dragon slide and the submarine. The park's **Cité des Sciences et de l'Industrie** is a large complex designed to make science more exciting to families (☎ **01-40-05-81-00**; Internet: `www.cite-sciences.fr`; Métro: Porte-de-la-Villette). There's something for every family member, from the planetarium to the Cité des Enfants, an adventure playground for 3- to 12-year-olds. In the Explora, interactive games demonstrate scientific techniques and present subjects including the universe, the earth, the environment, space, computer science, and health. Six films are shown daily in the gigantic sphere called the Géode, which has a huge hemispheric screen. Children can climb aboard an actual submarine in the l'Argonaute exhibit and see and participate in interactive demonstrations of the latest technological innovations in the Technocité exhibit. Admission to the exhibits, including the submarine Argonaut, is 50F ($7); admission to the Géode is 57F ($8), admission to Explora is 50F ($7), and admission to the Cité des Enfants is 25F ($3.60). The complex is open Tuesday to Saturday 10 a.m. to 6 p.m. and Sunday 10 a.m. to 7 p.m.

And on Your Left, Notre-Dame: Seeing Paris by Guided Tour

If this is your first time in Paris, an orientation tour can help you quickly get a grip on the city's geography. But even if you've been coming to Paris for 25 years, a well-executed walking or architecture tour can introduce you to sides of the city you never knew existed.

When you're lucky enough to be shown around by a guide whose enthusiasm makes the city come to life, it can be the high point of your entire trip.

Seine cruises

One of the most romantic and beautiful ways to see Paris is by one of the sightseeing boats that cruise up and down the Seine.

I don't advise taking one of the overpriced dinner or lunch cruises — they cost 350 to 500F ($50 to $71) per person. Instead, opt for an evening cruise. With its dramatically lit monuments and romantic bridges, the City of Light is truly breathtaking at night.

Three companies offer one-hour tours that are similar and cost about the same price:

- ✔ **Bateaux-Mouches:** Perhaps the best-known sightseeing boats are those of the Bateaux-Mouches, sailing from the pont de l'Alma on the Right Bank (8e; ☎ **01-42-25-96-10** or 01-42-76-99-99 for reservations; Métro: Alma-Marceau), and offering recorded commentary in up to six languages. From March to mid-November, 10 a.m. to 11 p.m., and late November to February, 11 a.m. to 9 p.m., the tours depart every 45 minutes, until noon, and every half an hour afterward. The cost is 40F ($6) adults and 20F ($2.90) children 5 to 13 and adults over 65; children under 5 ride free.

- ✔ **Bateaux-Parisiens:** Located at port de la Bourdonnais, 7e (☎ **01-44-11-33-44**; Métro: Bir-Hakeim), tours sail from the pont d'Iéna on the Left Bank. March to October, departures are every half an hour 10 a.m. to 10 p.m.; November to February, departures are every hour 10 a.m. and 9 p.m. The cost is 52F ($7) adults and 26F ($3.70) ages 12 and under.

- ✔ **Vedettes Pont Neuf:** Located at square du Vert-Galant, 1er (☎ **01-46-33-98-38**; Métro: Pont-Neuf), Vedettes Pont Neuf sail from the riverside, where the pont Neuf crosses Ile de la Cité. Vedettes boats are smaller and more intimate, and not all of them are covered. The commentary is live. March to October, departures are every half an hour 10:30 a.m. to 11 p.m.; November to February, departures are every 45 minutes from 10:30 a.m. to 10 p.m. (Saturdays and Sundays to 10:30 p.m.). The cost is 50F ($7) adults and 25F ($3.60) ages 4 to 12.

For a boat ride without commentary, take one of the **Bat-o-bus** shuttles that stop at Trocadéro, the Musée d'Orsay, the Louvre, Notre-Dame, and the Hôtel de Ville. (Signs on the quais will point you to the docking area.) A 12-hour ticket costs 65F ($9.30) adults and 35F ($5) children under 12, and you can jump off and on when you want.

You can also try a more unusual tour with **Paris Canal** (☎ 01-42-40-96-97; Métro: Bastille). Its three-hour cruises leave the Musée d'Orsay at 9:30 a.m. and end at Parc de la Villette. The boat passes under the Bastille and enters the Canal St-Martin for a lazy journey along the tree-lined quai Jemmapes. You'll cruise under bridges and through many locks. The boat leaves Parc de la Villette at 2:30 p.m. for the same voyage in reverse. Reservations are essential. The trip costs 100F ($14) for adults, 75F ($11) for those over 60, and 55F ($8) for children 4 to 11.

If you have restless young children, the Paris Canal trip may not be the best idea. The wait for each lock to let the boat pass may prove too long.

Bus tours

The biggest bus tour company is **Cityrama** (4 place des Pyramides, 1er; ☎ 01-44-55-61-00; Métro: Palais-Royal–Musée du Louvre), but its two-hour orientation tour is a bit pricey at 150F ($21) for those 12 and over. Its guided half- and full-day tours are 290F ($41) and 500F ($71), respectively. The tours to Versailles at 200F ($29) and to Chartres at 275F ($39) are a better bargain, because they take the hassle out of visiting these monuments. Nighttime illumination tours start at 150F ($21).

Paris's public transportation system, the RATP, offers the **Paris l'Open Tour** (☎ 01-43-46-52-06), which has quickly come to rival Cityrama. Its bright-yellow convertible buses take you to city highlights, while recorded commentary in French and English plays over the speakers. The 2¼-hour circuit covers all the sights in central Paris and offers extensions south to Bercy and north to Montmartre. A two-day pass is 135F ($19) or 110F ($16) with a Paris Visite pass (see the beginning of this chapter), and you can get on or off the bus as many times as you want, making this the more worthwhile tour. The buses run daily every 25 minutes from around 9:30 a.m. to 6:30 p.m. You can buy the pass at the tourist office (see Chapter 11) and at the RATP visitor center on place de la Madeleine.

The **RATP** (☎ 08-36-68-41-14) also runs **Balabus,** orange-and-white buses that run only from April to September on Sundays and holidays between noon and 8 p.m. Routes run between the Gare de Lyon and the Grand Arche de la Défense, in both directions, and cost one Métro ticket. Look for a "Bb" symbol across the side of the bus and along signs posted beside the route.

Walking tours

Comprehensive walking tours of Paris are given through **WICE** (20 bd. du Montparnasse, 15e; ☎ 01-45-66-75-50; Fax: 01-40-65-96-53; E-mail: wice@wice-paris.org; Internet: www.wice-paris.org), a **nonprofit** cultural association for Paris's English-speaking community. These are in-depth tours for those who want to do more than skim the surface. Recent tours have included "The Royal Squares of Paris," "Creative Writing Walks" of the Left and Right banks, and a Halloween tour of Père-Lachaise Cemetery. Tours vary in length and cost, but most run 90 to 150F ($13 to $21) for a two- to three-hour tour. WICE's tours are so popular with Paris residents that you'll need to book a few weeks ahead.

Peter and Oriel Caine are the founders of **Paris Walking Tours** (☎ 01-48-09-21-40; Internet: http://ourworld.compuserve.com/homepages/ParisWalking/), a popular English-language outfit whose guided walks cost 60F ($9). Some tours concentrate on a single neighborhood (Montmartre, the Marais, and so on), others are geared toward a theme (like Hemingway's Paris), and still others focus on a single sight (such as the Hôtel des Invalides, Château de Vaux-le-Vicomte, and the Paris Sewers). There's at least one tour given every day, and you don't need to make a reservation. Call for the designated meeting place. The Caines also offer a good Paris orientation tour (reservations required) that includes bus, Métro, and riverboat travel for 260F ($37).

Paris Contact (☎ 01-42-51-08-40) also offers two-hour guided walks built around themes ("In Jefferson's Footsteps," "The Origins of Paris") or neighborhoods (St-Germain-des-Prés, Le Marais, Montmartre). The tours cost 60F ($9) per person and don't have to be booked in advance — call ahead and ask for the full program to be faxed to your hotel. Paris Contact will also do custom tours at 80F ($11.45) per person, but these tours require 48 hours advance notice and have a two-person minimum. **Paris à Pied** (☎ 800-594-9535; E-mail: parisapied@aol.com; Internet: www.parisapied.com) has three three-hour tours geared to first-time visitors. Tours cost 200F ($28.60) and are made up of no more than six people. Tours have included "The Heart of Old Paris," "The Latin Quarter," and "The Marais."

If you don't want to join a group tour, you can follow the varied selection of strolls in *Frommer's Memorable Walks in Paris* (Hungry Minds, Inc.).

Cycling tours

For cyclists, **Paris à Vélo C'est Sympa** (☎ 01-48-87-60-01; Métro: Bastille) offers half-day tours of Paris for 170F ($17). Reservations are required. You can rent a bike for 80F ($11) per day, 60F ($9) per half-day, or 150F ($21.40) from Saturday morning until Sunday evening. At **Bullfrog Bike Tours** (☎ 01-06-09-98-08-60), friendly guides from Texas will take you on day or night bike tours lasting three to four hours. The cost is 150F ($21) for a day tour (reservations optional) and 170F ($24) for a night tour (reservations required). Look for the Bullfrog Bikes flags under the Eiffel Tower at the edge of the Champs-du-Mars. From May 5 to August 25, tours are at 11 a.m. and 3:30 p.m.; from August 26 to September 15, tours are at 11 a.m. only. Closed July 14 and on the final day of the Tour de France.

Suggested One-, Two-, and Three-Day Sightseeing Itineraries

There's so much to see and do in Paris that first- and even second-time visitors can feel overwhelmed just trying to figure out where to begin. If you're short on time or have children with you, you'll want to make the most of your trip. The following itineraries were designed to help you figure out where to start and what to do. But feel free to branch out and explore those interesting alleyways and pretty green spaces that you're sure to encounter. That's what is so much fun about Paris — it reveals itself in all kinds of ways, making the trips of each independent visitor different — and special.

If you have one day

Start early by having coffee and croissants at a cafe. Then begin at Kilometer 0: All distances in France are measured from the square in front of **Notre-Dame,** on the **Ile de la Cité.** The cathedral, with its glorious stained-glass windows, stands right in the center of Paris, and it's a great starting point for any tour. From there, it's just a short walk to the island's other Gothic masterpiece, **Sainte-Chapelle,** in the **Palais de Justice.** Afterward, cross the Seine to the **Musée du Louvre.** Select just a few rooms in a particular collection for your first visit — this is one of the world's largest and finest museums, and it would take months to see everything.

From the museum, stroll through the beautiful **Jardin des Tuileries** to **place de la Concorde** (where the guillotine stood during the French Revolution), with its Egyptian obelisk. Walk up the **Champs-Elysées** to the **Arc de Triomphe;** you can have lunch at one of several good restaurants near the Champs-Elysées. You can also get to the Arc de Triomphe by taking Métro Line 1, which runs in a straight line from the Louvre to the Arc de Triomphe (Métro: Charles-de-Gaulle–Étoile), or by climbing aboard bus 73 at the Concorde and riding up the Champs-Elysées.

From the Arc de Triomphe, walk down avenue Kléber to **place du Trocadéro** for splendid views of the **Tour Eiffel** (buses 22 and 30 also go to Trocadéro, as does Métro Line 6). Visit the tower, then head for the Left Bank. You can catch an express subway (RER) at **Champ-de-Mars,** southwest of the Eiffel Tower on the Seine (a long walk), to the St-Michel station in the heart of the **Latin Quarter.** Bus 63 from Trocadéro runs along the Seine and drops you off at the St-Germain-des-Prés church, right next to the famous **Café des Deux Magots** and

Café de Flore. Stroll down the lively boulevard **St-Germain-des-Prés** to **place St-Michel** and soak up the atmosphere along the boulevard and its maze of colorful side streets. This is an excellent area for dinner.

If you have two days

On the first day, follow the above itinerary from Notre-Dame to the Arc de Triomphe, but take a little more time in the Louvre. From the Arc de Triomphe, either walk south on avenue Marceau or take bus 92 to Alma-Marceau and board the **Bateaux-Mouches** for a **Seine boat ride.** Afterward, walk up posh avenue Montaigne to the Champs-Elysées and take Métro Line 1 to St-Paul, in the heart of the Marais. Walk east on rue St-Antoine and turn left on rue de Brague to see Paris's oldest square, the aristocratic **place des Vosges,** bordered by seventeenth-century town houses. After some refreshment at one of the many bars and bistros in the neighborhood, wander the quiet lamp-lit streets, which are built just wide enough for a horse and carriage.

Explore the **Left Bank** on your second day. Start at the Tour Eiffel and follow the Seine past the domed **Hôtel des Invalides** (which contains the **Tomb of Napoléon**) to the **Musée d'Orsay.** Spend a few hours with the Impressionist masters before heading to St-Germain-des-Prés and the Latin Quarter. On the way, you'll pass through the **Faubourg St-Germain,** a district of stately eighteenth-century mansions, many of which have been converted into government offices and embassies. Relax in Parisians' favorite park, the **Jardins du Luxembourg** near boulevard St-Michel. The **Musée Rodin** is also in this neighborhood.

If you have three days

On Day 3, you can combine the above itineraries with visits to **Père-Lachaise cemetery** and then **Montmartre** and **Sacré-Coeur.** Get up early and hop on the Métro to St-Paul, in the heart of the Marais. Walk over to Paris's oldest square, the aristocratic **place des Vosges,** bordered by seventeenth-century town houses. Then it's over to rue Thorigny for the **Musée Picasso.** Try to be there when it opens at 9:30 a.m. and allow two hours for your visit. Afterward, follow rue du Vieille-du-Temple to rue des Rosiers and pick up lunch from Jo Goldenberg (see Chapter 11). Browse the stores here and on rue des Francs-Bourgeois, then explore the wonderful **Centre Pompidou.** Afterward, jump on the Métro and head for Père-Lachaise. Spend the afternoon searching out the cemetery's famous residents with the map sold outside the gates. Then take the Métro to **Abbesses.** Walk down rue Tardieu to the base of Sacré-Coeur. Take the funicular (one Métro ticket) to the top, then spend 15 to 20 minutes inside the basilica before climbing to its dome. After climbing down, head behind the church to **place du Tertre,** to see how much it still resembles the picture painted of it by van Gogh. Even though the cafes are picturesque — and more expensive — save your appetite for **Au Poulbot Gourmet,** which is located at 39 rue Lamarck (follow rue Lamarck down the hill).

Shopping

Shopping in Paris has never been better. A recent upswing in France's economy has seen many new stores open and older ones expand. And a recent influx of American brands into the City of Light — Tommy Hilfiger, Ralph Lauren, Calvin Klein, MAC and Bobbi Brown cosmetics, Donna Karan — has Parisians looking stylish wearing American clothes. As for non-European Union visitors, a surging dollar and a falling euro at press time means that everything is much more afford-able than in the recent past.

Remember that a 20.6% **value-added tax** (**VAT** — **TVA** in French) has been tacked onto the price of most products, which means that many things cost less at home. In fact, Paris is probably the worst place to buy an American or a British label. (And why would you want to? You're after French style, after all.) Even French-made goods aren't nec-essarily cheaper here than elsewhere. Appliances, paper products, housewares, computer supplies, CDs, and women's clothing are notori-ously expensive in France, though the cost of computers is beginning to come down. On the other hand, you can often get good deals on cos-metics like Bourjois (a low-priced line made in the same factory as Chanel); skin-care products from Lierac, Galenic, Roc, and Vichy; and some luxury goods.

To recognize a bargain, it helps to check out the prices of French prod-ucts before your trip.

Probably the best time to find a bargain in Paris is during the twice-annual *soldes* (sales) in January and July, when merchandise can be marked down 30–50%. If you can brave the crowds, you just may find the perfect designer outfit at a fraction of the retail price.

Store hours are Monday to Saturday 9 or 9:30 a.m. (sometimes 10 a.m.) to 7 p.m. (later on Thursday evenings), without a break for lunch. Some smaller stores are closed on Monday or Monday mornings and break for lunch for one to three hours, beginning at around 1 p.m. Small stores also may be closed for all or part of August and on some days around Christmas and Easter. Sunday shopping is gradually making inroads in Paris but is limited to tourist areas. Try **rue de Rivoli** across from the Louvre, **rue des Francs-Bourgeois** in the Marais, the **Carrousel du Louvre,** and the **Champs-Elysées.**

Getting your VAT refund

If you spend more than 1,200F ($171) in a single store, you'll be able to get some of that 20.6% value-added tax back. The discount, however, isn't automatic. Food, wine, and tobacco don't count, and the refund is granted only on purchases you take with you out of the country — not on merchandise you ship home. To apply for a refund, you must show the clerk your passport to prove your eligibility. You'll then be given an export sales document (in triplicate — two pink sheets and a green one), which you must sign, and usually an envelope addressed to the store. Travelers leaving from Charles de Gaulle Airport may visit the Europe Tax-Free Shopping (ETS) refund point, operated by CCF Change, to receive an immediate VAT refund in cash; there's a 30F ($4.30) fee if you take your refund in cash. Otherwise, when you depart, arrive at the airport as early as possible to allow for lines at the détaxe (refund) booth at French Customs. If you're traveling by train, go to the détaxe area in the station before boarding — you can't get your refund documents processed on the train. Give the three sheets to the Customs official, who'll stamp them and return a pink and a green copy to you. Keep the green copy and mail the pink copy to the store. Your reimbursement will either be mailed by check (in French francs) or credited to your credit card account. If you don't receive your tax refund in four months, write to the store, giving the date of purchase and the location where the forms were given to Customs officials. Include a photocopy of your green refund sheet. Department stores that cater to foreign visitors, like Au Printemps and Galeries Lafayette, have special détaxe areas where clerks will prepare your invoices for you.

The best shopping neighborhoods

It seems that every Paris neighborhood has something to offer — even the tiniest pâtissiers in some of the most remote arrondissements will have exquisite, enticing window displays to lure you inside. Listed in this section are the more central Paris neighborhoods, where you'll be able to shop to your heart's content all day. Just make sure to wear comfortable shoes!

Fantasy land: The 8e

Paris has a well-deserved reputation as a bastion of over-the-top luxury; all you have to do is head for the 8e arrondissement to see why. Practically every one of the elite French design houses is based here on two streets that positively breathe haute couture — **avenue Montaigne** (Métro:Alma-Marceau or Franklin-D.-Roosevelt) and **rue du Faubourg St-Honoré** (Métro: Concorde). As you can expect, the snob quotient is high. But even if you don't have a platinum card, you can still have a good time window-shopping here.

While these streets boast some of the same big designer names, they're completely different in temperament. **Avenue Montaigne** is wide, graceful, and lined with chestnut trees. It's become undeniably hip, attracting the likes of **Dolce & Gabbana** at no. 2 (☎ 01-47-20-42-43) and **Prada** at no. 10 (☎ 01-53-23-99-40). **Rue du Faubourg St-Honoré** is narrower, with small sidewalks that are always jammed with shoppers. Here you'll find **Gucci** at no. 2 (☎ 01-53-05-11-11), **Hermès** at no. 24 (☎ 01-40-17-47-17), and **Yves Saint-Laurent** at no. 38 (☎ 01-42-65-74-59). Begin at the rue Royale intersection and head west.

Artsy eclecticism: The 4e

The Marais (Métro: Hôtel-de-Ville) is an idyllic postcard setting crammed with artists' studios, secret courtyards, magnificent Renaissance mansions, and some of the most original shops in the city. **Rue des Francs-Bourgeois** is the neighborhood's main artery, full of jewel-box-size shops selling everything from fashion to jewels. **Rue des Rosiers** is a fashion destination in its own right, with white-hot designers standing shoulder to shoulder with Jewish delis. And **rue Vieille-du-Temple** is home to many gay boutiques, as well as bars. Everything is really close in the Marais, so don't be afraid to ramble down the tiniest lane whenever whim dictates. Part of the fun of this neighborhood is that it's such a mixed shopping bag.

Marais highlights are **Paule Ka** (20 rue Mahler; ☎ 01-45-44-92-60), for the sort of timeless womenswear Grace Kelly and Audrey Hepburn used to wear; **Autour du Monde Home** (8 rue des Francs-Bourgeois; ☎ 01-42-77-06-08), a clothing/housewares store with everything from relaxed and sporty linen dresses to delicate linen sheets and nifty tableware; **Anne Sévérine Liotard** (7 rue St-Merri; ☎ 01-48-04-00-38), for candles that double as objets d'art and burn forever; **Lunettes Beausoleil** (28 rue Roi du Sicile; ☎ 01-42-77-28-29), for glamorous sunglasses that flatter any face; **Extrem Origin** (10 rue Ferdinand-Duval; ☎ 01-42-72-70-10), for ultrachic interior design that uses only natural elements; and **Plein Sud** (21 rue des Francs-Bourgeois; ☎ 01-42-72-10-60), for sexy French women's fashion that's carried only in exclusive stores in the United States.

BCBG chic: St-Germain-des-Prés (6e)

Bon Chic Bon Genre is what the French call the young moneyed class, and you'll see plenty of them sipping coffee or shopping in this area on boulevard St-Germain, between rue des St-Pères and rue de Tournon (Métro: Mabillon or St-Germain-des-Prés). Literary institutions **Café de Flore** and **Café des Deux Magots** are located here in case you get hungry, and there are lots of trendy stores in case you get bored. **Louis Vuitton** has opened a huge store behind Deux Magots on 6 place St-Germain (☎ 01-45-49-62-32), and **Christian Dior** and **Cartier** are nearby at 18 rue de l'Abbaye (☎ 01-56-24-90-53) and 41 rue de Rennes (☎ 01-45-49-65-80), respectively. Other big names here are **Emporio Armani** (149 bd. St-Germain; ☎ 01-53-63-33-50); **Céline** (58 rue de Rennes; ☎ 01-45-48-58-55); **Christian Lacroix** (2 place St-Sulpice;

☎ 01-46-33-48-95); **Stefanel** (54 rue de Rennes; ☎ 01-45-44-06-07); and **Comptoir des Cotonniers** (59 rue de Bonaparte; ☎ 01-43-26-07-56). And if you thought you could escape **The Gap,** you were sadly mistaken. The Gap and other international chain stores have taken up residence in the **Marché St-Germain,** a modern shopping mall that's out of place in a neighborhood known for bookstores and upscale boutiques. Visit if you need to experience air conditioning; otherwise, don't waste your time.

Young and branché: 2e

In this technological age, *branché* means "plugged in" or hip, and this is where hip young Parisians head for the season's funkiest looks. While it lacks atmosphere, the area doesn't lack for stores selling knock-off trends. The cheapest shopping is in the **Sentier** area, around the Sentier Métro stop. It's Paris's garment district, which overlaps parts of the 3e and 1er arrondissements. It's also an area frequented by prostitutes later in the day and evening. The best, but not cheapest, shops are within a square formed on the south by **rue Rambuteau,** on the west by **rue du Louvre,** on the north by rue Réamur, and on the east by **rue St-Martin.** This is where you'll find hot second-hand clothes, funky clubwear, and "stock" boutiques selling last season's designs at a discount.

Don't miss **Barbara Bui** (23 rue Etienne-Marcel, 1er; ☎ 01-40-26-43-65), for sophisticated contemporary fashion (she also has a trendy cafe two doors down); **Le Shop** (3 rue d'Argout, 2e; ☎ 01-40-28-95-94), for two floors of clubwear by France's hottest designers; **Kiliwatch** (64 rue Tiquetonne, 2e; ☎ 01-42-21-17-37), for cool retro looks that'll be on next year's runways (designers come here for inspiration); and **agnès b.** (3–6 rue du Jour; ☎ 01-45-08-56-56), for timeless chic for men and women.

The department stores

Two of Paris's major department stores, **Au Printemps** and **Galeries Lafayette,** offer tourists a 10% discount coupon, good in most departments. If your hotel or travel agent didn't give you one of these coupons (they're sometimes attached to a city map), you can ask for it at the stores' welcome desks — the clerks speak English.

Au Printemps (64 bd. Haussmann, 9e; ☎ 01-42-82-50-00; Métro: Havre-Caumartin) is one of Paris's larger department stores, but it's not very well organized, with merchandise sold in three buildings. Fashion shows are held under the 1920s glass dome at 10:15 a.m. every Tuesday, year-round, and every Friday, March to October. Near the Marais, **BHV (Bazar de l'Hôtel de Ville),** located at 52 rue de Rivoli, 1er (☎ 01 42 74 90 00; Métro: Hôtel-de-Ville), sells the usual clothing, cosmetics, luggage, and leatherware, but stop in to check out its giant basement-level hardware store that has everything you need to decorate your home.

The crowds of tourists at **Galeries Lafayette** (40 bd. Haussmann, 9e; ☎ 01-42-82-34-56; Métro: Opéra or Chaussée-d'Antin) attest to the fact that it makes shopping easier for foreigners — the store's VAT refund office is always packed. Much of the merchandise is of excellent quality, and the January sales are famous. The sixth-floor self-service cafeteria, Lafayette Café, offers tasty food and has good views of the Opéra and nearby rooftops. Probably the best thing about **La Samaritaine** (19 rue de la Monnaie, 1er; ☎ 01-40-41-20-20; Métro: Pont-Neuf or Châtelet–Les Halles), besides the fact that it's less expensive than Galeries Lafayette and Au Printemps, is its views. Look for signs in its main building that point to the panorama, a free observation point with a wonderful view that actually takes in the Eiffel Tower. Between the Louvre and the pont Neuf, La Samaritaine is housed in four buildings with art nouveau touches and has an art deco facade on quai du Louvre. The fifth floor of store no. 2 has a nice inexpensive restaurant, Le Toupary.

Au Bon Marché (24 rue de Sèvres, 7e; ☎ 01 44 39 80 00; Métro: Sèvres-Babylone) is the Left Bank's only department store and Paris's oldest. It's elegant and small enough to be manageable, and much of its merchandise is exquisite. (Check out the lingerie on the third floor.) The prices, however, often reflect this. If you're lucky enough to be here during the sales, you can find tons of deals. Make sure to visit the huge supermarket (in a building next door) — it's the city's largest *épicerie*. A small antiques market, a cafe, and a cafeteria are on the second floor. Monoprix and Prisunic were once fierce competitors, but they recently merged into **Monoprix-Prisunic,** with various locations (☎ 01-40-75-11-02), and have passed on the advantages — mainly low prices — to customers. The clothing is stylish, and the stores are great for accessories, low-priced cosmetics, lingerie, and housewares. Many locations also have large grocery stores. There's one Monoprix-Prisunic in the heart of St-Germain at 50 rue de Rennes (Métro: St-Germain-des-Prés).

The outdoor markets

I don't think a trip to Paris is complete without a visit to the vast **Marché aux Puces de la Porte de St-Ouen de Clignancourt** (18e; Métro: Porte-de-Clignancourt). Open Saturday to Monday 9 a.m. to 8 p.m., it's a real shopping adventure; you need to arrive early to snag the deals — if there are any. The market, also known as the Clignancourt flea market, features several thousand stalls, carts, shops, and vendors selling everything from vintage clothing to antique chandeliers, paintings, and furniture. The best times to find bargains are right at opening time and just before closing. Don't be put off by the stalls selling cheap junk on the market's periphery; it gets much better the farther you walk. Watch out for pickpockets. The **Marché aux Puces de la Porte de Vanves** (14e; Métro: Porte-de-Vanves) is probably the smallest of the fleas, but it's a bit more upscale — so are its prices. It's open Saturday and Sunday 8:30 a.m. to 1 p.m.

The prettiest of all the markets is the **Marché aux Fleurs** (4e; Métro: Cité), the flower market on place Louis-Lépine on Ile de la Cité. Visit Monday to Saturday to enjoy the flowers, even if you don't buy anything. On Sunday, the market becomes the **Marché aux Oiseaux,** selling birds and more unusual furry creatures — on a recent visit I saw hedgehogs, a skunk, and a raccoon, as well as ferrets, mice, guinea pigs, and rabbits. If you don't mind seeing creatures in cages, it can be fascinating.

Of course, you shouldn't miss the food markets, including the ones on **rue Mouffetard** in the Latin Quarter (6e; Métro: Monge or Censier-Daubenton); **rue de Buci** in St-Germain (6e; Métro: St-Germain-des-Prés); and **rue Montorguiel,** near the Bourse (1er; Métro: Les Halles). All three sell the freshest fruits, vegetables, meats, and cheeses. Most open-air food markets are open Tuesday to Sunday 9 a.m. to 1 p.m.

What to look for and where to find it

Le Louvre des Antiquaires (2 place du Palais-Royal, 1er; ☎ 01-42-97-27-00; Métro: Palais-Royal–Musée du Louvre) is an enormous mall filled with an amazing diversity of shops selling everything from Jean Cocteau sketches to silver older than the United States. The items are pricey, but rumors have it that some good deals exist here. A cafe and toilets are located on the second floor. On Sundays at **Le Village Suisse** (54 av. de la Motte-Picquet, 15e; no phone; Métro: La Motte-Picquet), about 150 stores in a two-block radius sell antiques in the middle- to high-priced range.

One of the city's leading English-language bookstores, **Brentano's** (37 av. de l'Opéra, 2e; ☎ 01-42-61-52-50; Métro: Opéra) offers a big general fiction and nonfiction stock that includes guides and maps. Brentano's usually has a shelf of discounted books. In St-Germain-des-Prés, quality fiction in English is the highlight of the **Village Voice** (6 rue Princesse, 6e; ☎ 01-46-33-36-47; Métro: Mabillon), along with an excellent selection of poetry, plays, nonfiction, and literary magazines. Owner Odile Hellier hosts free poetry and fiction readings with celebrated authors and poets. No, this isn't the original, but English-speaking residents of Paris still gather in the cluttered **Shakespeare & Co.** (37 rue de la Bûcherie, 5e; no phone; Métro or RER: St-Michel), named after Sylvia Beach's legendary literary lair. Shakespeare & Co. has poetry readings on Sundays. **Les Mots à la Bouche** (6 rue Ste-Croix-la-Bretonnerie, 4e; ☎ 01-42-78-88-30; Métro: Hôtel-de-Ville) is Paris's largest and best-stocked gay bookstore, where you can find French- and English-language books, as well as gay info magazines like *Illico, e.m@le,* and *Lesbia.* You can also find lots of free pamphlets advertising gay/lesbian venues and events.

The crystal at **Baccarat** (30 bis rue de Paradis, 10e; ☎ **01-47-70-64-30** or 01-40-22-11-00; Métro: Château-d'Eau, Poissonnière, or Gare-de-l'Est) is world-renowned, and has been since the eighteenth century. This store is also a museum, so even if its prices are too high, you can still enjoy browsing. Shop duty-free for Lalique, Baccarat, and more at **Cristal Vendôme,** in the Hôtel Intercontinental (1 rue de Castiglione, 1er; ☎ **01-49-27-09-60;** Métro: Concorde). The store will even ship purchases. The charming **La Maison Ivre** (38 rue Jacob, 6e; ☎ **01-42-60-01-85;** Métro: St-Germain-des-Prés) sits in the heart of the antiques-and-gallery district on the Left Bank. La Maison carries an excellent selection of handmade pottery from all over France, with an emphasis on Provençal and southern French ceramics.

If you don't mind synthetics or blends, head to **1 2 3** (42 rue Chaussée-d'Antin, 9e; ☎ **01-40-16-80-06;** Métro: Chaussée-d'Antin) for stylish women's suits, blouses, sweaters, and accessories at moderate prices; occasionally you'll find an all-wool or all-cotton product. You can find another 1 2 3 branch at 30 av. d'Italie, 13e (☎ **01-45-80-02-88;** Métro: pl. d'Italie). If you want a basic but classic French outfit, you can't do better than **agnès b.** (3–6 rue du Jour, 1er; ☎ **01-45-08-56-56;** Métro: Les Halles). Other agnès b. locations around the city sell men's and children's wear. At **Cacharel** (64 rue Bonaparte, 6e; ☎ 01-40-46-00-45; Métro: St-Sulpice), you'll find beautiful, reasonably priced women's, children's, and men's clothes, some with Liberty prints. The most cutting-edge fashion — much of it American (thus cheaper in the States) — is for sale at **Colette** (213 rue St-Honoré, 1er; ☎ **01-55-35-33-90;** Métro: Tuileries) in *trés* artistic displays. Colette also has artsy tchotchkes, art magazines, and art exhibits. The French love this store, so it's nice to visit to see what all the fuss is about. The **Etam** chain has dozens of stores all over Paris, with recent fashions at low prices. The merchandise is mostly made from synthetic or synthetic blend fabrics. Try the branch at 9 bd. St-Michel, 5e (☎ **1-43-54-79-20;** Métro: St-Michel); for lingerie, go to 47 rue de Sèvres, 6e (☎ 01-45-48-21-33; Métro: Sèvres-Babylone). And at **Rodier** (72 av. Ternes, 17e; ☎ **01-45-74-17-17;** Métro: Ternes) the prices are high, but the quality of the stylish knits is good, and you can often find bargains during sales. You can find other Rodier branches at 23 bd. de la Madeleine, 1er (☎ **01-40-15-06-80;** Métro: Madeleine), and 47 rue de Rennes, 6e (☎ **01-45-44-30-27;** Métro: St-Germain des Près).

You can find some quality men's shirts and pants at **Façonnable** (9 rue du Faubourg St-Honoré, 8e; ☎ **01-47-42-72-60;** Métro: Sèvres-Babylone), in addition to jackets, suits, and other men's wear. Another Façonnable branch is located at 174 bd. St-Germain, 6e (☎ **01-40-49-02-47;** Métro: Odéon). The huge **Madelios** (23 bd. de la Madeleine, 1er; ☎ **01-42-60-39-30;** Métro: Madeleine) offers one-stop shopping for men, selling everything from overcoats to lighters. If companions get bored waiting, Madelios is part of a small mall and has some nice stores for browsing.

The Swedish **H&M** (118 rue de Rivoli, 1er; ☎ 01-55-34-38-00; Métro: Hôtel-de-Ville), the "IKEA of fashion," has low-cost clothing for men and women and a hip atmosphere. **Kiliwatch** (64 rue Tiquetonne, 1er; ☎ 01-42-21-17-37; Métro: Etiene-Marcel) stocks a bright mish-mash of club clothes and vintage clothes in a slightly psychedelic setting. You can find surprisingly good prices at Kiliwatch. It has everything from wigs to coats, plus a few new designers. **Kookaï** (35 bd. St-Michel, 5e; ☎ 01-46-34-75-02; Métro: St-Michel) gets fun and funky with the latest styles — most in synthetics. You can find other Kookaï branches all over the city. **Mango** (3 place 18 Juin 1940, 6e; ☎ 01-45-48-04-96; Métro: Montparnasse-Bienvenue) is popular with young Parisian women for its inexpensive fashion-conscious clothes. Mango has lots of other locations throughout the city.

When I worked as an au pair, **Jacadi** (256 bd. St-Germain, 7e; ☎ 01-42-84-30-40; Métro: Solférino) was where my chic employer shopped for her very proper children's clothes. Jacadi has many branches all over the city, including one at 17 bd. Poissonière, 2e (☎ 01-42-36-69-91; Métro: Bone Nouvelle). Part of a French chain with a dozen stores in Paris, **Natalys** (92 av. des Champs-Elysées, 8e; ☎ 01-43-59-17-65; Métro: Franklin-D.-Roosevelt) sells children's wear, maternity wear, and related products. Your children will look *très mignons* (very cute) in the very sweet but pricey clothes sold at **Tartine et Chocolat;** stores are located at 105 rue du Faubourg-St-Honoré, 8e (☎ 01-45-62-44-04; Métro: Concorde), and 266 bd. St-Germain, 7e (☎ 01-45-56-10-45; Métro: Solférino).

In the basement of the men's store at Galeries Lafayette, the well-stocked large **Lafayette Gourmet** (52 bd. Haussmann, 9e; ☎ 01-48-74-46-06; Métro: Chaussée-d'Antin) is a terrific spot to browse for gifts or shop for yourself. The wine selection is wonderful, and the house-brand merchandise, often cheaper than other labels, is of very good quality. Lafayette Gourmet has prepared-food counters — ideal for picnics or train meals — and several eat-on-the-premises areas for quick meals or snacks. In Au Bon Marché department store, **La Grande Epicerie** (38 rue de Sèvres, 7e; ☎ 01-44-39-81-00; Métro: Sèvres-Babylone) is one of the best luxury supermarkets in Paris. It's a great place to look for gourmet gifts, such as olive oils, homemade choco-lates, and wine. La Grande Epicerie also makes for great one-stop picnic shopping, offering a wide array of prepared foods, meats, and cheeses. Alas, it doesn't come cheap. And they don't know the meaning of cheap over at **Fauchon** either (26–30 place de la Madeleine, 1er; ☎ 01-47-42-60-11; Métro: Madeleine). This is probably Paris's most famous gourmet store; you can buy everything from truffles to wine, then relax with a delicious pastry and a cup of tea in Fauchon's tea salon. Fauchon is overrun with tourists in the summer.

La Maison du Chocolat (225 rue du Faubourg-St-Honoré, 8e; ☎ 01-42-27-39-44; Métro: Ternes) is one of the best places in Paris to buy choco-late, with racks and racks of chocolate priced individually or by the kilo. Each is made from a blend of as many as six kinds of South American and African chocolate, flavored with just about everything imaginable. All the merchandise is made on the premises. If the smell doesn't lure you in, the view through the windows will. The petite **La Maison du Miel** (24 rue Vignon, 9e; ☎ 01-47-42-26-70; Métro: Madeleine or Havre-Caumartin) has varieties of honey that you never dreamed were possible (lavender, for example), identified according to the flower to which the bees were exposed. Lemon flower and pine tree have distinct tastes and make fine gifts. Don't visit **Jacques Papin, Prestige et Tradition** (8 rue de Buci, 6e; ☎ 01-43-26-86-09; Métro: Odéon), when you're hungry — unless you want to walk out with hundreds of dollars worth of wonderful stuff. This butcher shop has some of the most exquisite foods you'll ever see, including trout in aspic, exquisite pâtés and salads, lobsters, and smoked salmon.

Go to **Alessi** (14 rue du Faubourg St-Honoré, 8e; ☎ 01-42-66-14-61; Métro: Madéleine or Concorde) for bright and affordable kitchen implements, like magnetized salt and pepper shakers and wine openers that look a tad — well — *human.* You can also find cutlery, dishes, and linens at Alessi. Cooks love **Déhillerin** (18–20 rue Coquillière, 1er; ☎ 01-42-36-53-13; Métro: Les Halles), especially because its prices are discounted. Déhillerin is filled with copper cookware, glasses, dishes, china, gadgets, utensils, pots, and kitchen appliances. All the accoutrements of the kitchen are available at **Verrerie des Halles** (15 rue du Louvre, 1er; ☎ 01-42-36-80-60; Métro: Louvre-Rivoli) at discount prices usually reserved for professionals.

Go to **Bijoux Burma** (50 rue François 1er, 8e; ☎ 01-47-23-70-93; Métro: Franklin D. Roosevelt) for some of the best costume jewelry in the city. It's the secret weapon of many a Parisian woman. Bijoux Burma has branches at 14 rue Castiglione, 1e (☎ 01-42-60-35-52; Métro: Tuileries), and 23 bd. de la Madeleine, 1er (☎ 01-42-96-05-00; Métro: Madeleine). In the arty Passage du Grand Cerf, **Eric et Lydie** (7 Passage du Grand Cerf, 2e; ☎ 01-40-26-52-59; Métro: Etienne-Marcel) contains unusual, beautiful, and surprisingly reasonable-priced costume jewelry and accessories. At **Tati Or** (19 rue de la Paix, 2e; ☎ 01-40-07-06-76; Métro: Opéra), you can find 18-karat gold jewelry for up to 40% less than at traditional jewelers. More than 3,000 bracelets, earrings, necklaces, rings, and pins are offered, with about 500 items at less than 400F ($68).

Au Nain Bleu (406 rue St-Honoré, 8e; ☎ 01-42-60-39-01; Métro: Concorde) is filled with toy soldiers, stuffed animals, games, model airplanes, model cars, and puppets. Au Nain Bleu has been in business for over 150 years. **FNAC Junior** (19 rue Vavin, 6e; ☎ 01-56-24-03-46; Métro: Vavin) has books, videos, and music for children, as well as story hours and activities.

At **Le Jardin des Vignes** (91 rue de Turenne, 3e; ☎ 01-42-77-05-00; Métro: St-Sébastien-Froissart), you'll find very interesting bottles of rare wine, champagne, and cognac, all at reasonable prices. The owners are really excited about wine and also offer lessons about the wines of France. Perhaps the ultimate shop for oenophiles, the crowded **Lescene-Dura** (63 rue de la Verrerie, 4e; ☎ **01-42-72-08-74;** Métro: Hôtel-de-Ville) is a good bet for gifts. Lescene-Dura sells an amazing array of corkscrews, glassware, and pocketknives, as well as everything you may need to make wine at home. **Nicolas,** at 31 place de la Madeleine, 8e (☎ **01-42-68-00-16;** Métro: Madeleine), is the flagship store of the wine chain, with more than 110 branches in and around Paris. Nicolas offers good prices for bottles that you may not be able to find in the United States.

Nightlife: From the Comédie-Française to the Buddha Bar

It's always fun to party in Paris. You'll find that each neighborhood makes a different contribution to Paris's nightlife scene: The Marais is the center of gay clubs and bars — as well as some of the best dance clubs; the Bastille attracts bohemian types and clubgoers; and Ménilmontant has a white-hot bar scene. The side streets of the Champs-Elysées are home to upscale bars and discos, and a new generation of trendsetters is turning Pigalle into a rock music lovers' paradise. Jazz lovers will find it easy to club-hop around Les Halles or on the Left Bank. Bars usually close around 2 a.m., but most clubs don't open until 11 p.m., and the music doesn't stop pumping until dawn. Check the listings in *Night Life, Nova* magazine, or the English *Time Out Paris* section of the weekly *Pariscope* magazine for information on special theme nights at clubs.

For those desiring culture, Paris's performing arts scene is world class. Over the last couple of decades, the mega-expensive construction of the Opéra Bastille and Cité de la Musique, and the multimillion-dollar renovation of the Opéra Garnier and Châtelet (home to Théâtre Musical de Paris) are examples of the interest the citizens of Paris take in enlightening themselves — with many performances selling out in advance.

Several local publications provide up-to-the-minute listings of performances and other entertainment. *Pariscope: Une Semaine de Paris* (3F/42¢) has thorough performing-arts listings. *L'Officiel des Spectacles* (2F/30¢) is another weekly guide in French. **Paris Nuit** (30F/$5) is a French monthly that contains good articles, as well as listings. You can pick up the free music monthlies, *La Terrasse* and *Cadences,* outside concert venues. The *Paris Free Voice* is a free monthly spotlighting events of interest to English speakers, including poetry readings, plays, and literary evenings at English-language bookstores and libraries.

The performing arts

Paris is a great place to pursue culture.

You can use the Internet to get information from the **French Government Tourist Office** (www.francetourism.com), the **Office de Tourisme et de Congrès de Paris** (www.paris-touristoffice.com), and the **Maison de la France** (www.franceguide.com). You can also try **Culture Kiosque** (www.culturekiosque.com) for excellent magazine-style sites about opera and dance. The *Paris Free Voice's* Web site (http://parisvoice.com) features an events calendar and reviews of current opera, dance, and theater.

Ticket prices in this chapter are approximate; costs vary depending on who's performing what on which day. Call the theaters for information or consult *Pariscope* and other entertainment listings. Many concert, theater, and dance tickets are sold through **FNAC** stores, as well as at the box office. There are a dozen or so FNAC outlets throughout Paris; the most prominent is the one located at 74 av. des Champs-Elysées (Métro: George V). You can also reserve tickets by phone at ☎ **01-49-87-50-50** Monday to Friday 9 a.m. to 8 p.m. and Saturday 10 a.m. to 5 p.m. The **Virgin Megastore** (52 av. des Champs-Elysées; ☎ **01-49-53-50-00;** Métro:Franklin-D.-Roosevelt) is another reputable ticket seller. The store is open Monday to Saturday 10 a.m. to midnight.

Classical and organ concerts

Innumerable classical music and organ concerts are performed throughout the year, and many are quite affordable — if not free. Look for flyers, attached to most of the churches, announcing schedule times, prices, and locations.

More than a dozen Parisian churches schedule inexpensive or free organ recitals and concerts on a regular basis. Among them are **Notre-Dame** (☎ **01-42-34-56-10;** Métro: Cité or St-Michel); **St-Eustache** (1 rue Montmartre, 1er; ☎ **01-42-49-26-79;** Métro: Châtelet); **St-Sulpice,** place St-Sulpice (☎ **01-46-33-21-78;** Métro: St-Sulpice), which has the largest organ; **St-Germain-des-Prés** (place St-Germain-des-Prés; ☎ **01-44-62-70-90;** Métro: St-Germain-des-Prés); **La Madeleine** (place de la Madeleine; ☎ **01-42-77-65-65;** Métro: Madeleine); and **St-Louis en l'Ile** (19 bis rue St-Louis-en-l'Ile; ☎ **01-46-34-11-60;** Métro: Pont-Marie). In a less magnificent setting, the 6 p.m. Sunday concerts at the **American Church** (65 quai d'Orsay; ☎ **01-47-05-07-99;** Métro: Invalides) are friendly and inviting.

Free concerts are occasionally staged in the parks and gardens. Call ☎ **01-40-71-75-95** for information. The **Maison de la Radio** (116 av. du Président-Kennedy, 16e; ☎ **01-56-40-15-16;** Métro: Passy) offers free tickets to the recordings of some concerts. Tickets are available on the spot, an hour before the recording starts. The **Conservatoire National de Musique** in the Cité de la Musique (209 av. Jean-Jaurês, 19e;

☎ **01-40-40-46-46;** Métro: Porte de Pantin) also stages free concerts and ballets performed by students at the conservatory.

The Orchestre de Paris, under the direction of Christophe Eschenback, plays at the **Salle Pleyel** (252 rue du Faubourg-St-Honoré, 8e; ☎ **01-45-61-53-00;** Métro: Ternes), its official concert hall, from September to the end of June. The hall also welcomes internationally renowned orchestras and soloists. Tickets run from 50 to 400F ($7 to $57).

Opera and ballet

Designed by Charles Garnier, the radiantly rococo **Opéra Garnier** (place de l'Opéra, 9e; ☎ **08-36-69-78-68** for reservations; Fax: 01-40-01-25-60; Internet: www.opera-de-paris.fr; Métro: Opéra; RER: Auber), with its Chagall ceiling, has a 2001 program schedule dazzling enough to match its newly cleaned facade, with operas like *The Magic Flute* and *La Clémence de Titus* and ballets from choreographers Jerome Robbins and Jiri Kylian. The Ballet de l'Opéra de Paris and the Opéra National de Paris also schedule some performances at the Opéra Bastille. Opera tickets run 30 to 670F ($4.30 to $96) and dance tickets 30 to 395F ($4.30 to $57). Box office hours are Monday to Saturday 11 a.m. to 6:30 p.m.

While not as impressively *grand* as the Garnier, the **Opéra Bastille** (place de la Bastille, 12e; ☎ **08-36-69-78-68** for reservations; Fax: 01-40-01-16-16; Internet: www.opera-de-paris.fr; Métro: Bastille) offers first-class comfort and magnificent acoustics at each level of the auditorium. *Nabucco, Tosca, Don Giovanni,* and *Parsifal* are just some of the operas scheduled for the 2001 season, as well as ballet favorites like *The Nutcracker* and *Romeo and Juliet.* Opera tickets and dance tickets both run 45 to 670F ($6 to $96). The box office at 130 rue de Lyon (Métro: Bastille) is open Monday to Saturday 11 a.m. to 6:30 p.m.

The 2001 season offers operas such as *Othello* and *Falstaff* and Verdi's *Requiem,* and ballets choreographed by Pina Bausch and Charles Jude, performed at the **Châtelet, Théâtre Musical de Paris** (1 place du Châtelet, 1e; ☎ **01-40-28-28-40;** Internet: www.chatelet-theatre.com; Métro: Châtelet). You can also check out the concert series performed on Mondays, Wednesdays, and Fridays at 12:45 p.m. for only 55F ($8). Tickets for opera and ballet run 70 to 670F ($10 to $96) and tickets for concerts and recitals 30 to 595F ($4.30 to $85). The box office is open daily 11 a.m. to 7 p.m.

The **Opéra-Comique** (5 rue Favart, 2e; ☎ **08-25-00-00-58** for reservations; Fax: 01-49-26-05-93; Internet: www.opera-comique.com; Métro: Richelieu-Drouot) offers magnificent shows in an early-nineteenth-century building known as the Salle Favart. The theater is smaller than its counterparts — the auditorium is so intimate you can hear people whispering on stage. A new program by Jerome Savary promises highly entertaining shows. Tickets run 50 to 370F ($7 to $53), and the box office is open daily 11 a.m. to 7 p.m.

Saving money on theater tickets

On Thursdays, the four national theaters in Paris sell all seats for 50F ($7). You can also get half-price theater tickets for same-day performances to the national theaters and all other venues Tuesday to Saturday by visiting the Kiosque-Théâtre at the northwest corner of La Madeleine church (Métro: Madeleine) and buying tickets for same-day performances. The panels all around the kiosk indicate whether the performance is sold out (little red man) or tickets are still available (little green man). The Kiosque-Théâtre is open Tuesday to Saturday from 12:30 to 8 p.m. and Sunday from 12:30 to 4 p.m. A second branch of the discount-ticket counter can be found in front of the Gare Montparnasse. It's wise to arrive no later than noon, because lines are usually long. Students may be able to pick up last-minute tickets by applying at the box office an hour before curtain time. Have your International Student Identity Card (ISIC) with you.

Theater

The theaters listed in this section are "national theaters," supported by the government, but there are also many private ones. For full listings, consult *Pariscope*.

The classic tragedies and comedies of Corneille, Racine, Molière, and other French playwrights come alive in wonderful performances at the **Comédie-Française** (2 rue de Richelieu, 1er; ☎ 01-44-58-15-15; Métro: Palais-Royal–Musée du Louvre). Foreign playwrights, like Shakespeare, weren't performed at the Comédie-Française for nearly a century. These days, you'll find a good mix of classic and modern works and plays, translated from other languages. If you don't understand advanced French, chances are you won't enjoy the performances. Tickets are 70 to 190F ($10 to $27), with last-minute seats (on sale 30 minutes before the performance) at 30F ($4.30); box office hours are daily 11 a.m. to 6 p.m. For popular contemporary plays, go to the **Théâtre National de Chaillot** (place du Trocadéro, 16e; ☎ 01-53-65-30-00; Métro: Trocadéro), part of the art deco Palais de Chaillot, directly across the Seine from the Eiffel Tower. Tickets are 160F ($23) for adults, 120F ($17) for people under 26, and 80F ($11) for students. Box office hours are Monday to Saturday 11 a.m. to 7 p.m. and Sunday 11 a.m. to 5 p.m.

If you like modern drama from around the world, the **Théâtre National de la Colline** (15 rue Malte-Brun, 20e; ☎ 01-44-62-52-52; Métro: Gambetta) is the place to see it. Performances are from French and European names. The Petit Théâtre upstairs has short plays and offerings from international theater's less famous and up-and-coming playwrights. Tickets are 160F ($23) for adults, 130F ($19) for seniors, and 80F($12) for students. Box office hours are Wednesday to Saturday and

Monday 11 a.m. to 7 p.m., Tuesday 11 a.m. to 6 p.m., and Sunday 2 to 5 p.m. The **Odéon, Théâtre de l'Europe** (place de l'Odéon, 6e; ☎ 01-44-41-36-36;** Métro: Odéon) is in a beautiful early-nineteenth-century building, and its row of columns overlooks a pretty semicircular square near bustling boulevard St-Germain. Home of the Comédie-Française until the Revolution, the Odéon is now very much a European stage. Recent events at the Odéon included a poetry reading by Robert Wilson, set to music by Lou Reed. Tickets run 30 to 180F ($4.30 to $26). Box office hours are Monday to Saturday 11 a.m. to 6:30 p.m.

Summer is a good time to catch English-language theater in Paris. Try the **Théâtre de Nesle** (8 rue de Nesle, 6e; ☎ 01-46-34-61-04; Métro: St-Michel) or the **Théâtre des Déchargeurs** (3 rue des Déchargeurs, 1er; ☎ 01-42-36-00-02; Métro: Châtelet). For comedy in English, try **Laughing Matters,** in the historic Hôtel du Nord (102 quai de Jemmapes, 10e; ☎ 01-53-19-98-98; Métro: Jacques-Bonsergent). This company is thriving; the line-ups are always terrific, featuring award-winning comics from the United States, the United Kingdom, Ireland, and Australia. Shows start at 8:30 p.m., and admission is 100F ($14) at the door.

Cabarets

Even before Josephine Baker stunned Paris with her bananas, Paris's cabarets had a reputation for sensual naughtiness. Though the names Lido, Folies Bergère, Crazy Horse Saloon, and Moulin Rouge conjure up images of Maurice Chevalier and Mistinguett, it's the saucy cancan dancers that still draw in the crowds. The entertainers themselves have been replaced by light shows, special effects, and recorded music. If you're expecting to see lots of flesh in today's Parisian revues, you won't be disappointed — breasts and bums abound. In fact, it's rumored that Crazy Horse dancers are chosen for the uniformity of their breast size. If you must see a Paris cabaret show, do yourself a favor and have dinner somewhere else. For the extra $35 to $45, you could have a wonderful meal, and then head to the show.

Of the acts I've listed, none is suitable for children. Don't be surprised if every other member of the audience is from another country — these are some of the least Parisian experiences you can have in Paris.

The sexiest acts go on at **Crazy Horse, Paris** (12 av. George V, 8e; ☎ 01-47-23-32-32; Métro: George V). Dancers (who have names like Chica Boum, Pussy Duty-Free, and Zany Zizanie) appear on swing seats or slithering and writhing in cages . . . you get the picture. Cover and two drinks are 290F ($41). Shows start at 8:30 and 11 p.m. Award-winning chef Paul Bocuse designed the above-average menu for the **Lido** (116 bis av. des Champs-Elysées, 8e; ☎ 01-40-76-56-10; Métro: George V), but it's still not worth the money to have dinner there. Its revue, *C'est Magique,* offers "flying" dancers and an ascending stage that periodically delivers feathered women, fountains, and an ice rink, as well as high-tech laser lighting and video projections. Other acts include a magician who does astonishing bird tricks. A bar seat costs 385F ($55); the show with a half-bottle of champagne is 560F ($80) on Friday and Saturday and 460F ($66) Sunday to Thursday (midnight shows only). Dinner with a half-bottle of champagne is 815F ($116) nightly. Shows start at 10 p.m. and midnight.

The **Moulin Rouge** (place Blanche, Montmartre, 18e; ☎ **01-53-09-82-82;** Métro: Place-Blanche) is probably the most famous of the cabarets. It's been packing in crowds since 1889; Edith Piaf, Yves Montand, and Charles Aznavour made their reputations here. The Moulin Rouge's show, *Formidable,* features comedy, animal, and magic acts with the requisite scantily clad women bumping and grinding. A bar seat and two drinks is 370F ($52.85) Sunday to Thursday; the revue and champagne are 560F ($80) at the 9 p.m. show and 500F ($715) at the 11 p.m. show; dinner runs 790F ($113) at 7 p.m., but otherwise is 990F ($141). Even the waiters get into the act at **Paradis Latin** (28 rue Cardinal-Lemoine, 5e; ☎ **01-43-25-28-28;** Métro: Cardinal-Lemoine). A genial master of ceremonies encourages audience participation during a show less filled with gimmicks than the others. The revue and a half-bottle of champagne are 465F ($66); dinner runs 680F ($97). Performances are Wednesday to Monday beginning at 9:30 p.m.

Jazz

Parisians love American music (especially jazz), and the scene is vibrant, as a new generation develops a taste for the sound. You can look through the current *Pariscope* for the artists you admire. If you don't care who's playing, and you're just out for a night of good music, follow my suggestions.

A noisy crowd of foreigners and locals appreciates **Caveau de la Hûchette** (5 rue de la Hûchette, 5e; ☎ **01-43-26-65-05;** Métro or RER: St-Michel) for what it is — a terrific time. The music starts at 9:30 p.m. The cover is 65F ($9) Sunday to Thursday and 75F ($11) Friday and Saturday. **Le Baiser Sale** (56 rue des Lombards, 1er; ☎ **01-42-33-37-71;** Métro: Châtelet) specializes in fusion jazz, and is a good value too. The cover on Tuesday and Thursday to Sunday is 50 to 80F ($7 to $11); admission is free Monday to Wednesday. At **Le Duc des Lombards** (42 rue des Lombards, 1er; ☎ **01-42-33-22-88;** Métro: Châtelet–Les Halles), the crowd is casual and down to earth, and the sound is some of the most interesting jazz around. The cover is 80 to 120F ($11 to $17).

You can dine, as well as drink, at **Le Petit Journal St-Michel** (71 bd. St-Michel, 5e; ☎ **01-43-26-28-59;** Métro: Cluny–La Sorbonne; RER: Luxembourg), with its relaxed French atmosphere. The Claude Bolling Trio visits regularly, as do the Claude Luter Sextet and the Benny Bailey Quartet. The cover, including a drink, is 100F ($14). **New Morning** (7–9 rue des Petites-Ecuries, 10e; ☎ **01-45-23-51-41;** Métro: Château-d'Eau) is one of Paris's best jazz clubs, and you'll see everyone from Archie

Shepp, Bill Evans, and Elvin Jones to Kevin Coyne and Koko Ateba from Cameroon. The cover is 120F ($17).

Classy cocktails

In Paris, bars aren't reserved solely for drinking or nighttime entertainment. Parisians frequent cafes and bars at all hours of the day and are as likely to drop into a cafe or wine bar for a brandy at breakfast as they are to hang out in one at night. You'll never be far from a bar serving a classy concoction; below are just a few of the places where patrons go to see and be seen.

 You'll never be at ease in shorts and sneakers in these places, so don't even try it. Men should try khakis and a button-down shirt and/or jacket or the latest Hugo Boss; women should go with stylish dresses or skirts.

At **Buddha Bar** (8 rue Boissy d'Anglas, 8e; ☎ 01-53-05-90-00; Métro: Concorde), the music is spacey and the atmosphere electric, and you can see the prettiest people in Paris. A giant, impassive Buddha presides over the very un-Zenlike doings in this cavernous bar/restaurant. From the upstairs balcony, you can observe the fashionable diners below or mix with the swanky international crowd at the balcony bar. The point is to see and be seen — and then say you saw it. At **Alcazar** (62 rue Mazarine, 6e; ☎ 01-53-10-19-99; Métro: Odéon), elements of traditional brasserie style (like banquettes and mirrors) are slicked up and mixed with innovations (like a glassed-in kitchen theatrically installed along the left wall). The comfortable upstairs bar is great for a view over the bustling downstairs restaurant.

The entrance to **Man Ray** (34 rue Marbeuf, 8e; ☎ 01-56-88-36-36; Métro: Franklin-D-Roosevelt), the restaurant backed by American actors Johnny Depp, Sean Penn, and John Malkovich, is marked only by a Chinese character and big wrought-iron doors — so don't look for a sign. The vast downstairs restaurant is dominated by statues of two winged Asian goddesses who appear concerned — possibly about the food. The upstairs bar area is spacious, and the music leans toward jazz early in the evening. As the restaurant winds down around 11 p.m., the music takes on a harder edge and a sleek international crowd stands shoulder-to-shoulder along the curving bar. American artist and photographer Man Ray's photos adorn several walls.

Beautiful people dressed in black come to **La Fabrique** (53 rue du Faubourg St-Antoine, 11e; ☎ 01-43-07-67-07; Métro: Bastille) to see and be seen, drink at the minimalist bar, and eat the delicious Alsatian specialty, *Flammekueche* — large, square, thin-crusted pizzas topped with cream, herbs, and toppings of your choice, including salmon, ham and goat's cheese. Although the bar is open until around 5 a.m.(depending on the crowds), food is served only until midnight. Be ready to stand in line on the weekends, and look out for private parties, when the restaurant is closed to the public. At **The Lizard Lounge** (18 rue du Bourg-Tibourg, 4e; ☎ 01-42-72-81-34; Métro: Hôtel-de-Ville), the music is loud, but the heavy-gauge steel balcony overlooking the main bar offers a chance for quieter conversation. This stylish but easygoing bar is a pleasant place to hang out with an artsy international crowd. You can also arrive early in the evening for a reasonably priced, light meal prepared in the open kitchen. A DJ spins dance music in the refurbished basement Wednesday to Saturday.

Harry's New York Bar (5 rue Danou, 2e; ☎ 01-42-61-71-14; Métro: Opéra or Pyramides) is as popular with Americans today as it was in the days of F. Scott Fitzgerald and Gertrude Stein. It's not cheap — prices start at 45F ($7) — but you may want to splurge and raise a glass to the ghost of another famous customer, Ernest Hemingway.

Dance clubs

You may find that Paris clubs change their programming from night to night. At press time the fad was salsa music. One fun addition to the club scene are the barges, playing everything from house to blues, that are springing up in Paris's south. You can have a rip-roaringly good (though often crowded) time right on the Seine. But whether you like dancing to techno, house, salsa, world, classic rock, or swing, you're sure to find your type of music somewhere in Paris.

To club on a budget, go out during the week when cover charges may be (officially or unofficially) waived. Women often get in free — especially if they're dressed in something slinky, low-cut, or short (or all three). Black clothes are de rigueur for men and women, and the later one goes to a club, the better.

Many American students frequent the tri-level **La Locomotive** (90 bd. de Clichy, 18e; ☎ 08-36-69-69-28; Métro: Place-Clichy), especially on Sundays. At La Locomotive, people usually dance to rock and techno, although metal concerts are occasionally performed here. Graffiti art and psychedelic flowers decorate the walls. This is a very big place; on the lower level you can even see an old railway line. Including one drink, the cover Monday to Thursday and Sunday is 55F ($8) and 70F ($10) after midnight; Friday before midnight is 60F ($9) and after midnight it's 100F ($14); and the cover on Saturday is 100F ($14). Women get in free on Sunday before 12:30 a.m.

The Irish light ship **Batofar** (11 quai François Mauriac, 13e; ☎ 01-56-29-10-00; Métro: Bibliothèque François-Mitterrand or Quai de la Gare) has concerts Tuesday to Sunday starting around 8 p.m., and the party can go on all night. A young 20-something crowd packs the place, but it's still a lot of fun for other age groups. The music can be anything from drum and bass to rock and happy house. The cover is 20 to 60F ($2.90 to $8.60). Well-dressed French yuppies make up the crowd at

Bus Palladium (6 rue Fontaine, 9e; ☎ **01-53-21-07-33;** Métro: Pigalle), which used to play Motown but now concentrates more on house and techno. They like to party, and everyone gets down as the night goes on. The cover on Tuesday is 100F ($14) for men, while women enter free (with free champagne); the cover Thursday to Saturday, including one drink, is 100F ($14).

A festive tropical ambience and diverse music — everything from salsa to reggae — attract a lively crowd to the hip but cramped **La Chapelle des Lombards** (19 rue de Lappe, 11e; ☎ **01-43-57-24-24;** Métro: Bastille). To really enjoy this place, you have to dress the part, which means no sneakers or jeans, but rather your sophisticated best. The cover is 100F ($14) on Thursday and 120F ($17) on Friday and Saturday. The basement dance hall at **La Coupole** (102 bd. du Montparnasse, 14e; ☎ **01-43-27-56-00;** Métro: Montparnasse-Bienvenüe), a retro venue with plush banquettes and old-fashioned sounds, is a big draw for tourists. Come on Friday to hear the orchestra hum out some rhythm and blues; on Tuesday, salsa swings out the evening, with dance classes starting at 8:30 p.m. for 140F ($20, including a drink). The cover, including 2 drinks, is 80F ($11) on Sunday 3 to 9 p.m., 40F ($6) on Saturday 5 to 7 p.m., 100F ($14) on Saturday 9:30 p.m. to 4 a.m., 100F ($14) on Tuesday 9:30 p.m. to 3 a.m., and 100F ($14) on Friday 9:30 p.m. to 4 a.m.

Le Gibus (18 rue du Faubourg-du-Temple, 11e; ☎ **01-47-00-78-88;** Métro: République) was formerly one of Paris's most famous rock dance clubs, but this place has changed its style. Artistic director Bitchy José books top-level DJs who spin house music to a predominantly, but not exclusively, gay crowd. Watch for the monthly "Queer Nation" and "Nuits Blanches" parties. The cover, including one drink, is 100F ($14) on every night but Wednesday, when the cover is free. Le Gibus is open from midnight until noon.

Gay and lesbian bars

Open Monday to Saturday 2 to 8 p.m., the **Centre Gai et Lesbien** (3 rue Keller, 11e; ☎ **01-43-57-21-47;** E-mail: cglparis@cglparis.org; Internet: www.cglparis.org; Métro: Bastille) is a good source of info for general questions about Paris's gay community. The Marais, Les Halles, and the Bastille are the main gay/lesbian neighborhoods. Gay male bars are concentrated in the Marais — as is the hottest lesbian bar, Les Scandaleuses— but the liveliest gay club, Queen, is on the Champs-Elysées. For fuller details, see *Frommer's Gay & Lesbian Europe* (Hungry Minds, Inc.).

Queen (102 av. des Champs-Elysées, 8e; ☎ **01-53-89-08-90;** Métro: George V) is the busiest gay disco in Paris and one of the hottest clubs in town, with crowds so thick, it's difficult to get a drink. The patrons are about two-thirds gay, with the remaining third composed of attractive couples, models trying to escape the pickup scene, and straight men clever enough to have figured out where the beautiful women are. To get past stringent admission control at the door, it helps to have a great face and body — or at least the ability to disguise your faults with great clothes. Women can usually only get in with male friends. The cover is 50F ($7) on Sunday, Monday, and Thursday (including one drink); 30F ($4.30) on Wednesday (including one nonalcoholic drink); and 100F ($14) on Friday and Saturday (including one drink).

Both **Open Café** (17 rue des Archives, 4e; ☎ **01-42-72-26-18**) and **Café Cox** (15 rue des Archives, 4e; ☎ **01-42-72-08-00**) get so busy in the early evening that the crowd stands out on the sidewalk. These clubs are where you can find the most mixed gay crowd in Paris. The ambience at **Amnesia Café** (42 rue Vieille-du-Temple, 4e; ☎ **01-42-72-16-94;** Métro: Hôtel-de-Ville) is more friendly than "meat-markety," and the drinks and food are reasonably priced.

Le Pulp (25 bd. Poissonnière, 2e; ☎ **01-40-26-01-93;** Métro: Grands-Boulevards) is probably the hippest lesbian dance club in Paris. It resembles a nineteenth-century French music hall, and the music is cutting edge. No one shows up until after midnight. The presence of men is discouraged — although, if you're a gay male, you can go to the side, "separate but equal," entrance of **Le Scorp** (☎ **01-40-26-28-30**). At **Les Scandaleuses** (8 rue des Ecouffes, 4e; ☎ **01-48-87-39-26;** Métro: St-Paul), the proprietor, Nicole, sets a relaxed tone for a diverse mix of women, and at happy hour (6 to 8 p.m.), you get two beers for the price of one. The club is jammed on weekends. A few blocks east of avenue de l'Opéra, **La Champmeslé** (4 rue Chabanais, 2e; ☎ **01-42-96-85-20;** Métro: Bourse, Pyramides, Quatre-Septembre, or Opéra) is a comfortable bar for women. Cabaret night on Thursday draws a large crowd.

Fast Facts

American Express

The grand Paris office (11 rue Scribe, 9e; ☎ **01-47-14-50-00;** Métro: Opéra Chaussée-d'Antin or Havre-Caumartin; RER: Auber) is open Monday to Friday 9 a.m. to 6 p.m. The bank is open 9 a.m. to 5 p.m. on Saturday, but the mail pickup window is closed.

ATMs

ATMs are widely available; there's a bank on many a Paris corner. If you'd like to print out a list of ATMs that accept MasterCard or Visa cards, visit www.visa.com/pd/atm or www.mastercard.com/atm or ask your bank.

Business Hours

The **grands magasins** (department stores) are generally open Monday to Saturday 9:30 a.m. to 7 p.m.; **smaller shops** close for lunch and reopen around 2 p.m., but this is rarer than it used to be. Many stores stay open until 7 p.m. in summer; others are closed on Monday, especially in the morning. Large **offices** remain open all day, but some also close for lunch. **Banks** are normally open weekdays 9 a.m. to noon and 1 or 1:30 to 4:30 p.m. Some banks also open on Saturday morning. Some currency-exchange booths are open very long hours; see "Currency Exchange."

Currency Exchange

Banks and *bureaux de change* (exchange offices) almost always offer better exchange rates than hotels, restaurants, and shops, which should be used only in emergencies. For good rates, without fees or commissions, and quick service, try the **Comptoir de Change Opéra** (9 rue Scribe, 9e; ☎ 01-47-42-20-96; Métro: Opéra; RER: Auber). It's open Monday to Friday 9 a.m. to 6 p.m. and Saturday 9:30 a.m. to 4 p.m. The bureaux de change at all train stations (except Gare de Montparnasse) are open daily; those at 63 av. des Champs-Elysées, 8e (Métro: Franklin-D-Roosevelt), and 140 av. des Champs-Elysées, 8e (Métro: Charles-de-Gaulle–Etoile), keep long hours.

Doctors

Call your consulate and ask the duty officer to recommend a doctor, or call **SOS Médecins** (☎ 01-43-37-51-00), a 24-hour service. Most doctors and dentists speak some English.

Embassies/Consulates

If you have a passport, immigration, legal, or other problem, contact your consulate. Call before you go — they often keep strange hours and observe both French and home-country holidays. Here's where to find them: **Australia** (4 rue Jean-Rey, 15e; ☎ 01-40-59-33-00; Métro: Bir-Hakeim); **Canada** (35 av. Montaigne, 8e; ☎ 01-44-43-29-00; Métro: Franklin-D-Roosevelt or Alma- Marceau); **New Zealand** (7 ter rue Léonard-de-Vinci, 16e; ☎ 01-45-00-24-11, ext. 280 from 9 a.m. to 1 p.m.; Métro: Victor-Hugo); **Great Britain** (35 rue Faubourg St-Honoré, 8e; ☎ 01-44-51-31-02; Métro: Madeleine); **United States** (2 rue St-Florentin, 1er; ☎ 01-43-12-22-22; Métro: Concorde).

Emergencies

Call ☎ **17** for the **police.** To report a **fire,** dial ☎ **18.** For an **ambulance,** call ☎ **15,** or call ☎ **01-45-67-50-50** for **SAMU** (Service d'aide médicale d'urgence, or "emergency services"). For help in English, call **SOS Help** at ☎ **01-47-23-80-80** between 3 and 11 p.m. The main police station (9 bd. du Palais, 4e; ☎ **01-53-71-53-71;** Métro: Cité) is open 24 hours.

Hospitals

Two hospitals with English-speaking staff are the **American Hospital of Paris** (63 bd. Victor-Hugo, Neuilly-sur-Seine; ☎ 01-46-41-25-25; Métro: Les Sablons or Levallois-Perret), just west of Paris proper, and the **British Hospital of Paris** (3 rue Barbes Levallois-Perret; ☎ 01-46-39-22-22; Métro: Anatole-France), just north of Neuilly, over the city line northwest of Paris. Note that the American Hospital charges about $600 a day for a room, not including doctor's fees. The emergency department charges more than $60 for a visit, not including tests and x-rays.

Internet Access

To surf the net or check your e-mail, open an account at a free-mail provider, such as **Hotmail** (hotmail.com) or **Yahoo! Mail** (mail.yahoo.com) and all you need to check e-mail while you travel is a Web connection, available at Net cafes around the world. After logging on, just point the browser to your e-mail provider, enter your username and password, and you'll have access to your mail. The following Paris Web bars charge modest fees (25–60F/$3.60–$9 per hour): **Cristal Palace** (43 bd. de Sebastopol, 1er; ☎ 01-42-36-22-22; Métro: Châtelet), **Cybercafé de Paris** (11 and 15 rue des Halles, 1er; ☎ 01-42-21-11-11; Métro: Châtelet), **Web Bar** (32 rue de Picardie, 3e; ☎ 01-42-72-66-55; Métro: République or Temple), **Cyberia** (Centre Pompidou, 4e; ☎ 01-44-54-53-49. Métro: Rambuteau or Hôtel-de-Ville), **Village Web** (18 rue de la Bûcherie, 5e; ☎ 01-44-07-20-15; Métro: St. Michel), **Cyber Cube** (5 rue Mignon, 6e; ☎ 01-01-53-10-30-50; Métro: Odéon or St-Michel), **Virgin Megastore** (52 ave. des Champs Elysées, 8e; ☎ 01-49-53-50-00; Métro: Palais Royal-Musée du Louvre), **Planet Cyber Café** (173 rue de Vaugirard, 15e; ☎ 01-45-67-71-14; Métro: Rennes).

Laundry and Dry Cleaning

To find a laundry near you, ask at your hotel or consult the Yellow Pages under *Laveries pour particuliers.* Take as many 10F, 2F, and 1F pieces as you can. Washing and drying 6 kilos (13¼ lbs.) usually costs about 35F ($5.85). Dry cleaning is *nettoyage à sec;* look for shop signs with the word *pressing.*

Mail

Large **post offices** are normally open Monday to Friday 8 a.m. to 7 p.m. and Saturday 8 a.m. to noon; small post offices may have shorter hours. There are many post offices (PTT) scattered around the city; ask anybody for the nearest one. Airmail letters and postcards to the United States cost 4.40F (65¢); within Europe, 3F (45¢); and to Australia or New Zealand, 5.20F (75¢). The city's **main post office** is at 52 rue du Louvre, 75001 Paris (☎ 01-40-28-20-00; Métro: Louvre-Rivoli). It's open 24 hours a day for urgent mail, telegrams, and telephone calls. It handles Poste Restante mail — sent to you in care of the post office and stored until you pick it up; be prepared to show your passport and pay 3F (45¢) for each letter you receive. If you don't want to use Poste Restante, you can receive mail in care of **American Express.** Holders of American Express cards or traveler's checks get this service free; others have to pay a fee.

Maps

Maps printed by the department stores are usually available free at hotels, and they're good if you are visiting Paris for only a few days and hitting only the major attractions. The best maps are those of the *Plan de Paris par Arrondissement,* pocket-sized books with maps and a street index, available at most bookstores. They're extremely practical, and prices start at around 40F ($6).

Police

Dial ☎ **17** in emergencies; otherwise, call ☎ 01-53-71-53-71.

Post Office

See "Mail," earlier in this section.

Rest Rooms

Public rest rooms are plentiful, but you usually have to pay for them. Every cafe has a rest room, but they are supposed to be for customers only. The best plan is to ask to use the telephone; it's usually next to the *toilette.* For 2F (29¢) you can use the street-side toilets, which are automatically flushed out and cleaned after every use. Some Métro stations have serviced rest rooms; you are expected to tip the attendant 2F (29¢).

Safety

Paris is a relatively safe city, and violent crime is rare. Your biggest risks are pickpockets and purse snatchers, so be particularly attentive on the Métro and on crowded buses, in museum lines, and around tourist attractions. Women should be on guard, in crowded tourist areas and the Métro, against overly-friendly men who seem to have made a specialty out of bothering unsuspecting female tourists. Tricks include asking your name and nationality, then sticking to you like a burr for the rest of the day. They're usually much more harassing than harmful, but if you're too nice, you may be stuck spending time with someone with whom you prefer not to. A simple "leave me alone" (laissez-moi tranquille ["lay-say mwa tran-*keel*"]) usually works.

Taxis

For a taxi, contact **Alpha Taxis** (☎ 01-45-85-85-85), **artaxi** (☎ 01-42-03-50-50), **TaxisG7** (☎ 01-47-39-47-39), or **Taxis Bleus** (☎ 01-49-36-10-10). Be aware that the meter starts running as soon as you call a cab, so they're more expensive than regular cabs.

Telephone/Telex/Fax

Most **public phone booths** take only telephone debit cards called **télécartes,** which can be bought at post offices and at *tabacs* (cafes and kiosks that sell tobacco products). You insert the card into the phone and make your call; the cost is automatically deducted from the "value" of the card recorded on its magnetized strip. The télécarte comes in 50- and 120-unit denominations, costing 49F ($7) and 96F ($14), respectively, and can only be used in a phone booth. For placing **international calls from France,** dial 00, then the country code (for the United States and Canada, 1; for Britain, 44; for Ireland, 353; for Australia, 61; for New Zealand, 64), then the area or city code, and then the local number (for example, to call New York, you'd dial 00 + 1 + 212 + 000-0000). **To place a collect call to North America,** dial 00/33-11, and an English-speaking operator will assist you. Dial 00/00-11 for an American AT&T operator. For **calling from Paris to anywhere else in France** (called *province*), the country is divided into five zones with prefixes beginning 01, 02, 03, 04, and 05; check a phone directory for the code of the city you're calling. If you're **calling France from the United States,** dial the international prefix, 011; then the country code for France, 33; followed by the number but leaving off the initial zero (for example, 011 + 33 + 1-00-00-00-00). Avoid making phone calls from your hotel room; many hotels charge at least 2F (29¢) for local calls, and the markup on international calls can be staggering. You can send **telex** and **fax** messages at the main post office in each arrondissement of Paris, but it's often cheaper to ask at your hotel or to go to a neighborhood printer or copy shop.

Trains

The telephone number for reservations on France's national railroads (SNCF) is ☎ 08-36-35-35-35 (2.23F/32¢/minute). Open 7 a.m.–10 p.m. daily. Remember, you must validate your train ticket in the orange ticket *composteur* on the platform or pay a fine.

Water

Tap water in Paris is perfectly safe, but if you're prone to stomach problems, you may prefer to drink mineral water.

Weather updates

Call ☎ 08-36-70-12-34 (2.23F/32¢/minute) for France and abroad; ☎ 08-36-68-02-75 (2.23F/32¢/minute) for Paris and Ile de France.

Chapter 13

Five Great Side Trips from Paris

· ·

In This Chapter

▶ Seeing the palaces of Versailles and Fontainebleau

▶ Marveling at the stained glass at Chartres cathedral

▶ Spending a day at Disneyland Paris

▶ Visiting Monet at Giverny

· ·

*T*earing yourself away from the glories of Paris is no easy task, but once you see Louis XIV's stunning palace and awe-inspiring gardens of Versailles, Napoléon's smaller Fontainebleau palace, and the haunting medieval cathedral of Chartres, you'll be glad you did. If you have children, you'll also want to give your regards to Mickey Mouse and the pirate Jean Lafitte at Disneyland Paris. These four sights are the most widely visited attractions in the Ile de France, the suburbs and countryside surrounding Paris. If you have more time, you may also want to visit the house of painter Claude Monet, with its spectacular gardens and famous lily pond. Though it's technically in the Normandy region, a visit to Monet's house is only about an hour away by car. All of the adventures in this chapter can be experienced in one day — giving you plenty of time to make it back for a good dinner and a night on the town.

Visiting Louis XIV at Versailles

When you first see the **Château de Versailles** (☎ **01-30-84-74-00;** Internet: www.chateauversailles.fr) you won't be able to take it all in. This enormous palace, 20 km (13 miles) southwest of Paris, attests to the incredible privilege enjoyed by royalty during the 72-year reign of Louis XIV — the Sun King. Louis XIV thought that his greatness would be proven with a château that was the wonder of Europe.

The **tourist office** is at 7 rue des Réservoirs, which runs parallel to the palace (☎ **01-39-24-88-88**).

Getting there

However you travel to Versailles, be sure to get an early start from Paris — you'll need an entire day to see everything there is to see. I also suggest that you bring along a picnic lunch to enjoy in the fabulous gardens.

To get to the palace, catch **RER Line C5** at the Gare d'Austerlitz, St-Michel, Musée d'Orsay, Invalides, Pont de l'Alma, Champs-de-Mars, or Javel station and take it to the Versailles Rive Gauche station. The fare is 14.50F ($2.25) one-way, and the trip takes about half an hour. From there it's a short walk to the Château. Holders of a rail pass (see Chapter 7) can use it for the trip. For the same price, a **regular train** leaves the Gare Montparnasse for the Versailles Chantier station, where a free shuttle bus takes you to the palace.

If you're **driving,** head west on A13 from Porte d'Auteuil toward Rouen. Take the Versailles-Château exit, which is about 20 km (13 miles) from Paris. Park in the visitor's parking lot (paying) at place d'Armes. The drive takes about a half hour, but it can take more than an hour in traffic.

If driving out of Paris is out of the question, consider taking a tour bus to the Ile de France. The biggest company is **Cityrama** (4 place des Pyramides, 1er; ☎ 01-44-55-61-00; Internet: www.cityrama.com; Métro: Palais-Royal–Musée du Louvre), which offers various trips to Versailles costing 200 to 530F ($27 to $76). **Paris Vision** (214 rue de Rivoli, 1er; ☎ 01-49-27-00-06; Internet: www.parisvision.com; Métro: Palais-Royal–Musée du Louvre) offers an all-day excursion that leaves Paris at 8:30 a.m. Tuesday to Sunday for 390F ($56) and includes an entrance ticket to the palace. **France Tourisme** (33 quai des Grands Augustins, 6e; ☎ 01-53-10-35-35; Internet: www.parisavenue.com/sites/thebarber/thebarber/174/index.html; Métro/RER: St-Michel) has a 195F ($28) tour that includes an audioguide.

Seeing the palace and gardens

Versailles started out as Louis XIII's simple hunting lodge. Upon becoming king, Louis XIV decided to enlarge his predecessor's lodge and turn it into a spectacular palace. To accomplish this, he hired the best: Louis Le Vau and Jules Hardouin-Mansart, France's premier architects; André Le Nôtre, designer of the Tuileries Gardens in Paris; and Charles Le Brun, head of the Royal Academy of Painting and Sculpture, for the interior. Construction to turn the lodge into a palace began in 1661. In 1682, Louis transferred his court from the Palais du Louvre in Paris to Versailles and summoned his nobles to live with him — in order to prevent plots against him. It's estimated that anywhere from 3,000 to 10,000 people (including servants) lived, flirted, played, and plotted at Versailles. When you realize that Louis XIV truly believed that all of this over-the-top magnificence was simply his due, you'll also understand the volatile anger of the revolutionaries that arose a century later.

The Île de France

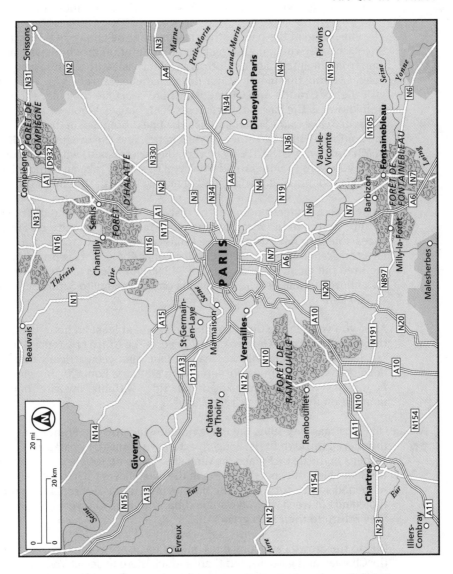

Louis XIV died in 1715 and was succeeded by his great-grandson, Louis XV, who continued the outrageous pomp and ceremony by making interior renovations and redecorations until a lack of funds forced him to stop. His son, Louis XVI, who married the Austrian princess Marie Antoinette, had simpler tastes and made no major changes to the palace. On October 6, 1789, a mob marched on the palace and forced the royal couple to return to Paris, and Versailles ceased to be a royal residence. Louis-Philippe, who reigned from 1830 to 1848, prevented the Château's destruction by donating his own money to convert it into a museum dedicated to the glory of France. John D. Rockefeller also contributed to the restoration of Versailles, which continues to this day.

The sheer size of the palace, the crowds, and the choice of tours can be totally overwhelming, so pick up an orientation brochure with a map from the information booth. Start your visit with the **Château** itself, entering through the Cour de la Chapelle (Entrance A). You can visit the six **Grands Appartements,** where court life took place (the best known is the Salon of Hercules, which houses Veronese's painting *Christ at Supper with Simon* and has the finest fireplace in the Château), the gold-and-white two-story **Royal Chapel,** and the breathtaking **Hall of Mirrors** (where the Treaty of Versailles was signed) without a guide, but if you want to understand what you're seeing, take an audioguide tour. The commentary is fascinating and well worth the 25F ($3.60).

To help your understanding of the history of Versailles (and of France), be sure to stop in the recently reopened **Musée de l'Histoire de France,** accessible through Porte D in the Château. Portraits of those who affected French history line the walls; Louis XIV is, not surprisingly, pictured the most. Admission is 20F ($2.90) for adults and half-price for children under 18. The museum is open Tuesday to Saturday 9 a.m. to 5:30 p.m.

After you've seen the Château, plan to spend at least an hour strolling through the **Formal Gardens.** On 250 acres, Le Nôtre created a Garden of Eden using ornamental lakes, canals, fountains, geometrically designed flowerbeds, and avenues bordered with statuary. Louis XV, imagining he was in Venice, used to take gondola rides with his "favorite" of the moment on the mile-long Grand Canal.

On Christmas Day 1999, the most violent windstorm in France's history thundered through Paris, causing extensive damage to parks and gardens in the Ile de France. At Versailles, the wind toppled ten thousand trees and blew out some windows at the magnificent Château. The palace reopened soon after the storm, but the difficult task of replanting the thousands of trees may take some time, and it may be years before they return to their lush grandeur.

Due to the crowds and long lines, most guests are content to visit only the Château and gardens, but there's much more to see at Versailles. The most important of the remaining sights are the **Grand Trianon** and the **Petit Trianon,** both opulent love nests constructed for the mistresses of kings. A long walk across the park takes you to the pink-and-white-marble Grand Trianon, designed in 1687 by Hardouin-Mansart for Louis XIV. It has traditionally served as a lodging for the country's important guests, though former French president Charles de Gaulle wanted to turn it into a weekend retreat for himself. Napoléon I spent the night here, and former U.S. president Richard Nixon slept in the room where Mme de Pompadour died. Gabriel, the designer of place de la Concorde, built the Petit Trianon in 1768 for Louis XV, whose mistress, Mme de Pompadour, inspired its construction. She died before it was

Versailles

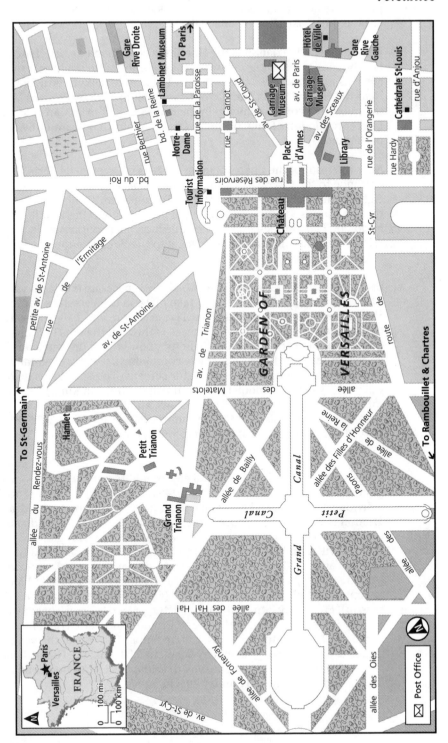

complete, so Louis XV used it for his trysts with Mme du Barry. Marie Antoinette adopted it as her favorite residence, where she could escape the constraints of palace life.

Behind the Petit Trianon is the **Hamlet,** a collection of small thatched farmhouses and a water mill where Marie Antoinette could pretend she was a shepherdess enchanted by the simple tasks of farm life. Near the Hamlet is the **Temple of Love,** built in 1775 by Richard Mique, the queen's favorite architect. In the center of its Corinthian colonnade is a reproduction of Bouchardon's *Cupid* shaping a bow from the club of Hercules.

Near the front of the Château, in the stables off avenue de Paris, is the entrance to the **Carriage Museum,** which houses coaches from the eighteenth and nineteenth centuries. The museum's collection includes the coaches used at the coronation of Charles X and the wedding of Napoléon I and Marie-Louise. The collection also contains a sleigh that rests on tortoiseshell runners. A ticket to the Petit Trianon admits you to this museum.

Each summer, the **Grandes Eaux Musicales** (baroque music plays while 24 fountains do their thing) take place in the Versailles gardens. Shows are Saturday and Sunday at 11 a.m., noon, and 2:30 p.m., with tickets available at 33F ($4.70). Access is through the court of the Château or near the Grand Canal. Better, however, is the **Fêtes de Nuits de Versailles,** a nighttime spectacle combining fireworks, fountains, music, and projected images on water screens. The 2001 Fêtes de Nuits will portray the best moments from the life of the Sun King, reenacted with help from costumed figures, horses, and hounds. Shows are scheduled to take place at the Neptune Fountain July 7, 21, and 28 at 10:30 p.m., August 25 at 9:30 p.m., and September 1, 8, and 15 at 9:30 p.m.

Admission to the palace is 45F ($6.45) for adults until 3:30 p.m. — the price drops to 35F ($5) after 3:30 p.m. — and 35F ($5) for ages 18 to 24, individuals over 60, and everyone on Sunday. Admission to the Grand Trianon is 25F ($3.60), reduced to 15F ($2.15) after 3:30 p.m. Admission to the Petit Trianon is 15F ($2.15), lowered to 10F ($1.45) after 3:30 p.m. A ticket with combined admission to both Trianons is 30F ($4.30), reduced after 3:30 p.m. to 20F ($2.90). An all-day "passport" allowing combined entry to the Château and the Trianons is 90F ($12.90) May 2 to September 30 (high season), or 70F ($10) from October to April (low season). From May 2 to September 30, the palace is open Tuesday to Sunday 9 a.m. to 6:30 p.m.; the Grand Trianon and Petit Trianon are also open Tuesday to Sunday 10 a.m. to 6 p.m. The rest of the year, the palace is open Tuesday to Sunday 9 a.m. to 5:30 p.m.; the Grand Trianon and Petit Trianon are open Tuesday to Friday 10 a.m. to noon and 2 to 5 p.m., and Saturday and Sunday 10 a.m. to 5 p.m.

Where to dine

The town of Versailles has no shortage of places where you can break for lunch, but once you're on palace grounds, it's infinitely more convenient to just stay put — otherwise you have to hike into town and back out to the palace again. Consider bringing a picnic or trying one of the following options: in the Château, there's a cafeteria just off the Cour de la Chapelle; in the Formal Gardens, there's an informal restaurant, **La Flotille,** on Petite Venise (to get there from the Château, walk directly back through the Gardens to where the canal starts and you'll see Petite Venise and the restaurant to your right); and finally, there are several snack bars in the Gardens near the Quinconce du Midi and the Grand Trianon. All of the dining options are open the same hours as the chateau (May 2 to September 30 Tuesday through Sunday 9 a.m. to 6:30 p.m.; October to April Tuesday to Sunday 9 a.m. to 5:30 p.m.).

Calling on Napoléon at Fontainebleau

About 60 km (37 miles) south of Paris, the **Palais de Fontainebleau** (☎ **01-60-71-50-70**) contains more than 700 years of royal history — from the enthronement of Louis VII in 1137 to the fall of the Second Empire. The Palais de Fontainebleau is probably most famous for Napoléon's farewell to his Imperial Guard, which he delivered on the grand exterior horseshoe staircase before leaving for exile. If you get tired of the palace's splendor, you can walk around the beautiful gardens and rent bikes to ride in the 42,000 acres of the kings' old hunting grounds, the Forêt de Fontainebleau.

The **tourist office** is at 4 rue Royale, near the palace (☎ **01-60-74-99-99**).

Getting there

The **Montargie line** to Fontainebleau departs hourly from the Gare de Lyon in Paris. The trip takes 35 minutes to an hour and costs 47F ($7). The Fontainebleau Avon station is located in Avon, a suburb of Paris. From the station, the **town bus** makes the 2-mile trip to the château every 10 to 15 minutes, Monday through Friday, and every 30 minutes on Saturday and Sunday. The bus ride costs 8F ($1.15).

Cityrama (4 place des Pyramides, 1er; ☎ **01-44-55-61-00;** Métro: Palais-Royal–Musée du Louvre) has bus tours combining both Fontainebleau and Barbizon for 335F ($47.90) per person.

If you're **driving,** take the A6 in the direction of Evry-Lyon-Chilly Mazarin for 40 km (25 miles). Exit Fontainebleau Montargis Par Fontainebleau Milly-La-Foret. Take the N37 in the direction of Fontainebleau for 8 km

(5 miles), then take the N7 in the direction of Fontainebleau for 6 km (4 miles) and exit at Fontainebleau.

Seeing the palace

François I built Fontainebleau for his mistress. His successor, Henri II, added a beautiful **ballroom** as a memorial to the woman he loved, his mistress, Diane de Poitiers: The ballroom is decorated with their inter-twined initials. The *Mona Lisa* once hung here (François I bought the painting from Leonardo himself). Stucco-framed paintings now hanging in the **Gallery of François I** include *The Rape of Europa* and depictions of mythological and allegorical scenes related to the king's life.

 Make sure to see the racy paintings (originally painted for the bedroom of a duchess) above the **Louis XV Staircase.** The stairway's architect simply ripped out her floor and used her bedroom ceiling to cover the stairway. One fresco depicts the Queen of the Amazons climbing into Alexander the Great's bed.

When Louis XIV ascended to the throne, Fontainebleau was largely neglected because of his preoccupation with Versailles. The palace found renewed glory under Napoléon I. You can walk around much of the palace on your own, but most of the **Napoleonic Rooms** are acces-sible only on guided tours, given in French. Napoléon had two bed-chambers; mirrors adorn either side of his bed in the grand chamber (look for his symbol, a bee), while a small bed is housed in the aptly named **Small Bedchamber.** A red-and-gold throne with the initial N is displayed in the **Throne Room.** You can also see Napoléon's **offices,** where the emperor signed his abdication, though the document exhib-ited is only a copy.

After a visit to the palace, wander through the **gardens,** paying special attention to the lovely carp pond and its fearless swans. If you'd like to promenade in the **forest,** a detailed map of its paths is available for 35F ($5) from the tourist office (for contact information, see earlier in this section). You can also rent bikes from nearby **A la Petite Reine** (32 rue des Sablons; ☎ **01-60-74-57-57**), for 80F ($11) per day or 100F ($14) on weekends, with a credit card deposit. The **Tour Denencourt,** about 5 km (3 miles) north of the palace, makes a nice ride and has a pretty view.

Fontainebleau is open Wednesday to Monday: July and August 9:30 a.m. to 6 p.m.; May, June, September, and October 9:30 a.m. to 5 p.m.; and November to April 9:30 a.m. to 12:30 p.m. and 2 to 5 p.m. Admission to the Grands Appartements is 35F ($5) for adults and 23F ($3.30) for ages 18 to 24, individuals over 60, and everyone on Sunday. Separate admission to the Napoleonic Rooms is 16F ($2.30) for adults and 12F ($1.70) for students 18 to 25; children under 18 enter free.

Fontainebleau

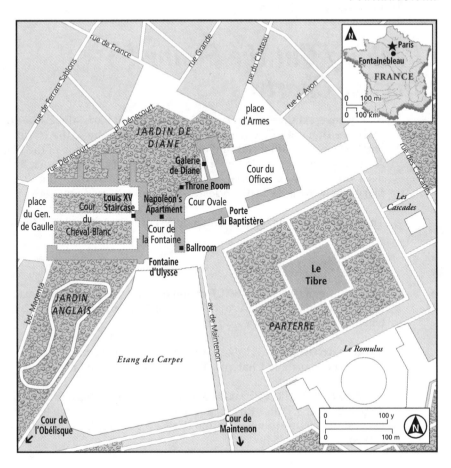

Where to dine

If you're arriving by train and plan to visit only Fontainebleau, consider bringing a picnic from Paris. In fine weather, the château's gardens and the nearby forest beckon. If you have a car, save your appetite for Barbizon. You can drive to Barbizon by taking the N7 in the direction of Paris for 8 km (5 miles), then the D64 for one mile to the Barbizon exit.

On the western edge of France's finest forest lies the village of **Barbizon,** home to a number of noted nineteenth-century landscape artists — Corot, Millet, Rousseau, and Daumier, among others. The colorful town has a lively mix of good restaurants, boutiques, and antiques shops — the perfect place to while away an afternoon.

For lunch, try the **Relais de Barbizon** (2 av. Charles-de-Gaulle; ☎ **01-60-66-40-28**), whose 145F ($20.70) lunch menu features hearty home-style dishes, such as duckling in wild-cherry sauce and braised lamb with thyme. It's open Thursday to Tuesday noon to 3 p.m. and Thursday to Monday 7 to 10 p.m.

Checking Out the Stained Glass at Chartres

Ninety-seven kilometers (60 miles) southwest of Paris, the **Cathédrale de Notre-Dame de Chartres** (☎ 02-37-21-56-33), one of the world's greatest Gothic cathedrals and one of the finest creations of the Middle Ages, has come second in importance to a majority of its visitors. Instead, it's a small scrap of material — said to have been worn by the Virgin Mary when she gave birth to Jesus — that draws so many here.

The **tourist office** is located outside the cathedral (☎ 02-37-21-50-00).

Getting there

Pick up one of the hourly **SNCF trains** from Paris's Gare Montparnasse to the town of Chartres. A round-trip ticket costs about 144F ($21); the trip takes about an hour.

If you're **driving,** take A10/A11 from Porte d'Orléans and follow the signs to Le Mans and Chartres. The drive takes about 75 minutes.

The bus tour outfit, Cityrama (4 place des Pyramides, 1er; ☎ 01-44-55-61-00; Métro: Palais-Royal–Musée du Louvre), offers five-hour excursions by bus that leave from Paris every Tuesday, Thursday, and Saturday for 285F ($40).

Seeing the cathedral

The cathedral you see today dates principally from the thirteenth century, when it was built with the combined efforts and contributions of kings, princes, church officials, and pilgrims from all over Europe. This Notre-Dame was among the first to use flying buttresses.

Take one of the excellent **guided tours** (40F/$6) of the cathedral — especially those offered by Englishman Malcolm Miller (☎ 02-37-28-15-58). He gives fascinating tours Monday to Saturday at noon and 2:45 p.m., from Easter to November (he's sometimes available in winter as well).

A good time to visit the cathedral is on Sunday afternoon, when **free organ concerts** (4:45–5:45 p.m.) and the filtered light coming in from the western windows make the church come wonderfully alive.

Notre-Dame de Chartres

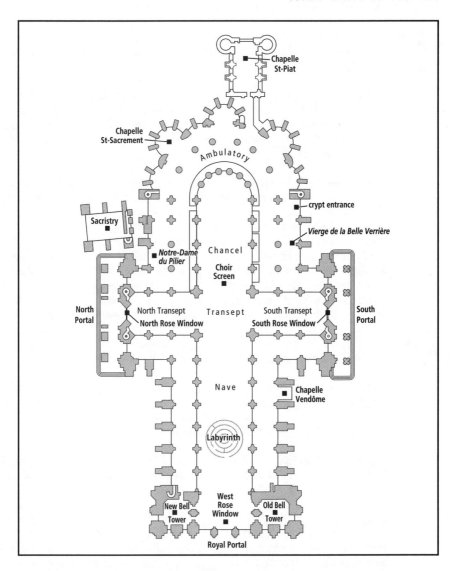

It's said that the sculptor Rodin sat for hours on the edge of the sidewalk, contemplating the portal outside the entryway, spellbound by its sculptured bodies draped in long, flowing robes with amazingly lifelike faces. Before entering, walk around to both the north and the south portals (dating from the thirteenth century). The bays depict such biblical scenes as the expulsion of Adam and Eve from the Garden of Eden and episodes from the life of the Virgin.

Next, just inside, you'll find the towers: **Clocher Vieux** (a 350-foot, twelfth-century steeple) and the **Clocher Neuf** (built in 1134). The Clocher Neuf's elaborate ornamental tower was added between 1507 and 1513 following one of the many fires that swept over the cathedral.

You can climb to the top of the Clocher Neuf, but make sure your shoes aren't slippery — parts of the tower are without a railing. And it's quite steep and narrow.

The cathedral is also known for its celebrated **choir screen.** Don't let the term fool you — this is a carved wood structure that took nearly 200 years to complete. The niches, 40 in all, contain statues illustrating scenes from the life of Mary. The choir screen is located in the middle of the cathedral toward the back.

Few of the rushed visitors ever notice the choir screen because they're transfixed by the **stained-glass windows.** The glass is unequaled anywhere in the world and is truly mystical. It was spared in both world wars because of a decision to remove it — piece by piece. Most of the stained glass dates from the twelfth and thirteenth centuries. It's difficult to single out one panel or window of particular merit; however, the oldest is the twelfth-century **Vierge de la belle verrière** (translated, this means "Virgin of the Beautiful Window," sometimes called the Blue Virgin) on the south side. The colors from the glass are such a vibrant startling blue, that it's hard to believe the window is 1,000 years old.

Bring a pair of binoculars to allow you to focus on the stained-glass panes that cover more than 3,000 square yards.

Look down in the **nave** (the widest in France) at the thirteenth-century labyrinth. It was designed for pilgrims to navigate on their hands and knees as a form of penance — all 1,000 feet of it. These days, much of it is covered with fold-up chairs for mass.

The **Sancta Camisia,** the holy relic that Mary allegedly wore during the birth of Jesus, is behind the choir screen in a chapel to the left of the church's treasury.

Entrance to the cathedral is free. It's open daily: from April to September 7:30 a.m. to 7:30 p.m., and October to March 7:30 a.m. to 7 p.m. In summer, French-language tours of the cathedral are given Tuesday to Saturday at 10:30 a.m. and daily at 3 p.m.; in winter, tours are daily at 2:30 p.m. French-language tours of the crypt are given daily at 11 a.m. and 2:15, 3:30, and 4:30 p.m. (also at 5:15 p.m. in summer). The crypt tour costs 10F ($1.45) for adults and 7F ($1) for ages 18 to 24 and individuals over 60. Ask at the Chartres tourist office outside the cathedral for information about tours in English and a schedule of masses open to the public. April to September, the tower is open Monday to Saturday 9:30 to 11:30 a.m. and daily 2 to 5:30 p.m.; October to March, hours are Monday to Saturday 10 to 11:30 a.m., and daily from 2 to 4 p.m. Admission to the tower is 25F ($3.60) for adults, 15F ($2.15) for seniors and students, and free for children under 12.

If you have extra time, spend it exploring the medieval cobbled streets of the **Old Town.** At the foot of the cathedral are lanes with gabled and turreted houses and humped bridges spanning the Eure River. One house, on rue Chantault, dates back nine centuries. Stop in at the **Musée de Beaux-Arts de Chartres** (29 Cloître Notre-Dame; ☎ 02-37-36-41-39), to see paintings by old masters such as Watteau, Brosamer, and Zurbarán. The museum is open Wednesday to Monday 10 a.m. to noon and 2 to 5 p.m. Admission is 10F ($1.45).

Where to dine

There are plenty of restaurants, cafes, and snack bars around town, but **Le Buisson Ardent** (10 rue au Lait; ☎ 02-37-34-04-66) is just a stone's throw from the cathedral. The restaurant serves up great fare made with farm-fresh ingredients, in a wood-beamed dining room. There is a variety of fresh fish dishes to choose from, though the roast pigeon with lemon juice, with potato pancakes and vegetables, is recommended. Calvados, an apple brandy, is a speciality of the Normandy region, so for dessert, try the crispy hot apples with sorbet and Calvados-flavored butter sauce. There are three fixed-price menus at 138F, 188F, and 225F ($20, $27, and $32). The restaurant is open daily noon to 2:30 p.m. and Monday to Saturday 7 to 10:30 p.m.

Spending the Day with Mickey at Disneyland Paris

Disneyland Paris (☎ 01-64-74-30-00) — which opened in 1992 to much controversy — has grown to become France's number-one attraction, with more than 50 million visitors per year: 40% of them French and half of those Parisian. Set on a 5,000-acre site (about one-fifth the size of the capital) in the suburb of Marne-la-Vallée 32 km (20 miles) east of Paris, the park incorporates the elements of its Disney predecessors but gives them a European flair. Allow yourself a full day to see Disneyland Paris (officially called Euro Disney).

Getting there

Take the **RER Line A** from the center of Paris (Invalides, Nation, or Châtelet–Les Halles) to Marne-la-Vallée/Chessy, a 45-minute ride. The fare is 38F ($6.35) one-way or 76F ($10.90) round-trip. Trains run every 10 to 20 minutes between 6 a.m. and 1 a.m., depending on the time of year. The station is located at the entrance to the park.

Shuttle buses, arriving every 45 minutes, connect the resort's hotels with Orly Airport (daily 9 a.m. to 7 p.m.) and Charles de Gaulle Airport (daily 8 a.m. to 8 p.m.). One-way transport to the park from either airport is 80F ($11). Within the park, a free shuttle bus connects the various hotels with the theme park. The bus stops every 6 to 15 minutes, depending on the time of year. Service begins an hour before the park opens and stops an hour after closing.

If you're **driving,** take A4 east and exit at *Park Euro Disney.* Guest parking at any of the thousands of spaces costs 40F ($6). A series of moving sidewalks speeds up pedestrian transit from the parking areas to the theme park entrance.

Getting information and taking a tour

For more information, contact the **Disneyland Paris Guest Relations office** (located in the park in City Hall on Main Street, U.S.A.; ☎ **01-64-74-30-00**). Guided tours in English cost 45F ($6) for adults and 35F ($5) for children 3 to 11. Tours last 3½ hours, and group size is generally 20 or more. The tours offer one of the best opportunities for a complete visit. Ask someone at the information desk for details.

Exploring the park

Disneyland Paris is divided into five major areas. The following list gives you an idea of what each area has to offer.

- ✔ **Main Street, U.S.A.,** is replete with horse-drawn carriages and street-corner barbershop quartets to give visitors a taste of the USA in the good old days. There are plenty of souvenir shops and even a train station, where you can take a steam-powered railway car for a trip through a Grand Canyon diorama to Frontierland.

- ✔ **Frontierland** evokes America's days of the Wild, Wild West family-style. There are paddle-wheel steamers, the "Critter Corral at the Cottonwood Creek Ranch" petting zoo, and "The Lucky Nugget Saloon," straight from the gold-rush era. There, visitors find an array of cancan shows (which, ironically, originated in the cabarets of early-1900s Paris). One of the best roller coasters in the park is here, too, Big Thunder Mountain. Go early to avoid its lines. Hop back on the steam train to Adventureland.

- ✔ **Adventureland** brings to life some tales popular with children. In Pirates of the Caribbean, kids will see (and perhaps be scared by) true-to-life looking eighteenth-century pirates, and climb a "Swiss Family Robinson" tree house, while legends from the Arabian Nights are re-enacted. The Indiana Jones and the Temple of Doom roller coaster is here, too. Afterward, take the steam train to Fantasyland.

- ✔ **Fantasyland** is home to the Sleeping Beauty Castle (Le Château de la Belle au Bois Dormant), with soaring pinnacles and turrets that are an idealized interpretation of the châteaux of France. Parading within its shadow are time-tested, though Europeanized, versions of Snow White and the Seven Dwarfs, Peter Pan, Dumbo (the flying elephant), Alice in Wonderland's Mad Tea Party, and Sir Lancelot's magic carousel. Board the train for passage to the final Disney "land," Discoveryland.

✔ **Discoveryland,** where visions of the future are exhibited and tributes paid to inventors such as Leonardo da Vinci, and to Jules Verne and H. G. Wells, the modern masters of science fiction. The latest attraction here is Space Mountain, a roller coaster that sends riders on a virtual journey from the earth to the moon through the Milky Way.

In addition to the theme park, Disney maintains an entertainment center, **Le Festival Disney,** the layout of which might remind visitors of a mall in California. Illuminated inside by a spectacular grid of lights suspended 60 feet above the ground, the complex contains dance clubs, shops, restaurants, bars, a French government tourist office, post office, baby-sitting service, and marina. Outside the park are pools, tennis courts, and a 27-hole golf course.

If you have kids under 7, they'd be best suited for Main Street, U.S.A., Fantasyland, Sleeping Beauty's Castle, and the afternoon parade. Children 7 to 12 may enjoy Frontierland, the Phantom Manor ghost house, the Big Thunder Mountain roller coaster, Adventureland, Indiana Jones and the Temple of Doom roller coaster, and the Pirates of the Caribbean ride. Teens may like Discoveryland, the Space Mountain roller coaster, and the Star Tours simulated spacecraft ride.

Admission to the park for one day is 210F ($30) for anyone over 11 and 170F ($24) for children 4 to 11; children under 4 enter free. Admission for two days is 385F ($55) for adults and 330F ($47) for children. From early November to late March, prices for one day are 160F ($23) for adults and 130F ($19) for children; prices for two days are 310F ($44) for adults and 250F ($36) for children. Entrance to Le Festival Disney (the consortium of shops, dance clubs, and restaurants) is free; there's usually a cover charge for the dance clubs. June 12 through September 12, Disneyland Paris is open daily 9 a.m. to 11 p.m.; September 13 through June 11, hours are Monday to Friday 10 a.m. to 6 p.m. and Saturday and Sunday 9 a.m. to 8 p.m. Hours vary with the weather and season, so call ☎ 01-64-74-30-00 before setting out.

You can rent wheelchairs and children's strollers for 30F ($4.30) per day, with a 50F ($7) deposit.

Where to stay

If you want to stay at Disneyland overnight or for a few days, you'll need to book your hotel room well in advance. Disneyland has plenty of hotels at different price levels. You can explore your options and book a room on the park's Web site (www.disneylandparis.com). The smallest but most luxurious choice is the four-star **Disneyland Hotel,** followed by the elegant four-star **Hotel New York.** The three-star

Disneyland Paris

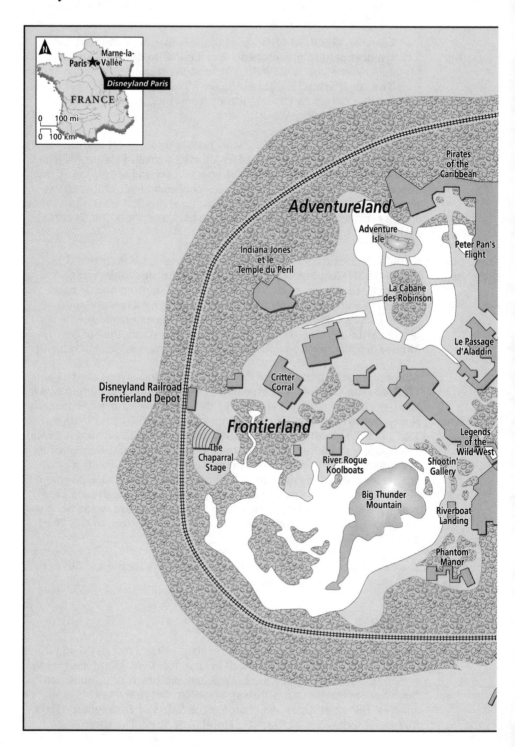

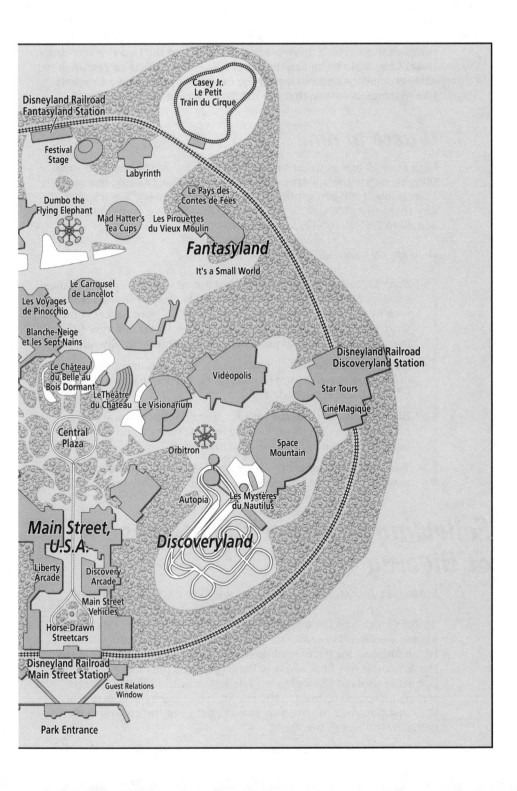

Sequoia Lodge resembles a giant home in the Rocky Mountains; while the three-star **Newport Bay Club** looks like the Hotel El Dorado in San Diego. The two-star **Hotel Santa Fe** looks like a southwestern adobe complex topped by a drive-in movie screen, and the two-star storefront **Hotel Cheyenne** looks like the set of a Western. Guests can camp in the campgrounds or rent out one of the log cabins at the **Davy Crockett Ranch.** Note, however, that the ranch is 15 minutes from the park.

Where to dine

With over 50 places to eat in Disneyland Paris, there should be something to satisfy the appetite of even the most finicky eater. Ignore the French food (you can get the real thing back in Paris). You'll spend anywhere from 100 to 300F ($14 to $43) for a two- or three-course meal and 50 to 70F ($7 to $10) for fast food.

Here are some standout restaurants:

✔ **Buzz Lightyear's Pizza Planet Restaurant** (Discoveryland). Named for the cartoon astronaut in Disney's *Toy Story,* this restaurant won't disappoint the movie's fans. There's a giant rocket launcher with three-eyed aliens, and the house special Pizzaburger (a hamburger with a mini-pizza on top) is quintessentially American.

✔ **Lucky Nugget Saloon** (Frontierland). This restaurant offers plenty of Western-themed food (hamburgers, barbeque), as well as a bilingual, Old West–style show.

✔ **Blue Lagoon Restaurant** (Adventureland). You can watch the pirates of the Caribbean float by in their boats while you enjoy seafood in tropical, romantic surroundings.

✔ **Toad Hall Restaurant** (Fantasyland). This is the place to go for reasonably priced English pub food, most notably fish-and-chips.

Following in Monet's Footsteps at Giverny

In 1883, Claude Monet moved to **Giverny** (☎ 02-32-51-28-21; www.giverny.org), — 80 km (50 miles) northwest of Paris — where the flower garden and the waterlilies beneath the Japanese bridge in the garden became his regular subjects until his death in 1926. Giverny lay abandoned for years until the Monet family donated the ruins to the Académie des Beaux-Arts in Paris (perhaps the most prestigious fine arts school in France) in 1966. It wasn't until 1977 that Giverny was restored and opened to the public. It has since become one of the most popular attractions in France, but even the crowds can't completely obscure the magic.

Even before you arrive at Giverny, you may have some idea of what you're going to see if you are familiar with at least a few of Monet's paintings of the gardens and the waterlilies. The gardens are usually at their best in May, June, September, and October. Should you yearn to have them almost all to yourself, plan to be at the gates when they open. You may spend at least a half day at Giverny — longer if you plan to eat lunch and visit the American Museum.

April to October, the gardens are open Tuesday to Sunday 10 a.m. to 6 p.m. Admission to the house and gardens is 35F ($6) for adults, 25F ($4.15) for students, and 20F ($3.35) for children 7 to 12; admission to the gardens only is 25F ($4.15).

It's estimated that at one point, more than 50 American artists lived in Giverny with their families. You can see much of their work at the **Musée d'Art Américain Giverny** (☎ 02-32-51-94-65), just 100 yards from Monet's house and gardens. Some say Monet's influence was responsible for the influx of American artists into the village in the late 1880s. Others say that Monet had little contact with the Americans, and it was Giverny's beauty that captured the hearts of painters like John Singer Sargent and William Metcalf, who spent their summers there. April to October, the museum is open Tuesday to Sunday 10 a.m. to 6 p.m. Admission is 35F ($5) adults and 25F ($3.60) students and 20F ($2.90) seniors and children.

Getting there

Pick up an **SCNF train** at the Gare St-Lazare in Paris — approximately every hour — for the 45-minute trip to Vernon, the town nearest the Monet gardens. The round-trip fare is about 134F ($22). From the station in Vernon, buses make the 3-mile trip to the museum for 12F ($2), or you can go on foot — the route along the Seine makes for a nice walk.

If you're **driving,** take A13 from the Porte d'Auteuil to Bonnières, then D201 to Giverny. The whole trip takes about an hour.

Cityrama (4 place des Pyramides, 1er; ☎ 01-44-55-61-00; Internet: www.cityrama.com; Métro: Palais-Royal–Musée du Louvre), offers two trips to Giverny: a five-hour trip at 350F ($42.90) Tuesday to Saturday and an all-day Giverny–Auvers-sur-Oise trip at 600F ($90) on Sunday or Wednesday, which includes lunch at the American Museum. Call for specific dates. **Paris Vision** (214 rue de Rivoli, 1er; ☎ 01-49-27-00-06; Internet: www.parisvision.com; Métro: Palais-Royal Musée de Louvre) also offers two trips: a Versailles-Giverny all-day trip on Tuesday, Thursday, and Saturday that includes lunch at the Moulin de Fourges for 795F ($113) and trips Tuesday to Sunday without lunch for 440F ($63) per person. From March to October, **France Tourisme** (33 quai des Grands Augustins, 6e; ☎ 01-53-10-35-35; Internet: www.parisavenue.com/sites/thebarber/174/index.html; Métro ad RER: St-Michel) has a 280F ($40) tour Tuesday to Sunday.

Where to dine

Your entry ticket is no longer valid once you leave Monet's home, so think ahead about whether you want to eat lunch before or after your visit. Most people arrive in early afternoon, so crowds are slightly lighter in the mornings.

The square directly across from Monet's house, as well as the adjacent street, has many little cafes and crêperies. But if you're in the mood for more substantial fare, walk back to town and treat yourself to **Le Relais Normand,** an old Norman manor house with a fireplace and terrace. It serves delicious dishes like Neufchâtel cheese in pastry, stewed beef à la Provençal, and young rabbit in green peppercorn sauce. The four-course prix-fixe menu is the best deal in the house at 175F ($25). The restaurant is open Tuesday to Sunday noon to 3 p.m.

Part IV
Tours and the Loire Valley Châteaux

The 5th Wave   By Rich Tennant

"Now THAT was a great meal! Beautiful presentation, an imaginative use of ingredients, and a sauce with nuance and depth. The French really know how to make a 'Happy Meal.'"

In this part...

The Loire Valley is undoubtedly France's most romantic region, where some two dozen of the most impressive châteaux in Europe are contained within a 113-km (70-mile) radius. In Chapter 14, I take you to Tours, the valley's principal city and the traditional place to base yourself for an exploration of the castles. The other good base city is Orléans, which I cover in Chapter 15 along with the eight most beautiful châteaux. The Loire Valley is where the kings and nobles of France chose to live for several centuries, and each castle has witnessed its share of bliss and bloodshed. You can visit two or three castles in one day or spend a week exploring the region and visiting a dozen or more. This area dazzles with examples of the flowering of Renaissance architecture in France, and the images of fierce medieval battlements set against soaring Renaissance turrets and towers will be the ones you remember for years to come.

Chapter 14

Tours: Gateway to Châteaux Country

● ●

In This Chapter

▶ Choosing where to stay and dine in Tours

▶ Exploring the historic sites in Tours

▶ Doing Tours by night

● ●

*W*riter Honoré de Balzac once proclaimed that **Tours**, 231.7 km (144 miles) southwest of Paris, was "laughing, loving, fresh, flowered, perfumed better than all the other cities of the world." I can't vouch for the perfumed part, but I can say that the city feels especially lively, perhaps because of the 32,000 students who call it home along with the 135,000 other residents. Above all, Tours is the ideal place to base yourself for an exploration of the Loire Valley's famed châteaux (see Chapter 15). At the junction of the Loire and Cher Rivers, it's the capital of the Touraine region, which was France's political/religious capital for 80 years in the 15th and 16th centuries. As a result, the region near Tours is now a showcase of royal and noble residences built during the Renaissance. Writers like François Rabelais, Balzac, and René Descartes owned homes here, and artists from Leonardo da Vinci to Alexander Calder have drawn inspiration from the area.

Getting There

Tours is an hour from Paris by **TGV,** the fast train, departing from Gare Montparnasse. About ten trains per day make the trip, costing 290 to 410F ($41 to $59) each way. Call the national train company, **SNCF,** at ☎ **08-36-35-35-35** for schedules and reservations. Trains arrive in Tours at the magnificent beaux-arts **Gare S.N.C.F.** on place du Général-Leclerc (☎ **02-47-20-50-50**). There's a suburban train station at St-Pierre-des-Corps, 5 km (3.1 miles) from Tours, where you may need to change trains. The **bus** station, **Gare Routière** (☎ **02-47-05-30-49**), is also on place du Général-Leclerc. For bus schedules (there's an information kiosk on rue de la Dolve in Tours), call ☎ **02-47-66-70-70** or the

Sampling the region's cuisine

A number of gastronomic specialties of the Loire Valley go particularly well with the region's wines. While exploring, look for menu items like *rillons* or *rillettes* (cooked pork chunks), *geline* (traditional free-range chicken), *coq au vin* (chicken stewed in wine), writer François Rabelais's favorite *fouaces* (traditionally prepared bread rolls), and *poires tapées* (dried pears steeped in wine). A special cheese of the region is Ste-Maure-de-Touraine. Local wines that you may want to try include Vouvray, Montlouis-sur-Loire, Amboise, Azay-le-Rideau, Chinon, Bourgueil, and St-Nicholas-de-Bourgueil.

bus station. The **Aéroport de Tours** is 6 km (3.7 miles) northeast of the city; for information, call ☎ **02-47-49-37-00.** There are direct flights to Tours from Lyon but not from Paris. If you're **driving** from Paris, you can take A10 southwest to Tours; it's about a 2¼-hour trip.

Getting Information and Getting Around

You exit the **train station** at Tours onto wide place du Général-Leclerc, planted with lilac trees. Across the street is a modern conference center, and next door, on the right, is the **tourist office** (78–82 rue Bernard-Palissy; ☎ **02-47-70-37-37**; E-mail: info@ligeris.com; Internet: www.ligeris.com), with maps, details on guided tours of the city and nearby châteaux, and other useful information. In addition, the office's staff can book a hotel room for you. From Mid-April to mid-October, the office is open Monday to Saturday 8:30 a.m. to 7 p.m. and Sunday 10 a.m. to 12:30 p.m. and 2:30 to 5 p.m.; from mid-October to mid-April, hours are Mon-day to Saturday 9 a.m. to 12:30 p.m. and 1:30 to 6 p.m., and Sunday 10 a.m. to 1 p.m.

It's easy to walk from one end of central Tours to the other, and most of the good hotels are about a 10-minute walk from the train station. For taxi service, call **Allo Taxi** at ☎ **02-47-20-30-40.** There are several car rental offices in or near the train station, including **Avis** (inside the station; ☎ **02-47-20-53-27**), open daily 8 a.m. to noon and 1:15 to 7:00 p.m., and **Hertz** (57 rue Marcel-Tribut; ☎ **02-47-75-50-00**), open daily 8 a.m. to noon and 2 to 7 p.m. You can rent a bike at **Vélomania** (109 rue Colbert; ☎ **02-47-05-10-11**) for 95F ($14) per day. The shop is open Monday 3:30 to 7:30 p.m., Tuesday to Friday 10:30 a.m. to 1:30 p.m. and 2:30 to 7:30 p.m., and Saturday and Sunday 10:30 a.m. to 7:30 p.m.

Tours

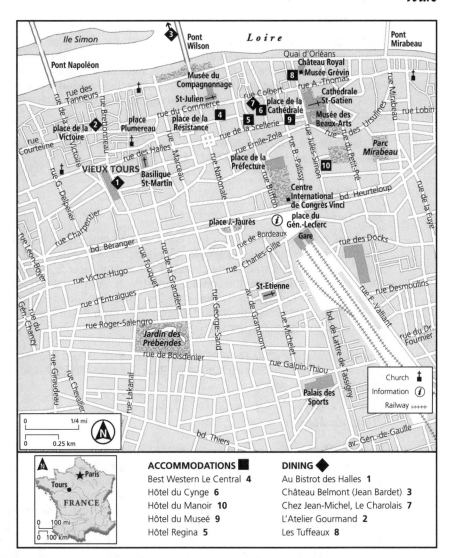

Church ✝
Information ⓘ
Railway ⊦⊦⊦⊦

ACCOMMODATIONS ■
Best Western Le Central **4**
Hôtel du Cynge **6**
Hôtel du Manoir **10**
Hôtel du Museé **9**
Hôtel Regina **5**

DINING ◆
Au Bistrot des Halles **1**
Château Belmont (Jean Bardet) **3**
Chez Jean-Michel, Le Charolais **7**
L'Atelier Gourmand **2**
Les Tuffeaux **8**

Where to Stay

If you want to experience life on a seventeenth-century country estate, think about staying and/or dining at the three-star **Château de Beaulieu** (67 rue de Beaulieu; ☎ **02-47-53-20-26**; Fax: 02-47-53-84-20) in Joue-les-Tours, 7.2 km (4½ miles) southwest of Tours. Another upscale restaurant/ hotel choice is the **Château Belmont** (see "Where to Dine" later in this chapter).

Best Western Le Central

$$$ Tours

Although it occupies an early-1900s building, the Best Western is fully modern — the interior was gutted and refurbished within the last few years. This full-service hotel has 40 rooms, decorated with tasteful reproductions and offering loads of amenities, as well as a good location near the center of town. In good weather, breakfast is served in the extensive gardens.

21 rue Berthelot. ☎ *02-47-05-46-44. Fax: 02-47-66-10-26. Rack rates: 340–680F ($49–$97) double. Breakfast: 55F ($8). AE, DC, MC, V.*

Hôtel du Cynge

$$ Tours

You pass through a mosaic-floored courtyard to enter the Cynge, an 18-room four-floor hotel (no elevator) well run by Christian and Nicole Langlois. This hotel, one of the oldest in Tours, is located in a handsome eighteenth-century building on a quiet side street near the center of town. While all the rooms are decorated in a simple contemporary style, the rooms on the lower floors are much larger than those above, which are considerably less expensive.

6 rue du Cygne. Tel 02-47-66-66-41. Fax: 02-47-66-05-13. E-mail: hotelcynge. tours@wanadoo.fr. *Parking: 30F ($4.30). Rack rates: 260-380F ($37–$54) double. Breakfast: 35F ($5). MC, V.*

Hôtel du Manoir

$$ Tours

This 20-room hotel is in a residential neighborhood a couple of blocks from the train station, but you may prefer to be a little closer to the center of town. Although the exterior is an attractive nineteenth-century town house that you enter through a beautiful courtyard, the interior is somewhat dowdy. Most of the generic small rooms come with small French balconies; rooms facing the street get lots of sunlight but can be noisy. The Manoir is run by the same management as the Hôtel du Musée (see later in this section), a more historically interesting property.

2 rue Traversière. ☎ *02-47-05-37-37. Fax: 02-47-05-16-00. Rack rates: 290F ($41) double. Breakfast: 30F ($4.30). MC, V.*

Hôtel du Musée

$$ Tours

This 22-room hotel offers a lot of old-world style, from the gracious welcome to the high-ceilinged rooms decorated with antiques. The Musée gets my vote for the most charming medium-priced hotel in Tours, with its winding stone staircase and tapestried walls. Though it's a good ten-minute walk from the train station, the hotel is close to the cathedral and museums, as well as the medieval section of town.

2 place François-Sicard. ☎ *02-47-66-63-81. Fax: 02-47-20-10-42. Rack rates: 240–270F ($34–$39) double. Breakfast: 25F ($3.60). MC, V.*

Hôtel Regina

$ Tours

Annie and Gérard Lachaize run the best budget hotel in Tours, and it's close to the center of town, between rue Colbert and rue de la Scellerie, near antiques shops, restaurants, and museums. The 20 rooms, which vary in size, are simple and homey — not to say homely — but clean and often quite sunny. Some rooms have showers and toilets, but most require you to use the bathrooms in the halls. The management is particularly friendly and accommodating.

2 rue Pimbert. ☎ *02-47-05-25-36. Fax: 02-47-66-08-72. Rack rates: 140–205F ($20–$29) double. Breakfast: 26F ($3.70). MC, V.*

Where to Dine

Au Bistrot des Halles

$$ Tours FRENCH

Bring the family to this informal brasserie for authentic old-style cuisine like *grand-mère* used to make. The decor is classic bistro, with an early-1900s zinc bar and lively wall murals. The reasonable prices and informal yet colorful atmosphere make this a good kid-friendly option. You'll find all of the region's specialties here, prepared with skill and flair, so be adventurous.

31 place Gaston-Pailhou. ☎ *02-47-26-07-23. Reservations recommended. Meals: Main courses 90–140F ($13–$20); menus 95F ($14) and 150F ($21). MC, V. Open: Daily noon to 2 p.m. and 7:30–11 p.m. Closed Sun and Thurs nights in low season.*

Château Belmont (Jean Bardet)

$$$ Tours FRENCH

Occupying an elegant Napoléon III mansion outside the town center in a parklike setting, this Michelin-lauded restaurant serves the cuisine of chef Jean Bardet. The grand home also serves as a select hotel (750 to 1,500F/$107 to $214 double). Because Bardet is one of France's most famous chefs, his varying Michelin stars are closely watched and analyzed; critics can't find much to fault here besides the stuffy service endemic to fancy French restaurants. Bardet's dramatic menus feature liberal doses of foie gras and truffles, as well as vegetables and herbs from his own gardens. One favorite of his is a lobster dish prepared with Vouvray wine and spiced fresh ginger.

57 rue Grolson. ☎ *02-47-41-41-11. E-mail:* sophie@jeanbardet.com. *Reservations required far in advance. Meals: Main courses 210–380F ($30–$54); menus 250–750F ($36–$107). AE, DC, MC, V. Open: Daily noon to 2 p.m. and 7:30–9:30 p.m. Closed Sun nights and Mon all day Jan–Apr and Nov–Dec; closed Mon lunch Apr–Nov.*

Chez Jean-Michel, Le Charolais

$$ Tours   FRENCH

This restaurant in the antiques quarter specializes in matching local cuisine, like *coq au vin* and *matelote d'anguille* (stewed eel), with fine Loire Valley wines (the owner is a former sommelier, so he knows his vintages). This is one of those small, well-priced restaurants where you may end up having one of your trip's most memorable meals; the management is clearly keeping an eye on the details while turning out sophisticated fare.

123 rue Colbert. ☎ *02-47-20-80-20. Reservations recommended. Meals: Main courses 95–165F ($14–$24); menus 75F ($11) at lunch, 180F ($26) at dinner. MC, V. Open: Tues–Sat noon to 2 p.m. and 7:30–10:30 p.m.*

L'Atelier Gourmand

$$ Tours   FRENCH

You may have trouble getting a seat at this popular spot near hopping place Plumereau; this is a well-run restaurant offering creative gourmet cuisine at reasonable prices. You can't go wrong sticking with the fixed-price menus offering Loire Valley classics like *rillettes* (pork) or *andouille* sausage dishes as a first course and fresh salmon from the Loire as a main course. In good weather, try for a seat on the terrace.

37 rue Etienne-Marcel. ☎ *02-47-38-59-87. Reservations recommended. Meals: Main courses 60–120F ($9–$17); menus 97F ($14) and 130F ($19). MC, V. Open: Daily noon to 2 p.m. and 7:30–9:30 p.m.*

Les Tuffeaux

$$ Tours   FRENCH

This small restaurant, a couple of blocks north of the cathedral, offers some intriguing gourmet choices, as well as a romantic dining room, with Oriental rugs on the tiled floors, lace curtains, beamed ceilings, and stone walls. Chef/owner Gildas Marsollier has created extensive menus offering good value with lots of little extras, like a little plate of sweets in addition to dessert. Popular dishes are the diced artichoke and green beans with red mullet, the sautéed crayfish in sweet peppers, and the duckling fillet with tomato purée and savory tiny beans.

19 rue Lavoisier. ☎ *02-47-47-19-89. Meals: Main courses 80–140F ($11–$20); menus 150F ($21), 210F ($30), and 250F ($36). MC, V. Open: Daily noon to 2 p.m. and 7:30–9:30 p.m. Closed Sun and Mon lunch.*

Exploring Tours

You may notice right away that Tours is a college town, with a hip young populace strolling the avenues and hanging out in cafes and bars with names like Mr. Cool, Route 66 Café, and Le Fly.

For a short walking tour of the town, begin in front of the cathedral (see the entry later in this section). Continue north on rue Lavoisier and make a left on rue Colbert, where you'll pass old cafes and shops, as well as fifteenth- and sixteenth-century houses. A couple of blocks up on your right is the passageway **Coeur Navre,** which was used to lead the condemned to the place of public execution. Fans of antiquarian books and antiques will enjoy **rue de la Scellerie,** a block south of rue Colbert; this antiques quarter is also home to the Grand Théâtre, built in 1869. Continue west on rue de la Scellerie to wide **rue Nationale,** a main boulevard containing every shop you could want, including major department stores like La Samaritaine and Au Printemps. Turn left on rue Nationale and walk south. In one block, rue Nationale becomes a pedestrian-only street with boutiques and outdoor cafes. In a few more short blocks, you'll reach the base of rue Nationale and the heart of town, **place Jean-Jaurès,** where you can see the imposing nineteenth-century facades of the law courts and town hall. Retrace your steps back up rue Nationale to rue du Commerce and take a left. In several blocks, you'll reach the restored medieval district, **place Plumereau,** called "place Plume" by locals. This area features cobblestone pedestrian streets surrounded by half-timbered buildings. You can find a host of fine boutiques and small shops on **rue du Grand-Marché,** just south of "place Plume." Rue du Grand-Marché leads to **place de la Victoire,** the location of an antiques/flea market.

More than 30 markets are held in Tours. Here are the most animated: The **gourmet market** is held the first Friday of every month 4 to 10 p.m. at place de la Résistance; the **flower market** takes place Wednesday and Saturday 8 a.m. to 6 p.m. on boulevard Béranger; the **antiques/flea market** is held on Wednesday and Saturday 7 a.m. to 5 p.m. at place de la Victoire; and the **craft market** takes place on Saturday 9 a.m. to 6 p.m. at place des Halles. **Traditional food markets** take place Tuesday to Sunday mornings at different spots in the city; ask the tourist office for details. The covered market, **Les Halles et Grand Marché,** with a huge selection of fresh meat, cheese, and produce from the region, is held at place Gaston-Pailhou Monday to Saturday 6 a.m. to 7 p.m. and Sunday 6 a.m. to 1 p.m.

In this section, I list the best sights, but there are half a dozen other attractions in Tours. If you're interested in seeing everything, you'll find it cost-effective to stop at the tourist office to buy the 50F ($7) **Carte Multi-visites**, which will get you into seven sights (Musée des Beaux-Arts, Musée St-Martin, Musée du Compagnonnage, Musée Grévin, Musée d'Histoire Naturelle, Musée des Vins de Touraine, and Centre de Création Contemporaine) and a guided city tour. Call ☎ 02-47-70-37-37 for details.

Tours runs a **tourist train** that leaves from in front of the cathedral, on the hour, about six times daily; the 40-minute trip costs 30F ($4.30) for adults and 15F ($2.15) for children under 11. In addition, the tourist office offers special themed, two-hour **guided pedestrian tours.** Contact the office for details. In July and August, you can take a **horse-and-buggy tour** through the ancient city center. For details, contact **Touraine en Roulotte** at ☎ 02-47-55-04-06.

The top sights

Musée des Beaux-Arts

Tours

Next to the Cathédrale St-Gatien, the Museum of Fine Arts is housed in a beautiful gated mansion (the former Palais des Archevêques), with colorful formal gardens. Inside, you can find eighteenth- and nineteenth-century paintings depicting the Loire Valley region, as well as a good selection of sixteenth- and seventeenth-century Dutch and French pictures. You won't want to miss the seventeenth-century painted **wood chimney** and the circa-1600 iron-and-bronze **alarm clock.** The third floor offers modern art, including a **Calder mobile.** The ground floor has a medieval collection and, behind glass, two paintings by Mantegna (*Christ in the Garden of Olives* and *Resurrection*), as well as an unattributed *Flight to Egypt* thought to be painted by Rembrandt.

18 place François-Sicard. ☎ 02-47-05-68-73. Admission: 30F ($4.30) adults, 15F ($2.15) students and seniors, free for children under 13. Open: Wed–Mon 9 a.m.– 12:45 p.m. and 2–6 p.m. Closed Jan 1, May 1, July 14, Nov 1 and 11, and Dec 25.

Cathédrale St-Gatien

Tours

Soaring up to a clerestory and three rose windows, this Flamboyant Gothic cathedral took 300 years to construct, beginning in 1236. Before entering the cathedral, take note of the gorgeous **stained-glass windows,** which have been compared to those of Paris's Sainte-Chapelle (see Chapter 12). An explanation of the images represented on the windows is given in several languages, including English; this explanation can be found on the right as you enter. A sculpted **tomb** containing the children of Charles VIII and Anne de Bretagne (Anne of Brittany) is in the chapel, and in the church's northeast corner is a remarkable **spiral staircase** similar to one at the Château de Blois (see Chapter 15). Don't miss the **cloisters,** built from 1442 to 1524, which you can visit with or without a guide. During August and September, free classical music concerts are performed on Sundays at 5 p.m.

Place de la Cathédrale. ☎ *02-47-70-21-00. Admission: Free. Open: Daily 9 a.m.–6 p.m.*

Musée Grévin

Tours

Waxworks museums are always a little corny, but you and the kids will like this one: It's an entertaining introduction to the history of France and the region, tracing events from A.D. 371 to the present in 31 elaborate tableaux. The museum is housed in the Château Royal, built on a Gallo-Roman site; it was the home of the comtes d'Anjou in the eleventh century, and a royal residence from the thirteenth to the fifteenth century. The castle has seen a couple of grand royal marriages (Charles VII married Marie d'Anjou in 1413 and Louis XI married Margaret of Scotland in 1436) and also welcomed Joan of Arc, who stopped here on her way back from her victory in Orléans. In fact, one tableau shows Joan looking stylish in a chain-mail miniskirt, selecting her armor in Tours in 1429. And there's François I with an elderly Leonardo da Vinci in 1516 showing the king the *Mona Lisa* at Amboise. And could that be Henri III dressed in drag at a sixteenth-century ball? Of course, not all history is pretty. You may want to steer young kids away from the tableaux depicting hangings (1560, the duc de Guise suppressing a Huguenot plot) and torture (1634, the evil Cardinal Richelieu looking for a confession).

25 av. André-Malraux (in the Château Royal). ☎ *02-47-61-02-95. Admission: 35F ($5) adults, 20F ($2.85) ages 7–16. Open: Mid-Mar to mid-June and Sept–Oct daily 9 a.m to noon and 2–6 p.m.; late June–Aug daily 9 a.m.–6:30 p.m.; Nov to early Mar daily 2–5:30 p.m. No admittance 45 minutes before closing. Closed Dec 25 and Jan 1.*

Other cool things to see

In case the top sights aren't enough, here are some more things to see in Tours:

- ✔ While wandering up rue Nationale toward the river, you can stop in at the **Musée des Vins de Touraine,** housed in the vaulted cellar storerooms of the twelfth-century Abbaye St-Julien at 16 rue Nationale (☎ 02-47-61-07-93). Interesting displays are grouped by themes like mythology, archaeology, religion, social rites, brotherhoods, and wine-making occupations. The museum is open Wednesday to Monday 9 a.m. to noon and 2 to 6 p.m., and admission is 15F ($2.15) for adults and 10F ($1.40) for students and seniors.

✔ Also in the St-Julien Abbey, you can find the **Musée du Compagnonnage,** highlighting local artisans' guild associations (☎ 02-47-61-07-93). The museum, which displays documents, paintings, tools, and masterpieces of stone and carpentry, is devoted to the journeymen who travel France after trade apprenticeships. Mid-September to mid-June, the museum is open Wednesday to Monday 9 a.m. to noon and 2 to 6 p.m.; late June to early September, hours are daily 9 a.m. to 12:30 p.m. and 2 to 6 p.m. Admission is 25F ($3.60) for adults and 15F ($2.15) for students and seniors.

✔ Next door to the Musée Grévin, in the same building, is the **Aquarium Tropical** (☎ 02-47-64-29-52), whose 35 tanks house 200 species of fish (some quite rare) from all over the world. It's open daily: July and August 9 a.m. to 7 p.m., mid-March to June and September to mid-November 9:30 a.m. to noon and 2 to 6 p.m., and late November to early March 2 to 6 p.m. Admission is 30F ($4.30) for adults, 22F ($3.15) for students and seniors, and 18F (2.60) for children under 12.

✔ You can't help but notice the beautiful Renaissance residence that houses the **Musée Archeologique de l'Hôtel Gouin** (25 rue du Commerce; ☎ 02-47-66-22-32). Inside are archaeological displays of every period of Tours history, from prehistoric and Gallo-Roman times through the medieval and Renaissance periods to the eighteenth century. The museum is open daily: mid-March to June and September 10 a.m. to 12:30 p.m. and 2 to 6:30 p.m., July and August 10 a.m. to 7 p.m., and October to early March 10 a.m. to 12:30 p.m. and 2 to 5:30 p.m. Admission is 20F ($2.85) for adults and 10F ($1.40) for students and children.

And on your left, the Château de Chambord: Guided bus tours of the region

For 100 to 185F ($14 to $26), **Touraine Evasion** (☎ 06-07-39-13-31; Internet: www.tourevasion.com) offers trips by air-conditioned minibus to half a dozen of the nearby châteaux, including Azay-le-Rideau, Chenonceau, Amboise, and Chambord. You can also rent the minibus and chauffeur and design your own route. The trips, available by reservation, depart from near the Tours tourist office or from your hotel.

Nightlife

Just follow the crowds to **"place Plume,"** where there are densely packed cafes and bars, frequented especially by students. In summer, everyone sits outdoors in the square and then hits the post-11 p.m. club scene. The best of the clubs is the cover-free **Le Louis XIV** (37 rue Briçonnet; ☎ 02-47-05-77-17), for cocktails and karaoke. In the same building is **Le Duke Ellington** (for jazz) and **Le Pharaon** (for rock). **L'Excaliber** (35 rue Briçonnet; ☎ 02-47-64-76-78) may have the best disco scene (cover 70F/$10), but **Le Trois Orfevres** (6 rue des Orfevres; ☎ 02-47-64-02-73) is the place to go for live music (cover 50F/$7). Other fun clubs are **Le Florida,** a no-cover disco at 2 rue Gay-Lussac (☎ 02-47-20-65-52), and **Le Petit Faucheau,** a jazz club at 23 rue des Cerisiers (☎ 02-47-38-67-62), with a 100F ($14) cover. Irish pub fans can head to **Buck Mulligans** (37 rue du Grand-Marché; ☎ 02-47-39-61-69), which has no cover.

Fast Facts

Country Code and City Code

The **country code** for France is **33**. The **city code** for towns in the Loire Valley region is usually **02**. To call from the United States, dial 011-33 plus the final nine digits of the number (dropping the initial zero). From within France, you dial all ten digits of the number.

Currency Exchange

Tours has money-changing facilities in the train station, as well as at several nearby banks. For the best rate, go to major banks like Bank of France or Crédit Lyonnais.

Emergencies

For **police,** call ☎ **17**; for the **fire department,** call ☎ **18**.

Hospitals

The **Hôpital Bretonneau** (2 bd. Tonnele; ☎ 02-47-47-47-47) is just north of place de la Cathédrale.

Information

See "Getting Information and Getting Around" earlier in this chapter.

Internet Access

To check on or send e-mail messages, head to **L'☎ier du Web** (55 rue Nationale; ☎ 02- 47-20-64-40), which charges 15F ($2.15) per hour and is open Tuesday to Saturday 9:15 a.m. to 10 p.m. and Monday 2 to 10 p.m., or **Le Cybespace Espace Internet** (27 rue Lavoisier; ☎ 02-47-20-89-69), which charges 1F (15¢) per minute and is open Monday to Thursday 9 a.m. to 7 p.m. and Saturday 9 a.m. to 12:30 p.m. and 1:30 to 7 p.m. Neither serves food. If you want a Web pub, check out **Le Paradis Vert** (9 rue Michelet; ☎ 02-47-64-78-50), which has billiard tables in addition to computers and a full bar. It's open daily 10 a.m. to 2 a.m., and e-mail costs 1F (15¢) per minute.

Pharmacies

There are several pharmacies on rue Nationale near place Jean-Juarès; look for the green neon cross.

Post Office

The **main post office** is at 1 bd. Beranger (☎ 02-47-60-34-20).

Chapter 15

The Best of the Loire Valley Châteaux

• •

In This Chapter

▶ Exploring the châteaux

▶ Learning about kings, queens, and mistresses

▶ Discovering medieval villages

• •

*J*ust a couple of hours southwest of Paris lies the **Loire Valley,** a region famous for its crisp wines, pastoral countryside, and glorious castles. Besides Paris, the area offers the most historic sites, in the closest proximity to one another, in the whole of France. Among the countless châteaux in the Loire Valley are about 20 that are worthy of a visit; for this chapter, I've chosen the 7 châteaux that are the most beautiful and interesting. Die-hard French history buffs can certainly visit more — or even all of them (for additional choices, see the sidebar "Other Loire Valley favorites" later in this chapter). For most people, four places will be sufficient before châteauxphobia (extreme fear of turrets and audioguides) kicks in.

Because the châteaux locations are so concentrated (about a dozen within a 96.6 km/60-mile radius), you can easily visit four of them in a two-day trip. In high season, you may see plenty of bus-tour groups doing just that. The short distances also mean that biking enthusiasts can have fun pedaling from one town to the next. If you have the time, you may want to visit one château per day for three days, giving yourself the leisure to explore the towns and surrounding countryside, too.

If you have time for just one château, you may want to choose **Chenonceau** (the most beautiful) or **Chambord** (the largest).

The cities of **Tours** (see Chapter 14) and **Orléans** (see the end of this chapter), 112.7 km (70 miles) apart, serve as convenient boundaries to the district — to the west and east, respectively — and you'll enjoy spending a night in either of these lively centers.

What's Where?: The Loire Valley and its Major Attractions

The Loire region is the "Valley of Kings," where a thousand years of French monarchs feasted and entertained, seduced and betrayed, and schemed and plotted. Major events of French history have occurred at these sites, from marriages to births to infidelities to murders. Each castle has a juicy story to tell, and all are set up with tours (guided or self-guided with audioguides) so that you can get the most from the experience.

Southwest of Tours are the castles of **Azay-le-Rideau** (20.1 km/13 miles from Tours), **Chinon** (48.3 km/30 miles from Tours), and **Ussé** (33.8 km/21 miles from Tours). Between Tours and Orléans are the castles of **Chenonceau** (25.7 km/16 miles from Tours, 86.9 km/54 miles from Orléans), **Amboise** (35.4 km/22 miles from Tours, 77.2 km/48 miles from Orléans), **Chaumont** (40.2 km/25 miles from Tours, 72.4 km/45 miles from Orléans), **Blois** (59.5 km/37 miles from Tours, 53.1 km/33 miles from Orléans), and **Chambord** (77.2 km/48 miles from Tours, 17.7 km/11 miles from Orléans).

Although you can get to almost all the châteaux by public transportation (with the exception of Ussé), the most efficient way to explore the region is by rental car. That way you can give a smaller sight a quick once over in a couple of hours, and spend half a day or longer exploring some of the more interesting towns and châteaux. If you want to drive from Paris, see Chapter 11 about where to rent a car; if you want to drive from Tours, see the rental information in Chapter 14. If you want to set out from Orléans, see the rental information at the end of this chapter.

The Loire Valley is crossed by half a dozen rivers, and the castles sit beside them, between them, high above them, and (in the case of Chenonceau) over them. The countryside is picturesque, with tiny medieval villages and small towns connected by uncrowded country roads. Although the castles are undoubtedly the stars of these towns, some towns (like Amboise and Blois) are larger and provide other diversions, and some (like Chenonceaux and Chambord) are tiny, without much to offer. The region is famous for its wines, and most restaurants have a good selection of local vintages on hand.

The Loire Valley

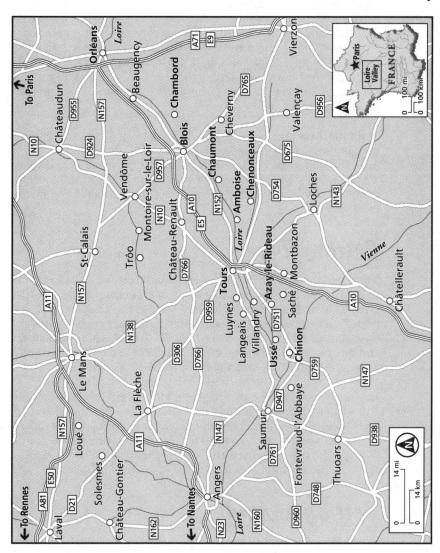

Azay-le-Rideau: A Renaissance Masterpiece

The only attraction in the pretty little village of **Azay-le-Rideau** (with houses from the tenth century onward) is the castle, and it's one of the Loire Valley's most beautiful, nestled between two branches of a sleepy river. The château presents a good sound-and-light show in summer. It'll take you about an hour to explore the village — a brochure, in

French, with a map showing the route of a **self-guided walking tour** is available from the **tourist office** (place de l'Europe; ☎ **02-47-45-44-40**; E-mail: otsi.Azay-le-Rideau@wanadoo.fr). The tour will lead you past half-timbered medieval houses, an eleventh-century church, and an ivy-covered mill along the slow-moving Indre River. March to October, the office is open daily 9:30 a.m. to 1 p.m. and 3 to 7 p.m.; November to February, the hours are Tuesday to Saturday 2 to 6 p.m. Because Azay is only about 20.9 km (13 miles) from both Tours and Chinon, many people bike to this site.

Night markets take place in Azay-le-Rideau 5 p.m. to midnight on certain days in July and August (dates for 2001 are June 24, July 20, August 3, and August 31). Vendors of food, crafts, and wine display their wares on the streets in the medieval section of town, and tourists mingle with villagers as they sample regional products and taste local wines.

Getting there

If you're **driving** from Tours, take D759 southwest, 20.9 km (13 miles) to Azay-le-Rideau. You can take a **bus** or **train** from Tours or Chinon (see "Chinon: Three Castles in One" later in this chapter). The train from Tours (three per day) takes 30 minutes and costs 28F ($4); the bus takes 45 minutes and costs 47F ($7). From Chinon to Azay, the train and bus both take 20 minutes and cost 25F ($3.60). For train and bus schedules, call ☎ **08-36-35-35-35** or 08-36-35-35-39 in English.

Azay-le-Rideau is 260.7 km (162 miles) from Paris, and the drive takes 3 to 4 hours. If driving from Paris, take A10 to Tours and then D759 to Azay-le-Rideau. You can take an express train from Paris to either Tours or Chinon and change to a local train or bus that travels to Azay-le-Rideau. The trip from Paris to Chinon (changing trains in Tours) takes about 2½ hours and costs 230F ($33) or 392F ($56).

Getting around

Everything you want to see in Azay-le-Rideau is within walking distance of the center. The **bus** stop is across from the tourist office, which is next-door to the town's most historic hotel. Several other hotels, as well as restaurants, are within a few blocks. The castle is a three-minute stroll from the tourist office.

Be forewarned that the Azay **train station** (☎ **02-47-45-37-93**) is a 25-minute walk (2.5 km/1.6 miles) from the center of town (there's no taxi stand). The local taxi service is **Taxi Gailloux** (☎ **06-11-29-69-69**). Head to **Le Provost** (13 rue Carnot; ☎ **02-47-45-40-94**) for information about bike rentals, which cost 50F ($7) for half a day and 60F ($9) for a full day. July and August, it's open daily 9:30 a.m. to noon and 2:30 to 7 p.m.; September to June, hours are Tuesday to Saturday 8:30 a.m. to noon and 2:30 to 7 p.m.

Where to stay

Best Western Hôtel Le Val de Loire

$$ Azay-le-Rideau

This is the town's most modern hotel — although it's short on charm, it offers all manner of amenities (like hairdryers, safes, and minibars) in the 27 generic but comfortable rooms. An elevator will help you get to the higher floors. The hotel is on the main road into town and only a few minutes' walk from the castle, so rooms in the front are noisy. English is spoken here.

5–52 rue Nationale. ☎ *02-47-45-28-29. Fax: 02-47-45-91-19. Internet:* www.bestwestern.com/fr/hotelvaldeloire. *E-mail:* hvl@wanadoo.fr. *Parking: free. Rack rates: 280–385F ($40–$55) double. Breakfast: 42F ($6). Closed Dec. AE, DC, MC, V.*

Hôtel de Biencourt

$ Azay-le-Rideau

An inexpensive option in the old part of town close to the castle, the Biencourt features 17 simple rooms that will suit budget travelers. Innkeeper Isabelle Marioton's eighteenth-century hotel is on a semi-pedestrian street in the medieval section of town, so it's very quiet.

7 rue Balzac. ☎ *02-47-45-20-75. Fax: 02-47-45-91-73. Rack rates: 210–370F ($30–$53) double. Breakfast: 38F ($5). Closed late Nov to Feb. MC, V.*

Le Grand Monarque

$$ Azay-le-Rideau

Although this is the town's most historic and best located hotel (next to the tourist office and across from the bus stop, with the castle a three-minute walk away), the rooms and the greeting are somewhat somber, and the building doesn't have an elevator. The 23 rooms and 2 suites are fairly spacious, done in navy, burgundy, and fleur-de-lis patterns; the modern baths include hairdryers. The annex rooms out back are very quiet, while the front rooms are on the main road. The inn's good restaurant, with the same name as the hotel, serves creatively prepared local fare (see "Where to dine").

3 place de la République. ☎ *02-47-45-40-08. Fax: 02-47-45-40-08. Internet:* www.legrandmonarque.com. *E-mail:*monarq@club-internet.fr. *Parking: 45F ($6). Rack rates: 370–520F ($53–$74) double; 650–875F ($93–$125) suite. Breakfast: 50F ($7). Closed Dec 15–Jan 31. MC, V.*

If you're looking for ultra-upscale country living, reserve a room at the **Château d'Artigny,** along D17 (☎ **02-47-34-30-30;** Fax: 02-47-34-30-39; E-mail: artigny@wanadoo.fr), near Azay-le-Rideau in the hamlet of Montbazon. The castle was built in the early 1900s for perfume/cosmetic king François Coty and now offers 53 gorgeous rooms and serves superb food.

Where to dine

L'Aigle d'Or

$$$ Azay-le-Rideau   TOURAINE

Ghislaine and Jean-Luc Fevre operate L'Aigle d'Or, the best restaurant in town, serving traditional gourmet cuisine with fish dishes as a specialty. The pretty dining room on the village's main street is decorated with antiques, and in summer, dining is available in the garden. Favorite dishes include the house foie gras and lobster preparations. Expect formal service with lots of courses — they do-it-up here.

10 av. Adelaide-Riche. ☎ *02-47-45-24-58. Meals: Main courses 95–130F ($14–$19); menus 105F ($15) at lunch; 155F ($22), 220F ($31), and 350F ($50) at dinner, includes a glass of wine with each course; children's menu 55F ($8). V. Open: Thurs–Tues noon to 2 p.m. and 7:30–9:30 p.m. Closed Sun nights year-round and Tues nights in low season.*

Le Grand Monarque

$$$ Azay-le-Rideau   TOURAINE

This hotel restaurant features the accomplished cuisine of Frédéric Arnault, who caters his menus to the best seasonal products. The restaurant has two dining rooms; the nicer one with a stone hearth is on the left as you enter the building. Summer dining is available in a large courtyard. Your meal may begin with a caviar *amuse bouche* (pre-appetizer), and then move on to *marbre d'aile de raie aux pommes vertes* (a ray prepared with green apples) and the grilled fish called *filet de dorade royale.* The food is flavorful but not heavy, and the desserts are exceptional.

3 place de la République (in the hotel). ☎ *02-47-45-40-08. Reservations required. Meals: Main courses 102–175F ($15–$25); menus 155F ($22), 225F ($32), and 285F ($41); children's menu 69F ($10). MC, V. Open: Daily noon to 2 p.m. and 7:30–10 p.m.*

Seeing the castle

Nestled on an island between two branches of the slow-moving Indre River, the picturesque **Château d'Azay-le-Rideau,** located in the center of town, a few blocks from the tourist office (☎ 02-47-45-42-04), is a Renaissance masterpiece. Unlike some of the other châteaux, Azay was built and occupied by nobles rather than royalty, so it's less a fortress than a grand home. The castle was begun around 1515 by Gilles Berthelot, François I's finance minister, in part to display his social ascension. When Berthelot eventually fell out of favor, François seized the castle but allowed it to remain empty. In the late eighteenth century, Charles de Biencourt, a liberal-minded aristocrat, bought the property and restored it to its former glory. At the beginning of the twentieth century, the French government bought the property from an impoverished marquis, the last of the Biencourts. Before entering, circle the château to admire its perfect proportions. Highlights are the **Grand Staircase** and the Biencourt **drawing room,** decorated in nineteenth-century style. Among many interesting artworks, the castle contains a copy of the painting **Bathing Lady**, a semi-nude portrait believed to be of Diane du Poitiers, the mistress of Henri II.

A leisurely visit to the castle and grounds will take you about 1½ hours. There are no tours in English, but there are audioguides (25F/$3.60) and free brochures in English. Admission is 35F ($5) for adults and 23F ($3.30) for young people 18 to 25; free for children under 18. The castle is open daily (except January 1 and December 25): April, May, June, and September 9:30 a.m. to 6 p.m.; July and August 9:30 a.m. to 7 p.m.; October 9:30 a.m. to 5:30 p.m.; and November to March 9:30 a.m. to 12:30 p.m. and 2 to 5:30 p.m. The last entrance is 45 minutes before closing.

Nightly, from May to September, the castle presents **Les Imaginaires**, a sound-and-light show. The event begins with a promenade from a park in the medieval section of the village, near the château. You stroll at your own pace through the village and to the château, where the light show and piped-in music lasts from 10:30 p.m. to 12:30 a.m. in May, June, and July; 10 p.m. to 12:30 a.m. in August; and 9:30 p.m. to midnight in September. Tickets to the event cost 60F ($9) for adults and 35F ($5) for young people 12 to 25; children under 12 are free. Tickets for the castle and the nighttime performance cost 80F ($11) for adults and 50F ($7) for young people 18 to 25; free for children under 18.

Chinon: Three Castles in One

The small town of **Chinon** is home to one of the oldest châteaux in France and also boasts a good number of medium-priced hotels and restaurants, as well as a restored medieval quarter. A number of interesting sights are within biking distance of the town (like the Château d'Ussé), so this is a good place to base yourself. Chinon's château, perched on a bluff high above the town, is actually the ruins of three fortresses. Although the château is mainly ruins, there's plenty to see, so you should allow a couple of hours to explore the site.

You can best appreciate the beauty of Chinon by viewing it from across the river Vienne, where you can see how the castle ruins rise above the town. Another great view is from high up on the castle ramparts, where you can look out over the town rooftops (all pointed spires like in a fairy-tale village) and just beyond the town to the acres of vineyards where workers harvest grapes for the famous red Chinon wine (you can try this wine at any of the area cafes or vineyards).

Chinon's medieval quarter contains cobblestone streets and well-restored half-timbered buildings. If you wander around, you may happen on **rue de la Lamproie** and the sixteenth-century house where Chinon's most famous son, humanist writer François Rabelais, was raised. On **rue Voltaire,** a sign explains that Joan of Arc arrived in Chinon on March 6, 1429. Joan wowed the royal entourage at Chinon and proved her mettle when she was able to pick the dauphin, Charles VII, out of a crowd at the castle. Her correct choice was considered a miracle and led Charles to support her in her military quest. Joan is honored in town by various plaques, a small museum (on the castle grounds), and a waxworks representation of that famous moment in history. The **tourist office** is at 11 rue Voltaire (☎ 02-47-93-17-85; Internet: www.chinon.com). May to September, it's open daily 10 a.m. to 7 p.m.; October to April, hours are Monday to Saturday 10 a.m. to noon and 2 to 6 p.m. You can find the usual brochures, and the helpful staff will help you map out your bike route or direct you to the best restaurants.

Getting there

Because Chinon's train station handles only slow local trains, the fastest way to get to Chinon from Paris is to take the speedy TGV (6 to 11 times daily from Paris's Gare Montparnasse) to Tours and then take a bus from the Tours train station to Chinon. With a 20-minute layover in Tours, the trip will take 2½ hours and cost (including the train and bus) 237 to 404F ($34 to $58). If you want to take a train directly from Paris to Chinon, without changing to a bus in Tours, the trip on a slow train leaving from Paris's Gare d'Austerlitz will take four hours and cost 181 to 258F ($26 to $37). **Trains** and **buses** arrive frequently from Tours, a one-hour trip costing 48 to 75F ($7 to $11). For information and reservations, call ☎ 08-36-35-35-35. The train station and the first bus stop are a half-mile walk from town (ask the bus driver to drop you at place Jeanne d'Arc, the second bus stop, bordering the commercial district). If you're **driving** from Tours, take D759 southwest for 48.3 km (30 miles); the trip takes about 40 minutes. To drive the 283.2 km (176 miles) from Paris, which takes about 3 to 4 hours, take A10 to Tours and then D759 southwest to Chinon.

Getting around

It's easy to explore Chinon on foot, including the old section of town on the far east side. There are a number of things to see that are not far from town if you have a rented car or bike. The place to rent bikes is the **Hôtel Agnès Sorel,** located beside the river on the far east end of town (4 quai Pasteur; ☎ 02-47-93-04-37), open daily 9 a.m. to noon and

2 to 6 p.m. Bike rental is 50F ($7) for a half day and 90F ($13) for a full day. You need to remind the pleasant staff here to give you a lock and a helmet. The route out of Chinon is very steep and you may have to walk your bike for the first 15 minutes. It's about an hour bike ride (14.5 km/9 miles) to Ussé, passing several other châteaux, attractive villages, and wine-tasting opportunities.

Where to stay

Best Western Hôtel de France

$$$ Chinon

The most handsome hotel in Chinon, this Best Western is a central sixteenth-century residence that has been a hotel since the Revolution; today it offers 30 individually decorated rooms with modern amenities. Some rooms preserve the historic charm of the place, with stone walls and tapestries, and many have balconies with château views. The hotel has a wonderful inner courtyard planted with citrus trees. Au Chapeau Rouge, the hotel's restaurant with outdoor and indoor seating, is recommended under "Where to dine." English is spoken here.

47–49 place du Général-de-Gaulle. ☎ *02-47-93-33-91. Fax: 02-47-98-37-03. Internet:* www.bestwestern.fr. *E-mail:* elmachinon@aol.com. *Rack rates: 370–550F ($53@$79) double. Breakfast: 50F ($7). Closed mid- to late Nov and mid-Feb to early Mar. AE, DC, MC, V.*

Chris' Hôtel

$$ Chinon

This 33-room hotel is a budget option (no elevator) on place Jeanne d'Arc, where the bus lets you off on the edge of the town's commercial district. (The square is also the site of a large Thursday-morning market.) Some of the rooms are very small, but they're comfortable and attractive, with bold wallpaper and reproduction furniture. Breakfast is served in a separate small building behind the hotel. The staff is cheerful and English-speaking.

12–14 place Jeanne d'Arc. ☎ *02-47-93-36-92. Fax: 02-47-98-48-92. Internet:* www.chris-hotel.fr. *E-mail:* serviceinformation@chris-hotel.fr. *Parking: 25F ($3.60). Rack rates: 200–430F ($29–$61) double. Breakfast: 40F ($6). AE, DC, MC, V.*

Hostellerie Gargantua

$$$ Chinon

This special place is the best hotel in town, named after the writer Rabelais's fictional giant, and occupying the fifteenth-century Palais de Baillage. The hotel is loaded with atmosphere, and the staff will assure you a pleasant stay. The spiral stone staircase leads to eight individually decorated, large rooms with antique appointments; some have canopied beds, oriental rugs, and beamed ceilings. The hotel also has an excellent restaurant by the same name (see "Where to dine").

73 rue Voltaire. ☎ *02-47-93-04-71. Fax: 02-47-93-08-02. Internet: www. hostelleriegargantua.com. E-mail: hostelleriegargantua@ hostelleriegargantua.com. Parking: 20F ($2.85). Rack rates: 400–600F ($57–$86) double. Breakfast: 55F ($8). Closed early to mid-Jan and early to mid-Dec. MC, V.*

Hôtel Diderot

$$ Chinon

Theodore Kazamias has owned this charming 28-room inn, just off place Jeanne d'Arc, for over two decades. The hotel occupies an ivy-covered eighteenth-century home boasting comfortable rooms — some simple and small, others larger, with charming touches like antique beds. Rooms on the rue Diderot side are noisy, so ask for one facing the quiet courtyard. In the common areas, you'll find half-timbered ceilings, a winding eighteenth-century staircase, and a fifteenth-century chimney — but no elevator. Also on the grounds are a renovated building with more modern rooms, and a one-room cottage. At breakfast, you can sample Madame's famous homemade jams, like clementine and pumpkin. The staff speaks English.

4 rue Buffon. ☎ *02-47-93-18-87. Fax: 02-47-93-37-10. Free parking in courtyard. Rack rates: 260–410F ($37–$59) double. Breakfast: 40F ($6). AE, DC, MC, V.*

Where to dine

Au Chapeau Rouge

$$$ Chinon   TOURAINE

This pleasant popular restaurant, with outdoor tables in an attractive square, is in the Best Western Hôtel de France (see "Where to stay"). Inside, the formal dining area consists of several rooms separated by high arches. The cuisine is traditional, emphasizing local products, and the most requested dishes are the terrine of duck foie gras and the *dos de sandre au beurre blanc* (perch with white-butter sauce). Another favorite is the *filet mignon de veau* (veal prepared with mushrooms). For dessert, try the version of baked Alaska called *l'omelette d'origine*. Menus are available in English.

49 place du Général-de-Gaulle (in the Best Western Hôtel de France). ☎ *02-47-98-08-08. Meals: Main courses 89–198F ($13–$28); menus 135F ($19), 160F ($23), and 295F ($42) tasting menu. DC, MC, V. Open: Daily noon to 3 p.m. and 7:30–9:30 p.m. Closed Sun night and Mon lunch.*

Au Plaisir Gourmand

$$$ Chinon   TOURAINE

This is the best restaurant in Chinon, where Jean-Claude Ribollet produces his famous cuisine, which is served formally. The seventeenth-century house is located at the far east end of town, just off the busy main street, and isolated by a flower-filled courtyard. The restaurant is quite small, so you'll have to make reservations; it's also expensive, but worth every franc. The menu may include creative options like *cassolette de queues d'écrévistes tiedes à la nage* (tails of crayfish casserole) and *aiguilettes de canard au miel et poivre rose* (slices of duck with honey and red pepper), or simple items cooked to perfection, like *sandre au beurre blanc* (pickerel fish with white-butter sauce). For dessert, try the pear with cassis and almond ice cream.

Quai Charles VII. ☎ 02-47-93-20-48. Reservations required far in advance. Meals: Main courses 95–195F ($14–$28); menus 180F ($26), 250F ($36), and 360F ($51) tasting menu. AE, V. Open: Tues–Sun noon to 2 p.m.; Tues–Sat 7:30–9:30 p.m. Closed mid-Jan to mid-Feb.

Hostellerie Gargantua

$$$ Chinon   TOURAINE

Some may call the setup a little corny — waitresses wear medieval wench outfits on weekends — but the food is excellent at this charming restaurant that's part of a very fine inn (see "Where to stay"). Although the inside is set up like a modern version of a medieval banquet hall, you may prefer the outside seating in summer, where you can view the castle ruins. The gimmick is that ancient recipes are used to create the dishes. The menu is full of classics like local *sandre* (perch) prepared with Chinon wine and duckling with dried pears. The service is efficient and professional.

73 rue Voltaire (in the hotel). ☎ 02-47-93-04-71. Meals: Main courses 80–120F ($11–$17); menus 165F ($24) and 210F ($30). MC, V. Open: Daily noon to 2 p.m. and 7:30–9:30 p.m.

La Maison Rouge

$$ Chinon   TOURAINE

Not to be confused with Au Chapeau Rouge (see earlier in this section), this atmospheric bistro is where locals go for a good, reasonably priced meal. The large menu reads like a catalog of favorite French foods, some of which are uncommon in America, like *tête de veau* (veal's head) and *lapin du jour* (rabbit of the day). If you're adventurous, you'll have an authentic meal here, surrounded by locals. Be forewarned: It can get a little rowdy when customers start drinking out of the wine casks.

38 rue Voltaire. ☎ 02-47-98-43-65. Meals: Main courses 45–90F ($6–$13); menus 69–129F ($10–$18). MC, V. Open: July–Aug daily noon to 2 p.m. and 7–9:30 p.m.; Sept–Dec and Feb–June Tues–Sun noon to 2 p.m. and 7–9:30 p.m.

Les Années 30

$$ Chinon   TOURAINE

The theme of this small rustic restaurant is the 1930s — so Sinatra is on the tape player and art deco posters are on the walls. For me, this place gets an A for atmosphere, a B for service, and a C for food. Don't get me wrong, the food is pretty good, but it's better elsewhere in town, where you get more courses for similar prices. Your first course could be the rabbit and ham medallions, and your main course fricassée of duck and mushrooms with foie gras. The unusual desserts include blueberry and pear *blinis* (small, thin pancakes) with Chinon wine and raisin ice cream.

78 rue Voltaire. ☎ *02-47-93-37-18. Meals: Main courses 95–150F ($14–$21); menus 130F ($19) and 180F ($26). MC, V. Open: Fri–Tues noon to 2:30 p.m.; daily 7:30–9:30 p.m. Closed mid-Nov to early Dec and late Feb to mid-Mar.*

L'Oceanic

$$ Chinon FRENCH

This restaurant, owned and operated by Marie-Paule and Patrick Descoubes, specializes in seafood; the fish dishes are indeed fresh and delicious. Carnivores can order the steak. The restaurant is on main rue Rabelais, with a pleasing aqua-toned interior and cafe tables behind a turquoise balustrade. It fills up with locals, as well as visitors, because it offers good value and attention to every detail.

13 rue Rabelais. ☎ *02-47-93-44-55. Meals: Main courses 45–80F ($6–$11); menus 115F ($16) and 160F ($23). MC, V. Open: Tues–Sun noon to 2:30 p.m.; Tues–Sat 7:30–10 p.m.*

You'll find rows of cafes and restaurants along **rue Rabelais,** but some of the best restaurants are at the far east end of town, in the medieval district.

Seeing the castle and more

It's a steep walk to get to the **Château de Chinon** (☎ 02-47-93-13-45), which is actually the ruins of three castles going back to the Middle Ages, but this site is definitely worth seeing. From 1427 to 1450, Charles VII lived here almost continually, and Chinon briefly became his capital city and the most important castle in France. But the most famous event to occur here was in 1429, when a peasant girl named Joan arrived at the castle and inspired Charles to drive the English out of France.

The **Château du Milieu,** at the center of the site, includes the reconstructed **royal apartments,** with tapestries, antique furniture, illuminated manuscripts, and a waxworks tableau of the fateful meeting between Joan of Arc and Charles VII. Courtiers tried to test Joan by asking her to pick the disguised Charles out of the crowd. When she chose correctly, Charles was so impressed that he agreed to attempt to recapture his kingdom from the invading English. As presented here, Joan's choice doesn't appear too miraculous: Dopey-looking Charles is the one in the purple tunic and the pointiest shoes. The actual place of the meeting, the **Main Hall,** is a roofless ruin next to the restored building.

At the far western end of the site is what's left of the **Château de Coudray:** several towers and dungeons, including the cylindrical **Tour de Coudray,** one of the best-preserved examples of a keep in France. The **Donjon de Coudray** is where members of the order of Templars were imprisoned in 1308. The Templars were a wealthy community of military monks — yes, you read that right — founded to protect Christian realms. You can visit the dungeon if you don't mind going down about five flights of steps into the moldy depths of a cellar.

At the entrance to the site, the clock tower contains the **Joan of Arc museum** — three floors and seven small rooms of Joan collectibles, like postcards, dinner plates, and posters. It's a bit scattershot but still mildly interesting. All that remains of **Château de St-Georges,** built in the twelfth century, are ruins near the entrance to the site. After touring the buildings and towers, you may enjoy the view over the steeply pitched slate roofs in town, to the vineyards beyond.

Allow yourself an hour to see the site and wander the grounds. Admission to the site is 29F ($4.15) for adults and 20F ($2.85) for children 7 to 18. There are no audioguides, but tours are given in English at 9:55 a.m., 11:25 a.m., 2:25 p.m., 3:50 p.m., and 5:05 p.m. Tour times may change, so you'll need to call the castle at ☎ 02-47-93-13-45 to confirm. The château is open daily (except January 1 and December 25): July and August 9 a.m. to 7 p.m., mid-March to June and September 9 a.m. to 6 p.m.; October 9 a.m. to 5 p.m.; November to early March 9 a.m. to noon and 2 to 5 p.m.

A **tourist train** (☎ 05-49-22-51-91) travels a 40-minute route up to the castle, through the town's medieval quarter, and past some interesting churches. The commentary is in English or German. Easter to September, the train operates Saturdays, Sundays, and holidays (July and August, it operates daily) and departs about six times per day from place Charles-de-Gaulle. The tour costs 25F ($3.60) for adults, 20F ($2.85) for children 10 to 14, and 15F ($2.15) for children under 10.

In town, the musty **Musée du Vieux Chinon** (44 rue Haute St-Maurice; ☎ 02-47-93-18-12) has rather extensive and interesting collections detailing the history of Chinon. The museum is housed in a fifteenth-century building containing the Salle des Etats-Générale, the grand room where the Estates General met in 1428. In this second-floor room, you can pay homage to Chinon's favorite son, François Rabelais, at his 1833 portrait by Delacroix, which was recently restored by the Louvre.

On the first floor, chained leopards face off on the **cape of St. Mexme,** part of a twelfth-century silk fabric that's the largest textile from this period in France. The top floor displays the work of *compagnonnage* (master craftsmen) from the town. Don't miss the decorative parts of two porcelain heating units from the end of the *ancien régime.* Explanatory brochures, written in English, are available at the entrance. Admission is 15F ($2.15) for adults and 10F ($1.40) for children. Mid-April to mid-November, the museum is open daily 11 a.m. to 1 p.m. and 3 to 8 p.m.

The Syndicat des Vins Chinon, an organization of local wine producers, agreed in 2000 to allow visits to the **caves painctes,** which are simply wine-storage cellars containing bottles of local vintages on rue de Caves Painctes. July to September, tastings and tours were scheduled daily at 10:30 a.m. and 4 and 5 p.m., costing 15F ($2.15). You need to check with the tourist office to find out if tours and tastings will be offered in 2001.

Nearby, between Chinon and Ussé, is the fifteenth-century **Château de la Grille** (☎ 02-47-93-01-95), a 125-acre winery owned by the Gosset family, who've been winegrowers for 14 generations. Free tastings of the special Chinon wine are offered in July and August daily 10 a.m. to 7 p.m. and September to June Monday to Saturday 9 a.m. to noon and 2 to 6 p.m. English is spoken here.

Nightlife

Le River Rock Café (15 rue Rabelais; ☎ 02-47-93-94-94) is a large brasserie where everyone hangs out. In the back of Le River Rock Café are four pool tables, a piano bar, and a long bar; in the front are restaurant tables and booths. Bar specialties include "beers of the world," as well as quarter sizes of Chinon wine for 19F ($2.70), which you can sample with all the typical cafe fare served here.

Ussé: Fit for Sleeping Beauty

The tiny village of **Ussé,** near the intersection of the rivers Indre and Loire, is home to the privately owned château that was supposedly the inspiration for the story of *Sleeping Beauty,* written by Charles Perrault (rumor has it that he stayed here in the seventeenth century). The French call the castle, with its glistening white stone and wonderful soaring turrets and towers, the *Château de la Belle au Bois Dormant* (Castle of the Beauty of the Sleeping Woods). You can easily picture beautiful ladies and brave lords strolling through the long halls and monumental stairways. But the village of Ussé is really a blink-and-you-miss-it kind of place. Nevertheless, the château is worth a visit, particularly for children, who may enjoy the waxworks reconstruction of the sleeping beauty story that's set up in a tower.

Getting there

If you're **driving,** take D7 southwest from Tours, following it for about 30 minutes. From Chinon, follow the signs north out of town. Ussé is about a 5- to 10-minute drive from Chinon. If you're coming from Paris, take A10 to Tours and then D7 to Ussé (about a 3-hour drive). Ussé is a flat and easy 14.5 km (9 mile) **bike** ride from Chinon; the tourist office in Chinon can give you a map and brochures of the interesting sights you might find along the way and nearby.

Where to stay

Le Clos d'Ussé

$ Ussé

This is the only lodging option in the tiny village. You'll have more fun staying in neighboring Chinon, but if you must find a place to stay in Ussé, this hotel provides acceptable accommodations. The three rooms are very simple but clean and comfortable, with cheerful patterned curtains and pastel-colored walls. If you speak French, you might enjoy learning about the history of the castle from the kind proprietors.

Across the street from the château on D7, Rigny-Ussé. ☎ *02-47-95-55-47. Rack rates: 260–320F ($37–$46) double. Breakfast: 35F ($5). V.*

Where to dine

You can grab lunch or a snack at the cafe **Le Bois Dormant** (open daily 10 a.m. to 5:30 p.m.), which has outside tables under shade trees, across the street from the castle on D7. (For dinner options, check out Chinon.)

Seeing the castle

The privately owned **Château d'Ussé** (☎ 02-47-95-54-05; Internet: www. tourisme.fr/usse) is set on a hill overlooking the river Indre. The Blacas family has lived here since the nineteenth century, occupying the left wing. Work began on the castle in 1455 on the foundations of an eleventh-century fortress, but the castle today reflects its sixteenth-century conversion into a country château for gentry. You can see Gothic (fifteenth century), Renaissance (sixteenth century), and classical (seventeenth century) architectural influences. The grounds are beautifully landscaped, with formal seventeenth-century **gardens** designed by Le Nôtre, who designed the gardens at Versailles. Among other century-old trees is a majestic cedar of Lebanon that was a gift in 1808 from writer Châteaubriand, a friend of the castle owner.

Other Loire Valley Favorites

If you have extra time and are looking for another interesting castle or two to visit in the area, consider these:

- ✔ **Château de Châteaudun:** About 128.7 km (80 miles) from Tours, this castle is a mix of medieval and Renaissance architecture, with towering chimneys and dormers. Inside you'll find two carved staircases, tapestries, and a Sainte-Chapelle with robed statues. Call ☎ 02-37-94-02-90 for hours and admission.

- ✔ **Château de Loches:** About 40.2 km (25 miles) from Tours, this castle, actually a walled citadel, is notable for its connection to Agnès Sorel, the first official mistress of a French king (Charles VII). Her remains are entombed in the west wing, and a copy of a painting, showing her as a fetching Virgin Mary, hangs in the royal apartments, along with other artworks and tapestries. Call ☎ 02-47-59-01-32 for hours and admission.

- ✔ **Château de Villandry:** About 17.7 km (11 miles) from Tours, this privately owned site is famous for its extensive sixteenth-century Renaissance gardens, mosaics of flowers organized by symbolic meanings, and vegetables of the period. The three levels of gardens include a top level of water gardens with pools and waterfalls. Call ☎ 02-47-50-02-09 for hours and admission.

- ✔ **Château de Langeais:** About 25.7 km (16 miles) from Tours, this medieval fortress built in 1465 is decorated sumptuously in period decor that includes fine tapestries. Call ☎ 02-47-96-72-60 for hours and admission.

- ✔ **Château de Saumur:** About 67.6 km (42 miles) from Tours, this fortress overlooking the Loire contains an interesting regional museum with a collection of ceramics and Limoges enamels. There's also a museum devoted to the history of the horse through the ages. Call ☎ 02-41-40-24-40 for hours and admission.

- ✔ **Château d'Angers:** About 56.3 km (35 miles) from Tours, this moated ninth-century castle contains the famous Apocalypse Tapestries, masterpieces from the Middle Ages. The series of 77 panels, illustrating the book of St. John, stretches 335 feet. There are also prison cells, ramparts, a chapel, and royal apartments to visit. Call ☎ 02-41-87-43-47 for hours and admission.

- ✔ **Château de Cheverny:** About 61.2 km (38 miles) from Tours, this seventeenth-century castle, owned by a descendant of the original owner, is decorated in classic Louis XIII style, with antiques, tapestries, and objets d'art. The stone stairway, with carved fruit and flowers, is a standout. Call ☎ 02-54-79-96-29 for hours and admission.

- ✔ **Château de Valençay:** About 66 km (41 miles) from Tours, this grandiose Renaissance château is adorned with domes, chimneys, and turrets. Inside, the private apartments are decorated in the Empire style, with a little Louis XV and Louis XVI (think Versailles) thrown in for good measure. Call ☎ 02-54-00-10-66 for hours and admission.

There's no audioguide, but brochures, written in English, are available at the beginning of the tour. A French guide (there are three to five guided tours per day) will start the tour at the small 1528 **chapel,** which has a pretty Renaissance porch with 12 carved apostles. The stone used in the chapel is from the region and retains its sparkling white color without restoration. Among the exterior's decorative elements are two gargoyles. Inside the chapel, you can find ribbed vaulting and sixteenth-century carved wood choir stalls, as well as a collection of Luca della Robbia ceramics from Florence. The **écurie,** close to the entrance to the chapel, is a garage-type building holding six antique vehicles, including a dog chariot, a 1920s horse-drawn car, and a nineteenth-century wicker carriage. Behind the chapel, **caves** used to store wine are set up with wax figures in a basic and somewhat humorous explanation of winemaking at the castle.

The guide then leads you through half a dozen castle rooms fully decorated with interesting antiques. More than other Loire Valley châteaux, Ussé feels "lived in," as the owners have restored period details like the eighteenth-century silks on the walls and seventeenth-century oak parquet floors. Most of the furniture is original eighteenth-century pieces that were made for the château. There are also collections owned by the resident marquis de Blacas, like weaponry and oriental objects from the Far East, brought home by Comte Stanislas de Blacas. Mannequins set up in several of the rooms display items from the family's extensive antique clothing collection.

After the tour, you can climb the **round tower** on your own to see the elaborately set up waxworks of the *Sleeping Beauty* story, featuring the Wicked Fairy, as well as rooms displaying nineteenth-century children's toys and games. In the **Orangerie,** located on the grounds, is an artisan crafts shop selling unique gifts like woven scarves and jewelry.

The castle is open daily: mid-February to March and late September to mid-November 10 a.m. to noon and 2 to 5:30 p.m.; April, May, and early to late September 9 a.m. to noon and 2 to 6:45 p.m.; and June to August 9 a.m. to 6:30 p.m. Admission is 59F ($8) for adults and 19F ($2.70) for children 8 to 16 years.

Chenonceau: The Château des Dames

The small village of **Chenonceaux** consists of about half a dozen hotels, a few restaurants, a couple of shops, and the most beautiful castle in the Loire Valley, the Château de Chenonceau (note that the town's name ends with an *x* but the château's doesn't). You won't soon forget your first image of this grand edifice, with its graceful arches creating a covered bridge over the pastoral Cher River. After spending a couple of hours exploring the castle and gardens, you can wander a few blocks to your hotel and enjoy the serenity of Chenonceaux after the tour buses have left. Better yet, wander back to the castle for the nighttime sound-and-light show, which takes place daily in summer (see "Seeing the castle" for details). The **tourist office** is at 1 rue Bretonneau (☎ 02-47-23-94-45). Mid-April to October, it's open daily 10 a.m. to noon and 2 to 6 p.m.; November to early April, hours are Monday to Saturday 10 a.m. to noon and 2 to 6 p.m. and Sunday 2 to 6 p.m.

Getting there

There are four **trains** per day, as well as a couple of buses, that travel from Tours to Chenonceaux. The train trip from Tours takes 30 minutes and costs 40F ($6) each way. For information and reservations, call ☎ **08-36-35-35-35.** The train stop is located a block from the center of the village, next to the château entrance. Buses traveling between Tours and Chenonceaux cost 25F ($3.60) and take an hour. If you're **driving** from Paris, take A10 past Blois, then D31 south past Amboise to N76 east, which leads to Chenonceaux. The drive from Paris to Chenonceaux takes about 2½ hours. From Tours, take N76 east to Chenonceaux. The drive from Tours to Chenonceaux takes about half an hour.

Getting around

A **taxi/minibus service** (☎ 02-54-78-07-65; Fax: 02-54-78-32-80; E-mail: taxiradioblois@wanadoo.fr) will take you from the Blois train station to either the two castles at Chambord and Cheverny (420F/$60) or the three castles at Chaumont, Amboise, and Chenonceaux (670F/$96).

Where to stay and dine

Hostellerie de la Renaudière

$$ **Chenonceaux**

This elegant eighteenth-century house, high above the road, an eight-minute walk from the château, is an informal 15-room family hotel (no elevator) that has been cheaply, if lovingly, restored by Joel and Isabelle Camus. It's landscaped grounds contain a pool and plastic playground equipment. The comfortable rooms come with hairdryers, mini-refrigerators, and bowls of fruit; some have wonderful views of the castle grounds. Train tracks are located across the road, so you may hear night trains if you have a room in front. The restaurant, with seating outside or in a glass-enclosed porch, highlights regional dishes and ancient recipes like St-Maure *frais au chou vert*, a kind of coleslaw using green cabbage, and a special rabbit preparation with a heavy white sauce called *rable de lapin à la Tourangelle*. I also enjoyed the boozy strawberry soup. The wine list concentrates on Loire Valley vintages. English is spoken here.

24 rue du Docteur-Bretonneau. ☎ *02-47-23-90-04. Fax: 02-47-23-90-51. E-mail:* gerhotel@club-internet.fr. *Rack rates: 250–450F ($36–$64) double; 750–900F ($107–$129) apartment. Breakfast: 25F ($3.60). Closed mid-Nov to mid-Mar. AE, DC, MC, V.*

La Roseraie

$$$ **Chenonceaux**

This 17-room hotel, with beautifully landscaped grounds and rose gardens, is the best place to stay in Chenonceaux. The handsome old inn, a five-minute walk from the castle, drips with ivy and period charm. Friendly innkeepers Laurent and Sophie Fiorito have outfitted the rooms in French country style, with special windows that mean quiet nights even though you're on the town's main road. The cozy beamed restaurant serves three meals a day in the dining room or on the terrace beside the heated pool. You can rent bikes here for 80F ($11) per day.

7 rue du Docteur-Bretonneau. ☎ *02-47-23-90-09. Fax: 02-47-23-91-59. Internet:* www.charminghotel.com. *E-mail:* lfiorito@aol.com. *Rack rates: 280–550F ($40–$79) double; 450–750F ($64–$107) family room for 4; 1,000F ($143) apartment. Breakfast: 38F ($5). MC, V.*

Seeing the castle

The "château des dames," the sixteenth-century **Château de Chenonceau** (☎ 02-47-23-90-07; Internet: www.chenonceau.com), is the Loire Valley's most beautiful castle, set on graceful arches above the river Cher. Because this is everybody's favorite, it's always very crowded, but even with 30 buses full of tourists swarming around, it's still a magical place. You enter by walking down a long tree-lined path passing though a grand entrance framed by sphinxes, and then down another long path lined by orange trees. In front of the castle are two lush **formal gardens,** one commissioned by Henri II's queen, Catherine de' Medici, and the other by her rival and Henri's mistress, Diane de Poitiers.

About a dozen castle rooms are open, all decorated with elaborately painted beams, period antiques, and an extensive collection of Flemish tapestries. Downstairs, you can visit the kitchens and pantry. In other rooms, you'll see a number of fine paintings, including *Virgin with Child* by Murillo and *Archimedes* by Zurburan, and works thought to be by Rubens, Van Dyck, and Poussin. There's even a dour portrait of Catherine de' Medici, who brought her Italian influence to the architecture of the castle. Originally, Henri II gave Chenenceau to the enchanting Diane, 20 years his senior; but after the king's death in a 1559 jousting tournament, Catherine forced her husband's "favorite" to move to the less desirable Chaumont (see the next section). The castle contains Diane's bedroom and an alluring portrait of her as Diana the Huntress, as well as a case containing a copy of her signature. After ousting Diane, Catherine moved into Chenonceau and brought workmen from Italy to embellish it with Renaissance style. The château's signature **Gallery,** with its dramatic arches over the river, was built at this time; in Catherine's day, it was used as a ballroom, but today it's sometimes used to display the works of contemporary artists.

The **Galerie des Dames,** a waxworks museum, is housed in the former royal stables on the castle grounds. The exhibits feature the women who lived at Chenonceau, with special attention to fabrics and costumes. Also on the grounds are a **cafe,** a **restaurant,** a sixteenth-century **farm** with a tiny duck pond, a **playground,** and a **flower shop,** where you can buy one of the special rose bushes grown in the gardens. The castle property also features 40 hectares of **grapevines** that are handpicked. You can buy the wine produced from these grapes at a **wine shop** on site.

To avoid the scores of tour buses, try visiting the castle very late in the day, very early in the day, or at lunchtime.

Allow yourself a couple of hours to see the château and wander the glorious gardens. The château is open daily 9 a.m. to 7 p.m. (except January 1 and December 25). Admission is 50F ($7) for adults, 40F ($6) for children 7 to 18 and for students up to age 27. The waxworks museum costs an additional 20F ($2.85). July and August, a sound-and-light show called **Les Dames de Chenonceau** is presented nightly 10:15 to 11 p.m., costing 60F ($9). The castle is illuminated, and music, singing, and historic commentary are broadcast over loudspeakers.

Chaumont: Exile of Diane de Poitiers

High above the Loire, with sweeping views of the countryside, **Chaumont** is an interesting site. However, there's really nothing in the tiny village but the château, so you'll probably want to hit this one as a half-day stop on the way to Amboise (to the west) or Blois (to the east). Built as a fortress in the Middle Ages, the castle was reinvented as an aristocrats' manor house in the nineteenth century, and the interiors reflect this use. In between, it witnessed a lot of history, including the banishment of Diane de Poitiers, the mistress of Henri II. Henri's wife, Catherine de' Medici, forced Diane to move out of Chenonceau (see the previous section) and into Chaumont after Henri's death in 1559. The most unique part of this site is the luxurious stables.

The **tourist office** is on rue du Maréchal-Leclerc (☎ 02-54-20-91-73), open daily 9:30 a.m. to noon and 2 to 5 p.m.

Getting there

If you're **driving,** take A10 from Blois or D751 from Amboise (about 20 minutes from either). From Paris, take A10 to Blois and continue for another 24.1 km (15 miles) until you see signs for Chaumont. It's about 2½ hours from Paris by car. You have to park in the village and walk quite a distance up a tree-lined hill to the château. There are seven daily **trains** that travel from Paris to Onzain, 1½ miles north of the château, located on the other side of the Loire. You have to walk from the train station to the chateau. For information and reservations, call ☎ 08-36-35-35-35. The 1¼-hour trip costs 132F ($19) or 186F ($27).

Getting around

A **taxi/minibus service** (☎ 02-54-78-07-65; Fax: 02-54-78-32-80; E-mail: taxiradioblois@wanadoo.fr) will take you from the Blois train station to either the two castles of Chambord and Cheverny (420F/$60) or the three castles of Chaumont, Amboise, and Chenonceaux (670F/$96).

Where to stay

Hostellerie du Château

$$ Chaumont

This 20-room newly renovated half-timbered hotel, one of few lodging options in tiny Chaumont, is across from the château entrance. The hotel is on the bank of the Loire, and some rooms have river views. The pool is surrounded by terraces, where dinner is served in season.

2 rue du Maréchal Delatre-de-Tassigny. ☎ *02-54-20-98-04. Fax: 02-54-20-97-98. Rack rates: 350–760F ($50–$109) double. Breakfast: 55F ($8). Closed Feb. AE, V.*

Seeing the castle

The **Château de Chaumont** (☎ 02-54-51-26-26) is a delightful residence set high above the Loire. Its clear strategic position, with views to the east and west, betray its original use as a fortress stronghold constructed at the end of the Middle Ages. The original building was burned to the ground, and construction on the present château, with its battlements and turrets, began in 1465 and ended in the sixteenth century. This château's most famous occupant was Diane de Poitiers, beautiful mistress to Henri II. When Henri II died, his powerful and embittered wife, Catherine de' Medici, forced Diane to give up the exquisite Château de Chenonceau in exchange for exile at Chaumont, a lesser residence.

During the eighteenth and nineteenth centuries, various aristocrats used the château as a private residence; it maintains that air today. Most notably, Princesse Marie-Charlotte de Broglie, the heiress to the fortune of the Say (a huge sugar importer), supervised extensive restorations to the château in 1875 with her husband, Prince Amedée de Broglie. Marie-Charlotte, one of two daughters of an extremely wealthy sugar importer, first bought the castle, then married the prince. She commissioned the architect to turn it into a luxurious home. But the life of splendor caught up with her, and after the prince died, she lost her fortune in the stock market crash of 1929. The French government bought the castle in 1938. In the center of the library is a display case containing notable **terracotta medallions** by potter Jean-Baptiste Nini, who lived at Chaumont from 1772 to 1786. These medallions depict famous guests of the castle, like Benjamin Franklin, as well as royalty of the period, like Louis XV, Louis XVI, and Marie Antoinette. Don't miss the **Ruggieri Chamber,** where Catherine de' Medici's royal astrologer, Cosimo Ruggieri, stayed; a sinister portrait of him is near the door. The Broglies commissioned the elaborate **stables** on the property, which were equipped with the latest equine amenities. Prince and Princesse de Broglie were also responsible for laying out Chaumont's elaborate park. Formerly 6,000 acres, the park now encompasses 52 acres on the plateau surrounding the castle.

Allow yourself an hour to see the castle and stables. The château is open daily (except January 1, May 1, November 1 and 11, and December 25): April to September 9:30 a.m. to 6 p.m. and October to March 10 a.m. to 4:30 p.m. Admission is 32F ($4.60) for adults and 21F ($3) for students; free for children under 18. Brochures, written in English, are available for self-guided tours.

From mid-June to late October, the annual **Festival International des Jardins** presents the best of contemporary garden designers and attracts visitors from all over France. Admission is 48F ($7) for adults and 20F ($2.85) for children 8 to 12. For more information, call ☎ 02-54-20-99-22.

Blois: Château of Royalty

Blois is a good-sized town with wide shop-lined boulevards and winding medieval streets to explore. Lording over the town is the château, one of the primary residences of royalty in the Loire and the location of pivotal historic events. The **tourist office** is next to the chateau at 3 av. Jean-Laigret (☎ 02-54-90-41-41; Fax: 02-54-90-41-49; E-mail: blois.tourism@wanadoo.fr; Internet: www.loiredeschateaux.com). It's open Monday 10 a.m. to 12:30 p.m. and 2 to 6 p.m.; Tuesday to Saturday 9 a.m. to 12:30 p.m. and 2 to 6 p.m.; and Sunday and holidays 9:30 a.m. to 12:30 p.m. A light-board with a map, found next to the office, gives information on lodging if you're having trouble finding a place to stay. There are public toilets here too.

Getting there

Six **trains** per day travel from Paris and pass through Orléans on their way to the Blois train station on avenue Jean-Laigret. The trip from Paris takes two hours and costs 180F ($26). The trip from Orléans to Blois takes an hour and costs 120F ($17). Five trains make the 30-minute trip from Tours, costing 65F ($9) each way. Trains from Amboise take 20 minutes and cost 50F ($7). For schedules and reservations, call

☎ **08-36-35-35-35.** The bus station, across from the train station on avenue Victor-Hugo, services Chambord, among other nearby villages. If you're **driving** from Tours or Orléans, take N152 east or the speedy A10 west; it takes about 45 minutes to an hour from Tours or Orléans. From Paris, take about a two-hour drive along A10 to Blois.

Getting around

The castle of Blois occupies a high position on a ridge in the center of town, overlooking the town and the river. It's easy to walk up to the castle from anywhere in town.

If you want to rent bikes in Blois to travel to neighboring castles, go to **Cycles LeBlond** (44 levée des Tuilleries; ☎ 02-54-74-30-13), open daily 9 a.m. to 9 p.m. (closed October 29 to November 6 and December 24 to January 2). The rental rates (per day) are 35 to 80F ($5 to $11) for adults and 30 to 60F ($4.30 to $9) for children. Another choice is **Ets Bucquet** (33 av. Wilson; ☎ 02-54-78-12-94), open Tuesday to Saturday 8:30 a.m. to noon and 2 to 6 p.m. The rates are 70F ($10) per day. Car rentals are available at **Ecoto** (58 av. Vendôme; ☎ 02-54-42-77-77), open daily 9 a.m. to noon and 2 to 5 p.m.

The **bus** company (☎ 02-54-90-41-41) runs tours of Blois, Chambord, and Cheverny. From June to early September, tours depart from the train station in Blois at 9:10 a.m. and 1:20 p.m. and return about four hours later. The tours cost 65F ($9) for adults and 50F ($7) for children. You can buy tickets at the Blois tourist office. In addition, a **taxi/minibus service** (☎ 02-54-78-07-65; Fax: 02-54-78-32-80; E-mail: taxiradioblois@ wanadoo.fr) will take you from the Blois train station to the two castles of Chambord and Cheverny (420F/$60), or to the three castles of Chaumont, Amboise, and Chenonceaux (670F/$96).

For a **local taxi,** to take you from the train station to your hotel, call ☎ 02-54-78-07-65.

Taxi Jean-Louis (20 rue Porte-Chartraine; ☎ 02-54-74-00-40 or 06-07-90-77-93) will take you to Chambord and Cheverny for 450F ($64) on weekdays or 600F ($86) on weekends and holidays, or to Chenonceau, Amboise, and Chaumont for 700F ($100) on weekdays or 1,000F ($143) on weekends and holidays.

You can even take a 25-minute **horse-and-buggy ride** through the old town of Blois at a cost of 30F ($4) for adults and 20F ($3) for children 2 to 12. During May, June, and September, the carriage departs from place du Château on weekends and holidays 2 to 6 p.m.; July and August, it leaves daily 11 a.m. to 7 p.m. For more details, call the tourist office at ☎ 02-54-90-41-41.

Where to stay

Hôtel Anne de Bretagne

$ Blois

This 29-room hotel, very close to the castle and the train station, is a good budget option. The rooms are simple and small, but they're brightened by colorful patterned bedspreads. Although it's just the basics here, you'll find that the staff is particularly sunny. The hotel is on a busy road, but it's set back from the street. Nevertheless, request a room in the back.

31 av. Jean-Laigret. ☎ *02-54-78-05-38. Fax: 02-54-74-37-79. Free parking. Rack rates: 315–380F ($45–$54) double. Breakfast: 38F ($5). Closed Jan. MC, V.*

Hôtel de France et Guise

$$ Blois

This 50-room hotel boasts the best location in town, across the boulevard from the castle. Some rooms have views of the castle, which looks especially dramatic when lit at night. Alas, the lovely reception area, with its oriental rugs and antiques, is soured by the dour greeting of the proprietress. This is a city hotel on a busy road, so you'll hear cars at night and in the morning. The rooms come in a variety of sizes, from cozy to spacious, and the detailing befits the age of the hotel; some have elegant ceiling moldings and marble fireplaces. Be aware that room no. 1 is brightened all night by the hotel's neon sign. Breakfast is served in a room that has a gilded ceiling and attractive murals of nearby châteaux.

3 rue Gallois. ☎ *02-54-78-00-53. Fax: 02-54-78-29-45. Rack rates: 260–410F ($37–$59) double. Breakfast: 32F ($4.60). Closed Nov–Mar. MC, V.*

Ibis Blois Centre

$$ Blois

Although it occupies an eighteenth-century town house, this 56-room chain hotel is fully modern inside, with all the usual amenities, including cable TVs. The hotel is conveniently located near the château. The rooms are clean, comfortable, and relatively spacious.

3 rue Porte-Cote. ☎ *02-54-74-01-17. Fax: 02-54-74-85-69. E-mail:* H0920@ accor-hotels.com. *Parking: 30F ($4.30) in the château lot. Rack rates: 275–380F ($39–$54) double. Breakfast: 35F ($5). AE, DC, MC, V.*

Mercure Centre

$$$ Blois

This thoroughly modern 98-room chain hotel, a concrete box on the far east end of town beside the river, is a 20-minute scenic walk from the château. The spacious rooms have amenities like air conditioning, hairdryers, and minibars. You can also find a bar, restaurant, pool with Jacuzzi, and fitness center.

28 quai St-Jean. ☎ *02-54-56-66-66. Fax: 02-54-56-67-00. Internet:* www. mercure-blois.fr. *E-mail:* H1621@accor-hotels.com. *Rack rates: 595– 695F ($85–$99) double. Breakfast: 58F ($8). AE, DC, MC, V.*

Where to dine

Au Rendezvous des Pêcheurs

$$ Blois   TOURAINE

Get ready for a delightful evening at this seafood restaurant, down a narrow winding road on the far west end of town. Chef/owner Christophe Cosme greets you at the door, takes your order, and bids you adieu at the end of your meal. That service and consideration would be enough to bring me back, but it's the outstanding, creative food that makes this place most memorable. Get the market menu, for which the chef uses the freshest products to concoct superb dishes. Two highlights are the *flan d'écrévisses* (freshwater crayfish tart with Vouvray wine) and the pairing of *dos de cabillau* (cooked codfish) with sausage and black olives. Although the specialty is seafood, meat eaters will find a few choices on the menu.

27 rue du Foix. ☎ *02-54-74-67-48. Reservations necessary. Meals: Main courses 98–145F ($14–$21); menu 150F ($21). MC, V. Open: Tues–Sat 12:30–2 p.m.; Mon–Sat 7–10 p.m. Closed first week in Feb and three weeks in Aug.*

Les Banquettes Rouge

$$ Blois   TOURAINE

This little hole in the wall is on one of the atmospheric winding streets in the town's old section. The brightly lit interior, with color splashes on the walls and vibrant paintings, beckons passers-by to join the hip young atmosphere. You can't go wrong with the simple well-priced cuisine and friendly service. Favorites like foie gras, *pot au feu* (braised beef simmered with vegetables), and fresh sole are summer standards, and in fall you'll find several fresh game dishes.

16 rue des Trois-Marchands. ☎ *02-54-78-74-92. Meals: Main courses 70–125F ($10–18); menus 89F ($13) at lunch, 105F and 159F ($15 and $23) at dinner. MC, V. Open: Mon–Sat noon to 2 p.m. and 7–10 p.m.*

Le Triboulet

$$ Blois   TOURAINE

This casual restaurant, in the courtyard in front of the château, is a good option for a light meal before or after exploring the castle. Le Triboulet offers a nice selection of salads with meat and fish, omelets, and oysters, as well as lots of dessert crêpes and ice cream. Most of the seating is outside in the château courtyard under bright awnings, although there are a few tables inside.

18 place du Château. ☎ *02-54-74-11-23. Meals: Main courses 65–90F ($9–$13); menus 80–120F ($11–$17). MC, V. Open: May–Oct Tues–Sun noon to 3:30 p.m. and 7–10 p.m.; Nov–Apr Tues–Sat noon to 3:30 p.m. and 7–9:30 p.m. Closed Feb.*

L'Orangerie

$$$ **Blois**   TOURAINE

This restaurant, next to the château and entered through a large gated formal courtyard, is the fanciest option in Blois. While seated in the floral-themed dining room, you'll be served gourmet cuisine along the lines of filet mignon with truffles, a medley of *langoustines* and *noix St-Jacques* (shellfish and nuts in cream sauce), and *la queue de petite lotte rotie* (roast monkfish with thyme). The intriguing dessert menu includes unusual homemade concoctions like *fondant chaud chocolat et pistache* (melted chocolate and pistachio with crème fraiche).

1 av. Jean-Laigret. ☎ *02-54-78-05-36. Reservations required. Meals: Main courses 160–200F ($23–$29); menus 140–365F ($20–$52); children's menu 80F ($11). MC, V. Open: Thurs–Tues 12:10–1:45 p.m. and 7:15–9:15 p.m. Closed Sun night and sometimes Tues night, mid-Feb to mid-Mar.*

Louis XII Brasserie

$ **Blois**   CAFE

This restaurant, set at the foot of the château in front of the lively market, is a popular hangout for student types and others. It serves the usual fare of salads, omelets, crêpes, desserts, and ice cream. Children will enjoy sitting in this lively square where the market spreads out on Saturdays.

1 rue St-Martin. ☎ *02-54-78-13-81. Meals: Main courses 20–45F ($2.85–$6). AE, DC, MC. Open: Mon–Sat noon to 3 p.m. and 7–10 p.m. Closed Nov.*

There are several cafes and tearooms, serving the usual fare, on the square next to the château. You may find more interesting choices on the winding streets in the old section of town near the Eglise de St-Nicolas. Check out rue Foulerie, in the working-class east end of town, for ethnic food restaurants, including Moroccan cuisine.

Seeing the castle and town

Murder, mayhem, and intrigue — it all took place at the **Château de Blois** (☎ **02-54-90-33-33**), which 400 years of royalty called home. There's a lot to see here, including the history of French architecture from the Middle Ages to the seventeenth century. The château, constructed in the tenth century, is made up of four stylistically distinct wings joined by a large courtyard.

Located in the château is the medieval **Salle des Etats-Généraux,** a thirteenth-century Gothic construction containing a grand conference room and a lapidary museum with original carvings and sculptures from the castle. The **Aile de Louis XII** was built from 1498 to 1503 in the Flamboyant Gothic style; a fine arts museum is in the former royal apartments located in this wing. For fans of the grotesque: Don't miss the portrait of Antoinetta Gonsalvus called *L'Hirsutism* — this young girl was the victim of a horrible hereditary disease that causes long hair to grow on the face. You can also find a fine collection of ironwork and a display of keys and locks.

Architectural historians call the **Aile de François I,** built from 1515 to 1524, a French Renaissance masterpiece, particularly for this wing's exterior spiral staircase tower. François I was a king of extravagant tastes; he had the immense Château de Chambord (see later in this chapter) built to prove the supremacy of the monarchy. This wing at Blois contains apartments once lived in by François, his daughter-in-law Catherine de' Medici (wife of Henri II), and his grandson Henri III. Catherine's study contains hidden cabinets where she stored her poisons. The third floor contains the room where the infamous murder of the duc de Guise took place in 1588. Henri III, who wanted to prevent a coup attempt by the powerful duke, planned the murder. There's a whole room devoted to paintings of the dastardly deed, and it's explained in detail in the brochure. The **Galerie Gaston d'Orléans,** built from 1635 to 1637, is a tour de force of French classical architecture designed by François Mansart. Gaston d'Orléans was Louis XIII's brother and a powerful member of the court of Louis XIII.

Allow a couple of hours for your visit. The château is open daily (except December 25 and January 1): October to mid-March 9 a.m. to 12:30 p.m. and 2 to 5:30 p.m.; mid-March to June and September 9 a.m. to 6 p.m.; and July and August from 9 a.m. to 8 p.m. Last admittance is at 5 p.m. Admission is 35F ($5) for adults, 25F ($3.60) for students 12 to 20, and 20F ($2.85) for children 6 to 11. Brochures, written in English, are available for a self-guided tour. Parking is available on avenue Jean-Laigret across from the tourist office.

The château sponsors several events. During July and August, a **market of regional specialties,** with vendors selling delicious local foods, takes place on the square in front of the castle every Thursday noon to 5 p.m. and a free **classical music concert** takes place in the Hall of the Estates General three times per week at 6:30 p.m.; call the castle for dates. From late April to mid-September (except July 13), a **sound-and-light show** takes place nightly 10 to 10:30 p.m.; the show is presented in English on Wednesdays in May, June, and September. The show costs 60F ($9) for adults and 30F ($4.30) for children 6 to 20. For more information, call ☎ 02-54-78-72-76.

In the town of Blois, the **Cathédrale St-Louis,** built from the twelfth to the seventeenth century in a predominantly Gothic style, is a handsome church with a stormy history. It's the fifth church built on the site; the others were destroyed by one disaster after another. In 1678, a hurricane left the building in ruins. Underground, the eleventh-century Carolingian crypt St-Solenne is worth seeing — it was built to house the tomb of the saint, and enlarged several times to accommodate the numerous pilgrims who wanted to visit the site. As a result, it's one of France's largest medieval crypts. The cathedral is open daily 7:30 a.m. to 6 p.m., and admission is free. Also worth a visit is the twelfth-century **Eglise St-Nicolas** on rue St-Laumen in the medieval section of town, where you can see modern stained-glass windows in an ancient edifice. The old windows were destroyed during bombing in 1940. The brochure tactfully says that "this modern lighting plan is a subject open to discussion." I bet it caused quite a bit of discussion, but the windows are quite glorious, forming cubist-type patterns along the stone walls. The church is open daily 7:30 a.m. to 6 p.m., and admission is free.

Shopping

You'll actually find some good shopping opportunities in Blois, particularly on **rue St-Martin** and **rue du Commerce.** The best toy store is **L'Atelier de Gepetto** (19 rue Porte Côte; ☎ 02-54-56-84-83), which specializes in wood toys and puppets. A very cool art gallery, **3 Dégres St-Laumer** (off rue St-Laumer; no phone), is located in the old section of town near the Eglise St-Nicolas; the entrance can be found on the middle of a stairway between two winding streets just north of the church. Antiques hounds should try **Langlois Tapisseries** (1 rue de la Vouté du Château; ☎ 02-54-78-04-43). Chocoholics won't want to miss **Jeff de Bruges** (77 rue du Commerce; ☎ 02-54-74-26-44) and **Max Vauche** (50 rue du Commerce; ☎ 02-54-78-23-55), who elevates chocolate making to a fine art. On Saturday mornings, a terrific **food market** is held on rue St-Lubin, lining several blocks in the center of town at the foot of the château.

Nightlife

Night owls will enjoy **Les Boucaniers** (promenade du Mail; ☎ 02-54-74-37-23), a nightclub beside the Loire. The best bar is **Pub Mancini** (1 rue du Puits-Chatel; ☎ 02-54-78-04-36), and the town's cybercafe is **L'Etoile Tex** (7 rue du Bourg-Neuf; ☎ 02-54-78-46-93), which serves Mexican and Italian food. Other fun bars include **Le Maryland** (5 place de la Résistance; ☎ 02-54-78-08-80), which is also a brasserie, open daily 7 a.m. to 1 a.m.; **Au Bureau** (1 rue du Chant des Oiseaux; ☎ 02-54-56-81-81), an old-fashioned pub; and **Pub Riverside** (3 rue Henri-Drussy; ☎ 02-54-78-33-79), which specializes in beers and whiskies. The nearest disco (10 km/6.2 miles from Blois) is **Le Charleston** on Route de Nozieux (☎ 02-54-20-61-06).

Amboise: A Fortified Château and Leonardo's Mansion

One of the most charming towns in the Loire Valley is **Amboise,** with a stately fortified château perched above the village and wonderful cobblestone streets made just for strolling. This is also the town where Leonardo da Vinci spent his last years; you can visit his manor house, which remains pretty much as he left it when he died here in 1519. The **tourist office** (7 quai du Général-de-Gaulle; ☎ **02-47-57-09-28**) has a good walking-tour map and can help you plan day trips to nearby sites. During July and August, the office is open daily 9 a.m. to 8 p.m.; September to June, hours are Monday to Saturday 9:30 a.m. to 12:30 p.m. and 2 to 6:30 p.m. and Sunday 9:30 a.m. to 12:30 p.m.

Getting there

Amboise is centrally located between Tours and Blois, and there are 14 **trains** per day making the trip from each town, taking about 20 minutes and costing about 35F ($5). Trains also arrive in Amboise from Paris's Gare d'Austerlitz, taking 2½ hours and costing about 200F ($29). For schedules and information, call ☎ **08-36-35-35-35.** There are six **buses** that travel daily from Tours to Amboise, taking 30 minutes and costing 32F ($4.60). Call ☎ **02-47-37-81-81** for more information. The **driving** route to Amboise from Tours or Orléans is N152 east or west, respectively; the trip takes about 45 minutes from either town. From Paris, it's a two-hour drive, taking A10 to the exit for Château-Renault, and then D31 to Amboise.

Getting around

You can rent bikes by the day or the week at **Loca Cycle** (2 bis rue Jean-Jacques-Rousseau; ☎ **02-47-57-00-28**), open daily 9 a.m. to 12:30 p.m. and 2 to 7 p.m. Rentals cost 50F ($7) for half a day and 90F ($13) for a full day. A **taxi/minibus service** (☎ **02-54-78-07-65;** Fax: 02-54-78-32-80; E-mail: taxiradioblois@wanadoo.fr) will take you from the Blois train station to the two castles at Chambord and Cheverny (420F/ $64) or to the three castles at Chaumont, Amboise, and Chenonceaux (670F/$96).

Where to stay

Le Choiseul

$$$$ **Amboise**

The 32-room Le Choiseul (the area's premier hotel) boasts a Michelin star and occupies three eighteenth-century buildings joined by Italian-style gardens. In addition to rooms in the main building, known as the Hermit's House, five private apartments can be found in the Duke's House and Apothecary's House. The spacious rooms are elegantly decorated with oriental rugs, chandeliers, and antiques; most have comfortable seating areas. Alongside the heated outdoor pool is a raised terrace surrounded by gardens. The fine restaurant, with views of the Loire River, serves regional specialties like perch and Touraine chicken. The château is behind and above the hotel, though the actual entrance is a ten-minute walk down the road.

36 quai Charles-Guinot. ☎ *02-47-30-45-45. Fax: 02-47-30-46-10. Internet:* www. le-choiseul.com. *E-mail:* choiseul@wanadoo.fr. *Rack rates: 650–1,450F ($93–$207) double; 1,550–1,950F ($221–$279) apartment. Breakfast: Continental breakfast 90F ($13); buffet breakfast 140F ($20). Closed early Dec to early Feb. AE, DC, MC, V.*

Where to dine

Brasserie de l'Hôtel de Ville

$$ Amboise TOURAINE

This casual brasserie offers a convivial atmosphere in the village center near the Eglise St-Florentin. It specializes in local products, as well as grilled meats and fish. Families tend to fill the tables in the front of the restaurant, attracted by the wide range of affordable main courses on the menu. The convenient location means tourists tend to wander in for a late lunch after touring the sites, but unlike some of the other eateries in this part of town, there's good value for the franc here. English is spoken here.

1–3 rue François-1er. ☎ *02-47-57-26-30. Meals: Main courses 59–137F ($8–$20). MC, V. Open: Daily 1–3 p.m. and 7:30–10 p.m.*

Seeing the castle and Leonardo's home

Six successive kings of France, from Charles VII to Henri II, lived at and modified the glorious **Château d'Amboise** (☎ 02-47-57-00-98; E-mail: chateau.amboise@wanadoo.fr), set on a rock high above the town. Perhaps the most influential was François I, who befriended master artist Leonardo da Vinci and set him up domestically just down the road at Le Clos Lucé. (An underground tunnel united the two residences so the king could visit his court's genius, and vice versa, without mixing with the common people.) As originally built, the heavily fortified castle was a massive tower of stone evoking the dark ages, but it fell victim to successive attacks for hundreds of years. In the fifteenth century, French kings brought Renaissance improvements and embellishments, and renovations in the sixteenth century created a castle five times bigger than what exists today. But 400 years of battles and neglect left it a shadow of its former glory, and it was used mainly as a jail. France's last king, Louis-Philippe, presided over much the same edifice we see today.

The castle has been the setting for a host of historic events, including the rather undignified death of Charles VIII, who in 1498 fatally hit his head on a low doorway. His widow, Anne de Bretagne, didn't miss a beat — she married his successor, Louis XII, the following year. Then there was the Amboise Conspiracy in 1560, when Protestants stormed the castle in the name of reform. Leaders of the movement were hanged or beheaded within the château walls. And there was more bloody violence toward Protestants during the St. Bartholomew's Day Massacre at Amboise in 1572.

A brochure, written in English, assists you in a self-guided tour of the castle, where you'll wander through 11 rooms filled with an impressive collection of armor, tapestries (don't miss the tributes to Alexander the Great), paintings (note the portraits of Louis XIII and Henri IV), and antique furniture. The third floor features rooms with Restoration and First Empire antiques from the time Louis-Philippe spent at the château. You can find a portrait of Louis-Philippe in the music room. After wandering through the castle, head to the far northwest corner of the grounds near the entrance ramp to check out the beautiful Flamboyant Gothic **Chapelle de St-Hubert,** built in 1496, where Leonardo da Vinci was allegedly buried.

Allow yourself at least an hour to see Amboise. The château is open daily (except December 25 and January 1): December and January 9 a.m. to noon and 2 to 5 p.m.; February, March, and November 9 a.m. to noon and 2 to 5:30 p.m.; April to June 9 a.m. to 6:30 p.m.; July and August 9 a.m. to 8 p.m.; and September and October 9 a.m. to 6 p.m. Admission is 41F ($6) for adults, 33F ($4.70) for students, and 21F ($3) for children 7 to 14. From late June to early September, a **sound-and-light show** is held on Wednesdays and Saturdays beginning at dusk and lasting 1½ hours. Admission is 80F ($11) for adults and 40F ($6) for children.

Leonardo da Vinci lived out his final four years about half a mile from the castle at **Le Clos Lucé** (☎ **02-47-57-62-88),** a brick-and-stone mansion given to him by François I. He died at the house on May 2, 1519. The house contains Leonardo's fine Louis XV furniture, including the bed where he drew his last breath. A highlight can be found in the basement: 40 models based on Leonardo's drawings of airplanes, helicopters, parachutes, tanks, and other machines of war. You can sit in the Italian Renaissance rose garden behind the house and sip tea at the cafe. The house is open daily (except December 25 and January 1): January 10 a.m. to 5 p.m.; February to late March and November and December 9 a.m. to 6 p.m.; late March to June and September and October 9 a.m. to 7 p.m.; and July and August 9 a.m. to 8 p.m. Admission is 40F ($6) for adults, 32F ($4.60) for students, and 20F ($2.85) for children 6 to 15. It's a ten-minute walk from the castle to Le Clos Lucé.

If you're in the middle of your châteaux exploration and are trying to keep all those turrets and towers straight, give yourself a refresher course at the **Parc Mini Châteaux** (route de Chenonceaux, Amboise; ☎ 02-47-23-44-44), which features 43 marquettes of Loire Valley châteaux built at 1/25th scale and surrounded by 4,000 bonzai. Admission is 65F ($9) for adults, 45F ($6) for children 4 to 16, and 59F ($8) for students. From April to mid-November, it's open daily 9 a.m. to 7 p.m. The park is located about 4 km (2.5 miles) south of the castle of Amboise.

Chambord: The Loire's Largest Château

Most people's jaws drop when they first see the château at **Chambord,** a fantastic jumble of soaring turrets and belfries, graceful arches, and dormers. And that's just what François I wanted: the most impressive château ever built. Allow yourself plenty of time to explore the interior with its refined Renaissance spaces, which are in stark contrast to its colossal opulent facade. The pièce de résistance is the monumental double staircase, with a design helped along by Leonardo da Vinci. Next to the castle you won't find anything but a hotel/restaurant and a few little tourist shops. Chambord also claims Europe's largest enclosed forest, stretching for 13,000 acres. This castle is a must-see, and my pick for best château — if you can visit only one. April to September, the small **tourist office** (place St-Michel; ☎ 02-54-20-34-86) is open daily 10:30 a.m. to 12:30 p.m. and 2 to 7 p.m.

Getting there

Buses (☎ 02-54-58-55-44) make the circuit from Chambord to Blois (20 km/12.4 miles) three times a day. The trip takes 45 minutes and costs 20F ($2.85). If you're **driving** from Paris, take A10 south to Orléans and then D951 southwest from Orléans (about 2 hours). From Blois, take D951 east (about 15 minutes). If you're driving from Orléans, take D951 southwest (about 35 minutes) and follow the signs to Chambord.

Getting around

The castle is just about the only thing in the tiny village of Chambord. The village's only hotel/restaurant is a former out building of the castle and is just a hop, skip, and a jump from the castle entrance.

The **bus** company (☎ 02-54-90-41-41) gives tours of Blois, Chambord, and Cheverny, with buses departing from the train station in Blois. From June to early September, tours depart daily at 9:10 a.m. and 1:20 p.m., and return about four hours later. The cost is 65F ($9) for adults and 50F ($7) for children. You can buy tickets at the Blois tourist office. A **taxi/minibus service** (☎ 02-54-78-07-65; Fax: 02-54-78-32-80; E-mail: taxiradioblois@wanadoo.fr) will take you from the Blois train station to the two castles at Chambord and Cheverny (420F/$60) or to the three castles at Chaumont, Amboise, and Chenonceaux (670F/$96).

Where to stay and dine

Hôtel St-Michel

$$ Chambord

This 39-room hotel, a former royal dog kennel, is the only lodging in town. The area is renowned as a hunting park, and the St-Michel is decorated with some taxidermy, mostly stag heads. The rooms, some with château views, are quite spacious; even the smallest attic rooms are comfortable and cheery. The baths have above average space and modern fixtures. Before falling asleep, look out your window at the castle sparkling with delicate white lights; in the morning, watch the sun rise over the castle. The hotel restaurant is quite good, and in fine weather, meals are served on the terrace facing the château. The parking lot holds only about five cars, but you can also park in the nearby château lot.

Place St-Michel. ☎ 02-54-20-31-31. Fax: 02-54-20-36-40. Parking: free. Rack rates: 300–450F ($43–$64) double. Breakfast: 42F ($6). MC, V.

Seeing the castle

The **Château de Chambord** (☎ 02-54-50-40-00) is the region's largest and most elaborate castle (with 440 rooms, 365 chimneys, and 84 stairways). It was built by François I, the last of the kings from the Age of Chivalry. After a decisive military battle, François was crowned king in 1515; he believed the best way to show the power of the monarchy was through extravagance, so his castles overflowed with riches and courtiers (over 1,800 at Chambord). Constructed between 1519 and 1545, Chambord was François's hunting lodge, a kind of country house used for sporting activities of all kinds — including amorous pursuits. Some of the château's most innovative elements came from the king's pal, Leonardo da Vinci (see the preceding section on Amboise), and you'll see the innovative Italian's ideas reflected in the castle's symmetry, in its domes, and particularly in the double spirals used in its famous central staircase.

Inside the castle, there's much to explore, including a luminous **chapel,** designed partly by Jules Hardoin-Mansart. You first enter the **keep,** where you'll find the famous double spiral "corkscrew" staircase, a masterpiece of the French Renaissance — one person can descend and another ascend and they won't ever meet. There are three levels of **royal apartments** filled with important paintings, tapestries, sculpture, and furniture that's original to the residence. The third floor contains a **museum of hunting and animal art,** which plays up Chambord's history as a hunting lodge. Finally, you may want to climb up to the **roof** to see elements of the audacious architecture up close and to catch the beautiful views of the canals and forests of Chambord.

Long after François made Chambord his dream house, other powerful and rich men upheld its traditions. In the early eighteenth century, Stanislas Zeczinski, king of Poland, lived there. After him, well-connected Maurice de Saxe owned the residence for a couple of years. Saxe was chummy with Louis V and managed to receive items from Versailles (various paintings and a marble fireplace) as gifts to decorate the château. France eventually bought the property for 11 million francs, and still holds official hunts for wild boar on the grounds. In 1983, the property was designated a World Heritage site.

You'll have fun exploring the site, so allow yourself at least a couple of hours to do so. The château is open daily (except January 1, May 1, and December 25) 9 a.m. to 6:15 p.m. (last entrance at 5:45 p.m.). Admission is 40F ($6) for adults and 25F ($3.60) for anyone age 18 to 25. The audioguide costs 25F ($3), and brochures, written in English, are available. You can rent bikes and boats, next to the castle, to explore the grounds and waterways.

Les Metamorphoses de Chambord, a two-hour sound-and-light show beginning at dusk, is held here on weekends from late April to June and in September, and Monday to Saturday in July and August. Admission is 80F ($11) for adults and 60F ($9) for children 6 to 14. **Les Ecuries du Maréchal de Saxe,** an equestrian spectacle, takes place on Saturdays and Sundays (May, June, and September at 11:45 a.m. and 4 p.m. and July and August at 11:45 a.m. and 5 p.m.). It costs 45F ($5) for adults and 30F ($4.30) for children under 12.

Orléans: Saved by Joan of Arc

Orléans, sitting beside the mighty Loire River, is one of the oldest cities in France. French kings established their dynasties in Orléans in the Middle Ages before deciding to make Paris their capital. Royals in the fifteenth and sixteenth centuries were particularly fond of the Loire Valley, as it was only two days' ride on horseback from Paris. You can feel and see the thousands of years of history here. The city has also had its share of misfortune over the ages. Attila the Hun came to Orléans to make mischief in 451. Though that siege was unsuccessful, there were many more to come. The city's heroine is the Maid of Orléans, Joan of Arc, who saved it from a seven-month siege by the English on May 8, 1429, a major turning point in the Hundred Years' War. Several sites are devoted to Joan, and the city commemorates her bravery annually at the Jeanne d'Arc Festival on May 7 and 8.

Orléans

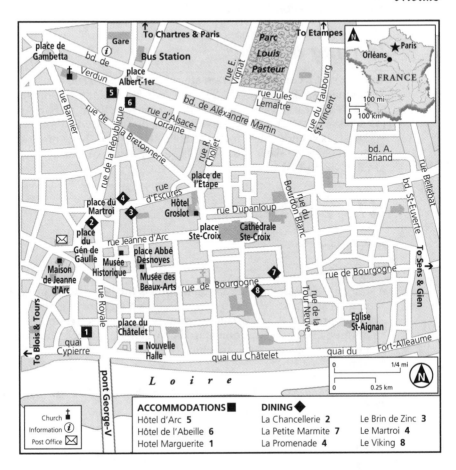

The **primary tourist office** is at 6 rue Albert-1er. The office is open daily: May to September 9 a.m. to 8 p.m., and October to April 9 a.m. to 1 p.m. and 2 to 6:30 p.m. The **secondary tourist office** is at 6 rue Jeanne-d'Arc (☎ 02-38-24-05-05). It's open daily: May to September 9 a.m. to 1 p.m. and 2 to 7 p.m., and October to May 10 a.m. to 6 p.m.

Getting there

The one-way **train** fare from Paris's Gare d'Austerlitz is 92F ($13), and the trip could be as short as an hour nonstop, or as long as 1¾ hours with lots of stops. There are also about 12 trains per day that travel from Tours, taking about 1½ hours and costing 90F ($13). For information and reservations, call ☎ 08-36-35-35-35.

Don't get off the train one stop too soon at Les Aubrais Orléans — it's the suburban stop about 11.3 km (7 miles) from the city.

If you're **driving,** the trip takes about 1½ hours from Paris on A10. From Tours, head east on A10 for about 1½ hours.

Getting around

You can rent a car near the train station at **Budget** (5 rue des Sansonnières; ☎ 02-38-54-54-30), and **Avis** (13 rue des Sansonnières; ☎ 02-38-62-27-04). **Ecoto** has an office nearby at 19 av. de Paris (☎ 02-38-77-92-92). The **Hertz** office (rue de Bannier; ☎ 08-03-86-18-61) is several miles from the train station and the center of town, so you'll have to take a cab to get there. For a cab, call **Taxi d'Orléans** at ☎ 02-38-53-11-11.

Where to stay

Hôtel d'Arc

$$$ Orléans

A stately 1902 building, this 35-room hotel is the best choice in the town center, located a stone's throw from the train station. Régine and Alain Guilgaut provide the finest in hospitality. The attractive lobby boasts an antique elevator. The rooms are fairly generic in decor but are very comfortable, and most are spacious. All have minibars, and some have balconies.

37 rue de la République. ☎ *02-38-53-10-94. Fax: 02-38-81-77-47. Rack rates: 390F ($56) double. Breakfast: 50F ($7). AE, DC, MC, V.*

Hôtel de l'Abeille

$$ Orléans

This 31-room hotel near the train station is a little worn at the seams, but it has a lot of style, from the burgundy lobby with a terra-cotta Joan of Arc statue and art deco posters to the individually decorated rooms. The same family has run the place since 1919. Some rooms have been recently renovated (they freshen up a few every year), and some have French balconies fronting this busy section of town (those in the back are much quieter). Even the tiny rooms may have an added touch like a marble fireplace. Beware of the steep staircase (there's no elevator).

64 rue Alsace-Lorraine (at the corner of rue de la République). ☎ *02-38-53-54-87. Fax: 02-38-62-65-84. E-mail:* hotel-de-labeille@wanadoo.fr. *Rack rates: 290–380F ($41–$54) double. Breakfast: 35F ($5). AE, DC, MC, V.*

Hôtel Marguerite

$$ Orléans

This 25-room hotel is a budget option, and if everything is booked in town, as often happens, they probably have a place for you. Some rooms have shared baths in the hallways, but they're spacious and clean. Most of the rooms on the second and third floors are more commodious than the simpler rooms on the first floor, and those on the upper floors have nice city views. The hotel's location on the market square isn't bad — it's fairly quiet. The owner is very gracious.

14 place du Vieux-Marché. ☎ *02-38-53-74-32. Fax: 02-38-53-31-56. Rack rates: 160–310F ($23–$44) double. Breakfast: 35F ($5). MC, V.*

Where to dine

La Chancellerie

$$ Orléans   ORLÉANAIS

This popular place run by Max and Jean-Luc Erta is a brasserie/restaurant. As you enter the restaurant, you may notice the fresh fish and shellfish on ice displayed outside (oysters are indeed a specialty). For good value, check out the daily special — like *tête de veau* with *sauce gribiche* (head of veal with caper mayonnaise) or *jambon à l'os fermie* (farm-fresh ham) — which comes with a complimentary glass of wine for only 73 to 79F ($10 to $11). The brasserie fare includes omelets and steak tartare. You can dine out on the square or at marble-topped tables inside.

95 rue Royale (place du Martroi). ☎ *02-38-53-57-54. Reservations recommended. Meals: Main courses 78–160F ($11–$23); menu 175F ($25); children's menu 48–50F ($7–$8). MC, V. Open: Mon–Sat noon to midnight.*

La Petite Marmite

$$ Orléans   ORLÉANAIS

Traditional cuisine rules at this little cafe on bustling rue de Bourgogne. The signature dishes are *coq au vin* (chicken stewed in red wine), *canard du maison* (roasted duck with cognac), and *lapin Lyonnais* (rabbit garnished with onions). For dessert, everyone orders *tarte tatin,* a caramelized apple pie that's a specialty of the region.

178 rue de Bourgogne. ☎ *02-38-54-23-83. Meals: Main courses 75–125F ($11–$18); menus 118–188F ($17–$27). MC, V. Open: Mon–Fri 7–10:30 p.m.; Sat–Sun noon to 2 p.m. and 7–10:30 p.m.*

La Promenade

$$ Orléans ORLÉANAIS

This elegant restaurant is located on the second floor of the building that houses Le Martroi (see later in this section), so you have a nice view of a major square. Seafood is a specialty here, and a standout is the mosaic of chilled fish with bouillabaisse and aïoli sauce. Try the lovely *cabillaud roti* (roasted codfish served with mussels) for a main course and the light pear dish with caramel sauce for dessert.

12 place du Martroi. ☎ 02-38-81-12-12. Reservations recommended. Meals: Main courses 65–97F ($9–$14); menus 90F ($13), 120F ($17), 160F ($23) with wine and coffee, 180F ($26) with aperitif, wine, and coffee. AE, V. Open: Tues–Sat noon to 2:30 p.m. and 7–11 p.m. Closed mid-Aug.

Le Brin de Zinc

$$ Orléans ORLÉANAIS

Mussels are a specialty here, and the extensive selection of mussels dishes are priced at 67 to 72F ($10 to $11). The house mussels dish has lardons, mushrooms, onions, white wine, and crème fraîche. Besides vegetarian choices, there are bistro specialties like duck confit. Outdoor seating is available, but the inside, with stone walls, feels very cozy.

62 rue Ste-Catherine. ☎ 02-38-53-38-77. Meals: Main courses 78–95F ($11–$14); menus 109F ($16) and 149F ($21). MC, V. Open: Daily noon to 2:30 p.m. and 7–11 p.m. Closed Tues in winter.

Le Martroi

$$ Orléans ORLÉANAIS

This brasserie is located on the first floor of a grand building on place Martroi, below La Promenade (see earlier in this section). A specialty of the house is the pork pâté *rustique* with Armagnac; they also serve a very good guacamole of tuna (don't ask, just eat). Popular main courses are zucchini caviar and grilled trout, with exceptional profiteroles for dessert. The restaurant also offers an after-10:30 p.m. menu.

12 place du Martroi. ☎ 02-38-42-15-00. Reservations recommended. Meals: Main courses 67–97F ($10–$14); menu du garçon with wine 90F ($13) not served Fri night or Sat all day. MC, V. Open: Daily noon to 3 p.m. and 7:30–11 p.m.

Le Viking

$ Orléans ORLÉANAIS

If you're looking for a simple place to have crêpes, look no further. This popular crêperie, with a beamed medieval atmosphere, has a good 109F ($16) fixed-price menu and yummy food. The restaurant also has more elaborate and expensive fare, including a lovely duck dish with foie gras.

233 rue de Borgogne. ☎ *02-38-53-12-21. Meals: Main courses 45–125F ($6–$18); menus 59–200F ($8–$29). AE, V. Open: Mon–Sat noon to 2 p.m. and 7–11 p.m. Closed Mon lunch.*

Seeing the town

Orléans is an easily navigated metropolis with several Romanesque churches and a score of Renaissance buildings. The city's train station is located in a modern shopping mall. When you exit the shopping mall, you can look down the impressive **rue de la République,** a wide boulevard (laid out with cable-car tracks in the eighteenth century) that leads down to the Loire River. Walk a few blocks down rue de la République to **place du Martroi,** where you'll find a large 1855 statue of Joan of Arc (her exploits are carved in bas-relief on the statue base). Beyond place du Martroi, rue de la République becomes **rue Royale,** which has many fine shops. Most of the city's interesting sites and museums are on the left side of rue de la République/rue Royale if you're facing the river.

The **Cathédrale Ste-Croix** (place Ste-Croix; ☎ 02-38-77-87-50) was built from 1607 to 1829 in a neo-Gothic style. Look for the seventeenth-century organ and early eighteenth-century woodwork (some by Man-sart) in the chancel. You'll need a guide to visit the crypt, which contains a treasury with Byzantine enamels. The church is open daily 10 a.m. to noon and 2 to 5 p.m., and admission is free. Across the street is the **Musée des Beaux-Arts** (1 rue Ferdinand-Rabier; ☎ 02-38-79-21-55), with five stories of sixteenth- to nineteenth-century French, Dutch, and Flemish works, plus a very fine twentieth-century art collection in the basement. The museum also has a Velasquez painting, **Apostle St. Thomas.** The fine arts museum is open Thursday to Saturday 10 a.m. to 6 p.m. and Wednesday 10 a.m. to 8 p.m. (closed January 1, May 1, November 1, and December 25), and admission is 20F ($2.85) for adults and 10F ($1.40) for children.

Around the corner from the fine arts museum is the Renaissance **Hôtel Groslot,** the former city hall on place de l'Etape just north of the cathedral. Built in 1550, the building has been considerably altered over the years and is now used for receptions and weddings. The interior decoration is known as "Gothic Troubadour" style (try throwing that phrase around at a cocktail party). In November 1560, François II, the 17-year-old king of France, died in this mansion after suffering a "fainting fit" during vespers at the nearby Eglise St-Aignan. Admission is free, and the house is open Sunday to Friday 10 a.m. to noon and 2 to 6 p.m. and Saturday 4:30 to 6 p.m. You can also stroll through the harmonious and romantic gardens, where there are fragments of a fifteenth-century chapel.

After visiting the Groslot, you can backtrack to the cathedral square and walk all the way down rue Jeanne-d'Arc, across rue Royale, to see a small museum dedicated to Orléans's favorite mademoiselle. The **Maison**

Jeanne-d'Arc (3 place de Gaulle; ☎ 02-38-52-99-89) is a twentieth-century reproduction of the fifteenth-century house where Joan of Arc, the liberator and patron of Orléans, stayed during her local heroics. The original house was much modified, then destroyed by bombing in 1940. The first floor has temporary exhibitions, and the second and third floors contain Joan-related models and memorabilia. The house is open Tuesday to Sunday: May to October 10 a.m. to noon and 2 to 6 p.m. and November to April 2 to 6 p.m. Admission is 14F ($2) for adults and 7F ($1) for children.

You may gain a better appreciation of Orléans if you take a self-guided tour of some of the city's historic sites and gardens. At the tourist office, pick up a brochure in English called the **Orléans Architectural and Historical Trail.** Two of the 43 sites on the trail — Louis Pasteur Park on rue Jules-Lemaitre and the gardens of the Vieille Intendance at the corner of rue Alsace-Lorraine and rue des Hugenots — are great places that you might not stumble across if you wandered around without guidance.

Shopping

One of the city's main industries, from the Middle Ages to well into the twentieth century, was vinegar making. You can buy some of the famous Orléans vinegar north of Orléans at **Vinaigre Martin Pouret** (236 Faubourg Bannier in Fleury-les-Aubrais; ☎ 02-38-88-78-49). Carrying on his family's business founded in 1797, M. Pouret, owner of Vinaigre Martin Pourret, is the only person left carrying on the slow, traditional vinegar-making method in the region. You can do a wine tasting at the **Cave de Marc & Sebastien** (1 rue Pierre-Percée; ☎ 02-38-62-94-11), which is located just north of the Loire, west of rue Royale.

Nightlife

Everyone feels right at home in **St. Andrews Pub** (15 rue Croix de Malte; ☎ 02-38-54-44-00). **Bel Air,** located at 44 rue du Poirier, a block south of rue de Bourgogne (☎ 02-38-77-08-06), is a hip cocktail bar near the Halles Châtelet, the old market building. Nearby is **George V,** alongside the Halles Châtelet (☎ 02-38-53-08-79), with a DJ and small dance floor (50F/$7 cover). **Paxton's Head** (264 rue de Bourgogne; ☎ 02-38-81-23-29) has live jazz on Saturday nights. For those who'd like to check their e-mail while they sip a café, there's **Odysseus Cyber Café** (32 rue du Colombier; no phone), with Internet access costing 30F ($4) per hour. It's open Monday to Wednesday 9 a.m. to 9 p.m., Thursday and Friday 9 a.m. to 1 a.m., and Saturday 11 a.m. to 1 a.m.

Part V
Normandy and Brittany

The 5th Wave   By Rich Tennant

"Funny—I just assumed it would be Carreras too."

In this part...

Touring Normandy and Brittany on France's west coast is a way to see some quintessential French country- side, charming towns, and famous sights. In Chapter 16, I lead you to the highlights of Normandy: rolling green hills, farmland, half-timbered houses, medieval churches, and even the D-Day beaches where 135,000 brave troops from the United States, Canada, and Great Britain managed against all odds to charge ashore and save Europe from the Nazis. It's a dramatic story that's told and retold in small and large monuments and museums along the coast- line. Perhaps the most moving site is the 173 acres of simple white crosses at the Normandy American cemetery near Omaha Beach. Nearby you can see the renowned Bayeaux Tapestry, the medieval scroll telling the story of when William the Conqueror of Normandy invaded England and was crowned king. One of France's most famous sights is also in Normandy: Mont-St-Michel, an abbey built on a rock just off the coast, has been a pilgrimage site for over a thousand years.

When French people talk of going to the shore, they often mean the rugged coast of Brittany on the Atlantic Ocean. In Chapter 17, I explore this fiercely proud, independent region, which has its own language, as well as folk customs and costumes. A region of fishers and artisans, Brittany is a place to eat oysters, buy Quimper pottery, and appreciate the traditions of a distinct community. Also in Brittany are France's largest prehistoric rock formations, hundreds of huge stones aligned like obedient soldiers in Carnac, which is also a seaside resort.

Chapter 16

Normandy

● ●

In this chapter

▶ Following in the footsteps of Joan of Arc in Rouen (without getting burned at the stake!)

▶ Deciphering the medieval Bayeux Tapestry, the story of William the Conqueror

▶ Paying homage at the D-Day beaches of World War II

▶ Climbing Mont-St-Michel to see one of Europe's great marvels

● ●

*N*ormandy is one of France's most appealing regions, and it's just a couple of hours from Paris by car or train. The capital is charming **Rouen,** where half-timbered houses (see the sidebar "Why all the half-timbered houses?" later in this chapter) and ancient churches line pedestrian streets paved with cobblestone. This was also the final resting place of France's favorite teenager, Joan of Arc, who was burned at the stake here by the English; her ashes were thrown in the Seine. In the town of **Bayeaux,** you can find the famous tapestry that tells the story of how France came to rule England for a brief time in the eleventh century. Nearby are the **D-Day beaches,** where on June 6, 1944, about 135,000 soldiers from England, the United States, and Canada landed in preparation for the seminal battle of World War II. The ensuing Battle of Normandy led to the liberation of Europe from the Nazis. Normandy also boasts one of France's most popular attractions, the abbey at **Mont-St-Michel.** Known for years by pilgrims journeying to the site as La Merveille (The Marvel), the abbey is set high on a rock just off the coast of Normandy.

Rouen: Capital of Normandy

Rouen, the ancient capital of Normandy, has been rebuilt after suffering extensive bombing during World War II. But even if some of the half-timbered houses are "merely the mock," this is definitely a charming town, offering wonderful museums and historic sites. The lively center has pedestrian streets with shops and restaurants. The fourteenth-century **Gros Horloge** is a big clock set in a Renaissance gateway that straddles the main pedestrian thoroughfare. Nearby is the **Cathédrale Notre-Dame,** which impressionist artist Claude Monet painted many times, in fog, rain, and snow. The cathedral and the impressive Gothic

Sampling the region's cuisine

Traveling through Normandy, you may see the sleepy-eyed cows that produce some of this region's delicious dairy products: cream, milk, and cheeses. Of the many special cheeses from Normandy, Camembert is the most famous, but there's also Livarot and Pont-l'Evêque. When food is prepared à la normande, it usually means the meat or seafood is prepared with cream, cider, or Calvados. Befitting Normandy's coastal location, menus often include Norman sole, Courseulles and Isigny oysters, Grandcamp scallops, and Honfleur prawns and cockles. Special meats to look for include Vallée d'Auge chicken, andouillé sausage from Vire, and Isigny lamb. The region is also known for apples, so local cider, the apple-based aperatif called pommeau, and Calvados (an apple brandy) are popular drinks. For dessert, an apple tart is the perfect ending to any meal.

churches of **St-Maclou** and **St-Ouen** form a triangle of spires that dominate the town. In the ancient **market square,** a modern church was built in memory of Joan of Arc; it's a clever design incorporating a market, a monument to St. Joan, and the ruins of the former church that long stood on the site but was destroyed during World War II. Rouen has long been famous for its *faïence* (painted pottery): If you're interested in this local craft, you can visit the *faïence* museum, as well as the many shops and antiques stores that sell fine pieces.

Getting there

Trains leave hourly from Paris's Gare St-Lazare for Rouen's **Gare SNCF** at place Bernard-Tissot at the end of rue Jeanne-d'Arc. The trip takes from 70 minutes to 1¾ hours and costs 78 to 120F ($11 to $17). For train info, call ☎ **08-36-35-35-39** or 08-36-35-35-35. The **Gare Routière** (bus station) is at 25 rue des Charrettes. **CNA buses** (☎ **02-35-52-92-00**) travel from Rouen to the Abbaye de Jumièges (see "Exploring the town" later in this chapter). The trip takes 45 minutes and costs 35F ($5).

The **Aéroport de Rouen** is in Boos, 10 km (6.2 miles) southeast of Rouen (☎ **02-35-79-41-00**). There are no direct flights from Paris to the Rouen airport, although there are direct flights from Marseille, Nice, and Bordeaux. To get to the center of the city from the airport, you need to take a **taxi** costing about 50F ($7).

If you're **driving** from Paris, take A13 west for 133 km (83.6 miles). The trip from Paris to Rouen is 1½ hours.

Normandy

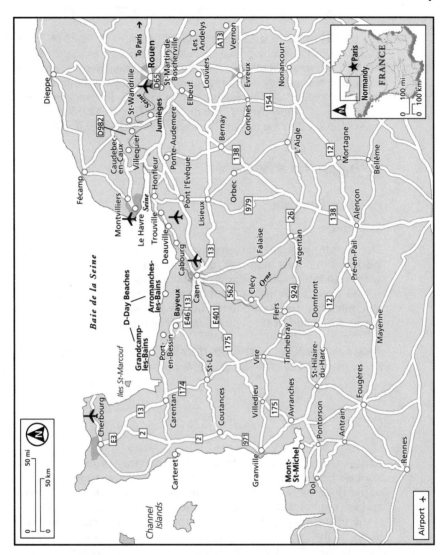

Getting around and getting information

If you want to rent a car, try **Avis** at the Gare SNCF (place Bernard-Tissot; ☎ **02-35-88-60-34**) next to the info counter; it's open daily 9:00 a.m. to 12:15 p.m. and 2 to 6 p.m. Avis's main booking number is ☎ **08-02-05-05-05**. **Hertz** is across the street at 130 rue Jeanne-d'Arc (☎ **02-35-70-70-71**), and is open daily 9 a.m. to noon and 2 to 6 p.m. You can rent a bike at **Rouen Cycles** (45 rue St-Eloi; ☎ **02-35-71-34-30**) for 70F ($10) per half day and 125F ($18) per day. For a **taxi,** call ☎ **02-35-88-50-50.**

The **tourist office** is at 25 place de la Cathédrale (☎ **02-32-08-32-40;** Fax: 02-32-08-32-44; E-mail: otrouen@mcom.fr; Internet: www.mairie-rouen.fr). Housed in a magnificent Renaissance building across from the cathedral, this office offers hotel booking, money exchange (no commission), and guided 2-hour walking tours (35F/$5). To check on or send e-mail, head to **Place Net** (37 rue de la République; ☎ **02-32-76-02-22**), open Monday 2 to 8 p.m. and Tuesday to Saturday noon to 8 p.m.

Where to stay

Hôtel de Bordeaux

$$ Rouen

The friendly staff and marvelous views from the upper-floor rooms in this modern hotel go a long way toward making up for the generic smallish accommodations and depressing facade of this cinder-block building across from the Seine. Most of the 47 rooms have access to communal balconies that wrap around the building; some have panoramic views of the rooftops and Gothic spires, as well as the greenish Seine.

9 place de la République. ☎ *02-35-71-93-58. Fax: 02-35-71-92-15. Parking: 36F ($5). Rack rates: 320-360F ($46–$51) double. Breakfast: 38F ($5) downstairs or 58F ($8) in room. MC, V.*

Hôtel de Dieppe

$$$ Rouen

Across from the train station, this reasonably priced Best Western is Rouen's best lodging option. It's on a busy road, so request a room on an upper floor in the rear. Some rooms are small, but all have modern decor and are comfortable. The great attached restaurant, Les Quatre Saisons, is the pride and joy of the Guéret family, who've been running it and the hotel for five generations. The chef's favorites are *sole Michel à la arête* (sole prepared on the bone in the chef's style) and *caneton Rouennais à la presse "Félix Faure" préparé devant le client par un maître canardier* (pressed duckling prepared tableside). For dessert, there's *soufflé du Président* (apple soufflé).

Place Bernard-Tissot. ☎ *800-528-1234 in the U.S. and Canada, or 02-35-71-96-00. Fax: 02-35-89-65-21.Free parking. Rack rates: 520–620F ($74–$89) double. Breakfast: 50F ($7). AE, DC, MC, V.*

Rouen

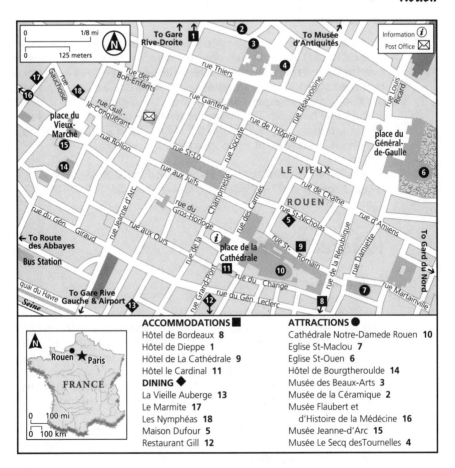

ACCOMMODATIONS ■
Hôtel de Bordeaux **8**
Hôtel de Dieppe **1**
Hôtel de La Cathédrale **9**
Hôtel le Cardinal **11**
DINING ◆
La Vieille Auberge **13**
Le Marmite **17**
Les Nymphéas **18**
Maison Dufour **5**
Restaurant Gill **12**

ATTRACTIONS ●
Cathédrale Notre-Damede Rouen **10**
Eglise St-Maclou **7**
Eglise St-Ouen **6**
Hôtel de Bourgtheroulde **14**
Musée des Beaux-Arts **3**
Musée de la Céramique **2**
Musée Flaubert et
  d'Histoire de la Médécine **16**
Musée Jeanne-d'Arc **15**
Musée Le Secq desTournelles **4**

Hôtel de la Cathédrale

$$ Rouen

The Cathédrale, an eighteenth-century house tucked into a narrow pedestrian side street paved with cobblestone, really feels like old Rouen; this is definitely the most charming medium-priced hotel in town. The hotel, located in an area that's very quiet at night, is built around a beautiful interior courtyard filled with flowers and surrounded by half-timbered facades. (The courtyard serves as a tearoom in good weather.) The 24 cheerful rooms, painted in bright colors, are comfortable, although some are small.

12 rue St-Romain. ☎ *02-35-71-57-95. Fax: 02-35-70-15-54. Internet:* www. hotel-de-la-cathedrale.com. *Parking: 35F ($5). Rack rates: 320–380F ($46–$54) double. Breakfast: 35F ($5). MC, V.*

Hôtel le Cardinal

$$ Rouen

This is a hotel for sound sleepers or those who want to admire the beautiful cathedral all night: It's on the cathedral square, and most rooms overlook the ornate facade, which is brightly lit at night. But be aware that the cathedral bell chimes every 15 minutes (and more jubilantly on the hour), and the square is noisy with late-night cafes on the first floor of the hotel building. The 20 rooms are fairly spacious and comfortable, decorated in a plain contemporary style. The staff can be rather brusk. Parking is somewhat of a problem in this busy area.

1 place de la Cathédrale. ☎ *02-35-70-24-42. Fax: 02-35-89-75-14. Parking: 31F ($4.40). Rack rates: 300–410F ($43–$59) double. Breakfast: 38F ($5). Closed mid-Dec to early Jan. MC, V.*

Where to dine

La Vieille Auberge

$$ Rouen FRENCH

This unassuming little restaurant near the Seine is family owned/operated and serves well-priced local specialties that are consistently tasty and appealing. All the usual regional dishes are featured, including *carnard Rouennais* (pressed duck), *marmit de poisson* (fish casserole), *escalopes de veau* (thin slices of veal), and, for dessert, *pomme Calvados au crème Normand* (apples with apple-brandy sauce and local whipped cream).

37 rue St-Etienne-des-Tonneliers. ☎ *02-35-70-56-65. Reservations recommended. Meals: Main courses 85–135F ($12–$19); menus 98–198F ($14–$28). Open: Tues–Sun noon to 2:30 p.m. and 7:30–9:30 p.m. MC, V.*

Le Marmite

$$$ Rouen FRENCH

This is a very romantic fine dining restaurant tucked into a side street just north of the *Vieille Marché* (old market) square. Elegant service and beautifully presented plates of traditional foods combine to assure a delightful meal. The menu offers all the region's specialties, like *foie gras de canard* (duck foie gras), *marmite de pomme* (apple casserole), and *camembert rôti* (roasted camembert). The wine list offers a range of affordable options.

3 rue Florence. ☎ *02-35-71-75-55. Reservations recommended. Meals: Main courses 110–155F ($16–$22); menus 125–198F ($18–$28). Open: Tues–Sun noon to 2:30 p.m.; Tues–Sat 7:30–9:30 p.m. MC, V.*

Les Nymphéas

$$$$ **Rouen FRENCH**

Set in an ancient half-timbered house near the Vieille Marché, this is one of Rouen's top restaurants, decorated with stylish contemporary flair. Chef Patrice Kukurudz is most interested in combinations of subtle flavors. His signature dishes are *foie gras chaud de canard au vinaigre de cidre* (hot duck foie gras with cider vinegar), *civet de homard au Sauternes* (lobster stew with sweet white wine), and, for dessert, *soufflé chaud aux pommes et Calvados* (hot apple soufflé with Calvados). In summer, lunch is served on the terrace.

7–9 rue de la Pie. ☎ *02-35-89-26-69. Internet:* www.lerapporteur.fr/ nymphàas. *Reservations required. Meals: Main courses 160–260F ($23–$37); menus 165–380F ($24–$54). AE, DC, MC, V. Open: Tues–Sun noon–2 p.m.; Tues–Sat 7:30–9:30 p.m. Closed late Aug to mid-Sept.*

Maison Dufour

$$$ **Rouen FRENCH**

Occupying a restored half-timbered corner building, this softly lit restaurant feels wonderfully cozy. The decor is rustic, with stone walls, beamed ceilings, hanging copper pots, and intimate rooms off the main room. The service is exceptional under the stern eye of Mme Dufour, whose family has run the restaurant since 1904. The food is high quality, especially at these reasonable prices. Besides the usual Normandy favorites, the restaurant features *moules de Bouchots à la crème* (mussels in cream sauce) and *sole frit, citron et persil* (sole fried with lemon and parsley). The perfect dessert is the *soufflé au Calvados.*

67 bis rue St-Nicholas. ☎ *02-35-71-90-62. Reservations accepted. Meals: Main courses 85–165F ($12–$24); menu 150–230F ($21–$33). AE, MC, V. Open: Tues–Sun noon to 2 p.m.; Tues–Sat 7:30–9:30 p.m.*

Restaurant Gill

$$$$ **Rouen FRENCH**

In a sleek modern dining room on the busy road beside the Seine, Gill is Rouen's top restaurant. Expect an elaborate multicourse meal; you may have to pace yourself. Specialties of chef Gilles Tournadre are *salade de queues de langoustines poëlées, chutney de tomate et poivron rouge* (salad of pan-fried prawn with tomato–and–red pepper chutney), *dos de cabillaud rôti, pommes et onion rouge* (roasted cod with apples and red onions), *pigeon à la Rouennaise avec sa raviole de foie gras* (guinea fowl with foie gras ravioli), and, for dessert, *millefeuille de minute* (pastry of the moment) or the traditional *soufflé au Calvados.*

9 quai de la Bourse. ☎ *02-35-71-16-14. Reservations required far in advance. Meals: Main courses 280–360F ($40–$51); menus 350–500F ($50–$71). AE, DC,*

MC, V. Open: May–Sept Tues–Sat noon to 2 p.m. and 6–10 p.m.; Oct–Apr Wed–Sun noon to 2:30 p.m., Tues–Sat 6–10 p.m. Closed two weeks in mid-Apr, three weeks in Aug and two weeks in early Jan.

Dishes you'll see frequently on Rouen menus include duck pâté, Normandy sole, pressed Rouen duck, Rouen sheep's foot, local cheese, apple tart, and soufflés. To drink, you'll find bottled cider and Calvados, the locally bottled apple brandy. One of Rouen's best restaurants is Les Quatre Saisons at the Hôtel de Dieppe (see "Where to stay" earlier in this section).

Exploring the town

The **petit train (little train)** runs 40-minute tours through the city, leaving daily from in front of the tourist office (25 place de la Cathédrale), at 10 and 11 a.m. and 2, 4, and 5 p.m. It costs 35F ($5).

Rouen is fairly compact — it'll take you about 15 minutes to walk from one end of the old center to the other. **Rue Jeanne-d'Arc** is the main thoroughfare, leading from the train station to the center. Not far from the station are Rouen's top two museums. The **Musée des Beaux-Arts** (square Verdrei; ☎ 02-35-71-28-40) contains a fine collection of paintings, drawings, and sculptures from the Middle Ages to the twentieth century, including works by Caravaggio, Velasquez, Delacroix, and Géricault (born in Rouen), all the way up to Monet (*Rouen Cathedral in Gray Weather*) and Helen Frankenthaler. Impressionist paintings are particularly well represented. The museum is open Wednesday to Monday 10 a.m. to 6 p.m. Admission is 20F ($2.85) for adults and 13F ($1.85) for students and children. The entertaining **Musée Le Secq des Tournelles** (rue Jacques-Villon; ☎ 02-35-88-42-92) displays the greatest European collection of ironworks, including signs, tools, and keys and locks from the third to the nineteenth century. The collection — housed in the former Eglise St-Laurent — was donated to the city by one collector in 1920. The museum is open Wednesday to Monday 10 a.m. to 1 p.m. and 2 to 6 p.m. Admission is 15F ($2.15) for adults and 10F ($1.40) for children and students.

Walking south down rue Jeanne-d'Arc from the train station, you'll first come to an interesting little museum, specializing in the most famous craft of the region: *faïence*. The **Musée de la Céramique** (1 rue de Faucon; ☎ 02-35-07-31-74) is dedicated to Rouen *faïence* and ceramics from the sixteenth to the eighteenth century, when Rouen was a major pottery center. The collection is housed in an elegant mansion called the Hôtel d'Hocqueville and is open Wednesday to Monday 10 a.m. to 1 p.m. and 2 to 6 p.m. Admission is 15F ($2.15) for adults and 10F ($1.40) for children and students.

Why all the half-timbered houses?

Those old buildings you see with the visible wood framing filled in by masonry are called half-timbered houses. Of the approximately 1,000 half-timbered houses (from the 14th to the nineteenth century) in Rouen's center, about 200 have been restored since World War II bombings. This style of building was popular because builders didn't have access to a lot of stone, the most common building material, but did have access to lots of oak in surrounding forests. After the war, the city used extensive records to restore buildings and builders researched ancient construction methods in order to be as authentic as possible.

Continue down rue Jeanne-d'Arc and take a right on the main street of the pedestrian shopping district, **rue de Gros Horloge,** admiring its many half-timbered buildings on your way to **place du Vieux-Marché,** the market square surrounded by cafes and restaurants. The ancient church on the square (the Eglise St-Vincent) was destroyed during World War II bombing and replaced in 1979 with a remarkable modern building that's a church (the Eglise Ste-Jeanne-d'Arc), a market with food shops, and a monument to Joan of Arc. The building's north side features a large cross on the site of the stake where Joan was burned to death for heresy. The church boasts many echoes of the sea, including scale-like roof tiles in slate and copper, fish-shaped windows, and a wooden boat-shaped ceiling. The sixteenth-century stained-glass windows from the former church were saved and installed in the new church.

True devotees of Joan of Arc won't want to miss the **Musée Jeanne-d'Arc,** located in a cellar off the central square (33 place du Vieux-Marché; ☎ **02-35-88-02-70**), just steps from the spot where she was burned alive at the stake on May 30, 1431. This is a musty place filled with cheesy waxworks, but it's hard not to be moved by Joan's story. There's a recorded commentary in English. The museum is open daily: June to August 9 a.m. to 7 p.m. and September to May 10 a.m. to noon and 2 to 6 p.m. Admission is 25F ($3.60) for adults and 13F ($1.85) for children and students.

Continue west several blocks along rue de Crosne, which turns into avenue Gustave-Flaubert. Several more blocks (a 15-minute walk from place du Vieille-Marché) will take you to a museum devoted to author Gustave Flaubert. The **Musée Flaubert et d'Histoire de la Médecine,** in the Hôtel-Dieu at 51 rue de Lecat (☎ **02-35-15-59-95**), displays souvenirs of the *Madame Bovary* author and Rouen native. In December 1821, Flaubert was born in this hospital building, where his father was the resident surgeon. The museum also features the tools of Flaubert's father, including medical and surgical instruments, documents, and hospital furnishings. Admission is 15F ($2.15), and the museum is open Tuesday to Saturday 10 a.m. to noon and 2 to 6 p.m.

On the other end of rue de Gros Horloge is the famous **Cathédrale Notre-Dame** (place de la Cathédrale; for info, call the tourist office at ☎ 02-32-08-32-40). Its complex asymmetrical facade just barely escaped total destruction during World War II bombing. The Flamboyant Gothic tower (with flamelike shapes) on the left is known as Tour de Beurre and contains a carillon of 55 bells. Legend has it that the money for the tower came from wealthy residents willing to pay for the privilege of eating butter during Lent. The Tour Lanterne contains a cast iron–and–copper spire, the tallest in France, added in the nineteenth century. Impressionist artist Claude Monet painted the harmonious west facade countless times in inclement weather. (You can see several of his paintings, including one of the cathedral, in the Musée de Beaux-Arts.) Inside is stained glass from the thirteenth to the sixteenth century, as well as Renaissance tombs of the Cardinals d'Amboise and Louis de Brézé. The church is open Monday to Saturday 8 a.m. to 7 p.m. and Sunday 8 a.m. to 6 p.m. Guided visits to the crypt (built in A.D. 1000 and containing a well that's nine centuries old) and the fourteenth-century Chapel of the Virgin (which has a medieval nativity painting and numerous magnificent tombs) take place June to August daily at 4 p.m. and September to May Saturday and Sunday at 3 p.m.

Behind the cathedral is the Flamboyant Gothic **Eglise St-Maclou** (☎ 02-35-71-71-72). The entrance is unusually elaborate with five porches containing five doors covered with Renaissance carvings. The church was badly damaged by a World War II bomb; photos inside detail the destruction. It's open Monday to Saturday 10 a.m. to noon and 2 to 6 p.m. and Sundays 3 to 5 p.m. (closed January 1, May 1, July 14, and November 11). East of the cathedral, the **Abbatiale St-Ouen** (once part of a major Benedictine Abbey) was built from the fourteenth to the sixteenth century and is one of France's most beautiful churches. It's notable for its unity of the Flamboyant Gothic style, a refined architecture that incorporates lots of light. Inside are eighteenth-century wrought-iron choir gates and a superb 1630 organ with over 3,000 pipes (renovated in the nineteenth century). St-Ouen is where Joan of Arc was sentenced to life imprisonment, though that sentence was later altered to death. Mid-March to October, the church is open Wednesday to Monday 10 a.m. to 12:30 p.m. and 2 to 6 p.m.; November to mid-December and late January to mid-March, hours are Wednesday, Saturday, and Sunday 10 a.m. to 12:30 p.m. and 2 to 4:30 p.m. For more information on the Abbatiale St-Ouen, call the tourist office at ☎ 02-32-08-32-40.

Mont-St-Michel (see "Mont-St-Michel: A Wonder Indeed" later in this chapter) isn't the only famous abbey in these parts, but the others draw far less tourists. Drive the **Route des Abbayes,** a 140 km (87-mile) driving route that roughly follows the Seine and passes half a dozen abbeys. The two most interesting abbeys are less than 64.4 km (40 miles) from Rouen. Leave Rouen west on D982 and then south on D65 to reach the first abbey. Many say France's most beautiful ruin is the **Abbaye de Jumièges** (☎ 02-35-37-24-02), eleventh-century remains surrounded by ancient yew trees. The Romanesque nave and two pillars, along with sixteenth-century chapels and stained glass, are all that's left from the Eglise St-Valentin. The abbey is open daily (except January 1, May 1, November 1, November 11, and December 25): late April to mid-September 9:30 a.m. to 7 p.m. and late September to mid-April 9:30 a.m. to 1 p.m. and 2:30 to 5:30 p.m. (last ticket sales are half an hour before closing). Admission is 32F ($4.60) for adults and 21F ($3) for anyone 12 to 25. Another 16.1 km (10 miles) down D982 is the **Abbaye St-Wandrille de Fontenelle,** built in the 13th and 14th centuries. The Gothic cloisters from the fourteenth to the sixteenth century are the highlights. Guided tours are given on Saturdays at 3:30 p.m. and Sundays and holidays at 11:30 a.m. and 3:30 p.m. Gregorian chant services are held on Sundays at 10 a.m. and weekdays at 9:45 a.m. Admission is 20F ($2.85).

Shopping

A **food-and-produce market** is held at place St-Marc on Tuesday, Friday, and Saturday 8 a.m. to 6:30 p.m.; on Sundays 8 a.m. to 1:30 p.m., it's a **flea market.** At place du Vieux-Marché, you find a **food market** Tuesday to Sunday 6 a.m. to 1:30 p.m. Place des Emmurées hosts a **food market** on Tuesdays and Saturdays and a **flea market** on Thursdays 8 a.m. to 6:30 p.m.

Rouen offers some very fine antiques shops, and anyone who's hunting for authentic *faïence* will enjoy perusing these colorful stores. Be aware that while antique *faïence* is quite expensive, contemporary versions are affordable and abundant. The best streets for antiques are **rue St-Romain, rue Damiette,** and **rue Eau-de-Robec,** which hosts an antiques fair on the first Saturday of every month. **Michel Carpentier,** (26 rue St-Romain; ☎ 02-35-88-77-47) sells high-quality contemporary *faïence* made in his shop.

Nightlife

Most of Rouen's nightlife is centered around place du Vieux-Marché. **Le Scottish** (21 rue Verte; ☎ 02-35-71-46-22) has live jazz and no cover. A popular beer pub is **La Taverne St-Amand** (11 rue St-Amand; ☎ 02-35-88-51-34). You can find high-brow entertainment at the **Théâtre des Arts** (22 place des Arts; ☎ 02-35-98-50-98), with classical music concerts, as well as opera and ballet. For plays, check out the **Théâtre des Deux Rives** (48 rue Louis-Ricard; ☎ 02-35-70-22-82).

The brochure *Cette Semaine à Rouen,* available free from the tourist office, lists all the current events.

Other Normandy favorites

If you have some additional time, check out these interesting spots:

✔ **Caen:** This mostly modern city, 103 km (64 miles) from Rouen, serves as a convenient transportation hub and is the capital of Lower Normandy. The bustling city is about a 15-minute drive from the D-Day beaches. The World War II Mémorial de Caen, located at esplanade Dwight-Eisenhower, is the region's most impressive. There are also a pair of noteworthy medieval abbeys, the Abbaye aux Dames on place de la Reine-Mathilde and the Abbaye aux Hommes on esplanade Jean-Marie-Louvel.

✔ **Deauville:** A stylish seaside resort since the mid-nineteenth century, Deauville, 70.8 km (44 miles) from Rouen, sports a number of diversions, including casinos, golf courses, polo grounds, and racetracks for wealthy vacationers. The sandy beach, lined by a wooden boardwalk, can be quite crowded in summer. Those looking for chic accommodations may want to contact the Hôtel Normandy (38 rue Jean-Mermoz; ☎ 02-31-98-66-22; Fax: 02-31-98-66-23; Internet: www.normandy@lucienbarriere.com), with rack rates at 1,100 to 2,200F ($157 to $314) double.

✔ **Etretat:** This picturesque seaside village, 87 km (54.1 miles) from Rouen, is the site of the unusual cliffs that Monet painted many times. The wide pebbly beach is accessed via a long concrete boardwalk. You can walk along the grassy tops of the cliffs and explore the tiny nineteenth-century Chapelle Notre-Dame de la Garde on top of the cliff on the east side of the beach. This is also a great place to eat crêpes or *moules frites* (mussels and french fries) at one of the beach cafes.

✔ **Honfleur:** You'll be completely charmed by this fishing village at the mouth of the Seine, 66 km (41 miles) from Rouen. Sit at a cafe by the harbor, take a spin on the carousel, catch a harbor boat ride, or visit the interesting historic house museums. There are a host of fine shops and art galleries on the streets near the port.

✔ **Pont de Normandie:** Drive over the spectacular cable bridge Pont de Normandie (33F/$5), which connects Le Havre to Honfleur over the Seine estuary in a daring feat of engineering. The bridge, completed in 1995, is 856 meters long.

✔ **Trouville:** More picturesque and simple than its flashy neighbor Deauville across the river Touques, Trouville, 70.8 km (44 miles) from Rouen, has long been a popular seaside resort, but it more closely resembles a fishing village. Plage de Trouville is the resort's one beach, lined by the requisite boardwalk with cafes and shops nearby.

Bayeaux and the Famous Tapestry

The picturesque town of **Bayeaux** is famous for displaying the tapestry that tells how the French conquered England in 1066. Now with a story line like that, you know this will be an impressive display — and indeed it is. But Bayeux is also a pleasant place to spend the night, with a number of fine hotels and restaurants and handsome cobblestone streets for strolling. At just 9.7 km to 19.3 km (6 to 12 miles) from the D-Day beaches, the town is a good place to base yourself for tours of those sites.

The first weekend in July is the two-day **Fêtes Médiévales,** a lively affair with costumed entertainers, parades, large markets, and late-night partying. The streets in the center of town are blocked off to cars during the festival.

Getting there

Trains traveling from Paris's Gare St-Lazare to Bayeaux take 2½ hours and cost 190F ($27). Six to twelve trains make the journey each day and most stop in Caen, where you may have to change trains, but the total trip time will still be 2½ hours and cost 190F. Twelve trains per day travel from Caen to Bayeux, with the trip taking 20 minutes and costing 35F ($5). The Bayeux **train station** is at place de la Gare, about a 15-minute walk from the town center. For train reservations and information, call **SNCF** at ☎ **08-36-35-35-39** or 08-36-35-35-35.

To **drive** from Paris to Bayeux, take A13 to Caen and E46 west to Bayeux. It's about a three-hour trip.

Getting around and getting information

For a **taxi,** call ☎ **02-31-92-92-40.** The **tourist office** is at pont St-Jean (☎ **02-31-51-28-28;** Fax: 02-31-51-28-29; Internet: www.bayeux-tourism.com; E-mail: bayeux-tourisme@mail.cpod.fr). June to mid-September, it's open Monday to Saturday 9 a.m. to noon and 2 to 6 p.m. and Sunday 9:30 a.m. to noon and 2:30 to 6:00 p.m.; late September to May, hours are Monday to Saturday 9 a.m. to noon and 2 to 6 p.m.

Where to stay

Hôtel Churchill-Clarine

$$$ Bayeux

The Churchill, in a handsome nineteenth-century stone building, claims a terrific location on the main street, a cobblestone pedestrian way lined with shops and restaurants. The property is well run by M. and Mme Silmi, who've recently completed extensive renovations. The 32 rooms offer a cheerful decor along with some antiques and large windows, some of which overlook the majestic cathedral. In the center of the hotel is a flower-filled, glassed-in courtyard — the site of the restaurant serving breakfast and dinner.

14 rue St-Jean. ☎ **02-31-21-31-80.** _Fax: 02-31-21-41-66. Free parking. Rack rates: 370–550F ($53–$79) double. Breakfast: 40F ($6). Closed Dec to mid-February. AE, DC, MC, V._

Hôtel d'Argouges

$$ Bayeux

The elegant exterior and lobby of this eighteenth-century mansion don't exactly jibe with the dowdy decor, small size of most rooms, and lack of an elevator. But if you're willing to pay more (and reserve far ahead), you can get one of the handsome suites. The hotel is in a fine location, facing central place St-Patrice. All 26 rooms have minibars; rooms in the back are quiet and look out on pretty gardens, while rooms in the front, though set back from the street by a courtyard, can be noisy. The staff, headed by the gracious Mme Auregan, is English-speaking and helpful. The continental breakfast is particularly good.

21 rue St-Patrice. ☎ **02-31-92-88-86.** _Fax: 02-31-92-69-16. E-mail:_ dargouges@ aol.com. _Free parking. Rack rates: 300–460F ($43–$66) double; 560–670F ($80–$96) suite. Breakfast: 45F ($6). Closed two weeks in Dec and two weeks in Jan. AE, MC, V._

Le Lion d'Or

$$$ Bayeux

Bayeux's best hotel is on the town's main pedestrian street in a seventeenth-century stone coaching inn. This has been the top place to stay in town for over 70 years, so reservations need to be made far in advance. The 25 rooms are individually decorated and possess a charm that comes from attention to detail. All of the rooms have minibars. Half pension is required here, meaning you must pay for lunch or dinner at the hotel restaurant, which serves traditional Norman cuisine.

71 rue St-Jean. ☎ **02-31-92-06-90.** _Fax: 02-31-22-15-64. E-mail:_ lion.d-or. bayeux@wanadoo.fr. _Rack rates: 420–510F ($60–$73) double. Half pension: 390–460F ($56–$66). Closed late Dec to late Jan. MC, V._

Where to dine

La Rapière

$$ Bayeux   NORMAN

The fifteenth-century mansion called the Hôtel de Croissant is the setting for this popular restaurant serving traditional food. Its central location and small size mean that the place fills up early and fast, so your best bet is to call ahead for reservations. The menu features local oysters followed by Normandy sole served with garden vegetables, and a fine apple tart for dessert.

53 rue St-Jean. ☎ *02-31-51-05-15. Reservations suggested. Meals: Main courses 65–125F ($9–$18); menus 80–150F ($11–$21). MC, V. Open: Wed–Mon noon to 2 p.m. and 7:30–9:30 p.m. Closed mid-Dec to Jan.*

Le Petit Normand

$$ Bayeux NORMAN

This simple restaurant, offering very good value for home-cooked hearty meals, is near the cathedral in an ancient building. Traditional Norman food washed down with cider is the way to go here. The chef recommends duck foie gras to start, followed by tripe cooked in Caen style or Vallé d'Auge chicken (free range). They serve a good selection of wonderful Normandy cheeses here too.

35 rue Larcher. ☎ *02-31-22-88-66. Reservations accepted. Meals: Main courses 48–98F ($7–$14); menus 60–135F ($9–$19). MC, V. Open: Late April to Sept daily noon to 2 p.m. and 7:30–9:30 p.m.; Oct to mid-Apr Fri–Wed noon to 2 p.m. and 7:30–9:30 p.m.*

Les Amaryllis

$$ Bayeaux NORMAN

The unusual aspect (for France) of this quaint restaurant is that the entire front room, with several booths and large picture windows facing the street, is a no-smoking area. The service is very efficient and the restaurant caters to locals, who appreciate the quality food, as well as to tourists, who can order from an English menu. Depending on availability, the restaurant has local meats and fish, like Honfleur prawns and salt meadow Isigny lamb. The wine list offers many reasonably priced options, as well as several good vintages by the glass.

32 rue St-Patrice. ☎ *02-31-22-47-94. Reservations accepted. Meals: Main courses 80–135F ($11–$19); menus 95–190F ($14–$27). MC, V. Open: June–Aug Tues–Sun noon to 2 p.m. and 8–10 p.m.; May–Sept Tues–Sun noon to 2 p.m., Tues–Sat 8–10 p.m. Closed late Dec to late Jan.*

Exploring the town

Bayeux is very compact and easy to walk through. The main road through the center is the pedestrian **rue St-Jean.** The tapestry and several smaller museums are south of rue St-Jean, as is the eleventh-century **Cathédrale Notre-Dame** (rue du Bienvenu; ☎ 02-31-92-01-85), which is an example of the Norman Renaissance style.

The eleventh-century **Tapisserie de Bayeux** is displayed in the **Centre Guillaume le Conquérant** (rue de Nesmond; ☎ 02-31-51-25-50). The

58 panels of the Bayeaux Tapestry (actually an embroidery in wool on a background of linen), measuring 230 feet long and 20 inches high, tell the story of the Norman Conquest — when William the Conqueror invaded England, resulting in the Battle of Hastings on October 14, 1066 — and William being crowned king of England. Born Billy the Bastard, William rose from rather ignoble beginnings and went on to rule England along with Normandy until his death in 1087. The plot of the story involves the hapless Prince Harold, a Saxon earl, who tried to crown himself king of England against the wishes of the previous ruler, Edward the Confessor, who had promised the throne to William from across the Channel. It's believed that the tapestry was commissioned in 1077 by William's half-brother Odon, the bishop of Bayeux, for display in his cathedral.

The tapestry's survival is a story in itself. The first historical mention of the tapestry was in 1476, when it was said that the canons of the Bayeux Cathedral would unroll it every year for display. The tapestry may have been stolen during the French Revolution in 1789. In 1792, a local man was using it as a tarp to hold down the belongings in his cart. A lawyer, sensing the value of the piece, traded some rope for the tapestry, saving it from certain destruction. Thankfully, the tapestry eventually ended up back in the hands of the town authorities.

After viewing much preliminary material to the tapestry (including a full copy with play-by-play translation, interpretation, and analysis), you'll get to see the real thing, behind thick glass in a dark tunnel-like room. Everything has English translations — there's an audioguide in English and a 14-minute film shown in English and French. Admission is 40F ($6) for adults and 16F ($2.30) for children and students; the ticket also includes admission to the **Musée Baron Gérard** and the **Hôtel du Doyen,** which display collections of religious artwork and local crafts-manship. Signs at the Tapestry Museum direct you to these smaller museums, which are within 200 yards and have the same hours as the Tapestry Museum. The Bayeux Tapestry Museum is open daily (except January 1, December 25, and the mornings of January 2 and December 26): May to August 9 a.m. to 7 p.m., late March to April and September to mid-October 9 a.m. to 6:30 p.m., and late October to mid-March 9:30 a.m. to 12:30 p.m. and 2 to 6 p.m. Entry is allowed up to 45 minutes before closing.

Southwest of the cathedral, at the **Musée Mémorial de la Bataille de Normandie 1944** (boulevard Fabian-Ware; ☎ 02-31-92-93-41), Bayeux commemorates its role as the first French town to be liberated from the Nazis. The startlingly modern building looks like a UFO bunker and uses soldier waxworks, as well as weapons, military equipment, and memo-rabilia, to outline all aspects of Operation Overlord (the code name for the invasion of Europe) and the Battle of Normandy, the decisive mili-tary operation of World War II. Admission is 32F ($4.60) for adults and 15F ($2.15) for children and students. The museum is open daily (closed late January): May to mid-September 9:30 a.m. to 6:30 p.m., and late September to April 10:00 a.m. to 12:30 p.m. and 2 to 6 p.m.

The D-Day Beaches

Some of World War II's most dramatic events took place on the coast of Normandy. Allied generals started plotting "Operation Overlord," the invasion of Europe, in 1943. On June 6, 1944, code-named **D-Day,** the allied troops invaded Normandy and started in motion the liberation of the European continent from the Nazis. More than 100,000 soldiers were killed in the ensuing battles. Today there's not much left on the beaches to remind us of these dramatic events besides some German bunkers, but small museums and memorials are placed all along the coast, explaining in detail each critical event and battle.

Off the coast of Arromanches, you can see the remains of an artificial harbor that was constructed by the allies and code-named Mulberry Harbor. And, of course, there are the cemeteries with their acres of white crosses to remind us of the heavy cost of freedom. The Battle of Normandy continued until August 21. Soon Paris was liberated, and a year later, when allied troops entered Berlin, Germany surrendered.

Getting there

If you're **driving** from Paris to the D-Day beaches, take A13 to Caen and E46 to Bayeaux and then go north on D6 to the coastal road D514. The trip takes about 3 hours. Following coastal D514 will take you past all the relevant D-Day sites. You can also drive the **Voie de la Liberté,** which follows the path of General Eisenhower and his troops as they liberated one village after another, from Utah Beach all the way to Belgium.

Bus Verts du Calvados (☎ 02-31-44-77-44 or 08-01-21-42-14) runs buses that travel to many of the villages along the coast. The **Carte Liberté,** a day pass allowing unlimited travel on the buses, costs 100F ($14). From July to September 4, bus no. 75 runs a tour that leaves from Caen's Gare Routière (bus station) at 9:30 a.m. and travels to Arromanches (the Musée du Debarquement, artificial harbor, and 360-degree film), Omaha Beach (the American Cemetery), and Pointe du Hoc (the place of the daring feat by Lt.-Col. James Rudder's American rangers, who took this German strongpoint on June 6), returning to Caen at 5:50 p.m.

Getting around and getting information

To rent a car, head to **Lefebvre Car Rental** (boulevard d'Eindhoven, Bayeux; ☎ 02-311-92-05-96). To rent a bike, go to **Roué** (14 bd. Winston-Churchill, Bayeux; ☎ 02-31-92-27-75); bikes cost 40F ($6) for half a day and 75F ($11) for a full day. Though the distances are short, bikers should be aware that travel along the D-Day beaches coastal route is a hilly and windy trek.

If you don't have access to a car, the best way to see the D-Day beaches is by tour. **Normandy Tours,** at the Hôtel de la Gare in Bayeaux (☎ 02-31-92-10-70), runs tours (in English) to Juno Beach, Arromanches, Omaha Beach, the American Military Cemetery, and Pointe du Hoc for 150F ($21) per person. **Bus Fly,** located in Bayeaux (☎ 02-31-22-00-08; Internet: www.busfly.com), also runs English-speaking tours of the D-Day beaches. A half-day trip costs 160F ($23) for adults and 140F ($20) for students and a full-day trip costs 300F ($43) for adults and 280F ($40) for students. Bus Fly will pick you up at your hotel in Bayeux.

The tourist offices in Bayeux and Caen have an abundance of info for those wishing to visit the beaches. The **Caen tourist office** is on place St-Pierre (☎ 02-31-27-14-14). July and August, the office is open Monday to Saturday 10 a.m. to 7 p.m. and Sunday 10 a.m. to 1 p.m. and 3 to 5 p.m.; September to June, hours are Monday to Saturday 10 a.m. to 1 p.m. and 2 to 6 p.m. and Sunday 10 a.m. to 1 p.m. The **Bayeux tourist office** is on pont St-Jean (see the preceding section for more details). You can pick up a brochure called *The D-Day Landings and the Battle of Normandy* at all local tourist offices.

Exploring the beaches

The beaches' code names, from west to east, are **Utah** and **Omaha** (where the Americans landed), **Juno** (where the Canadians landed), and **Gold** and **Sword** (where the British landed). **Ste-Mère-Eglise,** the first village liberated, has installed on the roof of the church a model of a U.S. paratrooper who became entangled in the steeple. The village's museum, which honors the paratroopers, is the **Musée des Troupes Aéroportées** (place 6 Juin; ☎ 02-33-41-41-35). It's open daily: May to mid-September 9:00 a.m. to 6:45 p.m., April and late September 9 a.m. to noon and 2:00 to 6:45 p.m., and October to March 10 a.m. to noon and 2 to 6 p.m. Admission is 25F ($3.60) for adults and 15F ($2.15) for students. The **American Cemetery** (☎ 02-31-21-97-44), with 9,000 white crosses and stars of David, is located near Omaha Beach at **Colleville-sur-Mer.** The cemetery is open daily: April to November 8 a.m. to 6 p.m. and December to March 9 a.m. to 5 p.m.

The most impressive contemporary D-Day museum/monument is the **Mémorial pour la Paix,** at esplanade Dwight-D.-Eisenhower in Caen (☎ 02-31-06-06-44; Internet: www.unicaen.fr/memorial). This comprehensive museum explains all of the major battles and explores themes like German Fascism, the French Resistance, and French collaboration. The museum is open daily (except the first half of January and December 25): July and August 9 a.m. to 9 p.m., late February to June and September and October 9 a.m. to 7 p.m., and November to mid-February 9 a.m. to 6 p.m. Last entrance is an hour before closing. Admission is 69F ($10). June to September, the museum runs tours (in English) of the beaches: The three-hour Montgomery Tour, which covers Gold, Juno, and Sword, leaves at 9 a.m. and 2 p.m. and costs 340F ($49); the six-hour Eisenhower Tour of Omaha and Utah beaches leaves at 9 a.m. and costs 480F ($69).

In the village of Ste-Marie du Mont, near Utah Beach, you can find the **American Commemorative Monument** and the **Musée du Debarquement d'Utah-Beach** (☎ 02-33-71-53-35), which traces the American landing at Utah. July and August, the museum is open daily 9:30 a.m. to 7:30 p.m.; April to June, hours are daily 9:30 a.m. to 7:00 p.m.; and December to March, hours are Saturday and Sunday 9:30 a.m. to 6:30 p.m. Admission is 30F ($4.30) for adults and 25F ($3.60) for students. In Arromanches, near Gold Beach, the **Musée du Debarquement** (☎ 02-31-22-34-31) explains the use of **Mulberry,** the allies' concrete artificial harbor. The harbor, which the British constructed off the coast, can be seen from the museum windows. May to September, the museum is open daily 9:00 a.m. to 6:15 p.m.; September to May, hours are Monday to Saturday 9:00 to 11:30 a.m. and 2:00 to 5:30 p.m. and Sunday 10:00 to 11:30 a.m. and 2:00 to 5:30 p.m. Admission is 35F ($5) for adults and 22F ($3.15) for children and students. Nearby, the **Arromanches 360 Cinéma** (chemin du Calvaire; ☎ 02-31-22-30-30) projects, on a circle of screens, an 18-minute film about the allied landings called *Le Prix de la Liberté* (The Price of Freedom). The cinema is open daily: June to August 9:10 a.m. to 6:40 p.m., May and September 10:10 a.m. to 5:40 p.m., and October to December and February to April 10:10 a.m. to 5:40 p.m. There are two shows per hour at 10 past and 40 past the hour. Admission is 24F ($3.40) for adults and 21F ($3) for children age 10 to 18 and students.

Mont-St-Michel: A Wonder Indeed

One of France's most popular attractions, the medieval abbey of **Mont-St-Michel** rises 260 feet from the primordial quick sands of the bay, just off the coast of Normandy. A causeway allows the steady stream of visitors to walk to the village, which doesn't allow cars. A steep road leads past souvenir shops and restaurants to the abbey itself, with its flower-filled cloister and soaring chapel perched close to heaven at the top of the rock. Despite all the tourists and hype, you can't help but be awed by this site. Mont-St-Michel is also famous for having the highest tides of continental Europe. The tide can rise as high as 50 feet in a few hours; at its fastest, it's said to be the speed of a galloping horse.

Getting there

From Paris's Gare Monparnasse, fast **TGVs** run frequently to Rennes in Brittany (2 hours; 289–505F/$41–$72). For reservations and information, call **SNCF** at ☎ 08-36-35-35-39 or 08-36-35-35-35. You can then take a bus (75 minutes) to Mont-St-Michel. For bus information, call **Les Couriers Bretons** at ☎ 02-33-58-03-07. The nearest train station (slow trains only) is at **Pontorson,** 9 km (5.6 miles) from Mont-St-Michel; a connecting bus (30F/$4.30) makes the ten-minute trip to the abbey.

Driving is the most convenient way to get to Mont-St-Michel. From Paris, take A13 to Caen, then N175 southwest to Pontorson and D976 to Mont-St-Michel (4½ hours). From Rouen, drive to Caen on A13 and follow directions from Paris. From Bayeux and the D-Day beaches, drive briefly southeast to Caen on E46, then southwest to Mont-St-Michel. Try to park (15F/$2.15) as close as possible to the abbey, because you have a long walk ahead of you. Be aware that the spaces just below the abbey entrance are covered by water at high tide. Announcements are made by loudspeakers to assure that everyone moves their cars in time.

It's not unusual to see 75 tour buses parked in the lots at Mont-St-Michel. To avoid the crowds, arrive late in the day. Tourists staying overnight on the Mont are allowed to park in the best spots closest to the entrance, and they have the additional luxury of visiting the abbey after all the others have left. In summer, the last regular tour of the abbey is at 5 p.m., and nighttime visits start at 9 p.m. Avoid Mont-St-Michel in August, when the crowds are at their worst.

Getting information

The **Mont-St-Michel tourist office** is on the left as you enter the fortified gate of the Mont (☎ **02-33-60-14-30;** Fax: 02-33-60-06-75; E-mail: OT.Mont. Saint.Michel@wanadoo.fr). From late June to mid-September, the tourist office is open Monday to Saturday 9 a.m. to 7 p.m. and Sunday 9 a.m. to noon and 2 to 6 p.m.; late September to mid-June, hours are daily 9 a.m. to noon to 2 to 6 p.m. Check with the office for the times of English-language tours of the abbey. Next to the Mont-St-Michel tourist office are public bathrooms and a fountain where you'll see lines of hearty pilgrims washing thick gray mud off of their legs.

Where to stay

Hôtel du Mouton Blanc

$$ Mont-St-Michel

The 15 rooms at this medieval hotel/restaurant about halfway up Grande Rue are just average; some are small, dark, and a little depressing. And there's no elevator. But the prices are good, and the restaurant is a charming place, serving some of the best food on the Mont, with views of the bay. Popular fare at the restaurant is a variety of seafood, including mussels from the bay and lobster served in a creamy casserole.

Grande Rue. ☎ *02-33-60-14-08. Fax: 02-33-60-05-62. Rack rates: 390–580F ($56–$83) double. Breakfast: 45F ($6). Half pension: 295–365F ($42–$52). Closed Jan. AE, MC, V.*

Mont-St-Michel

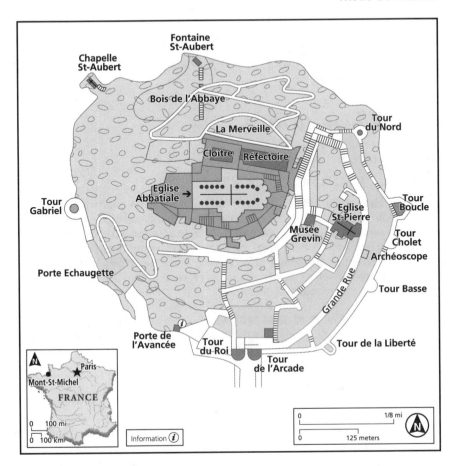

Terrasses Poulard

$$$ Mont-St-Michel

Several flights of steep stone steps lead up to this hotel and there's no elevator, so if you have a lot of baggage, you may have a difficult time getting to the entrance. The staff is very friendly. The 30 rooms, all with minibars, range from wonderful to depressing, with a difference of about 100F ($14) between the two. If you're willing to pay a bit more and reserve ahead, you can get a spacious room with a fireplace, sculpted moldings, and bay views. If you're traveling with children, ask for one of the larger rooms — reasonable prices and rooms with thick walls make this a good choice for families. Guests are served breakfast at the hotel's restaurant, a little farther up Grande Rue. Alas, tables for breakfast guests are grouped as far as possible from the windows that offer a wonderful view. At lunch and dinner, the restaurant serves average fare with a great view.

The specialties are *moules frites* (mussels and french fries), grilled seafood, crêpes, and *galettes* (buckwheat pancakes).

Grande Rue. ☎ *02-33-60-14-09. Fax: 02-33-60-37-31. Internet:* www.mere. poulard.fr. *E-mail:* mere.poulard.mtst.michel@wanadoo.fr. *Rack rates: 300–950F ($43–$136) double. Breakfast: 50F ($7). Half board: 350–620F ($50–$89). AE, MC, V.*

Where to dine

Crêperie La Sirène

$ Mont-St-Michel   CRÊPES

The restaurants on Mont-St-Michel tend to be overpriced, so it's nice to find this unassuming crêperie with friendly service, good food, and reasonable prices. The second-floor dining room, with a beamed ceiling and stone walls, offers great views of the bustling Grande Rue teaming with tourists. You have a huge choice of crêpes filled with vegetables and meat, as well as salads. For dessert, succumb to the banana crêpe smothered in chocolate sauce.

Grande Rue. ☎ *02-33-60-08-60. Reservations not accepted. Meals: Main courses 12–40F ($1.70–$6); menus 60–120F ($9–$17); children's menu 38F ($5). MC, V. Open: Daily noon to 2:30 p.m. and 6–9:30 p.m.*

La Mère Poulard

$$$ Mont-St-Michel   NORMAN

Is La Mère Poulard a tourist trap best avoided or a restaurant serving the best omelets in the world? Because it's nearly impossible to get a reservation, I guess most people think the latter. At any rate, this is certainly the most expensive and most famous restaurant on Mont-St-Michel, located in the busiest square, right at the entrance into town. The omelets, made in long-handled copper skillets and served by women in Norman costume, are indeed fluffy and delicious. The menu also features *agneau du pré salé* (lamb raised on the adjacent salt marshes) and seafood from the bay.

Grand Rue. ☎ *02-33-60-14-01. Reservations necessary at least 3 days in advance. Meals: Main courses 98–215F ($14–$31); menus 250–350F ($36–$50). AE, DC, MC, V. Open: Daily noon to 2:30 p.m. and 7:30–10 p.m.*

Exploring the abbey

You can see the famous silhouette of **Mont-St-Michel** (☎ **02-33-89-80-00**) from miles away, and many visitors cherish their first glimpse of La Merveille (The Wonder). After walking across the causeway, you enter the island of Mont-St-Michel through the **Porte Bavole,** built in 1590, and follow **Grande Rue,** a steep and narrow pedestrian street up to the abbey. On your left as you pass through the gate is the **Corps de Guard des Bourgeois,** a fifteenth-century building that now houses the tourist office.

There's a seemingly endless series of steep stone steps up to Mont-St-Michel, so you need to be well rested and in good shape to make the trek. This is definitely not a attraction for travelers with disabilities.

Mont-St-Michel is a sore subject in Brittany, and you're better off not bringing it up if you plan on visiting that region (see Chapter 17). Ancient Bretons coined the verse, "The River in its folly gave the Mont to Normandy," referring to the fact that the Selune changed beds in A.D. 933, making Mont-St-Michel fall within the boundary of Normandy instead of Brittany. Bretons are still peeved about it.

If you think Mont-St-Michel is crowded now, you should've seen it in 5000 B.C., when the dramatic pointed rock just off the coast was a pagan place of worship. The site was first consecrated in A.D. 708 and dedicated to the archangel Michael, who's considered the protector of faith and the one who weighs the souls. His job of weighing the souls made Michael one influential archangel. That explains why pilgrims would risk their lives walking through the patches of quicksand in the bay, braving the deadly tides, through thick fog and heavy rains, in order to visit the abbey.

Building and rebuilding the abbey (after several collapses) took about 500 years, so the site combines architectural styles from the Middle Ages to the sixteenth century. Construction began in the eighth century, when Aubert, a bishop of Avranches, claimed the archangel told him to build a monastery here. In 966, Richard, duc de Normandy, agreed to construct a Benedictine monastery over a set of crypts built at the peak of the rock, but it partially burned down in 1203. Later that century, Philippe Auguste of France made a donation that enabled the work to begin on the abbey's Gothic section, the part of the complex known to countless pilgrims as La Merveille. The two three-story buildings, crowned by the cloister and the refectory, are truly a marvel. In the fourteenth century, during the Hundred Years' War, fortifications were built to protect the abbey during a 30-year siege. The fortifications came in handy during World War II, when the Mont was the only part of France that didn't to fall to the Germans. In the fifteenth century, a Flamboyant Gothic chancel was built for the abbey church. The abbey was used as a prison during the French Revolution and was finally turned over to France's Historic Monuments department in 1874. The steeple, spire, and bronze statue of the archangel were added in 1897. On the abbey's 1,000th anniversary in 1966, a monastic community moved back into it; a Benedictine mass is held daily at 12:15 p.m.

Crowds gather in the **North Tower** after the last tour of the day to watch the tide creep and then rush in. The fastest tides take place during the equinoxes in March and September.

Among the highlights of the site are the thirteenth-century **cloister,** with its delicate zigzagging granite columns. The **center courtyard** has been planted with a medieval herb garden. Also interesting is the thirteenth-century **réfrectoire,** a large dining room with Romanesque and Gothic elements, where 30 monks would eat daily in silence. While exploring the abbey, you can occasionally get a glimpse of the actual rock, which is green with lichens. Don't miss the huge nineteenth-century **treadmill** that was manned by six prisoners in order to bring supplies up to the site. Admission to the abbey is 40F ($6) for adults and 25F ($3.60) for ages 18 to 25. It's open daily (except January 1, May 1, November 1, November 11, and December 25): May to mid-September 9:30 a.m. to 6:00 p.m. and late September to April 10 a.m. to 4 p.m. Most days in summer, hour-long tours are given (in English) at 10 and 11 a.m. and 2, 3, 4, and 5 p.m. The tour is included with the price of admission.

The **Musée Maritime** (Grande Rue; ☎ 02-33-60-14-09) bills itself as a Science and Environment Center and actually contains some interesting information about Mont-St-Michel Bay and the work being undertaken to prevent it from silting up. A major engineering project scheduled to start in the near future will tear down the causeway and turn Mont-St-Michel back into an island, reachable by bridge. This is the best of the ancillary attractions on the Mont. Admission is 45F ($6) for adults and 30F ($4.20) for children under 16. May through October, it's open daily 9:30 a.m. to 6 p.m.; November through April, hours are Tuesday to Sunday 9:30 a.m. to 6 p.m. You can skip the waxworks museum and the 15-minute French film hosted by the archangel.

Chapter 17

Brittany

The rugged coast of **Brittany** is lined with seaside resorts and windswept cliffs overlooking the Atlantic. Brittany is a proud region with its own culture and traditions. More than 200,000 people speak the Breton language, which is more similar to Welsh than to French. Thanks to the skills of the hearty Breton fishermen, you'll find excellent seafood in the region, particularly Belon oysters, which are world famous. This is also the home of hand-painted Quimper pottery, which features bright colors and simple patterns and is made in the small town of Quimper near Brittany's west coast. Brittany's earliest residents were Neolithic tribes who left their megaliths behind. You can see these ancient stone formations in Carnac. The Celts first arrived in the sixth century B.C., and Brittany's separate identity evolved from those tribes from the British Isles. The region didn't become part of France until 1532 — it has been fiercely guarding its independence ever since.

Bretons love it when you acknowledge their language, which is closer to Welsh than it is to French. Here are three common words:

✔ **Hello:** *brav an amzer* (brahv ahn *ahmzer*)

✔ **Goodbye:** *kenavo* (*cay*-nah-voh)

✔ **Thank you:** *trugarez* (*true*-gahr-ez)

Sampling the region's cuisine

Besides oysters, lobsters, scallops, and other fresh fish, Bretons love to eat *gallettes,* buckwheat pancakes rolled around vegetables, cheese, meat, or fish. The *galette complète* contains ham, cheese, and egg. The perfect drink to accompany *galettes* is local cider. Cornouaille cider from the Cornouaille region in Brittany is considered the highest quality. A *bolées* is a traditional large mug of cider. Breton beer is also a popular beverage in the region. The best-known brands are Coreff from Morlaix, Lancelot barley beer, and Telenn Du buckwheat beer. The most basic ingredient in Breton cooking is salted butter. Breton cows graze on the lush fields and marshes near the Atlantic Ocean, which gives the butter an innate saltiness. For dessert, try the *far Breton,* a prune tart with the consistency of a sturdy custard. You'll find the famous Brittany butter cookies with the brand name Traou Mad in stores throughout the region.

Nantes: Brittany's Ancient Capital

With half a million residents, **Nantes,** the former capital of Brittany, is a handsome and bustling town at the intersection of three rivers: the Loire, Erdre, and Sèvre. Though officially part of the Loire region, Nantes has always been historically linked to Brittany. The town gained a place in history books with the 1598 Edict of Nantes, in which Henri IV granted religious freedom to France's Protestant minority (however, Louis XIV revoked the edict in 1685). The huge château where the edict was signed still occupies a central place in the city. Nantes today is a lively college town with about 30,000 students. There's plenty to see and do, including excellent shopping and hopping nightlife, and it's a fine first stop on the way to exploring the region.

Getting there

The **TGV (fast train)** from Paris's Gare Montparnasse takes about 2¼ hours to get to Nantes and costs 297 to 345F ($42 to $49). Beware of slow trains that can take up to 5½ hours. For information, call ☎ 08-36- 35-35-39 or 08-36-35-35-35. Nantes's **Gare SNCF** (train station) is at 27 bd. de Stalingrad, a five-minute walk from the town center. Trains from Nantes to Quimper (only two or three per day) take 2¾ to 4 hours (depending on how many stops the train makes) and cost 182 to 267F ($26 to $38). See "Quimper and Its Hand-Painted Pottery" later in this chapter.

If you're **driving,** take A11 for 384.6 km (239 miles) west of Paris. The trip takes about 3 hours.

Brittany

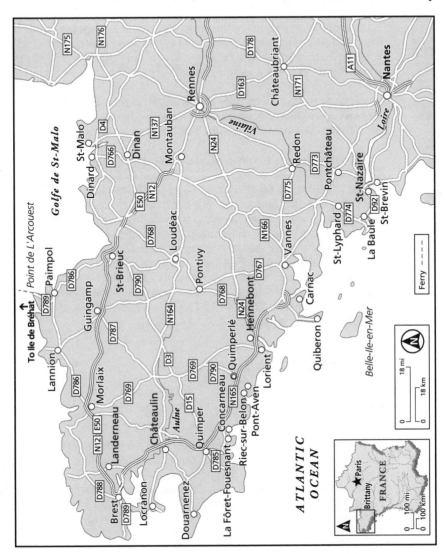

The **Aéroport Nantes-Atlantique** is 12 km (7.5 miles) southeast of town (☎ 02-40-84-80-00), and **Air Inter** (☎ 02-51-88-31-08) offers daily flights from Paris. A shuttle bus between the airport and the Nantes's train station takes 20 minutes and costs 40F ($6). If you take a taxi from the airport, it'll cost from 130 to 150F ($19 to $21) and will take about 15 minutes.

Getting around and getting information

Nantes offers an extensive bus system, as well as a metro and tram system, but all the major sights, restaurants, and hotels are within walking distance from the center of town. The tourist office has public transportation maps and schedules.

If you want to rent a car, note that **Budget, Hertz,** and **Europcar** have offices inside the train station. You can also find a taxi stand at the station. Call **Allô Taxi** at ☎ **02-40-69-22-22** to order a cab.

The **tourist office** is in the neoclassical Bourse (stock exchange) building, which is also occupied by a FNAC record store, at place du Commerce (☎ **02-40-20-60-00;** Fax: 02-40-89-11-99; Internet: www.reception.com/Nantes). July and August, it's open daily 10 a.m. to 7 p.m.; September to June, hours are Monday to Saturday 10 a.m. to 7 p.m. and Sunday 10 a.m. to noon and 2 to 6 p.m. The office will change money on days when banks are closed and organize walking tours of the city for 40F ($6) for adults and 25F ($3) for students and children. An **annex** at the château is open Wednesday to Sunday 10 a.m. to 1 p.m. and 2 to 6 p.m. If you want to check on or send e-mail, head to **Cyberhouse Café** (8 quai de Versailles; ☎ **02-40-12-11-84**), open daily 2 p.m. to 2 a.m.; it serves food and drinks.

Where to stay

Hôtel de France

$$$ **Nantes**

This beautiful eighteenth-century hotel, on a pedestrian street lined with the city's best shops, is full of character and charm. In fact, it's classified a historic monument. All 74 rooms have been recently renovated and have soundproof windows; many are decorated with ornate Louis XV and Louis XVI antiques, and some are large, with high ceilings. The hotel offers a piano bar and a restaurant called L'Opéra, which servers regional specialties. The staff is friendly and most speak English.

24 rue Crébillion. ☎ *02-40-73-57-91. Fax: 02-40-69-75-75. Rack rates: 355–590F ($51–$84) double. Breakfast: 50F ($7). MC, V.*

La Duchesse Anne

$$ **Nantes**

A five-minute walk from the train station and across from the Château des Ducs de Bretagne, this hotel offers comfortable rooms at reasonable prices. You can tell from the formal exterior and contrasting simple lobby that this is a grand hotel that has seen better days. Nevertheless, it offers 70 above-average rooms. They vary in style, with some of the larger

Nantes

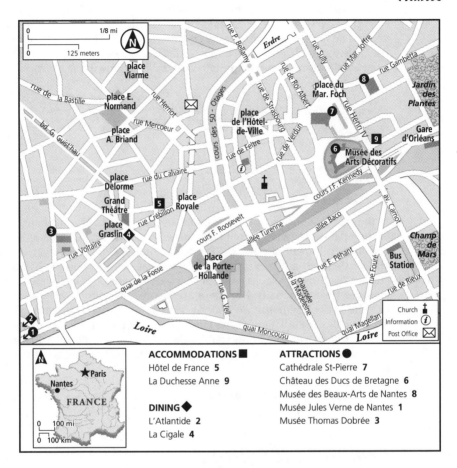

ACCOMMODATIONS ■
Hôtel de France **5**
La Duchesse Anne **9**

DINING ◆
L'Atlantide **2**
La Cigale **4**

ATTRACTIONS ●
Cathédrale St-Pierre **7**
Château des Ducs de Bretagne **6**
Musée des Beaux-Arts de Nantes **8**
Musée Jules Verne de Nantes **1**
Musée Thomas Dobrée **3**

rooms containing antiques and smaller rooms containing modern furniture. Some have views of the château, but since this is a noisy boulevard,
you may prefer a room facing the back or side of the hotel. A large breakfast buffet is served.

3 place de la Duchesse Anne. ☎ *02-51-86-78-78. Fax: 02-40-74-60-20.* www.
hotel-duchesse-anne.com. *E-mail:* contact@hotel-duchesse-anne.
com. *Parking: 30F ($4.30). Rack rates: 310–480F ($44–$69) double. Breakfast: 42F ($6).*

Where to dine

L'Atlantide

$$$ Nantes   FRENCH

Nantes's best restaurant, L'Atlantide, is an ultramodern glass-enclosed
dining room on the fourth floor of an office building, with panoramic

Seine views. Chef Jean Yves Guého prides himself on his menu's reflection of the seasons and the best market produce. Highlights are the starter of *oursin au petite coquillage* (sea urchin) and the main course of *tronçon de turbot rôti aux rattes et coques du croisic* (thick slices of turbot fish roasted with potatoes and cockles). The best dessert is *the petit banane rôti leger* (banana lightly roasted). The wine list is exemplary.

16 quai Ernest-Renaud. ☎ 02-40-73-23-23. Reservations required. Meals: Main courses 150–165F ($21–$24); menus 144–350F ($21–$50); children's menu 90F ($13). AE, MC, V. Open: Mon–Fri noon to 2:30 p.m.; Mon–Sat 7:30–10:30 p.m. Closed the first three weeks of Aug.

La Cigale

$$ Nantes   FRENCH

At this gorgeous 1895 art nouveau brasserie, the dining rooms boast elaborately painted towering ceilings, multicolored tile arches, stained glass, and huge gilt-framed mirrors. Try to get one of the blue velvet booths and settle in for a fun evening. This is a great place to sample Brittany's famous oysters — you can get a platter with six kinds. Chef Gilles Renault changes the menu daily, but there are always beautiful seasonal soups, like the *soupe crémeuse de potiron aux coques* (creamy pumpkin soup with cockles) in fall. One of the classic brasserie dishes is the *magret de canard rôti au miel, pommes sautées persillées* (roasted duck with honey and sautéed apples). The star among the homemade desserts is the black forest cake.

4 place Graslin. ☎ 02-51-84-94-94. Reservations recommended. Meals: Main courses 69–119F ($10–$17); menus 100–150F ($14–$21). MC, V. Open: Daily 7:30 a.m.–12:30 a.m.

Exploring the city

The **Nantes City Card,** good for one (90F/$13), two (160F/$23), or three (200F/$29) days, gives you admission to all the major museums, as well as free access to all the bus and metro lines. The pass is available at the tourist office on place du Commerce. For info, call ☎ 02-40-20-60-00.

Occupying the symbolic center of the city is the **Château des Ducs de Bretagne** (4 place Marc-Elder; ☎ 02-40-41-56-56), where the Edict of Nantes was signed in 1598. François II, duc de Bretagne, built the château in 1466 and his daughter, Anne de Bretagne, was born there in 1477. Protected by a moat and thick fortified walls, the château is an imposing edifice. It has served over the years as a prison, and its most famous prisoner was Gilles de Retz, known to all as Bluebeard, the fifteenth-century mass murderer. The building is currently undergoing extensive renovations until 2008. You're free to walk around or picnic on the grounds, and there's usually a temporary exhibit at the museum inside the walls. July and August, the museum is open daily 10 a.m. to noon and

2 to 6 p.m.; September to June, hours are Wednesday to Monday 10 a.m. to noon and 2 to 6 p.m. Admission is 20F ($2.85) for adults and 10F ($1.40) for students and children.

Just north of the castle, past a large public park, is the grand fifteenth-century Flamboyant Gothic **Cathédrale St-Pierre** (place St-Pierre; ☎ 02-40-47-84-64). Inside is the ornate Renaissance tomb of François II, duc de Bretagne, who ruled from 1458 to 1488. From the cathedral square, you can stroll down Nantes's best shopping streets to the commercial center. Take **rue de Verdun** to **rue de la Marne** to **rue d'Orléans** to **place Royale.** Continue on **rue Crebillon** to place Graslin, with its magnificent **Grand Théâtre.** Along the way, don't forget to walk through the beautiful nineteenth-century shopping arcade **passage Pommeraye.** Walking toward the Loire River will bring you to **place du Commerce,** with a lively cafe scene.

One block east of the cathedral in a gorgeous belle-époque building, the very impressive **Musée des Beaux-Arts** (10 rue Georges-Clemenceau; ☎ 02-40-41-65-65) contains sculptures and paintings from the twelfth to the nineteenth century. Among the highlights are *Nymphéas* by Monet, *Madame de Senonnes* by Ingres, and *Le Joueur de Vielle* by Georges de la Tour. The most bizarre work is an 1887 statue of a gorilla carrying off a damsel. The museum is open Monday, Wednesday, Thursday, and Saturday 10 a.m. to 6 p.m.; Friday 10 a.m. to 9 p.m.; and Sunday 11 a.m. to 6 p.m. Admission is 20F ($2.85) for adults and 10F ($1.40) for students and children; entrance to the museum is free on Sundays.

If you walk a couple blocks east, you can visit one of France's most beautiful botanical gardens, the **Jardin des Plantes.** While the northern entrance to the park is close to the Musée des Beaux-Arts, the southern border is across from the train station. Admission is free, and it's open daily 8 a.m. to 8 p.m.

If you walk about half a mile to the west end of town, you'll pass Nantes's lively shopping district on **rue de la Marne, rue d'Orléans,** and **rue Crebillon.** You'll finally reach **place Graslin**, anchored by the imposing **Grand Théâtre.** Two blocks farther on rue Voltaire is the **Musée Thomas-Dobrée** (18 rue Voltaire; ☎ 02-40-71-03-50), housed in a fifteenth-century palace. The museum displays a collection of Roman antiquities, medieval paintings, and Renaissance decor. It's open Tuesday to Sunday 10 a.m. to noon and 1:30 to 5:30 p.m., with an admission of 20F ($2.85) for adults and 10F ($1.40) for students and children. Walking south to the Loire River and another half a mile west will take you to the **Musée Jules-Verne** (3 rue de l'Hermitage; ☎ 02-40-69-72-52), with documents relating to the life of the nineteenth-century author, born in Nantes, who wrote *20,000 Leagues Under the Sea* and other classics. The museum is open Wednesday to Saturday and Monday 10 a.m. to noon and 2 to 5 p.m. and Sunday 2 to 5 p.m. Admission is 8F ($1.15) for adults and 4F (60¢) for children.

Shopping

One of France's most beautiful shopping plazas is the enclosed early-1900s tri-level **passage Pommeraye,** decorated with statuary, gilded columns, gas lamps, and elaborate moldings. Nearby are the wide pedestrian shopping streets: **rue de la Marne, rue d'Orléans,** and **rue Crebillon.** The market is held at the **Marché de Talensac** and at **place du Buffay,** Tuesdays to Saturdays 9 a.m. to 1 p.m.

Nightlife

There are many bars on **place du Bouffay** and on the ancient streets near the château, including **Buck Mulligan's** (12 rue de Château; ☎ 02-40-20-02-72) and **London's Bar** (2 rue de Charmelites; ☎ 02-40-89-30-56). **Paddy Dooley's** (9 rue Franklin; ☎ 02-40-48-29-00) is an Irish pub that sometimes has live bands. The disco scene reigns at **L'Evasion** (3 rue de l'Emery; ☎ 02-40-47-99-84). Check out what's happening in the free brochure, **Le Mois Nantais,** from the tourist office.

Quimper and Its Hand-Painted Pottery

Set in a valley where the Odet and Steir Rivers meet, the traditional town of **Quimper** (pronounced cam-*pair*) is the capital of the Cornouaille area of Brittany. Quimper's claim to fame is its brightly colored hand-painted pottery, which has been made here since the seventeenth century. Quimper is also the oldest Breton city — it was settled between A.D. 400 and 700. The medieval section of town, west of the cathedral, is a maze of cobblestone pedestrian streets lined with pricey boutiques.

Quimper is a fairly quiet town. A lively time to visit is during the week-long **Festival de Cornouaille** in late July. You'll need to book your hotel way in advance, as this is one of Brittany's largest celebrations. For details, call the tourist office at ☎ 02-98-53-04-05.

Getting there

TGVs from Paris's Gare Montparnasse make the trip to Quimper in 4½ hours and cost 384 to 463F ($55 to $66). Two or three trains per day travel to Nantes, taking 2¾ to 4 hours (depending on how many stops the train makes) and costing 182 to 267F ($26 to $38). For train information call ☎ 08-36-35-35-39 or 08-36-35-35-35. Quimper's **Gare SNCF** (train station) is on avenue de la Gare, 1 km (0.6 miles) east of the town center.

Quimper is 570 km (354.2 miles) from Paris, and the trip takes 5 to 6 hours. If you're **driving,** take A11 to A81 west to Rennes. From Rennes, take E50 west to Montauban and continue west on N164 to Châteaulin, and then south on N165 to Quimper. Driving from Rennes to Quimper takes 2 to 3 hours.

Getting around and getting information

If you want to rent a car, try the branch of **Hertz** across from the train station (19 av. de la Gare; ☎ **02-98-53-12-34**). Nearby is **Europcar** (14 av. de la Libération; ☎ **02-98-90-00-68**), and **ADA** (2 av. de la Gare; ☎ **02-98-52-25-25**). An **Avis** office is inside the train station (☎ **02-98-90-12-72**). To order a **taxi,** call ☎ **02-98-90-21-21**.

The **tourist office** is on place de la Résistance (☎ **02-98-53-04-05**; Fax: 02-98-53-31-33; E-mail: office.tourisme.quimper@ouest-mediacap. com; Internet: www.bretagne-4villes.com.). July and August, it's open Monday to Saturday 9 a.m. to 7 p.m. and Sunday 10 a.m. to 1 p.m. and 3 to 6 p.m.; September to June, hours are Monday to Saturday 9 a.m. to noon and 1:30 to 6 p.m. and Sunday 10 a.m. to 1 p.m. July and August, walking tours of Quimper leave from the tourist office on Tuesdays at 2 p.m. The office also runs day trips to Point du Raz (120F/$17) and Pont-Aven (110F/$16). If you go to Point du Raz, the westernmost point of France, you can have a grilled lobster dinner at the wonderful **L'Etrave** (place de l'Eglise, Cléden-Cap-Sizun; ☎ **02-98-70-66-87**).

Where to stay

Hôtel Gradlon

$$$ Quimper

This is the best place to stay in the town center, a nineteenth-century hotel on a side street with a new annex in the back (no elevator in either building). The Gradlon has been in Mme Coller's family since 1929, and, with her British husband, she runs a very fine establishment. In the center of the hotel is a pretty rose garden with the glass-enclosed breakfast room beside it. Attention has been paid to the 23 rooms, which are individually decorated with stylish touches like Breton posters on the walls. One of the best rooms is off the garden, with a separate entrance. The reasonable prices, central location, and relatively spacious rooms make this hotel popular for families. The Collers are always redecorating and updating the hotel.

30 rue de Brest. ☎ *02-98-95-04-39. Fax: 02-98-95-61-25. E-mail:* gradlon@ destination-bretagne.com. *Rack rates: 490–590F ($70–$84) double; 950F ($136) suite. Breakfast: 60F ($9). Closed late Dec to mid-Jan. MC, V.*

La Tour d'Auvergne

$$$ Quimper

La Tour d'Auverge is in a good location, two blocks from the cathedral. The 38 rooms are badly in need of an update; however, they're comfortable and clean. The hotel has been in the same family since 1920, when the great-great-grandmother of the present owner bought it. Pluses, besides its location, are its friendly staff, good restaurant, lobby bar, and breakfast room, where a buffet is set out.

13 rue des Réguaires. ☎ *02-98-95-08-70. Fax: 02-98-95-17-31. Internet:* www. la-tour-dauvergne.fr. *E-mail:* latourdauvergne@wanadoo.fr. *Free parking. Rack rates: 555–595F ($79–$85) double. Breakfast: 59F ($8). MC, V.*

A fancy option about 12.9 km (8 miles) north of Quimper is the **Manoir du Stang** in La Forêt-Fouesnant, off N783 (☎ **02-98-56-97-37**). May to September, this sixteenth-century manor rents 24 rooms, decorated with antiques, for 590 to 930F ($84 to $133) double. Credit cards aren't accepted.

Where to dine

L'Ambroisie

$$$ Quimper   BRETON

This attractive Michelin-starred restaurant near the cathedral gets the best reviews in town, although the quality of the food can be inconsistent. The dining room is certainly lovely, with large paintings of Breton scenes. Chef Guyon prides himself on a "light and sophisticated" touch, and the menu is filled with intriguing Breton dishes with a contemporary twist — like *blé noir* (crab rolled in buckwheat crêpes), *sauté de langoustines aux artichauts* (sautéed prawns and artichokes), and *filet St-Pierre* (John Dory fish). They serve wonderful chocolate desserts here, as well as *fraises de Plougastel* (local strawberries) in summer.

49 rue Elie-Fréron. ☎ *02-98-95-00-02. Reservations recommended. Meals: Main courses 85-120F ($12-$17); menus 120-360F ($17-$51); children's menu 70F ($10). MC, V. Open: Tues-Sun noon to 2 p.m. and 7:30–9:30 p.m. Closed late June to early July.*

Rive Gauche

$$ Quimper   BRETON

On lively rue Ste-Catherine, Rive Gauche stands out for its excellent prices matched with good food. The decor is hip and modern, and the waitstaff has a sense of fun and a hint of attitude. The *menu de terroir* (of the earth), which features foods from local farms, starts with a dozen oysters served on seaweed with a vinegar sauce. As a main course, there's *escalope de saumon* (thin slice of salmon served with a light cream sauce) and *andouillette des eleveurs d'armor, gillé au cidre* (special local sausage, prepared with a cider sauce).

9 rue Ste-Catherine ☎ *02-98-90-06-15. Reservations recommended. Meals: Main courses 75–100F ($11–$14); menus 88–170F ($13–$24). MC, V. Open: 12:30–2:30 p.m. and 7:30–10:30 p.m.*

La Tour d'Auvergne (see "Where to stay") contains a good restaurant also called La Tour d'Auvergne, serving Breton cuisine with menus at 135 to 290F ($19 to $41). For an excellent breakfast or snack, you can't do much better than the **Pâtisserie Boule de Neige/Larnicol** (14 rue des Boucheries; ☎ 02-98-95-88-22), whose display case is filled with pastries that are works of art. The restaurant has seating in the rear and in the garden courtyard.

Exploring the town

The **Cathédrale St-Corentin** (place St-Corentin; ☎ 02-98-95-06-19) sits at the center of town. A stone equestrian statue of King Gradlon (legendary founder of Quimper) is set between the two 250-foot spires. Built between the thirteenth and the fifteenth century, the cathedral has recently undergone extensive renovations of its stonework, paintings, and fifteenth-century stained-glass windows. Admission is free, and the church is open daily 9 a.m. to 6 p.m. To the west are a maze of pedestrian streets with some of the best shopping in Brittany. Cross the river on one of the tiny pedestrian bridges to reach the tourist office. Another five minutes by foot will bring you to *faïence* heaven, with the museum, tours, and shops devoted to this colorful local pottery.

For a good introduction to the Breton way of life, stop at the **Musée des Beaux-Arts** (4 place St-Corentin; ☎ 02-98-95-45-20) to see its large collection of paintings of the Brittany countryside and genre scenes of the Breton people. The museum also has a fine collection of paintings from the sixteenth to the twentieth century, including works by Rubens, Boucher, Fragonard, and Corot. A room is devoted to the Pont-Aven school, made famous by Gauguin; another room is devoted to Max Jacob, born in Quimper. July and August, the museum is open daily 10 a.m. to 7 p.m.; September to June, hours are Wednesday to Monday 10 a.m. to noon and 2 to 6 p.m. Admission is 25F ($3.60) for adults and 15F ($2.15) for students and children.

The **Musée de Faïence Jules Verlinque** (14 rue Jean-Baptiste-Bosquet; ☎ 02-98-90-12-72) displays a fun collection of the city's signature pottery. May to October, the museum is open Monday to Saturday 10 a.m. to 6 p.m. Admission is 26F ($3.70) for adults, 21F ($3) for those 18 to 25, and 15F ($2.15) for those 7 to 17.

Other Brittany favorites

Belle Ile: Consider visiting this bucolic island 15 km (9.3 miles) off the southern coast of Brittany, reachable by a 45-minute ferry (107F/$15 for adults, 66F/$9 for children, 468F/$67 for cars round-trip). This is the place to try thallasotherapy, a seawater therapy popular at coastal resorts. Treatments lasting 2 to 4 hours cost 270 to 550F ($39 to $79). The island's top place to try a treatment and spend the night is the **Castel Clara:** This hotel (☎ **02-97-31-84-21;** Fax: 02-97-31-51-69; E-mail: castelclara@relaischateaux.fr; Internet: www.relaischateaux.fr/castelclara), a Relais & Châteaux overlooking the sea, has rooms and half board costing 1,750 to 2,250F ($250 to $321) for a double or 2,950 to 3,950F ($421 to $564) for a suite. The restaurant is very expensive and has an excellent reputation. The hotel is closed from late November to mid-February. Next door is the less expensive **Manoir de Goulphar** (☎ **02-97-31-80-10;** Fax: 02-97-31-80-05; Internet: www.manoir-de-goulphar.fr), with rooms at 450 to 1,185F ($64 to $169) for a double or 1,690 to 2,030F ($241 to $290) for a suite; half pension is 635 to 2,090F ($91 to $299).

Presqu'île de Crozon: A drive around the Crozon Peninsula (58 km/36 miles from Quimper, 260.7 km/162 miles from Nantes) on Brittany's west coast offers wild and quintessential Brittany landscapes and seascapes. You'll find jagged cliffs at Chèvre, an ancient stone church at Rocamadour, grottoes at Morgat, and prehistoric stone alignments at Camaret.

Pont-Aven: Fans of painter Paul Gauguin will want to visit this pretty little village, 32.2 km (20 miles) from Quimper and 173.9 km (108 miles) from Nantes. Stone houses and mills along the river Aven make a picturesque scene. The small Musée de l'Ecole de Pont-Aven displays a couple of Gauguin prints, as well as paintings by less well known artists of the time, and many photos of the artists' colony that formed in the late nineteenth and early twentieth century. Artistic types are still drawn to this village, whose streets are lined with galleries. This is also the home of the cookie company Traou Mad, which makes the famous Brittany butter cookies.

St-Malo: This walled town is on the northern coast of Brittany, 170.6 km (106 miles) from Nantes. The charming town, with its pricey boutiques and lively cobblestone streets, is very popular with day-trippers and tour buses. You can walk all the way around the town's ramparts and sunbathe on the brown-sand beaches below. Children in particular enjoy frolicking in the shallow warm waters surrounding St-Malo.

Shopping

If you're looking to immerse yourself in the world of Quimper pottery, you can take a factory tour, see the museum, and spend time in shops devoted to this local craft.

The main factory/*faïence* store is **HB Henriot** (rue Haut; ☎ 02-98-90-09-36). July and August, 30-minute guided visits in English (20F/ $2.85 for adults and 10F/$1.40 for children) take place Monday to Thursday 9 to 11:30 a.m. and 1:30 to 5:30 p.m., and Friday 9 to 11:30 a.m. and 1:30 to 4:15 p.m.; September to June, visits are Monday to Thursday 9 to 11:30 a.m. and 1:30 to 4:30 p.m., and Friday 9 to 11:30 a.m. and 1:30 to 3:15 p.m. After the tour, you can visit the factory store with the largest selection of Quimper pottery in town. Nearby is a store selling "seconds" (slightly damaged or imperfect pieces at bargain prices).

Other good shops for Breton wares are **Bed Keltiek** (2 rue de Roi Gradlon; ☎ 02-98-95-42-82), which sells pottery, jewelry, and books; and located next door, **François Le Villec** (4 rue de Roi Gradlon; ☎ 02-98-95-31-54), which offers traditional *faïence*. **Heoligou** (16 rue du Parc; ☎ 02-98-95-13-29) has Brittany sweaters and other clothing. The **food market** is held at Halles St-François on rue Astor every Monday to Saturday 7 a.m. to 8 p.m. and Sunday 9 a.m. to 1 p.m.

Nightlife

Check out **rue St-Catherine** for a good sampling of bars. **Le Coffee Shop** (26 rue de Frout, behind the cathedral; ☎ 02-98-95-43-30) is a popular gay spot. **St. Andrews Pub** (11 place Stivel; ☎ 02-98-53-34-49) attracts an English-speaking crowd that enjoys the 45 kinds of beer available here. **Café des Arts** (on the corner of rue St-Catherine and blvd Dupleix; ☎ 02-98-90-32-06) is a nightclub with a huge drink menu and no cover. And **The Blue Note** (7 rue de Douarnenez; ☎ 02-98-53-47-47) has live jazz some nights, with no cover.

Carnac and Its Prehistoric Stones

Carnac boasts France's biggest prehistoric site, where thousands of huge stones stand sentinel over miles of rolling fields near the seaside. There are actually three major groupings, all within a mile of each other: the Alignements du Ménec, Alignements de Kermario, and Alignements de Kerlescan. Estimated to be from 4500 to 2000 B.C., the stones predate Stonehenge and even the Egyptian pyramids. Carnac is also a popular seaside resort; most visitors combine sun and fun with rock gazing.

Carnac is very quiet from October to May; this is the best time to wander around the ancient rocks without the distraction of crowds.

Getting there

The best way to get to Carnac is by **driving.** From Quimper, take N165 east to Auray, and then D768 south to Carnac. Driving the 486 km (302 miles) from Paris to Carnac takes about 5 hours. Take A11 southwest from Paris to Le Mans and then A81 west to Rennes. From Rennes, take N24 and then N166 southwest to Vannes. Drive west on E60 to Auray and south on D768 to Carnac.

The nearest **TGV (fast train)** station is in Auray, 14 km (8.7 miles) from Carnac. Trips from Paris's Gare Montparnasse to Auray by train take 3½ hours and cost 339 to 398F ($49 to $57). From Auray, you can take a bus costing 24F and taking 30 minutes to Carnac. You can also take a taxi to Carnac, which takes 15 minutes and costs about 70F ($10). In summer, you can take a train from Auray to Plouharnel, located 4 km from Carnac. From Plouharnel, seven buses per day make the five-minute trip from Plouharnel to Carnac in summer only for 5F (70¢). There are also taxis at the Plouharnel train station that'll take you to Carnac center in five minutes for about 35F ($5). For train information, call ☎ **08-36-35-35-35** or 08-36-35-35-39.

Getting around and getting information

You can rent bikes at **Le Randonneur** (20 av. des Druides, Carnac Plage; ☎ **02-97-52-02-55**), open April to September daily 9:30 a.m. to noon and 2:30 to 6:30 p.m. The cost is 60F ($9) per half day and 100F ($14) per full day.

The **tourist office** is at 74 av. des Druides (☎ **02-97-52-13-52**). July and August, it's open Monday to Saturday 9 a.m. to 7 p.m. and Sunday 3 to 7 p.m.; September to June, hours are Monday to Saturday 9 a.m. to noon and 2 to 6 p.m. April to September, an **annex** on place de l'Eglise is open Tuesday to Saturday 9:30 a.m. to 12:30 p.m. and 2 to 6 p.m.

Where to stay

Hôtel Celtique

$$$ **Carnac Plage**

This modern Best Western, a block from the beach, has 53 mostly spacious, comfortable rooms (some with balconies offering beach views). From the brightly lit lobby to the handsome bar, this is a well-run place. Amenities include a heated pool, hot tub, sauna, fitness room, and large commons room with a billiard table. The restaurant, An Daol, serves Breton specialties with an emphasis on seafood.

17 av. de Kermario or 82 av. des Druides. ☎ 02-97-52-14-15. Fax: 02-97-52-71-10. Internet: www.ot-carnac.fr/hotels/celtique. *Rack rates: 295–730F ($42–$104) double. Breakfast: 50–70F ($7–$10). MC, V.*

Hôtel le Diana

$$$$ Carnac Plage

Across from the main beach, this modern hotel is Carnac's top lodging. Most of the 32 individually decorated, comfortable rooms have balconies and ocean views. The restaurant overlooking the beach specializes in seafood. There's a large heated pool and sauna adjacent to the popular hotel bar.

21 bd. de la Plage. ☎ *02-97-52-05-38. Fax: 02-97-52-7-91. Internet:* www.ot. carnac.fr/hotels/diana. *E-mail:* diana@ot-carnac.fr. *Rack rates: 600–1230F ($86–$176) double; 1,330–1,750F ($190–$250) suite. Breakfast: 90F ($13). Half pension: 1,990–2,410F ($284–$344) for two. Closed late Oct to mid-Apr. AE, DC, MC, V.*

Where to dine

Auberge le Ratelier

$$ Carnac Ville   BRETON

M. and Mme Mobe run this ancient ivy-covered inn, located down a cul de sac close to the center of town. It's a warm rustic setting serving delicious Breton cuisine, with fresh local fish a highpoint. Your meal may begin with a *gaspacho de langoustines au basilic* (gazpacho with prawns and basil). As a main course, try *filet de dorade à la citronnelle, pommes de terre écrasées à l'huile d'olive* (dorade fish with lemongrass, served with potatoes with olive oil). For dessert, there's *nougat glacé au miel et rosace de fraises* (candied-fruit ice cream with honey and strawberries). The auberge also offers eight small, simple rooms upstairs at 250 to 350F ($34 to $48) for a double.

4 chemin Douët. ☎ *02-97-52-05-04. Reservations necessary. Meals: Main courses 85–125F ($12–$18); menu 95–185F ($14–$26). MC, V. Open: Daily noon to 2:30 p.m. and 7:30–9:30 p.m.*

Exploring the town and the mysterious stones

Carnac is divided into two sections: **Carnac Plage** is the beachfront resort with modern hotels lining the coast, and about 2.4 km (1½ miles) inland is **Carnac Ville,** with shops, restaurants, and several nightclubs. The prehistoric rock formations are on the north side of the city a few miles from the beach. A Celtic burial chamber dating from 5000 B.C., the **Tumulus St-Michel,** is on rue de Tumulus, less than a mile east from Carnac Ville. Built above the chamber is a sixteenth-century church. The chamber is closed indefinitely for excavations.

While the purpose of the **Alignments de Carnac** (☎ 02-97-52-89-99) remains a mystery, they can be dated to Neolithic times. Over thousands of years, villagers have used the rocks as a quarry, so it's impossible to know what the original formation was. What is visible now are rows of about 2,000 standing stones, some as high as 60 feet and weighing many tons. The most common hypotheses about the stones are that they marked burial sites, charted the course of the moon and planets, or were part of a religious ritual. Legend has it that the rocks represent a Roman army turned to stone.

The three major sites from west to east are the **Alignements du Ménec, Alignements de Kermario,** and **Alignements de Kerlescan.** At Ménec, the site that's on route des Alignements to the west of rue des Korrigans, most of the 1,100 stones are less than 1 meter high. About a mile east on route des Alignements is the Kermario site, with about 1,000 stones in 10 lines; there's a viewing platform here. About half a mile farther is Kerlescan, with 555 stones in 13 lines.

Because of the sheer number of visitors trampling and damaging the site, the area is fenced off and access is restricted. October to April, admission is free and visitors can walk through the site. But May to September, admission is limited to 25 people at a time (180 per day maximum), and 90-minute tours cost 33F ($5). The **visitor center** at the Alignements de Kermario is open daily 9 a.m. to 6 p.m. To reach the center from the direction of Carnac, take a right off rue des Korrigans onto route des Kerlescan.

The **Musée de Préhistoire** (10 place de la Chapelle; ☎ 02-97-52-22-04) displays interpretations of the alignments, as well as Paleolithic and Neolithic artifacts dating back to 450,000 B.C. It also offers a helpful English-language brochure. Late June to mid-September, the museum is open daily 10 a.m. to 6:30 p.m.; late September to mid-June, hours are Wednesday to Monday 10 a.m. to noon and 2 to 6 p.m. Admission is 30F ($4.30) for adults and 15F ($2.15) for students.

Nightlife

Les Chandelles (avenue de l'Atlantique; ☎ 02-97-52-90-98) is the most popular disco in these parts. There's a 60F cover. Nearby is the **Whiskey Club** (8 av. des Druides; ☎ 02-97-52-10-52), with live music and dancing. And at **Le Petit Bedon** (106 av. des Druides; ☎ 02-97-52-11-62), a 30-something crowd dances to oldies.

Part VI
Provence and the French Riviera

"I'M PRETTY SURE YOU'RE SUPPOSED TO JUST SMELL THE CORK."

In this part...

Provence and the French Riviera are sun-kissed regions in the southeast corner of France, where the air is perfumed by lavender and fresh herbs and the country-side is dotted with olive groves and vineyards that you may remember seeing in van Gogh and Cézanne paintings. In Chapter 18, I explore the top towns of Provence — Arles, Aix-en-Provence, Avignon, and St-Rémy-de-Provence — and teach you how to stay safe in wild Marseille. This is perhaps France's most written about region; its warm, dry weather and scenic countryside offer an idyllic vacation. You'll come across ancient Roman ruins, medieval towns, and sophisticated cities. The region's food and wines are world famous, and you're sure to enjoy some of your most memorable meals here, enlivened by the colorful Provençal herbs and olive oil.

In Chapter 19, I move along to where the coastline meets the warm Mediterranean near the border of Italy — the part of Provence known as the magical French Riviera, also called the Côte d'Azur. With lots of beaches, charming hill towns, hot nightlife, wonderful art museums, glamorous casinos, and seaside boardwalks, the Riviera is a festive playground. This is where artists like Picasso, Matisse, Léger, and Renoir chose to work and live, and the region's museums are full of their colorful canvases. I take you to the Riviera's top ten towns, all lined up along the coast. The big cities of Nice and Cannes, with their frenetic nightlife, contrast with the small towns of Beaulieu and St-Jean-Cap-Ferrat. The beautiful ports of St-Tropez and Antibes are a contrast to the hill towns of Biot, Vence, and St-Paul-de-Vence. My last stop along the French Riviera isn't really in France at all — it's the tiny principality of Monaco, where Grace Kelly once reigned at the side of Prince Rainier III, gamblers now head to try their luck at the famous casino, and visitors go to see the royal palace.

Chapter 18

The Best of Provence

In This Chapter

▶ Discovering the historic towns of Provence

▶ Exploring Avignon's Palais des Papes

▶ Following in the footsteps of van Gogh and Cézanne

*P*rovence, with its ancient towns, verdant countryside, and mild climate, is one of the most popular regions of France for visitors. Whether idling away the sunbaked afternoons in picturesque cafes and shops or seeking out major attractions like the grand Palais des Papes in Avignon or the impressive Roman ruins of Glanum in St-Rémy, your time spent in Provence is bound to be some of the most memorable of your trip. This is a region that has long been popular with artists, and you may enjoy following the footsteps of van Gogh in Arles and St-Rémy or seeking out the favorite landscapes of Cézanne in Aix-en-Provence. Aix is also be one of France's most beautiful cities, where eighteenth-century mansions of golden-colored stone line the Cours Mirabeau, a magnificent boulevard, and sculpted fountains seem to gurgle around every corner.

The fastest TGV train service to France's south coast will debut in June 2001: from Paris to Avignon in 2 hours and 38 minutes, Paris to Marseille in 3 hours, and Paris to Aix in 3 hours!

Avignon and the Palais des Papes

The glorious walled city of **Avignon,** capital of Christianity in the fourteenth century and home of the regal Palais des Papes, is a good base from which to tour the region. Due to its strategic site in the Rhône valley, the city became a Roman outpost and major stop on trading routes, and rose to prominence until reaching its pinnacle in the fourteenth century. Instability in Rome made Pope Clement V move to France, and for the next 65 years, Avignon became the papal seat and capital of the Christian world. Seven French popes ruled over Christendom from the Palais des Papes, and the city's diplomatic, artistic, and commercial life prospered. Then during the Great Schism (1376–1417), French cardinals decided to make trouble by continuing to elect French popes even after the papacy had returned to Rome. Soon all was sorted out and Rome was back on top. The period of prosperity forever changed Avignon, which, with its sumptuous mansions, grand squares, and towering palace, retains a look of pride and strength. But Avignon also has a resolutely modern side. In fact, the city is most famous today for its summer arts festival — this has helped turn Avignon into a year-round cutting-edge arts community.

The popular children's ditty *"Sur le pont d'Avignon, on y danse; on y danse"* ("On the bridge of Avignon, we dance, we dance") may actually have a very sinister meaning. Some historians think the lyrics were originally *"sous le pont"* ("under the bridge"), referring to a hermit who lived under the pont St-Benezet on the spit of land now known as Ile de la Barthelasse. Because the bridge was quite narrow at that time, people frequently fell off and either drowned in the fast-moving Rhône, or landed near the hermit's lair. The song may then refer to the hermit dancing for joy at the tragic fate of those falling into the river — close enough for him to scavenge clothes or other belongings.

Avignon was named a European City of Culture in 2000 (along with eight other cities). Because of that designation, the city tackled a number of projects that post-2000 visitors can enjoy: a new Museum of Contemporary Art housing works from the 1960s to the present (see "Exploring the town and environs" later in this chapter), a walking path along the former boat-towing path on Ile de la Barthelasse, a river boat shuttle to Ile de la Barthelasse, the renovation of place Pie, and renovations to the train station.

Sampling the region's cuisine

Avignon is capital of the Côtes du Rhône region, in which fine wines have been cultivated for 2,000 years. The famous *grand crus* (top wines) are Châteauneuf-du-Pape, Gigondas, Vacqueras, Lirac, Tavel, and Côtes du Rhône.

Regional food specialties available throughout Provence are *friandise composée de chocolat fin, sucre et liqueur d'origan* (petit fours of chocolate, sugar, and liqueur), *fruits confits d'Apt* (fruit preserved in sugar, a specialty of Apt), *berlingots de Carpentas* (soft candy, a specialty of Carpentas), *riz et sel de Camargue* (rice and salt from the Camargue region), *nougat de Sault* (nougat from Sault), and *calissons d'Aix* (almond-paste candy from Aix). Other food specialties include olive oil pressed in the village of Les Baux and *miel de Ventaux* (honey from Ventaux), as well as olives, *ail* (garlic), *fromage de chèvre* (goat cheese), *pastis* (anise-flavored liqueur), *fougasse* (flavored bread), and of course, *herbes de Provence*.

Provence

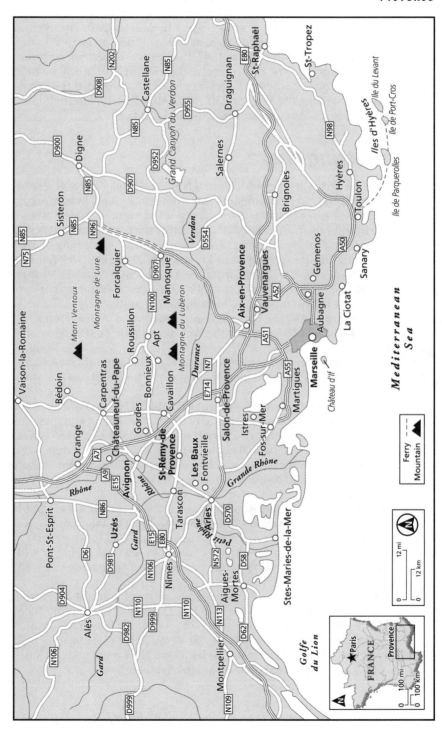

Mediterranean Sea

Golfe du Lion

Ferry
Mountain

12 mi
12 km

N

FRANCE
★ Paris
Provence
100 mi
100 km

The **Festival d'Avignon** (☎ 04-90-27-66-50; Internet: www. festival-avignon.com) is one of France's premier arts festivals — officials claim it's the world's biggest theater festival. The events at this festival aren't as expensive as those at the arts festival in nearby Aix-en-Provence. Created in 1947, the Festival d'Avignon features performances of theater, music, and dance. In 2001, it will be held July 6 through 28. Several ancillary festivals are held at the same time, including the **Festival Off** (☎ 01-48-05-01-19; Internet: www. avignon-off.org) featuring experimental fare.

Getting there

Trains arrive at Avignon's **Gare S.N.C.F.** on boulevard St-Roch, just outside the old city ramparts and a ten-minute walk from most hotels and the center of town. If you have a lot of luggage, there's a taxi stand in front of the train station. If you're traveling from Paris, TGVs depart from Paris's Gare de Lyon. New trains and tracks debuting in 2001 cut the trip time to Avignon from 3 hours and 20 minutes to 2 hours and 38 minutes. One-way trips from Paris to Avignon cost 345F ($49) in second class and 435F ($62) in first class. From Avignon, there are frequent trains traveling to Marseille (70 minutes, 92F/$13) and Arles (30 minutes, 40F/$6). For train reservations and information, call ☎ 08-36-35-35-39, or check the Web site at www.scnf.fr.

Avignon is infamous for attracting pickpockets and thieves. Keep a close eye on your bags, particularly at the train and bus stations.

The **Aéroport Avignon-Caumont** (☎ 04-90-81-51-51) is 8 km (5 miles) southeast of Avignon. There are direct flights, taking about an hour, from Paris's Orly Airport. In order to get from the airport to town, you'll need to take a taxi, which costs 80 to 100F ($11 to $14), depending on traffic. At the airport, you can find rental car offices for Hertz, Europcar, Avis, Budget, and National Citer.

Avignon's seedy **Gare Routière** (bus station) is on boulevard St-Michel, next to the train station (☎ 04-90-82-07-35). The information desk is open Monday to Friday 8 a.m. to noon and 1:30 to 6 p.m., and Saturday 9 a.m. to noon. Buses connect to Aix (one hour, 89F/$13), Arles (45 minutes, 48F/$7), and Pont du Gard (45 minutes, 35F/$5).

If you're **driving** from Paris, take A6 south to Lyon and A7 south to Avignon. Avignon is 683 km (425 miles) south of Paris. From Nice, Marseille, or Lyon, take A8 and A7 to Avignon. Orange is 30 km (18.6 miles) away from Avignon, St-Rémy 20 km (12.4 miles), Les Baux 25 km (15.5 miles), Arles 35 km (21.7 miles), Aix 60 km (37.3 miles), and Marseille 99 km (61.5 miles).

Getting around and getting information

It's easy to walk from one end of the walled city of Avignon to the other. Many hotels, restaurants, and sights, including the famous Palais des Papes, are clustered in the center of the city. However, you'll need to use some sort of public transportation or a car to get to the nearby walled suburb of Villeneuve-lez-Avignon, a lovely medieval village with several interesting historic sites (see later in this section).

To go to the walled suburb of Villeneuve-lez-Avignon (about 10 minutes), catch a no. 10 or 11 **bus** (Villeneuve puis Les Angles) from the main post office or the porte de l'Oulle on the west side of the city (Sundays and holidays it's the no. 10D bus). Buses run every 20 minutes (less frequently on Sunday) 7 a.m. to 8 p.m. and cost 7F ($1). The 100-seat **Bateau Bus** (☎ 04-90-85-62-25) goes from Avignon to Ile de la Barthelasse and then to Villeneuve six times per day in July and August (1¼-hour round-trip). Tickets are 40F ($6) for adults (32F/$4.60 with pass) and 20F ($2.85) for children under 12 (16F/$2.30 with the tourist pass called Avignon Passion; see "Seeing Avignon" later in this section for details).

You can pick up city bus info and tickets across from the train station at the **Tourelle Porte de la République** (☎ 04-90-82-68-19) or at the **bus stop** at place Pie (☎ 04-90-85-44-93).

You can rent a car at **Hertz** (4 bd. St-Michel; ☎ 04-90-82-37-67). To rent a bike, try **Holiday Bikes,** next to the tourist office on cours Jean-Jaurès (☎ 04-90-95-57-81), or **Cycles Peugeot** (80 rue Guillaume-Puy; ☎ 04-90-86-32-49). Rentals are 70 to 85F ($10 to $12) for a half day or 100 to 120F ($14 to $17) for a full day. For a **cab** from the place Pie taxi stand, call ☎ 04-90-82-20-20.

In 2000, a free **riverboat shuttle** began taking visitors from Avignon to the Ile de la Barthelasse, the island in the middle of the Rhône River. May through October, the company **Mireio** (☎ 04-90-85-62-25) runs the 10-minute shuttle daily from the harbor on the east side of the pont St-Bénézet, also known as the pont d'Avignon. The shuttle runs nonstop 11 a.m. to 9 p.m. in the middle of summer and less frequently on the shoulder season. After you reach the island, you can walk on the impressive new walking trail along the river called the promenade du Chemin des Berges, which has wonderful views of Avignon.

The **Avignon tourist office** is at 41 cours Jean-Jaurès (☎ 04-32-74-32-74; Fax: 04-90-82-95-03; E-mail: information@ot-avignon.fr; Internet: www.avignon-tourism.com). April to September, it's open daily 9 a.m. to 1 p.m. and 2 to 5 p.m.; October to May, hours are Monday to Saturday 9 a.m. to 1 p.m. and 2 to 5 p.m. and Sundays and holidays 10 a.m. to noon. During the July arts festival, hours are Monday to Saturday 10 a.m. to 8 p.m. and Sunday 10 a.m. to 5 p.m. Guides from the office lead tours of the city. The **Villeneuve-lez-Avignon tourist office** is at place Charles-David (☎ **04-90-25-61-33;** Fax: 04-90-25-91-55; E-mail: `Villeneuve.lez.avignon.tourisme@wanadoo.fr`; Internet: `www.villeneuve-lez-avignon`). July hours are daily 10 a.m. to 7 p.m.; August hours are daily 9 a.m. to 1 p.m. and 2 to 6 p.m.; and September to June hours are Monday to Saturday 9 a.m. to 1 p.m. and 2 to 6 p.m. To check or send e-mail, head to **CyberHighway** (30 rue des Infirmières; ☎ **04-90-27-02-09**), between place des Carmes and rue Cabassole, open Monday to Saturday 10 a.m. to 9 p.m. and Sunday 10 a.m. to 2 p.m. No food is served.

Where to stay

Frantour Primotel Horloge

$$$ Avignon

Just off place de l'Horloge and close to the Palais des Papes, this handsome 67-room hotel is part of a large French chain. The classical nineteenth-century facade belies the unabashedly modern guest room decor. The high-ceiling rooms come with minibars and hairdryers; the more expensive ones have terraces overlooking the square. Because the hotel is located in a busy area, the rooms facing the street have soundproof windows. A continental breakfast buffet is served on the glassed-in veranda.

1–3 rue Félicien-David. ☎ *04-90-16-42-00. Fax: 04-90-82-17-32. Internet:* `www.hotels-primotel.com`. *E-mail:* `avignonfrantour@hotels-primotel.com`. *Parking: Guests get a special rate at a nearby public lot of 45F ($6) per day. Rack rates: 450–800F ($64–$114) double. Breakfast: 60F ($9). AE, MC, V.*

Hôtel Clarion Cloître St-Louis

$$$$ Avignon

One of Avignon's best hotels, this is a pleasing combination of modern and antique styles. Located just inside the south city walls (close to the train station), the hotel was built as a Jesuit school in 1589 and became a military hospital during the Revolution. The lobby ceiling is constructed of ancient vaulting and the furniture is black and sleek. The 80 spacious rooms and suites are decorated in a contemporary style and come with minibars, safes, and hairdryers. Their large windows overlook the cloister courtyard or the hotel gardens. The large modern wing, with tinted windows, looks like a Manhattan office tower; rooms in this wing have balconies. On top of the modern wing are a pool and sun deck, open from May to September. The restaurant serves all meals under the ancient cloister vaults or in the garden.

20 rue du Portail-Boquier. ☎ *04-90-27-55-55. Fax: 04-90-82-24-01. Internet:* `www.cloitre-saint-louis.com`. *E-mail:* `hotel@cloitre-saint-louis.com`. *Parking: 50F ($7). Rack rates: 475–995F ($68–$142) double; 850–1,160F ($121–$66) suite. AE, MC, V.*

Avignon

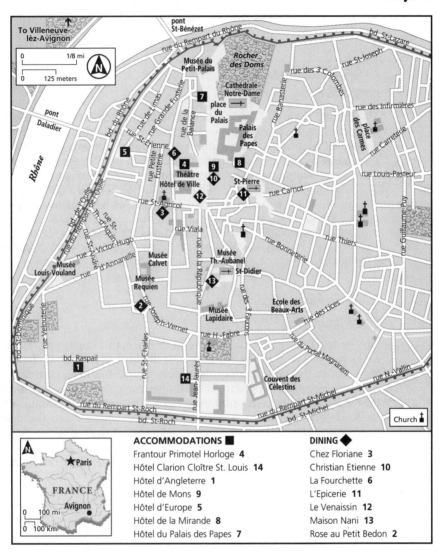

To Villeneuve-lèz-Avignon

0   1/8 mi

0   125 meters

pont Daladier

Rhône

pont St-Bénézet

rue du Rempart du Rhône

bd. St-Lazare

Musée du Petit-Palais

Rocher des Doms

rue des 3 Colombes

rue St-Joseph

Cathédrale Notre-Dame

bd. du Rhône

rue de Limas

rue de la Grande-Fusterie

rue de la Balance

place du Palais

Palais des Papes

rue Banasterie

rue des Infirmières

place des Carmes

rue Carreterie

rue St-Étienne

rue Petite Fusterie

7

5

6

4   **9**
     10

8

Théâtre
Hôtel de Ville

St-Pierre

rue Louis-Pasteur

rue de l'Ouille

bd. du Rempart de l'Ouille

rue St-Agricol

12

11

rue Carnot

rue St-Agricol

3

rue Viala

rue de la République

rue Bonneterie

rue Thiers

rue Guillaume-Puy

rue St-Victor-Hugo

rue d'Annanelle

rue St-André

rue St-Aquin

Musée Louis-Vouland

Musée Calvet

Musée Th.-Aubanel

St-Didier

Musée Requien

13

Musée Lapidaire

Ecole des Beaux-Arts

rue des Lices

bd. St-Dominique

rue Velouterie

rue Joseph-Vernet

rue St-Charles

2

rue H.-Fabre

rue des 3 Faucons

rue du Portail Magnanen

rue N.-Vallin

bd. Raspail

1

14

rue Jean-Jaurès

Couvent des Célestins

rue du Rempart St-Roch

bd. St-Roch

rue du Rempart St-Michel

bd. St-Michel

Church ⚱

★ Paris

FRANCE

Avignon

0   100 mi

0   100 km

ACCOMMODATIONS ■	DINING ◆
Frantour Primotel Horloge **4**	Chez Floriane **3**
Hôtel Clarion Cloître St. Louis **14**	Christian Etienne **10**
Hôtel d'Angleterre **1**	La Fourchette **6**
Hôtel de Mons **9**	L'Epicerie **11**
Hôtel d'Europe **5**	Le Venaissin **12**
Hôtel de la Mirande **8**	Maison Nani **13**
Hôtel du Palais des Papes **7**	Rose au Petit Bedon **2**

Hôtel d'Angleterre

$$ Avignon

This 40-room hotel is a little far from the action, in the southwest corner of the city, not far from the train station and tourist office. The standard contemporary rooms are comfortable and clean — if on the small and plain side. The building, built around 1929 in the art deco style, has four floors. A tasty continental breakfast is served next to the lobby. The friendly English-speaking staff will cheerfully recommend a restaurant or describe a tourist sight.

29 bd. Raspail. ☎ *04-90-86-34-31. Fax: 04-90-86-86-74. Internet:* www.
hoteldangleterre.fr. *E-mail:* info@hoteldangleterre.fr. *Parking: 40F
($6). Rack rates: 300–450F ($43–$64) double. Breakfast: 40F ($6). Closed late Dec to
late Jan. MC, V.*

Hôtel de la Mirande

$$$$ Avignon

The beautiful Mirande, occupying a Renaissance palace near the Palais
des Papes, is the top lodging choice. Each of the 20 rooms is individually
decorated in grand style; a famous Paris decorator was given unlimited
resources to search out the most exceptional antiques, oriental rugs,
handmade wallpapers, and damask curtains. All rooms have minibars.
The hotel has a Michelin-starred restaurant, as well as a cooking school.
The inner courtyard, a secret garden, is lush with plants and sculpture.

4 place de l'Amirande. ☎ *04-90-85-93-93. Fax: 04-90-86-26-85. Internet:* www.
la-mirande.fr. *Parking: 90–115F ($13–$16). Rack rates: 1,850–2,700F ($264–
$386) double; 4,200–6,050F ($600–$864) suite. Breakfast: 150F ($21). AE, MC, V.*

Hôtel de Mons

$ Avignon

On a quiet street off central place de l'Horloge, this family-run hotel, with
its 11 simple and odd-shaped rooms, is the best of Avignon's cheap lodgings. An atmospheric thirteenth-century chapel has been converted into
a rough-around-the-edges hotel that nevertheless possesses a homey —
if homely — charm. The real treat here is the ancient building with its
vaulted ceiling and old stone staircase that winds up to the beamed
rooms. Breakfast is served in a vaulted nook off the lobby.

5 rue du Mons. ☎ *04-90-82-57-16. Fax: 04-90-85-19-15. Rack rates: 270–290F
($39–$41) double. Breakfast: 35F ($5). MC, V.*

Hôtel d'Europe

$$$$ Avignon

The Europe caters to a crowd that appreciates overstated elegance. Built
in 1580, the mansion of the marquis de Graveson has been a hotel since
1799. Guests have included Napoléon, Châteaubriand, Victor Hugo,
Tennessee Williams, Salvador Dalí, and Picasso. The 47 spacious rooms
are decorated with antiques, oriental rugs, chaises, and chandeliers, and
boast marble fireplaces, paneled walls and doors, and classical moldings.
The three top-floor suites have balconies: two with views of the Palais des
Papes, one with a river view. La Vieille Fontaine restaurant is decorated
with tapestries. In summer, meals are served on the terrace near a fountain.

12 place Crillon. ☎ *04-90-14-76-76. Fax: 04-90-14-76-71. Internet:* www.
hoteldeurope.fr. *E-mail:* reservations@hotel-d-europe.fr. *Parking:*

60F ($9). Rack rates: 690–2,200F ($99–$314) double; 3,000–3,300F ($429–$471) suite. Breakfast: 98F ($14). AE, DC, MC, V.

Hôtel du Palais des Papes

$$$ Avignon

Considering the location and amenities, this hotel is a great deal in Avignon. For those who like to be in the heart of the city, the location couldn't be better — it's across the square from the Palais des Papes. (Keep in mind, that means it's a half-mile walk from the train station.) The 23 rooms are charming and stylish, with antique fixtures and stone walls. Some have a view of the Palais des Papes, which is particularly magnificent at night. Breakfast can be served in the room for a couple extra francs. The hotel also has a reasonably priced provençal restaurant. The English-speaking staff is welcoming.

1 rue Gérard-Philippe. ☎ *04-90-86-04-13. Fax: 04-90-27-91-17. Internet:* www. avignon-et-provence.com/hotel-le-lutrin-palais-des-papes. *Parking: 40F ($6). Rack rates: 380–850F ($54–$121) double. Breakfast: 40F ($6). MC, V.*

During the festival, hotel rooms are scarce. Here are a few more good medium-priced choices: **Citodel de Garlande** (20 rue Galante; ☎ 04-90-85-08-85); **Hôtel Blauvac** (11 rue de la Bancasse; ☎ 04-90-86-34-11); and **Hôtel Médiéval** (15 rue Petite Saunerie; ☎ 04-90-86-11-06).

Where to dine

Chez Floriane

$$ Avignon   PROVENÇAL

This lovely restaurant is set in a secluded courtyard in the center of town, but there's also seating inside, where the modern decor blends with the ancient building. The cuisine is Mediterranean with Italian influences. For the first course, try the excellent antipasta, a sampling of wonderful meats and vegetables, or the *légumes grillés à la mozzarella* (grilled vegetables with mozzarella). As a main dish, look no further than the homemade pastas, served provençal-style with understated sauces containing herbs from the region. The hip waitstaff, looking for a chuckle, is likely to take your order with a Cockney accent.

23 rue St-Agricol. ☎ *04-90-27-12-66. Meals: Main courses 95–145F ($14–$21); menus 70F ($10) at lunch, 150F ($21) at dinner. MC, V. Open: Mon–Sat noon to 2:30 p.m.; Tues–Sat 7:30–10 p.m.*

Christian Etienne

$$$$ Avignon   PROVENÇAL

This is fine dining at its most opulent. About half the tables are out on a narrow street near the Palais des Papes, but the atmospheric frescoed interior of this twelfth-century building is almost worth the (very steep) price. Daring chef Christian Etienne specializes in tomatoes, truffles, and fish: He bases entire menus on tomatoes in summer, creates wonderous truffle-studded concoctions in winter, and uses great imagination with fresh fish. A typical first course is *bouillon de lentilles aux saucisses de couenne* (lentil-and-sausage soup). Main dishes include *tronçon de baudroie poêlé au vin rouge des Côtes du Rhône, poire aux épices* (monkfish slices panfried with red wine and spiced pear), and *caille farcie d'une brunoise de céleri, ragoût de muscat aux lardons* (celery-stuffed quail with bacon ragout). A homemade ice cream or sorbet with an unusual flavor is the perfect way to round out a rich meal like this.

10 rue de Mons. ☎ *04-90-86-16-50. Reservations recommended. Meals: Main courses 170–325F ($24–$46); menus 180–500F ($26–$71). AE, DC, MC, V. Open June–Sept Mon–Sat noon to 2:30 p.m. and 8–10:30 p.m.; Oct–May Tues–Sat noon to 1:30 p.m. and 7:30–10 p.m.*

La Fourchette

$$$ Avignon   PROVENÇAL

Long a favorite with locals, this intimate restaurant run by Philippe and Danièle Hiely fills up early, so you'll need to make a reservation. What attracts people are the relatively low prices for the high-quality cuisine. Basically, this is updated bistro fare prepared with finesse. The big difference here is that there are more choices on the fixed-price menu than at most restaurants, and the dishes are quite elaborate for the price. A good first course choice is the *sardines marinées à la coriandre* (sardines marinated in coriander); for a main course, look for the special *agneau grillé au romarin* (grilled lamb with rosemary).

17 rue Racine. ☎ *04-90-85-20-93. Reservations necessary. Meals: Main courses 90–120F ($13–$17); menus 100F ($14) at lunch, 150F ($21) at dinner. MC, V. Open: Mon–Fri noon to 2:30 p.m. and 7:30–10 p.m.*

L'Epicerie

$$ Avignon   PROVENÇAL

Offering seating on picturesque place St-Pierre (with its ornate Gothic church), L'Epicerie has no trouble attracting customers. This is a well-run place, and you can bet the food is of the freshest quality and well presented. The cuisine is proudly provençal and features traditional fare like *croustillants de cabillaud au thym et à la tomate* (codfish in a pastry with thyme and tomato) and *confit d'agneau aux abricots et aux épices* (duck confit with apricots and spices). The chef's signature dish is the top-notch fish soup *bourride de poissons de la place St-Pierre*. The most popular dish on the menu is the *mignon de porc caramélisé à la moutarde* (marinated pork caramelized with mustard).

10 place St-Pierre. ☎ *04-90-82-74-22. Reservations preferred. Meals: Main courses 60–100F ($9–$14). MC, V. Open: Mon–Sat noon to 2:30 p.m.; daily 7:30–11 p.m.*

Le Venaissin

$$ Avignon   PROVENÇAL

Of the many terrace restaurants and cafes on place de l'Horloge, this one fills up first. That's because it has the most varied menu and the lowest prices. The square is beautiful, particularly at night, when the city hall's beaux-arts facade is lit up and the nearby carousel spins to calliope tunes. Expect faster-than-usual service and tables crammed so tightly you're likely to compare dishes with your neighbors. There are English menus and English-speaking waiters. A popular appetizer is the *salade mistral,* a chef-concocted mélange that includes melon, crab, and avocado. As a main course, the *loup au safran, courgette provençal* (seabass with saffron and eggplant provençal style) and *éstouffade de noix de joue de boeuf à la provençal riz pilaf* (beef stew provençal style with rice pilaf) are standouts. For dessert, try the *crème caramel* or *compote de pêche à la menthe fraîche* (peach compote with fresh mint). Kids will enjoy popular choices like *steak frites* (steak with french fries) for 35F ($5).

Place de l'Horloge. ☎ *04-90-86-20-99. Reservations accepted. Meals: Main courses 65–125F ($9–$18); menus 74F ($11) and 94F ($13); children's menu 35F ($5). MC, V. Open: Daily 9 a.m.–11 p.m.*

Maison Nani

$ Avignon   FRENCH

This cheerful little corner restaurant is a great place for a light lunch. Tables are outside, facing busy rue de la République, and inside, where brightly painted murals and original artwork are displayed. Salads and pastas dominate the menu. The best salad is the vegetarian Gargentua — a heaping portion of fresh greens and vegetables served with tapenade (olive spread) on toast. There are also several cold pasta salad dishes and plates of wonderful smoked salmon with capers and toast. The best main courses are hot pasta dishes like a mound of linguini with aioli, a light garlicy sauce that's a specialty of the region. The professional waitstaff is unusually friendly and considerate. The menu has English translations.

Rue Theodore-Aubanel (just off rue de la République). ☎ *04-90-14-04-30. Reservations accepted. Meals: Main courses 53–58F ($8–$9). No credit cards. Open: July–Sept Mon–Sat 11:30 a.m.–2:30 p.m. and 7–11 p.m.; Oct–June Mon–Sat 11:30 a.m.–2:30 p.m., Thurs–Sat 7–11 p.m.*

Rose au Petit Bedon

$$ Avignon   PROVENÇAL

From the outside, this looks like a small nothing-special restaurant; but when tables fill up by 7:30 p.m., you know something wonderful is happening in the kitchen. There are two floors, so even if it looks full, you should inquire (better yet, make a reservation). The decor is understated elegance lit by romantic candles. The menu, with English translations, highlights seafood. Your best bet is the "catch of the day," usually prepared with provençal herbs in a light sauce. The presentation of this dish is always artistic, with the chef creating patterns from the colors and textures of fresh vegetables and sauces.

70 rue Joseph-Vernet. ☎ 04-90-82-33-98. Reservations accepted. Meals: Main courses 90–145F ($13–$21); menus 165–220F ($24–$31). MC, V. Open: Tues–Sun noon to 2:30 p.m.; Mon–Sat 7:30–10:30 p.m. Closed Aug 1–15.

For cheap ethnic food, head to **rue des Teintures.** Around town, you'll find Cuban cuisine at **Cubanito Café** (51 rue Carnot; ☎ 04-90-27-90-59), open Monday to Friday 11 a.m. to 3 p.m. and daily 6:30 p.m. to midnight; Spanish cuisine at **Tapalocas** (15 rue Galante; ☎ 04-90-82-56-84), open daily noon to 1:30 a.m.; and Tunisian cuisine at **L'Empreinte** (33 rue des Teintures; ☎ 04-32-76-81-84), open April through October daily noon to 2 p.m. and 7:30 to 10 p.m. For a quick inexpensive meal, try one of the many cafes on **place de l'Horloge,** which stay open all day about 9 a.m. to 11 p.m. There are great wine bars in Avignon, like the **Cave de Bancass** (25 rue Bancass; ☎ 04-90-86-97-02), open Tuesday to Saturday 11:30 a.m. to 2 p.m. and Thursday to Saturday 7:30 p.m. to 3 a.m., and **Caveau du Théâtre Le Chevalier Thierry Piedoie** (rue des Trois Faucons; ☎ 04-90-86-51-53), open daily 7:30 p.m. to 2 a.m.

Exploring the town and environs

Avignon itself has a host of interesting sights, including one of France's biggest tourist attractions, the Palais des Papes. Nearby is Villeneuve-lez-Avignon, a medieval walled city where the wealthy cardinals affiliated with the Pope's Palace had their homes.

Seeing Avignon

The main road through the center of the city, **cours Jean-Jaurès,** becomes **rue de la République** and leads from the train station outside the city's fourteenth-century ramparts to the **Palais des Papes** about a half mile away. In summer, musicians and other entertainers perform on the cobblestone squares, particularly **place du Palais** (in front of the Palais des Papes). Next to the palace is the twelfth-century **Cathédrale Notre-Dame des Doms.** From the back exit of the cathedral, you find the **promenade du Rocher des Doms,** a lovely garden with views of Villeneuve across the river. Just south of place du Palais is **place de l'Horloge** (a handsome square with outdoor cafes), the imposing **Hôtel de Ville** (which houses town offices), and the beaux-arts **Opéra d'Avignon.** In the area west of here, you can find exclusive stores like **Christian Lacroix** and **Hermès,** along with excellent houseware, pottery, and antiques stores. Avignon also has good bargain-clothing and gift shops, particularly in the funky area of **rue de la Bonneterie** near Les Halles. Even farther east is **rue des Teinturiers,** where many of the city's ethnic restaurants, bars, and nightclubs are located. Just 3 km (1.9 miles) west of the city, across the Rhône River, is **Villeneuve-lez-Avignon,** a walled suburb of Avignon (where the court of the pope and the cardinals lived). The best way to reach Villeneuve is to drive across the Rhône (and Ile de la Barthelasse) on pont Edouard-Daladier and head north. There are several interesting sights here, including one of the biggest Carthusian monasteries in Europe.

From April to October, two-hour **guided walking tours of Avignon** leave Tuesdays and Thursdays at 10 a.m. from the tourist office (41 cours Jean-Jaurés; ☎ **04-32-74-32-72**). They cost 50F ($7), or 30F ($4.30) with an Avignon Passion pass (see details later in this section). During July and August, two-hour **guided tours of Villeneuve-lez-Avignon** leave Tuesdays and Thursdays at 5 p.m. from the tourist office and cost 25F ($3.60), or 20F ($2.85) with an Avignon Passion pass.

From mid-March to mid-October, the **tourist train** (☎ **04-90-82-64-44**) takes in the old city, with main roads and famous monuments, as well as lesser known roads that lead to more remote parts of the ancient city. It departs every 35 minutes daily (10 a.m. to 7:30 p.m.) from place du Palais and costs 35F ($5), or 30F ($4.30) with an Avignon Passion pass. The train travels one of two routes: through the old town or through the Rocher des Doms gardens.

At the first sight you visit (or at the tourist office), pick up a special free pass called **Avignon Passion.** You pay full price for the first sight, then you can get reduced rates on all the other attractions (and on the tours above).

The world's most important Gothic palace, the **Palais des Papes** (place du Palais; ☎ **04-90-27-50-74**), is certainly monumental. It's one of the most visited historic sights in France. In the fourteenth century, popes ruled Christendom from this palace and caused a brief crisis in the Catholic church, as Avignon and Rome competed for dominance. Rome won, but Avignon got to keep the palace; in fact, Rome owned the site until the French Revolution. Allow at least an hour to see everything, as there are 25 rooms to visit, and special exhibits are often set up (for example, during the July arts festival, the Grande Chapelle is used for an art show). Of the many sections of the palace, the standouts are the **Chapelle St-Jean,** on the ground floor, with beautiful fourteenth-century frescoes; the **pope's bedroom** (*chambre à coucher*), on the first floor, decorated with murals of birds and foliage; and the adjacent **Studium,** also known as the Stag Room, which is a pope's study with frescoes of hunting scenes. Take a look at the large central courtyard known as the **Grande Cour** or the **Cour d'Honneur,** where plays are performed during the Avignon Festival. There isn't a lot of decor here because the townspeople stripped the decadent interiors during the Revolution. So you mainly get to look at large-scale spaces and frescoes while hearing about the exploits that took place here. Visits are by free guided tour, or self-guided tour using an audioguide — by far the best method (the tour guide tends to hurry you through). Although the audioguide doesn't dwell on scandalous papal activities, it does include plenty of tidbits. Admission is 45F ($6) for adults and 36F ($5) for students and children. Combined admission for the palace and pont St-Bénezet is 55F ($8) for adults and 45F ($6) for students and children. The palace is open daily:

Palais des Papes

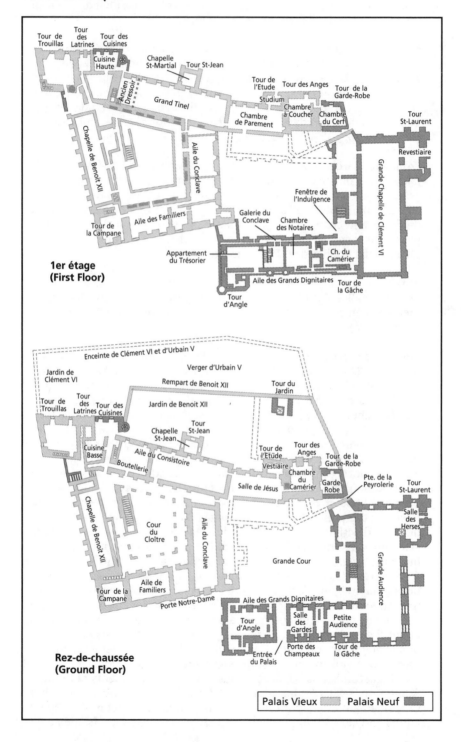

July to September 9 a.m. to 9 p.m., April to June, and October 9 a.m. to 7 p.m., and November to March 9:30 a.m. to 5:45 p.m. Admittance is not allowed an hour before closing.

Located in the fourteenth-century Palais des Archevêques, next to the Palais des Papes, is Avignon's best art museum, the **Musée du Petit Palace** (place du Palais; ☎ 04-90-86-44-58). This huge collection of medieval and Renaissance paintings focuses on Italian paintings from the thirteenth to the sixteenth century, Roman and Gothic sculpture from Avignon, and paintings of the school of Avignon from the fourteenth to the sixteenth century. A highlight is the *Virgin and Child* by Botticelli. From the palace windows, you can find wonderful views of Villeneuve across the river. The museum is open Wednesday to Monday (except January 1, May 1, July 14, November 1, December 25): June to September 10 a.m. to 1 p.m. and 2 to 6 p.m. and October to May 9:30 a.m. to 1 p.m. and 2 to 5:30 p.m. Admission is 30F ($4.30), or 15F ($2.15) with the Avignon Passion pass.

The **Musée Angladon** (5 rue Laboureur; ☎ 04-90-82-29-03) features a small collection of minor Impressionist paintings by major painters. It's worth a look for fans of the genre and those who enjoy seeing works in situ — that is, in the grand mansion of collector Jacques Doucet, the flamboyant Parisian fashion designer. Artists represented include Degas, Daumier, Manet, Sisley, van Gogh, Cézanne, Picasso, and Modigliani (usually one painting apiece). Most of these works are on the ground floor. On the second floor are eighteenth-century–style salons with antique furniture and artworks from various periods. It's open Wednesday to Sunday 1 to 6 p.m., and admission is 30F ($4.30) for adults and 20F ($2.85) with the Avignon Passion pass and for students and children.

The **Musée Calvet** (65 rue Joseph-Vernet; ☎ 04-90-86-33-84) is Avignon's fine arts museum set in a magnificent eighteenth-century mansion. It displays a broad collection of paintings and sculptures from the fifteenth to the twentieth century, as well as faïences (pieces of handpainted pottery from the region), silverware, and bronzes. The modern art room has works by Soutine, Manet, Sisley, and Camille Claudel. Admission is 30F ($4.30), or 15F ($2.15) with the Avignon Passion pass. It's open Wednesday to Monday 10 a.m. to 1 p.m. and 2 to 6 p.m. In the seventeenth-century baroque chapel of the College of Jesuits is Avignon's archaeological museum, the **Musée Lapidaire** (27 rue de la République; ☎ 04-90-86-33-84). The exquisite antique sculpture collection includes Egyptian, Etruscan, Greek, Roman, and Gallo-Roman works, plus antique vases, bronzes, and glassware. Admission is 10F ($1.40), or 5F (70¢) with the Avignon Passion pass. It's open Wednesday to Monday 10 a.m. to 1 p.m. and 2 to 6 p.m. The town's decorative arts museum, the **Musée Louis-Vouland** (17 rue Victor-Hugo; ☎ 04-90-86-03-79), features a superb collection of seventeenth- and eighteenth-century works, including tapestries and faïences. There's also a beautiful garden. Admission is 20F ($2.85), or 10F ($1.40) with the Avignon

Passion pass. The museum is open daily: May to October 10 a.m. to noon and 2 to 6 p.m., and November to April 2 to 6 p.m.

Medieval people had a funny saying about the **pont St-Bénezet** (rue Ferruce; ☎ 04-90-85-60-16): When crossing the bridge, you'd always meet two monks, two donkeys, and two prostitutes. The saying offers a glimpse into the medieval world, a heady mix of the sacred and the profane. Legend and lore whirl around this twelfth-century bridge that leads to nowhere, complete with a Romanesque chapel perched over the raging river. Because of constant flooding by the mighty Rhône, the bridge was destroyed many times during the Middle Ages and finally abandoned in the seventeenth century. In fact, it's said that Louis XIV was the last to cross the bridge. What's left now are just 4 arches from the bridge's original 22 arches that stretched all the way across the river. The bridge once led conveniently to Villeneuve on the other side of the river. The bridge was built because of the insistence of the shepherd Bénezet, who allegedly received word from on high that a bridge should be built here. Locals laughed until the scrawny shepherd suddenly turned into Charles Atlas and started lifting boulders over to the river side. The bridge's Chapelle de St-Nicolas is dedicated to the patron saint of bargemen: Bargemen have long plied the river's banks. The little museum below the bridge contains photos of paintings and engravings that have to do with the history of the bridge and what it looked like in the eighteenth and nineteenth centuries. An entertaining audioguide recounts the bridge's history. Admission is 19F ($2.70) for adults (15F/$2.15 with the Avignon Passion pass) and 15F ($2.15) for students and children. It's open daily: May to September 9 a.m. to 7 p.m., July 9 a.m. to 9 p.m., August to September 9 a.m. to 8 p.m., April to June and October 9 a.m. to 7 p.m., and November to March 9:30 a.m. to 5:45 p.m. Admittance is not allowed a half an hour before closing.

Opened in mid-2000, the **Collection Lambert at the Musée d'Art Contemporain** (5 rue Violette; ☎ 04-90-16-56-20) features art from the 1960s to today. The museum is housed in a former private mansion, the Hôtel de Caumont, in the center of Avignon, and the 400 works on display had been in storage for 20 years. The collection includes minimal art, conceptual art, photography, and video, with the work of artists like Brice Marden, Carl Andre, Anselm Kiefer, Cy Twombly, Andres Serrano, and Nan Golden. Admission is 25F ($3.60) for adults and 15F ($2.15) with the Avignon Passion pass and for students and children. The museum is open Tuesday to Sunday 11 a.m. to 7 p.m.

You can try the famous Châteauneuf-du-Pape wine at the **Musée des Outils de Vignerons** (avenue Bienheureux-Pierre-de-Luxembourg; ☎ 04-90-83-70-07). It's open daily 9 a.m. to noon and 2 to 6 p.m. for a visit and "free and tutored tasting" of the Laurent-Charles Brotte and Père Anselme cuvée. Of course, you can also buy wine here. You can catch a bus from Avignon to Châteauneuf-du-Pape or drive 12.9 km (8 miles) north on A9.

One of Provence's top sights is a great Roman aqueduct, the **pont du Gard** (☎ **04-66-37-51-12**), about 20 km (12.4 miles) from Avignon and 22.5 km (14 miles) northeast of Nîmes, with its triple row of arches spanning the Gard River. You can walk across the aqueduct, built in 19 B.C., and around a nearby arboretum. Bring a picnic and a bottle of wine. There are also restaurants nearby. Parking costs 20F ($2.85) for the first two hours and 5F (70¢) for each additional hour. The visitor centers on either side of the bridge show films. The center on the east side, called **Le Portal**, also has children's activities and an exhibit about the bridge. From Avignon, exit the city from the southwest on the pont de l'Europe on A9 and head toward Nîmes. Take N100 to N86 and cross the Gard River. Take D981 north to the parking area for the pont du Gard. Several buses depart Avignon each day and arrive at a stop that's about a ten-minute walk from the pont du Gard (45 minutes, 35F/$5)

Seeing Villeneuve-lez-Avignon

Only 3 km (1.9 miles) from Avignon, the suburb of Villeneuve is a long walk or a quick bike ride across the river. You can also take a city bus (see "Getting around and getting information" earlier in this chapter) or a taxi.

Founded in the fourteenth century by Innocent VI (the fifth pope of Avignon), the **Chartreuse du Val de Bénédiction** (60 rue de la République; ☎ **04-90-15-24-24**), is one of the biggest Carthusian monasteries in Europe. Inside the monastery, you find a church, three cloisters, a chapel full of frescoes, gardens, and 40 monk cells. You're free to walk around and take in the atmosphere without tour guides. Don't miss Pope Innocent VI's Gothic tomb inside the church. The monastery is the location of the Centre National des Ecritures du Spectacle and provides a lodging retreat for writers. Admission is 36F ($5) for adults, 23F ($3.30) with the Avignon Passion pass, and 21F ($3) for children. It's open daily: April to September 9 a.m. to 6:30 p.m. and October to March 9:30 a.m. to 5:30 p.m.

The fourteenth-century Gothic **Fort St-André** (Mont Andaon; ☎ **04-90-25-45-35**) was built to protect the city of Villeneuve and show the popes in Avignon a little French muscle. The fort, ordained by Phillippe le Bel, once sheltered a tenth-century abbey, but now there are pretty gardens from which you get a great view of the Rhône Valley and Avignon. Admission is 26F ($3.70) for adults, 16F ($2.30) with the Avignon Passion pass and 15F ($2.15) for children. It's open daily: April to September 10 a.m. to noon and 2 to 6 p.m. and October to March 10 a.m. to noon and 2 to 5 p.m.

When the pont St-Bénézet stretched all the way across the Rhône River, the **Tour Philippe le Bel** (rue Montée-de-la-Tour; ☎ **04-32-70-08-57**) stood conveniently at the base of the bridge once marking the entrance to the Gothic town of Villeneuve. The guardians of the citadel effectively controlled access to the bridge for all those approaching Avignon from the north in the fourteenth century. Climb the steep spiral staircase for the best view of Avignon and the Rhône Valley. Admission is 10F ($1.40) for adults and 6F (85¢) with the Avignon Passion pass and for students and children. April to September, it's open daily 10 a.m. to 12:30 p.m. and 3 to 6 p.m. (October to March, open Tuesday to Sunday only).

Shopping

Most markets in Avignon are open 7 a.m. to 1 p.m. The big covered market is **Les Halles** on place Pie, open Tuesday to Sunday. Other smaller **food markets** are on rampart St-Michel on Saturdays and Sundays, and on place Crillon on Fridays. The **flower market** is on place des Carmes on Saturdays, which becomes a **flea market** on Sundays. A more upscale **antiques market** fills up rue des Teinturiers all day on Saturdays.

Nightlife

Avignon sports a lively nightlife. You'll notice lots of people strolling up and down **rue de la République** as the young and restless decide where to make a night of it. The **Auberge de Cassagne** (450 allée de Cassagne; ☎ 04-90-31-04-18) is a piano bar, as is the **Brasserie Le Cintra** (44 cours Jean-Jaurès; ☎ 04-90-82-29-80), which also has live jazz. The **Red Zone** (27 rue Carnot; ☎ 04-90-27-02-44) offers live concerts featuring rock, country, and jazz. And **Le Woolloomooloo** (16 rue des Teinturiers; ☎ 04-90-85-28-44) is a funky place serving "food of the world" and featuring live music with no cover.

St-Rémy-de-Provence and Its Roman Ruins

At the foot of the Alpilles mountains, ancient **St-Rémy-de-Provence** retains a *soupçon* (a tiny bit) of the small-town flavor of Provence that some of the more touristy towns have lost. The downside is that there's not much to see or do, and it's difficult to get there by public transportation (there's no train station). The main attraction there is just outside town: The **Ruines de Glanum** — extraordinary Roman ruins that are still being excavated — include finds dating back to the first millennium B.C. Famous residents of St-Rémy have included French astrologer Michel de Nostredame (better known as Nostradamus), whose enigmatic predictions have been a source of debate for centuries. Dutch artist Vincent van Gogh checked into a mental hospital in St-Rémy in 1889 and painted some of his most famous works there. More recently, St-Rémy has become a destination for shopping for the home, with many antiques and interior decorating stores.

A great time to visit St-Rémy is during the **Fête de la Transhumance.** On Whit Monday (around June 11), all the shepherds of the surrounding area march their flocks into town; they arrive around 10:30 a.m. and are

St-Rémy-de-Provence

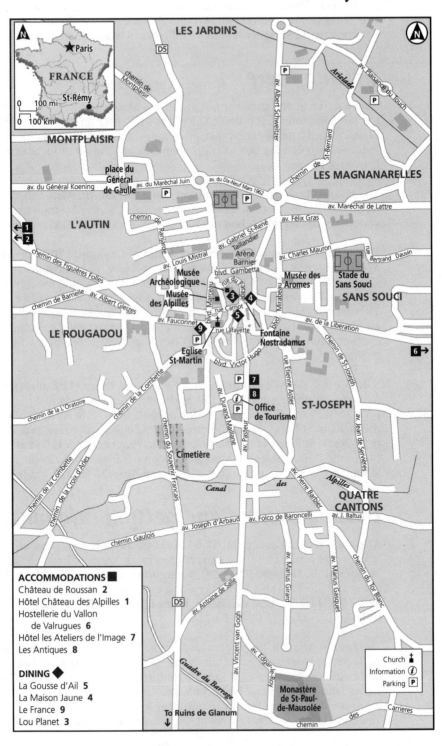

N

Paris

FRANCE

St-Rémy

0   100 mi
0   100 km

LES JARDINS

MONTPLAISIR

D5

chemin de Montplaisir

av. Albert Schweitzer

av. Plaisance du Touch

P

P

Ariolade

chemin de St-Bernard

place du
Général
de Gaulle

av. du Général Koening   av. du Maréchal Juin

av. du Dix-Neuf Mars 1962

P

LES MAGNANARELLES

P

av. Maréchal de Lattre

L'AUTIN

chemin de Ranjarde

chemin des Figuières Folles

av. Félix Gras

av. Louis Mistral

av. Gabriel St-René
Taillandier

Arène
Barnier

blvd. Gambetta

av. Charles Mauron

rue Bertrand Dauvin

1

2

Musée
Archéologique

Musée
des Alpilles

rue du Parage

Musée des
Aromes

Stade du
Sans Souci

SANS SOUCI

chemin de Barrielle   av. Albert Gleizes

blvd. Marceau

rue Carnot

3

4

rue Mirabeau

av. Fauconnet

rue Lafayette

5

av. de la Liberation

chemin de St-Joseph

LE ROUGADOU

9

P

Eglise
St-Martin

Fontaine
Nostradamus

blvd. Victor Hugo

6

rue Etienne Astier

chemin de la Comberte

chemin de la L'Oratoire

chemin de la Combette

P

7

av. Durand Maillane

av. Pasteur

8

Office
de Tourisme

ST-JOSEPH

av. Jean de Servières

P

chemin de la Croix d'Arles

chemin du Souvenir Français

Cimetière

Canal   des   Alpilles

QUATRE
CANTONS

av. Pierre Barbier

av. J. Baltus

chemin Gaulois

av. Joseph d'Arbaud   av. Folco de Baroncelli

D5

av. Antoine de Salle

av. Marius Girard

av. Marius Gasquet

chemin du Jor Blanc

av. Vincent Van Gogh

av. Edgar-le-Roy

Guadre du Barrage

Monastère
de St-Paul-
de-Mausolée

Carrières

des

chemin

To Ruins of Glanum

ACCOMMODATIONS ■
Château de Roussan **2**
Hôtel Château des Alpilles **1**
Hostellerie du Vallon
   de Valrugues **6**
Hôtel les Ateliers de l'Image **7**
Les Antiques **8**

DINING ◆
La Gousse d'Ail **5**
La Maison Jaune **4**
Le France **9**
Lou Planet **3**

Church
Information ⓘ
Parking P

driven twice around the center for about two hours. On August 15, there's the **Carreto Ramado,** where fifty horses pull an enormous cart loaded with local produce into town. Around that same date, the **Feria Provençale de St-Rémy** features bullfights in which the bull isn't killed.

Getting there

Buses arrive at and depart from St-Rémy's place de la République, near the large fountain just outside the old town center on the west side. Buses to and from Avignon take 40 minutes and cost 32F ($4.60). From Avignon, you can get bus or train connections to most other major Provence towns.

The nearest **train** station is **Avignon Gare.** For information, call ☎ 08-36-35-35-39. From Avignon Gare Routière (next to the Avignon train station), you can take a **bus** to St-Rémy (45 minutes; 36F/$5).

The nearest airport is the **Aéroport Avignon-Caumont** (☎ 04-90-81-51-51), which is 18 km (11.2 miles) from St-Rémy. The **Aéroport Nîmes-Garons** (☎ 04-66-70-49-49) is 40 km (24.9 miles) away, and the **Aéroport Marseille Provence** (☎ 04-42-14-14-14) is 85 km (52.8 miles) away. There are no buses from these airports to St-Rémy, so if you arrive by air, you'll need to rent a car. All three airports have rental car offices for Hertz, Avis, Europcar, National Citer, and Budget. See below for driving directions.

St-Rémy is 705 km (438.1 miles) from Paris and 18 km (11.2 miles) from Avignon. To **drive** from Paris, follow the directions to Avignon, then take D571 to St-Rémy. From the direction of Nice, take A8 to A7 and follow the signs to St-Rémy. From the direction of Nîmes and Arles, take A9 to St-Rémy. St Rémy is centrally located in Provence. Aix is 50 km (31.1 miles) from St-Rémy, Marseille 90 km (55.9 miles), Avignon 21 km (13 miles), Les Baux 10 km (6.2 miles), and Arles 22 km (13.7 miles).

Getting around and getting information

Abrivado (20 av. Fauconnet; ☎ 04-90-92-06-34) is the location for Avis and Budget rental cars. You can rent mountain bikes at **Ferri** (35 av. de la Libération; ☎ 04-90-92-10-88), where the prices are 60F ($9) for half a day and 95F ($14) for a full day. For a cab, call **Taxi E. Grimauld** at ☎ 06-09-31-50-38, **Taxi des Baux, Louis Brunet** at ☎ 06-80-27-60-92, or **Dalgon Taxi** at ☎ 06-09-52-71-54.

The **tourist office** is on place Jean-Jaurès (☎ 04-90-92-05-22; Fax: 04-90-92-38-52; Internet: www.saintremy-de-provence.com). Late June to mid-September, it's open Monday to Saturday 9 a.m. to noon and 2 to 7 p.m., and Sundays and holidays 9 a.m. to noon; late September to mid-June, hours are Monday to Saturday 9 a.m. to noon and 2 to 6 p.m. You can check and send e-mail at the tourist office, but you need to buy a 49F ($7) phonecard at a nearby tobacconist. The office also has a wide range of brochures, including self-guided tours of locations where van Gogh painted. Ask about walking tours (in English) of the town center. You can also send e-mail at **Compo Secretariat Services** (6 bis bd. Marceau; ☎ **04-90-92-48-11**), open Monday to Friday 9 a.m. to noon and 2 to 5 p.m.

Where to stay

Château de Roussan

$$ St-Rémy (west of town)

Set in a large landscaped park with sculpture gardens and fountains, this quirky manse, about a mile from St-Rémy, is for those who want to stay in a château with an amusing down-on-its-luck quality and pay bargain rates. The elegant neoclassical facade belies the neglected interior, and the atmosphere is casual to the extreme (to enter, you have to step over plastic dog toys on the mosaic floor). The upside is that the toys belong to a cute family of black labs; a family of cats lives on the second floor (when I stayed here, nursing kittens swung from the antique tapestries and rolled down the marble staircase). The 21 rooms are decorated with an unusual combination of interesting antiques and flea market finds, and the housekeeping is somewhat hit and miss. The common room has a billiards table, piano, and many board games. You can rent bikes for 100F ($14) per day. The restaurant serves average fare that's on the pricey side.

Route de Tarascon. ☎ *04-90-92-50-59. Fax: 04-90-92-50-59. E-mail:* chateau. de.roussan@wanadoo.fr. *Rack rates: 460–790F ($66–$113) double. Breakfast: 70F ($10) in restaurant or 80F ($11) in room. Half pension: 220F ($31). AE, MC, V.*

Hostellerie du Vallon de Valrugues

$$$$ St-Rémy (east of town)

An exquisite hotel east of the old town, the Vallon de Valrugues is one of the region's top choices, featuring a blend of modernity and tradition on a large estate. The 38 spacious rooms and 14 grand apartments offer mountain views (Alpilles, Luberon, and Mont Ventoux), deluxe amenities like bathrobes and fine toiletries, safes, and minibars; 18 have Jacuzzis. The prestige suite has its own pool. Also on site are a large heated pool, a driving range and putting green, a sauna, a billiards table, and a children's garden. The restaurant — one of the best in town — specializes in provençal fare.

Chemin de Canto Cigalo. ☎ *04-90-92-04-40. Fax: 04-90-92-44-01. Internet:* www. valrugues-cassagne.com. *E-mail:* vallon.valrugues@wanadoo.fr. *Rack rates: 780–1,650F ($111–$236) double; 5,300F ($757) suite; 2,280–2,980F ($326–$426) apt. Breakfast: 110F ($16). Half pension: 500F ($71). Closed Feb. AE, MC, V.*

Hôtel Château des Alpilles

$$$$ **St-Rémy (west of town)**

The Bon family has renovated this nineteenth-century bourgeois mansion, restoring it to its former grandeur. A private 10-acre park, with 300-year-old trees, surrounds the hotel. Spacious and decorated with antiques, the 15 rooms, 3 suites, and 2 apartments are spread among the castle, the nineteenth-century farmhouse, and La Chapel (a recent addition). Hotel amenities include a pool, two tennis courts, a bar, a sauna, and massages on request. The dining room features gourmet provençal cooking; Meals are served next to the pool for lunch in summer and in the lavish dining room in winter. The agreeable staff speaks English.

D31, Ancienne Route du Grès. ☎ *04-90-92-03-33. Fax: 04-90-92-45-17. E-mail:* chateau.alpilles@wanadoo.fr. *Rack rates: 945–1,200F ($135–$171) double; 1,490–1,520F ($213–$217) suite; 1,590–2,100F ($227–$300) apt. Breakfast: 68–95F ($10–$14). Closed mid-Nov to late Dec and mid-Jan to mid-Feb. AE, DC, MC, V.*

Hôtel les Ateliers de l'Image

$$$ **St-Rémy**

Near the tourist office and a short walk from the old town's center, this hip hotel with a photography theme includes an art gallery, a photo lab, and a photo shop. The owners converted the old St-Rémy music hall into a very contemporary hotel with 16 rooms. Though it's on a busy street, this hotel is set back from the road down a narrow alley and is surprisingly tranquil. In the front terrace, you find a small heated pool. Inside the glass-fronted lobby, the architecture is all about light and space, with soaring ceilings and lots of glass. The rooms are simple, modern, and stylish, with personal fax machines, modem sockets, and hairdryers; some offer mountain views. There's a billiards table and a bar, as well as bike rentals. The English-speaking staff is very friendly and will pick you up at the Avignon train station or airport.

Traverse de Borry, 5 av. Pasteur. ☎ *04-90-92-51-50. Fax: 04-90-92-43-52. Internet:* www.hotelphoto.com. *E-mail:* ateliers-images@pacwan.fr. *Rack rates: 560–660F ($80–$94) double. Breakfast: 70F ($10). MC, V.*

Les Antiques

$$$ **St-Rémy**

This hotel occupies an elegant nineteenth-century mansion near the tourist office — a few minutes' walk from the old town. The beautifully landscaped 7-acre grounds contain a pool and garden paths. The hotel's entrance leads to a refined foyer decorated with period antiques; the commons rooms off the main hall are similarly stylish. The hotel has 27 rooms — some are located in a more modern annex. All of the rooms are comfortable, but those in the annex are somewhat generic, while those in the main building have old-world charm. Ten rooms have air condition-ing. English is spoken here.

15 av. Pasteur. ☎ *04-90-92-03-02. Fax: 04-90-92-50-40. Free parking. Rack rates: 370–800F ($53–$114) double. Breakfast: 66F ($9). Closed mid-Oct to mid-Apr. MC, V.*

Just outside the medieval walls of Les Baux (a pedestrian-only hilltop village 12.9 km/8 miles from St-Rémy) is a fancy Relais & Châteaux hotel, **L'Oustau de Beaumanière** (☎ 04-90-54-33-07; Fax: 04-90-54-40-46; E-mail: oustau@relaischateaux.fr; Internet: www.oustaudebeaumaniere. com), known for serving some of the best food in the region. Don't be fooled by the bland exterior — the rooms are opulent, renting for 1,390F to 1,490F ($199 to $213) double and 2,100F to 2,200F ($300 to $314) suite.

Where to dine

La Gousse d'Ail

$$$ St-Rémy   PROVENÇAL

This small restaurant, a typical family-run place, serves delicious fresh food at reasonable prices. Specialties include *escargot à la provençal* (snails served with garlic and herbs from the region) and vegetarian dishes featuring colorful vegetables from the market, prepared with light sauces and local herbs. On Tuesday, the chef prepares the restaurant's famous bouillabaisse, and on Wednesdays, there's live jazz all evening. The waitstaff speaks English.

25 rue Carnot. ☎ *04-90-92-16-87. Reservations recommended. Meals: Main courses 75–120F ($11–$17); menus 90F ($13) at lunch, 175–210F ($25–$30) at dinner. MC, V. Open: Daily noon to 2:30 p.m. and 7:30–10 p.m. Closed Nov–Mar.*

La Maison Jaune

$$$ St-Rémy   PROVENÇAL

This is the best restaurant in the town center, serving memorable meals every time. It occupies an eighteenth-century building, and the decor is spare yet stylish, with huge casement windows providing lots of light and views. In summer, diners like to sit on the shady terrace and take in views of the old town and the Hôtel de Sade, which houses the archaeological museum. The specialties of chef François Perraud include *anchois frais marinés* (marinated anchovies), *semoule de blé épicés* (spiced wheat pasta), and a hearty *soupe de poisson* (fish soup). For dessert, try the *fraises et granité au safran et citron* (strawberries and saffron-and-lemon sherbert). The best deal is a Provençal Menu for a fair 265F ($38). English is spoken here.

15 rue Carnot. ☎ *04-90-92-56-14. Reservations necessary. Meals: Main courses 90–215F ($13–$31); menus 120F ($17) at weekday lunch, 180–305F ($26–$44) at other times. MC, V. Open: June–Sept Wed–Sun noon to 2:30 p.m., Tues–Sun 7:30–9:30 p.m.; Oct–May Tues–Sun noon to 2:30 p.m., Tues–Sat 7:30–9:30 p.m. Closed early Jan–Feb.*

Le France

$$ St-Rémy   PROVENÇAL

This pretty little restaurant, an institution among locals, features fine provençal cooking in an intimate atmosphere. This place offers a good opportunity to try some local specialties you're not likely to find anywhere else, like *pieds et paquets* (literally feet and packages, a dish of lamb tripe and feet cooked in white-wine sauce). They make a hearty Camargue bull stew here, as well as bouillabaise and bourride (two types of fish stew). The menus have English translations.

2 av. Fauçonnet. ☎ *04-90-92-11-56. Reservations recommended. Meals: Main courses 45–135F ($6–$19); menus 82–148F ($12–$21). MC, V. Open: Tues–Sun noon to 2:30 p.m. and 7:30–10 p.m. Closed Nov–Jan.*

Lou Planet

$ St-Rémy   CRÊPES

If you're looking for a light lunch, you'll enjoy this little crêperie located in a pretty square in the center of town. The tables are all outside under shady trees near a statue of Nostradamus. The menu features a wide range of crêpes and salads, including a good version of the classic *salade Niçoise*.

7 place Favier. ☎ *04-90-92-19-81. Meals: Main courses 43–84F ($6–$12). No credit cards. Open: Daily 11:30 a.m.–3:30 p.m. Closed mid-Oct to mid-Mar.*

Exploring the town

St-Rémy **walking tours** (☎ 04-90-92-05-22) leave the tourist office at place Jean-Jaurès on Fridays at 10 a.m.; with a minimum of 10 people, the tours last 1½ hours and cost 35F ($5) for adults and 20F ($2.85) for ages 12 to 18 and students. **Van Gogh tours** (☎ 04-90-92-05-22) leave the tourist office every Tuesday, Thursday, and Saturday at 10 a.m. and last 1½ hours; the cost is 35F ($5) for adults and 20F ($2.85) for ages 12 to 18 and students. The cost of the van Gogh tour includes reduced admission to the Centre d'Art Présence Van Gogh and St-Paul de Mausole (see later in this section). Guides take you to the locations painted by van Gogh in the St-Rémy area. You can arrange your own **self-guided tour** of locations painted by van Gogh by picking up a brochure with map from the tourist office.

One of southern France's major classical sites, the **Ruines de Glanum** (avenue Van Gogh), is about a mile south of St-Rémy. The earliest findings from the ruins date back to the Iron Age, around the 1st millennium B.C., when a fortified settlement supposedly occupied this site. Then the Celts arrived, and they eventually came under Greek influence, turning Glanum into a religious and commercial center. It later fell under Roman rule, which explains the characteristic thermal baths, villas, basilica, and temples. Wander through the ruins of the first-century Roman town, complete with a main street and house foundations, and feel yourself transported back in time. Excavations began here in 1921 and are ongoing. Archaeologists believe the site is actually about six or seven times the size of what has been uncovered so far. Many of the findings from Glanum are displayed at the Musée Archéologique (see later in this section). The site is open daily (except January 1, May 1, November 1, November 11, and December 25): April to September 9 a.m. to 7 p.m. and October to March 9 a.m. to noon and 2 to 5 p.m. Admission is 32F ($4.60) for adults and 21F ($3) for ages 12 to 25; combined admission for Glanum and the Archaeological Museum is 36F ($5).

The **Musée Archéologique** (rue du Parage; ☎ **04-90-92-64-04**), located in the Hôtel de Sade — a beautiful fifteenth-century town house that belonged to the Sades, an old provençal family — displays sculptures and objects found at Glanum (see earlier in this section), including pottery, coins, and jewelry. The museum is open Tuesday to Sunday (except January 1, May 1, November 1, November 11, and December 25): April to September 10 a.m. to noon and 2 to 6 p.m. and February, March, and October to December 10 a.m. to noon and 2 to 5 p.m. Admission is 15F ($2.15); combined admission for Glanum and the Archaeological Museum is 36F ($5).

The **Monastère de St-Paul-de-Mausolée** (avenue Edgar-le-Roy off avenue Van Gogh; ☎ **04-90-92-77-00**) is the twelfth-century monastery where van Gogh checked himself in for mental health reasons from May 1889 to May 1890. He loved the place and painted prolifically there, executing over 150 paintings, including his famous *Starry Night.* The ancient building still serves as a psychiatric hospital, but you can walk around the chapel and cloisters. It's open Tuesday to Saturday 9 a.m. to 7 p.m. Admission is 10F ($1.40) for adults and 5F (70¢) for students and children.

Occupying a beautiful old mansion, the **Centre d'Art Presence van Gogh** (8 rue Estrine; ☎ **04-90-92-34-72**) is a small art museum that hosts three or four exhibits per year. The permanent collection is diverse, with works from ancient Egypt and Rome, as well as seventeenth- to nineteenth-century paintings. A room devoted to van Gogh has reproductions of some of the works he painted in the region. A few contemporary artists are represented in the museum as well. A French film about the artist Poussin is shown a few times daily. Late March to December, it's open Tuesday to Sunday 10:30 a.m. to 12:30 p.m. and 2:30 to 6:30 p.m. Admission is 20F ($2.85) for adults.

If you're looking for more Roman ruins, you can check out **Les Antiques,** the name given to two ancient sculptured monuments marking the southern entrance to St-Rémy on avenue Van Gogh across from the entrance to Glanum. The **Mausolée des Jules** is a funerary monument from 30 to 20 B.C. and the triumphal arch next to it, the **Arc de Triomphe,** is from around 20 B.C.

Other Provence favorites

If you have the time and the interest, you can extend your exploration of Provence with the following sites:

Apt: Centrally located in the hilly Lubéron region (54 km/33 miles from Avignon), Apt is worth a visit particularly for its Saturday market, which features itinerant musicians in addition to the usual fresh produce, cheese, and meats from the region. The town's eleventh-century cathedral is famous for a relic known as the veil of St. Anne. The nearby Parc Naturel Régional du Lubéron is well suited for hiking and biking.

Cavaillon: Home of famous melons, Cavaillon (21 km/13 miles from Avignon) is an ancient town that's now an important farming area. Neolithic remains have been found on St-Jacques hill, which overlooks the town and provides wonderful views of the Lubéron region. The two Roman arches that sit on place François-Tourvel represent the Roman roots of the town.

Châteauneuf-du-Pape: One of the most famous wines of France is grown around the medieval village of Châteauneuf-du-Pape (12.9 km/8 miles from Avignon), which was the summer home of the popes of Avignon. You can see the ruins of the fourteenth-century Château des Papes, from where there are terrific views of the valley. You can taste the famous wine at Père Anselme's cellar and Musée des Outils de Vigneronsm.

Grand Canyon du Verdon: The gorges of the Ardèche in the Rhône Valley (40.2 km/ 25 miles from Avignon) are known as the Grand Canyon of France. This is nature at its wildest and most beautiful — 950-foot canyons dotted with grottoes and caves. The scenic D290 runs along the rim of the canyon, providing spectacular views, and there are plenty of places to park near well-marked footpaths. The north part of the canyon is less touristy than the southern section.

Les Baux: Most people take a day trip to Les Baux (12.9 km/8 miles from Avignon), a pedestrian-only village perched on the white rocks of the Alpilles and capped by castle ruins. You can visit thirteenth-century castle ruins, and troubadour concerts are held in the church at the top of the hill in July and August.

Orange: Take in an outdoor concert, perhaps Pavarotti, at the impressive Roman **Théâtre Antique.** For ticket information, call ☎ 04-90-34-24-24. Mid-July to mid-August, a theater, music, and dance festival is held here. Nearby is the gracious **Château de Rochegude** (☎ 04-75-97-21-10), a Relais & Châteaux, with tennis courts, a pool, and a gourmet restaurant. Orange is 25.7 km (16 miles) from Avignon.

Roussillon and Bonnieux: These two quaint hilltop villages (both about 40 km/ 24.9 miles from Avignon) are quintessential Provence. Roussillon is well known for the ochre rock surrounding the area, which boasts 17 shades, from golden yellow to bright red. Bonnieux still has parts of its ancient ramparts surrounding the town. Both villages offer extraordinary views of the countryside. Near Bonnieux is a well-preserved Roman bridge called the pont Julien, with three arches spanning the Calavon River.

Tarascon: This town on an island in the center of the Rhône River (23 km/14.3 miles from Avignon) is worth a visit to see the most impressive Gothic castle in Provence, the fifteenth-century Château de Tarascon. The heavily fortified structure sits right on the edge of the river. The castle has a medieval apothecary, a collection of tapestries, and a provençal garden. From the terrace, there are wonderful views of the surrounding countryside. Tarascon's most famous legend concerns a sea monster that was tamed by St. Martha. The town holds an annual festival in honor of the legend on the last weekend in June.

Toulon: This bustling French town (67.6 km/42 miles from Marseille) is the head-quarters of a French naval base. There's a large pretty harbor surrounded by hills topped with forts. Near the harbor are traditional markets and the Cathédrale Ste-Marie-Majeure, built in the Romanesque style in the twelfth century. Two interesting museums are the Musée de la Marine, with figureheads and ship models, and the Musée de Toulon, with artworks from the sixteenth century to the present, including a good collection of provençal and Italian paintings.

Uzès: The center of this medieval village (38 km/24 miles from Avignon) is the thirteenth-century castle called Duché, with apartments decorated in a Renaissance style. Nearby is the unique Tour Fenestrelle, a 42m (138-foot) round tower with six levels of windows that used to be part of an early Romanesque cathedral. Seventeenth-century playwright Jean Racine lived here for a short time, and the village and countryside influenced him.

Shopping

St-Rémy is a center of home decorating, with many antiques shops and fabric stores on the boulevards surrounding the old town, as well as on the old town's narrow streets. **Le Cypres Bleu** (3 place Favier; ☎ 04-32-60-05-14), has a good selection of faïences and ceramics. **La Boutigo** (12 rue Lafayette; ☎ 04-90-92-03-31) specializes in painted *santons* (collectible hand-painted clay figurines of medieval villagers that are designed to be grouped into Nativity scenes), faïences, and fabrics. You can find a couple of good antiques stores on the outskirts of town: **Au Broc de St-Ouen** (route d'Avignon; ☎ 04-90-51-72-62) has several dealers, and **Rotes Anciennes** (route d'Avignon; ☎ 04-90-92-13-13) sells a good selection of antiques and flea-market finds.

Pierre Leron-Lesure has devoted his life to making what he calls *sylvistructures* (sculptures from juniper-tree trunks). You can see these unique sculptures in the workshop, on the marble spiral staircase, and in the garden of the **Chimères du Bois** — a gallery in an ancient mansion on rue de Parage across from the archaeological museum (☎ 04-90-92-02-28). April to October, it's open daily 10 a.m. to 12:30 p.m. and 2 to 6 p.m.

St-Rémy is known for having great **markets.** On Wednesday mornings on the streets of the old town, vendors spread out their wares, including spices, olives, fabrics, and crafts. On Saturday morning, a small market is held near the Eglise St-Martin on boulevard Marceau.

Arles: Following in the Steps of van Gogh

Boasting Roman ruins, medieval churches, eighteenth-century mansions, and tributes to nineteenth-century artist Vincent van Gogh, **Arles** is rich with history. Its strategic position on the Rhône River has long made it popular. Greeks first settled in the area around the sixth century B.C. In the first century B.C., Julius Caesar gave the city prominence in his empire after the citizens of Arles assisted the Romans in their capture of Marseille. It experienced a Golden Age when it was known as *Rome of the Gauls.*

In the early years of Christianity, Arles became a great religious center, but invasions throughout the Middle Ages ravaged the town. It was revived in the twelfth century, and you can see a number of impressive Romanesque buildings from that period, including the Eglise St-Trophisme, which was once a cathedral. In the seventeenth and eighteenth centuries, noblemen built mansions in the city center; the mansions surrounding place du Forum are now elegant hotels. Today, Arles is most famous for being one of the final homes of Impressionist painter Vincent van Gogh. Fans of the tormented artist will find many reminders of him.

Getting there

Trains leave from Paris's Gare de Lyon and arrive at Arles's **Gare S.N.C.F.** (avenue Paulin-Talabot), a short walk from the town center. One high-speed direct TGV travels from Paris to Arles each day (3½ hours, 593F/$85 for first class, 379F/$54 for second). For other trains, you must change in Avignon. There are hourly connections between Arles and Avignon (25 minutes, 53F/$8 for first class; 36F/$5 for second), Marseille (one hour, 106F/$15 for first class, 71F/$10 for second), and Aix-en-Provence (1¾ hours, change in Marseille, 150F/$21 for first class, 113F/$16 for second). For rail schedules and information, call ☎ **08-36-35-35-39.**

The **Aéroport International de Nîmes-Garons** (☎ **04-66-70-49-49**) is 25 km (15.5 miles) northwest of Arles (five flights per day arrive from Paris). The bus company **Société Ceyte Tourisme Méditerranée (CTM)** runs buses between Arles and the airport. Buses arrive at, and leave from, boulevard Clemenceau near the tourist office (see "Getting around and getting information"). The **Aéroport International Marseille/Provence** is 70 km (43.5 miles) from Arles. From there, you'll need to rent a car to drive to Arles. The major rental car companies — Hertz,

Arles

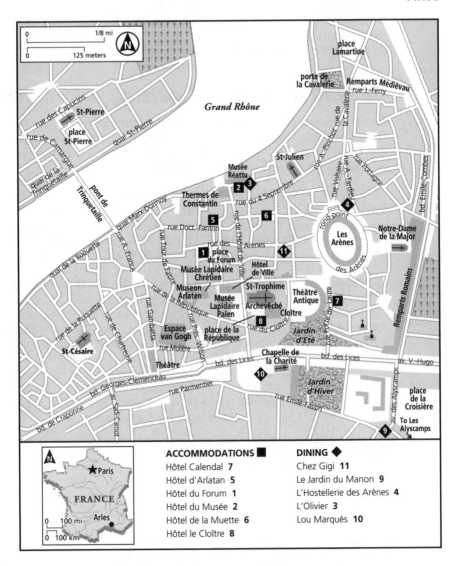

place Lamartine

porte de la Cavalerie

Remparts Médiévau
rue J.-Ferry

Grand Rhône

St-Pierre
rue des Capucins
place St-Pierre
rue de Camargue
quai St-Pierre

rue de la Cavalerie
rue de la Cavalerie

St-Julien

rue A.-Pichot
rue Voltaire
rue A.-Tardieu

rue A.-Portagne
bd. Emile-Combes

Musée Réattu
2 **3**

rue du 4 Septembre

4
rond-point

quai de la Trinquetaille
pont de Trinquetaille
quai Marc-Dormoy

Thermes de Constantin

Notre-Dame de la Major

rue Doct.-Fanton
5
6

Les Arènes

rue de l'Hôtel de Ville

rue des Arènes
place du Forum
1
11

des Arènes

Remparts Romains

Musée Lapidaire Chrétien

Hôtel de Ville

quai de la Roquette
rue A.-France
rue Tour-de-Fabre

Museon Arlaten
rue de la République
Musée Lapidaire Païen

St-Trophime
Archevêché
Cloître

Théâtre Antique
7

rue de la Roquette
rue Gambetta
rue de Chartreuse

Espace van Gogh
place de la République
rue du Cloître

rue Molière
rue Prés.-Wilson

Jardin d'Eté

rue de la Porte de Laure

St-Césaire

Théâtre

Chapelle de la Charité

bd. des Lices
bd. des Lices
av. V.-Hugo

10

Jardin d'Hiver

place de la Croisière

bd. Georges-Clemenceau
bd. de Craponne
bd. Salit-Ernot
rue Parmentier

rue Emile-Fassin

av. des Alyscamps

To Les Alyscamps
9

ACCOMMODATIONS ■
Hôtel Calendal **7**
Hôtel d'Arlatan **5**
Hôtel du Forum **1**
Hôtel du Musée **2**
Hôtel de la Muette **6**
Hôtel le Cloître **8**

DINING ◆
Chez Gigi **11**
Le Jardin du Manon **9**
L'Hostellerie des Arènes **4**
L'Olivier **3**
Lou Marquès **10**

★Paris

FRANCE

Arles

0   100 mi
0   100 km

Avis, Europcar, National Citer, and Budget — can all be found at the Marseille Airport.

Arles's **Gare Routière** (bus station) is in front of the train station. For information, call ☎ **04-90-49-38-01.** Arles is on one end of a bus line to Marseille, with stops including Les Baux (25 minutes, 29F/$4.15), Aix-en-Provence (1¾ hours, 70F/$10), and Marseille (2½ hours, 85F/$12). Bus service to Avignon is also available (45 minutes, 39F/$6). For details, call the **Société Ceyte Tourisme Méditerranée** at ☎ **04-90-93-74-90.**

If you're **driving,** note that D570 and N113 and A54 (between A9 and A7) lead to Arles. From Avignon, take A7 to A54 to N113. Driving time from Avignon to Arles is about 25 minutes. Driving from Paris to Arles would take about 7 hours. Arles is 740 km (450 miles) from Paris and 35.4 km (22 miles) from Avignon.

Getting around and getting information

All of the major sights in Arles are within walking distance from the center of town. The only sight that's inconvenient to walk to is the Musée de l'Arles Antiques (about 15 minutes away); it's an awkward walk past major roadways (with sidewalks).

For a rental car, try **Avis** (avenue Paulin-Talabot; ☎ **04-90-96-82-42**), **Hertz** (boulevard Victor-Hugo; ☎ **04-90-96-75-23**), or **Europcar** (boulevard Victor-Hugo; ☎ **04-90-93-23-24**). You can rent bikes at **Peugeot** (15 rue du Pont; ☎ **04-90-96-03-77**) for 35F ($5) per half day and 60F ($9) per day. For a cab, call **Arles Taxi** at ☎ **04-90-49-69-59** or 04-90-93-31-16.

The **tourist office** is on esplanade Charles-de-Gaulle (☎ **04-90-18-41-20**; E-mail: ot.accueil@visitprovence.com; Internet: www.arles.org). April to September, it's open Monday to Saturday 9 a.m. to 7 p.m. and Sunday 9 a.m. to 1 p.m.; October to March, hours are Monday to Saturday 9 a.m. to 6 p.m. and Sunday 10 a.m. to noon. A **small annex** is open at the train station Monday to Saturday 9 a.m. to 1 p.m. and 2 to 6 p.m. The tourist offices will book accommodations for a small fee and change money. If you want to check or send e-mail, head to **Point Web** (10 rue du 4 Septembre; ☎ **04-90-18-91-54**), open Monday to Saturday 8:30 a.m. to 7:30 p.m. No food or beverages are served.

Where to stay

Hôtel Calendal

$$ Arles

Mme Cécile Lespinasse-Jacquemin runs this attractive hotel — the best medium-priced lodging in Arles. Built in the seventeenth century, the Calendal is very centrally located, near the Roman Arena and next to the Roman Theater. The English-speaking staff lays out the breakfast buffet in the large shady courtyard, which also operates as a tearoom serving light meals. The cheerful reception area includes a computer on which you can check e-mail and a fax machine. The 38 recently renovated rooms are cozy, with provençal-style decor; some have terraces with seating areas. The front rooms offer views over the ruins, while the rooms overlooking the garden courtyard offer a quiet setting.

5 rue porte du Laure. ☎ *04-90-96-11-89. Fax: 04-90-96-05-84. Internet:* www.lecalendal.com. *E-mail:* contact@lecalendal.com. *Parking: 40–60F ($6–$9). Rack rates: 380–450F ($54–$64) double. Breakfast: 40F ($6). MC, V.*

Hôtel d'Arlatan

$$$ Arles

The Arlatan, the ancient town house of the comtes d'Arlatan de Beaumont, perfectly combines the antique with the modern. Built in the fifteenth century and accessible from a narrow alley, this hotel near place du Forum is loaded with charm. Tasteful antique furnishings decorate the public areas and guest rooms. Huge windows ensure that the 48 individually decorated rooms and apartments are filled with light; views are of the roofs of the old city, the garden, or the terrace. In the courtyard is a garden patio where breakfast is served in good weather. Archaeologists found a first-century Roman drain and statue plinth while digging under the hotel. Both of these items are available for you to admire.

26 rue du Sauvage. ☎ *04-90-93-56-66. Fax: 04-90-49-68-45. Internet:* www. hotel-arlatan.fr. *E-mail:* hotel-arlatan@provnet.fr. *Parking: 60–70F ($9–$10). Rack rates: 598–850F ($86–$121) double; 980–1,450F ($140–$207) suite. Breakfast: 62F ($9). AE, MC, V.*

Hôtel de la Muette

$$ Arles

The pleasant staff and good location make the Muette a solid bargain in the medieval section of town, a few minutes' walk from the Arena. This ancient hotel has sections built in the twelfth and the fifteenth centuries. Access to the rooms is up a steep, narrow, winding stone stairway. The 18 rooms are on the small side, but they're brightened by provençal fabrics on the bedspreads and curtains. Fans help to alleviate the summer heat. Breakfast is served on the terrace in front of the hotel.

15 rue des Suisses. ☎ *04-90-96-15-39. Fax: 04-90-49-73-16. Internet:* http: //perso.wanadoo.fr/hotel-muette. *E-mail:* hotel.muette@wanadoo. fr. *Parking: 50F ($7) in public parking garage across from the hotel. Rack rates: 320–360F ($46–$51) double. Breakfast: 38F ($5). MC, V.*

Hôtel du Forum

$$$ Arles

Although this is one of Arles's most elegant hotels (right on the central square), the reasonable rates make it a great value. The 38 spacious and attractive rooms are decorated with antiques and luxurious fabrics. The windows are soundproof, but if you like it extra quiet, request a room in the rear. The commons rooms are comfortable. The hotel also has a bar and a heated pool.

10 place du Forum. ☎ *04-90-93-48-95. Fax: 04-90-93-90-00. E-mail:* forumarles@ compuserve.com. *Parking: 60F ($9). Rack rates: 350–700F ($50–$100) double. Breakfast: 65F ($9). AE, MC, V.*

Hôtel du Musée

$$ Arles

You'll love the atmosphere of this hotel located in a sixteenth-century mansion on a tranquil street across from the Musée Réattu. The quiet location guarantees a good night's sleep, and the 20 rooms feature provençal decor and comfortable beds. Breakfast is served on the garden patio behind the building.

11 rue du Grand Prieuré. ☎ *04-90-93-88-88. Fax: 04-90-49-98-15. Parking: 40F ($6). Rack rates: 290–450F ($41–$64) double. Breakfast: 38F ($5). Closed Dec to mid-Feb. MC, V.*

Hôtel le Cloître

$$ Arles

A wonderful English-speaking couple runs this cozy hotel. It's difficult to find — tucked away on a steep side street between the Roman Theater and a medieval cloister. One side of the hotel is held up by thirteenth-century vaults from the adjacent cloister. The rooms in the back of the hotel have views of the cloister garden, while the other rooms have views of the Romanesque Eglise St-Trophisme. The 30 rooms boast antique details like beamed ceilings and stone walls.

16 rue du Cloître. ☎ *04-90-96-29-50. Fax: 04-90-96-02-88. E-mail:* `hotel_ cloitre@hotmail.com`. *Rack rates: 250–410F ($36–$59) double. Breakfast: 35F ($5). Closed mid-Nov to mid-Mar. AE, MC, V.*

Where to dine

Chez Gigi

$$ Arles PROVENÇAL

A few steps from the Arena, this popular neighborhood restaurant offers home-cooking at reasonable prices. The setting is casual, with families of several generations squeezed next to young dating couples. The menu is heavy on regional specialties, using provençal herbs, and prepared with care. Noteworthy dishes are the *soupe des poissons* (fish soup served with crusty breads and cheese) and the authentic *dorade provençal* (an ocean fish grilled with provençal herbs). For dessert, there's a lovely *crème brûlée*.

49 rue des Arènes. ☎ *04-90-96-68-59. Reservations recommended. Meals: Main courses 70–120F ($10–$17). MC, V. Open: Tues–Sun noon to 2 p.m. and 7:30–11 p.m.*

Le Jardin du Manon

$$$ Arles PROVENÇAL

A short walk from the old town center, this traditional restaurant with garden seating provides solid fine dining in an attractive setting filled with locals. The menu features provençal specialties served with the freshest ingredients. The best entree is the *millefeuille de brousse et tomate confit basilic* (pastry of goat's cheese and tomato-basil confit). As a meat dish, the chef recommends the *suprême de poulet farci à la tapenade, roti à la broche* (guinea fowl breast stuffed with olive paste and spit roasted). For dessert, there's a special *croustade de poire amande* (pear-and-almond pastry).

14 av. des Alyscamps. ☎ 04-90-93-38-68. Meals: Main courses 85–135F ($12–$20); menus 100–210F ($14–$30). AE, MC, V. Open: Thurs–Tues noon to 2 p.m. and 7:30–9:30 p.m. Closed Feb.

L'Hostellerie des Arènes

$$ Arles PROVENÇAL

Here you can dine alfresco across from the majestic Roman Amphitheater. The simple provençal fare is served by friendly English-speaking waiters, and the prices are low considering the quality. Locals know about the good value here, so the small restaurant frequently needs to turn diners away as the night wears on. Recommended are the *salade Arlesienne,* with salmon, pinenuts, cucumbers, and olives, and the *superbe bouillabaisse,* fish-and-shellfish stew. The dishes are presented with a flourish and sides like ratatouille. For dessert, try the *crème caramel.*

62 rue du Refuge. ☎ 04-90-96-13-05. Meals: Main courses 75–130F ($10–$18); menus 80F ($11) and 110F ($16). MC, V. Open: Wed–Mon noon to 2 p.m. and 7:30–10 p.m.

L'Olivier

$$$ Arles PROVENÇAL

The chef at L'Olivier, one of the top restaurants in town, assembles wonderful products from local farms and markets. Dining in the courtyard next to the gurgling fountain is a perfect way to spend a summer evening in Arles. The interior dining rooms are also attractive, with murals of the Camargue region and ancient stone walls. Expect to find beautifully presented dishes like the first course *filet de rouget poêlés à la l'huile d'olive, risotto d'épeautre au safran* (red mullet pan-fried with olive oil, and rissotto with shallots and saffron). The restaurant celebrates the nearby Camarague region with the unusual main course *pavé de taureau de Camargue, grillée d'échalotes beurre de câpres* (a thick slice of bull from the Camargue with grilled shallots and caper butter). There's also an excellent large menu of local wines.

1 bis rue Réattu. ☎ *04-90-49-64-88. Reservations recommended. Meals: Main courses 108–280F ($15–$40); menus 168–298F ($24–$43). MC, V. Open: Tues–Sat noon to 2:30 p.m. and 7:30–9:30 p.m.*

Lou Marquès

$$$$ Arles PROVENÇAL

Lou Marquès, part of a Relais & Châteaux hotel, has the highest reputation in town for its quality cuisine. Seating is in the formal dining room or on the terrace. The cuisine features creative twists on provençal specialties. A first course could be *queues de langoustine en salade vinaigrette d'agrumes et basilic* (crustacean and a salad with citrus-and-basil vinaigrette) or *risotto de homard aux truffes* (lobster risotto with truffles). As a main course try *pavé de loup en barigoule d'artichaut et à la sauge* (a thick slice of wolf fish with sage-stuffed artichokes) or *filet mignon de veau et ragoût fin de cèpes et salsifis* (veal with a stew of mushrooms and oyster plant). For a light dessert, there's *biscuit glacé au miel de lavande* (a small cake glazed with lavender honey).

At the Hôtel Jules-César, 9 bd. des Lices. ☎ *04-90-52-52-52. Reservations recommended. Meals: Main courses 180–250F ($26–$36); menus 105F ($15) at lunch, 240–340F ($34–$49) at dinner. AE, DC, MC, V. Open: Thurs–Tues noon to 2 p.m. and 7:30–10 p.m. Closed Nov–Dec.*

If you're looking for a light meal, head to **place du Forum,** where you can find several cafes with tables spilling into the square (including the cafe made famous by van Gogh in his *Café at Night, Place du Forum*).

Exploring the town

The historic center of Arles is **place de la République,** with a monumental obelisk towering over a fountain. Facing the fountain are the ornate seventeenth-century **Hôtel de Ville,** the town hall, and the Romanesque **Eglise St-Trophisme.** A block east are the first-century ruins of the **Théâtre Antique** and, close by, the even more impressive first-century **Amphithéâtre** (also called the **Arènes**) where bullfights are held. All that remains of the old Roman forum in **place du Forum** are a couple of columns (part of the Hôtel Nord-Pinus), but the area is now a pretty square filled with cafes and surrounded by deluxe hotels.

Easter to October, the **Petit Train d'Arles** (☎ 04-93-41-31-09) tours the town in 35 minutes at a cost of 30F ($4.30) for adults and 15F ($2.15) for children 3 to 10. The train leaves from the Arena entrance daily 10 a.m. to noon and 2 to 7 p.m.

If you plan to see a lot of sights, you can save money by purchasing one of two special tickets at the first museum you visit or at the tourist office. The **Visite Générale** ticket (65F/$9 for adults, 50F/$7 for students and children under 18) gets you into the Amphithéâtre, Théâtre Antique,

Cryptoportique, Thermes de Constantin, St-Trophisme, Les Alyscamps, Musée Reattu, Musée de l'Arles Antique, and Musée Arlatan. The **Circuit Arles Antique Pass** (55F/$8 for adults, 40F/$6 for students and children under 18) gets you into the Amphithéâtre, Théâtre Antique, Thermes de Constantin, Cryptoportique, and Musée de l'Arles Antique.

Many of the sights in Arles (Amphithéâtre, Théâtre Antique, Thermes de Constantin, Cryptoportique, St-Trophime, Les Alyscamps, and Musée Réattu) follow these daily hours: December to January 10 a.m. to noon and 2 to 4:30 p.m., February 10 a.m. to noon and 2 to 5 p.m., March 9 a.m. to 12:30 p.m. and 2 to 5:30 p.m., April to mid-June and late September 9 a.m. to 12:30 p.m. and 2 to 7 p.m., late June to mid-September 9 a.m. to 7 p.m., October 10 a.m. to 12:30 p.m. and 2 to 5:30 p.m., and November 10 a.m. to 12:30 p.m. and 2 to 5 p.m. These sights also share the same admission: 20F ($2.85) for adults and 15F ($2.15) for students and children under 18.

The A.D. 80 **Amphithéâtre (Arènes)** (rond-point des Arènes; ☎ 04-90-49-36-86), is Arles's most dramatic Roman ruin. The space was used in Roman times for brutal gladiator-type sporting events (using wild animals). In the Middle Ages, the Arena became a fortress and, later, a squatters' camp. Though the steps and seats have been ravaged by time, the theater, built for 20,000 spectators, can still hold about half of its original capacity. Today, the city uses the space to host the Arles version of a bullfight (which is not bloody like the Spanish version) during Les Dix Jours du Toro from mid- to late April and the Fêtes d'Arles in early July and mid- to late September. There are also occasional Spanish-style bullfights during these festivals. The most popular bullfighting event in Arles is more of a pageant-type spectacle in which bulls raised in the nearby Camargue region are taunted but not harmed. In this event, called a *cocarde*, the bull is outfitted with colorful ribbons tied to its horns and the *razeteurs* are the men in the ring who try to remove the ribbons. If you don't want to see the occasional Spanish-style bullfights where the bull is killed, avoid events with the description *mise-à-mort*. The Arena is dramatic when lit at night. For details on the events held here, call ☎ 04-90-96-03-70. See earlier in this section for hours and admission.

Fans of van Gogh and contemporary art may enjoy the **Fondation van Gogh** (26 rond-point des Arènes; ☎ 04-90-49-94-04). The homages to van Gogh are conceived in paintings, sculptures, photos, mixed media, letters, and musical scores — all loaded with van Gogh colors and motifs, like ragged shoes, cane chairs, sunflowers, cypresses, and ears. Artists represented include Alex Katz, Francis Bacon, Larry Rivers, David Hockney, Jasper Johns, Robert Motherwell, and Roy Lichtenstein. The works contemplate his sorrow and solitude and pay tribute to his energy and his vision's intensity. There are English translations throughout. The museum is open daily: late March to November 10 a.m. to 7 p.m. and December to mid-March 9:30 a.m. to noon and 2 to 5:30 p.m. Admission is 30F ($4.30) for adults and 20F ($2.85) for students and children.

In search of van Gogh

In February 1888, Dutch artist Vincent van Gogh (1853–90) took the train to Arles to escape dreary Paris. Although he arrived to find snow and ice, he decided to stay. That fall, his friend and fellow artist Paul Gauguin visited, but the two had a terrible falling out and Gauguin left. A drunken van Gogh then cut off his own left earlobe and presented it to a prostitute at a nearby brothel. The townspeople were concerned about this "lunatic from the North," so van Gogh allowed himself to be hospitalized at the Hôtel Dieu in Arles. He continued to paint prolifically, but soon transferred to a rest home in St-Rémy. In July 1890, van Gogh attempted suicide and died two days later. However, during those 18 months in Arles, he produced over 200 paintings and over 100 drawings and watercolors, including some of his most famous works (*The Yellow House, The Bedroom at Arles, Vincent's Chair, The Night Café,* and *Café at Night, Place du Forum*). He also wrote hundreds of letters.

Though there are no van Gogh paintings in Arles, fans of the artist will enjoy seeing some of the sites he painted, as well as some of the tributes to him. A statue of the artist with one ear can be found in the **Jardin d'Eté**, just south of the Théâtre Antique. The Hôtel Dieu where van Gogh was institutionalized is now a cultural center called the **Espace Van Gogh** (place Félix-Rey; ☎ **04-90-49-39-39**). In this cultural center, you can admire the flower-filled cloister he painted. The building also houses a library and an art gallery and shows free films. Admission is free to the Espace Van Gogh, which is open Tuesday 12:30 to 7 p.m., Wednesday and Saturday 10 a.m. to 12:30 p.m. and 2 to 5 p.m., and Friday 12:30 to 6 p.m. True van Gogh fans should visit **Les Alyscamps,** the Roman cemetery that the artist painted several times. The **cafe** made famous in the painting *Café at Night* is in the southeast corner of place du Forum. Perhaps the most rewarding site for van Gogh buffs is the **Fondation Van Gogh** next to the Arèna, displaying homages to van Gogh by artists like David Hockney, Jasper Johns, and Roy Lichtenstein (see later in the chapter for more details).

When the **Théâtre Antique** (rue du Cloître; ☎ **04-90-49-36-25**) was built in the first century B.C., it could hold 10,000 spectators. Alas, all that remains are lots of ancient rubble and two sad-looking Corinthian columns nicknamed the *Deux Veuves* (two widows). For hundreds of years, beginning in the fifth century, the theater was used as a rock quarry, helping to build churches, homes, and fortifications. But the space is now back to its original use as an open-air theater: July brings a performing-arts festival and a costume festival called the Festival of the Queen of Arles. See earlier in this section for hours and admission.

Built from the twelfth to the fourteenth century, the **Eglise et le Cloître St-Trophisme** (place de la République; ☎ **04-90-49-33-53**), with its elaborately carved facade, is one of the most beautiful Romanesque churches in Provence. A famous Last Judgment image is sculpted above the imposing brick-red doors. The most beautiful part of the church is the cloister, with two Romanesque and two Gothic galleries and many evocative stone carvings. See earlier in this section for hours and admission.

The entire family may enjoy the comprehensive **Museon Arlaten** (29 rue de la République; ☎ 04-90-96-08-23), a museum of provençal culture (the name is in the provençal language) founded in 1896 by Nobel Prize–winner Frédéric Mistral. The large museum staffed by costumed docents contains clothing, furniture, toys, ironworks, guns, farm equipment, documents, photos, paintings, pottery, musical instruments, and model ships. Don't miss the two nineteenth-century iron bikes (velocipedes) or the thrones for Napoléon III and his empress, Eugénie (c. 1860). The Dodekatheion, the ruins and statuary of a Roman temple, can be found in the central courtyard. The museum is open daily (except January 1, May 1, November 1, and December 25): July and August 9:30 a.m. to 1 p.m. and 2 to 6:30 p.m.; April, May, and September 9:30 a.m. to 12:30 p.m. and 2 to 6 p.m.; and October to March 9:30 a.m. to 12:30 p.m. and 2 to 5 p.m. Admission is 25F ($3.60) for adults and 20F ($2.85) for students and children under 18.

You have a long, dusty walk over major roadways and past a skateboard park to get to the **Musée de l'Arles Antiques** (avenue de la 1ère Division Française Libre; ☎ 04-90-18-88-88), located about half a mile from town, but it's well worth it. This modern air-conditioned museum contains the extraordinary archaeological finds of Arles from prehistory to the sixth century. There's a large collection of sculptures, sarcophagi (elaborate tombs), and amphores (double-handled jars), as well as scaled models of all of Arles's Roman monuments, including the extraordinary circus (currently being excavated next door) where chariot races were held. The museum has even set up catwalks over ancient mosaics so you can better see them in their entirety. The museum is open daily (except January 1, May 1, November 1, December 25): March to October 9 a.m. to 7 p.m. and November to February 10 a.m. to 5 p.m. Admission is 35F ($5) for adults and 25F ($3.60) for students and children under 18.

Les Alyscamps (avenue des Alyscamps; ☎ 04-90-49-36-87), an ancient necropolis, is really a unique site and well worth the ten-minute walk southeast of the city center. The area has been an inspiration to many artists, including van Gogh, who described Les Alyscamps in a letter to his brother, Theo; the text is reproduced at the site. Van Gogh and his friend Gauguin both painted Les Alyscamps several times. The name Alyscamps is believed to be a derivation of Elysian Fields. Alyscamps was used as both a Roman burial site and an early Christian cemetery from the fourth to the twelfth century. By the Middle Ages, there were 17 churches here; now all that remains are the ruins of one Romanesque chapel — St-Honorat. During the Renaissance, royals, nobles, and even monks were in the habit of giving away the most beautifully sculpted sarcophogi as gifts, so only the plainest of stone coffins line this sacred path. See earlier in this section for hours and admission.

In the fifteenth-century priory of St. Gilles (Knights of Malta), you can find the **Musée Réattu** (10 rue du Grand-Prieuré; ☎ 04-90-49-37-58), which features the paintings of local artist Jacques Réattu, drawings by Picasso, and a collection of sixteenth-century Flemish tapestries. The museum also houses Henri Rousseau drawings of the region (including images of the Arles arena), a collection of paintings by nineteenth- and twentieth-century artists, and temporary exhibits of photography. See earlier in this section for hours and admission.

If you haven't had your fill of Roman ruins, here are two more: the **Thermes de Constantin** and the **Cryptoportique.** The Thermes de Constantin (rue D.-Maïsto next to the Rhône River) are the ruins of a huge bathhouse and are all that remains of the Emperor Constantine's fourth-century palace. The Cryptoportique (next to the Arleten Museum) are double underground galleries in the shape of a U dating from 30 to 20 B.C. See earlier in this section for hours and admission.

Shopping

A colorful **market** takes place Wednesdays 7:30 a.m. to 12:30 p.m. on boulevard Emile-Combes and Saturdays 7:30 a.m. to 12:30 p.m. on boulevard des Lices. For provençal fabrics and gifts, head to **Les Olivades** (2 rue Jean-Jaurès; ☎ 04-90-96-22-17), and **Souleiado** (4 bd. des Lices; ☎ 04-90-96-37-55).

Aix-en-Provence and the Cours Mirabeau

Writers and artists drawn to **Aix-en-Provence** have long heralded this exquisite place, calling it the "Queen of Sweet Provence" and the "Athens of Southern France." This cosmopolitan city, founded in 122 B.C., is distinguished by its numerous sculptured fountains and golden-hued mansions, and by the regal boulevard cours Mirabeau and the winding streets of the old town. Its cafes are packed with students and its markets overflow with colorful produce. These qualities are quintessentially Aix (pronounced simply as "ex"). It's a town rich with discoveries — every corner you turn, you'll see an intriguing shop, a new restaurant, and a gurgling fountain. Aix's favorite painter is Paul Cézanne, who loved to paint the countryside around Aix, and whose last studio is just outside town.

Aix is also a major university town (the Université Aix-Marseille, founded in the fifteenth century) and home to the famous **Festival Provençal d'Aix** (☎ 04-42-63-06-75), a deluxe fete held in July, featuring classical music, opera, and ballet. Ancillary festivals and lots of street musicians fill the town from late June to early August, so summer is a fun time here. Visitors in 2001 are in for a treat because a major construction project on the **cours Mirabeau,** France's most beautiful boulevard, is due to be completed. Because Aix doesn't have the "must see" sights of

Aix-en-Provence

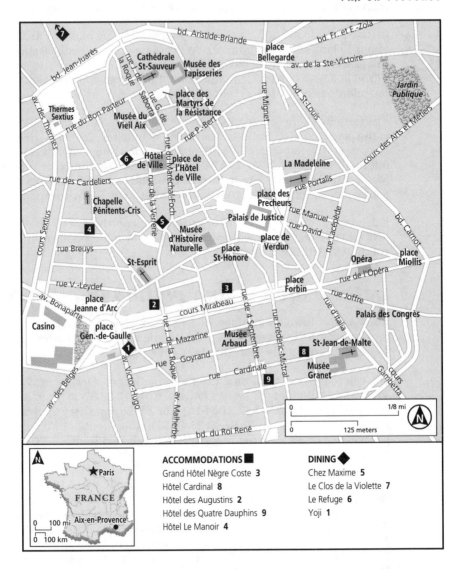

ACCOMMODATIONS ■	DINING ◆
Grand Hôtel Nègre Coste **3**	Chez Maxime **5**
Hôtel Cardinal **8**	Le Clos de la Violette **7**
Hôtel des Augustins **2**	Le Refuge **6**
Hôtel des Quatre Dauphins **9**	Yoji **1**
Hôtel Le Manoir **4**	

some other towns, you can relax into Provence time here and spend a day or two wandering this lovely town that seems kissed by the sun.

Getting there

The **Gare S.N.C.F.** (train station) is on rue Gustave-Desplaces at avenue Victor-Hugo. If you want to take a train to Aix from Paris, you need to change trains in Marseille. The trip from Paris to Marseille is about 3½ hours, and it's another half an hour to Aix from Marseille. The cost of a train ticket from Paris to Aix is 400 to 656F ($57 to $94). There are frequent connections from Aix to Marseille (35 minutes, 40F/$6). For train information or reservations, call ☎ **08-36-35-35-39** or 08-36-35-35-35.

In time for summer 2001, a new TGV station is being built in Vitroll, about 15 km (9.3 miles) from Aix. At press time, the schedules and prices were still being decided, but the train will run from Paris to Vitroll in 3 hours and 10 minutes. From the station, you can take a ten-minute taxi ride to the center of Aix.

The **Gare Routière** (bus station), on rue Lapierre (off avenue des Belges), is the place to catch buses to Marseille (40 minutes, 28F/$4), Arles (1 hour and 50 minutes, 68F/$10), and Avignon (1 hour, 100F/$14). For information, call ☎ **04-42-27-17-91.** July and August, the office is open Monday to Saturday 7:30 a.m. to 6:30 p.m. and Sunday 9 a.m. to 5 p.m.; September to June, hours are Monday to Saturday 8 a.m. to 6 p.m.

If **driving** to Aix from Avignon or other points north, take A7 south to RN7 and follow it into town. From Marseilles or other points to the south, take A51 north into town.

Getting around and getting information

Aix is a great town for strolling, so be sure to give yourself some free time to explore. Don't miss the atmospheric medieval walkways, like **passage Agard** off the east end of the cours Mirabeau.

You can rent a car at **National Citer** (32 rue Gustave-Desplaces; ☎ **04-42-93-10-14**), **Budget** (16 av. des Belges; ☎ **04-42-38-37-36**), and **Avis** (11 rue Gambetta; ☎ **04-42-21-64-16**). For a bike rental, try **Cycles Zammit** (27 rue Mignet; ☎ **04-42-23-19-53**), where rentals cost 39F ($6) per half day or 60F ($9) per day. For a taxi, call **Taxi Radio** at ☎ **04-42-27-71-11** or 04-42-27-62-12.

The **tourist office** (2 place du Général-de-Gaulle; ☎ **04-42-16-11-61;** Fax: 04-42-16-11-62; E-mail: infos@aixenprovencetourism.com; Internet: www.aixenprovencetourism.com) is open Monday to Saturday 8:30 a.m. to 7 p.m. and Sunday and holidays 10 a.m. to 1 p.m. and 2 to 6 p.m. To check on or send e- mail, head to **Hub Lot Cybercafe** (15–27 rue Paul-Bert; ☎ **04-42-21-37-31**), serving cafe fare. It's open Monday to Saturday 7 a.m. to 10 p.m.

Where to stay

Grand Hôtel Nègre Coste

$$$ Cours Mirabeau

Staying at this grand eighteenth-century hotel on the cours Mirabeau puts you in the center of the action, but the soundproof windows mean you don't have to stay up all night — unless you want to. The Nègre Coste has long been an important address and has played host to some important guests, including royalty and celebrities. The formal public rooms include the Provençal Salon and Salon Louis XV, as well as a gleaming bar. All 37 spacious guest rooms are furnished with antiques and boast a historic flavor, with touches like beamed ceilings and attractive moldings. Rooms look out on the busy and beautiful central boulevard or the narrow streets of the old town.

33 cours Mirabeau. ☎ *04-42-27-74-22. Fax: 04-42-26-80-93. Parking: 50F ($7). Rack rates: 420–800F ($60–$114) double. Breakfast: 50F ($7). MC, V.*

Hôtel Cardinal

$$ Mazarin

Natalie Bernard has owned this eighteenth-century townhouse for several years, and every year she renovates and restores several of the 31 units (24 rooms, 7 suites). The restored rooms tend to be more exactingly decorated, but all of the rooms, with fireplaces and cozy sitting areas, have a certain bohemian charm and are larger than those in comparable hotels. The suites have kitchenettes. The Cardinal, across from the house where writer M. F. K. Fisher lived in the 1950s, has been an address for writers and artists for decades. The windows give you a view of this pretty residential area, where the aristocracy of Aix built their mansions. Just a few blocks away is the cours Mirabeau.

22 rue Cardinale. ☎ *04-42-38-32-30. Fax: 04-42-26-39-05. Rack rates: 350–420F ($50–$60) double; 480F ($69) suite. Breakfast: 38F ($5). MC, V.*

Hôtel des Augustins

$$$ Vieil Aix

Because of its historic atmosphere (it occupies a fifteenth-century convent that once hosted Martin Luther), central location, and sound management, this is my favorite pricey hotel in Aix. It has been a hotel since 1892, although it was fully restored in 1984. The careful restoration kept a lot of historic details, like the stone walls and vaulting, stained glass, and wood paneling. The 29 rooms are spacious and soundproof — crucial for this busy part of town — and come with minibars; some have Jacuzzis and terraces. The decor is provençal, with colorful bedspreads, curtains, and wallpapers. The hotel has views of the rooftops of Aix and the famous cours Mirabeau.

3 rue de la Masse (at the corner of cours Mirabeau). ☎ *04-42-27-28-59. Fax: 04-42-26-74-87. Parking: 50f ($7.15). Rack rates: 600–1,500F ($86–$214) double. Breakfast: 50F ($7). MC, V.*

Hôtel des Quatre Dauphins

$$ Mazarin

A charming small hotel in the quiet residential Mazarin district, the Quatre Dauphins is a solid choice. This hotel is named after one of Aix's most memorable fountains, located nearby, which has water cascading from the mouths of four finely carved dolphins. Set on a quiet street, the hotel is a short walk from both the train station and cours Mirabeau (the main boulevard). The 12 rooms, some of which are on the small side, are decorated in a contemporary style with provençal fabrics; all have minibars.

54 rue Roux-Alphéran. ☎ *04-42-38-16-39. Fax: 04-42-38-60-19. Rack rates: 335–490F ($48–$70) double. Breakfast: 42F ($6). MC, V.*

Hôtel Le Manoir

$$ Vieil Aix

This lovely hotel is a real value considering you're staying in an atmospheric fourteenth-century cloister on a quiet street in the heart of the old town, near rue Tanneurs — a street lined with a large number of inexpensive restaurants. The 40 rooms are attractive and decorated with contemporary or antique furniture. The rooms have high ceilings (some with beams); ancient vaulting is evident throughout the hotel. Most rooms look out on the quiet interior garden courtyard. The staff is exceedingly friendly.

8 rue Entrecasteaux. ☎ *04-42-26-27-20. Fax: 04-42-27-17-97. E-mail:* Ltr@ hotelmanoir.com. *Internet:* www.hotelmanoir.com. *Free parking. Rack rates: 325–490F ($46–$70) double. Breakfast: 35F ($5). MC, V.*

Where to dine

Chez Maxime

$$$ Vieil Aix PROVENÇAL

This long-running hit with locals and tourists alike is set on bustling place Ramus. Most people sit on the square, but the inside is attractive and cozy — especially the tables by the front windows. This restaurant specializes in meats, thickly sliced and prepared with provençal herbs. A popular entree is the *terrine de légumes rôti au provençal* (a vegetable terrine that comes with tapenade, an olive paste that's a regional specialty). The best main courses are the *pavé d'agneau aux herbes provençal* (lamb with fresh herbs) and *pavé de boeuf à la fondue de foie gras et au cèpes* (beef served with foie gras and white mushrooms). For dessert, look no further than the *parfait glacé au fruit confit* (ice cream parfait with fruit). Menus are available in English.

12 place Ramus (a couple blocks north of cours Mirabeau). ☎ *04-42-26-28-51. Reservations recommended. Meals: Main courses 75–165F ($11–$22); menus 100F ($14) at lunch, 138–270F ($20) at dinner. MC, V. Open: Tues–Sat noon to 2:30 p.m.; Mon–Sat 7:30–10 p.m. Closed mid- to late Jan.*

Le Clos de la Violette

$$$$ **Northern Aix PROVENÇAL**

This restaurant, located on the northern edge of town, is Aix's best. To get there from the center of town, you can take a long walk or a short taxi ride. In this cozy yet elegant setting, you can sample truly innovative cuisine; the chef has received a well-earned Michelin star. The menu changes depending on the season and best market fare. Two of the chef's favorites are the *queues de langoustines rôti ravioli fourré au courail* (roast langoustine tails with ravioli stuffed with shellfish eggsack) and *carré d'agneau rôti en croûte au chevre frais et champignons* (roast rack of lamb with a pastry of goat cheese and mushrooms). For dessert, you may choose a platter of cookies like the *gros calissons d'Aix* (large almond-paste cookies) or *biscuit friable aux noisettes et brousse battue à la vanille, aux longs copeaux de chocolat* (vanilla-nut cookies with chocolate shavings). The very complete wine list boasts unusual and special selections from exclusive small wineries in the region. Ask the sommelier for his advice.

10 av. de la Violette. ☎ *04-42-23-30-71. Reservations necessary. Meals: Main courses 300–375F ($43–$54); menus 300F ($43) at lunch, 600F ($86) tasting menu. AE, DC, MC, V. Open: April–Oct Tues and Thurs–Sat noon to 2 p.m., Tues–Sat 7:30–10 p.m.; Nov–Mar Tues–Sat noon to 2:20 p.m. and 7:30–10 p.m. Closed late Dec to early Jan, Feb, and early Aug.*

Le Refuge

$ **Vieil Aix SMOKED MEAT AND FISH**

This is a very specialized place, but if you like smoked salmon and/or smoked duck, you'll be in heaven. Although most of the seating is on hip place des Cardeurs, the setting inside the tiny restaurant is après-ski, with snowshoes hanging on the wood-paneled walls. As the cheerful waiter explained to me, "We are in a mountain cabin." Whatever. The menu is very limited, but what they do, they do well. You choose from 14 fixed-price menus that include salad, main course, dessert, and a glass of wine. Basically, you have a choice among salmon, lobster, and duck, mostly smoked. The duck also comes barbecued, and there's homemade foie gras too. The meals are served with fries, salad, delicious homemade coleslaw, and a cup of hot mulled wine. Jazz and blues play on the tape box, and the atmosphere is very relaxed and fun.

13 place des Cardeurs. ☎ *04-42-96-17-23. Reservations recommended. Meals: Menus 46F ($7) at lunch, 75–80F ($11–$12) at dinner. MC, V. Open: Daily noon to 3 p.m. and 7:30 p.m. to midnight.*

Yôji

$$$ south of Cours Mirabeau   JAPANESE

This is the best Japanese restaurant in Aix — an excellent alternative for those looking to escape from French cuisine for a night. Although the restaurant is on busy avenue Victor-Hugo, the dining room has a calm aura, with a sleek decor and low lighting. It serves authentic Japanese and Korean cuisine, including wonderful combinations of sushi and sashimi that are reasonably priced and delicious.

7 av. Victor-Hugo. ☎ 04-42-38-48-76. Reservations recommended. Meals: Main courses 110–160F ($16–$23); menus 125–200F ($18–$29). AE, MC, V. Open: Tues–Sun noon to 2 p.m. and 7:30–10 p.m.

Aix is a great restaurant town, with lots of ethnic choices — along with the typical mouth-watering provençal cuisine. On **place Ramus** in the old town, you can find Cuban, Thai, Japanese, Senegalese, and Chinese restaurants. Other good restaurant streets are **rue de la Verrerie** and **rue des Tanneurs.** Aix is also a wonderful town for cafe-lingering. The king of all cafes is **Les Deux Garçons** (53 cours Mirabeau; ☎ 04-42-26-00-51). You may want to sit outside and people-watch along the avenue, but don't forget to check out the beaux-arts interior of this classic establishment.

Exploring the town

The recently renovated **cours Mirabeau,** a gorgeous wide boulevard lined with lush 150-year-old plane trees, is the main intersection of town. Cafes, shops, and hotels line the north side of the street, while eighteenth-century mansions stand on the south side. The boulevard is bookended by two huge fountains. The 1860 **Fontaine de la Rotonde,** on the west end of the street, has statues representing Justice (facing cours Mirabeau), Agriculture (facing Marseille), and Fine Arts (facing Avignon). On the east end of the street, the nineteenth-century **Fontaine du Roi René** shows the medieval King René (who brought the Muscat grape to Provence) with a bunch of grapes in his hand. Also on the cours Mirabeau are the 1691 **Fontaine des Neuf Canons,** displaying nine cannons, and the 1734 **Fontaine d'Eau Chaude,** said to be fed by thermal sources.

The neighborhood south of the cours Mirabeau is the **quartier Mazarin,** designed in the seventeenth century, with streets in a grid pattern. This is where the aristocracy of Aix lived. Walk down rue 4 Septembre to see **place des Quatre Dauphins** with its wonderful dolphin fountain. On the way, you'll pass the **Musée Paul-Arbaud,** displaying faïence. A left at the fountain down rue Cardinale will bring you to the **Eglise St-Jean-de-Malte,** a fortified twelfth-century Gothic church, and the **Musée Granet,** with works by Cézanne and other artists upstairs and Roman excavations, including mosaics and statuary, in the basement. North of cours Mirabeau is **Vieil Aix,** the old town, with its maze of semi-pedestrian streets and wonderful large squares. Take spooky passage Agard at the east end of cours Mirabeau to reach the nineteenth-century **Palais de Justice** on **place de Verdun,** where the flea market is held three times a week. Two blocks north and one block west is the eighteenth-century **Ancienne Halle aux Grains** (the old Corn Exchange, now a post office) on **place Richelme,** where there's a fruit-and-vegetable market every morning on the square. A couple blocks up rue Gaston de la Saporta is the **Musée du Vieil Aix,** displaying a history of the town. **Place de l'Archevêché** is where you'll find the seventeenth-century **Palais de l'Archevêché,** a grand residence where the prestigious music festival called Festival International d'Art Lyrique (☎ 04-42-17-34-00; Internet: www.aix-en-provence.com/festartlyrique/) is held every year in July. On the first floor of the palace is a **Musée des Tapisseries** displaying beautiful tapestries. Just beyond is the **Cathédrale St-Sauveur,** unique because it contains architectural styles from the fifth to the seventeenth century.

To save money on museum admissions, buy a **Passport 1** covering the Musée Granet, Pavillon de Vendôme, Musée des Tapisseries, and Ecole d'Art for 50F ($7) for adults and 40F ($6) for students and children. The **Passport 2** covers the Musée Granet, Pavillon de Vendôme, Musée des Tapisseries, Ecole d'Art, and Atelier de Cézanne for 70F ($10) for adults and 60F ($9) for students and children. The passes are sold at all the sights covered by the passes, as well as at the tourist office.

The tourist office runs a **free two-hour walking tour** (in English) of the city on Wednesdays at 9:30 a.m. and on Sundays and public holidays at 9:30 a.m. from July to October. From November to June, there are walking tours of Aix on Saturdays at 9:30 a.m. Theme tours of Aix (literary, architecture, Cézanne, Zola, fountains, history) are given on other days depending on the time of year. Check with the tourist office at ☎ 04-42-16-11-61. The office also organizes full-day and half-day tours of the region costing 160 to 250F ($23 to $36). Among the tours are Lavender Roads; Marseille; Les Baux and St-Rémy; Arles; and Cassis and its deep rocky inlets. Call the tourist office for reservations.

If you want to follow in the footsteps of painter Paul Cézanne, who was born and died in Aix, walk along the **Circuit de Cézanne;** the sidewalk markers bearing his name begin at the tourist office. The walk highlights the places Cézanne used to frequent, the school where he studied, images he painted, and the shop where his father worked. The tourist office has a free accompanying brochure called "In The Footsteps of Paul Cézanne." Another choice is driving or walking the **route de Cézanne** along D17 (Route de Tholonet), which leaves Aix from the southeast and travels for about 6.4 km (4 miles) toward Mont St-Victoire (Cézanne's favorite peak). The route shows images that Cézanne painted and places where he used to set up his easel.

Paul Cézanne is considered an artists' artist. At the **Atelier de Cézanne** (9 av. Paul-Cézanne; ☎ 04-42-21-06-53), about a mile north of town, you're likely to encounter artists that are making the pilgrimage to see the painter's milieu, as well as his motifs and the views of the country-side he painted continuously. Cézanne's last studio was built on a hill outside Aix, in 1901, in full view of Mont St-Victoire — one of his favorite subjects. In 1906, Cézanne died of pleurisy contracted while painting outdoors. Today the studio is set up as though Cézanne had just stepped out — with paints, a glass of wine, and a pipe perched near an easel. It's a place to "witness the unfolding of his sensations," according the curator of the space. The studio is open Wednesday to Monday (except January 1, May 1, and December 25): April to September 10 a.m. to noon and 2:30 to 6 p.m. and October to March 10 a.m. to noon and 2 to 5 p.m. Admission is 16F ($2.30) for adults and 10F ($1.40) for students and children. To get there, take the no. 1 bus, leaving from La Rotonde (place Général-de-Gaulle) in Aix every 20 minutes, to stop Cézanne.

Located on the first floor of the grand Archbishop's Palace, the **Musée des Tapisseries** (28 place des Martyrs de la Résistance; ☎ 04-42-23-09-91) contains a rich collection of textiles from the seventeenth and eighteenth centuries. Highlights are "The Grotesque," a seventeenth-century theatrical series depicting musicians, dancers, and animals, and "The History of Don Quixote," a series of ten works showing scenes from the Cervantes story. The contemporary art section displays colorful abstract and figurative tapestries by living artists. It's open Wednesday to Monday 10 a.m. to noon and 2 to 6 p.m. (closed January 1, May 1, and December 25). Admission is 20F ($2.85) for adults and 15F ($2.15) for students and children.

Set in the eighteenth-century Hôtel d'Estienne de St-Jean, the **Musée du Vieil Aix** (17 rue Gaston-Saporta; ☎ 04-42-21-43-55) displays a mildly interesting collection of ephemera relating to Aix, including early maps and a large collection of santons — the folklore doll figures popular in Provence. It's open Tuesday to Sunday: April to September 10 a.m. to noon and 2:30 to 6 p.m. and October to March 10 a.m. to noon and 2 to 5 p.m. Admission is 20F (2.85) for adults and 15F ($2.15) for students and children.

Many people head to the **Musée Granet** (place St-Jean-de-Malte; ☎ 04-42-38-14-70), which occupies a seventeenth-century Knights of Malta palace, to see the only Cézanne works in town. The museum also has an interesting collection of eighteenth- and nineteenth-century paintings, including works by Van Dyck, David, Delacroix, and Ingres, as well as many paintings by its namesake, the academic provençal painter François Marius Granet. In the basement is perhaps the most interesting part of the museum: archaeological finds from the area, including glorious Roman statues and mosaics. It's open Wednesday to Monday 10 a.m. to noon and 2 to 6 p.m. (closed January 1, May 1, May 8, May 21, July 14, August 15, November 1, November 11, and December 25). Admission is 20F ($2.85) for adults and 15F ($2.15) for students and children.

Fans of faïence, locally made hand-painted pottery, should head to the Mazarin quarter to check out the **Musée Paul-Arbaud** (2 rue du

4 Septembre; ☎ **04-42-38-38-95**). This eighteenth-century mansion houses an interesting collection of provençal earthenware, as well as paintings, illuminated manuscripts, and other rare books. The museum is open Monday to Saturday 2 to 5 p.m. (closed January). Admission is 20F ($2.85) for adults and 15F ($2.15) for students and children.

Shopping

Aix offers the best markets in the region. Place Richelme is filled with a **fruit-and-vegetable market** every morning. This is the place to buy all the exquisite products of Provence, like olives, lavender, local cheeses, and fresh produce. There's a **flower market** on Sunday mornings at place des Prêcheurs, and on Tuesday, Thursday, and Saturday mornings on place de l'Hôtel-de-Ville. The **fish market** is held mornings on rue des Marseillais.

La Cure Gourmande (place de l'Hôtel-de-Ville; ☎ **04-42-21-26-48**) stocks all the classic Provence sweets, like *provençaux biscuits* (Provence cookies), *artisanaux chocolats* (handmade chocolates), *calissons d'Aix* (the classic almond-paste cookie), *caramels à l'ancienne* (old-fashioned caramels), and *confiseries traditionelles* (traditional sweets). Another excellent candy shop is **Calissons du Roy René** (rue Clemenceau; ☎ **04-42-26-67-86**), specializing in calissons — those yummy almond-paste sweets. **La Blanche Boutique** (4 rue Gibelin; ☎ **04-42-21-34-82**) is a beautiful gift shop selling handmade baskets and wonderful things to put in them. **Quant aux Hommes** (18 rue Fauchier; ☎ **04-42-38-55-82**) sells clothing, gifts, and unusual items for travelers. And **Papiers Plumes** (8 rue Papassaudi; ☎ **04-42-27-74-56**) is a stationery shop selling papers, pens, and stylish notebooks.

Nightlife

A student town, Aix is particularly lively at night. You may see roving groups of young people looking for the nearest hot spot. The **Forum des Cardeurs,** a lively square in the center of Old Aix, has a high concentration of bars attracting students and 30-somethings. **Le Scat** (11 rue de la Verrerie; ☎ **04-42-23-00-23**) is a good jazz club with an 80F ($11) cover. There's also the dance club **Le Mistral** (3 rue Mistral; ☎ **04-42-38-16-49**) with a 100F ($14) cover. Musicians entertain strollers on summer evenings — look for them on the cours Mirabeau and place d'Albertas west of the Palais de Justice in the old town.

Marseille: Crime and Bouillabaisse

Most people steer clear of **Marseille** because of its reputation as a seething haven of iniquity. Alas, this city's bad reputation, which has existed for at least 2,000 years, is highly deserved. Visitors tend to be limited to those looking for drugs and/or sex, or young people into adventure-type tourism — where they go to dangerous places and look for trouble. They'll probably find it in Marseille, whose streets are crawling with shady characters. It's all a shame really, because there are interesting historic sites here.

If you're determined to brave seeing Marseille, you need to be on guard at all times. Tourism literature claims that Marseille (like Naples in Italy) is experiencing a renaissance and has improved much over the last few years, but the city seems worse to me these days.

Marseille is both an ancient city and a thoroughly modern one, as well as a cosmopolitan center and a huge metropolis of a million residents. The city's center is the Vieux Port, the old port claimed by Greek sailors in 600 B.C. Romans took over in 49 B.C. Staunchly independent, Marseille didn't become a part of France until 1660. The Black Plague in 1770 decimated the population, but by 1792 residents rose to prominence when they marched into Paris singing what's now called *La Marseillaise* (the French national anthem). Today, Marseille is looking boldly into the future while planning the celebration of its 26th centennial.

Marseille is a town of intriguing religious **pilgrimage festivals.** Here are the major dates and locations: February 2 at St-Victor, August 15 at Notre-Dame de la Garde, September 8 at Notre-Dame de Galine, and June 18 at Sacré-Coeur. Pastoral festivals take place from the end of December to the end of January.

Getting there

The grand **Gare St-Charles** train station (place Victor-Hugo; ☎ 08-36-35-35-39; Internet: www.sncf.fr) is at the top of a huge stone staircase. If you have a lot of luggage, it's best to take a cab to your hotel. The information and ticket windows are on the lower level of the station. Ten to twelve fast TGVs travel from Paris to Marseille each day, costing 370 to 455F ($53 to $65). Beginning in June 2001, the train trip from Paris to Marseille will be reduced to 3½ hours (from 4 to 5 hours). Hourly trains to Nice take 2½ hours and cost 148F ($21). Trains also go to Avignon (70 minutes, 92F/$13) and Aix (40 minutes, 41F/$6).

If you're walking from the train station, go down the huge staircase and walk straight on boulevard d'Athènes to the McDonald's. Then take a right onto La Canebière, which leads to the old port, the location of the largest concentration of hotels, restaurants, and shops, as well as the tourist office. It's a ten-minute walk.

The **Aéroport Marseille-Marignane,** also called the Marseille-Provence Airport (☎ 04-42-14-14-14; Internet: www.marseille.aeroport.fr), is 28 km (17.4 miles) northwest of the city. A shuttle bus (45F/$6) between the airport and the Gare St-Charles departs every 20 minutes daily from 6 a.m. to 10 p.m. (later if there are late flights). You can buy tickets

Marseille

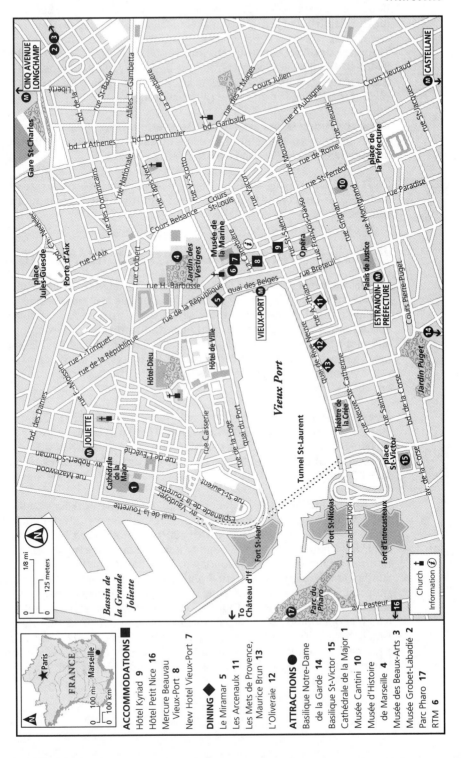

ACCOMMODATIONS ■
Hôtel Kyriad **9**
Hôtel Petit Nice **16**
Mercure Beauvau
Vieux-Port **8**
New Hotel Vieux-Port **7**

DINING ◆
Le Miramar **5**
Les Arcenaulx **11**
Les Mets de Provence,
Maurice Brun **13**
L'Oliveraie **12**

ATTRACTIONS ●
Basilique Notre-Dame
de la Garde **14**
Basilique St-Victor **15**
Cathédrale de la Major **1**
Musée Cantini **10**
Musée d'Histoire
de Marseille **4**
Musée des Beaux-Arts **3**
Musée Grobet-Labadié **2**
Parc Pharo **17**
RTM **6**

at the ticket office in the airport between terminals 1 and 2. For information, call ☎ **04-42-14-31-27.** The shuttle bus leaves the Gare St-Charles for the airport every 20 minutes daily 5:30 a.m. to 9:50 p.m.

The **Gare des Autocars** (bus station) is on place Victor-Hugo (☎ **04-91-08-16-40**). The station has frequent buses to Aix (40 minutes, 27F/$3.85), Arles (3 hours, 85F/$12), Avignon (1 hour, 93F/$13), Cannes (2½ hours, 127F/$18), and Nice (3 hours, 138F/$20).

If you're **driving** from Paris, follow A6 south to Lyon, then continue south along A7 to Marseille. The drive takes about 7 hours. From towns in Provence, take A7 south to Marseille.

Don't plan on bringing a car to Marseille; it'll likely be broken into or stolen. Your best bet is to take the train into town and rely on public transportation.

Getting around and getting information

This is one town where you feel practically obligated to rely on the **tourist train** (see "Exploring the city" later in this section), because walking around Marseille isn't that safe and the attractions are quite spread out. You can also take local **buses** and **subways.** Information and maps for the public transportation system are available at **Espace Info** (6 rue des Fabres; ☎ 04-91-91-92-10). Tickets for the bus and subway system, available at the tourist office, are 9F ($1.30); day passes are 25F ($3.60).

Two rental-car agencies near the train station are **Europcar** (7 bd. Maurice-Bourdet; ☎ 04-91-99-40-90) and **Thrifty** (8 bd. Voltaire; ☎ 04-91-05-92-18). For a cab, call **Marseille Taxi** at ☎ 04-91-02-20-20, **Taxi Blanc Bleu** at ☎ 04-91-51-50-00, or **Radio Taxi France** at ☎ 04-91-85-80-00.

The **tourist office** is at 4 La Canebière (☎ **04-91-13-89-00;** Fax: 04-91-13-89-20; E-mail: accueil@marseille-tourisme.com; Internet: www.marseille-tourisme.com): July to September, it's open Monday to Saturday 9 a.m. to 8 p.m. and Sunday and holidays 10 a.m. to 7 p.m.; October to June, hours are Monday to Saturday 9 a.m. to 7 p.m. and Sunday and holidays 10 a.m. to 5 p.m. This large office has a souvenir shop, runs guided tours, and sells bus and metro passes. There's a **small annex** at the Gare St-Charles (on the left as you exit the station), which is open Monday to Friday 10 a.m. to 5 p.m. To check on or send e-mail, head to **Info Web Café** (1 quai de Rive-Neuve; ☎ 04-91-33-74-98), a hip cafe/bar on the north side of the old port. Info Web Café is open Monday to Saturday 9 a.m. to 10 p.m. and Sunday 2 to 7 p.m.

Where to stay

Hôtel Kyriad

$ Old Port

This is the least expensive of the many standard hotels on the old port. The Kyriad was formerly part of the Climat franchise, so the rooms have a chain-hotel quality. The location is good — on the border of the old port and the historic center of Marseille. The 49 rooms have radios and hairdryers, and the hotel has a bar.

6 rue Beauvau. ☎ ***04-91-33-02-33.*** *Fax: 04-91-33-21-34. E-mail:* kyriad. vieux-port@wanadoo.fr. *Internet:* www.hotelscie.fr/climatde-france.
Rack rates: 340–380F ($49–$54) double. Breakfast: 42F ($6). MC, V.

Hôtel Petit Nice

$$$$ 7e Arrondissement

This Relais & Châteaux member is the top lodging choice. The Passédat family has turned two Greek villas on the coast into a luxurious destination and an oasis of tranquillity in hectic Marseille. The 12 light and airy rooms are all individually decorated in a modern style with deluxe amenities. The hotel has a large pool and a terrace where meals are served in good weather. Gérald Passédat runs the kitchen — the best in Marseille — and serves specialties from the region. Diners have views of the coast.

Anse de Maldormé, Corniche J.-F. Kennedy. ☎ ***04-91-59-25-92.*** *Fax: 04-91-59-28-08. E-mail:* passedat@relaischateaux.fr. *Internet:* www.relaischateaux. fr. *Parking: 100F ($14). Rack rates: 1,200–2,600F ($171–$371) double; 4,300–5,500F ($614–$786) suite. Breakfast: 120F ($17). AE, DC, MC, V.*

Mercure Beauvau Vieux Port

$$$ Old Port

This classic hotel, part of the Mercure chain, is currently undergoing a renovation to restore some of its former grandeur. Most of the 61 rooms have port views, and some have balconies. All have large windows that let in lots of light and air. The lobby is pretty, with antiques and oriental rugs.

4 rue Beauvau. ☎ ***04-91-54-91-00.*** *Fax: 04-91-54-15-76. E-mail:* H1293@ accor-hotels.com. *Rack rates: 660–1,600F ($94–$229) double. Breakfast: 67F ($10). AE, MC, V.*

New Hotel Vieux-Port

$$ Old Port

Part of a new hotel chain, this high-rise has 47 rooms — most with terraces overlooking the old port. The terraces are shared by several rooms. The room decor is uninspired and generic, with stucco walls and maybe a tired print or tourist poster; some rooms are quite large, with high ceilings. All rooms have minibars and hairdryers. The hotel is in a busy part of town, but the soundproof windows make the rooms fairly quiet. A large buffet breakfast, including hardboiled eggs and ham, is served in the breakfast room (with port views).

3 bis rue Reine-Elisabeth. ☎ *04-91-90-51-42.* Fax: 04-91-90-76-24. E-mail: marseillevieux-port@new-hotel.com. *Internet:* www.new-hotel.com. *Rack rates: 375–470F ($54–$67) double. Breakfast: 55F ($8). MC, V.*

Where to dine

Le Miramar

$$$$ Old Port PROVENÇAL

This is the best restaurant in Marseille. Le Miramar is set on the north side of the old port, with views of the hilltop Notre-Dame de la Garde. Prepare for a hearty meal, especially if you order the restaurant's special *bouillabaisse,* which comes in two courses and is exquisitely prepared with fresh herbs and fish. The restaurant also has wonderful lobster preparations, including the *fricassée de homard* (lobster stewed provençal-style with fresh herbs).

12 quai du Port. ☎ *04-91-91-10-40. Reservations necessary. Meals: Main courses 190–260F ($27–$37); bouillabaisse 275F ($39). AE, DC, MC, V. Open: Mon–Sat noon to 2:30 p.m. and 7:30–10 p.m. Closed two weeks in Jan and three weeks in Aug.*

Les Arcenaulx

$$$ Old Port PROVENÇAL

This restaurant/bookstore features excellent provençal cooking in a charming atmosphere. Look for friendly, sophisticated service, as well as generous helpings. The regional specialties include *pieds et paquets* and *bouillabaisse* and a simple grilled catch of the day. The restaurant also serves pizza and salads. The desserts are homemade delicacies — it's worth saving room for them.

25 cours d'Estienne d'Orves. ☎ *04-91-90-63-35. Reservations necessary. Meals: Main courses 60–140F ($9–$20); menu 135F ($19). MC, V. Open: Mon–Fri noon to 2:30 p.m.; Mon–Sat 7–10:30 p.m. Closed late July to late Aug.*

Les Mets de Provence, Maurice Brun

$$$ Old Port PROVENÇAL

At this family-run dining spot (opened in 1935), a meal is still an event that takes up the better part of the day — the entire day if digestion is included — so don't plan on rushing if you come here. The basic five-course menu includes a platter of grilled fish prepared provençal style, as well as a serving of either chicken or meat with seasonal vegetables, a cheese course, and dessert.

18 quai de Rive-Neuve, 2nd floor. ☎ *04-91-33-35-38. Reservations necessary. Meals: Main courses 175–230F ($25–$33); menus 215F ($31) at lunch, 285F ($41) at dinner. MC, V. Open: Tues–Sat noon to 2:30 p.m.; Mon–Sat 7:30–10:30 p.m. Closed Aug 1–15.*

L'Oliveraie

$$ Old Port PROVENÇAL

You can expect a warm welcome here. The waitstaff is happy to recommend or explain dishes. L'Oliveraie is a busy place and the atmosphere can be somewhat frantic, but diners usually enjoy sitting by the window and watching all the strollers on the busy square. All the specialties of the region are offered, as well as bistro fare. Good choices are any of the regional fish dishes like baked cod or grilled red mullet, served with market fresh vegetables and herbs. The reasonably priced wine list features wines of the region.

10 place aux Huiles. ☎ *04-91-33-34-41. Reservations recommended. Meals: Main courses 95–135F ($14–$19); menus 100F ($14) at lunch, 165F ($24) at dinner. MC, V. Open: Mon–Fri noon to 2:30 p.m; Mon–Sat 7:30–11 p.m. Closed Aug.*

Marseille is the birthplace of *bouillabaisse*. The city's pride in this classic fish stew has necessitated the bouillabaisse contract — a guarantee of quality and authenticity that many chefs, who make the soup, have signed. The other famous dish here is *pieds et paquets* (literally feet and packages). To make this dish, small squares of lamb stomach are rolled into packets and garnished with bacon, garlic, and parsley with lamb "trotters" (feet), and cooked in a sauce of white wine and tomatoes.

Exploring the city

Like Paris, Marseille is divided into arrondissements (Marseille has 16). **La Canebière,** nicknamed Can o' Beer by World War II GIs, is the main intersection, leading to the old port with its many hotels and restaurants. Just east of the old port is the huge covered shopping mall **Centre Bourse.** The streets a block in from the port, on the port's south side, are lined with restaurants with outdoor terraces. The old quarter, called **Panier,** is on the north side of the port.

The **Histobus** offers a guided English tour of Marseille's main sights (old port, Notre-Dame de la Garde, St-Victor Abbey, and so on). Tours run daily from July to September and Sundays from October to June. The cost is 50F ($7) for adults and 25F ($3.60) for children. For details, call the tourist office at ☎ **04-91-13-89-00.**

The **Petit Train de la Bonne Mère** (tourist train) makes two circuits around town. January to November, train no. 1 makes a 50-minute round-trip to Notre-Dame de la Garde via the old port and the St-Victor Abbey. Easter to October, train no. 2 makes a 40-minute round-trip of old Marseille via the cathedral, Vieille Charité, and the Quartier du Panier. The trains depart from quai des Belges and cost 30F ($4.30) for adults and 15F ($2.15) for children for one trip, or 50F ($7) for adults and 30F ($4.30) for children for both trips. For details, call ☎ **04-91-40-17-75.**

The tourist office can arrange a **taxi tour** that ranges from 1½ to 4 hours (200F to 570F/$29 to $81). A taxi tour is a great way for three adults, or two adults and two children, to see the major sights. The tourist office distributes **"Le fil de l'histoire"** ("The Red Line of History"), which includes a map and self-guided tour brochure for the Panier district, Marseille's colorful old quarter. Markers have been placed throughout the district for you to follow as you walk.

You should exercise caution in Marseille. Here are some tips for staying safe: Stay near the old port; travel in groups of at least two if possible; avoid deserted streets; avoid the Panier district at night; and take taxis to tourist destinations.

Just 4.8 km (3 miles) from the port of Marseille, the small rocky island of If (pronounced *eef*) contains an imposing fortress prison, the **Château d'If** (☎ **04-91-55-50-09**). François I built this fortress off the coast in 1524. The fortress became a prison soon after it was built. The prison has harbored many unfortunate souls — many jailed on political and religious grounds. The Château d'If has become especially famous for the fictional prisoner, the Count of Monte Cristo, from the novel by Alexandre Dumas. The château is open Tuesday to Sunday (except January 1 and December 25): April to September 9:30 a.m. to 6:30 p.m. and October to March 9:30 a.m. to 5:30 p.m. Admission is 25F ($3.60) for adults and 15F ($2.15) for children. You can get to the château by taking a 20-minute boat ride that departs from the quai des Belges. The ride costs 55F ($8).

The basilica **Notre-Dame de la Garde** (☎ **04-91-13-40-80**) was constructed on the highest point in the city in 1853. With its strategic location, the site has always been a lookout post, fortification, and place of worship all rolled into one. It's also a popular pilgrimage site. The church is Romanesque Byzantine style, with domes, multicolored stripes of stone, and lots of gilding, marble, and mosaics. The lower church features the vaulted crypts; the upper church houses the sanctuary. You can find wonderful views of the city from the garden in front of the church. It's open daily: May to October 7 a.m. to 8 p.m. and November to April 7 a.m. to 7 p.m. Admission is free. To get to Notre-Dame de la Garde, take bus no. 60 or the tourist train (see earlier in this section), or walk through the Jardin de la Colonne at the top of the cours Pierre-Puget (about a half-hour walk).

Shopping

Here's a sampling of the best markets in Marseille (unless indicated, they're open Monday to Saturday): The **Capucins Market** on place des Capucins is open daily 8 a.m. to 7 p.m. This market has fruit, herbs, fish, and food products. **Quai des Belges** is a fish market on the old port, open daily 8 a.m. to 1 p.m. The **Allées de Meilhan on La Canebière** is where you can find flowers on Tuesday and Saturday 8 a.m. to 1 p.m.; it has vendors selling santons from the last Sunday in November to December 31 daily 8 a.m. to 7 p.m. On **cours Julien** near Notre-Dame du Mont, you'll find a market with fruits, vegetables, and other foods. At the same location on cours Julien, there are vendors with stamps on Sundays 8 a.m. to 1 p.m.; Every other Sunday 8 a.m. to 7 p.m. there are vendors with secondhand goods. Every other Saturday, there are vendors with old books; on Fridays 8 a.m. to 1 p.m. there are vendors with organic products; and on Saturdays and Wednesdays 8 a.m. to 1 p.m. there's a flower market.

Marseille is the place to buy *santons* — those clay Nativity figurines that are popular throughout Provence. The elaborately decorated figurines, many of which are villagers outfitted for the common trades and professions of the Middle Ages, are highly collectible. You'll find countless stores along **La Canebière** selling these colorful dolls. There's also a good santon store called **Carbonel** (49 rue Neuve-Sainte-Catherine; ☎ 04-91-13-61-36), near the old port. You can also find a famous soap made in Marseille, which is stamped with the city's name. The soap is sold in all the city's large department stores, in the **Centre Bourse,** or at **La Licorne** (Cours Julien; ☎ 04-96-12-00-91).

Nightlife

A good late-night cafe/bar near the old port is **Brasserie Vieux-Port New-York** (33 quai des Belges; ☎ 04-91-33-91-79). For cabaret performances, there's **Le Chocolat Théâtre** (59 cours Julien; ☎ 04-91-42-19-29). Call for hours and information about performances and prices. A popular and reasonably safe disco is **Café de la Plage** in Escale Borély, a mall on avenue Mendès-France (☎ 04-91-71-21-76).

Chapter 19

The Riviera

. . . .

In This Chapter

▶ Visiting the top ten towns along the French Riviera

▶ Hitting the beaches and modern art museums

▶ Making the scene: The Riviera's hottest nightlife

. . . .

*B*esides Paris, France's most popular draw for tourists is the **French Riviera,** known as the **Côte d'Azur.** And it's no wonder. Sophisticated resorts lined along the Azure Coast boast top-notch amenities and cultural activities, and miles of warm-water beaches beckon sun worshipers of all ages. In fact, these chic seaside towns and charming hillside villages have been attracting sun bathers, socialites, and artists for over a century. The artists have left their legacy in the many top-notch museums focusing on twentieth-century works and featuring artists like Picasso, Matisse, Léger, Chagall, and Renoir.

There's a lot to see and do on the Riviera, and you could easily spend a couple of weeks here. You can base yourself in Nice or Cannes and make day trips to the surrounding towns, or rent a car and hop from village to village along the coast. Either way, you'll want to allow yourself plenty of time for wallowing in the sunshine and taking in the exciting nightlife of this special corner of France.

What's Where: The French Riviera and Its Major Attractions

The Riviera occupies the southeast corner of the country, near where France meets the border of Italy. Its capital city is the multifaceted **Nice,** a good base for exploring the region, with many attractions of its own. East of Nice, the glamorous principality of **Monaco** occupies a small slice of mountainous coastline close to the Italian border. Between Nice and Monaco are the village of **Beaulieu,** nestled into a coastal inlet, and the exclusive peninsula of **St-Jean-Cap-Ferrat.** To the west of Nice, the flamboyant **Cannes** (famous for the annual Film Festival) is the largest center. Between Cannes and Nice are **Antibes,** a lively town that has become a yachting base; **Cap d'Antibes,** the exclusive tip of the peninsula; tiny **Biot,** famous for crafts like glass blowing and pottery; **Vence,** a circular cobblestone village; and **St-Paul-de-Vence,** a pedestrian-only village built on a steep rock. Last but certainly not least, **St-Tropez** is perhaps the most famous village on the Riviera and a must-see for anyone in search of the hectic heart and sassy soul of this region.

To help you find Web sites for hotels, restaurants, and other businesses along the Riviera, check out **www.cote.azur.fr**.

The **Carte Musées Côte d'Azur** gives you free access to 62 museums, monuments, and gardens in the region. A three-day pass (to be used over three consecutive days) costs 80F ($11) and a seven-day pass (to be used over seven consecutive days) 150F ($21). You can buy the passes at any participating sight, as well as at the individual tourist offices. For more information and details on which sights offer the pass, call ☎ 04-93-13-17-51 or check on the Net at www.cmca.net.

To get to the Riviera, you can catch one of the frequent daily flights from Paris to Marseille (see Chapter 18) or Nice (see later in this chapter), or hop on one of the fast TGV trains leaving about six times daily from Paris's Gare de Lyon to Marseille (three hours), Cannes (six hours), and Nice (6 hours).

Debuting in June 2001 will be the fastest TGV train service yet to France's south coast: from Paris to Marseille in three hours! See Chapter 18 for details.

Sampling the region's cuisine: French meets Italian

The Riviera's cuisine is certainly one of the high points of a visit. Here you can dine on classic French fare prepared in the light and flavorful provençal manner, with liberal use of olives and olive oil. You can also find wonderful authentic Italian cuisine — you can't go wrong by making a beeline to any restaurant advertising *pate fraîche* (fresh homemade pasta). As befits such a sophisticated region, many towns on the Riviera boast a range of good ethnic restaurants, including Asian and African cuisines. And it's no coincidence that the birthplace of the thong offers the best selection of vegetarian restaurants in France. The region's proximity to the Mediterranean means fish is always on the menu: Plan to feast on steamy fish stews like *bourride* and *bouillabaisse,* sauces like *tapenade* (olive paste) and *aïoli* (a garlic mayonnaise), and lots of freshly caught fish and shellfish.

The French Riviera

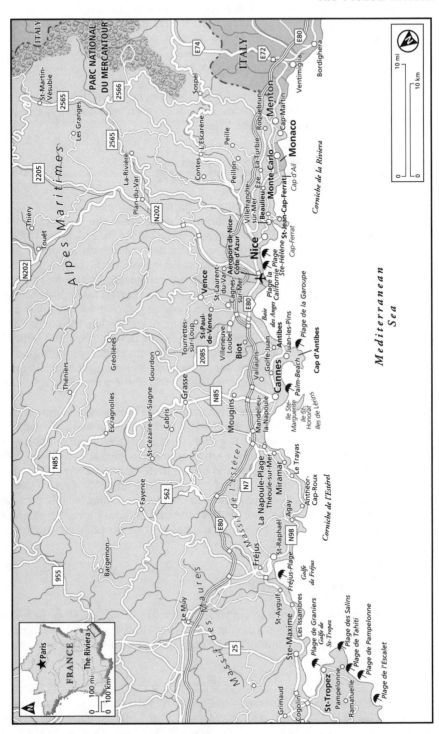

Pokey regional trains run along the coast from Marseille all the way to Italy, making stops at St-Raphaël (where you can take boats to St-Tropez in season), Cannes, Antibes, Biot (the train station is about 8 km/5 miles from the village), Nice, Beaulieu, and Monaco, as well as a dozen other towns. For details on getting to each town on the Riviera, see the individual town sections in this chapter.

When taking trains and buses on the Riviera, sit on the right side if you're going east and on the left side if you're going west in order to get the spectacular coastal view.

St-Tropez: Sun and Fun

Forget all the hype about topless bathing, hedonistic bar scenes, and preening celebrities — **St-Tropez** is hands down the Riviera's most charming town, a pastel-colored fishing village that happens to be one of the most glamorous spots on earth. Just don't come in July or August, when dense crowds make even a stroll in front of the yacht-filled harbor nearly impossible. Unlike other Riviera towns, St-Tropez has a perfectly preserved center — a picturesque port unmarred by high-rise hotels and virtually unchanged for over a century. (For evidence, visit the portside Impressionist museum L'Annonciade to see the early-1900s images of St-Tropez.) Bustling cafes crowd the old port, and behind them the winding village streets beckon with exclusive boutiques and romantic restaurants. All paths seem to lead up to the citadel, a sixteenth-century fort perched at the top of the town.

The beaches of St-Tropez are a lively scene — a not-to-be-missed part of the Tropezienne experience. The most famous beaches are located several miles from town and lined with restaurants and clubs. **Pampelonne Beach,** on the peninsula's southeast coast, is perhaps the most famous (or notorious) stretch of sand on the Riviera. After a day on the beach, it's time to gear up for a great dinner and a taste of St-Tropez after dark. The crowd is young and starts out late: Dinner is at 10 p.m. and bar hopping begins shortly thereafter. If you aren't into the bar scene, you may enjoy strolling along the old port or people watching from one of the portside cafes.

Getting there

St-Tropez is difficult to get to without a car (no trains stop there) or even with a car, so plan on at least a half-day of travel to reach this popular resort. Summer traffic onto the peninsula can be bumper-to-bumper for miles.

The closest major bus-and-train hub is **St-Raphaël,** 38 km (23.6 miles) east of St-Tropez. **Buses** from Cannes to St-Raphaël take 70 minutes and cost 36F ($5), and buses to St-Tropez from St-Raphaël take an additional 50 minutes and cost an additional 52F ($7). St-Raphaël is on the main

St-Tropez

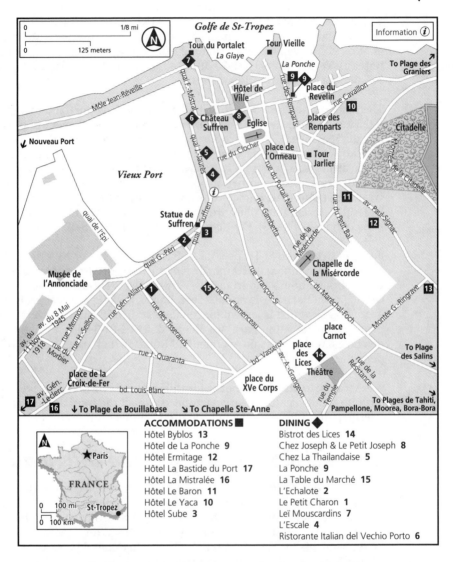

ACCOMMODATIONS ■	DINING ◆
Hôtel Byblos **13**	Bistrot des Lices **14**
Hôtel de La Ponche **9**	Chez Joseph & Le Petit Joseph **8**
Hôtel Ermitage **12**	Chez La Thailandaise **5**
Hôtel La Bastide du Port **17**	La Ponche **9**
Hôtel La Mistralée **16**	La Table du Marché **15**
Hôtel Le Baron **11**	L'Echalote **2**
Hôtel Le Yaca **10**	Le Petit Charon **1**
Hôtel Sube **3**	Leï Mouscardins **7**
	L'Escale **4**
	Ristorante Italian del Vechio Porto **6**

coastal train line for the Riviera. A train from Nice to St-Raphaël takes 50 minutes and costs 59F ($8); trains from Cannes to St Raphaël take half an hour and cost 37F ($5). Other nearby train stations are at Toulon (60 km/37.3 miles), Cannes (82 km/51 miles), Nice (103 km/64 miles), and Marseille (134 km/83.3 miles). For train information, call ☎ **08-36-35-35-39** or 08-36-35-35-35. For bus info, call Forum bus at ☎ **04-94-95-16-71.**

Transports Maritimes Raphaëlois (☎ **04-94-95-17-46**) runs a shuttle boat service between St-Raphaël and St-Tropez. Boats run daily (in season), taking 50 minutes and costing 60F ($9) one way. From April to June, September, and October, only a couple of shuttle boats travel between St-Raphaël and St-Tropez each week. St-Tropez is about 20 minutes by boat from St-Maxime, and two companies make frequent shuttle boat trips between them daily (in season): **Transports Maritimes M.M.G.** (☎ 04-94-96-51-00), running from April to November 4, and **Les Bateaux Verts** (☎ 04-94-49-29-39). Both charge 64F ($9) for adults and 32F ($4.60) for children 12 and over.

The major airports nearest to St-Tropez are the **Aéroport Toulon-Hyères** (56.3 km/35 miles away), **Aéroport International de Nice–Côte d'Azur** (91 km/56.5 miles), and **Aéroport International de Marseille-Provence** (115 km/71.5 miles). There are offices for all major car-rental agencies at the airports. A taxi from Nice airport to St-Tropez is 1,300F ($176). The distance from the other airports to St-Tropez makes a rental car your best option. Air France runs a **boat shuttle** from Nice's airport to St-Tropez, three times daily, from June to October, with the 1¼-hour trip costing 200F ($29). For details, call ☎ 08-02-80-28-02.

If you're **driving** to St-Tropez, take A8 from Marseille or Nice and follow the signs. Depending on traffic, driving to St-Tropez from Marseille takes about 2 hours and from Nice Airport takes about 1½ hours. Driving from Paris takes about seven hours. Parking is a real problem in St-Tropez, which is known for the fastest towing on the Riviera. The best parking lot is the **Parc des Lices** (☎ 04-94-97-34-46) beneath place des Lices, with access on avenue Paul-Roussel. It charges 12F ($1.70) per hour.

A great time to visit St-Tropez is for the **Voilles de St-Tropez,** a weeklong antique yacht regatta in early October. Contact the tourist office (see "Getting around and getting information" in this section) for details.

Getting around and getting information

The area around St-Tropez is somewhat hilly, but you can bike to most of the beaches on the peninsula. A scooter is a good way to get to the beaches of Pampelonne, which are further away. You can rent bikes, scooters, and motorbikes at **Holiday Bikes** (15 av. du Général-Leclerc; ☎ 04-94-97-09-39); **Scooter Station** (12 av. du Général-Leclerc; ☎ 04-94-97-62-40), scooters only; **Espace 83** (2 av. du Général-Leclerc; ☎ 04-94-80-00), scooters and motorbikes only; or **Mas** (3 rue Quaranta; ☎ 04-94-97-00-60). Rentals start at 50F ($7) per day for bikes; motorbikes and scooters start at 99F ($14) per day. These shops are open daily 9 a.m. to 12:30 p.m. and 3 to 7 p.m.

You can rent a car, scooter, or bike at **Locazur,** located at route des Plages, near the Plage de Bouillabaisse (☎ 04-94-97-57-85). Car rentals start at 350F ($50) per day.

About every half-hour daily 8 a.m. to 5 p.m. in summer, and mornings only during the off-season (October to May), free **beach shuttles** leave from place des Lices to the beaches of Pampellone and Salins. If you drive to the beaches, you'll have to pay around 22F ($3.15) for parking. You should keep in mind that taxi fees in St-Tropez are very high. You can also take a **water taxi** to the beaches: **Taxi de Mer "Le Royale"** (☎ 06-09-53-15-47) runs service to and from the beaches daily from June to September 9 a.m. to midnight (in season). The water taxi, which will pick you up at the port and drop you at any beach, costs 1,200F ($171) one way and 1,800F ($257) round-trip. The boat seats a maximum of 6 people, and the price is the same no matter how many passengers make the trip. The boat ride takes about 35 minutes.

The **tourist office** is at quai Jean-Jaurès (☎ 04-94-97-45-21; E-mail: tourisme@nova.fr; Internet: www.nova.fr/saint-tropez). It's open daily: July and August 9:30 a.m. to 1 p.m. and 2 to 10 p.m. and September to June 9 a.m. to noon and 2 to 6 p.m. If you want to send or check on e-mail, head to **Cyber-FCDCI Internet** (2 av. Paul-Roussel; ☎ 04-94-54-84-81), where access costs 35F ($5) per half-hour. It's open Monday to Saturday 9 a.m. to 1 p.m. and 2:30 to 7 p.m.

Where to stay

Hôtel La Bastide du Port

$$$ St-Tropez

This 26-room hotel is located across from the bay, near the new port, within walking distance of Bouillabaisse beach and a five-minute walk from the center of town. Don't let the bland exterior fool you: The high-ceiling rooms are very cheerful, with tile floors, large windows, and wrought-iron chandeliers. The rooms in the front of the hotel face the harbor and have balconies with bay views. But despite soundproof windows, these rooms are definitely noisier, as the hotel is on the main road into town. The rooms in the rear look out on the palm-tree-lined courtyard where breakfast is served in good weather.

Port du Pilon. ☎ *04-94-97-87-95. Fax: 04-94-97-91-00. E-mail:* HOTEL-LA-BASTIDE-DU-PORT@wanadoo.fr. *Free parking. Rack rates: 650–800F ($93–$114) double. Breakfast: 50F ($7). MC, V.*

Hôtel Byblos

$$$$$ St-Tropez

This four-star hotel, a cluster of stucco buildings painted in cool Mediterranean colors high above the village near the citadel, is St-Tropez's most exclusive. The 112 rooms and suites are elegant, as you'd expect, decorated with antiques and statuary. The staff can be a tad snooty — the better to handle the demanding clientele. The complex includes boutiques, restaurants, a bar, and the Cap du Roi disco, which attracts the elite of St-Tropez. The centerpiece of the garden courtyard is a large pool, where you may want to spend the day while the staff caters to your every whim.

Av. Paul-Signac. ☎ *04-94-56-68-00. Fax: 04-94-56-68-01. Internet:* www.byblos. com. *E-mail:* saint-tropez@byblos.com. *Parking: 170F ($24). Rack rates: 2,500–3,850F ($357–$550) double; 4,700–9,000F ($671–$1,286) suite. Breakfast: 140F ($20). Closed mid-Oct to mid-Apr. AE, DC, MC, V.*

Hôtel de La Ponche

$$$$ St-Tropez

This 22-room hotel is on a narrow winding street in the heart of historic St-Tropez. The rear overlooks the fisherman's port, and the simple cottages have an authentic charm. The pretty rooms sport designer linens and antique lamps, and many have large private balconies with sea views; others look out over the church tower and tiled roofs of the village. There are four suites that are ideal for families. On-site is a popular restaurant whose large terrace overlooks the harbor. The Ponche is popular with Americans, who seem to prefer its understated elegance to the more blatant luxury at the Byblos. The hotel offers an unusual amenity for late sleepers: Breakfast is served until 3 p.m.

3 rue des Remparts (place du Revellin). ☎ *04-94-97-02-53. Fax: 04-94-97-78-61. Internet:* www.laponche.com. *E-mail:* hotel←ponche.com. *Parking: 100F ($14). Rack rates: 1,200–2,000F ($171–$286) double; 2,800 ($400) suite. Breakfast: 100F ($14). MC, V.*

Hôtel Ermitage

$$$ St-Tropez

The most common comment among Americans about this hotel is that the 27 rooms are too small. Nevertheless, the English-speaking staff is particularly welcoming, the prices are good, and the hotel is well situated at the top of the hill near the exclusive Byblos. Some rooms have views over the gardens and a distance view out to sea; others look toward the citidel, past a noisy road. All of the rooms are simple and clean, although they're undoubtedly small; the larger rooms are light and airy, with large arched windows looking out over the rooftops and to the sea. The hotel has a pretty bar area with a stone fireplace and a patio that overlooks the harbor.

Av. Paul-Signac. ☎ *04-94-97-52-33. Fax: 04-94-97-10-43. Free parking. Rack rates: 590–990F ($84–$141) double. Breakfast: 65F ($9). MC, V.*

Hôtel la Mistralee

$$$$ St-Tropez

This seven-room hotel may be the most unique option in St-Tropez. The Mistralee is also the newest hotel in St-Tropez, as it was converted from a private manor into a luxury hotel in 2000. This 1850 villa is the former vacation home of Alexandre, a famous Parisian hairdresser born and raised in St-Tropez. His tastes ran to the baroque (the home is full of opulent details), from elaborate ceiling moldings to festive wall murals to gilded paneled walls. The rooms are spacious and decorated with unusual antiques. The grounds are unique: You follow the red ochre columns through a lush garden to a tiled pool with chaises under Japanese umbrellas. Thick pool towels are stacked in wicker baskets in the Roman villa–style pool house.

1 av. du Général-Leclerc (near place des Lices). ☎ *04-98-12-91-12. Fax: 04-98-12-91-13. Internet:* www.mistralee.fr. *E-mail:* mistralee@infonie. fr. *Free parking in courtyard. Rack rates: 1,800–3,000F ($257–$429) double; 5,500F ($786) suite. Breakfast: 120F ($17). MC, V.*

Hôtel le Baron

$$ St-Tropez

This 11-room hotel at the top of the hill near the entrance to the citadel gardens has an ultracool feeling about it. The building also serves as a cafe, restaurant, and bar with an African-themed decor, including such decorations as wooden sculptures and a surprisingly lifelike elephant head. The rooms are light and airy, although they are small, and some have French doors leading to tiny balconies. The location is good, as there are a number of funky little restaurants, shops, and galleries on the old winding streets nearby. The management here also runs the Key West beach concession, with a restaurant at the Pampelonne beach and the Pub Café Barock on rue de la Citadelle near the hotel.

23 rue de l'Aioli. ☎ *04-94-97-06-57. Fax: 04-94-97-58-72. E-mail:* hotel.le.baron@ wanadoo.fr. *Rack rates: 450–650F ($64–$93) double. Breakfast: 45F ($6). MC, V.*

Hôtel Sube

$$$ St-Tropez

You can't get any more centrally located than this 28-room second-floor hotel on the old port behind the bronze statue of Vice-Admiral Pierre André de Suffren. The rooms are simple and small with perfect harbor views. Dashing young sailors hang out in the nautical-themed bar, where the balcony has a panoramic bay view. Alas, you won't get a room here unless you book way ahead. And don't plan on getting to sleep until the wee hours; your fellow guests like to party.

15 quai Suffren (on the old port). ☎ *04-94-97-30-04. Fax: 04-94-54-89-08. Rack rates: 590–1,500F ($84–$214) double. Breakfast: 65F ($9). AE, MC, V.*

Hôtel Le Yaca

$$$$ St-Tropez

This quintessentially Mediterranean hotel, which is elegant yet cozy, consists of 27 rooms and suites in four adjoining historic houses. All rooms are individually decorated in a modern style, with touches like marble fireplaces; some have terraces or balconies with water views, and others overlook St-Tropez's winding streets. The least expensive rooms are small but just as pretty as the expensive rooms. A very fine Italian restaurant with terrace seating in summer, as well as a good bar, can be found on-site. Breakfast is served in the poolside garden in summer, or in your room. The English-speaking management is extra-accommodating and professional. In July and August, a shuttle service is available for both the local beaches (free) and from airports (charge).

1 bd. d'Aumale. ☎ *04-94-55-81-00. Fax: 04-94-97-58-50. E-mail:* hotel-le-yaca@ hotel-le-yaca.fr. *Rack rates: 1,350–2,500F ($193–$357) double; 3,700F ($529) suite; 5,400F ($771) duplex suite. Breakfast: 100–150F ($14–$21). Closed mid-Oct to mid-Apr. AE, DC, MC, V.*

Where to dine

Bistrot des Lices

$$ St-Tropez   PROVENÇAL

On bustling place des Lices (a great people-watching spot), Bistrot des Lices is a reasonably priced choice with indoor and outdoor seating. The best bargain is the lunch menu that gives you a first course and second course or a *plat du jour* plus dessert. Provençal cuisine is featured, but you can choose from a number of good Italian choices as well. Chef Christophe Jourdren's most popular dish is *salade de langoustines rôties à la fleur de thym* (prawn salad), and he makes a lovely ratatouille. Chocolate fans will drool over the moist cake called *moelleux minute tout chocolat.*

3 place des Lices. ☎ *04-94-55-82-82. Meals: Main courses 160–190F ($23–$27); menus 99F ($14) at lunch, 195F ($28) at dinner. AE, MC, V. Open: Daily noon to 2:30 p.m. and 6–11 p.m.*

Chez Joseph and Le Petit Joseph

$$ St-Tropez   PROVENÇAL

These side-by-side restaurants are serviced by the same kitchen, and the menus are quite similar. Le Petit Joseph, which doesn't take reservations, is quieter and more romantic, with low beamed ceilings, an Asian decor, and cozy banquettes. Chez Joseph, where you sit with other patrons at long tables, tends to be completely booked and packed at 10 p.m. Both restaurants have outdoor seating, but while Le Petit has just a few tables, Chez has a large terrace. The traditional yet creatively presented cuisine emphasizes fish, and the menu changes often. For dessert, the *parfait léger* is a treat — vanilla custard with chocolate powder on a cherry crumble with a scoop of cherry-vanilla ice cream and fresh fruit.

1 place de l'Hôtel-de-Ville. ☎ *04-94-97-01-66. Meals: Main courses 180–250F ($26–$36); menus 180F ($26) and 245F ($35). AE, MC, V. Open: Daily noon to 2 p.m. and 7:30–10:30 p.m.*

Chez la Thailandaise

$$ St-Tropez   THAI

For something a little different, try this atmospheric restaurant on the harbor. The entrance is flanked by little stone elephants, and the decor includes plenty of Asian touches, like bamboo chairs. House specialties include sautéed duck with mushrooms and oyster sauce, chicken salad with fresh ginger, and fresh squid and prawns with Thai herbs and garlic. There are also the usual Thai dishes, like crispy spring rolls and pad Thai. Dessert is a plate of exotic fruit. They have menus in English.

Quai Jean-Jaurès (on the old port). ☎ *04-94-97-88-22. Reservations recommended. Meals: Main courses 130–170F ($19–$24); tasting menu 340F ($50). AE, MC, V. Open: Apr–Oct daily noon to 2 p.m. and 7:30–10:30 p.m.*

La Ponche

$$ St-Tropez   PROVENÇAL

This stylish restaurant in the chi-chi Hôtel de La Ponche is exceptional — boasting great food, service, and views — and it's actually not as expensive as you may think. The locale can't be beat, on the city's ancient ramparts next to an old stone city gate, overlooking the sea and fishing port. Chef Christian Geay highlights summery dishes like *salade de crustaces à la vinaigrette de truffes* (seafood salad with truffles) and *moules à la marinière* (mussels with red sauce). The chicken preparations tend to be creative. The special dessert is *nougat glace au coulis de framboise* (nougat ice cream, which has almonds and honey, with puréed strawberries).

3 rue des Ramparts (in the Hotel de La Ponche). ☎ *04-94-97-02-53. Meals: Main courses 110–210F ($16–$30); menus 130F ($19) at lunch, 190F ($27) and 250F ($36) at dinner. AE, MC, V. Open: Apr to mid-Nov daily noon to 2:30 p.m. and 7:30–10:30 p.m.*

La Table du Marché

$$ St-Tropez   PROVENÇAL

The pastries in the window display cases look so exquisite, you may be tempted to stop for a bite. Give in to your temptation. Christophe Leroy runs this épicerie, bistro, and sushi bar. The sushi is fairly expensive: A plate of sashimi, maki, and sushi will set you back 290F ($41). But the *marché* (market) menu is a pretty good value. On the 99F ($14) set menu you get a *plat du jour*, dessert, and glass of wine. The most expensive item on the menu is penne pasta with truffles. The restaurant also serves salads, quiches, and sandwiches.

38 rue Georges-Clemenceau. ☎ *04-94-97-85-20. Meals: Main courses 90–180F ($13–$26) sushi menu, 50–220F ($7–$31) market menu; menu 99F ($14). AE, V. Open: Daily 10 a.m.–3 p.m. and 7–10 p.m. Closed Jan–March and mid-Nov to mid-Dec.*

L' Echalote

$$ St-Tropez PROVENÇAL

This port-side restaurant draws crowds to its gardenlike terrace. The menu emphasizes delicacies of the land and sea — for example, the *terrine pêcheur* is light and fluffy, prepared with freshly caught fish. The *andouillette de Troyes au tomate provençal et pomme au four* is a special sausage from the region served with a garlic and tomato sauce and baked apples. Foie gras fans will want to try the "trilogy," three types of foie gras grandly presented. They make a mean chocolate cake, too.

35 rue du G. Allard (on the port). ☎ *04-94-54-83-26. Meals: Main courses 80–165F ($11–$24); menus 105F ($15) and 165F ($24). AE, MC, V. Open: Daily noon to 2 p.m. and 7–9 p.m. Closed Thurs lunch in season and closed Thurs all day off-season.*

Le Petit Charon

$$ St-Tropez PROVENÇAL

Anne Violaine and Christian Benoit own this charming little restaurant. The small menu is not so much limited as it is focused on a few items prepared perfectly. The fish soup and gazpacho with mussels and herbs are fine summer fare. The main courses always include freshly caught fish of the day simply prepared, as well as a scallop risotto with truffles. If you're looking for heartier fare, you may want to choose lamb, beef, or duck served with delicacies like cèpe mushrooms and homemade gnocchi.

6 rue des Charrons. ☎ *04-94-97-73-78. Reservations recommended. Meals: Main courses 90–115F ($13–$16). MC, V. Open: Daily noon to 2 p.m. and 7:30–9:30 p.m.*

Leï Mouscardins

$$$$ St-Tropez PROVENÇAL

Chef Laurent Tarridec runs the fanciest and most expensive restaurant in town, and because it's set on the second floor of a port-side building, all tables have harbor views. You can splurge on regional dishes like *bourride,* the hearty fish stew made here with apples, onions, and pears. Other recommendable dishes are *grenouilles menunière* (frogs' legs) and *épaule de lapin* (rabbit), but preparations of fresh fish, locally caught, are the specialty. The special Grand Marnier soufflé is a must-try. In good weather, seating is available on the terrace.

Tour du Portalet (on the old port). ☎ *04-94-97-29-00. Reservations required. Meals: Main courses 180–245F ($26–$35); menus 280F ($40) at lunch, 335f ($48) at dinner.*

AE, DC, MC, V. Open: June–Sept Mon–Sat noon to 2 p.m. and 7:30–10 p.m.; Oct–May Tues–Sat noon to 2 p.m. and 7:30–9:30 p.m.

L'Escale

$$ St-Tropez PROVENÇAL

Fish lovers will be attracted by the sight of the live fish and lobsters in tanks at the entrance. Most of the seating at this large harbor-side restaurant is in a glass-enclosed terrace, so you can do some people watching in any weather; however, the banquettes and wicker chairs are packed close together. Try one of the multitiered seafood plates — the three-tiered seafood plate (loaded with oysters, shrimp, clams, mussels, lobster, and more) is an excellent choice for four people. You can get the famous *tarte tropezienne* here, made just down the street at Sénéquier. And for after your meal, the restaurant offers special coffees from New Guinea, Ethiopia, Guatemala, and Haiti.

9 quai Jean-Jaurès (on the port). ☎ *04-94-97-00-63. Meals: Main courses 85–185F ($12–$26); menus 195F ($28) and 310F ($44). AE, DC, MC, V. Open: Daily noon to 2:30 p.m. and 7:30–10:30 p.m. Closed Mon off-season.*

Ristorante Italian del Vechio Porto

$$ St-Tropez ITALIAN

This lively restaurant, with a large outdoor seating area on the port, has excellent prices and good food. The huge sizzling pan of paella out front attracts many customers to the restaurant. Waiters rush by, juggling pizzas delivered to the long family-style tables, along with *moules* (mussels) done ten ways and homemade pasta. The menus are in English.

Quai Jean-Juarès (on the old port). ☎ *04-94-97-58-04. Meals: Main courses 60–160F ($9–$23); menu 145F ($20). MC, V. Open: Daily noon to 2:30 p.m. and 7–10 p.m.*

Exploring the town and the beaches

After you walk around St-Tropez's old port, head to the beautiful small **L'Annonciade, Musée de St-Tropez** (place Grammont; ☎ 04-94-97-04-01) to see how artists painted this port about 75 years ago. As it turns out, the port hasn't changed much. The museum is housed in a former chapel, an austere church built next to the port in 1568. The highlights among the colorful, cheerful collection of Impressionist and fauvist works are paintings by Derain, Van Dongen, Seurat, Braque, Matisse, Signac, Bonnard, Utrillo, and Dufy. It's open Wednesday to Monday (except January 1, May 1, and December 25): June to September 10 a.m. to noon and 3 to 7 p.m., and October and December to May 10 a.m. to noon and 2 to 6 p.m. Admission is 30F ($4.30) for adults and 15F ($2.15) for students and seniors.

If you walk past the old port and up quai Jean-Jaurès, you'll soon come to the **Château Suffren,** built in 980. The building is now an attractive art gallery with large plate-glass windows overlooking the port. Pass through place de l'Hôtel de Ville to rue de la Ponche and follow it for several blocks. Take a right on rue des Remparts, which turns into rue Aire du Chemin and eventually dead ends at rue Misericorde. Walk left for two blocks to reach the **Chapelle de la Misércorde,** which has a brightly colored tiled roof.

Port Grimaud, 4 miles northwest of St-Tropez, is an attractive village made to look old, where stone houses sit beside canals and people moor their boats practically right outside their doors. There are a number of fine shops and restaurants. You can get there by driving 3 miles west on A98 and 1 mile north on route 98.

In St-Tropez, and along most of the French Riviera, going to the *plage* (beach) means setting up camp at a concession location that provides beach chairs, umbrellas, snacks, a restaurant, a bar, and sometimes water sports. When you choose a beach, you're choosing a business to patronize for the day. The most popular St-Tropez beaches are Bouillabaisse, Graniers, Salins, Pampellone, and Tahiti.

Here's what you'll find at each of these popular beaches:

- ✔ **Bouillabaisse:** An easy walk from town, this beach offers **Golf Azur** (☎ 04-94-97-07-38), a restaurant that specializes in grilled fish. A section of beach at Bouillabaisse, just west of town, has clean shallow waters, making it a good choice for kids. Parking costs 22F ($3.15) per day.

- ✔ **Les Graniers:** This is one of the best beaches for families and is within walking distance of town. There's free parking and **Les Graniers** (☎ 04-94-97-38-50), the main restaurant at the beach, is one of the better beach concessions. It serves the usual provençal cuisine, lots of grilled fish, and *moules frites* (mussels and french fries). Its 100F ($14) *plat du jour* is reasonably priced when compared to most restaurants.

- ✔ **Pampelonne:** Here, there are about 35 businesses on a 4.8 km (3-mile) stretch, located about 10 km (6.2 miles) from St-Tropez. You'll need a car, bike, or scooter to get from town to the beach. Parking is about 22F ($3.15) for the day. Famous hedonistic spots along Pampelonne include the cash-only club **La Voile Rouge,** which features bawdy spring break–style entertainment and actively excludes kids and seniors (its legal problems may close it before the summer of 2001), and **Le Club 55** (☎ 04-94-79-80-14), a large, expensive nightclub set up like an exclusive garden cafe on the beach. **Plage des Jumeaux** (☎ 04-94-79-84-21), another popular Pampelonne beach spot, is a good place for families with young kids because it has playground equipment. **Marine Air Sports** (☎ 06-07-22-43-97) rents boats; **Team Water Sports**

(☎ 04-94-79-82-41) rents jet-skis, scooters, water-skiing equipment, and boats.

✔ **Salins:** Located just north of Pampelonne and closer to the village of St-Tropez (3 km/1.9 miles from St-Tropez), this is a wide sandy beach, whose popularity is evident by how fast the parking lot fills up. Arrive early to get a good spot on the sand. Parking costs about 22F. The most popular restaurant on Salins beach is **Leï Salins** (☎ 04-94-97-04-40).

✔ **Tahiti:** This wild spot permits topless, and even nude, sunbathing. Tahiti beach is 5 km (3.1 miles) from St-Tropez and parking costs about 22F. This is known as the region's most decadent beach and tends to attract a young crowd interested in cruising.

The gulf of St-Tropez is so beautiful that you may be tempted to take a **boat ride.** Captain Henri (☎ 06-09-50-60-72) has been offering harbor cruises on his classic 1936 gaff-rigged wooden sailboat **Thule** since 1993. The 1½-hour cruise, with narration in English and other languages, costs 80F ($11) for adults and 40F ($6) for children under 10. From April to early October, tours leave daily at 2:30 and 4:30 p.m., cruising past oceanfront houses of celebrities like George Michael, Arnold Schwarzenegger, and Sylvester Stallone. You'll also pass Pampelonne Beach, where director Roger Vadim set the film *And God Created Woman,* which skyrocketed Brigitte Bardot to worldwide fame. If you like to participate, you can help to haul the sails as the boat cruises around the gulf.

Shopping

When strolling in St-Tropez, don't miss the **pedestrian alleys,** which are usually lined with exclusive shops. A rough guide: Shops on the harbor sell cheap sexy clothes and shops a few blocks from the harbor sell expensive sexy clothes. **Hermès** (☎ 04-94-97-04-29) is tucked into an old building on rue de la Ponche. The best shoe store (selection and price) is **Les Tropeziennes** on rue Georges Clémenceau near place des Lices (☎ 04-94-97-19-55). There are also a number of good housewares stores, like **HM France** (12 rue Georges Clémenceau; ☎ 04-94-97-84-37), a chain specializing in fine linens.

Jacqueline Thienot (12 rue Georges-Clémenceau; ☎ 04-94-97-05-70), situated down an ancient alley, is a very fine antiques shop whose proprietor speaks English. Perhaps the most surprising store in St-Tropez is **Le Jardin de Zita** (12 aire du Chemin; ☎ 04-94-97-37-44), a sort of high-class junk shop filled with odds and ends for decorating your bohemian yet stylish home. You can find a large selection of beautiful pottery at **Poterie Augier** (22 rue Georges Clémenceau; ☎ 04-94-97-12-55).

The **fish, vegetable, and flower market** is located down a tiled alley around the corner from the tourist office. It operates daily 8 a.m. to noon in summer and Tuesday to Sunday 8 a.m. to noon in winter. On Tuesday and Saturday mornings on place des Lices, there's an **outdoor market** with food, clothes, and *brocante* (flea-market finds).

Nightlife

St-Tropez is famous for its nightlife, and you'll have no problem finding a fun spot here. From partying at bars and clubs to people watching at cafes along the old port, there's something for everyone. The key words are *loud* and *late,* so take a disco nap and get ready to hit the town. Besides the in-town venues, there are also the beach clubs that stay rowdy until the wee hours (see "Exploring the town and the beaches" earlier in this section).

Live music adds to the merriment at the friendly **Kelly's Irish Pub** (quai F. Mistral; ☎ **04-94-54-89-11**), which serves Guinness and Irish whiskey, among other beverages. **Papagayo** (in the Résidence du Port, next to the harbor; ☎ **04-94-97-76-70**) is where the yachting crowd gathers for meeting and greeting. At the cool Hôtel Sube, partyers practically hang off the balcony of the second-floor **Bar Sube** (15 quai Suffren; ☎ **04-94-97-30-04**). **Chez Fuchs** (7 rue des Commercants; ☎ **04-94-97-01-25**) is popular with the younger crowd and stays open 'til midnight year-round. English is spoken here. Stop by cozy **Chez Palmyre** (2 rue du Petit Bal; ☎ **04-94-97-43-22**) during its 7 to 9 p.m. happy hour for cocktails and tapas.

In the Hôtel Byblos, **Les Caves du Roi** (avenue Paul Signac; ☎ **06-12-77-73-31**) is a swank hot disco. **Le Pigionnier** (13 rue de la Ponche; ☎ **04-94-97-36-85**) is a popular gay club. The **VIP Room** (Résidence du Port; ☎ **04-94-97-14-70**) is a bar and lounge, attracting all ages, next to the new port. A central cafe on the old port, **Sénéquier** (quai Jean-Jaurès; ☎ **04-94-97-00-90**) offers prime people watching and serves famous desserts. The **Café de Paris** (15 quai Suffren; ☎ **04-94-97-00-56**) is a popular brasserie/sushi bar beneath the Hôtel Sube. And the **Café des Arts** (place des Lices; ☎ **04-94-97-17-29**) is one of St-Tropez's most famous cafes.

Cannes: More Than Just the Film Festival

Cannes, famous for the annual International Film Festival, is the Riviera at its most gaudy and banal — and for some people that's reason enough to stop here. Overdevelopment has erased much of this seaside city's beauty, but it certainly has a fun quality and offers unrivaled people watching, as well as excellent shopping. The famous La Croisette board-walk along the beach is lined with "palaces," the four-star grand hotels that have long attracted the rich and famous.

Cannes

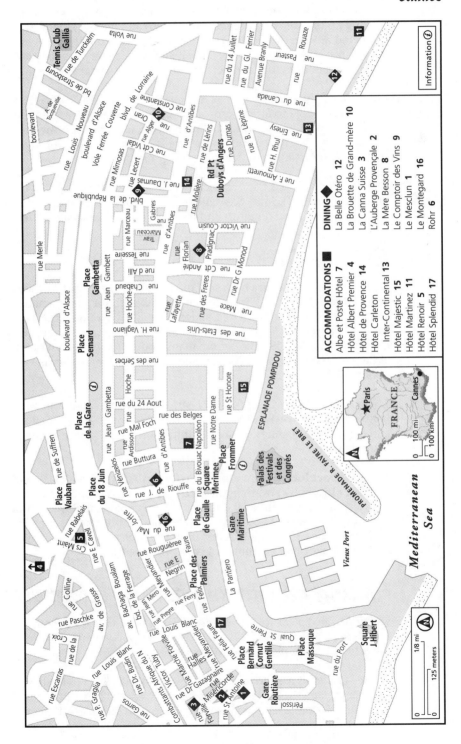

ACCOMMODATIONS
Albe et Poste Hôtel **7**
Hôtel Albert Premier **4**
Hôtel de Provence **14**
Hôtel Carleton
  Inter-Continental **13**
Hôtel Majestic **15**
Hôtel Martinez **11**
Hôtel Renoir **5**
Hôtel Splendid **17**

DINING
La Belle Otéro **12**
La Brouette de Grand-mère **10**
La Canna Suisse **3**
L'Auberge Provençale **2**
La Mère Besson **8**
Le Comptoir des Vins **9**
Le Mesclun **1**
Le Montegard **16**
Rohr **6**

Most visitors make a beeline for the Film Festival palace, a huge concrete monstrosity set on the beach. During the festival in May, images of stars walking up the steps on the red carpet, surrounded by paparazzi, are projected around the world. The city also spreads out the famous carpet in July, August, and December, so tourists can pose for photos. Handprints of directors and actors line the square near the steps.

I suggest that you avoid Cannes during the 10-day Film Festival in May. You won't be able to attend any of the fabulous events, and the crush of media people will be overwhelming. If you must visit during the festival, your best bet for celebrity spotting is to eat lunch or dinner at one of the beach restaurants owned by the grand hotels.

The best time to visit Cannes, a city of 70,000 people, is April, May (not during the festival), June, September, and October. July and August are so crowded it'll be difficult to find a square of sand or a cafe table.

Getting there

Cannes is a major Riviera hub, so it offers frequent train and bus service. From Paris, the fast **TGV train** to Cannes takes about 5 hours and costs 464 to 739F ($66 to $106). The Cannes **Gare SNCF** (train station) is on rue Jean-Jaurès (☎ 04-93-99-19-77). For information and reservations, call ☎ 08-36-35-35-39. **Buses** from many spots along the Riviera arrive at Cannes's **Gare Routière** (bus station) on place Bernard Cornut-Gentille (☎ 04-93-39-18-71).

Trans Côte d'Azur (☎ 04-92-98-71-30) runs **boats** to and from Monaco (130F/$19 round-trip) and St-Tropez (130F/$19 round-trip). They arrive and depart from Cannes's Gare Maritime at the port, at the end of rue Maréchal-Joffre.

The **Aéroport International de Nice–Côte d'Azur** (☎ 04-93-21-30-30) is 27 km (16.8 miles) from Cannes. There are two bus options from the Nice airport to the center of Cannes. The bus company **Rapides Côte d'Azur** (☎ 04-93-39-11-39) runs from the airport to Cannes for 75F ($11) and takes 30 minutes. A taxi from the Nice airport to the center of Cannes takes half an hour and costs 420F ($60).

Getting around and getting information

You don't need a car to get around Cannes; the city is quite compact. **Allo Taxi** (☎ 04-92-99-27-27) will drive you from one end of town to the other or make pickups at Nice's airport.

Cannes is a good base for exploring the region. It's 9 km (5.6 miles) from Antibes, 25 km (15.5 miles) from St-Paul-de-Vence, 32 km (19.9 miles) from Nice, 50 km (31.1 miles) from Monaco, and 79 km (49.1 miles) from St-Tropez. To rent a car, try **Access Rent a Car** (5 rue Latour-Maubourg; ☎ **04-93-94-06-05**) or **Alliance Location** (19 rue des Frerer Pradignac; ☎ **04-93-94-61-94**).

For bike and scooter rentals, try **Cycles Daniel** (2 rue du Pont-Romain; ☎ **04-93-99-90-30**), **Holiday Bikes** (16 rue du 14 Juillet; ☎ **04-97-06-30-30**), and **Locations Mistral** (4 rue Georges-Clemenceau; ☎ **04-93-99-25-25**).

The **main tourist office** is in the Palais des Festivals (to the left of the famous steps on the ground floor) on boulevard de la Croisette (☎ **04-93-39-24-53**; Internet: www.cannes-on-line.com), open daily 9 a.m. to 7 p.m. There's also an **office** in the train station (☎ **04-93-99-19-77**), open Monday to Saturday 9 a.m. to noon and 2 to 5 p.m. If you want to check on or send e-mail, head to **Asher Cyber Espace** (44 bd. Carnot; ☎ **04-92-99-03-01**), open Monday to Thursday 9 a.m. to 7 p.m. and Friday to Sunday 9 a.m. to noon.

Where to stay

Albe et Poste Hôtel

$$ Cannes

This 24-room hotel is the best budget option in Cannes. The location is very good; it is situated opposite the main post office, close to place de Gaulle, and just a few short blocks from La Croisette (the waterfront boardwalk). The rooms are simple and small, but comfortable, and come with the usual stable of amenities. New owners Nelly and Marcel Moura are top-notch hoteliers who pride themselves on service.

31 rue Bivouac Napoléon. ☎ *04-97-06-21-21. Fax: 04-97-06-21-27. E-mail:* albe-et-poste-hotel@wanadoo.fr. *Rack rates: 350–500F ($50–$71) double. Breakfast: 35F ($5). MC, V.*

Hôtel Albert Premier

$$ Cannes

The 11-room Albert Premier is a good budget choice. The hotel is on the far side of the main highway into Cannes, which is not an ideal location, but the staff is sincerely friendly, there's a small garden, and you won't find a better price for a decent room. Some third-floor rooms have distant water views, and all rooms have soundproof windows. The hotel also provides a bowl of fruit in the rooms (which is unusual for a two-star hotel).

68 av. de Grasse. ☎ *04-93-39-24-04. Fax: 04-93-38-83-75. Internet:* www.cannes-hotels.com. *Free parking. Rack rates: 300–360F ($43–$51) double. Breakfast: 35F ($5). MC, V.*

Hôtel Carleton Inter-Continental

$$$$ **Cannes**

One of the famous palace hotels on the waterfront (its two shapely domes make it an unmistakable landmark), the Carleton has long been popular with Americans. The grand entrance and the lobby, with its marble columns and frescoed ceiling, wowed the upper classes in 1912, when the hotel opened, and continue to do so. The 338 rooms and suites are as luxurious as you'd expect them to be, and a number have balconies with sea views; the 12-room imperial suite boasts its own elevator and butler. The hotel has four restaurants, including the deluxe La Belle Otéro (see "Where to dine"), plus an elegant bar and casino. The private beach across from the hotel is perfect for celebrity sightings. Other amenities are an indoor pool, a hot tub, a health club, and a tennis court. Be aware that by June the Carleton is usually fully booked through July and August.

58 bd. de la Croisette. ☎ *04-93-06-40-06. Fax: 04-93-06-40-25. Internet:* `http://cannes@interconti.com`*. Parking: 180F ($26). Rack rates: 1,680–4,090F ($240–$584) double. Breakfast: 130–175F ($19–$25). AE, DC, MC, V.*

Hôtel de Provence

$$ **Cannes**

Located behind a private garden, this 30-room hotel is a good choice if you are looking for a relatively inexpensive hotel. The location isn't bad either: It's in a relatively quiet neighborhood, only a few blocks from La Croisette. The hotel has a homey feel to it — in the public rooms, as well as in the guest rooms. Rooms are decorated simply, but with attention to detail, and include safes. All double rooms have terraces that offer views of the garden, with its century-old palm trees.

9 rue Molière. ☎ *04-93-38-44-35. Fax: 04-93-39-63-14. Internet:* `www.hotel-de-provence.com`*. Parking: 50F ($7). Rack rates: 400–550F ($57–$79) double. Breakfast: 40F ($6). Closed mid-Nov to mid-Dec. MC, V.*

Hôtel Majestic

$$$$ **Cannes**

Its bright-white undulating facade distinguishes the Majestic from the other grand hotels along La Croisette. The hotel also boasts a classically inspired lobby with immense Greek-style statues, a casino, and a garden courtyard. Of the 305 rooms and suites, 140 have been renovated in the past few years. The hotel's beach is known for having the best water-sports program, with instructors and rentals available. There's also a pool, health club, and tennis court. The fancy restaurant, La Villa des Lys, has a new young chef, Bruno Oger, who has received a number of accolades.

14 bd. de la Croisette. ☎ *04-92-98-77-00. Fax: 04-93-38-97-90. E-mail:* `majestic@lucienbarriere.com`*. Parking: 170F ($24). Rack rates: 1,290–4,900F ($184–$700) double. Breakfast: 140F ($20). Closed mid-Nov to Dec. AE, DC, MC, V.*

Hôtel Martinez

$$$$ **Cannes**

The largest of the grand palaces along La Croisette, this 393-room art deco hotel is also the site of Cannes's most famous deluxe restaurant, La Palme d'Or. But perhaps because the Martinez has become popular with group tours and conventions, it feels less elegant than the other hotels along La Croisette, even though it offers the same deluxe room amenities, like high-quality linens and marble baths. The hotel also has a pool, a hot tub, and tennis courts.

73 bd. de la Croisette. ☎ **04-92-98-73-00.** *Fax: 04-93-39-67-82. Internet:* www. hotel-martinez.com. *Parking: 160F ($23). Rack rates: 1,300–4,800F ($186–$686) double. Breakfast: 160F ($23). AE, DC, MC, V.*

Hôtel Renoir

$$$ **Cannes**

This stylish 27-room hotel is a good medium-priced choice, offering big hotel amenities. The rooms are cheerfully decorated in provençal style, with colorful bedspreads and painted furniture. While the hotel is a 10-minute walk from the public beach, it does have a private beach, and south-facing rooms on the upper floors have distant water views. But ask for a room facing north, because the south rooms face a busy highway (although they do have double soundproof windows to temper the noise). The reception desk can also change money for you.

7 rue Edith-Cavell. ☎ **04-92-99-62-62.** *Fax: 04-92-99-62-82. E-mail:* renoir@ worldnet.fr. *Parking: 60F ($9) day. Rack rates: 400–900F ($57–$129) double. Breakfast: 75F ($11). AE, MC, V.*

Hôtel Splendid

$$$ **Cannes**

The Splendid is for people who want a grand water-view hotel but don't want to splurge on the famous palace hotels a few blocks away. This 62-room hotel has an excellent location, just a block from the Palais des Festivals. The pretty belle époque facade gives you a good idea of the rooms, which are beautifully decorated and full of luxurious touches. Considering the location and amenities, this is a good-value lodging for Cannes, particularly since many of the rooms have water views. The hotel is next to place de Gaulle, one of the busiest squares in Cannes, but rooms have soundproof windows, so it's very quiet.

4 rue Félix-Faure (across from the port). ☎ **04-93-99-53-11.** *Fax: 04-93-99-55-02. E-mail:* hotel.splendid.cannes@wanadoo.fr. *Rack rates: 450–1,000F ($64–$143) double. Breakfast: 75F ($11). Closed Nov–Dec. AE, MC, V.*

Hotels do book up in Cannes. If you're having trouble getting a reservation, try **Cannes Réservations** (8 bd. d'Alsace; ☎ **08-10-06-12-12;** Fax: 04-93-99-06-60; E-mail: `cannes-reservation@en-france.com`), open Monday to Saturday 9 a.m. to 7 p.m.

Where to dine

La Belle Otéro

$$$$ Cannes   PROVENÇAL

If it's swellegance you're after, muster the courage to march into the Carleton and take the elevator to the seventh floor ("*septième étage, s'il vous plaît*") for an extravagant meal at La Belle Otéro, named after a nineteenth-century courtesan. The dining room has a deluxe design, perfect for European royalty and Hollywood celebrities. If you like to dine incognito behind shades, the restaurant also has a magnificent terrace with sweeping coastal views. While every dish is special, chef François Chauveau would like to draw your attention to the *Milanaise de gnocchis aux asperges violettes de provence* (gnocchi with purple-tipped asparagus), *grillade de daurade royale du pays* (grilled sea bream), and *carré d'agneau de Sisteron en gratinée d'olives* (rack of lamb with a crusty top of olives).

58 bd. de la Croisette (in the Hôtel Carlton Inter-Continental). ☎ *04-92-99-51-10. Reservations required. Meals: Main courses 250–480F ($36–$69); menus 290F ($41) at lunch with wine and coffee, 410F ($59) and 620F (89) at dinner. AE, DC, MC, V. Open: Wed–Sat noon to 2 p.m.; Tues–Sat 7:30–9:30 p.m. Closed early June to early July and late Oct to mid-Nov.*

L'Auberge Provençale

$$$ Cannes   PROVENÇAL

The oldest restaurant in town, L'Auberge Provençale opened in Le Suquet in 1860 and has been serving traditional regional dishes ever since. The 150F ($21) menu, which has six main dish choices, is a good value. Although the cooking can be inconsistent, several dishes are always good, including *bouillabaisse* (the rich fish stew) and *carré d'agneau de Sisteron* (rack of lamb), a specialty of the region. For dessert, the best bet is *le petit crêpe flambé à la liqueur d'orange* (a flaming crêpe with orange liqueur). A terrace provides outdoor seating in summer.

10 rue St-Antoine. ☎ *04-92-99-27-17. Reservations accepted. Meals: Main courses 105–320F ($15–$46); menu 150F ($21). AE, DC, MC, V. Open: Daily noon to 2:30 p.m. and 7–11:30 p.m.*

La Brouette de Grand-mère

$$ Cannes   PROVENÇAL

Locals love this old-fashioned restaurant called "grandmother's wheelbarrow," serving homey, traditional food. The restaurant is very small and you must make reservations. The 200F ($29) menu may seem expensive, but it's actually a real bargain because wine and coffee are included. The few seats on the outdoor terrace fill up first. The menu is loaded with regional dishes like *bourride* (the traditonal fish soup) and *lottes niçoise* (monkfish prepared with herbs).

9 bis rue d'Oran (off rue d'Antibes). ☎ *04-93-39-12-10. Reservations necessary. Meals: Main courses 55–125F ($8–$18); menu 200F ($29). MC, V. Open: Mon–Sat 7:30–9:30 p.m. Closed Nov to mid-Dec.*

La Canna Suisse

$$ Cannes   SWISS

Two sisters own this little Le Suquet restaurant that's decked out like a Swiss chalet and specializes in fondue. The menu features all types of cheese fondues (particularly cheese of the region). This is the place to head to in the off-season when there's a bit of chill in the air.

24 rue Forville (Le Suquet). ☎ *04-93-99-01-27. Meals: Main courses 50–90F ($7–$13). MC, V. Open: Mon–Sat 7:30–9:30 p.m. Closed July.*

La Mère Besson

$$ Cannes   PROVENÇAL

The candlelit tables under the awning at La Mère Besson, located on a quiet street just a few blocks up from La Croisette, are among the best places to dine in Cannes. This classic restaurant has been dishing out homecooking to families since the 1930s. The daily specials here are like a course in provençal cuisine, featuring *osso bucco* (veal braised with tomatoes) and *lapereau farci aux herbes de Provence* (baked rabbit stuffed with meat and provençal herbs).

13 rue des Frères-Pradignac. ☎ *04-93-39-59-24. Reservations necessary. Meals: Main courses 70–140F ($10–$20); menus 100F ($14) and 170F ($24). AE, MC, V. Open: Tues–Fri noon to 2 p.m.; Mon–Sat 7:30–10 p.m.*

Le Comptoir des Vins

$$ Cannes   PROVENÇAL

This wine bar/restaurant in an atmospheric cellar is a favorite hangout for oenophiles, and a lively scene on most nights. There are daily hearty specialties, like fresh pastas and *blanquette de veau* (veal stew), as well as a large assortment of pâtés to be enjoyed with various wines, by the bottle or glass.

13 bd. de la République. ☎ *04-93-68-13-26. Meals: Main courses 49–150F ($7–$21); menu 140F ($20). MC, V. Open: Mon–Sat 7:30–10:30 p.m.*

Le Mesclun

$$$ Cannes   PROVENÇAL

You can dine fancy, without breaking the bank, at this beautiful little restaurant in Le Suquet. After the restaurants in the grand hotels along La Croisette, this is the best dining experience you can find in Cannes. Everything seems gilded in this bi-level dining room, from the chairs to the picture frames. The kitchen also has a golden touch, turning out traditional cuisine with gourmet inspiration (there's an English menu). For a starter, the chef recommends the sautéed duck liver with a salad, warm oysters, homemade ravioli with mushrooms and artichokes, or fish soup with scallop carpaccio. Promising main courses are the prime rib of veal gratinéed with dried fruit and sweet white-wine sauce; roasted sea bass with mushrooms, shallots, and watercress; and lamb cutlets with black-bean ragôut. The standout desserts are the warm apple tart with cinnamon ice cream and caramel custard ice cream with jasmine flavoring.

16 rue St-Antoine (Le Suquet). ☎ *04-93-99-45-19. Reservations accepted. Meals: Main courses 130–180F ($19–$26); menu 170F ($24); tasting menu 260F ($37). MC, V. Open: Thurs–Tues 6:30–11 p.m. Closed mid-Nov to Dec.*

Le Montegard

$$ Cannes   VEGETARIAN

This intimate restaurant, just north of place du Gaulle, is a real treat. The elegant little dining room is decorated with yellow tiles, provençal fabrics, and a few antiques. In addition to the menu, there are several fixed-price choices, including an all-vegetarian menu and two menus featuring fish. The restaurant features creative vegetarian cooking with wonderful preparations of fresh organic vegetables — some are quite unusual. Each dish looks like a work of art with colors, textures, and flavors combining in exciting ways. The wine list concentrates on organic wines. The homemade desserts, like the hot fig tart wrapped in pastry, are exceptional.

6 rue Maréchal-Joffre. ☎ *04-93-39-98-38. Reservations accepted. Meals: Main courses 85–145F ($12–$21); menus 100–170F ($14–$24). MC, V. Open: Tues–Sat noon to 2:30 p.m. and 7:30–10 p.m.*

Le Moulin de Mougins

$$$$$ Mougins   FRENCH

Renowned chef Roger Vergé's Moulin de Mougins is one of France's most famous restaurants, set in a sixteenth-century mill near the entrance of the charming hilltop village of Mougins, where Picasso and other artists once kept homes. Even though there are million-dollar paintings on the walls, the restaurant is very comfortable, almost homey. Specialties include the starter *poupeton de fleur de courgette à la truffe noire de Valréas, coulis de champignons* (zucchini blossoms stuffed with black truffles, served with puréed mushrooms). As a main course, try the *carré d'agneau, côte premières en croûte de parfums de saisons, jus d'aïado* (rack of lamb in an herb crust, stuffed with parsley, chervil, and garlic). Vergé also runs a cooking school on the premises and offers three deluxe rooms and four suites for 800F to 1,500F ($114 to $214) per night.

Avenue Notre-Dame de Vie, Mougins (4 miles from Cannes). ☎ *04-93-75-78-24. Reservations required. Meals: Main courses 200–475F ($29–$68); fixed-price menus 275–760F ($39–$109) at lunch, 550–775F ($79–$111) at dinner. AE, DC, MC, V. Open: Tues–Sun noon to 2:15 p.m. and 8–10 p.m. Closed late Jan to early Mar.*

Rohr

$ Cannes   TEAROOM

This distinguished establishment is Cannes's most famous *salon de thé*. The luxurious decor recalls the days of the belle-époque, when British ladies would gather every day at 4 p.m. for a spot of tea and a piece of cake. The cakes are indeed quite excellent here, as are the homemade chocolates and pasteries. They also serve specialty salads.

63 rue d'Antibes. ☎ *04-93-39-04-01. Meals: Main courses 45–85F ($6–12). MC, V. Open: Daily 8:30 a.m.–12:30 p.m. and 3–7 p.m.*

Cannes's small romantic restaurants are clustered in Le Suquet, the Old Town. In fact, on rue St-Antoine (the Old Town's main street), about 70 percent of the businesses are restaurants. The top three luxury restaurants can be found in the grand hotels along La Croisette: La Belle Otéro at the Carlton, La Palme d'Or at the Martinez, and La Villa des Lys at the Majestic. While all three offer superb fine dining, my favorite is La Belle Otéro because it has the best view (from the seventh floor of the hotel).

Exploring the town and the beaches

The tourist office runs two-hour **guided walking tours** of Le Suquet (Old Town), La Croisette (beach boardwalk), and the Palais des Festivals (where the Film Festival is held). The tours take place Wednesdays at 2:30 p.m. and cost 40F ($6) for adults; tours are free for children under 12. Meet at the tourist office at the Palais des Festivals. For details, call ☎ 04-93-39-24-53. Also be aware that a **tourist train** loops around Le Suquet and the Croisette. It costs 35F ($5) for adults and 15F ($2.15) for children and takes 40 minutes to complete the two-mile loop. For details, call ☎ 06-14-09-49-39.

You may want to explore Cannes on your own, and not on a formal walking tour. You'll get the best taste of the city by exploring the narrow streets of **Le Suquet** (its Old Town), which actually give you a feel for the walled town turned fishing village that rose up here in the Middle Ages. Just past the small restaurants and boutiques on rue St-Antoine, you can climb the ancient steps to a square where you'll find the impressive **Musée de la Castre** (☎ 04-93-38-55-26), housed in a twelfth-century former priest dormitory. The museum contains collections donated by nineteenth-century explorers and ethnographers, with a focus on Mediterranean and eastern archaeology and indigenous art; for instance, there's a mannequin dressed as a "funeraire rambaram" (a type of village elder who presides over funerals). The museum's Eskimo art collection is growing. There's also an interactive exhibit of musical instruments from all over the world that allows you to hear the sounds of the instruments. On the second floor is a collection of paintings by artists from Cannes and the region. In the painting *Le Suquet au coucher du soleil, vu du Nord,* which shows Cannes in 1864, the sky is the only thing that still looks the same. The museum is open Wednesday to Monday: October to March 10 a.m. to noon and 2 to 5 p.m.; April to June 10 a.m. to noon and 2 to 6 p.m.; and July to September 10 a.m. to noon and 3 to 7 p.m. Admission is 10F ($1.40), but free for students. From the ramparts surrounding the museum, you have a lovely view over the city, the old harbor, and the sea. Even in high season, you may be the only one enjoying this peaceful and romantic place — everyone else will likely be at the beach.

After exploring Le Suquet, you'll want to check out the famous markets. The **Marché Forville** on rue Meynadier (near to Le Suquet, just off rue St-Antoine) is the largest market in Cannes and is located in a block-long covered building. Vendors sell fruits, vegetables, and flowers Tuesday to Sunday, and it turns into a flea market on Mondays. Keep walking east on the pedestrian-only rue Meynadier, where you'll find some of the best shops, everything from bargain clothing stores to fancy food stores. Afterward, you can walk south a few blocks to the **old port,** where luxury yachts tie up next to local fishing boats. Next to the old port is the **Palais des Festivals,** which houses the tourist office (just left of the grand steps) and is the venue for the Film Festival events. When the Film Festival isn't in session, it serves as a conference hall year-round. Now you're on **La Croisette,** Cannes's boardwalk, officially known as boulevard de la Croisette, which stretches a couple of miles and is lined with grand hotels. Feel free to wander into a lobby, plop down on a plush wing chair, and watch the fancy folks come and go.

There are 33 **public and private beaches** in Cannes, and most are a combination of sand with pebbles. But going to the beach in Cannes isn't a back-to-nature experience. In fact, you can't really see the sand because the beach chairs cover almost every square inch of it. Really, the beach scene here is all about posing and checking out the poseurs. The private beaches cost money, which entitles you to a lounge chair for the day or half the day; umbrellas usually cost about 30F ($4.30) extra. There are also food concessions and a restaurant at all private beaches. If you have the francs (170F/$24 for half a day and 265F/$38 for a full day) and want to make the scene, go to one of the palace hotel beaches: the **Carleton** (☎ 04-93-06-44-94), **Majestic** (☎ 04-92-98-77-32), **Martinez** (☎ 04-92-98-74-22), and **Noga Hilton** (☎ 04-92-99-70-00). The private beaches of other hotels charge a little less for half day and full day rates at the beach. Children's rates are about 25F to 50F ($3.60 to $7) at most private beaches. The beach restaurants associated with the palace hotels usually have a dish of the day on a set-price lunch menu that's not too expensive (around 145F/$21). The palace hotel beaches also have the best water-sports concessions.

For a free public beach with lifeguards, head to **Midi Plage** (☎ 04-93-39-92-74), located on the west side of the old port. The beach also has a restaurant with reasonable rates serving lunch, dinner, and snacks.

Shopping

Most stores in Cannes are open Monday to Saturday 10 a.m. to noon and 2 to 7:30 p.m. A **Cartes Avantages,** costing 100F ($14), entitles you to reductions at many shops and restaurants. You can buy the card at the Gare Routière (bus station), at the port, or in shops that honor it.

Cannes is famous for its food, flower, and flea markets held in various squares all over town. The biggest market is the **Marché Forville,** just east of the Old Town (Le Suquet), and a few blocks north of the old port. This colorful market features produce and fish in a block-long covered building. Restaurateurs and other gourmands come from all over the region to buy fish here from the fishwives selling their husbands' catch of the day. It's open Tuesday to Sunday 7 a.m. to 12:30 p.m. On Mondays, a flea market takes over the space (October to June 8 a.m. to 6 p.m. and July to September 3 to 6 p.m.).

From July to September, a flower market is held at the **Allées de la Liberté** daily 7 a.m. to 1 p.m.; October to June, the hours are Tuesday to Sunday 7 a.m. to 1 p.m. Several markets specializing in clothes are held on Saturdays 8 a.m. to 12:30 p.m. at **place Gambetta, place du Commandant Maria,** and **place de Cannes la Bocca.** Flea markets are held in these locations on Thursdays 8 a.m. to 6 p.m.

The pedestrian **rue Meynadier** has the best selection of specialty food shops. **Ernest Traiteur** (52 rue Meynadier, at the corner of rue Louis-Blanc; ☎ 04-93-06-23-00) is a famous pâtisserie specializing in cakes, as well as a deli that handles Film Festival receptions; the prepared foods are expensive but good. **Ceneri** (22 rue Meynadier; ☎ 04-93-39-63-68) is a famous third-generation cheesemaker that sells to the region's most famous restaurants.

The town's best candymaker is **Maiffret** (31 rue d'Antibes; ☎ 04-93-39-08-29), making bonbons since 1885. The chocolate laboratory on the second floor is open to visitors Tuesday to Friday 2 to 3 p.m. The other top chocolatier is **Bruno** (50 rue d'Antibes; ☎ 04-93-39-26-63), which also makes marvelous *gelée de fruits.*

The wine store **La Cave de Forville** (28 rue Meynadier; ☎ 04-93-39-45-09) carries, among other fine vintages, La Vendage des Moines (Monks' Vintage), the wine made by monks on the nearby island of St-Honorat.

Cannelle at Galerie Gray-d'Albion (32 rue des Serbes; ☎ 04-93-38-72-79) is a deluxe specialty food store similar to Fauchon in Paris. It doubles as a *salon du thé,* serving wonderful teacakes at noon on the terrace.

If you are shopping for clothing, **rue Meynadier** has inexpensive shops, while **rue d'Antibes** has middle-range prices. The high-end designer shops are on or near **La Croissette.**

Nightlife

There are a variety of nightclubs, casinos, and clubs in Cannes. Next to the famous restaurant La Palme d'Or in the Hôtel Carleton is **Le Carlton Casino Club** (58 bd. de la Croisette; ☎ 04-93-68-00-33), which requires jackets for men and a passport to enter. The same requirements are enforced at the **Casino Croisette** (the largest casino in town) in the Palais des Festivals (1 jetée Albert-Edouard; ☎ 04-93-38-12-11). At the Casino Croisette is the nightclub **Jimmy's de Régine** (☎ 04-93-68-00-07), with a 100F ($14) cover.

In the cellar of the Hôtel Gray-d'Albion is the disco **Jane's** (38 rue des Serbes; ☎ 04-92-99-79-79), with a cover of 50 to 100F ($7 to $14). There's no cover at **Le Loft** (rue du Dr. Monod; ☎ 04-93-39-40-39). Another popular bar is **Les Coulesses** (29 rue du Commandant-André; ☎ 04-92-99-17-17). The hippest disco currently is **What Nots** (7 rue Marceau; ☎ 04-93-68-60-50), which has no cover. **Zanzibar** (85 rue Félix-Faure; ☎ 04-93-39-30-75) is a famous gay bar. Perhaps the most sublime place to have a drink is the Hôtel Carlton's **Le Bar des Célébrities** (58 bd. de la Croisette; ☎ 04-93-06-40-06).

Biot and the Léger Museum

In the tiny hilltop village of **Biot,** craftspeople specializing in pottery and glassmaking ply their ancient trades. Romans first settled the village in 154 B.C. In the Middle Ages, the Black Plague wiped out the population of Biot, and fifty families resettled it in 1470. Many current residents of the village are descendents of these early settlers.

Because Biot is so small and offers just one hotel in the Old Town, many people make this a half-day trip from Cannes or Nice. A walk from one end of the village to the other takes about 10 minutes. The renowned Ferdinand Léger Museum is located a couple of miles from the village, with signs to direct you there.

At Biot's pottery and glassblowing studios, you can watch the pieces being made. Most of the artisan studios are on the highway on your way to the village, so a car is helpful here. Because Biot is set on a hill, walkers have to trudge up very steep steps to get to town. Although the old village itself is pedestrian only, there is a parking lot at the top of the hill near the village center.

Getting there

Biot is 8 km (5 miles) inland from Antibes, 9 km (6 miles) from Cagnes (9.50F/$1.30 by bus), 15 km (9.3 miles) from Nice, and 15 km (9.3 miles) from Cannes. If you're **driving,** take N7 east from Antibes, or west from Nice.

The Biot train station lies on the main coastal rail route, though the actual village is inland. There is frequent service from Nice (17 minutes, 55F/$8) and Antibes (10 minutes, 35F/$5). For train information and schedules, call ☎ **08-36-35-35-39** or 08-36-35-35-35. The Biot train station is located about 8 km (5 miles) from the actual hilltop village of Biot. Between the station and the village is an unattractive highway with no sidewalks, so this is not a pleasant walk. Bus service to the village from the train station runs hourly on weekdays and less frequently on Sundays.

La Société Sabac (☎ **04-93-74-91-56**) runs buses between Biot and Antibes; trips take 20 minutes and cost 20F ($2.85). Monday to Saturday, ten buses leave hourly 7:20 a.m. to 6 p.m.; Sunday and holidays, there are seven buses per day 8 a.m. to 6 p.m. Buses leave from place Guynemer, the square at the entrance to town near the post office. Buses also stop at the Ferdinand Léger Museum and the Verrerie de Biot (glassblowing studio).

Getting around and getting information

The local taxi service is **Taxis Biot** (☎ **04-93-65-34-15** or 04-93-33-37-04).

The **tourist office** is located at 46 rue St-Sebastien, at place de la Chapelle (☎ **04-93-65-05-85**; Internet: www.biot-coteazur.com). From September to June, the office is open Monday to Friday 9 a.m. to noon and 2 to 6 p.m. and Saturday and Sunday 2 to 6 p.m.; July and August, hours are Monday to Friday 10 a.m. to 7 p.m. and Saturday and Sunday 2:30 to 7 p.m.

Where to stay

Domaine du Jas de Biot

$$$ **Biot**

This three-star hotel, a Spanish-style complex offering 17 rooms and suites with terraces, is along a dusty highway about half a mile from the entrance to the Old Town. It's conveniently situated about halfway between the old city and the Léger museum — within walking distance from each. The rooms are modern and good-sized, with lots of sunlight. The hotel also has a pool and bar.

625 route de la Mer. ☎ *04-93-65-50-50. Fax: 04-93-65-02-01. Rack rates: 700–950F ($100–$136) double; 1,000–1,400F ($143–$200) suite. Breakfast: 60F ($9). Closed Nov–Mar. MC, V.*

Hôtel des Arcades

$$ Biot

Under the medieval arches on the village's main square, this 12-room hotel, built in 1480, is the only lodging in the Old Town. With an ambience "très Greenwich Village," according to the owners, it serves as a hotel, bistro, tobacconist, and art gallery, as well as a hangout for locals. Alas, it's tough to get a room here because it's the only game in town and fills up fast. To reach the rooms in this ancient stone house, you climb a curving tiled stairway; the stairway's walls are covered with original abstract art. The rooms, which vary in size, are cheerfully decorated in a simple and artsy style (a tapestry may be used to cover the bath area) and have wonderful views over the rooftops. Some rooms have terraces or small balconies. The bistro is known for excellent homecooking. The Brothier family has run the hotel for 45 years.

16 place des Arcades. ☎ *04-93-65-01-04. Fax: 04-93-65-01-05. Rack rates: 300–500F ($43–$71) double. Breakfast: 40F ($6). AE.*

Where to dine

Café de la Poste

$$ Biot   PROVENÇAL

This is Biot's classic cafe, where visitors mingle with artists and locals. It was founded in 1885, and the decor is retro, with quaint antiques in the cozy dining room. The cafe dishes out authentic recipes from the old country, like *pot au feu grand-mère* (beef and vegetable stew), *tête de veau* (calves' heads), and rabbit with olives, as well as a large selection of salads. The children's menu features hamburgers, french fries, and ice cream. Sitting on the large shaded terrace on the village's main street allows you to monitor all the goings-on. In season, the cafe features live jazz in the evenings.

24 rue St-Sébastien. ☎ *04-93-65-19-32. Meals: Main courses 80–150F ($11–$21); children's menu 50F ($7). V. Open: Daily noon to 3 p.m. and 7:30–10 p.m. Closed Oct–Apr.*

Crêperie du Vieux Village

$ **Biot**   **CRÊPES**

For a cheap crêpe meal, you'll like the extensive selection of main course and dessert crêpes at this atmospheric hole in the wall, located near place des Arcades at the top of the village.

2 rue St-Sébastien. ☎ *04-93-65-72-73. Meals: Main courses 13–46F ($1.85–$7). No credit cards. Open: May to mid-Nov daily noon to 2 p.m. and 7:30–9:30 p.m.*

La Pierre à Four

$$ **Biot**   **PROVENÇAL**

Chef Guy Portelli has created a tribute to ancient cuisine in this atmospheric restaurant that offers excellent quality for the price. Most diners choose signature dishes like the roast duck with chevre, the famous brioche with escargots and foie gras, or the beef, served either provençal (grilled with herbs from Provence) or flambéed with cognac or butter. The extensive dessert menu includes the standout *charlotte aux poivres* (baked pears). English menus are available.

15 bis route de Valbonne. ☎ *04-93-65-60-00. Meals: Main courses 120–150F ($17–$21); menus 109F ($16), 139F ($20), and 239F ($34). MC, V. Open: July–Aug daily noon to 2:20 p.m. and 7:30 p.m. to midnight. Closed off-season Tues all day, Sat lunch, and Sun night.*

Le Restaurant Galerie des Arcades

$$ **Biot**   **PROVENÇAL**

The only hotel in town (see "Where to stay") is also the best place to eat dinner. People travel for miles for this homecooked Niçoise cuisine prepared by Mimi Brothier, a former model for Picasso. Patrons sit family style on long banquet tables. Specialities include quintessential dishes like *blettes* and *courgettes* (swiss chard and zuccini), *salade niçoise* (salad with tuna and potatoes), *soupe au pistou* (garlic soup), *bourride* (fish soup), and *ravioli tout nu* (homemade). The wines here are chosen by a special oenologue.

16 place des Arcades. ☎ *04-93-65-01-04. Meals: Main courses 160–180F ($23–$26). AE. Open: Tues–Sun noon to 2 p.m.; Tues–Sat 7:30–9:30 p.m. Closed mid-Nov to mid-Dec.*

Les Terraillers

$$$ **Biot**   **PROVENÇAL**

This is the best and most expensive restaurant in town, located down the hill from the medieval center in a sixteenth-century building that used to be a pottery studio. The dining room is decorated with antiques and majestic bouquets, and outdoor dining on the garden terrace is offered in season. Chantal and Pierre Fulci have been running this restaurant for over 20 years. Chef Jacques Claude is an expert at assembling unique and flavorful combinations. For instance, his *cougettes fleurs* (zuccini flowers) are served with truffle butter and his ravioli is made with foie gras. The fresh fish may be roasted and served on spaghetti. For dessert, try the light and fluffy *coco Suzette* (coconut crêpe). The wine cellar is extensive.

11 route du Chemin-Neuf. ☎ *04-93-65-01-59. Meals: Main courses 150–310F ($21–$44); menus 180–380F ($26–$54). MC, V. Open: June–Sept Fri–Wed noon to 2 p.m., daily 7–10 p.m.; Oct–May Fri–Tues noon to 2 p.m. and 7–10 p.m. Closed Nov.*

Exploring the village and the Léger museum

In the center of the village is **place des Arcades,** located at the very top of the hill. The arches around the square date from the thirteenth and fourteenth centuries. Also in this square are the sixteenth-century gates to the city and remains of medieval ramparts. At the far end is the fifteenth-century **Eglise de Biot.**

The tradition of glassmaking in Biot began only in 1956, when ceramic engineer Eloi Monod opened the **Verrerie du Biot** glass studio and museum (chemin des Combes; ☎ 04-93-65-03-00), which is still the largest glass studio in town. Admission is free. Local artisans take pride in practicing a craft that can be traced back 5,000 years to the Egyptians. Since Monad opened his studio, eight glass artists have opened their own galleries, including **Jean Claude Novaro** at place des Arcades (☎ 04-93-65-60-23), and **Jean-Michel Operto** at Silice Creation (173 chemin des Combes; ☎ 04-93-65-10-25). Each artist offers his own take on the contemporary stylings of glass, and it's fascinating to watch them, lit by flaming ovens, as they create the glassware.

For centuries, Biot has been associated with pottery — mainly large earthenware amphora containers called Biot jars. You'll find them at **La Poterie Provençale** (1689 route de la Mer; ☎ 04-93-65-63-30).

The **Musée National Ferdinand-Léger,** located at chemin du Val de Pome, on the eastern edge of town (☎ 04-92-91-50-30), houses an impressive collection devoted to the beloved cubist; people who aren't familiar with Léger's vibrant works are in for a treat. The building is an immense contemporary structure built after Léger's death, and designed especially to highlight his oeuvre. Huge colorful mosaics, stained-glass windows, and giant metal sculptures decorate the exterior. Inside, the building's large spaces give ample room for Léger's monumental paintings, as well as drawings, ceramics, and tapestries executed between 1905 and 1955. This is exciting, life-affirming work. A French film about Léger runs hourly, and a brochure in English is available. The ground floor hosts changing exhibits. The museum is open Wednesday to Monday 10 a.m. to 12:30 p.m. and 2 to

5:30 p.m. Admission is 38F ($5.40) for adults and 28F ($4) for children, but free on the first Sunday of each month.

Antibes and Cap d'Antibes

The town of **Antibes** manages to blend its ancient past and jazzy present in an appealing way. Antibes has a historic center of pedestrian streets ringed by a newer section of town, attractively laid out with smart shops and handsome squares, like place Général-de-Gaulle, where you can find the tourist office. As the unofficial capital of the yacht industry, Antibes is full of young people — mainly Brits, Americans, Australians, and Kiwis (New Zealanders) — looking to be crewmembers on yachts, and giving the town an anglicized feel. This youthful populace also distinguishes Antibes from some of the other Mediterranean towns that are popular with retirees. The town's two big yachting events are **Les Voiles d'Antibes** in June and the **Antibes Cup** in July. The **Jazz Festival,** which takes place for three weeks in July, is one of the most famous in France.

Antibes is actually one of the region's most ancient cities, founded by Greek seafarers around 400 B.C. as a convenient stopover between Corsica and Marseilles. The original city was called Antipolis ("opposite") because it was opposite Corsica. The region became a Roman province, and Antipolis was again an important stop along a trade route. When Nice and Cannes were only villages, the people of Antipolis erected temples, public baths, aqueducts, a triumphal arch, and large fortifications. In the eleventh century, the name of the city was changed to Antibes.

The picturesque old port of Antibes, with its ancient ramparts, is next to the new Port Vauban, where most of the colossal yachts are moored. Antibes is quite lively in season, and those wandering around town may be treated to impromptu entertainment, like a Dixieland jazz band playing on place Nationale. **Cap d'Antibes** (the tip of the peninsula) is an isolated residential area, with private estates and fancy hotels, located about 5 km (3.1 miles) uphill from town. There are crowded sandy beaches near town, but the Garoupe beaches, a couple of miles from town toward the tip of the peninsula, are the preferred spot for sunbathing or strolling along the beachfront pedestrian path.

Getting there

Antibes is 11.3 km (7 miles) east of Cannes and 20.9 km (13 miles) west of Nice. The bus station, Gare Routière, is centrally located on place Guynemer (☎ 04-93-34-37-60). It takes about 30 minutes (25F/$3.40) by **bus** from Cannes or Nice. The train station, Gare SNCF, is at place Pierre-Semard north in the Old Town. **Trains,** running every half-hour to and from Cannes, take ten minutes and cost 16F ($2.30); trains that run every half-hour to and from Nice take 20 minutes and cost 25F ($3.40). For information and reservations, call ☎ **08-36-35-35-39.**

If you're driving from Nice, take N98 west for about 15 minutes; from Cannes, it's an even quicker trip, about 10 minutes east on A8.

The **Aéroport de Nice–Côte d'Azur** (☎ 04-93-21-30-30) is 23 km (14.3 miles) from Antibes. For information on flights, call ☎ **08-36-69-55-55.** A bus to town costs 45F ($6) and takes 40 minutes. A taxi will take about half an hour and cost around 280F ($40).

Getting around and getting information

Frequent local **bus service** (☎ **04-93-34-37-60**) loops all the way out to the tip of the peninsula and back to town, costing 15.50F ($2.20) round-trip. You can pick up the bus at the Gare Routière (bus station), or along boulevard Albert-1er, where there are several stops marked along the wide sidewalk. The bus takes about 15 minutes to travel from the bus station to the Eden Roc hotel at the tip of the peninsula.

For a cab, call **Allo Taxi Antibes** at ☎ **04-93-67-67-67.** To rent a car, try **Avis** (32 bd. Albert-1er; ☎ **04-93-34-65-15**), **Budget** (40 bd. Albert-1er; ☎ **04-93-34-36-84**), or **Europcar** (2 bd. Foch; ☎ **04-93-34-79-79**). For bike or scooter rental, head to **Access FRL** (43 bd. Wilson; ☎ **04-93-67-62-75**) or **Auto Moto Location** (93 bd. Wilson; ☎ **04-92-93-05-06**). Bikes rent for 80F ($11) per day, and scooters for 140F ($20) per day.

The **tourist office** is at 11 place Général-de-Gaulle (☎ **04-92-90-53-00;** Internet: www.antibes-juanlespins.com). During July and August, the tourist office is open Monday to Sunday 9 a.m. to 7 p.m.; January to June and September to December, hours are Monday to Friday 9 a.m. to 12:30 p.m. and 2 to 6:30 p.m., and Saturday 9 a.m. to noon and 2 to 6 p.m. To check on or send e-mail, head to the **Workstation Cyber Café** (1 av. St-Roch; ☎ **04-92-90-49-39**), open Monday to Friday 8 a.m. to 8 p.m. and Saturday 8 a.m. to 5 p.m. The cafe serves coffee and sandwiches.

Where to stay

Auberge Provençale

$ Antibes

This family-run inn, located on the Old Town's busy place Nationale, has seven very basic rooms at bargain prices. The centrally located hotel/restaurant is about a two-minute walk from the port and beaches. This area stays loud late at night, as late diners mingle with bar hoppers. The very popular and reasonably priced restaurant, also called Auberge Provençale (see "Where to dine"), serves fresh fish, shellfish, and grilled meats in a shaded courtyard.

Place Nationale. ☎ *04-93-34-13-24. Fax: 04-93-34-89-88. Rack rates: 300–400F ($43–$57) double. MC, V.*

Hôtel Castel Garoupe

$$$ Antibes

This compound is nestled in palms and bougainvillea near the tip of the peninsula. While the hotel is a pleasant 10-minute walk from a good beach, it's a long walk (3 km/1.9 miles) down a steep hill to town, so you'll have to rely on the bus or a car. The 27 rooms, including 4 studios with kitchenettes (perfect for families), are mainly spacious and modern, with some antiques; 6 rooms have terraces with distant sea views. The hotel also has a good-sized pool and a tennis court (100F/$14 per hour). The restaurant serves breakfast and snacks, but not dinner.

959 bd. de la Garoupe. ☎ *04-93-61-36-51. Fax: 04-93-67-74-88. Internet:* www. castel-garoupe.com. *E-mail:* castel-garoupe@wanadoo.fr. *Free parking. Rack rates: 695–870F ($99–$124) double; 1,015–1,425F ($145–$204) studio. Rates include breakfast. Closed early Nov to mid-Mar. AE, MC, V.*

Hôtel du Cap–Eden Roc

$$$$ Cap d'Antibes

Staying at the famous Hôtel du Cap is very pricey, and guests' most vivid memories tend to be of the creative additions to the bill. For example, you'll be charged extra to sit in a lounge chair by the pool, and if you order a kir royale (champagne and cassis), you'll pay $50 for the half bottle of champagne used to make the drink. But the world's wealthiest are content to stroll through the marble-columned lobby and take the elevator up to their antiques-filled gilded rooms. The manicured lawn, lined with palm trees, leads down to the pool house and heated seawater pool carved into a cliff above the Mediterranean. Built in 1870, the 130-room hotel promises luxury that never goes out of style. The hotel's isolation in a 22-acre park at the peninsula's tip is part of its appeal, as are amenities like five clay tennis courts, a fitness club, and one of the Riviera's top restaurants.

Bd. Kennedy. ☎ *04-93-61-39-01. Fax: 04-93-67-76-04. Internet:* www. edenrock-hotel.fr. *E-mail:* EDENROC-HOTEL@wanadoo.fr. *Rack rates: 2,500–4,500F ($357–$643) double; 5,500–6,500F ($786–$929) suite. Breakfast: 120F ($17). Personal checks must be accompanied by a letter from your bank vouching for the amount. Closed mid-Oct to Apr. No credit cards.*

Hôtel Mas Djoliba

$$$ Antibes

Although this pretty 13-room hotel is located in a kind of nowheresville (a steep residential area on the edge of town), it's not too far from the beach, with about a 15-minute walk to the historic center. *Mas* means "farmhouse," but this hotel surrounded by lush foliage feels more like a private villa. Some of the charming rooms have distant sea views, and one has a balcony. All of the rooms are relatively spacious. The top-floor two-bedroom suite can sleep five people and has a terrace and sea view. Families seem particularly at home at Djoliba, with the heated pool supplying hours of distraction for kids. The staff is particularly friendly. In summer, the management gives preference to demi-pension guests — those willing to eat dinner every night at the hotel.

29 av. de Provence. ☎ *04-93-34-02-48. Fax: 04-93-34-05-81. Internet:* www. hotel-pcastel-djoliba.com. *E-mail:* info@hotel-pcastel-djoliba. com. *Free parking. Rack rates: 430–590F ($61–$84) double; 720F ($103) suite. Breakfast: 50F ($7). Demi-pension: 430–550F ($61–$79). Closed Nov–Jan. MC, V.*

Hôtel Royal

$$$ **Antibes**

This 37-room waterfront hotel, with its own private beach, has been owned and operated by the Duhart family since 1950. Many of the modern motel-style rooms have French balconies or terraces, and almost all have sea views. The hotel has two eating spots, Le Dauphin, a restaurant in a glass-enclosed wing, and a more casual cafe on the hotel's beach. From July to September, half-pension rates (two meals at the hotel) are obligatory.

16 bd. Maréchal-Leclerc. ☎ *04-93-34-03-09. Fax: 04-93-34-23-31. Parking: 40F ($6). Rack rates: 570–750F ($81–$107) double. Breakfast: 55F ($8). Half pension: 430–550F ($61–$79). Closed Nov–Dec. AE, MC, V.*

Le Relais du Postillon

$$ **Antibes**

This former coaching inn, where stage coaches used to stop to pick up and drop off weary travellers, is a rarity in Antibes: a medium-priced hotel centrally located in the old city, with an excellent restaurant. Though the sheets and towels are very thin, the 15 rooms are pretty, with attractive bedding and curtains, and some have terraces facing the square. The rooms are definitely a good value, although they vary considerably in size. For instance, the room called Malte is a beautiful large room overlooking the square, while La Valette is a small room facing the rear of the building. The restaurant, also called Le Relais du Postillon, serves lunch and dinner (see "Where to dine").

8 rue Championnet (across from the post office park). ☎ *04-93-34-20-77. Fax: 04-93-34-61-24. Internet:* www.relais-postillon.com. *E-mail:* postillon@ atsat.com. *Rack rates: 255–478F ($36–$68) double. Breakfast: 42F ($6). MC, V.*

Where to dine

Izanami

$$ Antibes JAPANESE

This tiny sushi restaurant opened in the spring of 2000, and the buzz hasn't stopped. Serge and Ann Cecille prepare and serve wonderful sushi and sashimi rolls using fresh local fish, as well as tempura, yakitori, and teriyaki. The restaurant is located on a quiet street in the Old Town, not far from the bus station. The restaurant also prepares takeout food.

16 rue de Fersen. ☎ *04-93-34-57-17. No reservations. Meals: Main courses 100–115F ($14–$16); sushi 10–13F ($1.40–1.85) per roll. MC, V. Open: Daily noon to 2 p.m. and 7:30–10 p.m.*

L'Armoise

$$$ Antibes PROVENÇAL

Chef Laurent Brackenier runs this charming little restaurant near the market. The cuisine is classic provençal with Italian influence, and one glance at the menu will tell you that this is serious food. For instance, for a first course you can have *raviole de cèpes "maison" au beurre de truffes et aux pignons* (house ravioli with white mushrooms with truffle butter and pine nuts). Delicious main courses are the homemade *ravioli aux blettes sauce foie gras* (ravioli with swiss chard and foie gras), *noisettes d'agneau au parfum de truffes* (lamb chops with truffle oil), and *filet de boeuf au foie gras, sauce au jus de cèpes* (steak with foie gras and white mushroom sauce).

2 rue de la Touraque. ☎ *04-93-34-71-10. Meals: Main courses 95–130F ($14–$19); menus 120F ($17) and 160F ($23); special foie gras menu 280F ($40). MC, V. Open: Thurs–Tues 8–10 p.m.*

La Taverne du Saffronier

$$ Antibes PROVENÇAL

This traditional brasserie with garden terrace seating is a dependable choice for a good-quality, reasonably priced meal. The service is friendly, gracious, and efficient. All the provençal favorites are served, including *bouillabaisse* and fish soup. Grilled fish is the focus of the menu. The restaurant offers a kid's menu too.

Place Saffranier. ☎ *04-93-34-80-50. Meals: Main courses 60–130F ($9–$19). No credit cards. Open: Tues–Sun 12:15–2:15 p.m. and 7:15–9:15 p.m. Closed mid-Dec to mid-Jan.*

L'Auberge Provençale

$$ Antibes PROVENÇAL

Fish and grilled meats are the specialties at this family-owned traditional restaurant on hopping place Nationale, where there's usually strolling entertainment or a Dixieland jazz band entertaining passersby. Most diners head straight back to the restaurant's large garden courtyard, where tables are set up under brightly colored umbrellas.

61 place Nationale. ☎ *04-93-34-13-24. Meals: Main courses 75–125F ($11–$18). MC, V. Open: Daily 12:30–1:30 p.m. and 7:30–10 p.m.*

Le Brulot

$$ Antibes PROVENÇAL

On a tiny Old Town street lined with restaurants, this lively spot stands out for good food and good value. The moment you walk into the intimate dining room, you'll smell the raison d'être of the place: wood-grilled fish. The menu features catch of the day prepared on the grill with a variety of sauces and herbs. Perhaps the most popular dish, other than fish, is the *cochon de lait farci* (stuffed suckling pig). The restaurant also offers outside seating on a busy pedestrian street and a children's menu.

3 rue Frédéric-Isnard. ☎ *04-93-34-17-76. Meals: Main courses 55–125F ($7-$17); menus 140–198F ($20–$28). MC, V. Open: Tues–Sat noon to 2 p.m. and 7:30–10 p.m.; Mon 7:30–10 p.m. Closed early to mid-Jan and early to mid-Aug.*

Le Relais du Postillon

$$$ Antibes PROVENÇAL

Expect excellent food, creatively prepared and stylishly presented, at this small restaurant in the hotel also called Le Relais du Postillon off rue de la République. The menu changes daily as the masterful chef improvises, but what arrives on your plate inevitably consists of beautiful colors, shapes, and textures. Standbys are *foie gras de canard* (duck foie gras), *pot-au-feu de la mer* (seafood and vegetable stew), *feuillantine de caille* (quail wrapped in parchment), and *croustillant de langouste* (prawns in a pastry). *Panache de la mer* is a combination of seafood prepared in a variety of ways, including dumplings and tarts. The lunch menu is very limited, usually with a choice of one or two main courses, so check the chalkboard out front before sitting down. The restaurant has half a dozen tables outside on the square; inside is a romantically lit cozy dining room fronted by a long bar.

8 rue Championnet (across from the post office park). ☎ *04-93-34-20-77. Reservations preferred. Meals: Main courses 85–135F ($12–$19); menus 155–250F ($22–$36). MC, V. Open: Tues–Sun noon to 2 p.m.; Mon–Sat 7:30–10 p.m. Closed Nov.*

Restaurant Albert-1er

$$ Antibes   PROVENÇAL

This brasserie across from the beach is known for having the freshest fish in town. It specializes in oysters and other shellfish, and the paella prepared with locally caught fish is not to be missed. The restaurant also has a children's menu. In summer, everyone sits on the terrace, with views of the beach.

46 bd Albert 1er. ☎ *04-93-34-33-54. Reservations accepted. Meals: Main courses 75–145F ($11–$21); menus 100–250F ($14–$36). MC, V. Open: Thurs–Tues noon to 2:30 p.m. and 7–10:30 p.m. Closed mid-Nov to mid-Dec.*

Restaurant de Bacon

$$$$ Cap d'Antibes   PROVENÇAL

This is Antibes's most deluxe restaurant, located at the tip of the peninsula near the fanciest hotels. The dining room and shaded terrace offer views of the sweeping coast and sandy beaches. The menu is dependent each day on what's the freshest and best fish available. The creative preparations may be *fricassée de rougets* (braised red mullet in red wine sauce) or *chapon en papillote* (baked in parchment). But the restaurant prides itself on its preparation of that regional specialty *boullabaisse,* a hearty fish-and-shellfish soup. For dessert, the restaurant always has a selection of fresh tarts and other delicacies.

Bd. de Bacon. ☎ *04-93-61-50-02. Reservations necessary. Meals: Main courses 160–175F ($23–$25); menus 280–480F ($40–$69). AE, MC, V. Open: Tues–Sun noon to 2 p.m. and 8–10 p.m. Closed Nov–Dec.*

Exploring the town and the beaches

The peninsula containing the towns of Antibes on the east, Juan-les-Pins on the west, and Cap-d'Antibes at the tip is just east of Nice. The coastline, with sandy beaches and rocky embankments, is 24.1 km (15 miles) long.

Antibes has an easy layout. From central **place Général-de-Gaulle,** rue de la République leads to the **Old Town,** with its cobblestone pedestrian streets, and ends at **place Nationale,** the liveliest square in the Old Town. Rue Sade, on the south side of place Nationale, leads to **Cours Messena,** which is set up for several blocks with a covered market. One block south is the **Château Grimaldi,** housing the Musée Picasso, and the Cathédrale d'Antibes (see later in this section for details on both). Just beyond the ramparts of Château Grimaldi is the **old port,** crowded with pleasure yachts. To get to Cap d'Antibes at the tip of the peninsula, you need to drive or take a city bus. There are several bus stops along boulevard Albert-1er, stretching from place Général-de-Gaulle to the beach. Antibes's famous **Provençale Market,** with food and flowers, is held in the covered market building on Cours Messina daily 6:30 a.m. to 12:30 p.m. In the afternoon, crafts are displayed in the market building. A very good **flea market** is held every Thursday and Saturday 8 a.m. to 5 p.m. on place Audiberti.

Le Petit Train d'Antibes (☎ 04-93-67-43-59) runs frequent half-hour tours of Antibes and Juan-le-Pins. In Antibes, the train leaves from place de la Poste and passes by the pedestrian streets, provençal market, Old Town, port Vauban, and ramparts. Tickets are 35F ($5) for adults and 20F ($2.85) for children 3 to 10. The train runs daily: February and March 2 to 5 p.m., April to June 10 a.m. to 6 p.m., July and August 10 a.m. to 11 p.m., and September and October 10 a.m. to 7 p.m. A tour group called **Naturama** (☎ 06-60-05-58-46) organizes 1½-hour walking tours (35F/$5) of Cap d'Antibes and the Sanctuary of La Garoupe, with a minimum group size of eight people. On the tour, you'll see breathtaking views, small chapels, and a lighthouse. If you want to explore the area on your own, follow the 2-km (1.2-mile) round-trip, pine-tree-lined **footpath** along the shore on the southern tip of the peninsula. Take the small path at the end of the Garoupe beaches.

In the old stone Château Grimaldi, sitting high on a bluff overlooking the sea, the **Musée Picasso** (place Mariéjol; ☎ 04-92-90-54-20) is one of Riviera's loveliest museums. Prolific artist Pablo Picasso spent the fall of 1946 painting at the villa, which was owned by the town; in gratitude he donated to Antibes the 181 works he completed there, as well as ceramics and sculpture. The museum, which frequently hosts themed exhibits of modern and contemporary art, has a large collection of works by twentieth-century artists. Don't miss the sculpture garden on a balcony with a panoramic view. The museum is open Tuesday to Sunday: June to September 10 a.m. to 6 p.m. and October and December to May 10 a.m. to noon and 2 to 6 p.m. Admission is 30F ($4.30); an audioguide is available for 20F ($2.85).

The **Cathédrale d'Antibes,** on place Mariéjol (no phone), is one of the Riviera's most beautiful cathedrals — it's a baroque church whose graceful facade boasts stripes of burnt orange and yellow. The cathedral was built on the site of a Roman temple dedicated to Diana. Inside, you find a twelfth-century Roman choir, an eighteenth-century baroque nave, and the famous Brea altarpiece painted in 1515. It's open daily 9 a.m. to 6 p.m., and admission is free.

The imposing **Musée d'Archéologique,** located on Bastion St-André, just southwest of the Picasso Museum (☎ 04-92-90-54-35), contains an impressive collection of antiquities found in Antibes and in shipwrecks nearby (some dating back to 1200 B.C.) This museum tends to put on "fun" exhibits like images on ceramics of Dionysus (Greek god of wine) from the sixth to third century B.C. It's open Tuesday to Sunday: June to September 10 a.m. to 6 p.m. (Fridays to 10 p.m.) and October to May 10 a.m. to noon and 2 to 6 p.m. Guided visits are given on Fridays at 3 p.m. Admission is 20F ($2.85).

WORTH THE SEARCH

Other Riviera favorites

If you happen to have some extra time and a deep interest in this region, here are a few more wonderful places you can visit:

Grasse: This town, 23.3 km (14½ miles) from Antibes, is called the "Perfumed Balcony of the Riviera" for good reason: It's the center of the region's perfume business. Three factories are open for tours (Molinard; Gallard; and Fragonard, named after painter François Fragonard, who was born in Grasse), and 70 others operate in town. Grasse is a bustling place containing 45,000 residents, with an old city surrounded by ramparts and a twelfth-century cathedral boasting a painting by Rubens.

La Napoule-Plage: This secluded resort (8 km/5 miles from Cannes) has a pretty sandy beach. There's also the Musée Henry-Clews with collections and works of an eccentric American sculptor who died in 1937.

Mougins: The hilltop medieval village of Mougins, the longtime home of Picasso, contains one of the Riviera's most famous restaurants, Le Moulin de Mougins (☎ 04-93-75-78-24)— reserve far in advance. There's also a wonderful photography museum at the top of the hill featuring candid photos of Picasso.

Roquebrune and Cap-Martin: These two picturesque resorts, one in the hills and one beside the shore, are close to the Italian border. Roquebrune is 25.7 km (16 miles) east of Cannes and Cap Martin is 24.1 km (15 miles) east of Nice. Roquebrune is accessed by the Grande Corniche, the mountain road that runs along the eastern part of the French Riviera. It's a charming village where cobblestone streets are lined with boutiques, gift shops, and galleries. There's also the Château de Roquebrune, a tenth-century castle that houses a museum. Cap-Martin was once a popular resort for celebrities, royalty, and politicians and still attracts a wealthy crowd. The beach is rocky but scenic. A walking path here, the Promenade Le Corbusier, named after the artist who used to come to the resort, is one of the finest on the Riviera for coastal views.

Menton: Very close to the border of Italy, Menton (8 km/5 miles from Monaco) is said to enjoy more sunshine than any other town on the Riviera. There are pretty — though very crowded — beaches, and the old town close to the shore is charming with cobbled winding streets and interesting boutiques. There's also the Musée Jean-Cocteau, with works and memorabilia of the artist. Menton is particularly popular with retirees, who have apartments in many of the large residential hotels lining the shore.

At Cap d'Antibes, next to the Eden Roc hotel and surrounded by a 12-acre park, the **Musée Naval et Napoléonien** (avenue Kennedy; ☎ 04-93-61-45-32) contains Napoleonic memorabilia and is worth the trip for military history buffs. The museum also has a fine collection of model ships, paintings, and marine objects. November to September, the museum is open Monday to Friday from 9:30 a.m. to noon and 2:15 to 6 p.m. and Saturday from 9:30 a.m. to noon. Admission is 30F ($4.30) adults and 20F ($2.85) children.

Marineland, on route de Biot (RN7), just east of Antibes center (☎ 04-93-33-49-49), is Europe's largest marine zoological park and is home to killer whales, dolphins, sea lions, seals, penguins, and sharks, as well as aquariums of exotic fish. It's open year-round daily 10 a.m. to 5 p.m. but the last admission is at 4 p.m. Admission is 149F ($22) for adults and 99F ($14) for children.

Antibes has some of the best beaches on the Riviera, in terms of sand and cleanliness. The entire peninsula with Antibes and Juan les Pins has 25 km (15½ miles) of coastline and 48 beaches. The ones at the Cap are the prettiest and have the best sand. **Plage de la Salis** is located just south of town, within walking distance. On the eastern neck of the cape are the **Plages de la Garoupe,** which are the peninsula's nicest beaches, a long stretch of a couple of miles. All beaches have concessions with chairs and umbrellas to rent, as well as a variety of water sports. There's always a nearby restaurant, serving snacks and full meals.

Nightlife

There's a lot more nightlife in nearby Juan-les-Pins, a suburb of Antibes reachable in a few minutes by car, but Antibes does have its share of good bars, especially on **boulevard d'Aguillon** near the port. The **Hop Store** (38 bd. d'Aguillon; ☎ 04-93-34-15-33) is a good Irish pub. **La Siesta** (route du Bord de Mer; ☎ 04-93-33-31-31) is a disco and casino.

Vence and the Matisse Chapel

Most visitors come to **Vence** to see a masterpiece by Matisse — the Chapelle du Rosaire, the Dominican chapel he designed in the hills just outside the town center. But the town itself is a suitable stop for lunch and a stroll. Vence, with a population of 15,000, has a pedestrian-only medieval center surrounded by ramparts. Along the Old Town's narrow cobblestone streets are cafes, galleries, and small shops. Vence is much less touristy than neighboring St-Paul-de-Vence (see later in this chapter), but it offers its own understated charms.

Getting there

There are **buses** traveling frequently between Nice and Vence, and the one-hour (24.1 km/15-mile) trip costs 22F ($3.15). Buses arrive and depart from place du Grand Jardin, near the tourist office. For bus schedules, call **Bus S.A.P. (Societe Automobile de Provence)** at ☎ 04-93-58-37-60.

Vence has no train station, but the nearest train station is in Cagnes-sur-Mer about 7.2 km (4½ miles) away. From there, you can take an S.A.P. bus (see above for number).

To drive from Nice to Vence, take N7 west to Cagnes-sur-Mer, then D236 north to Vence.

If you fly into Nice's airport, you can rent a car and drive to Nice or take a bus or train from the center of Nice to Vence.

Getting around

The local bus service for Vence is **Bus Var Mer** (☎ 04-93-42-40-79). You can order a taxi by calling ☎ **04-93-58-11-14** or by going to the taxi stand on place du Grand Jardin.

To rent a car, try **Europcar** (840 av. Emile-Hugues; ☎ **04-93-58-00-29**) or **Budget** (avenue Rhin et Danube; ☎ **04-93-58-04-04**). You can rent bikes at **Vence Motos** (avenue Henri-Isnard; ☎ **04-93-58-56-00**). Rentals cost 60F ($8) for a half day and 100F ($14) for a full day.

The **tourist office** is at 8 place du Grand Jardin (☎ **04-93-58-06-38**). It's open Monday to Saturday: June to September 9 a.m. to 1 p.m. and 2 to 7 p.m. and October to May 9 a.m. to 12:30 p.m. and 2 to 6 p.m. To check on or send e-mail, go to **Internet Email** (147 av. des Poilus; ☎ **04-93-58-99-66**), open Monday to Friday 9:30 a.m. to 12:30 p.m. and 2 to 6 p.m.

Where to stay

Château St-Martin

$$$$ Vence

This is Vence's most deluxe dining/lodging option; it's also one of the region's top options. The hotel features 40 rooms and suites in the main house, and 5 villa-like cottages on the sprawling 35-acre property, with a pool and two tennis courts. Paths run through the landscaped property, set in the hills with distant views to the sea. The spacious rooms are decorated in an elegant style. At the acclaimed restaurant La Commanderie, chef Dominique Ferrière turns out poetic inspirations along the lines of *escalope de foie gras poêlée à la betterave rouge et au vinaigre de vin* (slices of foie gras pan-fried with red beets and wine vinegar) and *mignon de veau mariné au gingembre et miel de Provence, fricassée de légumes et soja* (veal marinated with ginger and provençal honey with fricasée of vegetables and soy beans).

Av. des Templiers (3 km/1.9 miles from the center of Vence, about a 20-minute drive from Nice's airport). ☎ *04-93-58-02-02. Fax: 04-93-24-08-91. Internet:* www. chateau-st-martin.com. *E-mail:* st-martin@webstore.fr. *Rack rates:*

2,000–4,500F ($286–$643) double; 3,200 ($457) suite. Breakfast 135F ($19). Closed Nov–Apr. AE, DC, MC, V.

Hôtel le Provence

$$ Vence

To reach Margaretha and Francis Sobata's simple 16-room hotel, you pass through a garden courtyard filled with roses and climbing bougainvillea — and that's perhaps the most memorable thing about this unassuming place. The hotel is situated in a fine location, across from the circular ramparts to the Old Town. The Sobatas, a young friendly couple who speak English, recently purchased the property and are planning a number of renovations. The rooms vary from quite small to medium size; some rooms have private balconies, while most have views of the garden or the village rooftops and the distant sea.

9 av. Marcellin-Maurel. ☎ *04-93-58-04-21. Fax: 04-93-58-35-62. Rack rates: 250–440F ($36–$63) double. Breakfast: 40F ($6). MC, V.*

Where to dine

Auberge des Seigneurs

$$ Vence   PROVENÇAL

At this rustic seventeenth-century hotel/restaurant, the dining room features beamed walls and ceilings, a long central table, and a huge fireplace where chickens and hams are roasted on spits. The combination of atmosphere and reasonable prices is popular with Americans and other tourists. The theme of the restaurant is the cuisine of François Premier (reigned 1515–47). In addition to the roasted chicken (which takes an hour to be roasted) and ham, the limited menu also features trout François-1er (a whole fish roasted with herbs and served with vegetables). Meals are brought to the table and served family-style from large platters. The service is friendly, if harried, and a shaggy dog (Monsieur Tim) sometimes greets guests. Before the check is presented, ladies are given a red rose. Live acoustic guitar provides entertainment on some nights. The hotel has six simple rooms renting at 280F to 400F ($38 to $54) for a double.

Place du Frene. ☎ *04-93-58-04-24. Reservations recommended. Meals: Main courses 75–150F ($11–$21); menus 165F ($24), 205F ($29), and 240F ($34). MC, V. Open: Thurs–Sun noon to 2 p.m.; Tues–Sun 7:30–9:30 p.m. Closed late Oct to mid-Mar.*

Jacques Maximin

$$$$ Vence   PROVENÇAL

This much-lauded restaurant, with its star chef, has been a destination of gourmands for over 20 years. Settle into the luxurious dining room for dishes like *filet de loup rôti à la niçoise* (roasted sea bass niçoise style) and *canard entier du lauragais rôti à l'ail, sauce poivrade* (whole duck roasted with garlic and a peppery wine sauce). Better yet, put yourself in Monsieur Maximin's capable hands and order the special of the day.

689 Chemin de la Gaude (about 3 km/1.9 miles from Vence along route Cagnes-sur-Mer). ☎ *04-93-58-90-75. Reservations necessary. Meals: Main courses 195–320F ($28–$46); menus 240F ($34) at lunch, 300–550F ($43–$79) at dinner. AE, MC, V. Open: Tues–Sun noon to 2 p.m.; Tues–Sat 7:30–9:30 p.m.*

La Farigoule

$$ Vence   PROVENÇAL

This the best restaurant in the village center, but it's small and fills up fast. The dining room is cheerful and cozy, with provençal fabrics decorating the tables and windows. In summer, the restaurant offers seating on the interior courtyard. English menus are available. The most requested dish is a special *bourride provençal*, a fish soup that is a specialty of the region. You can also order a yummy poached octopus in pepper-and-lemon broth as an appetizer. Main course specialties include sea bass with lemon-and-tomato marmalade, braised leg of lamb in aromatic juice for two, sea scallops with pasta salad, and La Farigoule's famous *tarte fine au caviar de cèpes* (mushroom pie). Another very special dish can be found in the cheese course: *millefeuille de pain d'épices au roquefort* (puff pastry of spiced bread with roquefort cheese).

15 rue Henri-Isnard. ☎ *04-93-58-01-27. Reservations necessary. Meals: Main courses 120–160F ($17–$23); menus 135F ($19) and 160F ($23); tasting menu 250F ($36). MC, V. Open: Thurs–Mon noon to 2 p.m. and 7:30–10 p.m.; Wed 7:30–10 p.m.*

Le P'tit Provençale

$$ Vence   PROVENÇAL

This small casual restaurant, within the Old Town ramparts, is the place locals go to when they want a good but not too expensive dinner. The cuisine has plenty of Italian influence. The best choice for an appetizer is the *risotto aux champignons des bois, jus de volaille à l'huile vierge* (risotto with forest mushrooms, chicken broth, and virgin olive oil). A standout main course is the *émincé de magret de canard rôti aux petits légumes au champêtre* (thin slices of roasted fatted duck breast with vegetables, rustically prepared). For dessert, you can have an excellent *mousseline de chocolat au Grand Marnier* (chocolate mousse with Grand Marnier).

4 place Clemenceau. ☎ *04-93-58-50-64. Meals: Main courses 90–110F ($13–16); menus 105F ($15) and 155F ($22); children's menu 60F ($9). MC, V. Open: Tues–Sat 12:15–2 p.m. and 7:15–9:30 p.m.*

Exploring the town

Place du Peyra, inside the ramparts (the thick stone walls of the town), contains the **Vieille Fontaine,** a huge urn-shaped fountain, and a tenth-century cathedral decorated with a Chagall mosaic on the left as you enter. At place du Frene near the town's west gate, the fifteenth-century **Château Villeneuve** (☎ 04-93-24-24-23) contains a private modern art museum, with a permanent collection that includes works by Matisse, Dufy, Dubuffet, and Chagall. It's open daily 10 a.m. to 6 p.m. Admission is 30F ($4) adults and 15F ($2) children.

In 1947, at age 77, Henri Matisse agreed to create a Dominican chapel in the hills near Vence. Two years later, after hundreds of preparatory drawings and many sleepless nights, Matisse had designed one of his most unusual works — the **Chapelle du Rosaire,** located at 468 av. Henri-Matisse, 1.5 km (.9 miles) from the center of town (☎ 04-93-58-03-26). On the building's completion, he said, "I want those entering my chapel to feel themselves purified and lightened of their burdens." The building has become somewhat of a pilgrimage site for thousands of Matisse-ophiles, who visit the chapel in different seasons and times of day in order to see the changes sunlight makes on the stained-glass reflections. Matisse designed every aspect of the building — not only the stained glass and tiles, but also elements like the altar and the priests' vestments. When driving or walking toward the building from Vence, you first see the 40-foot wrought-iron cross on a low-lying, unassuming whitewashed building. Inside, down a flight of stairs, is the chapel, a luminous space with black-and-white-tiled walls and bright stained-glass windows. There are three minimalist tile designs: a powerfully executed Stations of the Cross, an immense Madonna and Child, and a portrait of a faceless St. Dominic (to the right of the altar). After exiting the chapel, you'll find an exhibit area, **L'Espace Matisse,** displaying Matisse's drawings and samples of vestments in bright colors and starbursts designed by the artist. A brochure is available in English. Admission to the chapel is 15F ($2.15). From December to September, the chapel is open Tuesday and Thursday 10 to 11:30 a.m. and 2 to 5:30 p.m. and Monday, Wednesday, and Saturday 2 to 5:30 p.m. Sunday mass, which starts at 10 a.m., is followed by a visit at 10:45 a.m.

The **Galerie Beaubourg** (2618 route de Grasse; ☎ 04-93-24-52-00), which is a five-minute drive from the center of town, is an audacious contemporary art gallery housed in the Château Notre-Dame des Fleurs, a nineteenth-century mansion. The large formal garden features a number of surprising sculptures. Artists represented inside and out include Tinguely, Klein, Cesar, Stella, Rivers, and Warhol. From mid-June to mid-September, the gallery is open Monday to Saturday 11 a.m. to 7 p.m.; late September to early June, hours are Tuesday to Saturday 12:30 to 5:30 p.m. Admission is 30F ($4) adults and 15F ($2) for children.

Nightlife

The most popular bars and cafes are clustered around the main squares of the village. **Le Clemenceau** (☎ 04-93-58-24-70) is a cafe on place Clemenceau; **Henry's Bar** tends to have patrons spilling out onto place de Peyra; and **La Régence** is always full on place du Grand Jardin.

St-Paul-de-Vence and the Maeght Foundation

St-Paul-de-Vence, one of the most beautiful villages in France, is a small pedestrian-only medieval burg built into a steep hill, with dozens of art galleries lining the cobblestone streets. St-Paul-de-Vence is popular with tourists, who tend to make a day trip of strolling the narrow, steep streets and walking around the ramparts of this fortified town. After all the day-trippers leave, the village is very quiet and peaceful in the evenings.

St-Paul's history can be traced back to the sixth century B.C. when a fortified enclosure was built here. The site came under Roman rule in 154 B.C. and became prosperous as a key stop along an east-west trading route. The castle on the top of the hill was built in the twelfth century, as was the Romanesque church nearby. In the fifteenth and sixteenth centuries, the village became prosperous as a provincial capital and took on the look it retains today. In the twentieth century, celebrities discovered St-Paul, and artists, writers, and filmmakers flocked to the village. Expensive hotels and restaurants soon followed. A short walk from the entrance to the village is the Maeght Foundation, one of the best modern art museums in France.

Getting there

The best way to get to St-Paul is to **drive.** From Nice, take A8 to Cagnes-sur-Mer and then follow the signs and the route de la Colle (RD 436) to St-Paul-de-Vence. The drive from Nice to St-Paul takes about 40 minutes. The nearest **bus** stop is located on the route de Vence, ¼ mile from the town ramparts. Buses leave frequently from Nice (30.6 km/19 miles from St-Paul) and the neighboring town of Cagnes-sur-Mer (6.4 km/ 4 miles from St-Paul). The bus from Nice costs about 65F ($9), and the bus from Cagnes-sur-Mer costs about 22F ($3.15). Call the bus company **Cie SAP** at ☎ 04-93-58-37-60 for the schedule. The closest **train** station is in Cagnes-sur-Mer, 6.4 km (4 miles) away. The train from Nice to Cagnes-sur-Mer takes about 7 minutes and costs about 35F. For train schedules, call ☎ 08-36-35-35-39.

Getting around and getting information

St-Paul is small and easy to walk through. No cars are allowed within the ramparts, except for people who have reservations at one of the hotels within the ramparts. If you have a reservation, you can drive in and park at your hotel. The town has two local cab companies: **Taxi Gilbert** at ☎ **04-93-73-64-30** and **Taxi Jean-Luc** at ☎ **06-08-26-11-72.**

The **tourist office** is at 2 rue Grande (☎ **04-93-32-86-95;** Fax: 04-93-32-60-27; E-mail: artdevivre@wanadoo.fr). The office is open daily: October to May 10 a.m. to 6 p.m. and June to September 10 a.m. to 7 p.m. To send or check on e-mail, stop at **St-Paul Web** (4 rue de l'Etoile; ☎ **04-93-32-07-80**). It's open daily 10 a.m. to 7 p.m.

Where to stay

Hostellerie les Remparts

$$ St-Paul

How nice to find an affordable hotel in St-Paul. After all the day-trippers have left, you can wander the romantic streets in peace and make your way to this medieval house, located in the center of the village, for a candlelit dinner and quiet slumber. The rooms are on the small side, but they're unique, with arches, stoned walls, paintings, and antiques. Each room has a view of the village or the valley below, and some have floor-to-ceiling windows. The restaurant offers reasonably priced provençal cuisine.

72 rue Grande. ☎ *04-93-32-09-88. Fax: 04-93-32-06-91. Internet:* www.stpaulweb. com/remparts. *E-mail:* hr@saintpaulweb.com. *Rack rates: 320–520F ($46–$74) double. Breakfast: 40F ($6). MC, V.*

Hôtel le Hameau

$$$ St.-Paul-de-Vence

This former farmhouse, about half a mile from St-Paul, is a pleasant place to stay, with views of the village. The rooms are attractive — some have tiled floors and beamed ceilings, and all have antiques. The large garden has an orangerie, as well as jasmine and honeysuckle. The hotel also has a large pool with a Jacuzzi. Breakfast, in your room or on the terrace, includes homemade orange marmelade. When artist Marc Chagall visited St-Paul, he stayed here.

528 route de la Colle. ☎ *04-93-32-80-24. Fax: 04-93-32-55-75. Rack rates: 580–750F ($83–$107) double; 850F ($121) suite. Breakfast: 105F ($14). MC, V.*

Hôtel le St-Paul

$$$$ St-Paul

This member of the prestigious Relais & Châteaux group, occupying a sixteenth-century house in the heart of the village, offers St-Paul's most deluxe accommodations within the ramparts. The 15 rooms and suites are grandly decorated with antiques and the finest fabrics. The hotel has a fine provençal restaurant, featuring a charming patio with a fountain, where you're surrounded by flowering window boxes and ancient village buildings.

86 rue Grande. ☎ *04-93-32-65-25. Fax 04-93-32-52-94. Internet:* www. relaischateaux.fr/stpaul. *E-mail:* Stpaul@relaischateaux.fr. *Rack rates: 950–1,800F ($136–$257) double; 1,600–3,500F ($229–$500) suite. Breakfast: 105F ($15). Closed Dec–Jan. AE, DC, MC, V.*

Le Mas d'Artigny

$$$$ St-Paul

About 2 km (1¼ miles) from St-Paul, this exquisite 83-room hotel is set among acres of pine groves. All rooms have balconies with distant sea views, and there are 25 luxury suites. Amenities include a heated pool, tennis courts, mountain bikes, a golf driving range, billiards, and a fitness course. The expensive restaurant features the cuisine of chef François Scordel, who won the Toque d'Or (golden chef's hat) in 1999, an annual award presented by the National Academy of Cuisine.

Route de la Colle. ☎ *04-93-32-84-54. Fax: 04-93-32-95-36. Internet:* www. mas-artigny.com. *E-mail:* mas.artigny@wanadoo.fr. *Parking: 60F ($9). Rack rates: 1,200–2,200F ($171–$314) double; 2,050–3,000F ($293–$429) suite. AE, DC, MC, V.*

Where to dine

La Colombe d'Or

$$$$ St-Paul-de-Vence PROVENÇAL

This world-famous hotel/restaurant has been host to the rich and famous for decades. But over the years, the Golden Dove has become a bit of a tourist trap, with its food not measuring up to the high prices. Expect to find the most typical provençal cuisine, with first courses like foie gras and main courses like roasted monkfish with herbs and Sisteron lamb. Perhaps the most memorable aspect of the meal will be the remarkable art collection on the walls of the public rooms, with works by Matisse, Braque, Léger, and Calder among others. The hotel also has 26 very expensive rooms and suites (1,400F/$200 for a double; 1,600F/$229 for a suite), with access to a heated pool and sauna.

Place de Gaulle. ☎ *04-93-32-80-02. Reservations necessary. Meals: Main courses 150–300F ($21–43). AE, DC, MC, V. Open: Daily noon to 2 p.m. and 7–10 p.m. Closed Nov–Dec.*

Exploring the town

The tourist office offers one-hour **guided walking tours** of the village for 50F ($7) per person. Arrive at the tourist office (2 rue Grande; ☎ 04-93-32-86-95) any day between 10 a.m. and 5:30 p.m. for an almost immediate departure. The cost also includes admission to the Museum of Local History or a visit to an artist's studio.

The privately owned **Fondation Maeght,** located just outside the town walls (☎ 04-93-32-81-63), is dedicated to modern art. The building itself is a striking contemporary art statement; the grounds and building exterior display monumental sculptures, ceramics, and stained glass by artists like Giacometti, Miró, and Chagall. While the museum owns an important collection of works (by artists like Bonnard, Braque, Calder, Chagall, Giacometti, Matisse, and Miró), the museum is usually filled with special exhibits drawn from public and private collections. This is a large museum, so you may need to allow yourself a couple of hours to go through it. It's open daily: October to June 10 a.m. to 12:30 p.m. and 2:30 to 6 p.m. and July to September 10 a.m. to 7 p.m. Admission is 35 to 45F ($5 to $6) for adults and 25 to 35F ($3.60 to $5) for children 10 to 18.

Shopping

The village streets are chock full of expensive boutiques and galleries. Some top galleries are **Atelier Christian Choisy** (5 rue de la Tour; ☎ 04-93-32-01-80), **Galerie Lilo Marti** (La Placette; ☎ 04-93-32-91-22), and **Gallery 5** (5 place de l'Eglise; ☎ 04-93-32-09-71). Jewelry lovers will want to check out **Nicola's Tahitian Pearl** (47 rue Grande; ☎ 04-93-32-67-05).

Climb down some steep steps to a fourteenth-century wine cellar to visit **La Petite Cave de St-Paul** (2 rue de la Petite Sellerie; ☎ 04-93-32-59-54), which stocks an excellent selection of regional wine. Among the shop's most prized wines are bottles from Le Mas Bernard, the winery owned by the Maeght Foundation, which owns only 3 hectares of vineyards west of St-Paul. The wine from Le Mas Bernard is very good and unavailable in the United States because of the small production.

Nice: A Study in Contrasts

The seaside city of **Nice** (the Riviera's largest) is at once sophisticated and giddy, regal and honky-tonk, and dignified and disorderly. With a

Nice

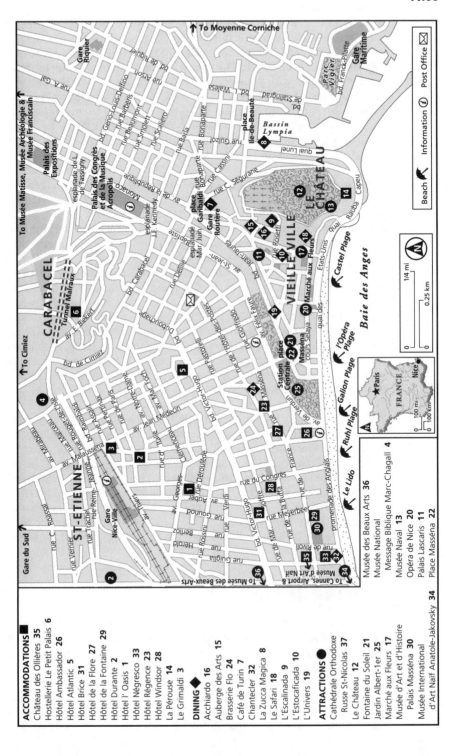

population of 400,000, Nice is large enough to offer many contrasting elements. You may be struck by the grace of the city, its buildings decorated with filigreed wrought-iron balconies and multicolored shutters, and also by its boisterous energy. The promenade des Anglais, along the crescent-shaped Baie des Anges, is the Riviera's most beautiful beachfront boardwalk. The Old Town, a maze of winding narrow streets crowded with vendors, is the heart of this city that cherishes its uniqueness. Street names in the Old Town are written in French and Nissart. Nissart is not a dialect but a real language that is closer to Italian than it is to French. Because Nice still holds tight to its traditions and history of independence, elderly Niçoise still speak the language, and some young people learn it in school.

Nice didn't actually become a part of France until 1860. The city's history stretches back to the fourth century B.C., when the Greeks settled on the Colline du Château (known as just Le Château). In 100 B.C., Romans built a town called Cemenelum on the hill of Cimiez. Barbarians and Saracens subjected the town to six centuries of invasions, until the counts of Provence resettled the Colline du Château in A.D. 500. In the fourteenth century, the Niçoise agreed to be under the sovereignty of the House of Savoy. But between 1691 and 1731, and 1792 and 1814, Nice fell briefly under French rule. In 1704, Louis XIV, annoyed with the Niçoise because they wanted their independence from France, destroyed all buildings on the Castle Hill. Finally, in 1860, Napoléon III and King Victor Emmanuel II of Sardinia signed the Treaty of Turin, which made Nice a part of France again and paved the way for it to become a popular winter resort during the early 1900s — and what is now the capital of tourism on the French Riviera.

There are many interesting tourist sights in Nice, but with 19 galleries and museums, Nice is most of all a city of art. One of the country's foremost modern art museums, the Musée d'Art Modern et d'Art Contemporain, occupies a dramatic contemporary building in the center of town. The city has museums devoted to Henri Matisse, who lived in Nice for many years and is buried here, and Marc Chagall, as well as the Museum of Fine Arts (in the building formerly owned by Russian aristocrats), the Museum of Naïve Art, a museum of decorative art (the Musée d'Art et d'Histoire Palais Masséna), and the Palais Lascaris with baroque art.

Getting there

Nice is a major transportation hub and a convenient base from which to explore the region. The **Aéroport International Nice–Côte d'Azur** (☎ 04-93-21-30-12) is France's second busiest airport, with up to 45 planes per day flying from Paris to Nice; there's also a flight from New York to Nice. Easy Jet is a budget airline that flies all over Europe, including a flight from London to Nice. The airport, with two terminals, is 7 km (4.3 miles) from the city center. Terminal 1 is used for international flights. For airport public transportation, call ☎ 04-93-21-30-83;

for airport taxis, call ☎ **04-93-13-78-78.** A taxi takes 20 minutes and costs about 170F ($23). A bus leaves the airport every 30 minutes for the town center and SNCF train station, costs 23F ($3), and takes 30 minutes.

From Paris's Gare du Lyon, the **TGV train** takes 6½ hours to get to Nice's **Gare S.N.C.F.** and affords beautiful views along the coast — particularly from Cannes to Nice. There are two trains per day from October to May and three per day from June to September. The train from Paris costs 565 to 739F. The slow trains that travel along the coast of the Riviera stop in Nice, so there is frequent service to Cannes, Monaco, and Antibes, among others. For train information, call ☎ **08-36-35-35-39.** Trains arrive in the center of the modern part of the city on avenue Thiers.

The **Gare Routière de Nice** is the bus station at promenade de Paillon (☎ **04-93-85-61-81**). Buses are a very cheap and practical way to visit nearby cities and towns. For instance, a one-way trip by bus to Monte Carlo is only 20F ($2.85).

If you're **driving** to Nice, you can take A8, the Route Napoléon, or national highway 7, 98, or 202. Nice is 931 km (578.5 miles) from Paris and 190 km (118 miles) from Marseille. Driving from Paris to Nice will take about 10 hours. The trip from Marseilles to Nice will take about 3 hours, depending on traffic.

Getting around and getting information

You don't need a car in Nice, as the Old Town and many attractions are within walking distance. City buses are a convenient way to see the museums in Cimiez, a suburb of Nice. The bus company is **Agence SUNBUS** (10 av. Félix-Faure; ☎ **04-93-16-52-10**), open Monday to Friday 7:15 a.m. to 7 p.m. and Saturday 7:15 a.m. to 6 p.m. You can pick up route maps in the office. Tickets, which you can buy on the buses, cost 9F ($1.30).

With the **Sun Pass,** you can travel freely on all regular bus lines in Nice and the hills of Cimiez for one day (25F/$3.60), five days (90F/$13), or seven days (115F/$16).

You can rent a car at the following offices: **Avis,** at the airport (☎ **04-93-21-36-33** terminal 1 or **04-93-21-42-80** terminal 2) or at the SNCF train station (☎ **04-93-87-90-11**); **Budget,** at the airport (☎ **04-93-21-36-50** terminal 1 or **04-93-21-42-51** terminal 2) and across the street from the SNCF train station at 9 av. Thiers (☎ **04-93-16-24-16**); **Hertz,** at the airport (☎ **04-93-21-36-72** terminal 1 or **04-93-21-42-72** terminal 2) or in the SNCF train station (☎ **04-93-16-10-30**). You can rent a bike at **Arnaud** (4 place Grimaldi; ☎ **04-93-87-88-55**), **JML** (34 av. Auber; ☎ **04-93-16-07-00**), or **Nicea Location Rent** (9 av. Thiers; ☎ **04-93-82-42-71**).

The main **taxi stands** are located at esplanade Masséna, promenade des Anglais, place Garibaldi, rue Hôtel des Postes, the SNCF train station, Nice's airport, and Acropolis, also known as the Palais des Congrès, which is half a mile north of the center of town. To summon a cab, call **Central Taxi Riviéra** at ☎ **04-93-13-78-78.** (Note that there's a higher rate 7 p.m. to 7 a.m.)

The **main tourist office** is at 5 promenade des Anglais (☎ **04-92-14-48-00** or 04-93-83-32-64; E-mail: otc@nice-coteazur.org; Internet: www.nice-coteazur.org). During July and August, the tourist office is open Monday to Saturday 8 a.m. to 8 p.m. and Sunday 9 a.m. to 6 p.m.; September to June, hours are Monday to Saturday 9 a.m. to 6 p.m. There are **branch offices** near the airport on promenade des Anglais (☎ **04-93-83-32-64**), open the same hours as the main office; at the airport in terminal 1 (☎ **04-93-21-44-11**), open daily 8 a.m. to 10 p.m.; and at the train station on avenue Thiers (☎ **04-93-87-07-07**), open mid-June to mid-September daily 7:30 a.m. to 8 p.m. and mid-September to mid-June daily 8 a.m. to 7 p.m. To check on or send e-mail, head to **La Douche** (34 cours Saleya; ☎ **04-93-62-81-31**), open daily 2 to 10 p.m., or **Web Nice** (25 bis promenade des Anglais; ☎ **04-93-88-72-75**), open Monday to Saturday 10:30 a.m. to 8:30 p.m.

Where to stay

Château des Ollières

$$$$ **Center**

The eight-room Château des Ollières, for many years the home of Prince Lobanov-Rostowsky, is the region's most luxurious small hotel, set in a landscaped 20-acre park. The hotel is decorated in baroque splendor, with sculpted woodwork and rich fabrics. The large extravagant rooms boast comfortable seating areas, antiques, and thick carpeting. The hotel provides exceptional service and an exclusive restaurant on site.

39 av. des Baumettes (just off promenade des Anglais). ☎ *04-92-15-77-99. Fax: 04-92-15-77-98. E-mail:* ollieres@riviera-isp.com. *Rack rates: 1,200F ($171) double; 1,700–2,000F ($243–$286) suite; 3,300F ($471) tower apartment. Breakfast: 90F ($13). AE, MC, V.*

Hostellerie Le Petit Palais

$$$ **North of Center**

Former home of French actor/writer Sacha Guitry, this belle-époque property is now a fine Best Western with 25 rooms. The hotel is set high in a residential district, about a five-minute drive up from the center of town and within walking distance of the Chagall Museum. The interior still retains its elegant details, like sculpted ceiling moldings and paneled walls. The commons rooms and guest rooms are furnished with antiques; some rooms have terraces and distant sea views. There's an attractive garden on the property.

10 av. Emile-Bieckert. ☎ *04-93-62-19-11. Fax: 04-93-62-53-60. E-mail:* petitpalais@ provence.riviera.com. *Parking: 55F ($8). Rack rates: 695–810F ($99–$116) double. Breakfast: 55F ($8). AE, MC, V.*

Hôtel Ambassador

$$$ Center

With a prestigious location overlooking central place Masséna, the 45-room Ambassador occupies a beautiful beaux-arts building. It offers all the modern amenities you'd expect. The rooms are spacious and comfortable, and many have balconies with views of the plaza and the beaches along the promenade des Anglais. The staff is efficient and friendly and speaks English.

8 av. de Suède. ☎ *04-93-87-75-79. Fax: 04-93-82-14-90. Rack rates: 590–850F ($84–$121). Breakfast: 50F ($7). Closed Nov–Jan. MC, V.*

Hôtel Atlantic

$$$$ Center

The grand beaux-arts Atlantic, with 123 rooms, has been wonderfully restored to preserve its elegant touches. You'll find stucco ceilings, decorative frescoes, sculpted woodwork, and period decor throughout the commons rooms. One highlight is the stained-glass ceiling in the hall. Most rooms are decorated in a practical modern style, but they're mainly spacious, with sitting areas; some have balconies. The rooms have views of a broad attractive street lined with shade trees. The lush garden is a quiet spot to wind down.

12 bd. Victor-Hugo. ☎ *04-93-88-40-15. Fax: 04-93-88-68-60. E-mail:* info@ atlantic-hotel.com. *Rack rates: 750–950F ($107–$136) double. Breakfast: 85F ($12). AE, MC, V.*

Hôtel Brice

$$$ Center

This Mediterranean-style hotel, part of the Tulip chain, claims an ideal location, a few blocks from the beaches and a short walk to the Old Town, and features a memorable colorful garden with a fountain and statuary. In the colonial-style sitting room, the friendly hotel staff is available to answer questions or help with special requests. Many of the 58 rooms are filled with light, and those looking out over the garden are the most desirable. All rooms have the usual amenities; some have French balconies with intricate wrought-iron work. The hotel offers a reasonably priced restaurant, as well as a sauna, gym, and solarium.

44 rue Maréchal-Joffre. ☎ *04-93-88-14-44. Fax: 04-93-87-38-54. Internet:* www. nice-hotel-brice.com. *E-mail:* brice@webstore.fr. *Parking: 30F ($4.30). Rack rates: 620–720F ($89–$103) double. Breakfast: 40F ($6). AE, MC, V.*

Hôtel de Flore

$$$ **Center**

A great location and standard rooms are what you get at this 63-room Best Western in the center of the modern part of Nice, a block from the promenade des Anglais. The rooms are compact but comfortable, and special windows keep out the city noise. While the rooms are somewhat generic, they do have comfortable beds with new mattresses. The staff is friendly and efficient and speaks English.

2 rue Maccarani. ☎ *04-92-14-40-20. Fax: 04-92-14-40-21. E-mail:* flore@aaacom.com. *Rack rates: 560–620F ($80–$89) double. Breakfast: 60F ($9). MC, V.*

Hôtel de la Fontaine

$$ **Center**

A block from the deluxe Négresco and the promenade des Anglais, this hotel rises above the competition by virtue of its friendly and attentive management, who recently bought the property. The 29 rooms are standard but comfortable, with attention paid to details like better-than-average sheets and towels. In summer, breakfast is served in the garden courtyard beside the handsome fountain.

49 rue de France. ☎ *04-93-88-30-38. Fax: 04-93-88-98-11. E-mail:* hotel-fontaine@webstore.fr. *Rack rates: 530–600F ($76–$86) double. Breakfast: 50F ($7). MC, V.*

Hôtel Durante

$$ **Center**

This lodging, an attractive hotel near the train station, has a serene quality about it. The 22 rooms look out onto a pretty landscaped garden, and the English-speaking management is exceedingly friendly. The rooms are simple but well appointed; some have kitchenettes.

16 av. Durante. ☎ *04-93-88-84-40. Fax: 04-93-87-77-76. E-mail:* 3soleils@informa.fr. *Free parking. Rack rates: 450–550F ($64–$79) double. Breakfast: 55F ($8). Closed Nov–Jan. MC, V.*

Hôtel l'Oasis

$$ **Center**

This small hotel, located in a busy area about halfway between the train station and the beach, is indeed an oasis; it's set in a lush garden and boasts a pool. The 38 rooms are on the small side, but they're clean and comfortable, and the rates are very reasonable. Ask the management about the hotel's most famous guests: Chekhov and Lenin apparently stayed here during the belle époque, when Nice was considered Moscow-by-the-Sea.

23 rue Gounod. ☎ *04-93-88-12-29. Fax: 04-93-16-14-40. Free parking. Rack rates: 430–500F ($61–$71) double. Breakfast: 45F ($6). MC, V.*

Hôtel Négresco

$$$$ Center

Built in 1913, Nice's most famous hotel, which has a pink dome, sits majestically on the promenade des Anglais facing the beach and the sea. The 145 posh rooms are individually decorated with museum-quality furniture and artwork, and many have balconies facing the sea. Each floor features rooms in a different style, from Louis XV to Empire to Napoléon III. The Salon Royal, with its glass dome, is where you have a drink before dining at the acclaimed Chantecler (see "Where to dine"). The beautiful brasserie La Rotonde, with a carousel theme, is used for less expensive dining. The highlight of the hotel is the lobby men's room, decorated in an uproarious Napoléon theme.

37 promenade des Anglais. ☎ *04-93-16-64-00. Fax: 04-93-88-35-68. E-mail:* negresco@nicematin.fr. *Parking: 170F ($24). Rack rates: 1,350–2,750F ($193–$393) double; 3,400–3,350F ($486–$479) suite. Breakfast: 130F ($19). AE, MC, V.*

Hôtel Régence

$$ Center

The Régence is situated on one of the busiest pedestrian streets in the modern part of Nice but within easy walking distance of the Old Town and beaches. The central location means there's street life outside your window 'til the wee hours, with a major strolling scene, as well as street performers and musicians. Fortunately, the 39 rooms, which are small but immaculate, have soundproof windows. Breakfast is served in a sunny room or on a small terrace. In the lobby, you can find a huge binder with extensive sightseeing information in English.

21 rue Masséna. ☎ *04-93-87-75-08. Fax: 04-93-82-41-31. E-mail:* HTLregence@ aol.com. *Rack rates: 310–380F ($44–$54) double. Breakfast: 35F ($5). MC, V.*

Hôtel Windsor

$$$ Center

Owner Bernard Redolfi-Strizzot transformed a nineteenth-century hotel near the promenade des Anglais into the highly original 60-room Windsor — a celebration of contemporary art. Local and nationally recognized artists have decorated the rooms with murals, paintings, and sculptures, and the result is sometimes ravishing, sometimes startling, but always unique. One room is decorated with works by Henri Olivier, who makes "living still-lifes"; another features the conceptual poetry of Lawrence Wiener (his poem about dreams is written in bright colors on the wall above the bed). Breakfast is served in the attractive dining room or the exotic garden. The fitness area has a sauna and massage room.

You can enjoy swimming in the pool, surrounded by colorful tropical plants, and listening to piped-in bird song. The hotel has a very fine restaurant, as well as an attractive bar with live piano music on some nights.

11 rue Dalpozzo. ☎ *04-93-88-59-35. Fax: 04-93-8-94-57. E-mail:* windsor@ webstore.fr. *Rack rates: 550–750F ($79–$107) double. Breakfast: 50F ($7). MC, V.*

La Pérouse

$$$$ near Castle Hill

The well-run La Pérouse is one of Nice's top hotels, with a special location on the side of the Colline du Château, overlooking the sea. The rooms have sweeping views of the coastline and the Old Town. The 64 low-ceilinged rooms are decorated luxuriously with the Mediterranean in mind, with blue and green florals predominating. The hotel has a heated pool in the garden, as well as a Jacuzzi. The restaurant is open for dinner from mid-June to mid-September only.

11 quai Rauba-Capeu. ☎ *04-93-62-34-63. Fax: 04-93-62-59-41. E-mail:* lp@hroy. com. *Parking: 70F ($10). Rack rates: 765–1,850F ($109–$264) double. Breakfast: 95F ($14). MC, V.*

Le Grimaldi

$$$ Center

This newly renovated hotel, with an elegant 1930s facade, is an excellent value in a good central location, about halfway between the train station and the beach. The 23 rooms are individually decorated with modern panache, using brightly colored Souleïado (Provençal) fabrics. The three types of rooms (regular, superior, and junior suite) all have huge windows, with some opening onto French balconies, and are bathed in light. You can choose between a breakfast buffet served in the sleek breakfast room or an American breakfast brought by room service. You'll need to book early for this one; it has become a hip place to stay.

15 rue Grimaldi. ☎ *04-93-16-00-24. Fax: 04-93-87-00-24. Internet:* www. le-grimaldi.com. *E-mail:* zedde@le-grimaldi.com. *Free parking. Rack rates: 470–870F ($67–$124) double; 1,200–1,400F ($171–$200) suite. Breakfast: 75–125F ($11–$18). MC, V.*

Where to dine

Acchiardo

$ Vieille Ville   NIÇOISE

This restaurant is where you can find one of the cheapest good meals in town. It's a small, unpretentious place in the Old Town that attracts locals, as well as visitors, who tend to wander in after perusing the inexpensive menu. Specialties are fish soup, homemade ravioli, and other fresh pastas. Your best bet is the *plat du jour,* which is bound to be a hearty traditional dish.

38 rue Droite. ☎ *04-93-85-51-16. Reservations recommended. Meals: Main courses 80–120F ($11–$17). MC, V. Open: Mon–Sat noon to 2 p.m.; Mon–Fri 7:30–10 p.m. Closed Aug.*

Auberge des Arts

$$ Vieille Ville   NIÇOISE

This locals' joint in the Old Town serving great regional specialties is a good choice for a reasonably priced lunch or dinner. The ambience is that of a casual cafe, with terrace seating on a busy narrow street. The kitchen turns out all the favorites, like *pissaladière, farcis, tartes des blettes,* and *salade niçoise.* The desserts are homemade.

9 rue Pairolière. ☎ *04-93-85-63-53. Reservations recommended. Meals: Main courses 85–225F ($12–$32); menus 150–330F ($21–$47). MC, V. Open: Tues–Sat 12:30–2:30 p.m.; Mon–Sat 7:30–11 p.m.*

Brasserie Flo

$$ Center   NIÇOISE

Across from the Galeries Lafayette department store and near place Masséna, Flo has a terrific central location. The hip brasserie is set in a converted nineteenth-century theater, meaning it positively drips with atmosphere, with the highlight being the soaring frescoed ceilings. There's something for everyone here. The menu offers typical brasserie fare, fresh shellfish, grilled fish, and excellent soups.

2–4 rue de Sacha-Guitry. ☎ *04-93-13-38-38. Reservations recommended. Meals: Main courses 85–190F ($12–$27); menus 120–160F ($17–$23); children's menu 50F ($7). AE, MC, V. Open: Daily noon to 3 p.m. and 7 p.m.–12:30 a.m.*

Café de Turin

$$ Center   NIÇOISE

The Turin, a bustling brasserie on central place Garibaldi, is known for its wonderful shellfish. Its solid reputation has borne the test of time, and for years locals and visitors have come here for towering seafood platters with oysters, clams, shrimp, and other shellfish. This is also a popular place to come for a drink or an aperitif before dinner, but it's never easy to find a table.

5 place Garibaldi. ☎ *04-93-62-66-29. Reservations recommended. Meals: Main courses 100–150F ($14–$21). MC, V. Open: July–Aug daily 5–11 p.m.; Sept–May daily 8 a.m.–10 p.m.*

Chantecler

$$$$ Center NIÇOISE

For the best and most expensive meal in Nice, head to the exquisite Chantecler. The setting is palatial — the ornately carved wood paneling was purchased from a château, as were many of the antiques. Chef Alain Llorca uses top-quality ingredients like black truffles, foie gras, giant prawns, and lobster to create enchanting dishes. A popular choice is a presentation of 11 tapas, delicate morsels bursting with flavor. The menu changes according to the freshest produce and meats, but a first course highlight is *pommes de terre nouvelles poêlées, anchois marinés et brochette de suppions* (pan-fried new potatoes, marinated anchovies, and skewered cuttlefish) and a main course highlight is *épigrammes d'agneau de lait* (lamb with breaded, braised, and grilled meat). Sommelier Jean-Max Haussy can help you select the perfect wine, though you may have trouble finding one for a reasonable price.

At the Hôtel Négresco, 37 promenade des Anglais. ☎ *04-93-16-64-00. Reservations required far in advance. Meals: Main courses 390–670F ($56–$96); menus 300F ($43) at lunch, 450F ($64) and 650F ($93) at dinner. AE, MC, V. Open: Daily 12:30–2:30 p.m. and 7:30–10:30 p.m. Closed mid-Nov to mid-Dec.*

La Zucca Magica

$$ Port VEGETARIAN/ITALIAN

The chef at this popular harborside restaurant was recently selected as the best Italian chef in Nice. That this honor should go to a vegetarian restaurant was the most startling part of the news. Chef Marco, who opened his restaurant in 1997 after cooking for many years in Rome, certainly has a fine pedigree — he's a relative of Luciano Pavarotti. He serves refined cuisine at reasonable prices, using recipes from Italy's Piedmont region and updating them with no meat or fish. The pumpkin decor will put you in the mood for the creative cuisine. You'll have to trust Marco, though, because everyone is served the same meal. You can count on savory cuisine using lots of herbs, Italian cheeses, beans, and pasta. Lasagna is a specialty.

4 bis quai Papacino. ☎ *04-93-56-25-27. Reservations recommended. Meals: Menus 85F ($12) at lunch, 150F ($21) at dinner. MC, V. Open: Tues–Sat 12:30–2:30 p.m. and 7:30–10:30 p.m.*

Le Safari

$$ Vieille Ville NIÇOISE

Arrive at Le Safari before 9 p.m. if you don't want to wait for a table. The crowds flock to this restaurant at the far east end of cours Saleya because the prices are reasonable and the food is good. The waiters must train like Olympic athletes the way they speed around the huge terrace. The restaurant also has seating inside, but you won't be able to enjoy the free entertainment from the traveling musicians, who tend to pause to play some tunes in front of Le Safari. The menu emphasizes pastas and grilled fish. The Niçoise *merda de can* (gnocchi with spinach) is a specialty, as well as beef stew. The staff speaks English, and there are English menus available.

1 cours Saleya. ☎ *04-93-80-18-44. Reservations recommended. Meals: Main courses 85–135F ($12–$19); menu 150F ($21). AE, MC, V. Open: Daily noon to 3 p.m. and 7:30–11:30 p.m. Closed Mon Nov–Apr.*

L'Escalinada

$$ Vieille Ville NIÇOISE

The terrace tables on this bustling street corner fill up first, because this is a prime people-watching section of the Old Town. This tiny restaurant, with its cheerful English-speaking staff, serves excellent specialties like homemade *socca*, *pissaladière*, and a variety of pastas. But the real standout is the homemade gnocchi, a melt-in-your-mouth version of the potato dumplings, which come heaped on a steaming platter. The authentic food is served in generous portions.

22 rue Pairolière. ☎ *04-93-62-11-71. Reservations recommended. Meals: Main courses 80–120F ($11–$17); menus 110F ($16) and 150F ($21). MC, V. Open: Daily noon to 2:30 p.m. and 7:30–11:30 p.m.*

L'Estocaficada

$$ Vieille Ville NIÇOISE

Tucked away on a side street in the Old Town, this restaurant is one of those places that you have to be looking for in order to find. As a result, patrons come in hungry for the homecooked traditional cuisine of Brigitte Autier. The restaurant is named after a popular Niçoise specialty that's a mix of codfish, olive oil, olives, tomatoes, potatoes, onions, and herbs. Begin your meal with a typical soup of the region like *bourride* (a fish stew). There are also a variety of pizzas on the menu.

2 rue de l'Hôtel-de-Ville. ☎ *04-93-80-21-64. Reservations recommended. Meals: Main courses 58–125F ($8–$18); menus 60–150F ($9–$21). MC, V. Open: Tues–Sat noon to 2:30 p.m.; Mon–Sat 7:30–10:30 p.m.*

L'Univers

$$$ Vieille Ville NIÇOISE

One star was recently awarded to prestigious chef Christian Plumail for this fine restaurant on the border of old Nice. The dining room's decor is deceptively simple considering the complex tastes being devised in the kitchen. Wrought-iron chairs surround glass-topped tables in the center of the room, but you'll want one of the tables on the perimeter — they're better for watching the gourmands of Nice come and go. The most famous dish here is the red mullet with asparagus. Other good choices are the summer special, *bouillon de petits gris et pistes à l'ail nouveau* (snail soup) and *morue fraîche aux artichauts* (fresh cod with artichokes). The restaurant offers an excellent strawberry tart for dessert.

54 bd. Jean-Jaurès. ☎ 04-93-62-32-22. Reservations necessary. Meals: Main courses 90–250F ($13–$36); menus 110F ($16) at lunch, 350F ($50) at dinner. MC, V. Open: Sun–Fri 12:30–2:30 p.m.; Mon–Sat 7:30–10:30 p.m.

The Niçoise pride themselves on their cuisine, which features a number of unique specialties. *Socca* is a steaming crêpe made of chickpeas that's sold from street vendors in the heart of the Old Town. *Pissaladière* (onion tart) and *farcis* (stuffed vegetables) are favorite appetizers. *Beignets de fleurs de cougettes* are fried zucchini flowers, and *tarte de blettes* is a tart garnished with Swiss chard. Visitors have a hard time ordering *merda de can,* which translates literally as dog excrement, but it's actually very delicious gnocchi with spinach. Small local olives, *poutine* (fried little fish), and preserved fruits are also specialties of Nice. Last but not least, there's the famous *salade niçoise,* made with tuna, potatoes, tomatoes, olives, anchovies, green beans, and capers.

Exploring the town

Nice has two distinct parts. The **modern area** in the center of the city and to the west of the old town boasts the famous **promenade des Anglais,** hands-down the Riviera's best beach boardwalk. Hotels in a wide range of price categories line the promenade. The **Vieille Ville,** on the east side, is home to Old Town, a magical place with winding ancient streets leading to charming cafes, markets, and unique shops. You can always find a lively street life here. While passing colorful markets, you may see a hurdy-gurdy player or other street performers along cours Saleya. Between the Old Town and the harbor is the **Colline du Château,** also known as just Le Château. This hill no longer has a castle but it does have a wonderful view over the bay. An elevator takes you to the top, or you can ride the tourist train to the top. The **tourist train** (☎ 04-92-14-48-00), which travels around the old city and up to Castle Hill, takes 40 minutes, costs 30F ($4.30), and leaves from the esplanade Albert-1er, across from the Hôtel Méridien. It operates daily: July and August 10 a.m. to 7 p.m., April to June and September to 6 p.m., and October to March to 5 p.m. On a hill north of town is a suburb of Nice called **Cimiez,** which also has a rich historical record as is evident from the **Roman ruins.** Next to the ruins is the famous **Musée Matisse,** the most popular museum in Nice.

Nice's wild **Carnaval** takes place the last two weeks in February and features parades, concerts, balls, fireworks, and general merriment. The Mardi Gras Parade goes from place Masséna down avenue Jean-Médecin, and the flower processions are on promenade des Anglais. The other big annual event is the **Festival du Jazz,** which takes place in July under the olive trees of the Cimiez Gardens and in the nearby Roman Arenas, on three stages simultaneously. For the event, the city hosts over 200 musicians from all over the world. Call the tourist office for details.

Beware of pickpockets in Nice, particularly near the train station and in the Old Town.

A guided English-language **walking tour of Nice's baroque art** (in the Palais Lascaris, Eglise du Gésu, Cathédrale Ste-Réparate, and Chapelle de la Misércorde) takes place Tuesdays and Sundays at 3 p.m., lasts 2½ hours, and costs 45F ($6). Tours leave from the Palais Lascaris, located at 15 rue Droite. Call ☎ 04-93-62-18-12 for details.

Walking around Nice

If you want to follow your own walking tour, begin on the **promenade des Anglais,** which was the grand idea of a vacationing Englishman, who saw many beggars here after the harsh winter of 1820–21 and set them to work building the boardwalk. The promenade follows the Baie des Anges along 15 pebbly private beaches, which are crowded with restaurants and concessions. On the other side of the boulevard, grand sea view hotels line the road. Be sure to check out one of the Riviera's top hotels, the Négresco, with its whimsical pink dome. In the evening, jazz, salsa, swing, and classical musicians give free performances along the promenade.

Then it's on to **Vieille Ville,** where the streets are lined with cafes, bars, and shops. Begin on **cours Saleya,** which, depending on the hour and day, is filled with a market of vegetables, flowers, or antiques. On the north side of the street is the **Chapelle de la Miséricorde,** a small eighteenth-century church with a jewel box of an interior. From mid-September to May, this baroque masterpiece is open for free tours on Tuesdays 10 a.m. to noon and 2 to 4 p.m.

Farther up cours Saleya, take a left on rue de la Poissonerie. Near the tops of buildings throughout the Old Town are interesting architectural flourishes, like multicolored murals, stucco friezes, and trompe l'oeil. For instance, on a building on the right side of rue de la Poissonerie is a 1584 fresco of Adam and Eve. Nearby is a lentil from the Middle Ages inscribed with the name of the family that lived in the house. Soon you'll reach the **Eglise Ste-Rita de l'Annonciation** (open daily 7:30 a.m. to 6:30 p.m.), built in the Middle Ages but "baroquialized" in the eighteenth century. This popular church is devoted to St. Rita, the patron saint of desperate causes. It's the most visited chapel in the Old Town and one of the oldest churches in Nice.

Take a left on rue de la Préfecture to reach the early-seventeenth-century **Palais de la Préfecture,** formerly the residence of the governors and princes of Savoy. Now it contains the office of the president of the General Council and the prefect of the Alpes-Maritimes region. Retrace your steps back on rue de la Préfecture to rue Droite, an ancient street used in medieval times to cross the Old Town from one city gate to the other. Take a left onto rue Droite and look for the **Eglise St-Jacques Le Majeur ou du Gésu.** After the Jesuits built this church in 1650, many wealthy families constructed palatial homes nearby. The beautiful church facade was used as a model for baroque churches throughout the region. The church is infrequently open, so seeing the facade will have to suffice.

Rue de Gésu, across from the church, leads to **place Rosetti,** which is the largest square in Old Town thanks to Monsieur Rosetti, a local who gave money to destroy all the buildings in front of the cathedral in order to improve the view from the cathedral steps. Rue Rossetti off the square leads again to rue Droite. Take a left onto rue Droite to see the **Palais Lascaris,** a museum of decorative arts (see later in this section for details). A cannon ball imbedded onto the corner building near the Palais Lascaris is from a 1543 siege of the town. Follow rue Droite to rue St-François and **place St-François,** where there's a fish market Tuesday to Sunday mornings.

Beyond the square is rue Pairoliere ("cauldron"), considered the belly of Nice, lined with food shops like *charcuteries* (pork butchers) and *boucheries* (butchers). A shortcut on tiny rue du Choeur leads to place St-Augustin with the **Eglise St-Martin et St-Augustin,** a baroque church containing a fine *Pietà* attributed to Ludovic Brea (a famous Niçoise artist of the Middle Ages). Rue Sincaire leads to rue Catherine-Ségurane, which leads to the **harbor,** the **flea market,** and a **monument to Catherine Ségurane,** Nice's most beloved heroine. This washerwoman became famous during a 1543 siege of Nice by the Turks. She climbed to the top of the ramparts that surrounded the town back then, pulled up her dress, and "mooned" the advancing Turks, thus allegedly slowing down the enemy (and/or boosting the morale of the Niçoise).

Seeing the top sights in Nice and Cimiez

You can get a **Passe-Musées** for museums in Nice or for the region. A one-week pass for all Nice museums is 70F ($10) and a one-week pass for all regional museums is 140F ($20).

In the Old Town, you can find a fine art collection housed in the **Palais Lascaris** (15 rue Droite; ☎ **04-93-62-72-40**), a seventeenth-century Genoese-style palace with a grand central staircase and baroque state-rooms. The palace was the home of the Lascaris-Ventimiglia family, who in 1648 combined four houses to make the residence. The family sold the palace in 1802, and it became a rabbit warren of squalid apartments until the city of Nice came to the rescue in 1942, purchasing the building and restoring it. On display are seventeenth- and eighteenth-century objects, including Flemish tapestries and faïence vases, as well as displays of crafts like weaving and pottery making. From December to October, it's open Tuesday to Sunday 10 a.m. to noon and 2 to 6 p.m.; guided tours are given Wednesdays, Fridays, and Sundays at 3 p.m. Admission is free.

Did you know?

Listen for a cannon shot from the Colline du Château every day at noon. Why? Well, in the late nineteenth century, the Englishman Lord Coventry retired from the army and came to live in Nice. He had an absent-minded wife, so he built a cannon on Castle Hill and fired it every day to remind her to prepare lunch for him.

Built from 1650 to 1680, the baroque **Cathédrale Ste-Reparate,** on place Rosetti in the heart of the Old Town (☎ **04-93-62-34-40**), is devoted to the patron saint of Nice, St. Reparate. Legend has it that her body was put on a barge out to sea and arrived back in the bay escorted by angels and doves (thus the name of Nice's bay, Baie des Anges, translated Bay of Angels). The church's 12 chapels, which belonged to wealthy families and corporations, are decorated in rich stucco and marble. The bell tower was added in the eighteenth century. The cathedral also has the designation "basilica," meaning a very important cathedral that hosted cardinals and bishops. It's open daily 9:30 to 11:45 a.m. and 3 to 5:30 p.m.; guided visits are Tuesdays 3 to 5 p.m. Admission is free.

Built in 1990, the enormous and daring **Musée d'Art Moderne et d'Art** (promenade des Arts; ☎ **04-93-62-61-62**) is highly entertaining as it follows the history of European and American avant-garde painting from the 1960s to the present. Quite a bit of space is devoted to the works of Yves Klein, a Niçois who made a big splash in the 1960s with his famous blue paintings and his "happenings." The museum also has a large collection of American pop art, with works by Warhol, Rauschenberg, and Lichtenstein. It's open Wednesday to Monday 10 a.m. to 6 p.m. (Fridays in season to 10 p.m.); it's closed January 1, Easter Sunday, May 1, and December 25. Admission is 25F ($3.60).

The beautiful **Musée Matisse** (164 av. des Arènes de Cimiez; ☎ **04-93-81-08-08**), situated in an Italianate villa high above Nice, houses a wonderful collection of monographs, drawings, and engravings by Matisse, as well as personal items of the artist, like furniture and vases that appear in his paintings, sculptures and paintings he cherished, and even a huge kouros (an ancient Greek statue) he owned. The museum also has Matisse's first painting, a dour 1890 still life, and one of his last gouaches from 1953. Matisse lived in Nice from 1917 until his death in 1954 and is buried in the cemetery nearby. To get to the museum, take the no. 15 or 17 bus to Cimiez and get off at the Arènes stop. The museum is open Wednesday to Monday: April to September 10 a.m. to 6 p.m. and October to March 10 a.m. to 5 p.m.; it's closed January 1, May 1, and December 25. Admission is 25F ($3.60).

Nice even has Roman ruins! Next to the Matisse Museum in Cimiez is the ancient **Baths of Cemenelum,** founded in 14 B.C. by Augustus. Admission is free and is open the same hours as the adjacent museum.

To find out more, visit the **Musée Archéologique de Nice-Cimiez,** located at 160 rue des Arènes on the western boundary of the ruins (☎ 04-93-81-59-57). The collections range from the Metal Ages (1100 B.C.) to the Middle Ages and include ceramics, glass, coins, jewelry, and sculptures. While in Cimiez, poke your head into the **Monastère de Cimiez,** located on place du Monastère next to the Matisse Museum (☎ 04-93-81-00-04). The interior is decorated with seventeenth-century frescoes, an ornate gilded wooden altarpiece, and paintings by Louis Brea. It's open daily 10 a.m. to noon and 3 to 6 p.m. The monastery's hilltop floral garden has the best view of Nice and is open until nightfall.

While living in nearby Vence, artist Marc Chagall worked on his Bible paintings between 1960 and 1966. His Bible paintings form the core of the collection at the **Musée National Message Biblique Marc Chagall,** on avenue du Docteur-Menard, at the corner of boulevard de Cimiez (☎ 04-93-53-87-20). The museum's collection, which is the largest public Chagall collection, spans the artist's life with works from the 1930s to his death in 1985 — paintings, drawings, engravings, mosaics, glass windows, and tapestries. The stark modern building that houses the works is set in a park, about a five-minute drive or short bus ride (no. 15) north of the center of town in Cimiez. The museum is open Wednesday to Monday: October to June 10 a.m. to 5 p.m. and July to September 10 a.m. to 6 p.m. Admission is 30F ($4.30); it's free the first Sunday of every month.

Nice's **Musée des Beaux-Arts** (33 av. des Baumettes; ☎ 04-92-15-28-28) is housed in an early-1900s Italianate mansion on the west side of town, the former residence of the Ukrainian Princess Kotchubey. The fine arts museum covers the seventeenth century to early twentieth century, with a collection of over 6,000 works. The seventeenth-century section was recently expanded and includes Italian paintings and Dutch landscapes. The late-nineteenth and early-twentieth-century collection has works by Dufy, Van Dongen, Monet, Degas, and Renoir. The large sculpture gallery contains works by Rodin and others. The museum is open Tuesday to Sunday 10 a.m. to noon and 2 to 6 p.m.; guided tours are given in English on Fridays at 3 p.m. Admission is 25F ($3.60).

A donation by art critic Anatole Jakovsky enabled the **Musée International d'Art Naïf** (avenue de Fabron; ☎ 04-93-71-78-33; Bus: 9, 10, 11, 12, 34) to open in the early 1980s in the attractive Château Ste-Hélène. The collection of 600 paintings, drawings, and sculptures traces the history of naïve painting from the eighteenth century to the present. The museum is open Wednesday to Monday 10 a.m. to noon and 2 to 6 p.m. Admission is 25F ($3.60) for adults and 15F ($2.15) for children.

The **Musée d'Art et d'Histoire Palais Masséna,** located at 65 rue de France, next door to Hôtel Négresco (☎ 04-93-88-11-34), was the home of Victor Masséna, an aristocrat. The museum, which is Nice's oldest art museum, houses a fine collection of decorative art and exhibits on local history. However, the Masséna is closed at press time and will remain closed for renovations until 2003 or even 2004. It should still be open Tuesday to Sunday 10 a.m. to noon and 2 to 6 p.m. Admission should still be 25F ($3.60) for adults and 15F ($2.15) for children.

In the late nineteenth century, the Russian aristocracy began wintering on the Riviera and transformed Nice in the process. You can't miss the soaring ornate onion domes at the top of the **Cathédrale Orthodoxe Russe St-Nicolas,** located on avenue Nicolas II off boulevard du Tzarévitch (☎ **04-93-96-88-02**). Built from 1902 to 1912, this magnificent church contains a large collection of icons, elaborate woodwork, and frescoes. The cathedral is open daily: May to September 9:30 a.m. to noon and 2:30 to 8 p.m. and October to May 9:30 a.m. to noon and 2:30 to 6 p.m.

Shopping

Nice's famous flower market, the **Marché aux Fleurs,** takes place on cours Saleya, the Old Town's pedestrian street, Tuesday to Saturday 6 a.m. to 5:30 p.m. and Sunday 6 a.m. to noon. A **fruit-and-vegetable market** takes place on the eastern side of cours Saleya Tuesday to Saturday 6 a.m. to 5:30 p.m. and Sunday 6 a.m. to noon. The antiques and flea market, **Marché à la Brocante,** is held on cours Saleya Mondays 8 a.m. to 6 p.m. The flea market, **Marché des Puces,** is at place Robilante (on the port) Tuesday to Saturday 10 a.m. to 6 p.m. And the fish market, **Marché aux Poissons,** is held on place St-François Tuesday to Sunday 6 a.m. to 1 p.m. The stretch of **rue Pairolière** to rue du Marché has shops specializing in cheeses, olives, fruits and vegetables, and herbs and spices.

Special things to look for in Nice include **glassware** from Biot, **pottery** from Vallauris, **perfumes** from Grasse, **faïence** from Moustier, **wine** from nearby Bellet, and **fougasse à la fleur d'oranger** (local bread made with orange blossoms).

You'll find the best olive oil at the **Maison de l'Olive** (18 rue Pairolière; ☎ **04-93-80-01-61**) and the best candied fruit at the **Confiserie Florian du Old Nice** (14 quai Papacino; ☎ **04-93-55-43-50**). On the north side of place Rosetti in the Old Town, you can find the best **ice cream** at **Finuccio** (☎ **04-93-80-62-52**), with original flavors like lavender flower, thyme, bière, rosemary, jasmine, and semolina. The **Caves Caprioglio** (16 rue de la Préfecture; ☎ **04-93-85-66-57**) is the oldest wine store in Nice and one of the oldest in France; the vineyard is only 50 hectares, and 12 families own it.

For gifts and souvenirs, head to the **Galeries Niçoises** (5 place Garibaldi; ☎ **04-93-85-36-83**) and **La Maïoun** (1 rue du Marché; ☎ **04-93-13-05-75**). At **Le Chandelier** (7 rue de la Boucherie; ☎ 04-93-85-85-19) and **Les Olivades** (8 av. de Verdun; ☎ **04-93-88-75-50**), you can browse through a great collection of Provençal fabrics.

If you're looking for arts and crafts, head to the **Atelier Contre-Jour** (3 rue du Pont Vieux; ☎ 04-93-80-20-50) for handicrafts in wood and clothing in silk and leather, and **Plat Jérôme** (34 rue Centrale; ☎ 04-93-62-17-09) for pottery. Many **artists' studios/galleries** are located on side streets near the cathedral in the Old Town.

Nightlife

Nice offers some of the best nightlife on the Riviera. You can go to the opera, hang out in an Irish pub, party at a disco, or wander along the promenade des Anglais, where itinerant musicians jam 'til the wee hours. For happenings about town, check out the free guides *Le Mois à Nice* and *L'Exés* and also *La Semaine des Spectacles* and *L'Officiel des Loisirs Côte d'Azur* (both are available at newsstands).

For highbrow entertainment, head to the **Opéra de Nice** (4 rue St-François-de-Paule; ☎ 04-92-17-40-44), an early-1900s palace designed by Charles Garner, architect of Paris's Opéra Garnier. Opéra de Nice presents a full repertoire of opera and concerts, with tickets at 50 to 400F ($7 to $57). On the other end of the scale are the 10 p.m. Vegas-style shows on Fridays and Saturdays at the **Casino Ruhl** (1 promenade des Anglais; ☎ 04-93-87-95-87), with a 120F ($17) cover that includes a drink. The casino is open for gambling noon to 4 a.m. for slot machines and 8 p.m. to 4 a.m. for the more formal gaming rooms. Entrance to the formal rooms is 75F ($11). If you play the slot machines, you don't need a passport, but for the formal gaming rooms, you do. Gentlemen are not required to wear a jacket and tie but sneakers are frowned upon.

Nice has many bars in the Old Town where Americans will feel right at home, including the **Scarlett O'Hara Irish Pub,** located on the corner of rue Rosetti and rue Droite ☎ 04-93-80-43-22; **Wayne's** (15 rue de la Préfecture; ☎ 04-93-13-46-99); and **William's Pub** (4 rue Centrale; ☎ 04-93-85-84-66), which has live music. If you'd rather hang out with French people, try **La Civette,** a popular spot for aperitifs at 29 rue de la Préfecture ☎ 04-93-62-35-51. **Butterfly** (2 quai des Etats-Unis; ☎ 04-93-92-27-31) is a hip nightclub with dancing right across from the beach; the cover is 50F ($7). Nice also has a big gay scene — the most popular club is **Blue Boy** (9 rue Spinetta; ☎ 04-93-44-68-24).

St-Jean-Cap-Ferrat and the Rothschild Villa

You may equate the name Cap-Ferrat with images of extreme opulence, but the village of **St-Jean-Cap-Ferrat** is really just a small touristy fishing port with a dozen reasonably priced restaurants bordering the harbor and a handful of little boutiques nearby. The real estate on this lush peninsula is among the Riviera's priciest. At the tip of the peninsula, a couple of miles from the port, is one of the area's most expensive and luxurious hotels, the Grand Hôtel du Cap-Ferrat. The Rothschild villa, on the highest and most central spot on the peninsula, is a fascinating museum that illustrates life in the belle époque and is surrounded by magnificent French gardens.

Getting there

The village of Cap-Ferrat is about a mile from the nearest train station at Beaulieu (see "Beaulieu and the Villa Kérylos" later in this chapter); it's a pretty walk along the bay. For train information, call ☎ 08-36-35-35-39 or 08-36-35-35-35. There's no bus from the center of Beaulieu to the village of Cap-Ferrat, so you need to take a **taxi** (60F/$9) if you don't have a car.

Nice is 3.7 km (6 miles) away, and **buses** frequently make the half-hour trip at a cost of 10.50F ($1.40). The bus between Nice and Cap-Ferrat, the no. 111, runs Monday to Saturday (not holidays). The **Aéroport Nice–Côte d'Azur** is about 20 minutes (20.9 km/13 miles) from Cap-Ferrat. You can rent a car from the airport or take an airport shuttle bus to the center of Nice and pick up a bus to Cap Ferrat from the Nice bus station. Monaco is 16 km (10 miles) away from Cap-Ferrat, while Cannes is 40 km (26 miles) away. To drive to Cap-Ferrat from Nice, take N7 east.

Getting around and getting information

You really need a car for Cap-Ferrat — mainly to arrive and depart from the peninsula. The Villa Ephrussi is technically within walking distance (about 20 minutes) from the village, but access is from a busy road with a narrow sidewalk and then up a long winding driveway with no side-walk. If you stay at a hotel near the harbor, you can walk to restaurants and shopping, but the car will come in handy if you want to explore the peninsula by driving through the steep residential area, out to see the Grand Hôtel. You can also take long walks along coastal paths on Cap-Ferrat. The **tourist office** is at 59 av. Denis-Séméria (☎ **04-93-76-08-90**; Internet: www.ville-saint-jean-cap-ferrat.fr). During July and August, the office is open Monday to Friday 8:30 a.m. to noon and 1 to 5 p.m. and Saturday 8:30 a.m. to 4 p.m.; September to June, hours are Monday to Friday 10 a.m. to noon and 1 to 5 p.m. and Saturday 10 a.m. to noon. The tourist office offers free trail maps for exploring the peninsula on foot.

Where to stay

Grand Hôtel du Cap-Ferrat

$$$$ St-Jean-Cap-Ferrat

This is one of the Riviera's grandest hotels, as reflected in its name and prices. They don't nickel and dime you here: Breakfast is included and so is admission to the pool, a mirror of heated salt water that seems to float just above the Mediterranean (admission is charged at the Eden Roc in Antibes). And the staff is actually friendly. All is palatial at the Grand, from the lobby, with its inlaid marble floor and soaring columns, to the 55 gorgeous rooms, many with terraces and sea views. The 14-acre estate features floral garden paths. The restaurant is superb, with dining outside on the sea-facing terrace or inside in the gilded dining room.

Bd. du Général-de-Gaulle. ☎ *04-93-76-50-50. Fax: 04-93-76-04-52. Internet:* www.grand-hotel-cap-ferrat.com. *E-mail:* reserv@grand-hotel-cap-ferrat.com. *Rack rates: 3,300–7,100F ($471–$1,014) double; 9,300–15,000F ($1,329–$2,143) suite. Ask about much-lower off-season (Mar, Apr, Nov, Dec) rates. Rates include breakfast. Closed Jan–Mar. AE, MC, V.*

Hôtel Belle Aurore

$$$ St-Jean-Cap-Ferrat

The English-speaking staff is accommodating at this hotel (no elevator), a pleasant seven-minute walk from town. While the lobby and bar area are somewhat dreary, just outside is a good-sized pool surrounded by a large terrace, where breakast is served. The pool includes the whimsical touch of a tiny island with a tall palm tree in the middle. The 20 rooms are motel-style, but comfortable, and many have terraces with views of the village and port. All rooms have extras like safes and minibars.

49 av. Denis-Séméria. ☎ *04-93-76-24-24. Fax: 04-93-76-15-10. Rack rates: 490–690F ($70–$99) double. Half pension: 220F ($32) per person. Breakfast: 49F ($7). MC, V.*

Hôtel Brise Marine

$$$ St-Jean-Cap-Ferrat

By virtue of its location in the Old Town, a few blocks up from the harbor, this is the best choice for a medium-priced hotel. The 17-room Brise Marine is a very attractive pale-yellow villa set high, with spectacular views of the Riviera coast all the way to Italy. It's also quite near Paloma Plage, one of the two public beaches. The high-ceilinged rooms are pretty and fresh, some with balconies; the eight rooms with views are more expensive. Breakfast is served in the large stone courtyard with sea views. The hotel has been owned and operated by the same family since 1945.

58 av. Jean-Mermoz. ☎ *04-93-76-04-36. Fax: 04-93-76-11-49. Internet:* www.hotel-brisemarine.com. *E-mail:* bmarine@nicematin.fr. *Rack rates: 750–810F ($107–$116) double. Breakfast: 60F ($9). MC, V.*

Hôtel Clair Logis

$$ St-Jean-Cap-Ferrat

This 18-room hotel is a lovely, large villa with three buildings. The location, high in the central part of the peninsula in a residential area, means you're somewhat isolated. It's a long walk to town or the beaches, so access to a car is critical if you choose to stay here. The rooms range in size: A modern annex has simple smaller rooms and the pavilion has the largest rooms, like Hibiscus, with a balcony and huge bath. The hotel is surrounded by a dense canopy of trees, so there are no water views.

12 av. Centrale. ☎ *04-93-76-04-57.* *Fax:* *04-93-76-11-85.* *Internet:* www. hotel-clair-logis.fr. *Free parking. Rack rates: 340–740F ($49–$106) double. Breakfast: 50F ($7). MC, V.*

Hôtel La Voile d'Or

$$$$ St-Jean-Cap-Ferrat

La Voile d'Or manages to be both luxurious and down-to-earth — perhaps it's the sight of the gregarious owner, who has run the hotel for over 40 years, walking around in casual clothes and checking up on the comfort of guests. Or it could be the dining room, which, though lovely, has a distinct beachy-ness. The 45 rooms, perched above the harbor, actually have more interesting views than those at the Grand Hôtel (see earlier in this section), because they look out over the sweep of coastline from Beaulieu to Monaco. The rooms are the height of elegance and comfort — all have antiques and French doors leading to terraces. You can easily walk to the village and portside restaurants. The hotel has garden terraces for dining, as well as a cheerful dining room with wraparound windows. The heated pool is set above the harbor and sea, and the private beach is a short walk down the embankment.

31 av. Jean-Mermoz. ☎ *04-93-01-13-13.* *Fax: 04-93-76-11-17. Internet:* www. lavoiledor.fr. *E-mail:* reservation←voiledor.fr. *Parking: 150F ($21). Rack rates: 1,980–3,500F ($283–$500) double. Rates include breakfast. High season (June-Sept). Ask about off-season rates. Closed Nov–Mar. AE, MC, V.*

Hôtel l'Oursin

$$ St-Jean-Cap-Ferrat

This is a cheap hotel with a difference: The 14 stylish rooms are decorated with artwork, photography, and antiques. The three rooms on the highest floors have harbor views. The rooms are small with stucco walls, but they do get lots of sunlight. The hotel is also very well located, in the heart of the village, across from the harbor.

1 av. Denis-Séméria. ☎ *04-93-76-04-65.* *Fax: 04-93-76-12-55. E-mail:* oursin@ wanadoo.fr. *Rack rates: 280–550F ($40–$79) double. Breakfast: 45F ($6). MC, V.*

Where to dine

Capitaine Cook

$$ St-Jean-Cap-Ferrat PROVENÇAL

Next door to the fancy Hôtel La Voile d'Or (see "Where to stay" earlier in this section), a few blocks uphill from the center of the village, this restaurant specializes in seafood served in hearty portions. You get a wonderful view of the coast from the restaurant's terrace, and inside the decor is rugged-sea-shanty style. Oysters, served simply on the half shell or in several creative ways with sauces and herbs, are a speciality. While roasted catch of the day is the mainstay, the filet mignon is also popular. The staff speaks English.

11 av. Jean-Mermosz. Tel **04-93-76-02-66.** *Meals: Main courses 45–140F ($6–$20); menus 120F ($17) and 150F ($21). MC, V. Open: Fri–Tues noon to 2 p.m.; Thurs–Tues 7:30–9:30 p.m. Closed mid-Nov to Dec.*

Grand Hôtel du Cap-Ferrat

$$$$ St-Jean-Cap-Ferrat PROVENÇAL

This is extravagance defined, and the stellar service can't fail to impress. The restaurant offers seating outside on the garden terrace or inside in the lavishly decorated dining room. Chef Jean-Claude Guillon has a solid reputation, and you'll have to put yourself in his hands because the menu detailing unusual ingredients and preparations is likely to leave even an expert translator perplexed. The famous lamb for two, *carré d'agneau des Alpes du sud rôti et gratinée au pistou* (rack of lamb from the Alps roasted and browned with basil-and-garlic sauce), costs 580F ($83), but it's worth it. Other exceptional dishes are the first course *truffles d'été en chausson feuilletée, meli-melo de salade au vinegre de Xeres* (summer truffles in a pastry with a salad of assorted seafoods and sherry vinegar) and the main course *tournedos de boeuf, poêlé au foie gras façon "Rossini"* (beef filet with pan-fried foie gras).

Bd. du Général-de-Gaulle. ☎ **04-93-76-50-50.** *Reservations required. Meals: Main courses 230–375F ($33–$54); menu 570F ($81). AE, MC, V. Open: Daily noon to 2 p.m. and 7:30–9:30 p.m. Closed Jan–Mar.*

Le Provençal

$$$ St-Jean-Cap-Ferrat PROVENÇAL

What distinguishes this restaurant, just up from the harbor in the village center, is that you get a very fancy meal in an elegant setting. The 250F menu is an excellent value: Instead of including the usual lesser choices, Le Provençal lets bargain hunters choose from impressive dishes like the first course *mille-feuille de caille en fouille de poireaux nouveaux, artichauts violets, fricassée de seiche* (puffed pastry with quail, new leeks, small artichokes, and braised squid), the main dish *épaule d'agneau confite miel et épices* (lamb shoulder with a confit of honey and spices), or *rouget rôti au cocofrais* (roasted red mullet with coconut). The most popular dessert is the rich *crème brûlée*. The restaurant's location gives you wonderful views of the harbor and coast.

2 av. Denis-Séméria. ☎ *04-93-76-03-97. Reservations required. Meals: Main courses 150–550F ($21–$79); menus 250F ($36), 350F ($50), and 650F ($93). MC, V. Open: May–Oct Fri–Sun noon to 2:30 p.m., daily 7:30–11 p.m.; Nov–Apr Fri–Sun noon to 2:30 p.m. and 7:30–11 p.m.*

Le Skipper

$$ St-Jean-Cap-Ferrat   PROVENÇAL

This harborside restaurant specializing in fish features the chef's famous fish soup with Parmesan rouille. The dense brown broth is served in a large bowl that you ladle into your soup dish and accompanied by toasted bread roundlets that you spread with a very hot sauce and dunk into the soup. As a main course, two standouts are sole fillets with whipped butter and monkfish with "famous" sauce, an herb-rich cream roux. But perhaps the most popular dish is the mussels marinara (the key is in the rich broth). For dessert, try the excellent *citron tart meringue*. The menu has English translations.

Port de St-Jean-Cap-Ferrat. ☎ *04-93-76-01-00. Meals: Main courses 67–180F ($10–$26); menus 98F ($14), 159F ($23), and 235F ($34). MC, V. Open: Fri–Wed noon to 2 p.m. and 7:30–10:30 p.m.*

Le Sloop One

$$$ St-Jean-Cap-Ferrat   PROVENÇAL

Of the dozen or so restaurants next to the harbor, this one gets the most favorable reviews year after year. It's a favorite of Andrew Lloyd Webber, as well as many guidebooks and *Gourmet* magazine, so it tends to fill up first. The decor is yacht-club attractive, with blue-and-white chairs and awning, and the waiters are snappily dressed in captain's jackets. Not surprisingly, fish is the thing here. The wonderful *quenelle de sole* (sole dumpling) is often on the menu, as is the whole roasted monkfish seasoned with provençal herbs. For dessert, the restaurant has home-made ice cream.

Port de St-Jean-Cap-Ferrat. ☎ *04-93-01-48-63. Reservations recommended. Meals: Main courses 145–165F ($21–$24); menu 155F ($22). MC, V. Open: Thurs–Tues noon to 2 p.m. and 7–10:30 p.m. Closed mid-Nov to mid-Dec.*

Exploring the villa and beaches

The **Villa Ephrussi de Rothschild** (avenue Denis-Séméria; ☎ 04-93-01-33-09; Internet: www.villa-ephrussi.com) is one of the Riviera's most beautiful villas. In 1912, the highly eccentric Béatrice Ephrussi, baronne de Rothschild (1864–1934), built this pink-and-white mansion, with Italian Renaissance influences, at the peninsula's highest point and named it the Ile de France, after her favorite ship. Béatrice, born a Rothschild, was the daughter of a Banque de France director and wife of the wealthy banker Maurice Ephrussi. She discovered Cap-Ferrat in 1905 and bought 18 acres on which to build her dream villa. The project took seven years, involving 20 to 40 architects. As money was no object, the baronne purchased exquisite antiques, frescoes, and artwork from all over the world. Equally remarkable are the property's seven gardens, created with themes: Spanish, Florentine, lapidary, Japanese, exotic, provençal, and the rosery. One irony is that Béatrice, with homes in Paris and Monaco (her preferred home), never really spent much time here. She had no children, so she left the villa, along with its collections, to the Académie des Beaux-Arts de l'Institut de France, which now runs the museum. You can have lunch or a snack in the lovely tearoom with views of the port of Villefranche, or on the terrace surrounded by the gardens. You can tour the downstairs with a brochure in English, but seeing the upstairs rooms requires a guide and costs an extra 14F ($2). During July and August, the villa is open daily from 10 a.m. to 7 p.m.; mid-February to October, hours are daily from 10 a.m. to 6 p.m.; and November to mid-February, hours are Monday to Friday from 2 to 6 p.m. and Saturday and Sunday from 10 a.m. to 6 p.m. Admission is 49F ($7); guided tours of the second floor (in French) are given at 11:30 a.m. and 2:30 and 3:30 p.m. and cost an extra 14F ($2).

You can spend the day at the **Grand Hôtel du Cap-Ferrat's pool,** open daily 10 a.m. to 7 p.m. for outside guests. The daily rate is 310F ($44) for adults and 190F ($27) for children, while the half-day rate is 200F ($29) for adults and 130F ($19) for children. Day rates for cabanas are 1,500F ($214) with four lounge "beds" (which include mattresses); a small cabana is 700F ($100) per day with two beds; a massage is 550F ($79) and a swimming lesson is 350F ($50). **Club Dauphine** is the poolside restaurant.

It's difficult to actually see the sandy beaches of Cap-Ferrat, because almost every inch of sand is taken up by the beach chairs that are lined up by the beach concession. Nevertheless, these are attractive warm water beaches with picturesque views of the sweeping coastline and mountains. **Plage de Passable** (chemin de Passable; ☎ 04-93-76-06-17) is on the west side of the peninsula, less than a mile from the village. Concessions include a bar, a restaurant open for lunch and dinner, and an ice-cream stand. **Plage Paloma** (route de St-Hospice; ☎ 04-93-01-64-71) is in a pretty spot on the east side of the island just past the port (500 meters), with views of the coastline and Beaulieu. Restaurants and concessions are beachside. The beach is an easy five-minute walk from town. Both beaches have free parking.

Beaulieu and the Villa Kérylos

Beaulieu, located between Monaco (3.7 km/6 miles east) and Nice (3.7 km/6 miles west), is a small beach resort that features side-by-side Relais & Châteaux deluxe hotels. Although there's not much to do in Beaulieu besides enjoy the beautiful Mediterranean beaches, it does have one must-see sight worth a special trip: the faux-Greek Villa Kérylos. The Berlugans (people from Beaulieu) are a friendly crowd, so this is a nice place to base yourself for day trips to Monaco, Nice, and Cap-Ferrat.

Getting there

Beaulieu is a stop on the Riviera's main coastal **train** line, which has frequent service to Nice and Monaco. The train station, **Gare SNCF,** is located at place Georges-Clémenceau in the center of town. For train information or reservations, call ☎ **08-36-35-35-39. Buses** traveling a coastal route to Nice stop in Beaulieu at the corner of boulevard Maréchal-Leclerc and boulevard Maréchal-Joffre. For bus information, call ☎ **04-93-85-61-81.** It's about a 30-minute **drive** from Nice to Beaulieu along the coastal highway or the Moyenne Corniche.

Getting around and getting information

You can walk from one end of Beaulieu to the other in about 10 minutes, but if you want a taxi, try the stand at place Georges-Clémenceau (☎ **04-93-01-03-46**). You can rent a car at **Avis** (garage de la Poste, 1 rue Georges-Clémenceau; ☎ **04-93-01-00-13**), **Hertz** (port de Plaisance; ☎ **04-93-01-62-30**), or **Locations Citer** (1 bd. Maréchal-Joffre; ☎ **04-93-01-65-65**).

The **tourist office** is on place Georges-Clémenceau (☎ **04-93-01-02-21;** Fax: 04-93-01-44-04; Internet: www.ot-beaulieu-sur-mer.fr). It's open daily: July and August 10 a.m. to 6 p.m. and September to June 10 a.m. to noon and 2 to 6 p.m.

Where to stay

Hôtel Frisia

$$$ Beaulieu

Americans feel right at home at the 32-room Frisia because owner Daniel Hoessly is American/Swiss. The hotel has a great location, across from the port and not far from Plage Petite Afrique, and 16 rooms have wonderful sea views. All rooms have been recently renovated and include mini-bars and safes; the family rooms fit four people comfortably. A pool is being installed for 2001, and the top floor has a terrace with panoramic views. The bar is a comfortable place to chat with your friendly hosts and meet other guests.

2 bd. Eugène-Gauthier. ☎ *04-93-01-01-04. Fax: 04-93-01-31-92. E-mail:* info@ hotel-frisia.com. *Rack rates: 500–710F ($71–$101) double. Breakfast: 50F ($7). Closed mid-Nov to mid-Dec. MC, V.*

Hôtel Le Havre Bleu

$$ Beaulieu

This whitewashed villa with bright-blue shutters (no elevator) is quite welcoming, but the neighborhood around it has a wrong-side-of-the-tracks quality. The 22 rooms are small and simple but very clean and dressed up with provençal fabrics. The amenties are a little nicer here than at most two-star hotels (higher-quality towels and linens, Galimard soap). For breakfast, you can choose in-room service or dining in the cheerful breakfast room. The staff is efficient though taxed. The hotel rents fans (10F/$1), bikes (40F/$5 per half day), and beach towels (25F/ $3 per day).

29 bd. Maréchal-Joffre. ☎ *04-93-01-01-40. Fax: 04-93-01-29-92. E-mail:* Pascal. Cheruy@wanadoo.fr. *Free parking. Rack rates: 320–370F ($46–$53) double. Breakfast: 20F ($2.85) continental or 35F ($5) full. MC, V.*

Hôtel Le Marcellin

$$ Beaulieu

This is Beaulieu's best budget option. Of the hotel's 19 rooms, five share bathrooms. The building has no elevator, so guests with lots of baggage will have to lug it up a steep winding staircase. But the simple rooms get lots of light. The hotel is in a decent location, a few blocks from the center of town and a five-minute walk to the beaches. It has a cozy feel about it and has been run by the same family since 1938.

18 av. Albert-1er. ☎ *04-93-01-01-69. Fax: 04-93-01-37-43. Rack rates: 160–300F ($23–$43) double. Breakfast: 35F ($5). MC, V.*

La Réserve de Beaulieu

$$$$ Beaulieu

Of the two four-star hotels on the waterfront, La Réserve boasts the more renowned reputation mainly because of its restaurant, which has two Michelin stars and is one of Les Grandes Tables du Monde (an organization of the world's top restaurants). The hotel is also a member of the prestigious Relais & Châteaux group. The Italianate rose-pink villa, built in 1881, contains sleek interiors with marble floors, gold damask curtains, and wrought-iron chandeliers. All 37 rooms and suites feature lush carpeting, antique furniture, and comfortable seating areas, as well as extras like CD players, VCRs, and two TVs. Many have balconies, where you can enjoy breakfast with a sea view. Beautiful gardens lead to the heated seawater pool, which sits just above a private beach and port. A health club was being added at press time.

5 bd Maréchal-Leclerc. ☎ *04-93-01-00-01. Fax: 04-93-01-28-99. Internet:* www. reservebeaulieu.com/. *E-mail:* reservebeaulieu@relaischateaux. fr. *Rack rates: 1,050–4,400F ($150–$629) double; 3,200–8,200F ($457–$1,171) suite. Breakfast: 140F ($20). Closed mid-Jan to Feb and mid-Nov to mid-Dec. AE, DC, MC, V.*

Le Métropole

$$$$ Beaulieu

Built in the early 1900s to resemble an Italian palace, this four-star Relais & Châteaux hotel is on the beach and practically next door to La Réserve. The hotel's 35 rooms and 5 apartments are more modern and less grand than those of its neighbor. The rooms are attractive and quite spacious, decorated with provençal fabrics, wicker, and overstuffed couches. Many have French doors that lead to balconies overlooking the sea (rooms with balconies and sea views are twice the price). The pool is heated to 86°F year-round. The restaurant, with a large terrace looking out over the sea, serves expensive provençal cuisine.

15 bd. Maréchal-Leclerc. ☎ *04-93-01-00-08. Fax: 04-93-01-18-51. Internet:* www. le-metropole.com/. *E-mail:* metropole@relaischateaux.fr. *Rack rates: July–Sept 1,700–3,400F ($243–$486) double; 4,600–5,900F ($657–$843) suite. Half pension: 450F ($64) per person. Breakfast: 135F ($19). Closed late Oct to late Dec. AE, DC, MC, V.*

Where to dine

La Pignatelle

$$ Beaulieu PROVENÇAL

This chef-owned/operated restaurant is a favorite with locals, who appreciate the good value represented by well-priced delicious food. In summer, seating is available on the terrace in the shady garden. The chef concentrates on simple, traditional preparations of fresh fish and vegetables. Let your waiter steer you to the best choices, which may include the classic *salade Niçoise,* and as a main course, the roasted sea bream with provençal herbs. The restaurant also serves homemade pastries.

10 rue de Quincenet. ☎ *04-93-01-03-37. Reservations recommended. Meals: Main courses 55–160F ($8–$23); menus 80F ($11), 138F ($20), and 188F ($27). MC, V. Open: Thurs–Tues noon to 2 p.m. and 7:30–10 p.m. Closed Nov–Dec.*

La Réserve de Beaulieu

$$$$ **Beaulieu** **PROVENÇAL**

"The king of restaurants and the restaurant of kings," La Réserve is one of France's finest restaurants, serving haute cuisine in a spacious room with Mediterranean views. The walls are decorated with Aubusson tapestries and the ceiling with Italianate frescoes. Chef Christophe Cussac received his second Michelin star in 1999, and is in top form. Lovely first courses include the *balico de petits rougettes aux artichauts* (small red-leaf lettuce with artichokes) and *salade de homard aux pousses d'épinards et panisses au parmesan* (lobster salad with spinach-and-Parmesan pancake). Main courses not to be missed are *palangre meunière aux tomates confites* (palangre fish pan-fried with tomato preserves) and *loup de Méditerranée au bellet rouge et poire épicée* (sea bass with spiced pear). Not surprisingly, the restaurant also offers a very special foie gras dish: *foie gras d'oie en coque de sel et côtes de blettes a l'orgeat* (foie gras in a shell of salt and special Swiss chard).

5 bd. Maréchal-Leclerc. ☎ 04-93-01-00-01. Reservations required far in advance. Meals: Main courses 165–370F ($24–$53); menus 300F ($43), 480F ($69), and 650F ($93); tasting menu 850F ($121). Open: Daily noon to 2:30 p.m. and 8–10:30pm. Closed mid-Jan to Feb and mid-Nov to mid-Dec. AE, DC, MC, V.

Les Agaves

$$ **Beaulieu** **PROVENÇAL**

Les Agaves, in the 1900 Palais des Anglais, is the best restaurant in town if you don't want to break the bank and go to Le Réserve. This bistro, situated in an attractive building that has been turned into storefronts, has been receiving laudatory press for a few years. The best surprise is that the prices are quite reasonable for the creative cuisine. Chef/owner Jacques Lelu's specialties are homemade ravioli and grilled dishes; his ultimate ravoili dish is served with *cèpes* (white mushrooms) and truffles. His *bouillabaisse,* famously hearty, is made with about half a dozen types of fresh fish. The restaurant also serves an excellent *coquilles St-Jacques,* the classic scallop dish, and *filet de rascasse à la crème de truffe* (scorpion-fish with truffle sauce). English is spoken here.

4 av. Maréchal-Leclerc. ☎ 04-93-01-13-12. Reservations recommended. Meals: Main courses 90–190F ($13–$27); menu 175F ($25); bouillabaisse 250F ($36). Open: Wed–Sun noon to 2:30 p.m.; Tues–Sun 7:30–10 p.m. Closed Nov.

Résidence Eiffel

$$$ **Beaulieu** **PROVENÇAL**

If you'd like a four-star sea view with your meal but the four-star hotels aren't in your budget, this is a decent choice. The restaurant, in a hotel that is set in a marvelous waterfront villa that used to belong to Gustave Eiffel (of tower fame), is located next to the Villa Kérylos (see "Exploring the villa and beaches" later in this section). The portions are small and the food quality is inconsistent, but the view of the coastline is perfect. The crowd, mainly hotel residents, tends to be on the older side. Stick to the simplest dishes, like *moules marinière* (mussels cooked in white wine with onions and herbs) as a first course, and for the main course *filet de pagne rôti, crème d'artichauts* (roast local fish with artichoke sauce) or a pasta dish like the *penne au crevettes* (shrimp). If they have the mandarin-and-chocolate soufflé, order it.

Rue Gustave-Eiffel. ☎ *04-93-76-46-46. Meals: Main courses 76–118F ($11–$17); menu 159F ($23). MC, V. Open: Daily noon to 2 p.m. and 7–9 p.m. Closed Nov to mid-Dec.*

Exploring the villa and beaches

Théodore Reinach (1860–1928) created his dream house at the tip of a rocky promontory jutting into the sea and named it the **Villa Kérylos** (rue Gustave-Eiffel; ☎ **04-93-01-01-44**). An archaeologist, man of letters, and scholar of ancient Greece, Reinach wanted his home to replicate a Greek villa from the second century B.C. So the house, built from 1902 to 1908, is a completely unique mingling of early-1900s techniques with ancient Greek sensibility; it's a fun and fascinating combination. Reinach wanted to eat, sleep, and party like the Greeks, so his dining room chairs are vertical chaise lounges for reclining, next to three-legged tables. His bed is framed by fluted columns, and his marble bathtub can fit ten men. The villa has mosaics, frescoes, and reproductions of artworks from Pompeii and ancient Greece. Luxurious materials like marble, bronze, ivory, and exotic woods are used liberally. You won't want to miss the gallery of antiquities in the stone basement, which is surrounded by windows level with the sea. You can watch windsurfers while admiring copies of famous statues like the *Venus de Milo* and the *Discus Thrower.* You can get a brochure in English. After touring the house, stroll through the garden and have a bite to eat at the cafe. From mid-February to mid-November, the villa is open daily 10:30 a.m. to 6 p.m.; July and August, hours are daily 10:30 a.m. to 7 p.m.; mid-December to mid-February, hours are Monday to Friday 2 to 6 p.m. and Saturday and Sunday 10:30 a.m. to 6 p.m.; the villa is closed January 1 and December 25. Admission is 40F ($6) for adults and 20F ($2.85) for children; guided visits in French are given at 2:15, 3:15, and 4:15 p.m. in spring and autumn, and also at 5 p.m. in summer. For a tour in English, you must make a reservation. A summer classical music concert series is held at the villa in late July and early August, featuring four concerts beginning at 8:30 p.m. and costing 100F ($14). Call for dates.

The two beaches with concessions are **Plage Petite Afrique** off promenade Pasteur (☎ **04-93-01-11-00**) and **La Calanque** at Baie des Fourmis (☎ **04-93-01-45-00**). These are attractive, if crowded, beaches. Plage Petite Afrique, the easternmost, is a crescent-shaped beach dotted with palm trees and lush vegetation.

Nightlife

At the **Grand Casino de Beaulieu** (4 av. Fernand-Dunan; ☎ 04-93-76-48-00), jackets are required for men at the fancy end, which has a 70F ($10) entrance fee. The slot machine section, where dress is more casual, is free to enter and doesn't require a passport. For the game rooms you need a passport. The casino also has a disco on site.

Monaco: Big Money on The Rock

Visitors flock to the principality of **Monaco** to ogle the ultra-rich gamblers, watch the changing of the guard at the Grimaldi Palace, and stroll through the exotic gardens. Looking for a quaint little place on a sliver of coast near the border of Italy, most people are struck by the overdevelopment — particularly the densely packed skyscrapers. This tiny country, with 30,000 residents and 371 acres (the size of a small town), is built into the side of a steep ridge. The roads and streets are in vertical layers that are difficult to navigate, so elevators take people from one level to the next. But most people don't bother to use them — they drive. Monaco and its Monégasques absolutely adore the automobile (the famous Grand Prix in late May or early June is the year's biggest event). The town is crisscrossed by fast roads with no sidewalks, or very narrow ones. If you don't have a car, the best way to get around is by bus.

Besides cars, the other thing worshiped in Monaco is money. The Monégasques don't pay income tax, and the whole principality, with its wall-to-wall condominium towers and casino culture, seems obsessed with lucre — filthy or otherwise. Two-thirds of its hotel rooms are contained within four-star deluxe hotels, so Monaco has always been a destination for the rich and famous.

There are pockets of beauty in this principality and a number of interesting sights. Orange trees line rue Grimaldi, the main road through the center, and you can catch a glimpse of the yacht-filled harbor from almost anywhere in Monaco. The Old Town surrounding the palace has narrow cobblestone streets and charming restaurants and shops. The parks and gardens of the principality, especially the Jardin St-Martin with views out to sea, are spectacular. And, if you're willing to scrub up and plop down a 100F ($14) cover charge, you can wander around the famed Monte Carlo Casino, with its gilded columns and frescoed ceilings, or have a drink at the terrace bar in the Hôtel Hermitage with breathtaking port views.

The Grimaldi family, originally from Genoa, acquired the lordship of Monaco in 1308, and since then, the title Prince de Monaco has been bestowed on the heirs. Prince Rainier III (in his late 70s) is the current head of the family — you probably know that in 1956 he married American actress Grace Kelly, who died in a car crash here in 1982. The

Monaco

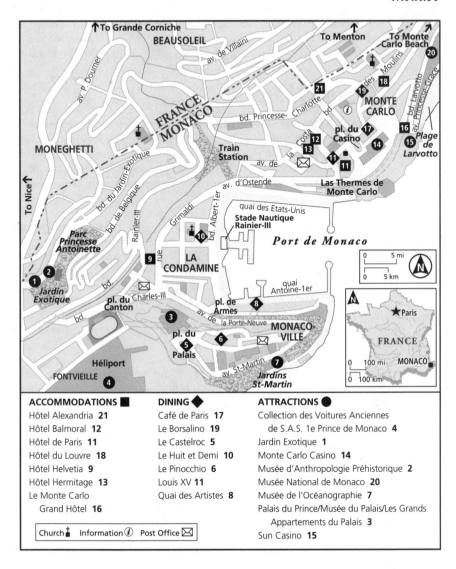

ACCOMMODATIONS ■	DINING ◆	ATTRACTIONS ●
Hôtel Alexandria **21**	Café de Paris **17**	Collection des Voitures Anciennes
Hôtel Balmoral **12**	Le Borsalino **19**	de S.A.S. 1e Prince de Monaco **4**
Hôtel de Paris **11**	Le Castelroc **5**	Jardin Exotique **1**
Hôtel du Louvre **18**	Le Huit et Demi **10**	Monte Carlo Casino **14**
Hôtel Helvetia **9**	Le Pinocchio **6**	Musée d'Anthropologie Préhistorique **2**
Hôtel Hermitage **13**	Louis XV **11**	Musée National de Monaco **20**
Le Monte Carlo	Quai des Artistes **8**	Musée de l'Océanographie **7**
Grand Hôtel **16**		Palais du Prince/Musée du Palais/Les Grands
		Appartements du Palais **3**
Church ⛪ Information ⓘ Post Office ✉		Sun Casino **15**

European tabloid press follows closely the exploits of Rainier and Grace's three children: Albert (will the heir to the throne ever get married?), Caroline (is her third marriage on the rocks?), and Stephanie (will she ever find true love?). Many tourists visit Monaco's cathedral to pay homage at Princess Grace's burial site.

Monaco has a heavy police presence, and rowdiness isn't tolerated in the principality. You can assume that most men you see riding scooters in Monaco are police.

Monaco's telephone numbers have eight digits, as opposed to France's numbers with ten digits. When calling Monaco from France, dial ☎ 00-377 plus the eight-digit number. To dial Monaco from the United States, dial ☎ 011-377 plus the eight-digit number. To call a number in France from Monaco, dial ☎ 011-33 plus the last nine digits of the number.

Getting there

With no border formalities, Monaco is easy to get to by car, bus, or train. There's frequent train service (every half-hour) to and from Cannes, Nice, Antibes, and Menton. Trips from Nice to Monaco cost 40F ($6) and take 20 minutes. There's one train per day from Paris costing 464 to 739F. It takes seven hours. For train schedules, call ☎ 93-10-60-01 in Monaco or 08-36-35-35-39 in France.

In late 1999, Monaco opened an enormous new train station ¼ of a mile east of the old station. This new station has three exits on three levels, and if you don't know which exit to use you may have trouble finding your hotel. Monaco is a confusing place to navigate, so you may want to pick up a free map at the station's tourist office (open daily 9 a.m. to 6:30 p.m.). Arriving at the Monaco train station after 9 p.m. is like arriving on Wall Street after 9 p.m. — it's desolate, and there's not a soul on the street. On the bright side, Monaco restaurants serve dinner late, so you can get a full meal after 10 p.m.

There's frequent bus service (every 15 minutes) to Nice, Beaulieu, and Menton on line no. 100 of the French bus company Rapides Côte d'Azur (☎ 04-97-00-07-00). The trip from Nice to Monaco by bus takes half an hour and costs 15.50F ($2.20) round-trip or 8.50F ($1.15) one-way. The times and prices are the same to Menton. The easiest place to catch a bus is in front of the Casino, but it also stops in front of the port (on boulevard Albert-1er at the Stade Nautique stop) and at several other spots around town.

If you're driving from Nice to Monaco, take N7 northeast. The 12-mile drive takes about 40 minutes because of heavy traffic; Cannes to Monaco takes about 55 minutes. If driving from Paris, take A6 to Lyon. In Lyon, take A7 south to Aix en Provence and A6 to Monaco.

Getting around and getting information

The best way to get around Monaco is by **bus,** and you can buy bus cards, which cost 8F ($1.15) per ride, at *tabacs* (tobacconists). Bus stops are set up every few blocks on the main streets in town, like boulevard Albert-1er, avenue St-Martin in Monaco Ville, and boulevard des Moulins in Monte Carlo. Buses go to all the major tourist sights; just look at the front of the bus to see the destination.

Monaco is considered the safest place in Europe. Lots of security forces are around to protect everyone's money, and the streets are safe at all hours. Children take buses alone. It's also one of the cleanest places in Europe, and you'll rarely see litter on the ground.

For a **taxi,** call ☎ 93-15-01-01. There are taxi stands in front of the Casino on avenue de Monte-Carlo, at place des Moulins in Monte Carlo; at the Port de Monaco on avenue Président J. F. Kennedy; and in front of the Poste de Monte-Carlo on avenue Henry-Dunant. There's a **Hertz** car rental office at 27 bd. Albert-1er (☎ 93-50-79-60), and an **Avis** office at 9 av. d'Ostende (☎ 93-30-17-53).

The **Corniches** are the three major scenic coastal highways of the Riviera stretching from Nice to Menton and passing around Monaco. The lower road is called the **Corniche Inférieure;** the middle road is the **Moyenne Corniche,** which runs through the mountains; and the **Grande Corniche** is the highest road over the top of the mountains bordering the Riviera.

If you're driving around Monaco, be *very careful* on the wicked curves of the corniches.

The changing of the palace guard takes place at 11:55 a.m., which creates a major traffic jam in Monaco between 10:30 and 11:30 a.m. If you're driving in or around Monaco during that time, you'll have major delays.

The **tourist office** is at 2A bd. des Moulins, Monte Carlo (☎ 92-16-61-66), and is open daily 9 a.m. to 6:30 p.m. The popular bar/restaurant **Stars 'N' Bars** (6 quai Antoine-1er on the port; ☎ 93-50-95-95), also serves as a Web cafe.

Where to stay

Hôtel Alexandra

$$$ Monte Carlo

Close to the casino, the early-1900s Alexandra has a great corner location. The friendly reception makes you feel right at home. A recent renovation cleaned up the beautiful facade and spruced up the 56 rooms, which are spacious and comfortable, although some are dark. They include modern modular wall units forming desks and closets and extras like soundproof windows, minibars, and hairdryers. The rooms with French balconies have street views. The continental breakfast is served only in the rooms.

33 bd. Princesse-Charlotte. ☎ 93-50-63-13. Fax: 92-16-06-48. Parking: 42F ($6). Rack rates: 580–890F ($83–$127) double. Breakfast: 75F ($11). MC, V.

Hôtel Balmoral

$$$ Monte Carlo

One of the great deals on the Côte d'Azur, the 64-room Balmoral is a few blocks from the casino; it's beside the Hermitage on a promontory, so you have the same view as those paying three times the rate next door. Many rooms have French balconies, where you can enjoy a perfect sunrise over the sea. If you don't require a sea view, you can get a large room facing the street for 450F ($64). Breakfast is served in a rather depressing basement room, but it is a pretty good buffet, with cheeses, meats, and pâtés, in addition to the usual fare. The large patio and garden overlooking the harbor are perfect for strolling or sitting. The restaurant is open for lunch and dinner.

12 av. de la Costa. ☎ *93-50-62-37. Fax: 93-15-08-69. Internet:* www.hotel-balmoral. mc. *E-mail:* resa@hotel-balmoral.mc. *Rack rates: 450–1,100F ($64–$157) double; 1,300–2,000F ($186–$286) suite. Breakfast: 90F ($13). AE, MC, V.*

Hôtel de Paris

$$$$ Monte Carlo

One of Europe's grandest hotels, the Paris, built in 1864, sits beside the famous casino on Monte Carlo's central square. The elaborate facade is a wonder surpassed only by the gilded lobby with marble columns, classical statuary, crystal chandeliers, and frescoes. The 197 sumptuous rooms include 19 large junior suites and 43 pricey apartments. The high-ceilinged rooms are individually decorated with antiques and stylish accessories, and many have balconies. The hotel features four restaurants, two of which have Michelin stars: Alain Ducasse's Louis XV (three stars), the Grill (one star), the Salle Empire, and the Côte Jardin. Le Bar Américain is a sophisticated jazz club. The hotel is connected to the Thermes Marins, an ultramodern seawater therapy spa. The hotel also has an indoor pool, saunas, and a fitness center. Guests are given a gold card allowing free access to the casino and the Monte Carlo Beach Club, with its private pool and beach. The card also offers a 50 percent discount at the Monte Carlo Country Club, with 23 tennis courts and the Golf Club.

Place du Casino. ☎ *92-16-30-00. Fax: 92-16-38-50. Internet:* www. montecarloresort.com. *E-mail:* hp@sbm.mc. *Parking: 150F ($21). Rack rates: 2,240–3,710F ($320–$530) double; 3,710–4,920F ($530–$703) suite; from 7,000F ($1,000) apartment. Breakfast: 170F ($24). AE, DC, MC, V.*

Hôtel du Louvre

$$$ Monte Carlo

A few blocks from the casino, the 33-room Louvre is a good medium-priced option. The hotel is located on a busy central road, but the rooms have soundproof windows, so it's relatively quiet. Most rooms are on the small side, but some have French balconies with distant sea views. All rooms have minibars. There's a bus stop in front of the hotel for city buses that travel to all the attractions in Monaco, including the palace and port.

16 bd. des Moulins. ☎ *93-50-65-25. Fax: 93-30-23-68. Internet:* www.monte-carlo. mc/louvre. *E-mail:* hotel-louvre@monte-carlo.mc. *Rack rates: 880–980F ($126–$140) double. Breakfast: 70F ($10). AE, MC, V.*

Hôtel Helvetia

$$ La Condamine

This is the best cheap hotel in Monaco, with a good location just steps from rue Princesse-Caroline, a 4-block-long cafe-lined pedestrian street leading to the port. The hotel is also a short walk from place d'Armes, where Monaco's outdoor food market is held Saturday mornings. Of its 25 rooms, 21 have private baths. For breakfast in the pleasant street-front dining room, you can choose from a continental or full breakfast, both with homemade jam.

1 bis rue Grimaldi. ☎ *93-30-21-71. Fax: 92-16-70-51. Internet:* www.monte-carlo. mc/helvetia. *E-mail:* hotel-helvetia@monte-carlo.mc. *Rack rates: 380–480F ($54–$69) double. Breakfast: 40F ($6). MC, V.*

Hôtel Hermitage

$$$$ Monte Carlo

Second only to the Hôtel de Paris (see earlier in this section), the Hermitage is a glistening beaux-arts palace, with a wonderful location high on the precipice. Like the Paris, the Hermitage is owned by the Société des Bains de Mer, an organization founded in 1863 to develop Monte Carlo. The facade, facing the port and the sea, has an Italian-style loggia and vaulting with ceiling frescoes. Inside is a Winter Garden, built by Gustave Eiffel, with a Tiffany-type stained-glass dome. The lovely 227 rooms, including 18 apartments and 14 junior suites, are decorated in period decor in the central part, or in a cheerful contemporary style in the newer wings. Many of the rooms have balconies with wicker furniture. You have access to the attached seawater therapy spa (also attached to the Paris), with a large pool. The restaurant and bar Le Vistamar, which recently received a Michelin star, opens onto a beautiful terrace that is the best place to have a drink in Monaco. Guests are given a gold card allowing free access to the casino and the Monte Carlo Beach Club, with its private pool and beach. The card also offers a 50 percent discount at the Monte Carlo Country Club, with 23 tennis courts and the Golf Club.

Square Beaumarchais. ☎ *92-16-40-00. Fax: 92-16-38-52. Internet:* www. montecarloresort.com. *E-mail:* hh@sbm.mc. *Rack rates: 2,370–3,120F ($339–$446) double; 3,020–4,200F ($431–$600) suite; from 4,500F ($643) apartment. Breakfast: Continental breakfast 160F ($23); buffet breakfast 190F ($27). AE, MC, V.*

Le Monte Carlo Grand Hôtel

$$$$ Monte Carlo

In a feat of daring engineering and questionable aesthetics, the 619-room Grand was built over the water at the edge of Monte Carlo. In order to fit six floors of rooms, the ceilings are on the low side, particularly in the lobby, so the impression of grandness is limited. Nevertheless, this is a top-notch hotel with a down-to-earth quality and a friendly staff. A country French decor and a liberal use of wicker brighten up the rooms, many of which have balconies overlooking the sea. There are four restaurants, a nightclub called Les Folies Russes, and the Sun Casino, as well as a pâtisserie and a cafe. A heated freshwater pool is situated on the roof.

12 av. des Spélugues. ☎ *93-50-65-00. Fax: 93-30-01-57. Internet:* www. montecarlograndhotel.com. *E-mail:* grandhotel@monaco.mc. *Rack rates: 1,450–2,750F ($207–$393) double; 2,400–4,200F ($343–$600) suite. Breakfast: Continental breakfast 120F ($17); English breakfast 170F ($24). AE, DC, MC, V.*

Where to dine

Café de Paris

$$$ Monte Carlo FRENCH

Most visitors have at least a drink at the Café de Paris, the prime people-watching spot in Monaco. It's located next to the casino and across from the Hôtel de Paris. There's an extensive overpriced menu (in English), and you can eat light (*salade Niçoise,* fish stew) or heavy (*foie gras,* roast pig). If you really want to splurge, get a sampling of caviar for 650F ($88). Most of the tables are outside, but inside you'll find an ice-cream vendor, tourist boutiques, and a gambling area with slot machines.

Place du Casino. ☎ *92-16-20-20. Reservations recommended. Meals: Main courses 120–220F ($16–$30). MC, V. Open: Daily 7 a.m.–2 a.m.*

Le Borsalino

$$ Monte Carlo ITALIAN

The Italian owners (who speak French, English, and Italian among other languages) make you feel at home at this inexpensive restaurant not too far from the casino. This is a simple place with outdoor tables on the busy main street. Inside is a large bar; behind the bar is a large-screen TV that usually shows an Italian soccer game. The menu holds few surprises, offering large portions of homemade pasta and pizza. For dessert, try the excellent tiramisu.

4 bd. de Moulins. ☎ *93-50-66-92. Reservations accepted. Meals: Main courses 65–145F ($9–$20). MC, V. Open: Daily noon to 2 p.m. and 7–11 p.m.*

Le Castelroc

$$$ Monaco Ville   MONÉGASQUE

The Bonadede family has been running this restaurant, across from the palace, for three generations. Prince Rainier is a regular, as are most of Monaco's elite who know that they can get excellent, reasonably priced homecooking and perfect service. François Bonadede and his son, Marc, specialize in authentic Monégasque cooking, and one or both are apt to stop by your table and ask what you think of it. All the local specialties are on the menu, including *stocafi*, *pissaladière*, and *barbagiuan*. For a main course, pasta dishes are a good choice, especially with a regional sauce like aïoli. Most of the seating is outdoors under umbrellas in a hibiscus-scented courtyard with views of the city, sea, and mountains.

Place du Palais. ☎ *93-30-36-68. Reservations necessary. Meals: Main courses 85–145F ($12–$21); menus 125F ($17) at lunch, 245F ($33) at dinner. MC, V. Open: Late May to Sept Sun–Fri noon to 3 p.m. and 7–10 p.m.; Feb to mid-May and Oct-Nov Sun–Fri noon to 3:30 p.m.*

Le Huit et Demi

$$ La Condamine   ITALIAN/MONÉGASQUE

This authentic restaurant, just off pedestrian rue Princesse-Caroline, is named after the seminal Fellini movie *8½,* and the patrons usually include several large tables of Italians. The movie theme extends to the interior walls, which are painted with names of classic movies. Most of the seating is outside, where you can sit on director's chairs under brightly colored umbrellas and enjoy a cool breeze blowing off the port. Skip the fish dishes and stick with the specialty: homemade pasta. The restaurant also serves good pizza, made the Italian way with thin crust, easy on the tomato sauce, and lots of garlic.

4 rue Langlé. ☎ *93-50-97-02. Reservations recommended. Meals: Main courses 75–135F ($10–$18). MC, V. Open: Mon–Sat noon to 2:30 p.m. and 7–11:30 p.m.*

Le Pinocchio

$$ Monaco Ville   ITALIAN

This restaurant near the palace has been serving hearty Italian home-cooking since 1973. The owner, Enzo, displays a certain sangfroid, not to say crankiness, but he means well. The restaurant has tables outside, under awnings, on this narrow street; inside seating is cozy, with tables forming two long rows along the walls. The specialties of the chef (whose ingredients are the freshest) are risotto, ravioli Pinocchio (homemade and stuffed with meat), and spaghetti with shrimp.

30 rue Comte-Félix-Gastaldi. ☎ *93-30-96-20. Reservations recommended. Meals: Main courses 70–110F ($9–$15); menus 110F ($15) at lunch, 180F ($24) at dinner. MC, V. Open: Thurs–Tues noon to 2 p.m. and 7:30–10:30 p.m. Closed mid-Dec to mid-Jan.*

Louis XV

$$$$ Monte Carlo PROVENÇAL/TUSCAN

This golden palace is one of the best restaurants in the world. The restaurant offers haute cuisine in a resplendent if imposing setting, and that means astronomical prices. Star chef Alain Ducasse, who has his hand in many other restaurants in Paris, London, New York, and Japan, is the maestro behind the operation. He calls the cuisine here "southern flavors and Mediterranean cuisine." You can choose from two menus at every meal or order à la carte: The more expensive menu, "Pour les Gourmands," offers meat and fish choices, and the "Jardin de Provence" is closer to a vegetarian menu. The menus change seasonally to reflect the freshest ingredients. A typically delectable first course is *légumes des jardins de Provence mijotés à la truffe noire rapée* (garden vegetables of Provence simmered with grated black truffles). For a main course, the chef recommends *poitrine de pigeonneau, foie gras de canard et pommes de terre au jus d'abats* (breast of pigeon with duck foie gras and potatoes with the juice of organ meats). A famous dessert is the *frais des bois, sorbet au mascarpone* (wild strawberries with mascarpone sorbet).

At the Hôtel de Paris, Place du Casino. ☎ *92-16-30-01. Reservations recommended. Jacket and tie required for men. Meals: Main courses 400–700F ($57-$100); menus 920F ($131) and 1,050F ($150). AE, MC, V. Open: Late June to Aug Wed–Mon noon to 2 p.m. and 7–10 p.m.; Sept to mid-June Thurs–Mon noon to 2 p.m. and 7–10 p.m.*

Quai des Artistes

$$ La Condamine BRASSERIE

Artists and creative types hang out at Quai des Artistes, a bar/brasserie/restaurant on the west side of the harbor. Not surprisingly, the restaurant has lots of outdoor seating so you can watch the yachts come and go. The inside is sleek and stylish, with a long inviting bar. Standouts include the special preparation of *suprême poulet fermier* (tender breast of farm-raised chicken roasted with lemon verbena and crisp young leeks) and the carpaccio of tuna Japanese style, served with eggplant caviar. For dessert, try the homemade sorbets, with raspberry being the most popular. English menus are available.

4 quai Antoine-1er. ☎ *97-97-97-77. Reservations recommended. Meals: Main courses 95–175F ($13–$24); menus 135F ($18) at lunch, 185F ($25) at dinner. MC, V. Open: Daily noon to 2 a.m.*

Monaco boasts quite a few food specialties. The national dish is *stocafi*, a heavy stockfish dish prepared with olive oil, onions, tomatoes, white wine, potatoes, black olives, and cognac. *Pissaladière* is a pizza with onions, and *barbagiuan* is a stuffed dumpling with rice, squash, leeks, eggs, and cheese. *Beignet de fleur de courgettes* are batter-fried zucchinis stuffed with veal and cheese. And a special Monaco aperitif is *pastis Casanis,* a local brand of pastis, which is an anise-flavored liqueur.

Exploring the principality

Monaco has five sections. **Monaco Ville** is the charming Old Town up on "The Rock," to the west of the harbor. Here you'll find the palace, where the changing of the guard takes place, the Oceanographic Museum/Aquarium, the cathedral, the St-Martin Garden, and lots of wonderful shops and restaurants. **Monte Carlo,** to the east of the harbor, is where you'll find the famous casino, fancy shops, and the luxury hotels like the Paris, the Hermitage, and the Monte Carlo Grand. West of the Old Town, **Fontvieille** is an industrial suburb that was created by filling in a marshy area. Monaco's car museum is located in this neighborhood. **La Condamine,** the center of Monaco in front of the Port d'Hercule, boasts lots of shops and restaurants and some inexpensive hotels. **Larvotto,** on the far east end of the principality, has a good stretch of public beach called Plage du Larvotto and the new Grimaldi Forum, where conferences and events are held.

With commentary in English, the red-and-white tourist train **Azur Express** winds through the Old Town and travels to Monte Carlo in 30 minutes round-trip. The train arrives at and departs from the Musée Océanographique in Monaco Ville every half-hour daily 10:30 a.m. to 6 p.m. The fare is 37F ($5).

The **Palais du Prince** (place du Palais; ☎ 93-25-18-31), where Prince Rainier lives, has a defensive appearance, betraying its beginnings as a thirteenth-century fortress. In the fifteenth century, the Grimaldis transformed it into a royal palace and in the late sixteenth century, hired Italian artists to decorate the property (the courtyard and interior still bear this heavy Italian Renaissance influence). A guide leads you on a half-hour tour through a dozen finely furnished rooms, including the throne room. You can see marble floors and stairways, sixteenth-century frescoes, paneled walls, and even a hall of mirrors (a smaller version of the one at Versailles). The large official portrait of the present-day Grimaldis is in one of the last rooms on the tour: Albert wears a tennis sweater, while Caroline and Stephanie are in ballgowns; the painting within the painting is a larger-than-life portrait of Princess Grace, looking supernaturally serene. These days just father and son (Prince Rainier and Albert) occupy the palace, and Caroline and Stephanie make their homes elsewhere. In season, you may find long lines here daily. The best time to visit is early or late in the day, and the worst time to visit is after the changing of the guard, when crowds are at their peak.

Crowds form early for the 11:55 a.m. changing of the guard in front of the palace, which lasts less than 10 minutes. For a good view, arrive at least 20 minutes before the event.

In another wing of the palace, the **Musée des Souvenirs Napoléoniens et Archives** (☎ 93-25-18-31) is a small museum containing some interesting Napoléon materials, like the hat he wore on Elba (the site of

Napoléon's first exile), a piece of mahogany from his coffin, and his death mask in bronze. There's an entertaining description by Napoléon of the harrowing birth of his son. While his second wife, Marie-Louise, endured 26 hours of hard labor, she shouted at Napoléon, "You want to sacrifice me for the sake of my son?" The museum also features exhibits about the history of Monaco. Most exhibits have English translations.

The palace and museum are open daily (except December 25 and January 1): June to September 9:30 a.m. to 6:30 p.m., October to November 10 a.m. to 5 p.m., and December to May 10:30 a.m. to 12:30 p.m. and 2 to 5 p.m. Admission for the palace's grand apartments is 30F ($4) for adults and 15F ($2) for children 8 to 14; admission for the museum is 20F ($3) for adults and 10F ($1) for children 8 to 14; and admission to both the apartments and the museum is 40F ($5) for adults and 20F ($3) for children. Guided tours are given in English.

Built on the edge of a cliff overlooking the sea, the **Musée de l'Océanographique et Aquarium** (avenue St-Martin; ☎ 93-15-36-00) occupies a beautiful beaux-arts building and includes one of Europe's largest aquariums. Prince Rainier I, great-grandfather of the present ruler, built this museum in 1910 to house his extensive collections from sea travels and explorations. The aquarium contains 3,000 fish, including many rare species and a coral reef from the Red Sea. Don't miss the elegant polka-dot grouper named after Grace Kelly (*merou de Grace Kelly*) and the aquarium's oldest fish, the fierce moray eel caught off Antibes in 1968. There's also the decisive Napoléon fish. In the oceanographic museum, the whale room shelters whaling boats and skeletons of their victims. One skeleton is from a fin whale that washed up on the Italian coast some months after the prince harpooned him in 1896. Other interesting exhibits are the "first submarine," a tortoise-shaped vessel built by American David Bushnell and used during the American Revolution. The museum also shows fun nineteenth-century films of the research ship *Princesse Alice* and its crew (the prince is the one in the straw boater and walrus mustache). The museum is open daily (except the Sunday of the Grand Prix race): July and August 9 a.m. to 8 p.m. and September to June 9:30 a.m. to 7 p.m. Admission is 60F ($9) for adults and 30F ($4.30) for children.

Two interesting attractions are located on the side of a rocky cliff on the west end of Monaco: the **Jardin Exotique** and the **Musée d'Anthropologie Préhistorique de Monaco** (62 bd. du Jardin-Exotique; ☎ 93-15-29-80). In 1912, Prince Albert I created, in the Jardin Exotique, a strange world with thousands of blooming cacti, including rare species and giant cacti over 100 years old. You wander over paths and bridges with panoramic views of Monaco and the sea. Among other unusual plants is the elephant-eared kalanchoe, with large velvety leaves used by mothers in Madagascar to carry their babies. Near the bottom of the gardens are caves reachable by 300 steps. You can visit the caves, filled with stalactites and stalagmites forming natural sculptures, by guided tour, on the hour daily 10 a.m. to 5 p.m. Also on the property is the Musée d'Anthropologie, containing more collections of the intellectually curious Albert I. These anthropology exhibits prove that even Cro-Magnon man liked the Côte d'Azur. Apparently archaeologists found prehistoric skeletons, including two people embracing, in the nearby caves, as well as cave paintings. The museum also houses taxidermy of bear, bison, and moose. Scientists discovered evidence that bears and panthers lived in the caves on the rocks. The garden and museum are open daily (except November 19 and December 25): mid-May to mid-September 9 a.m. to 7 p.m. and late September to early May 9 a.m. to 6 p.m.

Built in 1875, the **Cathédrale de Monaco** at 4 rue Colonel de Castro in Monaco-Ville (☎ **93-30-87-70**) is where Princess Grace is buried. You can pay homage at her tomb marked by an inscribed stone (*Gracia Patricia Principis Rainerii III*) and bushels of roses. The cathedral was built in 1875 in a part Romanesque, part Byzantine style.

The tiny **Musée de la Chapelle de la Visitation** (place de la Visitation; ☎ **93-50-07-00**) contains the personal collection of Barbara Piasecka Johnson — about 20 seventeenth-century paintings, including works by Rubens, Zubaran, and Ribera. The works are exhibited in a baroque style seventeenth-century chapel, a brightly lit room with marble floors and columns. The museum is open Tuesday to Sunday 10 a.m. to 4 p.m., and admission is 20F ($2.85).

Prince Rainier's antique car museum, the **Collection des Voitures Anciennes de S.A.S Prince de Monaco** (Les Terrasses de Fontvieille; ☎ **92-05-28-56**), contains about 100 shiny vehicles, including the 1956 Rolls-Royce Silver Cloud that Prince Rainier and Princess Grace rode on their wedding day. The museum is open daily 10 a.m. to 6 p.m. (except December 25). Admission is 30F ($4.30) for adults and 15F ($2.15) for children 8 to 14.

The **Musée National de Monaco** (17 av. Princesse-Grace; ☎ **92-16-73-21**) displays a large collection of dolls and automatons made in Paris in the late nineteenth century. The dolls are presented in show-cases with period furniture, chinaware, and other items of daily life. There's also a dollhouse villa designed by Charles Granier, the architect who designed the Paris and Monaco opera houses. The museum is open daily (except January 1, May 1, November 19, and December 25): April to September 10 a.m. to 6:30 p.m. and September to Easter 10 a.m. to 12:15 p.m. and 2:30 to 6:30 p.m. Admission is 30F ($4.30) for adults and 20F ($2.85) for children 6 to 14.

Shopping

Monaco's **food market** takes place Saturdays 7 a.m. to noon on place d'Armes at the top of rue Grimaldi. A **flea market** is held Saturdays from 10 a.m. to 5 p.m. at the Port de Fontvieille. All the fanciest designer boutiques, like **Chanel** and **Gucci,** are located in Monte Carlo near the grand hotels. The best shopping street, with unique stores, in La

Condamine is pedestrian **rue Princesse-Caroline,** starting at rue Grimaldi and stretching three blocks to the port.

The best of the interesting small boutiques are **Sorasio Fleurs,** an elegant flower shop at 6 av. des Beaux-Arts in the Hôtel de Paris (☎ 93-30-71-01); the **Boutique du Rocher,** at 1 av. de la Madone (☎ 93-30-91-17) and rue Emile de Loth (☎ 93-30-33-99), the official store of the Princess Grace charitable foundation, selling art and handcrafts; and **Yves Delorme,** at Centre Commercial le Métropole (☎ 93- 50-08-70), for luxurious lines.

Nightlife

The **Casino du Monte Carlo** (place du Casino; ☎ 92-96-21-21) was once a very formal place (perhaps you may remember its cameo appearance in the *I Love Lucy* episode where Lucy wins a fortune here by accident). Now you'll see busloads of disheveled tourists tripping up the marble steps to play the one-armed bandits. But the casino does have more formal "private" rooms, where there's no electronic gaming and a jacket and tie are required, after 9 p.m., for gentlemen. To enter the gaming rooms, you must be 21, present a passport or driver's license, and pay 50F ($7) for the Salons Européens (opening at noon) or 100F ($14) for the Salons Privés (opening at 3 p.m.). The Salons Privés are extraordinary, with muraled walls and frescoed ceilings; it's actually worth going in and gawking. The casino's **Cabaret** (☎ 92-16-36-36), around the left side of the building, hosts Vegas-style nightclub shows from mid-September to the end of June, Tuesday to Sunday 10 to 11:30 p.m. (admission is 250F/$36). Dinner plus the show costs 500F ($71).

If you prefer more sophisticated entertainment, the place to see concerts, ballet, and opera is the **Opéra de Monte-Carlo,** a beaux-arts opera house that's also part of the casino building. For tickets and information, call the Atrium du Casino at ☎ 92-16-22-99 or stop by the box office Tuesday to Sunday 10 a.m. to 7 p.m. Tickets run 150 to 720F ($21 to $103).

Fun bars in Monaco include **Sass Café** (11 av. Princesse-Grace; ☎ 93-25-52-00), which has a piano bar; **Quai des Artistes** (4 quai Antoine-1er on the port; ☎ 97-97-97-77), attracting a young after-dinner crowd to the large bar area (see "Where to dine"); and **Stars 'N' Bars** (6 quai Antoine1er on the port; ☎ 93-50-95-95), an American-style bar and restaurant with a sports bar and disco (after 11 p.m.) on the third floor. **Jimmy'z** is a disco at Le Sporting Monte-Carlo, an entertainment complex at 26 av. Princesse-Grace (☎ 92-16-22-77).

Part VII
The Part of Tens

The 5th Wave   By Rich Tennant

"Here's something. It's a language school that will teach you to speak French for $500, or for $200 they'll just give you an accent."

In this part...

In this part, I give you some French basics: Phrases, foods, and gifts you'll want to know about so that your trip will be easier and more fun. The fabulous food is one of the best things about France: You shouldn't leave the country without trying some of its specialties, so in Chapter 20, I list the foods you simply must try while in the gourmet capital of the world. In Chapter 21, I list ten special gift ideas for those jealous friends and family members that you left behind. And in Chapter 22, I give you a dozen or so phrases that'll get you through most situations.

Chapter 20

Bon Appétit: The Top Ten or So Foods You *Must* Taste While in France

*T*asting the amazing cuisine of France is one of the best reasons for visiting the country. Being adventurous is the key: Many of the best foods in France are rarely seen in the United States — and if they are, they taste better in France. You can put your trust in French chefs because they take great pride in the freshness and preparation of their food. Restaurant meals, with five to seven courses, last several hours, so you'll need to pace yourself (and don't fill up on bread, no matter how wonderful it is).

For more details on French cuisine and lots of great recipes to try before and after your trip, get a copy of *French Cooking For Dummies* (Hungry Minds, Inc.).

Café au Lait *(cafay oh lay)*

This is espresso with steamed milk (similar to a latte you'd order at any American coffee bar) and is the perfect eye-opener in the morning or pick-me-up in the afternoon. It's sometimes called a *café crème*. No, it isn't American coffee — it's much better. What many French people drink for a quick pick-me-up during the day and also after meals is *un espresso*, a tiny cup of very strong espresso coffee. For decaffeinated coffee, ask for *café decaffeiné* or *un déca*.

Croissant (kwah-sawnt)

These popular breakfast rolls are pretty much available all over the world now, but if you think you know all about croissants, think again. Croissants in France, a staple at every bakery in the country, taste very different from ones you get in other countries. They're light, flaky, and irresistibly buttery.

Pain au Chocolat (pan o shawk-oh-lot)

A kids' favorite, this delicious breakfast pastry is a square croissant filled with dark chocolate, and you can find one at every bakery (*pâtis-serie*) in the country. The French eat a light (continental) breakfast of a croissant and pastry with coffee. That way, they save up big appetites for lunch and dinner, which are multicourse extravaganzas.

Croque Monsieur (croak mis-syer)

This is ham and melted cheese on a croissant, usually served open-faced. Available at most cafes, it's the perfect light lunch sandwich. A *croque madame* is the same but with a grilled egg on top.

Escargots (es-car-go)

Yes, like Lucy Ricardo (remember that episode of *I Love Lucy*?), while in France you need to try snails, served in their shells with lots of butter, garlic, and parsley. They're luscious, tender little treats, but what you'll taste most is garlic. Snails are a true French delicacy.

Bouillabaisse (booh-ya-besse)

This hearty fish stew, considered a meal in itself, is the specialty of Provence and the Riviera (especially Marseille). At some restaurants, the fish (many types) is served separately from the broth. When you're served the soup, you may also be served round, toasted pieces of bread and a hot peppery sauce called *rouille*. What you do is spread the sauce on the bread and plop the bread into the stew or pour the broth over the bread. Then you can add the fish or eat it separately. A cousin of bouillabaisse is *bourride,* another authentic fish soup popular along the Mediterranean.

Cuisses de Grenouilles (cweess duh gre-noo-yuh)

Frogs' legs do taste a little like chicken, but they're more delicate and salty. You'll find the best examples of this classic French dish in the Loire Valley.

Pâté de Fois Gras (pat-ah dew fwoh grah)

A staple of every fancy restaurant in France is goose liver pâté, which is often *à la maison* (homemade) and *poêlé* (pan-fried). Rich and creamy, with dense flavor and a delicate texture, *pâté de foie gras* is a quintessential French food.

Truffes (troof)

France's most expensive food, delicious *truffes* are a rare kind of black fungus (like mushrooms) that need to be dug out of the ground by special dogs or pigs trained for the task of locating them. Truffle season is November to March. Truffles appearing on any dish (*aux truffes*) up the price of the meal by 20 or more dollars. Look for them particularly on omelets and pasta.

Chariot de Fromage (chair-ree-aht duh frwoh-mahg)

Ah, the chariot of cheese: brie, camembert, roquefort, chèvre, gruyère, and so on. At the best restaurants, the selection of cheeses is so enormous, it must be wheeled to you on a trolley. When the waiter brings it over, ask which are the best cheeses of the region *("Les fromages de la region?")* and choose which ones you want by pointing to several. The waiter will serve them and you can eat them with a knife and fork.

Tarte Tartin, Soupe de Fraises, Ile Flotant, Crème Brûlée, Mousse au Chocolat (tart tah-tihn, soup duh frez, eel flo-tahnt, krem bruh-lay, moose oh shawk-oh-laht)

Apple tart, boozy strawberry soup, floating island (meringue with a custard sauce), custard topped with caramel, chocolate mousse . . . and the list goes on. Don't ever skip dessert in France. *C'était bon!*

Chapter 21

The Art of the Souvenir: The Top Ten Gifts to Buy in France

In This Chapter

▶ Buying the perfect gift

▶ Bringing home a taste of France

▶ Finding the best crafts

Many people come to France specifically to shop (you know who you are), but this list is more for those who, in the midst of exploring this most special country, would like to bring home a thing or two for those less fortunate. These gift givers often need a bit of direction, so here are ten perfect gifts that whisper "France."

If you're truly a serious shopper, you may want to buy a copy of *Born to Shop Paris* or *Born to Shop France* (both by Hungry Minds, Inc.).

Scarves in Paris

The first thing you notice about Parisian women is that they're very stylish. The second thing you notice is that they all wear scarves. So buy a few for yourself or your significant other. And while you're at it, buy them for all your female friends and family. They come in all price ranges — from the priciest at Hermès to the best bargains at street vendors. And they're easy to pack. While searching for the perfect scarves, you may want to pick up a few neckties for the men on your list. Once again, a wide range of prices and styles are available, from vibrant silk Hermès ties to whimsical Eiffel Tower–patterned ties available at street vendors near — where else? — the Eiffel Tower.

Stationery in Paris

Although the art of the snail-mail letter is fading fast, you can still find exquisite papers and stationery sets in Paris's fine shops, including the big department stores like La Samaritaine, Au Printemps, Au Bon Marché, and Galeries Lafayette. You'll find the most original selections at boutiques on the Left Bank and the least expensive selection in the student area of St-Germain.

Quimper Pottery in Brittany

Quimper pottery has been a famous collectible for antiques buffs for many years. You can buy contemporary examples of the hand-painted craft at several shops in the town of Quimper, including the premier maker, H. B. Henriot, which also offers factory tours.

Fishermen's Sweaters in Brittany

After a day or two on the blustery coast of Brittany, you may be looking to buy one of those bulky fishermen's sweaters. The most common types have blue-and-white or red-and-white horizontal stripes. The best brands are St. James and Tricommer. These rugged sweaters will last a lifetime.

Santons in Provence

Made of clay or wood, *santons* are often hand-painted and highly individualistic renderings of ordinary townspeople and their professions, as well as saints and nativity cast members. These highly popular collectible figurines are available throughout Provence and the Riviera.

Fabrics in Provence

Nothing says Provence like those wonderful, brightly colored cotton fabrics sold all over the south of France. You'll see the Soulëiado brand and store name in most towns in Provence and the Riviera. Though the style is heavily imitated, the designs were originated in the eighteenth and nineteenth centuries. They make great tablecloths and napkins, as well as dresses and purses. You can find them at discount prices at markets in Provence and also at department stores in Paris.

Perfume in Grasse

The town of Grasse on the Riviera is the perfume-making capital of France. After touring one of the three factories open to tourists — Molinard, Galimard, and Fragonard — you can sign up for a class to make your own perfume or buy some of the specially packaged wares. In Paris, head to rue de Rivoli across from the Louvre for the best perfume shops, including those offering discounts. You can find all the top names here, as well as some boutique French perfume not easily found in the United States.

Lingerie on the Riviera

It's no surprise that the Riviera offers the best lingerie shops anywhere. You'll be able to buy a wide range of top-of-the-line teddies, nightgowns, and underwear for relatively good prices. Swimsuits (*maillot de bain*) are also fun to shop for here, and you'll find a variety of daring styles. Since the French practically invented sex appeal and spare no expense to achieve it, expect to splurge.

Handmade Glass Objects in Biot

The tiny hilltop village of Biot, located between Cannes and Nice on the Riviera, is France's capital of glass. You can watch about a dozen top artisans blowing and sculpting exquisite glass objects in its many studios and galleries. Among the names to look for are Novaro, Saba, and Pierini. Most of Biot's galleries will pack and ship internationally.

Cider and Calvados in Normandy

The apple orchards throughout Normandy's rolling green landscape are known for producing the exceptional fruits Normans use for a variety of beverages. They traditionally drink with their meals a light, refreshingly fizzy cider instead of wine. Bringing a bottle of this cider home will immediately transport you back to the region's half-timbered houses. And after a meal, Normans enjoy Calvados, a fiery brandy served with or in coffee. It takes 12 to 15 years to bring this famous liqueur to term.

Chapter 22

Pardon My *Français:* The Top Ten (Or So) Expressions You Need to Know

In This Chapter

▶ Greeting people

▶ Asking questions

▶ Interpreting the responses

*O*ne of the most important things to remember about France is that the people speak French there. Yes, that may seem obvious, but many tourists assume that all French people understand and speak English fluently, and this assumption often leads to bad feelings all around. Try using the basic phrases in this chapter to get what you need. When all else fails, there's always "*Parlez-vous anglais?*" ("Do you speak English?"). You'll be amazed at how French people appreciate it when you try to speak their language, which is, after all, one of the world's most elegant.

For more extensive coverage of French terms, see the Appendix at the end of this book. But if you want to immerse yourself in the language, a good start is buying *French For Dummies* (Hungry Minds, Inc.). Then go practice rolling those *r*'s.

Bonjour or Bonsoir

These are your basic hellos: *bonjour* (bohn-*jhoor*) — "good day" — and *bonsoir* (bohn-*swahr*) — "good night." Whenever you enter a shop or restaurant, greet the merchant with a hearty *bonjour* (or *bonsoir*, depending on the time of day) followed by — and this is very important — either *monsieur* (mister or sir) or *madame* (Mrs. or ma'am). You may note a slight look of surprise and then a look of pleasure. (The person is thinking: "Wow, I'm amazed this foreigner addressed me properly. That's very nice.") This is how French people address one another, and they're aware that other people (especially Americans) aren't as formal. In service situations (say in a shop or bakery), any female over 15 is addressed as *madame* (never *mademoiselle*). By the way, the word *allo* is used as a greeting when you answer the telephone.

Au Revoir

Au revoir (o ruh-*vwahr*) means "goodbye." It should be combined with the appropriate *monsieur* or *madame* (see the first entry). Variations on goodbye include *à bientôt* (ah byeh-*toh*), which means "see you soon," and *à tout à l'heure* (ah *toot* ah lair), which means "see you later." *Allons-y* (ahlohn-*zee*) or "let's go" is what you say when you and your companions are leaving a place together.

S'il Vous Plait

Meaning "please," the phrase *s'il vous plait* (seel voo *play*) is great for ordering at restaurants, asking questions, or merely gaining someone's attention. You can follow it by pointing to what you want on the menu, in the bakery case, or on the shop shelf. Spread your pleases thickly and follow each with the appropriate *monsieur* or *madame*.

Merci

Merci (mair-*see*), meaning "thank you," is the appropriate ending for any transaction, be it a meal or a shopping expedition. A big thank you is *merci beaucoup* (boh-*koo*), and a more casual big thank you is *merci bien* (bee-*ehn*). French people like to have the last word, and they'll always respond to *merci* in one of two ways: The more formal response is *"Je vous en prie"* ("You're welcome") and the casual response *"De rien"* ("It's nothing"). At this point, there's really nothing left for you to say, so just smile and wave.

Pardon or Désolée

Pardon (pahr-*dohn*) is a very useful word meaning "excuse me," but you can also use it to mean "I'm sorry," "I need to pass by," or "I need help." *Désolée* (day-zoh-*lay*) also means "I'm sorry," but is used when you've done something stupid like knocked over a display of glassware. Of course if you do that, you may also have to say *"C'est combien?"* (see entry later in this chapter).

Où Est?

Lost? Just ask for directions. *Où est* (ooh-*eh*) means "where is." Rather than just launching into it, though, it's much better if you start with *"Pardon, monsieur [or madame], où est . . ."* French people never just ask a stranger a question, they start with a formality. If you want to get a really positive reaction, say *"Excusez-moi de vous déranger* [duh voo day-rahn-*jay*], *monsieur [or madame], où est . . . ?"* which means "Excuse me for bothering you, sir [or ma'am], where is . . .?" The person will be so overjoyed at being addressed in the perfect polite manner, he or she will probably walk you to where you need to go.

C'est Combien?

In a shop, say *"C'est combien?"* (say comb-bee-*ehn*) — "How much is it?" — and point to whatever you want to buy. The French person will probably say the amount in French, which you probably won't understand (see the next entry). But then he or she will usually write down the amount and you can decide whether or not you want to buy whatever it is.

Je Ne Comprends Pas

Je ne comprends pas (jhuh neh kohm-*prahn* pah) means "I don't understand." If you think you may understand it the second time, say *"Repetez, s'il vous plait"* (reh-pe-*tez*, seel voo *play*), which means "Can you please repeat that?" To ask them to speak more slowly, say *"Pouvez-vous parler plus lentement"* (poo-vay-*voo* par-lay ploo lan-te-*ment*). You can also ask them if they speak English (see below). If you reach an impasse, try hand signals and pointing.

Ne Quittez Pas

Ne quittez pas (neh key-*tay* pah) is what French people say on the telephone to mean "hold on" or "just a minute" (literally "don't leave"). Sometimes it means they're getting someone who speaks English to talk to you. Alas, because of the brusque way the phrase is spoken, those who don't speak the language could misinterpret it as a goodbye phrase. Whatever you do, don't hang up.

Complet (cohm-play)

You didn't make reservations. It's late in the day and pouring rain. You see a hotel. It looks nice. You approach the desk with an inquiring look.

The woman shakes her head sadly and says *"Complet"* (cohm-*play*) — "Full" — or *"Je suis désolée. Nous sommes complet"* ("I'm sorry. We are full."). This means the hotel (or restaurant) is full and you should have made reservations.

C'était Bon

C'était bon (set-*tey* bohn) means "It's good." When the waiter comes over to see how you're doing and the food is good (and it usually is), say an enthusiastic *"C'était bon!"* Sometimes the waiter will even prod you into it. He'll say, *"C'était . . .?"* (literally, "It was ...?" or "How was it?") and that's when you respond *"C'était bon,"* smile, and pat your stomach for emphasis.

L'addition, S'il Vous Plait

L'addition, s'il vous plait (la-dis-see-*yoh*) means "The check, please." The French believe in long multicourse meals, and there's virtually no turnover of tables at restaurants. The waiters expect you to be there for hours, so you need to request a check if you want to leave. Another popular way to say this is *"La note, s'il vous plait."*

Parlez-vous Anglais?

Parlez-vous Anglais? (par-lay-*voo* ahn-*glay*) translates to "Do you speak English?" When all else fails, this is your fallback position. The most common response is *"A leetle,"* but that means they speak English better than you speak French, so between the universal language of hand signals and lots of smiles, you should be able to figure out just about anything.

Appendix

Quick Concierge

• •

Fast Facts

American Express

The **Paris office** (11 rue Scribe, 9e; ☎ 01-47-14-50-00; Métro: Opéra, Chaussée-d'Antin, or Havre-Caumartin; RER: Auber) is open weekdays 9 a.m. to 6 p.m. The bank is open 9 a.m. to 5 p.m. on Saturday, but the mail pickup window is closed. The **Nice office** (11 promenade des Anglais; ☎ 04-93-16-53-51) is open daily 9 a.m. to 9 p.m. The Monaco office (35 bd Princesse Charlotte; ☎ 93-25-74-45) is open from 9am to 5pm. There are also American Express offices in Aix-en-Provence, Cannes, Dijon, Marseille, Nantes, Orléans, Rouen, and Tours, among other cities. The tourist office in each town will be able to direct you to the nearest American Express office.

ATM locators

ATMs are widely available in towns and cities throughout the country. If you'd like to print out a list of ATMs that accept MasterCard or Visa, ask your bank or print out lists from www.visa.com/pd/atm and www.mastercard.com/atm.

Business Hours

In Paris, the **grands magasins** (department stores) are generally open Monday to Saturday 9:30 a.m. to 7:00 p.m.; **smaller shops** close for lunch and reopen around 2 p.m., but this is rarer than it used to be. Many stores stay open until 7 p.m. in summer; others are closed on Monday, especially in the morning. Large **offices** remain open all day, but some also close for lunch. Throughout the country, **banks** are normally open weekdays 9 a.m. to noon and 1 or 1:30 to 4:30 p.m. Some banks also open on Saturday morning. Some currency-exchange booths are open very long hours; see the "Currency Exchange" listing. In the rest of the country, most stores are open 9:30 a.m. to noon and 2 to 6 p.m., with later hours in summer. Department stores in cities throughout the country are open during lunch.

Collect calls

For an AT&T operator: ☎ 0800-99-00-11; MCI: ☎ 0800-99-00-19; Sprint: ☎ 0800-99-00-87. See also "Telephone/Telex/Fax," later in this Appendix.

Credit Cards

Visa, MasterCard, American Express, and Diners Club are all accepted throughout the country, but the most commonly accepted are Visa and MasterCard. See also "Lost Property" in this Appendix.

Currency Exchange

Banks and *bureaux de change* (exchange offices) almost always offer better exchange rates than hotels, restaurants, and shops, which should be used only in emergencies. You'll find them in central commercial areas of all towns and cities in France. (See Chapter 9 for exchange rates.)

Despite disadvantageous exchange rates and long lines, many people prefer to exchange their money at **American Express** (see the listing earlier in this Appendix).

Customs

Non-EU nationals can bring the following items into France duty-free: 200 cigarettes or 100 cigarillos or 50 cigars or 250 grams of smoking tobacco; 2 liters of wine and 1 liter of alcohol over 38.80 proof; 50 grams of perfume, one-quarter liter of toilet water; 500 grams of coffee, and 100 grams of tea. Travelers ages 15 and over can also bring in 1,200F ($171) in other goods; for those 14 and under, the limit is 600F ($86). **EU citizens** may bring any amount of goods into France, as long as it's for their personal use and not for resale.

Returning **U.S. citizens** who've been away for 48 hours or more are allowed to bring back, once every 30 days, $400 worth of merchandise duty-free. You'll be charged a flat rate of 10-percent duty on the next $1,000 worth of purchases; on gifts, the duty-free limit is $100. You cannot bring fresh foodstuffs into the United States; tinned foods, however, are allowed.

Citizens of the U.K. who are **returning from a European Union country** have no limit on what can be brought back from an EU country, as long as the items are for personal use (this includes gifts), and the necessary duty and tax has been paid. There are guidance levels set at 800 cigarettes, 200 cigars, 1 kg smoking tobacco, 10 liters of spirits, 90 liters of wine, and 110 liters of beer. **Canada** allows its citizens a $500 exemption, and you're allowed to bring back the following items duty-free: 200 cigarettes, 1.5 liters of wine or 1.14 liters of liquor, and 50 cigars. In addition, you may mail gifts to Canada from abroad at the rate of Can$60 a day, provided they're unsolicited and don't contain alcohol or tobacco or advertising matter. Write on the package "Unsolicited gift, under $60 value." All valuables should be declared on the Y-38 form before departure from Canada, including serial numbers of valuables you already own, such as expensive foreign cameras. *Note:* The $500 exemption can be used only once a year.

The duty-free allowance in **Australia** is A$400 or, for those under 18, A$200. Personal property mailed back from France should be marked "Australian goods returned" to avoid payment of duty. Upon returning to Australia, citizens can bring in 250 cigarettes or 250 grams of loose tobacco, and 1,125 ml of alcohol. If you're returning with valuable goods you already own, such as foreign-made cameras, you should file form B263.

The duty-free allowance for **New Zealand** is NZ$700. Citizens over 17 can bring in 200 cigarettes or 50 cigars or 250 grams of tobacco (or a mixture of all three if their combined weight doesn't exceed 250 grams), plus 4.5 liters of wine or beer or 1.125 liters of liquor.

Dentists

You can call your consulate and ask the duty officer to recommend a dentist. For dental emergencies in Paris, call **SOS Dentaire** (☎ 01-43-37-51-00) daily 9 a.m. to midnight. If you are not in Paris, you should go to the nearest hospital, which will always have a dentist on duty or know how to reach one.

Doctors

Call your consulate and ask the duty officer to recommend a doctor. In Paris, call **SOS Médecins** (☎ 01-43-37-51-00), a 24-hour service. If you are not in Paris, you can go to the local hospital or ask at the police station for the number of a doctor that speaks English. Remember: You need to have your health insurance card with you unless you want to pay cash for the services.

Drugstores

Pharmacies are marked with green crosses and are often upscale affairs that sell toiletries in addition to prescription drugs and over-the-counter remedies. If you're shopping for products other than drugs, it's almost always cheaper to buy them elsewhere, such as a *supermarché* (supermarket).

Electricity

The French electrical system runs on 220 volts. Adapters are needed to convert the voltage and fit sockets, and are cheaper at home than they are in Paris. Many hotels have two-pin (in some cases, three-pin) sockets for electric razors. It's a good idea to ask at your hotel before plugging in any electrical appliance.

Embassies/Consulates

If you have a passport, immigration, legal, or other problem, contact your consulate. Paris is the capital of France and therefore the seat of all embassies and consulates. Call before you go: They often keep strange hours and observe both French and home-country holidays. Here's where to find them: **Australia,** at 4 rue Jean-Rey, 15e (☎ **01-40-59-33-00;** Métro: Bir-Hakeim); **Canada,** at 35 av. Montaigne, 8e (☎ **01-44-43-29-00;** Métro: Franklin-D.-Roosevelt or Alma-Marceau); **New Zealand,** at 7 ter rue Léonard-de-Vinci, 16e (☎ **01-45-00-24-11,** ext. 280 from 9 a.m. to 1 p.m.; Métro: Victor-Hugo); **United Kingdom,** at 35 rue Faubourg St-Honoré, 8e (☎ **01-44-51-31-02;** Métro: Madeleine); **United States,** at 2 rue St-Florentin, 1er (☎ **01-43-12-22-22;** Métro: Concorde).

Emergencies

Call ☎ **17** for the **police.** To report a **fire,** dial ☎ **18.** For an **ambulance,** call ☎ **15,** or call ☎ **01-45-67-50-50** for **SAMU** (Service d'Aide Médicale d'Urgence). In Paris, for help in English, call **SOS Help** at ☎ **01-47-23-80-80** between 3 and 11 p.m. The main police station (9 bd. du Palais, 4e; ☎ **01-53-71-53-71;** Métro: Cité) is open 24 hours.

Information

Before you go, contact the **French Government Tourist Office** at 444 Madison Ave., 16th floor, New York, NY 10022-6903 (Fax: 212-838-7855; Internet: www.francetourism.com). This office does not provide information over the phone. When you arrive in Paris, head to the **Office de Tourisme de Paris** at 127 av. des Champs-Elysées, 8e (☎ **08-36-68-31-12** at 2.23F/32¢ min, or 01-49-52-53-35). Each town and village in France has its own tourist office and these are listed in the appropriate chapters.

Internet Access

To surf the Net or check your e-mail, open an account at a free-mail provider, such as Hotmail (hotmail.com) or Yahoo! Mail (mail.yahoo.com), and all you need to check e-mail while you travel is a Web connection, available at Net cafes around the world. After logging on, just point the browser to your e-mail provider, enter your username and password, and you'll have access to your mail. You can find Net cafes or places that offer Internet access in almost every town in France. Check with the local tourist office for locations. In addition, you can open up an e-mail account for reasonable fees at many post offices in larger towns in France, because they offer computers for e-mail and Internet access.

Laundry and Dry Cleaning

To find a laundry near you, ask at your hotel or consult the Yellow Pages under *Laveries pour particuliers.* Take as many 10F, 2F, and 1F pieces as you can. Washing and drying 6 kilos (13¼ lbs.) usually costs about 35F ($6). Dry cleaning is *nettoyage à sec;* look for shop signs with the word *pressing.*

Liquor Laws

Supermarkets, grocery stores, and cafes sell alcoholic beverages. The legal drinking age is 16. Persons under 16 can be served an alcoholic drink in a bar or restaurant if accompanied by a parent or legal guardian. Wine and liquor are sold every day of the year. *Be warned:* The authorities are very strict about drunk-driving laws. If convicted, you face a stiff fine and a possible prison term of 2 months to 2 years.

Lost Property

There are lost property (*objets trouvés*) offices in most big cities in France, and you can ask the tourist office for the location. In Paris, the central office is **Objets Trouvés** (36 rue des Morillons, 15e; ☎ **01-55-76-20-20**; Métro: Convention), at the corner of rue de Dantzig. The office is open Monday, Wednesday, and Friday 8:30 a.m. to 5 p.m. and Tuesday and Thursday 8:30 a.m. to 8 p.m. For lost and found on the Paris **Métro**, call ☎ **01-40-06-75-27**. You will also want to call the police by dialing **17**.

If you lose your **Visa** card, call ☎ **08-36-69-08-80**; for **MasterCard**, call ☎ **01-45-67-53-53**. To report lost **American Express** cards, call ☎ **01-47-77-72-00**.

Luggage Storage/Lockers

Most Paris hotels will store luggage for you for free, and that's your best bet, especially if you plan to return to Paris after a tour of the provinces. Otherwise, try the *consignes,* which are the luggage offices at large railway stations. Otherwise, you'll have to lug your luggage with you — all the more reason for packing light!

Mail

Large **post offices** are normally open weekdays 8 a.m. to 7 p.m. and Saturday 8 a.m. to noon; small post offices may have shorter hours. All towns in France have at least one post office. Airmail letters and postcards to the United States cost 4.40F (65¢); within Europe, 3F (45¢); and to Australia or New Zealand, 5.20F (75¢).

Paris's **main post office** is at 52 rue du Louvre, 75001 Paris (☎ **01-40-28-20-00**; Métro: Louvre-Rivoli). It's open 24 hours a day for urgent mail, telegrams, and telephone calls. It handles Poste Restante mail sent to you in care of the post office and stored until you pick it up; be prepared to show your passport and pay 3F (45¢) for each letter you receive. If you don't want to use Poste Restante, you can receive mail in care of **American Express.** Holders of American Express cards or traveler's checks get this service free; others have to pay a fee.

Maps

Maps of Paris, printed by the department stores, are usually available for free at hotels. The maps are good if you're visiting Paris for only a few days and hitting the major attractions. But if you plan to really explore all the nooks and crannies of Paris, the best maps are those of the *Plan de Paris par Arrondissement,* pocket-sized books with maps and a street index, available at most bookstores. They're extremely practical, and prices start at around 40F ($6). Free maps of other French cities, towns, and villages are available at local tourist offices.

Newspapers and Magazines

In major cities, newsstands carry the latest editions of the *International Herald Tribune,* published Monday to Saturday, and the major London papers. *Time* and *Newsweek* are readily available. So is *USA Today*'s International edition. The weekly entertainment guide *Pariscope,* which comes out on Wednesdays, has an English-language insert that gives you up-to-the-minute information on the latest cultural events. You can also get the *New York Times* in some of the bigger English-language bookstores.

Police

Dial ☎ **17** in emergencies.

Post Office

See "Mail," previously in this Appendix.

Rest Rooms

You can find public rest rooms at train stations, airports, tourist sites, and often tourist offices. Every cafe has a rest room, but it's supposed to be for customers only. The best plan is to ask to use the telephone; it's usually next to the *toilette.* For 2F (29¢) you can use the street-side toilets, which are automatically flushed out and cleaned after every use. Some Métro stations have serviced rest rooms; you're expected to tip the attendant 2F (29¢).

Safety

France, particularly in the provinces, is very safe. Exceptions are the heavily touristed areas of Provence and the Riviera, which tend to attract thieves, particularly at train and bus stations. Paris is a relatively safe city, and violent crime is rare. Your biggest risks are pickpockets and purse snatchers, so be particularly attentive on the Métro and on crowded buses, in museum lines, and around tourist attractions. Women should be on guard in crowded tourist areas and on the Métro against overly friendly men who seem to have made a specialty out of bothering unsuspecting female tourists. Tricks include asking your name and nationality, then sticking like a burr to you for the rest of the day. They're usually more harassing than harmful, but if you're too nice, you may be stuck spending time with someone with whom you prefer not to. A simple "leave me alone" (*laissez-moi tranquille* ["lay-say- mwa tran-*keel*"]) usually works. Special mention should be made of Marseille, which is a rough and tumble town. The very high unemployment means there seem to be a large number of men loitering around looking for someone to rob. Watch your back!

Smoking

Although restaurants are required to provide no-smoking sections, you may find yourself next to the kitchen or the rest rooms. Even there, your neighbor may light up and defy you to say something about it. Large brasseries, expensive restaurants, and places accustomed to dealing with foreigners are most likely to be accommodating.

Taxes

Watch out: You can get burned. As a member of the European Union, France routinely imposes a standard 20.6 percent value-added tax (VAT, in France known as the TVA) on many goods and services. The tax on merchandise applies to clothing, appliances, liquor, leather goods, shoes, furs, jewelry, perfume, cameras, and even caviar. You can get a refund — usually 13 percent — on certain goods and merchandise, but not on services. The minimum purchase is 1,200F ($171) in the same store for nationals or residents of countries outside the European Union.

Telephone/Telex/Fax

Most **public phone booths** take only telephone debit cards called **télécartes,** which can be bought at post offices and at *tabacs* (cafes and kiosks that sell tobacco products). You insert the card into the phone and make your call; the cost is automatically deducted from the "value" of the card recorded on its magnetized strip. The télécarte comes in 50- and 120-unit denominations, costing 49F ($7) and 96F ($14), respectively, and can only be used in a phone booth.

Cashiers will almost always try to sell you a card from France Télécom, the French phone company, but cards exist that give you more talk time for the same amount of money. Instead of inserting the card into a public phone, you dial a free number and tap in a code. The cards come with directions, some in English, and can be used from public and private phones, unlike France Télécom's card. Look for *tabacs* that have advertisements for Delta Multimedia or Kertel, or ask for a *télécarte international avec un code.* The coin-operated pay phones that are left are almost exclusively in bars, cafes, and restaurants and take 1F, 2F, and 5F pieces; the minimum charge is 2F (29¢).

To place **international calls from France,** dial 00, then the country code (for the United States and Canada, 1; for Britain, 44; for Ireland, 353; for Australia, 61; for New Zealand, 64), then the area or city code, and then the local number (for example, to call New York, you'd dial 00 + 1 + 212 + 000-0000). **To place a collect call to North America,** dial 00-33-11, and an English-speaking operator will assist you. Dial 00-00-11 for an American AT&T operator; MCI 0800-99-00-19; Sprint 0800-99-00-87.

To **call from France to anywhere else in France** (called *province*), you'll always dial ten digits. The country is divided into five zones with prefixes of 01, 02, 03, 04, and 05; check a phone directory for the code of the city you're calling.

If you're **calling France from the United States,** dial the international prefix, 011; then the country code for France, 33; followed by two-digit city code and the eight-digit local number, but leave off the initial zero on the two-digit city code (for example, 011 + 33 + 1-0-00-00-00-00).

Avoid making phone calls from your hotel room; many hotels charge at least 2F (29 ¢) for local calls, and the markup on international calls can be staggering.

You can send **telex** and **fax** messages at the main post office in any town, but it's often cheaper to ask at your hotel or go to a neighborhood printer or copy shop.

Time

Paris is 6 hours ahead of eastern standard time; noon in New York is 6 p.m. in France.

Tipping

Service is supposedly included at your hotel, but the custom is to tip the **bellhop** about 7F ($1) per bag, more in expensive hotels. If you have a lot of luggage, tip a bit more. Don't tip housekeepers unless you do something that requires extra work. Tip a few dollars if a reception staff member performs extra services.

Although your *addition* or *note* (restaurant bill) or *fiche* (cafe check) will bear the words *service compris* (service charge included), always leave a small tip. Generally, 5 percent is considered acceptable. Remember, service has supposedly already been paid for.

Taxi drivers appreciate a tip of 2F to 3F (29¢ to 43¢). On longer journeys, when the fare exceeds 100F ($14), a 5- to 10-percent tip is appropriate. At the theater and cinema, tip 2F (29¢) if an usher shows you to your seat. In **public toilets,** there is often a posted fee for using the facilities. If not, the maintenance person will expect a tip of about 2F (29¢). Put it in the basket or on the plate at the entrance. **Porters** and **cloakroom attendants** are usually governed by set prices, which are displayed. If not, give a porter 5F to 8F (70¢ to $1.15) per suitcase, and a cloakroom attendant 2F to 4F (29¢ to 57¢) per coat.

Trains

The telephone number for reservations on France's national railroads (SNCF) is ☎ **08-36-35-35-35,** or to get an English-speaking operator ☎ **08-36-35-35-39** (2.23F/32¢/minute). It's open daily 7 a.m. to 10 p.m. Remember, you must validate your train ticket in the orange ticket *composteur* on the platform or pay a fine.

Water

Tap water in France is perfectly safe, but if you're prone to stomach problems, you may prefer to drink bottled water.

Weather updates

Call ☎ **08-36-70-12-34** (2.23F/32¢/minute) for France and abroad; ☎ **08-36-68-02-75** (2.23F/32¢/minute) for Paris and the Ile de France.

Toll-Free Numbers and Web Sites

Major airlines

Air Canada
☎ 800-630-3299 in the U.S.
☎ 01-44-50-20-20 in France
www.aircanada.ca

Air France
☎ 800-237-2747 in the U.S.
☎ 08-02-80-28-02 in France
www.airfrance.com

American Airlines
☎ 800-433-7300 in the U.S.
☎ 01-69-32-73-07 in France
www.aa.com

British Airways
☎ 800-247-9297 in the U.S.
☎ 0-802-802-902 in France
www.british-airways.com

Continental Airlines
☎ 800-525-0280 in the U.S.
☎ 01-42-99-09-99 in France
www.continental.com

Delta Air Lines
☎ 800-221-1212 in the U.S.
☎ 01-47-68-92-92 in France
www.delta-air.com

Iceland Air
☎ 800-223-5500 in the U.S.
www.icelandair.com

Northwest/KLM
☎ 800-225-2525 in the U.S.
www.nwa.com

TWA
☎ 800-221-2000 in the U.S.
☎ 01-49-19-20-00 in France
www.twa.com

United Airlines
☎ 800-241-6522 in the U.S.
www.united.com

US Airways
☎ 800-428-4322 in the U.S.
☎ 01-41-40-30-30 in France
www.usairways.com

Car rental agencies

Auto Europe
☎ 800-223-5555
www.autoeurope.com

Avis
☎ 800-331-1212
www.avis.com

In Paris: place Madeleine, 8e;
☎ 01-42-66-67-58

Budget
☎ 800-527-0700
www.drivebudget.com

Information on Paris locations:
☎ 08-00-10-00-01; 1.29F/18¢ min

Hertz
☎ 800-654-3131
www.hertz.com

In Paris: 123 rue Jeanne d'Arc, 13e;
☎ 01-45-86-53-33

Kemwel Holiday Auto (KHA)
☎ 800-678-0678
www.kemwel.com

National
☎ 800-CAR-RENT
www.nationalcar.com
In Paris: 23 bd Arago, 13e.; ☎ 01-47-07-87-39

Getting More Information

The information sources I list in this section are the best of the bunch. Dig in before you go and you'll be well prepared for your trip.

Touring the tourist offices

For general information about France, contact an office of the **French Government Tourist Office** at one of the following addresses:

- ✔ **In the United States:** The **French Government Tourist Office** (Fax: 212-838-7855; Internet: www.francetourism.com), 444 Madison Ave., 16th floor, New York, NY 10022-6903; 676 N. Michigan Ave., Chicago, IL 60611-2819 (Fax: 312-337-6339); or 9454 Wilshire Blvd., Suite 715, Beverly Hills, CA 90212-2967 (Fax: 310-276-2835). Phone numbers aren't listed because offices prefer to be in touch via e-mail or fax.

- ✔ **In Canada: Maison de la France/French Government Tourist Office,** 1981 av. McGill College, Suite 490, Montréal PQ H3A 2W9 (Fax: 514-845-4868).

- ✔ **In the United Kingdom: Maison de la France/French Government Tourist Office,** 178 Piccadilly, London W1V 0AL (☎ 0891-244-123; Fax: 020-7493-6594).

- ✔ **In Australia: French Tourist Bureau,** 25 Bligh St. Level 22, Sydney, NSW 2000 Australia (☎ 02-231-5244; Fax: 02-231-8682).

- ✔ **In New Zealand:** You won't find a representative in New Zealand; contact the Australian representative.

- ✔ **In Paris: The Office de Tourisme et des Congrès de Paris,** 127 av. des Champs-Elysées, 75008 Paris (☎ **08-36-68-31-12** [2.23F/min]; Fax: 01-49-52-53-00; Métro: Charles-de-Gaulle–Etoile or George V).

Surfing the Web

You'll find a lot of excellent information about France on the Internet — the latest news, restaurant reviews, concert schedules, subway maps, and more.

France

- ✔ **All Things French** (www.allthingsfrench.com). Much of this site is concerned with shopping — glassware, toys, beauty products — but check out the vacation packages for ballooning holidays over Burgundy and Bordeaux, river barging, and alpine adventures.

- **Arthur Frommer's Budget Travel Newsletter** (www.frommers. com/newsletters). Click here for travel tips, reviews, online booking, "Ask the Expert" bulletin boards, travel bargains, and travel secrets for hundreds of destinations.

- **Avignon and Provence** (www.avignon-et-provence.com). Here you'll find restaurant reviews (many restaurants provide their menus), museum listings, ideas for outdoor activities, and lots of history about the popes of Avignon, in addition to practical information for emergencies and classified ads.

- **Beyond the French Riviera** (www.beyond.com). The Travel section of this guide deals with the regions of southeast France, explaining train, bus, air, and sea travel in detail. A directory of towns takes you to photos, history, and excursions.

- **Brittany Holiday Guide** (www.brittany-guide.com). Come here for thorough descriptions, with photos of places of interest, hotels and guest houses, transportation information (including roadwork), history, and an events calendar for the region.

- **Cannes Online** (www.cannes-on-line.com). The city's promotional site includes uncritical hotel listings, a city map, and an events calendar.

- **Châteaux and Country** (www.chateauxandcountry.com). Scroll down to the bottom of the home page and click on the American flag in the right corner for the English version. This is a comprehensive site with photos, driving directions, castle hours, and admission prices, and, where applicable, castle lodging prices.

- **France Way** (www.franceway.com). With lots of suggestions for your trip to France — especially Paris — this guide covers dining, lodging, and transportation. The detailed listings of restaurants in Paris don't appear to be paid ads.

- **French Government Tourist Office** (www.francetourism.com). Here you'll find information on planning your trip to France, as well as practical tips, family activities, events, and accommodations.

- **Giverny and Vernon** (www.giverny.org). Visitors to the region forever associated with Claude Monet will find loads of useful travel and transportation information. The site gives details on the area's castles, museums, and places of archaeological interest, as well as the artist's famous gardens.

- **Nice, French Riviera** (www.nice-coteazur.org). While this official tourism site is a little thin, it's helpful for its calendar of events and hotel search.

- **French Tourism Board for Normandy** (www.normandy-tourism. org). This site has hotel descriptions and information on museums and attractions organized by town. Check out the D-Day section that highlights Battle of Normandy places of interest. An interactive parks and gardens list takes you to photos and information about the many gardens in the region.

✔ **Mappy** (www.mappy.fr). This handy site will tell you the exact mileage, precise directions, toll prices, and amount of time it takes to drive anywhere in France. You can print out the maps or have them mailed to you.

✔ **Loire Net** (www.loire.net). With photos, descriptions, and reviews, this guide to the Loire Valley shows off the historic châteaux, museums, and other attractions.

✔ **Provence Touristic Guide** (www.provence.guideweb.com). Dig into the "Leisure and Culture" section for pictures, exhibit descriptions, and contact information for museums. The site also has a directory of hotels and guest houses that includes photos, and the ability to take online reservations.

✔ **Provence Web** (www.provenceweb.fr). This site gives the addresses for hotels, restaurants, and activities for 600 towns in Provence and Camargue, Luberon, and Verdon.

✔ **Riviera Côte d'Azur** (www.crt-riviera.fr). On this site, excursions and outdoor activities around the Côte d'Azur are arranged by season. Take a photo tour to see where you might go hiking or four-wheeling. Find out where you can get a Carte Musée Côte d'Azur, the pass is good at 62 museums on the Riviera.

✔ **SNCF (French Rail)** (www.sncf.fr). The official Web site of the French railway system, this site sells seats online for trips through France. You can also find timetables and prices here.

✔ **Subway Navigator** (metro.ratp.fr:10001/bin/cities/english). This site provides detailed subway maps for Paris and other French cities, plus 60 other cities around the world. You can select a city and enter your arrival and departure points, and then Subway Navigator will map out your route and estimate how long your trip will take.

✔ **Travel France** (www.bonjour.com). Here you can pick one of the country's regions and peruse a directory of links to attractions, tour operators, and city visitor bureaus. Check out the hints for getting around Paris.

Paris and environs

✔ **Aeroports de Paris** (www.paris-airports.com). Click the American flag on this site's home page for an English version that provides transfer information into Paris, and lists terminals, maps, airlines, boutiques, hotels, restaurants, and accessibility information for travelers with disabilities.

✔ **Bonjour Paris** (www.bparis.com). Utilize this fun and interesting site chock full of information about the city. You'll find everything from cultural differences to shopping to restaurant reviews, all written from an American expatriate point of view.

✔ **Channels Paris** (www.paris.cx). Centering on an elaborate virtual tour, this site offers hundreds of photos, maps, and links, and a search page for available hotels. Drop in on the chatbox and check out the Q&A on its Paris Forum.

✔ **Château de Versailles** (www.chateauversailles.com). Before visiting the country residence of Louis XIV, print out pages from this inventive reference, full of pictures of its works of art, its history, and its grounds. The site has appropriate music and moving 360-degree films of a few of the most important rooms.

✔ **Eiffel Tower** (www.tour-eiffel.fr). Read the history of the tower and practical information about its hours, tours, restaurants, and boutiques.

✔ **ISMAP** (address locator) (www.ismap.com). Type in an address in Paris on this site and ISMAP will map it, including nearby sights of interest and the closest Métro stops.

✔ **The Louvre** (www.louvre.fr). After checking out the descriptions of the guided tours, permanent collections, and temporary exhibits, download the free QuickTime VR software to take a virtual stroll through the museum. *Venus de Milo* and *Mona Lisa* are merely tastes of what lies ahead.

✔ **Paris.Com** (www.paris.com). The lodging section of this site includes photos of rooms; you can also find restaurant reviews and descriptions of the sights here.

✔ **Paris Digest** (www.parisdigest.com). Paris Digest selects "the best sights in Paris" and provides photos and links to them, as well as restaurants with views and good decor, and information on shopping, hotels, and things to do.

✔ **Paris France Guide** (www.parisfranceguide.com). This site has lots of useful information about Paris, with current nightlife, restaurant, music, theater, and events listings. This guide is brought to you by Eurorez, the publishers of the *Living in France, Study in France,* and *What's on in France* guides.

✔ **Paris Free Voice** (www.parisvoice.com or www.thinkparis.com). This is the online version of the free Paris monthly, *The Paris Voice.* It's hip and opinionated with lots of listings for performance art, music, and theater.

✔ **Paris Pages** (www.paris.org). There's so much information on this site, you won't know where to begin. Lodging reviews are organized by area and the monuments standing nearby, and you'll also find photo tours, shop listings, and a map of attractions with details.

✔ **Paris Tourist Office** (www.paris-touristoffice.com). The official site of the Paris Tourist Office provides information on the year's events, museums, accommodations, nightlife, and restaurants.

✔ **RATP (Paris Urban Transit)** (www.ratp.fr/index.eng.html). On this site, you can find subway and bus line maps, timetables, and information, as well as routes and times for Noctambus, Paris's night buses that run after the Métro closes.

✔ **Smartweb: Paris** (www.smartweb.fr/paris). The big attractions, such as the Louvre and the Eiffel Tower, are featured on this site, in addition to shop and gallery listings organized by arrondissement. Airport terminal information and click-on subway maps are also posted here.

Hitting the books

Most bookstores will have several shelves devoted entirely to Paris- and France-related titles. Here are a few other books that might be useful for your trip. All Frommer's guides are published by Hungry Minds, Inc.

✔ *Frommer's France,* updated every year, is an authoritative guide that covers the entire country.

✔ *Frommer's Provence & the Riviera* takes you to the best offerings in the south of France.

✔ *Frommer's Gay & Lesbian Europe* contains great chapters on Paris and Nice and the Riviera.

✔ *Frommer's Paris,* updated every year, covers everything you want to know about the City of Light.

✔ *Frommer's Paris from $80 a Day* is the guide for those of you who want to visit Paris comfortably but don't want to spend a fortune doing it.

✔ *Frommer's Portable Paris* is the pocket-sized version of *Frommer's Paris.*

✔ *Frommer's Memorable Walks in Paris* is for those who want to explore the city in-depth and on foot, with easy directions and descriptions of important sights.

✔ *Frommer's Irreverent Paris* is a fun guide for sophisticated travelers who want the basics without a lot of excess.

✔ *Paris For Dummies* focuses on the City of Light. It gives you all the information you need to visit this dynamic city in the easy-to-read Dummies format.

Brushing Up on Basic French

You're going to France, so why not try to learn a little of the language? At the very least, try to learn a few numbers, basic greetings, and —

above all — the life raft, *Parlez-vous anglais?* (Do you speak English?). As it turns out, many people do speak a passable English and will use it liberally if you demonstrate the basic courtesy of greeting them in their language. *Bonne chance!*

Basics

English	French	Pronunciation
Yes/No	**Oui/Non**	wee/nohn
OK	**D'accord**	dah-*core*
Please	**S'il vous plaît**	seel voo *play*
Thank you	**Merci**	mair-*see*
You're welcome	**De rien**	duh ree-*ehn*
Hello (during daylight hours)	**Bonjour**	bohn-*jhoor*
Good evening	**Bonsoir**	bohn-*swahr*
Good-bye	**Au revoir**	o ruh-*vwahr*
What's your name?	**Comment vous appellez-vous?**	ko-mahn-voo- za-pell-ay-*voo?*
My name is	**Je m'appelle**	jhuh ma-*pell*
Happy to meet you	**Enchanté(e)**	ohn-shahn-*tay*
How are you?	**Comment allez-vous?**	kuh-mahn-tahl- ay-*voo?*
Fine, thank you, and you?	**Trés bien, merci, et vous?**	tray bee-ehn, mair-*see*, ay *voo?*
So-so	**Comme ci, comme ça**	kum-*see*, kum-*sah*
I'm sorry/excuse me	**Pardon**	pahr-*dohn*
I'm so very sorry	**Désolé(e)**	day-zoh-*lay*
That's all right	**Il n'y a pas de quoi**	eel nee ah pah duh *kwah*

Getting around/Street smarts

English	French	Pronunciation
Do you speak English?	**Parlez-vous anglais?**	par-lay-voo-ahn-*glay?*
I don't speak French	**Je ne parle pas français**	jhuh ne parl pah frahn-*say*
I don't understand	**Je ne comprends pas**	jhuh ne kohm-*prahn* pas
Could you speak more loudly/more slowly?	**Pouvez-vous parler plus fort/ plus lentement?**	Poo-*vay* voopar-lay ploo for/ploo lan-te-*ment?*
Could you repeat that?	**Répetez, s'il vous plaît**	ray-pay-*tay*, seel voo *play*
What is it?	**Qu'est-ce que c'est?**	kess-kuh-*say?*
What time is it?	**Qu'elle heure est-il?**	kel uhr eh-*teel?*
What?	**Quoi?**	kwah?
How? or What did you say?	**Comment?**	ko-*mahn?*
When?	**Quand?**	kahn?
Where is?	**Où est?**	ooh-eh?
Who?	**Qui?**	kee?
Why?	**Pourquoi?**	poor-*kwah?*
here/there	**ici/là**	ee-*see*/lah
left/right	**à gauche/à droite**	a goash/a drwaht
straight ahead	**tout droit**	too-drwah
I'm American/	**Je suis / américain(e)**	jhe sweez a-may-ree-*kehn*/
Canadian/	**canadien(e)/**	can-ah-dee-*en*/
British	**anglais(e)**	ahn-*glay* (*glaise*)
Fill the tank (of a car), please	**Le plein, s'il vous plaît**	luh plan, seel-voo-*play*
I'm going to	**Je vais à**	jhe vay ah

I want to get off at	**Je voudrais descendre à**	jhe voo-*dray* day-son drah-ah
airport	**l'aéroport**	lair-o-*por*
bank	**la banque**	lah bahnk
bridge	**pont**	pohn
bus station	**la gare routière**	lah gar roo-tee-*air*
bus stop	**l'arrêt de bus**	lah-*ray* duh boohss
by means of a bicycle	**en vélo/par bicyclette**	uh *vay*-low, par bee-see-*clet*
by means of a car	**en voiture**	ahn vwa-*toor*
cashier	**la caisse**	lah *kess*
cathedral	**cathédral**	ka-tay-*dral*
church	**église**	ay-*gleez*
dead end	**une impasse**	ewn am-*pass*
driver's license	**permis de conduire**	per-*mee* duh con-*dweer*
elevator	**l'ascenseur**	lah sahn *seuhr*
entrance (to a building or a city)	**une porte**	ewn port
exit (from a building or a freeway)	**une sortie**	ewn sor-*tee*
gasoline	**du pétrol/de l'essence**	duh pay-*trol*/ de lay-*sahns*
ground floor	**rez-de-chausée**	ray-de-show-*say*
highway to	**la route pour**	la root por
hospital	**l'hôpital**	low-pee-*tahl*
insurance	**les assurances**	lez ah-sur-*ahns*
luggage storage	**consigne**	kohn-*seen*-yuh
museum	**le musée**	luh mew-*zay*
no entry	**sens interdit**	sehns ahn-ter-*dee*
no smoking	**défense de fumer**	day-*fahns* de fu-may
on foot	**à pied**	ah pee-*ay*

(continued)

(continued)

English	French	Pronunciation
one-day pass	**ticket journalier**	tee-kay jhoor-nall-ee-*ay*
one-way ticket	**aller simple**	ah-*lay sam*-pluh
police	**la police**	lah po-*lees*
rented car	**voiture de location**	vwa-*toor* de low-ka-see *on*
round-trip ticket	**aller-retour**	ah-*lay* re-*toor*
second floor	**premier étage**	prem-ee-*ehr* ay-*taj*
slow down	**ralentir**	rah-lahn-*teer*
store	**le magazin**	luh ma-ga-*zehn*
street	**rue**	roo
suburb	**banlieu, environs**	bahn-*liew,* en-veer-*ohn*
subway	**le métro**	le may-tro
telephone	**le téléphone**	luh tay-lay-*phone*
ticket	**un billet**	uh *bee*-yay
ticket office	**vente de billets**	vahnt duh bee-*yay*
toilets	**les toilettes/les WC**	lay twa-*lets*/les vay-*say*
tower	**tour**	toor

Necessities

English	French	Pronunciation
I'd like	**Je voudrais**	jhe voo-*dray*
a room	**une chambre**	ewn *shahm*-bruh
the key	**la clé (la clef)**	la clay
How much does it cost?	**C'est combien?/ Ça coûte combien?**	say comb-bee-*ehn?*/ sah coot comb-bee-*ehn?*
That's expensive	**C'est cher/chère**	say share
Do you take credit cards?	**Est-ce que vous acceptez les cartes decredit?**	es-kuh voo zaksep-*tay* lay kart duh creh-*dee?*

I'd like to buy	**Je voudrais acheter**	jhe voo-dray ahsh-*tay*
aspirin	**des aspirines/ des aspros**	deyz ahs-peer-*een*/ deyz ahs-*proh*
cigarettes	**des cigarettes**	day see-ga-*ret*
condoms	**des préservatifs**	day pray-ser-va-*teef*
dictionary	**un dictionnaire**	uh deek-see-oh-*nare*
dress	**une robe**	ewn robe
envelopes	**des envelopes**	days ahn-veh-*lope*
gift	**un cadeau**	uh kah-*doe*
handbag	**un sac**	uh sahk
hat	**un chapeau**	uh shah-*poh*
magazine	**une revue**	ewn reh-*vu*
map of the city	**un plan de ville**	unh plahn de *veel*
matches	**des allumettes**	dayz a-loo-*met*
necktie	**une cravate**	uh cra-*vaht*
newspaper	**un journal**	uh zhoor-*nahl*
phonecard	**une carte téléphonique**	uh cart tay-lay-fone-*eek*
postcard	**une carte postale**	ewn carte pos-*tahl*
road map	**une carte routière**	ewn cart roo-tee-*air*
shirt	**une chemise**	ewn che-*meez*
shoes	**des chaussures**	day show-*suhr*
skirt	**une jupe**	ewn jhoop
soap	**du savon**	dew sah-*vohn*
socks	**des chaussettes**	day show-*set*
stamp	**un timbre**	uh *tam*-bruh
trousers	**un pantalon**	uh pan-tah-*lohn*
writing paper	**du papier à lettres**	dew pap-pee-*ay* a *let*-ruh

In your hotel

English	French	Pronunciation
Are taxes included?	**Est-ce que les taxes sont comprises?**	ess-keh lay taks son com-*preez?*
balcony	**un balcon**	uh bahl-cohn
bathtub	**une baignoire**	ewn bayn-*nwar*
for two occupants	**pour deux personnes**	poor duh pair-*sunn*
hot and cold water	**l'eau chaude et froide**	low showed ay fwad
Is breakfast included?	**Petit déjeuner inclus?**	peh-*tee* day-jheun-*ay* ehn-*klu?*
room	**une chambre**	ewn *shawm*-bruh
shower	**une douche**	ewn dooch
sink	**un lavabo**	uh la-va-*bow*
suite	**une suite**	ewn sweet
We're staying for . . . days	**On reste pour . . . jours**	ohn rest poor . . . jhoor
with air-conditioning	**avec climatization**	ah-*vek* clee-mah-tee-zah-ion
without	**sans**	sahn
youth hostel	**une auberge de jeunesse**	oon oh-bayrge-duh-jhe-*ness*

In the restaurant

English	French	Pronunciation
I would like	**Je voudrais**	jhe voo-*dray*
to eat	**manger**	mahn-*jhay*
to order	**commander**	ko-mahn-*day*
Please give me	**Donnez-moi, s'il vous plaît**	doe-nay-*mwah,* seel voo play

an ashtray	**un cendrier**	uh sahn-dree-*ay*
a bottle of	**une bouteille de**	ewn boo-*tay* duh
a cup of	**une tasse de**	ewn tass duh
a glass of	**un verre de**	uh vair duh
a plate of breakfast	**une assiette de le petit-déjeuner**	ewn ass-ee-*et* duh luh puh-*tee* day-zhuh-*nay*
cocktail	**un apéritif**	uh ah-pay-ree-*teef*
check/bill	**l'addition/la note**	la-dee-see-*ohn*/la noat
dinner	**le dîner**	luh dee-*nay*
knife	**un couteau**	uh koo-*toe*
napkin	**une serviette**	ewn sair-vee-*et*
platter of the day	**un plat du jour**	uh plah dew jhoor
spoon	**une cuillère**	ewn kwee-*air*
Cheers!	**A votre santé!**	ah vo-truh sahn-*tay!*
Can I buy you a drink?	**Puis-je vous acheter un verre?**	*pwee*-jhe voo *zahsh*-tay uh *vaihr?*
fixed-price menu	**un menu**	uh may-*new*
fork	**une fourchette**	ewn four-*shet*
Is the tip/service included?	**Est-ce que le service est compris?**	ess-ke luh ser-*vees* eh com-*pree?*
Waiter!/Waitress!	**Monsieur!/ Mademoiselle!**	mun-*syuh*/mad-mwa-*zel*
wine list	**une carte des vins**	ewn cart day *van*
appetizer	**une entrée**	ewn en-*tray*
main course	**un plat principal**	uh plah pran-see-*pahl*
tip included	**service compris**	sehr-*vees* cohm-*pree*
wide-ranging sampling of the chef's best efforts	**menu dégustation**	may-*new* day-gus-ta-see-*on*
drinks not included	**boissons non comprises**	bwa-*sons* no com-*pree*

Making Dollars and Sense of It

Expense	Amount
Airfare	
Car Rental	
Lodging	
Parking	
Breakfast	
Lunch	
Dinner	
Babysitting	
Attractions	
Transportation	
Souvenirs	
Tips	
Grand Total	

Notes

Fare Game: Choosing an Airline

Travel Agency:_____ Phone:_____

Agent's Name:_____ Quoted Fare:_____

Departure Schedule & Flight Information

Airline:_____ Airport:_____

Flight #:_____ Date:_____ Time:_____ a.m./p.m.

Arrives in:_____ Time:_____ a.m./p.m.

Connecting Flight (if any)

Amount of time between flights:_____ hours/mins

Airline:_____ Airport:_____

Flight #:_____ Date:_____ Time:_____ a.m./p.m.

Arrives in:_____ Time:_____ a.m./p.m.

Return Trip Schedule & Flight Information

Airline:_____ Airport:_____

Flight #:_____ Date:_____ Time:_____ a.m./p.m.

Arrives in:_____ Time:_____ a.m./p.m.

Connecting Flight (if any)

Amount of time between flights:_____ hours/mins

Airline:_____ Airport:_____

Flight #:_____ Date:_____ Time:_____ a.m./p.m.

Arrives in:_____ Time:_____ a.m./p.m.

Notes

Sweet Dreams: Choosing Your Hotel

Enter the hotels where you'd prefer to stay based on location and price. Then use the worksheet below to plan your itinerary.

Hotel	Location	Price per night

Menus & Venues

Enter the restaurants where you'd most like to dine. Then use the worksheet below to plan your itinerary.

Name	Address/Phone	Cuisine/Price

Places to Go, People to See, Things to Do

Enter the attractions you would most like to see. Then use the worksheet below to plan your itinerary.

Attractions	Amount of time you expect to spend there	Best day and time to go

Going "My" Way

Itinerary #1

- ☐ _____
- ☐ _____
- ☐ _____
- ☐ _____

Itinerary #2

- ☐ _____
- ☐ _____
- ☐ _____
- ☐ _____

Itinerary #3

- ☐ _____
- ☐ _____
- ☐ _____
- ☐ _____

Itinerary #4

- ☐ _____
- ☐ _____
- ☐ _____
- ☐ _____

Itinerary #5

- ☐ _____
- ☐ _____
- ☐ _____
- ☐ _____

Itinerary #6

☐ _____
☐ _____
☐ _____
☐ _____

Itinerary #7

☐ _____
☐ _____
☐ _____
☐ _____

Itinerary #8

☐ _____
☐ _____
☐ _____
☐ _____

Itinerary #9

☐ _____
☐ _____
☐ _____
☐ _____

Itinerary #10

☐ _____
☐ _____
☐ _____
☐ _____

Notes

Index

•G•

•N•

Notes